Macroeconomic Policy in the European Monetary Union

This book collects contributions of distinguished researchers from different European countries and institutions which offer the reader a multifaceted assessment of the implementation of macroeconomic policies in the Euro zone five years after the launch of the common currency. Albeit this volume has a larger scope – how economic policy works inside a monetary union – it is very much focused on the functioning of fiscal policy under the Stability and Growth Pact (SGP).

The book begins by sketching a unified conceptual framework, providing the reader with a benchmark with which the conclusions of the individual chapters can be evaluated. The overall assessment is mixed. The SGP is considered both as an opportunity to strengthen macroeconomic stability across the countries belonging to the Euro area, and as an ill-designed institutional device to combine fiscal discipline with effective stabilization at the national level. The critical elements that emerge from the analyses presented here concern the monetary and fiscal policy-mix, the evolution and control of fiscal aggregates over the business cycle and their implications for the SGP rules, the accountability of debt evolution, the financial spill-over of national fiscal policies, and the measurement and assessment of automatic stabilizers. Through stressing country heterogeneity and considering how the size of the country impinges on the effectiveness of fiscal policy, these essays go some way in broadening the interpretative focus of the pros and cons of the SGP.

This book will be of great interest to students and researchers engaged with macroeconomic stabilization and monetary and fiscal policy interactions, as well as professionals in the public sector and the financial institutions of the EU.

Francesco Farina is a Professor of Economics at the University of Siena.

Roberto Tamborini is Head of the Department of Economics at the University of Trento.

Routledge Studies in the European Economy

1. **Growth and Crisis in the Spanish Economy, 1940–1993**
   Sima Lieberman

2. **Work and Employment in Europe**
   A new convergence?
   Edited by Peter Cressey and Bryn Jones

3. **Trans-European Telecommunication Networks**
   The challenges for industrial policy
   Colin Turner

4. **European Union - European Industrial Relations?**
   Global challenges, national developments and transnational dynamics
   Edited by Wolfgang E. Lecher and Hans-Wolfgang Platzer

5. **Governance, Industry and Labour Markets in Britain and France**
   The modernizing state in the mid-twentieth century
   Edited by Noel Whiteside and Robert Salais

6. **Labour Market Efficiency in the European Union**
   Employment protection and fixed-term contracts
   Klaus Schömann, Ralf Rogowski and Thomas Kruppe

7. **The Enlargement of the European Union**
   Issues and strategies
   Edited by Victoria Curzon-Price, Alice Landau and Richard Whitman

8. **European Trade Unions**
   Change and response
   Edited by Mike Rigby, Roger Smith and Teresa Lawlor

9. **Fiscal Federalism in the European Union**
   Edited by Amedeo Fossati and Giorgio Panella

10. **European Telecommunications Liberalisation**
    Edited by Kjell A. Eliassen and Marit Sjøvaag

11. **Integration and Transition in Europe**
The economic geography of interaction
Edited by George Petrakos, Gunther Maier and Grzegorz Gorzelak

12. **SMEs and European Integration**
Internationalisation strategies
Birgit Hegge

13. **Fiscal Federalism and European Economic Integration**
Edited by Mark Baimbridge and Philip Whyman

14. **Financial Markets in Central and Eastern Europe**
Stability and efficiency
Edited by Morten Balling, Frank Lierman and Andy Mullineux

15. **Russian Path Dependence**
Stefan Hedlund

16. **The Impact of European Integration on Regional Structural Change and Cohesion**
Edited by Christiane Krieger-Boden, Edgar Morgenroth and George Petrakos

17. **Macroeconomic Policy in the European Monetary Union**
From the old to the new Stability and Growth Pact
Edited by Francesco Farina and Roberto Tamborini

Macroeconomic Policy in the European Monetary Union

From the old to the new Stability and Growth Pact

Edited by
Francesco Farina and Roberto Tamborini

Routledge
Taylor & Francis Group
LONDON AND NEW YORK

First published 2008
by Routledge
2 Park Square, Milton Park, Abingdon, Oxfordshire OX14 4RN

Simultaneously published in the USA and Canada
by Routledge

711 Third Avenue, New York, NY 10017

First issued in paperback 2014

Routledge is an imprint of the Taylor & Francis Group, an informa business

Typeset in Times New Roman by
Newgen Imaging Systems (P) Ltd, Chennai, India

British Library Cataloguing in Publication Data
A catalogue record for this book is available from the British Library

Library of Congress Cataloging in Publication Data
A catalog record for this book has been requested

ISBN 978–0–415–42900–9 (hbk)
ISBN 978–1–138–80627–6 (pbk)
ISBN 978–0–203–93453–1 (ebk)

Contents

Figures

Tables

Contributors

M. Catenaro, *European Central Bank*

J. Creel, *OFCE, Paris*

F. Farina, *Univeristy of Siena, Italy*

E. Gaffeo, *University of Trento, Italy*

J. Le Cacheux, *OFCE, Paris*

J. Mélitz, *University of Strathclyde*, CREST-INSEE, and CEPR

R. Morris, *European Central Bank*

A. Muscatelli, *University of Glasgow, UK*

G. Passmani, *University of Trento, Italy*

R. Ricciuti, *University of Florence, Italy*

T. Ropele, *University of Milan – Bicocca, Italy*

F. Saraceno, *OFCE, Paris*

S. Schiavo, *University of Trento, Italy*

R. Tamborini, *University of Trento, Italy*

P. Tirelli, *University of Milan – Bicocca, Italy*

1 Introduction

F. Farina and R. Tamborini

On 1 January 2007, the euro celebrated its fifth anniversary of circulation as the single currency of twelve countries of the European Union (EU). On the same day, the euro club welcomed the thirteenth country, Slovenia. The protracted and sometimes confused debate on the costs and benefits of a single currency, on Europe as an optimum currency area, and on the accession parameters has become a matter for the historians. The task now is to understand the extent to which the common monetary house is robust, well-designed and in line with the aspirations of the citizens who inhabit it.

This book collects contributions of distinguished researchers from different European countries and institutions who met at the conference series organized by the Jean Monnet Chair in 'European Macroeconomics' at the University of Siena (Italy) in 2004–6. The contributions selected for this book focus on economic policy in the context of macroeconomic stabilization goals in the European Monetary Union (EMU). Taking stock of the long-lasting debate about the pros and cons of the design of the EMU, the general aim of the book is to provide the reader with a multifaceted assessment of the *implementation* of macroeconomic policies in the euro zone and of their effects five years after the inception of the euro.

The state of affairs

On the fifth anniversary, the press has given prominence to opinion polls about the citizens'sentiments towards the euro. An example, drawn from the Eurobarometer survey, is provided by Table 1.1, reporting on the perceived cost-benefit balance after adoption of the euro.

The picture is not particularly rosy, both in absolute terms (only 48% of the EMU citizens strike a positive cost-benefit balance) and in terms of trend over time (the percentage was 51 one year earlier). The most significant item on the cost side of the balance is the rise in the general price level (81% of respondents); at some distance followed by difficulties in adaptation and use (19%), higher unemployment (7%) and loss of sovereignty (5%).

The opinion of academics is well represented by Charles Wyplosz (2006), who sees some 'dark sides' in a 'major success'. Interestingly, the academic ranking of discontent is almost the reverse of that of the general public: low and stable inflation

Table 1.1 Percentage of respondents for whom the benefits of the euro are greater than the costs

	2006	*2005*
Ireland	75.4	72.0
Finland	64.7	67.0
Luxemburg	63.8	77.0
Austria	62.3	54.0
Belgium	58.4	68.0
Spain	54.6	61.0
France	51.0	57.0
EURO 12	48.0	51.0
Germany	46.0	47.0
Portugal	42.7	45.0
Italy	41.4	43.0
Netherlands	38.4	38.0
Greece	38.0	39.0

Source: Eurobarometer.

is ranked high on the positive side of the balance sheet; problems of acquaintance with the new currency are not even mentioned. The poor performance of the euro area in terms of growth and job creation is not charged to the single currency. On the other hand, prominent on the negative side of the balance sheet are some flaws in the institutional design of the area. These concern the transparency and accountability of the European Central Bank (ECB), and the trembling Stability and Growth Pact (SGP). As a matter of fact, the only major setback in the general functioning of the euro area in these five years has occurred at this junction, namely the suspension of the SGP excess deficit procedure obtained by Germany and France in November 2004 in opposition to the Commission's recommendation.

This event reminds us that, eventually, the most important opinions remain those of the political forces that alternate in power in the EMU sovereign states. These opinions, however, are not easily intelligible, and may be revealed more by deeds than words. In this respect we can only say that the SGP crisis is a representation of a more general tension in the EU among the three key actors on the stage of democracy: elected governments, public opinion and technocrats (Fitoussi, 2002). This tension has been tangible throughout the entire history of the EMU, from the Delors Report and the Maastricht Treaty, to the adoption of the SGP and the choice of the first group of euro countries (Wyplosz, 2006; Tamborini and Targetti, 2005). This complex triangle cannot be reduced to the caricature of 'good guys' (economists and technocrats) vs. 'bad guys' (governments) as is often perceived from economic analyses and prescriptions. Whatever the economists' opinion may be, the dissatisfaction of the majority of the public opinion with the euro, and with the EU more generally (as witnessed by the rejections of the 'constitutional' draft in different countries) can hardly be overemphasized when assessing finer institutional and operational aspects of the EMU. And if economists may, with some reason, wish to refrain from being involved in these matters, they should be aware that 'politics' amounts to much more than a white noise in models and forecasts.

Hence, introductorily we wish to remind the broader scenario where this epoch-making *political* creature should be framed, though what the reader will find in this book is a collection of self-contained, mostly empirical, economic analyses of the first five years of EMU and its prospects.

First and foremost, the EMU represents a major change in the 'political-economic regime' for its member countries.[1]

[1]By 'political-economic regime' we mean the set of constraints, goals and opportunities that face private and public agents in a given economic system. The liberalization of the circulation of goods, capitals and individuals, the adoption of a single currency and the devolution of monetary sovereignty to an independent supranational institution, the introduction of a common 'economic constitution' in the form of the Treaty of Maastricht, and self-imposed fiscal rules through the SGP, all have yielded profound consequences not only on economic magnitudes and structures but also on the economic institutions.

Following these changes, the EMU countries are shifting from a well-defined and consolidated political-economic regime – what we may call the *international regime* – to one still incipient, uncertain in shape, and with difficult to predict outcomes. The *ancien régime* was founded on the following premises: 1) The sovereignty of the policy makers – the monetary authorities (MAs) and the fiscal authorities (FAs) – had the same geographical extension as the state. 2) Geo-politics coincided with geo-economics, or, in other words, the geographical boundaries of the states and their organisms coincided with economic areas which were internally homogeneous, and mutually heterogeneous, as regards a) national identity and definition of national interests, and b) economic-social structures.

The time-honoured international regime in Europe was eroded over the last twenty years by numerous factors determining the collapse of both its premises. First, the experience of the European Monetary System of fixed exchange rates – and more in general the effects of the globalization of markets – has shown that substantial political-economic sovereignty, both in terms of independence and of effectiveness, has been lost, despite the formal sovereignty of the state (Padoa Schioppa, 1992). Second, the geo-economic map of Europe no longer exactly coincides with its geo-political map. Economically homogeneous areas (the 'macro-regions', in EU vocabulary) have boundaries which often cross two or more states, and this tends to disrupt the coincidence between nationality and economic interests, and the consistency of government actions defined solely by the geographical domain of the state.

In the presence of these phenomena, public economics suggests that policy-making should be articulated into 'levels of government' hierarchically arranged according to their ability to regulate and control the interdependences and spatial externalities of public and private economic choices. This suggestion has been followed in the past by those numerous nation-states that have devolved powers to their regions, as well as obviously by the federal states. At least from a normative point of view, the process ongoing in Europe is towards rearranging the national policy authorities into what we may call an *interregional regime*: that is, a system characterized by 1) a common currency, 2) the close integration of cross-border geo-economic areas which are internally homogeneous (but not necessarily homogeneous among each other), 3) the hierarchical organization of territorial economic policy competences, and therefore of policy agencies. The first manifest step in this direction has been taken with the single currency and the creation of the ECB. To a large extent, in the EMU the national MAs and the ECB are already operating in an interregional regime which may not yet be thoroughly defined as regards the allocation of functions between centre and periphery, but is nevertheless solidly established.

The framework in which the national FAs operate is much more uncertain. As yet, this framework is not even remotely interregional in nature; nor does it look like becoming so in the near future. In its present form it is a hybrid between the old and the new, one that might be called a *constrained international regime*. This institutional mismatch between MAs and FAs has caused much concern for scholars and politicians. It has led to the proposal of a complete interregional regime (to use our terminology) with the creation of a central FA to parallel the ECB. This view is by no means universally shared, however. Some argue that a 'monetary giant' surrounded by 'fiscal dwarves' is a better guarantee of the independence of the central bank, of monetary and financial stability, of restricted growth of the public sector, and of fiscal discipline. Yet, it cannot be overlooked that, so far, it is governments themselves that have resisted to a larger devolution of fiscal prerogatives to a supranational authority (Buti and Franco, 2005; Wyplosz, 2006). Hence, it comes as no surprise that the SGP, and fiscal policy more generally, appear as the weakest pillar of the EMU. It also seems reasonable to predict that improvements cannot only come from better economic engineering, and that they may take a long and troubled road to come.

Thus, albeit this volume has a larger scope – how economic policy works inside a monetary union – it is very much focused on the functioning of fiscal policy under the SGP. Particular emphasis is given to the constraints of the SGP on the one hand, and the presence of a single monetary policy on the other. In this respect, the focus is on the most recent advances in the literature, namely how the *fiscal-monetary policy mix* is actually working within the peculiar institutional setup of the EMU. The critical elements that emerge from the analyses presented here concern the evolution and control of fiscal aggregates over the business cycle and their implications for the SGP rules, the accountability of debt evolution, the financial *spillovers* of national fiscal policies, the measurement and assessment of automatic stabilizers, the relationship between fiscal performance and country size.

The overall assessment is mixed. In particular, the SGP is considered both as an opportunity to strengthen macroeconomic stability across the countries belonging to the euro area, and as an ill-designed institutional device to combine fiscal discipline with effective stabilization at the national level. Though the positive design of the EMU institutions and policy instruments is beyond the scope of the book, we are confident that the results presented here may allow for an informed judgement on the SGP reform introduced in March 2005 and on the prospective evolution of economic policy in the EMU. A more detailed presentation of the contributions to the volume follows in the next section.

Looking forward

We wish now to draw the reader's attention to three main prospective issues that we distil from this assessment of the first five years of EMU.

The first is that the new SGP remains silent about the problem of monetary and fiscal policy co-ordination, thus showing a difficulty to recognize the central role of monetary and fiscal interactions in the euro area (see also Wyplosz, 2006).

The 'consensus view' is that monetary and fiscal policy co-ordination can be waived as the ECB and national FAs are committed to the same inflation and output objectives (Dixit and Lambertini, 2003). There results the 'division of labour' between the ECB taking care of EMU-wide shocks and national FAs taking care of domestic asymmetric shocks. Yet the problem of the complex monetary and fiscal interactions which develop in a monetary union should not be downplayed. The recognition of this problem will probably have to go beyond the role of the SGP rules as a substitute for open co-ordination (Beetsma *et al.*, 2001). The role, if any, is in fact limited to the well known 'common pool problem'. Each government in a monetary union might free-ride on the common pool of financial resources and fail to endogenize the negative *spillovers* (higher interest rates) towards the other members stemming from its fiscal stance. Yet, the quest for a co-ordination of national fiscal policies in the EMU does not arise only from this problem. The real question is not just a possible co-ordination failure among the FAs, but, more importantly, the overall co-ordination between a single monetary stance and a plurality of fiscal stances.

First of all, the EMU countries differ both as for growth differentials and for persistent differences across business cycles. Symmetric shocks, or asymmetric shocks originating in one country and generating *spillover* effects throughout the euro area, may cause different weights put by the ECB and by the FAs in their respective loss functions become relevant (Tamborini, 2004: 154–5). One or more governments might then indulge in discretionary fiscal policies which are mutually compatible with the common inflation and output objectives, but possibly not compatible with overall macroeconomic conditions as shaped by the ECB and the other FAs. The ECB and the national FAs should therefore co-ordinate in order to avoid that the impulse on the euro interest rate resulting from the governments' fiscal stances clashes with the conduct of monetary policy.

There are reasons to think that the debate on policy co-ordination should be resumed soon. The substantial demise of co-ordinated macroeconomic policies of stabilization might not be unrelated to the large current account imbalances recently observed among EMU economies, following widening divergences across real effective exchange rates (Tamborini, 2001; De Grauwe, 2006), as well as to the structural current account surplus of the euro area as a whole vis-à-vis the rest of the world. The limitation of (unco-ordinated) fiscal policies to domestic fiscal shocks can also be questioned from a welfare point of view. As shown by Muscatelli *et al.* (this volume), the euro area displays conditions whereby welfare gains, in terms of consumption smoothing, can be obtained by combining monetary and fiscal stabilization in the area as a whole.

The new Pact has allowed the European Commission more room for discretionality in the evaluation of public budgets. This improved relevance of the specific state of public finances and of the overall macroeconomic conditions is probably a step forward in the direction of removing the stringencies created by a monetary and fiscal tightening during a recession, but not a clear recognition of policy co-ordination as a central question.

The second issue for the future that it is worth considering is that the shift of focus of the new SGP from current deficits to debt brings into light a new possible conflict between the two fiscal policy objectives of output stabilization and the stabilization or the decumulation of debt (depending on whether or not a country is presently respecting the 60% limit for the debt/GDP ratio). During Stage II of the pre-EMU procedures (1993–7), the credible threat of exclusion from the single currency was an effective enforcement device for the Maastricht criteria. In most EMU countries, both the deficit/GDP and the debt/GDP ratios were successfully reduced. The savings on interest expenditure helped in the consolidation of public finances, and compliance at least with the deficit/GDP Maastricht limit admission was successfully accomplished also by 'high debt' countries such as Italy and Belgium. Starting from Stage III, however, the sanction of exclusion from the monetary union has no longer been in place. After the inception of the EMU, public deficit and debts over GDP have begun to increase again.

The common wisdom in the debate on monetary integration in Europe is that the accumulation of public debt in the past decades was mainly the consequence of fiscal profligacy. The view has been put forward that the establishment of a 'monetary dominance' regime, whereby fiscal authorities abide by the restrictive monetary stance of the central bank, is hampered in Europe by the FAs' lack of compliance with the SGP (Buti and Franco, 2005). The 'fiscal indiscipline' which impaired the monetary and fiscal policy mix of the European countries throughout the 1980s was not completely dismissed in the 1990s and after, also considering that the fiscal retrenchment has then been conducted by raising tax pressure more than by cutting public expenditures. The Pact just relies on a penalty for 'excessive deficit' which is much lower than the threat of the pre-EMU period (the exclusion from the EMU). The end of the enforcement represented by the Maastricht clauses for admission to the monetary union has favoured the resurgence of large public deficits and provoked a sort of 'consolidation fatigue' (Huges-Hallett *et al.*, 2003).

In this view, the empirical evidence witnessing a long story of pro-cyclical fiscal policies should not be traced back to the ill-conceived design of the SGP. Quite the contrary, the accumulation of public debt was the direct consequence of continuously expanding public expenditures, as 'pro-cyclical behaviour seems to pertain mostly to good times' (European Commission, 2006: 187). After the recourse, during bad times, to discretional fiscal policies in addition to automatic stabilizers, many governments in the good times failed to engineer the fiscal retrenchment which was needed for the budget to stay 'close to balance or in surplus' (Buti and Franco, 2005). In this perspective, the constraints put on the fiscal stance – first by the Maastricht Treaty, and then by the SGP – did not represent an obstruction to the goal of output stabilization in the EMU. Econometric estimates of fiscal stances conducted by Galì and Perotti (2004) support this view. By using the cyclically adjusted public budget balance (CAPB) – the value that the public budget would have assumed 'if the output level would have not changed' – as a proxy of discretionary fiscal policy, they found for the EMU countries 'a clear trend towards a smaller value' of the co-efficient linking the cyclically adjusted primary deficit-GDP ratio to the output gap (*ibidem*: 547). Galì and Perotti interpret their estimates as indicating the FAs' switch from a pro-cyclical to an a-cyclical variation of fiscal stances and as a proof of lack of evidence that the 3% limit has impeded the full operation of automatic stabilizers during downswings.

However, the exclusive reliance of most empirical research on the CAPB obscures the problem of the possible conflict between output stabilization and debt reduction. In fact, the CAPB and the growth rate of the debt/GDP ratio respond to different variables. Whereas the former just cancels out the effect of the *cyclical* component of GDP on the *total* budget, the latter depends on the evolution of the *primary* balance in connection with the gap between the real interest on debt and the GDP growth rate.[2]

On the one hand, the alleged a-cyclicity of fiscal policy from Maastricht onwards could also stem from the strengthening of the consolidation effort, which obliged fiscal authorities to renounce to expansionary interventions during upswings and turn excess fiscal revenues to the reduction of the debt/GDP ratio. On the other hand, it may well happen that an upward leap in the interest rate (and then in interest payments) and/or a lower growth rate causes the rise of the deficit and debt above the planned figures for reasons different from deliberate expansionary interventions by the FAs. Since it measures the variation of the fiscal stance just as a *residual*, the CAPB is unable to indicate whether a violation of the SGP is due to a lack of 'fiscal discipline' or to a lack of 'room for manoeuvre' caused to the FAs by a non-expected squeeze of the fiscal revenues, following a slowdown in the growth rate of income, and/or an excessive absorption by interest payments after a rise in the interest rate provoked by international financial markets or by the ECB monetary stance. Whatever the origin of a deficit/GDP above the 3% limit, the SGP imposes on the FAs the obligation to compensate for any exogenous shock to the public budget. The fiscal retrenchment, which is needed in order to abide by the 3% limit and/or to impede the further accumulation of public debt, may come at the cost of suspending the operation of automatic stabilizers. Thus, the SGP requirements are potentially conducive to a deflationary bias in the overall macroeconomic governance. Disappointingly, this is not detected by the current method of evaluating the variation of fiscal stances by the EMU governments (Farina and Tamborini, 2001 and 2004).

The difficulty to reconcile the objectives of output stabilization and debt decumulation has to be traced back to the incompleteness of the institutional design of the Pact. The *Tax Smoothing* principle, to which the SGP is inspired, dictates that cyclical fluctuations in the primary budget should be averaged out in order to stick to a balanced budget in the medium term. Yet, no account is taken of exogenous shocks increasing the deficit/GDP ratio during bad times, which may cause the two objectives of output stabilization and debt decumulation to be in conflict.

Therefore, a weakness of the old and the new SGP is to be unable to differently evaluate and regulate the case in which a deviation from the CAPB in the medium term derives from excessive expenditure at the numerator of the public budget/GDP ratio, or from a sluggish growth at the denominator. The several failures manifested by the EMU governments in their attempts to abide by the public deficit and debt/GDP ratios not necessarily are a proof of a tendency to renege on the SGP commitments. The recent recession in the euro area has slowed down the formation of additional revenues, and the room for fiscal manoeuvre has narrowed accordingly. Some EMU governments proved unwilling to curb automatic stabilizers. FAs auto-absolved from the 'sin' of postponing debt decumulation and implementing the discretionary interventions needed for output stabilization through higher public expenditure and/or tax cuts. Some other EMU governments, instead, acknowledged that the SGP does not allow for a violation of the 3% limit due to an unexpected reduction in fiscal revenues. These FAs have been using fiscal revenues for debt consolidation in the rush to comply with the requirements for admission to the euro. Many 'high debt' EMU countries, however, even when refraining from discretionary fiscal policies during the recession following the 'Twin Towers', have been unable to reduce their public debt (Farina and Ricciuti, 2006).

Contrary to the presumption of the above-mentioned econometric estimates, Figure 1.1 shows that the average behaviour of the EMU governments' fiscal stances appears to be highly pro-cyclical, even using the CAPB, a method of measuring the FAs' behaviour we have questioned, as it might underestimate the width of fiscal restrictions. Furthermore, after that, pro-cyclical fiscal stances in bad times have been complemented by the turn to higher interest rates by the ECB. Figure 1.2 witnesses that the monetary *and* fiscal policy mix in the EMU have recently become restrictive.

The foregoing considerations lead us to the third question, only marginally tackled by the new SGP; that is, the lack of attention for the connections between fiscal policy and growth in the euro area. As stressed above (see also Gaffeo *et al.*, this volume), the growth rate is a major determinant of the room for fiscal manoeuvre within the SGP boundaries. As a matter of fact, it has been claimed that the lower-than-expected potential growth, which seems to have established in Europe after the deficit limit was set, calls for a corresponding adjustment from the 3% down to 1.8% (Gros, 2004). No doubt, fostering its poor growth is also imperative for Europe in order to relax the SGP constraint. In this perspective, the 'Frankfurt-Brussels consensus' subscribes to the view of 'the cycle around the trend' where the two phenomena are taken as independent. Stabilization policy (basically, aggregate demand management) is aimed at smoothing cyclical fluctuations but it is not

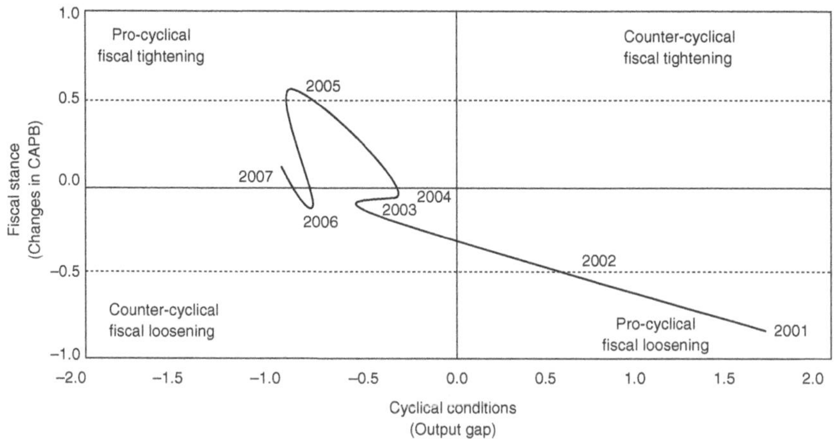

Figure 1.1 Euro-area fiscal stance and cyclical condition, 2001–7.

Source: European Commission Services, 2006.

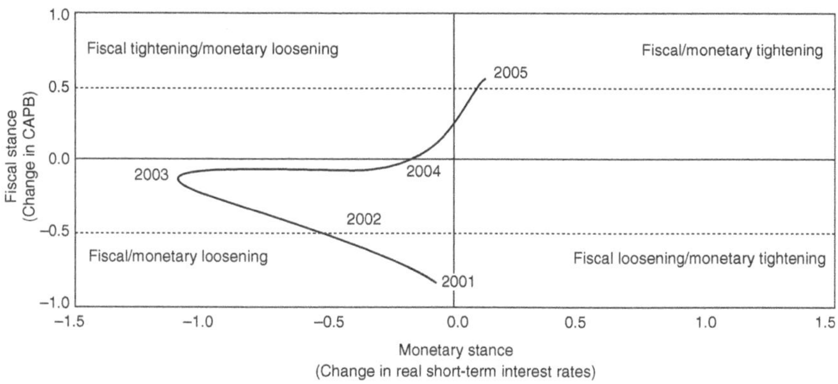

Figure 1.2 Euro-area policy-mix, 2001–5.

Source: European Commission Services, 2006.

(it should not be) regarded as a means to affect the trend. Fiscal policy is almost entirely confined within this dimension. After monetary unification, the tool-box of policy-makers has been left with fiscal policy as the sole instrument for adjustment, but under the constraint of the SGP, which discourages discretionary interventions.

This recommendation of the European Commission is also a consequence of (non-uncontroversial) empirical evidence showing so-called Non-Keynesian effects of fiscal policy (Giavazzi and Pagano, 1996), and a limited width of the fiscal multiplier (Blanchard and Perotti, 2002). As a result, the endogenous feedback of an expansionary fiscal policy on output is downplayed. Whatever the macroeconomic conditions, any deviation of the total balance from the condition of a zero structural total deficit/GDP ratio, different from the impact of the cycle on the primary balance/GDP ratio, should be compensated. Fiscal authorities are required to react by a fiscal retrenchment, disregarding that raising aggregate demand is an alternative source of improvement of public finances.

In order to raise the trend of output, the recommended strategy is to push the economic system towards the efficiency frontier by injecting more competition and flexibility into the economy. The EMU countries with a slow trend of total factor productivity are pressed to implement a wide range of supply-side policies. The objective is to sustain growth by eliminating rents and boosting the turnover of firms in order to prompt the adoption of new technologies. The competitive advantage conquered by the best performers as for liberalization is taken to act as incentive for reforms in the labour market and Welfare institutions by the more 'rigid' countries (Tabellini and Wyplosz, 2004).

On the other hand, it should not be overlooked that the recovery of potential growth in Europe is both a problem of market liberalization and of enhancement of the determinants of growth. In this perspective, the *composition* as well as the *extent* of the government budget do matter (e.g. Afonso *et al.*, 2005). It is now generally agreed that programmes of growth-friendly public expenditures (infrastructural investments, other expenses aimed at fostering innovation and improving human capital) should be resumed. True, a pro-growth *composition* of the government budget does not imply sustained deficits. Yet, there are at least three direct or indirect connections with deficits. The first is that, as a result of *hysteresis*, the extent and speed of stabilization may affect the average growth rate of output: unduly prolonged recessions that wear out physical and human capital displace the economy onto a lower growth path. A second and more specific one relates to capital market imperfections that prevent the private sector from keeping the economy on the efficient growth path after a shock: in some cases there are distinct gains from redistributing resources intertemporally by means of government's borrowing (Andersen and Dogonowsky, 1999). A third connection, widely discussed in the SGP debate, is that the so-called structural reforms may be quite costly in fiscal terms in the short run, whereas they produce social gains and fiscal revenues in the future: again, a welfare dimension of fiscal imbalances emerges that has no relation with the cycle but with the trend of GDP. The new Pact waives the obligation to consider expenditures in public investment in the computation of the public balance only for the EMU countries with sound finances. Yet, the economies which may be more in need of pro-growth public investments are those with a deficit/GDP ratio burdened by a sluggish growth. To this aim, the new methods of economic integration in Europe, in particular the Method of Enhanced Co-operation, could be fruitfully exploited. Joint ventures in R&D projects and networks among the European governments, oriented to boost the diffusion of the Information and communication technologies, should be soon organized in order to fuel convergence across the EMU economies.

Overview of the book

Vis-à-vis the enormous literature available, the major features of this book are that

- in the general assessment of the macroeconomic performance of the euro area, and in particular of fiscal policy under the SGP, the focus is on the most recent advance in the literature, namely how the *fiscal-monetary policy mix* is actually working within the peculiar institutional setup of the EMU;
- the book covers in an organized and compact manner the main issues and questions concerning fiscal and monetary policy, the SGP and macroeconomic performances in the EMU, that have proliferated in a vast and heterogeneous literature, such as: structural analyses of fiscal-monetary interactions, the evolution and control of fiscal aggregates over the business cycle and their implications for the SGP rules, the controllability of debt evolution, the financial *spillovers* of national fiscal policies, the measurement and assessment of automatic stabilizers, the relationship between fiscal performance and country size;
- all contributions are essentially empirical in nature, though firmly rooted in theoretical analyses that are aptly expounded and discussed; all the issues are examined and tested with a variety of up-to-date techniques and from multifaceted points of view.

The contributions are organized in three parts covering, respectively, macroeconomic governance in the EMU, empirical analyses of national fiscal stances, and other fiscal policy issues such as heterogeneity, interdependence and divergence.

Part I opens with an introductory, broad assessment of fiscal policy in the EMU provided by Marco Catenaro and Richard Morris ('Fiscal policy implementation in EMU: From Maastricht to the SGP reform and beyond'). Prior to EMU, fiscal policies in Europe exhibited severe deficit and debt biases. The Maastricht Treaty and the SGP introduced a fiscal framework aimed at correcting such biases and ensuring sound budgetary positions in EMU. However, following significant consolidation efforts in the run-up to EMU, recent years have witnessed a re-emergence of fiscal imbalances, and the SGP has come under increasing strain and criticism. Against this background, the authors examine the fiscal rules that have recently been revised, and conclude that they are now more tailored to economic and country-specific circumstances. This may not only enhance 'ownership' – that is, the political endorsement of the SGP – but also presents new implementation challenges. A rigorous implementation of these new rules will therefore be essential to restore credibility and ensure prudent fiscal policies.

In the subsequent chapter, 'Macroeconomic adjustment in the euro area: The role of fiscal policy', Anton Muscatelli, Tiziano Ropele and Patrizio Tirelli move from the 'Frankfurt-Brussels consensus', based on the view that the ECB alone should stabilize the union-wide economy, and address the question whether fiscal policy, modelled as feedback rules on output, that is, automatic stabilizers, adds value to the stabilization role played by monetary policy in the euro area as a whole. They perform this task by means of a small two-country model of EMU, estimated by using the synthetic euro-data collected over the period 1970–98. They find that the stabilizing effects of fiscal policy in response to EMU-wide shocks carry over to the case of asymmetric disturbances only if a significant home bias characterizes national consumption bundles. Thus, results suggest a novel approach to the philosophy of EMU macroeconomic policymaking. At the euro area level, the action of automatic stabilizers should be regarded as a useful complement to the ECB actions. The usual case for fiscal stabilization of within-EMU asymmetric shocks is confirmed only if the composition of national aggregate demand functions is sufficiently biased towards domestic production.

Part II presents three chapters devoted to the more specific issue of the correct measurement of fiscal stances, which is notoriously problematic in view of the correct implementation and assessment of fiscal rules. Jacques Melitz ('Measuring and assessing fiscal automatic stabilizers') compellingly argues that not just unemployment compensation, but many more categories of government spending (payments for pensions, sickness, subsistence, invalidity, childcare and subsidies of all sorts to firms), respond automatically and significantly to the cycle. In addition, if potential output is not deterministic but subject to supply shocks, the current practice that divides the official figures for cyclically adjusted budget balances by potential output produces inefficient estimates of discretionary fiscal policy. Accordingly, the paper provides separate estimates of the impact of the cycle on the levels of budget balances and the ratios of budget balances to output. The author concludes that the cyclical adjustments depend more on inertia in government spending on goods and services than they do on taxes (which are largely proportional to output), and still more on transfer payments. Besides calling for different series for discretionary fiscal policy, these results also raise questions about the general policy advice to 'let the automatic stabilizers work'.

'Getting measures of fiscal stance right for the new SGP', by Edoardo Gaffeo, Giuliana Passmani and Roberto Tamborini, casts the problem in a macroeconometric framework, their main point being that fiscal stances cannot be isolated from the concomitant evolution of the macroeconomic scenario, with particular regard to monetary policy, interest rates and the growth rate. The authors present an econometric estimate and simulations of a macroeconomic model of Italy and Germany which addresses three issues. First, interactions between monetary and fiscal rules are modelled and examined in a dynamic setting. Second, consistently with common perception and the new formulation of the SGP, the business cycle and the responses of policy variables are cast in terms of *growth gaps*, not gaps in levels, with respect to potential. Third, budgetary components (primary expenditure and total tax revenue) are examined as separate fiscal rules, which allows us to track the reaction of the fiscal stance to growth shocks more precisely. Then, simulations of negative growth shock highlight several pitfalls in current measures of fiscal ratios to GDP, and suggest more accurate assessment of fiscal stances.

Francesco Farina and Roberto Ricciuti ('Testing the fiscal theory of the price level for European countries: A cointegrated VAR approach') address the same issue from a different angle. They investigate the interaction, which took place in Europe during the last decades, between liabilities – the sum of public debt and monetary base – and budget surplus. Their econometric estimates confirm the hypothesis that the Ricardian Regime theorized by the Fiscal theory of the price level (FTPL) is even less likely to be found in the European countries than in the US case studied by Canzoneri *et al.* (2001). By analyzing the impulse part of the response functions through the estimate of cointegrated Vector autoregression (VAR), this econometric investigation finds that in European countries an innovation in surplus is not consistently correlated with the subsequent surpluses. Especially in 'high debt' countries, compliance with the *Tax Smoothing* principle is not found. By turning to the new SGP, the European Commission has pointed to a lessening of the obligations for the 'low debt' countries, while it keeps exerting a tough pressure on the 'high debt' countries for a rapid reduction of the liabilities/GDP ratio. For these latter FAs, no improvement in the rules, aimed to reconcile output stabilization and debt decumulation, has been envisaged.

Finally, Part III broadens the scope of macro-policy analysis to the dimensions of heterogeneity, interdependence and divergence within the euro area. To begin with, Jacques Le Cacheux and Francesco Saraceno ('one size does not fit all country size and fiscal policy in a monetary union') analyze the heterogeneous nature of the euro zone from the vantage point of the co-existence of small and large countries. Each group faces different incentives and constraints, thus adopting divergent strategies in the occurrence of common macroeconomic shocks. In particular, large countries have not been able, or willing, to abide by the HSGP rule for 'excessive deficits'. The authors propose a simple two-country model of the macroeconomics of a monetary union, in order to shed light on the role of size in the determination of fiscal policy stances. Since the re-interpretation of the Pact has not taken the size criterion into account, a comprehensive discussion of the EMU rules, starting with the SGP, cannot be further postponed.

The role of interdependence across EMU members due to the so-called financial spillovers of fiscal policy, which figures prominently in the traditional justifications for the SGP, is carefully examined by Stefano Schiavo in his paper 'Assessing financial spillovers of national fiscal policies'. By blending historical surveys and econometric tests, the chapter offers a multifaceted approach to this issue: encompassing the correct measure of financial spillover of fiscal imbalances (flow vs. stock), the marginal impact of national fiscal imbalances on EU total wealth, how national interest rate spreads over the bund rate react to news about national deficits. Overall, despite the strong co-movements displayed by European interest rates, empirical evidence does not support the idea that fiscal variables are a key determinant of these interrelations.

Jean Creel and Jacques Le Cacheux ('Inflation divergence and public deficits in a monetary union') reconsider the link between, on the one hand, domestic public debts and, on the other hand, average and domestic inflation rates in a monetary union. Introducing three realistic assumptions in a model recently proposed by

Beetsma and Vermeylen (2005), they show that the causation between inflation dynamics and public finances may go from the former to the latter. They conclude that inflation divergence may have been responsible for the diverging patterns of public finances in Europe, some countries having had to let their public deficits go adrift to cope with high inflation pressures. Despite the constitution of the euro area, homogeneous fiscal rules, like the ones considered in the SGP, are not optimal in this respect, at least insofar as inflation convergence has not been achieved.

Notes

1 We have developed this approach in Farina and Tamborini (2001).

2 In fact, denoting with d_t, b_t and b'_t the GDP ratios of debt, total balance and primary balance, respectively, the usual approximation for the change in the debt/GDP ratio yields

$$\Delta d_t \approx d_{t-1}(r_t - g_t) - b'_t$$

where r_t is the real interest rate and g_t is the the GDP growth rate. A typical SGP plan requires the government to commit itself to a certain $\Delta d^* \leq 0$ per year upon the estimated trend values of $\bar{r}$ and $\bar{g}$. This implies a path for the primary balance such that

$$b'^*_t = -\Delta d^* + d_{t-1}(\bar{r} - \bar{g})$$

As a conseqence, along this path the total balance will evolve according to

$$b_t \approx b'_t - r_t d_{t-1}$$
$$b^*_t = -\Delta d^* - d_{t-1}\bar{g}$$

Clearly, in a debt-control perspective, the year by year commitment on the decifit/GDP ratio has no connection with the 3% ceiling, but it is determined by the debt/GDP target and the estimated growth trend of GDP. For instance, along a debt reduction path, the prescription that the medium-term total budget should be ‘close to balance or in surplus’ only applies if the GDP growth trend is lower than the planned year rate of change of the debt/GDP ratio ($\bar{g} \leq -\Delta d^*/d_{t-1}$). On the other hand, *ceteris paribus*, a low growth trend requires more ambitious primary and total budget *surpluses*. At the same time, random shocks to the real interest rate or to the growth rate will give rise to deviations of the debt and total balance GDP ratios from their planned paths. This will occur by pure accounting factors, even if the government does not change its planned primary balances in response to shocks, as shown by the following expressions of the *actual* evolution of Δd_t and b_t upon introducing the planned primary balance b'^*_t and assuming that $r_t = \bar{r} + \varepsilon_{rt}$ and $g_t = \bar{g} + \varepsilon_{gt}$:

$$\Delta d_t - \Delta d^*_t = d_{t-1}(\varepsilon_{rt} - \varepsilon_{gt})$$
$$b_t - b^*_t = -d_{t-1}\varepsilon_{rt}$$

In this framework, positive shocks to the real interest rate and negative shocks to the growth rate bear the main responsibility for debt and budget GDP ratios worse than planned. These ratios will deteriorate to a greater extent if the primary balance also displays a cyclical component.

References

Andersen, T. M. and Dogonowsky, R. R. (1999), 'Social insurance and the public budget', in Hughes-Hallett, A. J., Hutchinson, M. M., Hougaard Jensen, S. E. (eds), *Fiscal Aspects of European Monetary Integration*, Cambridge: Cambridge University Press.

Beetsma, R., Debrun, X. and Klaassen, F. (2001), 'Is fiscal policy coordination in EMU desirable?', *Swedish Economic Policy Review*, 8: 57–98.

Blanchard, O. and Giavazzi, F. (2003), 'Macroeconomic effects of regulation and deregulation in goods and labour markets', *Quarterly Journal of Economics*, 118: 879–907.

Blanchard, O. and Perotti, R. (2002), 'An empirical characterization of the dynamic effects of shocks to government spending and taxes on output', *Quarterly Journal of Economics*, 117: 1329–68.

Buti, M. and Franco, D. (2005), *Fiscal policy in Economic and Monetary Union*, Cheltenham: Edward Elgar.

Canzoneri, M., Cumby, R. and Diba, B. (2001), 'Is the price level determined by the needs of fiscal solvency?', *American Economic Review*, 91: 1221–36.

De Grauwe, P. (2006), 'What have we learnt about monetary integration since the Maastricht Treaty?', *Journal of Common Market Studies*, 44: 711–30.

Dixit, A. and Lambertini, L. (2003), 'Symbiosis of monetary and fiscal policies in a monetary union', *Journal of International Economics*, 60: 235–47.

European Commission (2006), 'Public finances in EMU 2006', *European Economic Reports and Studies*, 3.

Farina, F. and Tamborini, R. (2001), 'Macroeconomic stabilization policies in Europe under the new regime of monetary union', Quaderni del Dipartimento di Economia Politica, Università di Siena, n. 317. [Social Science Research Network (SSRN), Macroeconomics, http://papers.ssrn.com.]

—— (2004), ' "Set a sufficiently ambitious budget target and let the automatic stabilizers work." Can it really work in the European Monetary Union?', *Open Economies Review*, 15: 143–68.

Farina, F. and Ricciuti, R. (2006), 'Fiscal rules and the evaluation of fiscal stances in Europe', *Revue de l'OFCE*, 4: 275–301.

Fitoussi, J. P. (2002), *La régle et la choix*, Paris: Editions de Seuil.

Galí, J. (2005), 'Modern perspectives on fiscal stabilization policies', *CESifo Economic Studies*, 51: 587–99.

Galí, J. and Perotti, R. (2003), 'Fiscal policy and monetary integration in Europe', *Economic Policy*, n. 37: 535–72.

Giavazzi, F. and Pagano, M. (1996), 'Non Keynesian effects of fiscal policy changes: international evidence and Swedish experience', *Swedish Economic Policy Review*, 3: 67–103.

Gros, D. (2004), 'The nine lives of the Stability Pact', Special Report of the CEPS Macroeconomic Policy Group, Bruxelles.

Hughes-Hallett, A., Lewis, J., and von Hagen, J. (2003), *Fiscal Policy in Europe, 1991–2003. An Evidence-based Analysis*, London: CEPR.

Padoa Schioppa, T. (1992), *l'Europa verso l'unione monetaria. Dallo Sme al Trattato di Maastricht*, Turin: Einaudi.

Tabellini, G. and Wyplosz, C. (2004), 'Supply-side policy coordination in the European Union', *Swedish Economic Policy Review*, 13: 101–56.

Tamborini, R. (2001), 'Living in the EMU: Interest rates, prices and the adjustment of payments in a monetary union', *Journal of Common Market Studies*, 39: 123–46.

—— (2004) 'The "Brussels Consensus" on macroeconomic stabilization policies in the EMU: A critical assessment', in F. Torres, A. Verdun, C. Zilioli, H. Zimmermang (eds) *Governing EMU: Political, Economic, Historical and Legal Aspects*, Florence: European University Press.

Tamborini, R. and Targetti, F. (2005), 'The crisis of the Stability Pact and a proposal', in Arestis, P., McCombie, J. and Vickerman, R. (eds), *Growth and Economic Development. Essays in Honour of A. P. Tirwall*, Aldershot: Edward Elgar, forthcoming.

Wyplosz, C. (2006), 'European Monetary Union: The dark sides of a major success', Economic Policy, 46: 207–61.

Part I

Macroeconomic governance in the EMU

2 Fiscal policy and implementation in EMU

From Maastricht to the SGP reform and beyond[1]

M. Catenaro and R. Morris

2.1 Introduction

Prior to Economic and Monetary Union (EMU), fiscal policies in Europe exhibited severe deficit and debt biases. The Maastricht Treaty and the Stability and Growth Pact (SGP) introduced a fiscal framework aimed at correcting such biases and ensuring sound budgetary positions in EMU. However, following significant consolidation efforts in the run-up to EMU, the early years of the millennium witnessed a re-emergence of fiscal imbalances, and the SGP came under increasing strain and criticism. Against this background, the fiscal rules have recently been revised and are now more tailored to economic and country-specific circumstances. This may enhance ownership but also presents new implementation challenges.

In the light of the SGP reform, this chapter examines how the EU fiscal rules have evolved over time and how they have been implemented from the adoption of the Maastricht Treaty to the present day, including initial experiences with the implementation of the reformed Pact. Section 2.2 starts by providing an overview of the EU fiscal rules and their implementation since the adoption of the Maastricht Treaty up until the reform of the Pact. Section 2.3 explains and assesses the Pact reform. Section 2.4 then makes an attempt to interpret the first experiences with the implementation of the new framework. All in all, it is concluded that implementation has been smooth and consistent, but with consolidation requirements that are rather lenient while fiscal targets and projections point to only slow and back-loaded progress towards sound public finances in many countries. The assessment of the implementation of the revised rules is therefore mixed and it remains to be seen whether the new rules will be implemented in a manner that is sufficient to ensure fiscal sustainability in EMU.

2.2 The EU fiscal rules and their implementation

2.2.1 From Maastricht to the SGP

In the decade and a half before the signing of the Maastricht Treaty (in 1992) the aggregate debt/GDP ratio of the euro area effectively doubled from around

30% to almost 60%. Similarly, large increases in debt ratios also occurred in other (non-European) industrialized countries, such as the United States and Japan.

Over time, persistently high deficits and rising debt levels such as those experienced in the late 1970s and 1980s are likely to have a detrimental impact on economic stability and growth. Profligate fiscal policies can also impede the effective conduct of a stability-oriented monetary policy. Among other things, high deficit and debt levels may reduce the scope for governments to use fiscal policy as a tool for stabilizing domestic demand, since deficits that are increasing from already high levels could spark fears concerning the sustainability of public finances. Excessive government borrowing may contribute to inflationary pressures and put upward pressure on interest rates, which would crowd out private investment. Higher debt also increases the interest payment burden with the result that government spending tends to be diverted from more productive uses.

In EMU, the sharing of a single currency implies that the deficit bias is likely to be greater than would otherwise be the case (as at least one disciplining mechanism, the nominal exchange rate, has been removed). Moreover, given the combination of a single monetary policy with decentralized fiscal policies, some kind of implicit co-ordination mechanism is needed to ensure fiscal policies are mutually consistent and do not threaten macroeconomic stability and cohesion of the euro area.[2]

To address concerns that large deficits and rising debt could threaten the smooth functioning of EMU, the Maastricht Treaty introduced into the European Community Treaty (henceforth the 'Treaty') a number of rules aimed at disciplining EU Member States' fiscal policies. These include the prohibition of monetary financing of deficits by the European System of Central Banks (ESCB) (Article 101) and the so-called no-bail-out clause, which states that European institutions or Member States shall not be liable for or assume another Member State's financial obligations (Article 103). The former contributes to a clear separation between monetary policy and fiscal policy, which should ensure that a stability-oriented monetary policy is not directly compromised by excessive government borrowing. The latter makes clear that in EMU, Member States do not have to bear the cost of financing other Member States' debt. This should, in principle, encourage financial markets to distinguish between different euro area governments' debt instruments, thereby strengthening financial market discipline on fiscal policies.

In addition to these basic safeguards, the Treaty obliges Member States to avoid 'excessive deficits' assessed against 'reference values' of 3% of GDP for the deficit and 60% of GDP for debt (Article 104). The sustainability of a government's financial position, in the sense of not having a deficit that is 'excessive' as defined by Article 104 of the Treaty, is one of the convergence criteria for adoption of the euro. Moreover, breaches of the reference values result in the initiation of an Excessive Deficit Procedure (EDP) with the aim of examining and, if necessary, correcting the situation. For Member States that have adopted the single currency, this procedure can ultimately lead to financial sanctions. However, the procedure as laid down in the Treaty is in no sense mechanistic, and ultimately leaves it to the discretion of the EU Council of Ministers of Economic Affairs and Finance (henceforth the 'ECOFIN Council') to decide whether to take action.

In the years that followed the signing of the Maastricht Treaty, the 3% reference value served as a relatively simple yardstick of the success of fiscal policy and received considerable prominence in the public debate. It greatly facilitated monitoring of fiscal performance by the public and by financial markets, since in most countries the objective of qualifying for adoption of the euro attracted widespread support. A number of governments staked their reputations on bringing deficits below 3% in time to be among the first wave of countries to adopt the euro. As a consequence, fiscal balances in most EU Member States improved significantly in the run-up to EMU (see Table 2.1).[3] For the euro area as a whole, the general government deficit was reduced from 4.5% of GDP in 1991 to below 3% in 1997. The structural improvement in the budget balance was even more significant, amounting to more than 3 percentage points of GDP.

Nonetheless, concerns remained that the fiscal rules as set out in the Maastricht Treaty would not provide enough of a 'stick' to ensure fiscal discipline once the 'carrot' of participation in the single currency had been eaten. There were concerns that compliance with the 3% of GDP reference value may not be sufficient to maintain or reduce debt to reasonable levels. There were also fears that fiscal

Table 2.1 Fiscal consolidation in the run-up to EMU (as a % of GDP)

	1991	*1992*	*1993*	*1994*	*1995*	*1996*	*1997*
General government budget balance							
Belgium	−6.0	−6.8	−7.0	−4.7	−4.4	−3.8	−2.0
Germany	−3.2	−2.7	−3.4	−2.5	−3.2	−3.3	−2.6
Greece	−11.4	−12.6	−13.6	−9.9	−10.2	−7.4	−6.6
Spain	−4.2	−3.9	−6.6	−6.0	−6.5	−4.8	−3.3
France	−2.0	−3.8	−5.6	−5.6	−5.5	−4.1	−3.0
Ireland	−2.2	−2.4	−2.3	−1.5	−2.0	0.0	1.3
Italy	−9.7	−9.2	−9.1	−8.8	−7.4	−7.0	−2.7
Luxembourg	1.5	0.6	1.3	2.3	2.4	1.2	3.7
Netherlands	−2.7	−3.7	−3.1	−3.6	−4.3	−1.9	−1.2
Austria	−2.9	−1.9	−4.1	−4.8	−5.6	−3.9	−1.7
Portugal	−5.5	−2.7	−5.6	−5.6	−5.2	−4.5	−3.4
Finland	−1.4	−5.6	−7.8	−6.0	−6.2	−3.5	−1.2
Euro area	**−4.5**	**−4.7**	**−5.5**	**−5.0**	**−5.0**	**−4.2**	**−2.6**
Cyclically adjusted budget balance							
Euro area	**−5.5**	**−5.2**	**−4.7**	**−4.3**	**−4.5**	**−3.5**	**−2.1**
General government debt							
Euro area	**57.5**	**59.3**	**65.1**	**67.8**	**72.4**	**74.1**	**73.6**

Source: European Commission, AMECO database.

Notes

1 The figures presented in the table are those available under the ESA 95 accounting framework at the end of 2006. They show that in 1997, the government deficit stood above the 3% of GDP reference value in two countries that entered EMU in 1999 (Spain and Portugal). The figures available at the beginning of 1998, when the decision on the countries entering EMU was taken, were based on ESA 79. Those figures showed deficits that complied with the 3% of GDP limit.

2 Euro area refers to the composition until 31 December 2006, thus comprising the 12 Member States listed in the table.

policies would become pro-cyclical if Member States were forced to increase taxes or reduce spending during recessions in order to keep their deficits below 3% of GDP. Such concerns led to the negotiation and signing of the SGP, which sought to put more "flesh on the bones" of the fiscal framework of the Maastricht Treaty.[4]

2.2.2 The 'original' SGP

The SGP aims to prevent excessive deficits through policy surveillance and co-ordination, and to deter as well as correct excessive deficits by providing clear rules for the application of the EDP. It is primarily based on two Council Regulations, which in accordance with their aims and functions are often referred to as the 'preventive arm' and the 'corrective arm' (or 'deterrent arm') of the Pact.[5] These were backed by a solemn declaration of the European Heads of State or Government, which expressed Member States' political commitment to implementing the rules in a strict and timely manner.[6]

Under the preventive arm, Member States submit annual stability and convergence programmes, which present information regarding their economic and fiscal policies.[7] These programmes include in particular the 'medium-term objective' of fiscal policy and, where applicable, the adjustment path towards it. In its original form, the SGP specified that the medium-term objective (MTO) should be a budget that is 'close to balance or in surplus'. The rationale was both to ensure fiscal positions that would be sustainable in the long run while also creating sufficient room for fiscal policy to help smooth output fluctuations in the short run without breaching the 3% of GDP deficit ceiling.[8] The generic term 'close to balance or in surplus' reflected the fact that while close-to-balance budgets should be, as a rule, sufficient to ensure sustainable fiscal positions, some countries might wish to target surpluses with a view to reducing debt ratios more rapidly and so create room to accommodate the future fiscal burden of ageing populations. The Member States' stability programmes are assessed by the Commission and may be examined by the ECOFIN Council, which can choose to make public its opinion on each programme. The preventive arm also includes an early-warning device whereby the Council can issue recommendations to Member States to take corrective measures if budgetary developments point to the risk of an excessive deficit. Overall, however, the emphasis of the preventive arm is on 'soft' procedures which foster fiscal discipline and policy co-ordination through multilateral surveillance and peer pressure.

By contrast, the corrective arm relies on stricter and more formal procedures designed to enforce fiscal discipline in countries where deficits have become excessive and are therefore giving rise to greater concern. To this end, the EDP already outlined in the Treaty was clarified and 'speeded up', in particular with regard to the following:

- *Exceptional circumstances*: The conditions under which a deficit above 3% could be deemed exceptional and temporary (and therefore not excessive) were defined strictly as cases in which a country experiences an annual fall in real GDP of at least 2%. A fall in real GDP of between 0.75% and 2% could also be deemed exceptional in the light of supporting evidence submitted by the Member State in question regarding the accumulated output loss and the abruptness of the downturn.

- *The deadline for the correction of excessive deficits*: It was specified that the correction of an excessive deficit should be completed 'in the year following its identification unless there are special circumstances', although the nature of such special circumstances was not explicitly defined.
- *The timing of procedural steps*: A timetable with precise deadlines for the various steps of the procedure was laid out whereby, in the event of non-compliance by a Member State with the recommendations and decisions of the Council, the time between the reporting of a deficit above 3% of GDP and the imposition of sanctions should be no more than ten months.
- *The nature of sanctions*: It was clarified that, if the Council were to impose sanctions on a Member State, a non-interest-bearing deposit would be required which, in the event of a further two years of non-compliance, would, as a rule, be converted into a fine.

With these clarifications, the corrective arm of the SGP provided for a strict and timely application of all elements of the EDP. Nonetheless, it fell short of the original proposal of the German government, which had supported a fully automatic sanctioning mechanism outside the standard Treaty framework (Stark, 2001). Such automatism was considered inappropriate by some Member States. The SGP that was finally agreed instead took the form of EU secondary legislation with decisions to be taken within the standard legislative framework (i.e. Council recommendations or decisions, adopted by qualified majority, on the basis of recommendations by the Commission). The Commission therefore preserved its 'right of initiative', while the Council ultimately retained discretion in taking decisions within an overall rules-based framework.

2.2.3 Experience under the original Pact

Notwithstanding the gradual fiscal consolidation made during the mid-1990s, by the time the SGP entered into force shortly before the introduction of the single currency in January 1999, most euro area Member States were still some way from achieving medium-term budgetary positions that were close to balance or in surplus. Further consolidation was therefore necessary in order to create room for the operation of the automatic fiscal stabilizers while maintaining a safety margin with respect to the 3% deficit ceiling (Buti *et al.*, 1998).

In the early years of Stage Three of EMU, nominal budget balances generally continued to improve and, by 2000, the euro area budget deficit was reduced to just 1% of GDP. However, fiscal consolidation slowed down and, from 2001 onwards, the euro area budget balance ratio started to deteriorate, increasing to above 3% of GDP by 2003, with only a small decline back below this level in 2004 (see Table 2.2). This return to higher deficits in the euro area needs to be seen in the context of the slowdown in economic growth and, more importantly, consolidation fatigue, which started soon after the launch of the single currency. In some countries, structural budgetary positions started to deteriorate as early

Table 2.2 Fiscal developments under the Stability and Growth Pact (as a % of GDP)

	1998	*1999*	*2000*	*2001*	*2002*	*2003*	*2004*
General government budget balance							
Belgium	−0.8	−0.5	0.1	0.4	0.0	0.0	0.0
Germany	−2.2	−1.5	−1.1	−2.8	−3.7	−4.0	−3.7
Greece	−4.3	−3.4	−4.0	−5.4	−5.2	−6.1	−7.8
Spain	−3.1	−1.3	−0.9	−0.5	−0.3	−0.0	−0.2
France	−2.6	−1.7	−1.5	−1.6	−3.2	−4.2	−3.7
Ireland	2.4	2.7	4.6	0.8	−0.6	0.3	1.5
Italy	−2.8	−1.7	−2.0	−3.1	−2.9	−3.5	−3.4
Luxembourg	3.4	3.4	6.0	6.1	2.1	0.3	−1.1
Netherlands	−0.9	0.4	1.3	−0.2	−2.0	−3.1	−1.8
Austria	−2.3	−2.2	−1.8	0.0	−0.5	−1.6	−1.2
Portugal	−3.0	−2.7	−3.2	−4.3	−2.9	−2.9	−3.2
Finland	1.7	1.6	6.9	5.0	4.1	2.5	2.3
Euro area	**−2.2**	**−1.3**	**−1.0**	**−1.8**	**−2.5**	**−3.1**	**−2.8**
Cyclically adjusted budget balance							
Belgium	−0.4	−0.8	−1.0	0.2	−0.1	0.5	0.0
Germany	−1.8	−1.3	0.6	−3.4	−3.6	−3.4	−3.2
Greece	−3.4	−2.6	−3.4	−4.8	−5.1	−6.4	−8.4
Spain	−2.8	−1.6	−1.8	−1.4	−0.7	−0.1	0.0
France	−2.5	−2.1	−2.6	−2.5	−3.6	−4.1	−3.7
Ireland	1.9	1.1	2.3	−0.9	−1.8	−0.3	1.4
Italy	−2.5	−1.6	−1.7	−4.1	−3.4	−3.5	−3.3
Luxembourg	4.1	2.9	4.1	5.1	1.4	1.0	−0.2
Netherlands	−1.3	−0.9	0.2	−1.4	−1.9	−2.1	0.9
Austria	−2.5	−2.8	−2.5	0.3	−0.3	−0.9	−0.7
Portugal	−3.4	−3.5	−4.2	−5.5	−3.5	−2.4	−2.6
Finland	0.6	0.6	5.4	4.1	4.1	3.3	3.0
Euro area	**−2.0**	**−1.5**	**−0.9**	**−2.6**	**−2.8**	**−2.7**	**−2.5**
General government debt							
Euro area	**73.2**	**72.0**	**69.3**	**68.3**	**68.2**	**69.3**	**69.8**

Source: European Commission, AMECO database. Data exclude receipts from the sale of Universal Mobile Telecommunications System (UMTS) licenses.

Note
The figures presented in the table are those available under the ESA 95 accounting framework at the end of 2006. They therefore include all the statistical revisions that have taken place since 1998 in the euro area countries (in particular, in Greece and Portugal).

as 2000 since, in a context of favourable economic growth, tax cuts were not matched by equivalent expenditure reductions. While the fiscal consolidation that was achieved during the 1990s was largely attributable to an increase in the revenue/GDP ratio, which, for the euro area as a whole, rose from 44% in 1991 to 47% in 1999 (see Figure 2.1), after 1999 about two-thirds of the earlier increase in the revenue/GDP ratio was reversed.[9] Meanwhile, primary expenditure, which had been reduced by more than 1% of GDP in the run-up to EMU, started to increase again after 1999.

A key mistake that was made by many Member States in the early years following the adoption of the euro was to fail to take advantage of 'good times' to achieve

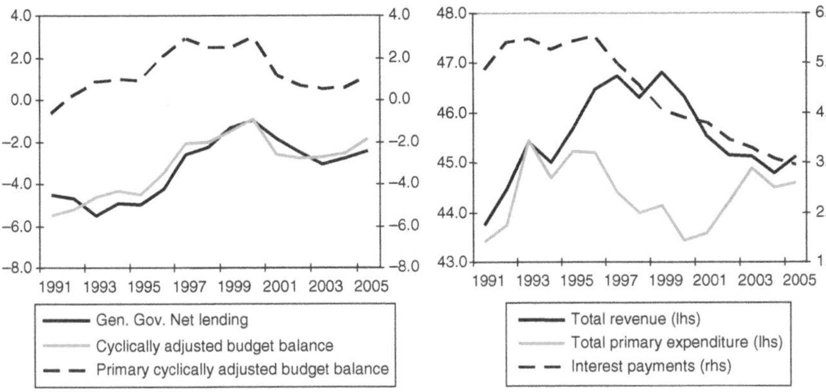

Figure 2.1 Euro area fiscal developments, 1991–2005: determinants and components (as a % of GDP).

Source: European Commission.

sound fiscal positions. This may have been partly because improving nominal budget balances in the early years of the Pact's implementation initially contributed to the false perception that fiscal positions were also getting better. In theory, the evolution of cyclically adjusted budget balances should have alerted policy-makers to the fiscal loosening that was taking place. In practice, however, estimates of the cyclically adjusted budget balance are prone to error due to the difficulty of measuring the cyclical position of the economy in real time and the sensitivity to the cycle of some budget items. This was especially true in the early years of the single currency when estimates of trend or potential output growth for many countries proved to be over-optimistic. In cases where potential growth is over-estimated, there is likely to be a bias towards estimating negative output gaps (i.e. concluding that actual output is below potential) and a corresponding tendency to underestimate (overestimate) the cyclically adjusted deficit (surplus). In addition, methods used for the cyclical adjustment of fiscal variables do not always capture all temporary influences on the budget balance. For example, the impact of asset prices on tax revenues is not well captured by current methods and hence there is a tendency for cyclically adjusted budget balances to paint an overly positive picture of the true state of the public finances during asset price booms such as that related to the 'dot.com bubble' of the late 1990s.

The deterioration of budget balances in many countries from 2001 onwards very quickly put the SGP to the test. Six euro area Member States have incurred excessive deficits since 1999: Portugal in 2001 (and again in 2005), Germany and France in 2002, the Netherlands and Greece in 2003, and Italy in 2004. Among these, only the Netherlands succeeded in correcting its excessive deficit in a timely and durable manner. Some Member States resorted to temporary measures to comply nominally with the rules. Moreover, owing to large statistical revisions, some excessive deficits were only identified several years after the 3% of GDP reference value was breached from an *ex post* perspective, after statistical corrections led to upward revisions of earlier deficit figures.[10] Typically, this took place when initially reported deficits coincided with significant adverse deficit-debt adjustments, notably in Greece, Italy and Portugal.

Faced with deteriorating fiscal positions in a number of countries, the ECOFIN Council appeared reluctant to implement the Pact in a strict manner. The first evidence of this came in early 2002, when the Council rejected Commission recommendations to issue 'early warnings' to Germany and Portugal to take action to prevent their deficits from exceeding the 3% reference value. Instead, the Council took the view that such a formal step was unnecessary in the light of commitments by these countries to take corrective measures.[11] In both cases, however, the 3% limit was breached and EDPs were subsequently launched.[12]

An even more significant deviation from the rules and procedures of the Pact came in November 2003, in the context of the EDPs against Germany and France. Having been given until 2004 to correct their excessive deficits, it became clear by autumn 2003 that the measures taken by both countries would not be sufficient to comply with the Council's recommendations. The Commission recommended that the Council should step up pressure on both countries by issuing 'notices' (i.e. one step in the EDP before sanctions), while also suggesting an extension of the 2004 deadline by one more year.[13] However, the Council failed to achieve the necessary qualified majority to adopt these decisions. Instead, it issued 'conclusions' in which it put the procedures in abeyance in the light of commitments expressed by Germany and France to take effective action to correct their excessive deficits by 2005.[14] These conclusions were subsequently challenged by the Commission and annulled by the European Court of Justice (ECJ) on the grounds that the Council had not followed the rules and procedures as set out in the Treaty. In particular, the ECJ made clear that the Council could not, by itself, take initiatives in the absence of an appropriate recommendation by the Commission and could not replace a 'procedure' with 'political conclusions'.[15]

It would be wrong, however, to paint a totally negative picture of the experience under the original SGP. Fiscal deficit ratios in the euro area did not return to their pre-Maastricht levels and earlier trends of rapidly rising public debt and expenditure ratios were mostly brought to a halt. A number of countries did moreover succeed in complying with the rules. Among these, Belgium, Spain and Austria all consolidated their fiscal positions further and managed to reach close to balance or in surplus budgetary positions. Meanwhile, Ireland, Luxembourg and Finland, while loosening fiscal policy, did so having entered EMU with large budget surpluses, and their fiscal positions have remained broadly sound. Also, the Netherlands, after breaching the deficit ceiling in 2003, has since turned this round to again reach a close-to-balance budgetary position. While overall fiscal consolidation may have largely stalled after 2000, there was no generalized or significant loosening of fiscal policies in the euro area. It can therefore be argued that, even if the original SGP did not fully attain its objectives, it did have a constraining effect on fiscal policies.

Another criticism that was made of the SGP in its original form was that it gave rise to pro-cyclical fiscal policies. This was due to the fact that its 'softer' preventive arm failed to ensure that countries reached sound fiscal positions in good times, while the much 'harder' corrective arm then forced fiscal retrenchment in bad times. In truth, however, this may be a criticism of the failure to implement the Pact correctly rather than any shortcoming in the rules themselves. To illustrate this point, Figure 2.2 plots changes of the fiscal stance as measured by the change in

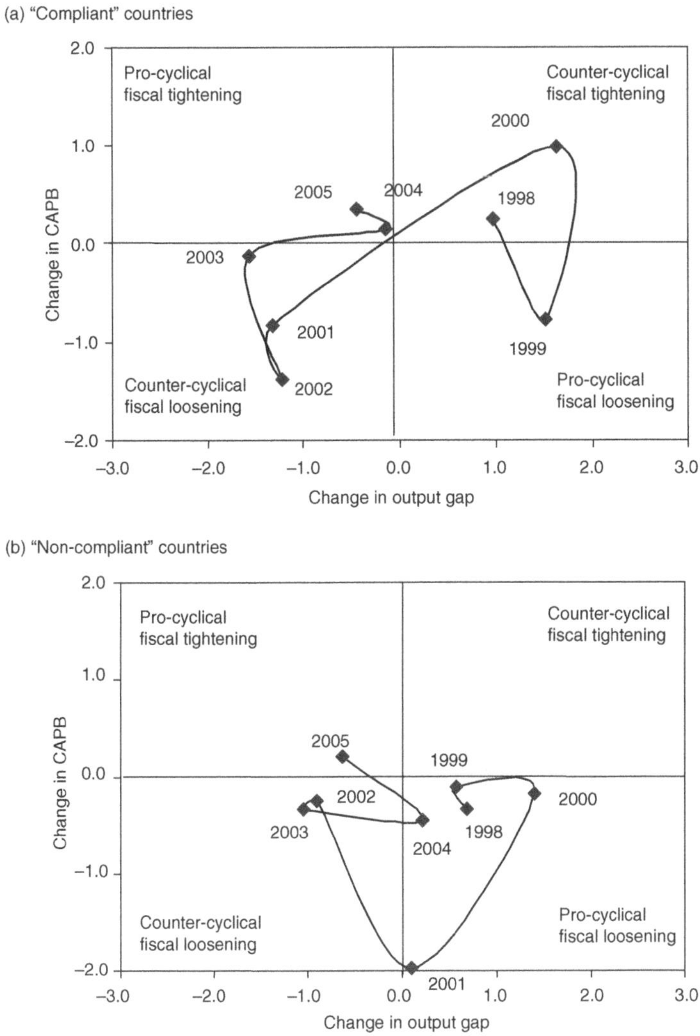

Figure 2.2 Fiscal policy stance under the SGP.

Source: European Commission and own calculations.

the cyclically adjusted primary balance (CAPB) in response to cyclical conditions, measured by the change in the output gap, distinguishing between seven 'compliant' countries (Belgium, Spain, Ireland, Luxembourg, the Netherlands, Austria and Finland) and five 'non-compliant' countries (Germany, Greece, France, Italy and Portugal) and taking the simple average for each group. Figure 2.2 shows that in the countries that have generally complied with the requirements of the SGP, this has created the necessary room for fiscal policy to play a role in smoothing output fluctuations. By contrast, in the countries that have struggled to respect the 3% deficit limit, fiscal policy has tended to respond less well to cyclical developments. More specifically, the difficulty that some countries have encountered in complying with the rules owes at least in part to a pro-cyclical loosening of fiscal policy during the upturn of 1999–2000.

2.3 The 2005 reform of the SGP

As actual fiscal developments moved budgetary positions further away from the Pact's requirements, and political commitment to the rules waned, criticisms of the SGP gained prominence and became more widely accepted.

A frequent criticism of the original SGP was that it placed too much emphasis on formal compliance with rules and took too little account of economic circumstances. It was argued that the close-to-balance or in-surplus objective, which was generally interpreted as implying the maintenance of a broadly balanced budget (in cyclically adjusted terms), failed to consider the specific circumstances of each Member State, in particular with regard to long-term fiscal soundness, public investment needs or the costs of structural reforms. According to this view, it does not make sense for countries with, for example, widely diverging debt levels to target exactly the same budget balance. The emergence of excessive deficits in a number of countries suggested that the mechanisms underlying the preventive arm (i.e. monitoring and peer pressure) were too weak to ensure progress towards sound fiscal positions. Meanwhile, when countries did incur excessive deficits, the Pact's corrective arm was criticized for requiring prompt corrective action regardless of economic growth considerations. In particular, some critics of the Pact found it inappropriate to require Member States to correct excessive deficits by tightening fiscal policy during periods of low growth, since this could dampen prospects for economic recovery. The Pact was also criticized for not paying sufficient attention to debt developments, as it did not clarify the application of the debt criterion of the Treaty.

According to advocates of reform, such shortcomings contributed to a lack of commitment and ownership on the part of Member States, the Commission and the ECOFIN Council, which could partly explain difficulties in applying the rules and procedures. To address this, numerous proposals to improve or amend the rules were put forward. Prominent among these have been those suggesting more focus on the quality of public finances (Fitoussi and Creel, 2002; Blanchard and Giavazzi, 2004), to shift the emphasis of the SGP away from deficits and onto debt and sustainability (Buiter and Grafe, 2002; Pisani-Ferry, 2002), or to replace numerical rules with stronger fiscal institutions and market discipline (Wyplosz, 2005).

While some commentators called for a complete overhaul of the rules, others defended the *status quo* or at most called for more incremental adjustment (Buti *et al.*, 2003; Bini Smaghi, 2004). Defenders of the existing rules argued that they were sufficient to preserve the sustainability of public finances in EMU while also allowing room for the full operation of automatic stabilizers (Marin, 2002). The importance of relatively simple rules and limited discretion under the original SGP was stressed in particular with a view to supporting market and public monitoring of fiscal policies (Schuknecht, 2004). According to this view, the problem was not the rules *per se*, but deficient enforcement that undermined the deterrent power of the Pact (such as the need for a qualified majority in the Council and the problem of 'sinners judging sinners'). This called for improvements in the implementation and enforcement of the rules rather than changes in the rules themselves (Gros *et al.*, 2004).

Prior to the SGP reform, there had already been a number of incremental refinements to the way the Pact was implemented. Over time, more attention came to be paid to the influence of the cycle, with cyclically adjusted budget balances acquiring greater prominence, at least under the preventive arm. In November 2002, the Commission issued a communication with a broad set of proposals, some of which were subsequently adopted by the ECOFIN Council.[16] In this context, the initial emphasis on setting target dates for the achievement of balanced budgets was replaced by a Eurogroup commitment to annual improvements of underlying fiscal balances by at least 0.5% of GDP (see below). Following the procedural impasse in the context of the EDPs against Germany and France, however, the Commission decided to launch a more wide-ranging discussion on reforming the SGP, including the option of changing the Council Regulations.[17] The Commission's proposals, along with other suggestions, were discussed at length by Member States in late 2004 and early 2005. The outcome of these discussions was an agreement to make changes to the SGP as set out in the ECOFIN Council Report of March 2005 and later implemented via amendments to Council Regulations 1466/97 and 1467/97.[18] The reform adopted by the ECOFIN Council left the structure of the SGP in place and did not alter the fundamental elements of the EU fiscal framework enshrined in the Treaty, such as the 3% and 60% reference values, which were outside its scope. Within this overall framework, however, the reform did introduce a number of significant changes.

As to the changes affecting the preventive arm, the reform has introduced various refinements to the earlier provisions concerning the setting of and progress towards sound medium-term budgetary positions and to the elements that are to be taken into account when assessing Member States' fiscal positions. These include:

The definition of the medium-term budgetary objective: Rather than being required to target 'close-to-balance or in-surplus' budgetary positions, each Member State now presents its own country-specific MTO in its stability or convergence programme, which is then assessed by the Council. These country-specific MTOs are differentiated and may differ from a position of close-to-balance or in-surplus. They should provide a safety margin with respect to the 3% of GDP reference value, ensure rapid progress towards sustainability and, taking this into account, should allow room for budgetary manoeuvre, particularly with regard to the need for public investment. For euro area and ERM II Member States, an initial range for country-specific MTOs, in cyclically adjusted terms and net of one-off and temporary measures, has been set between −1% of GDP and 'in balance or surplus'.

The adjustment path to the MTO: Member States that have not yet achieved their MTOs are expected to take steps to do so over the cycle. To this end, euro area and ERM II Member States should as a benchmark pursue an annual adjustment in cyclically adjusted terms, net of one-off and temporary measures, of 0.5% of GDP. The adjustment effort should be greater in good times, but could be more limited in bad times. Good times are defined as 'periods where output exceeds its potential level, taking into account tax elasticities', while the Code of Conduct specifies that the 'change in the output gap could also be considered, especially when the output gap is estimated to be close to zero'. Member States that do not follow the required adjustment path should explain the reasons for not doing so in their programme update, and the Commission is entitled to issue 'policy advice' to encourage Member States to stick to the adjustment path.

Taking into account structural reforms: Member States may be allowed to deviate from the MTO or the adjustment path towards it if they undertake structural reforms, and in this context special attention is paid to pension reforms which introduce multi-pillar systems that include a mandatory, fully funded pillar. However, 'only reforms which have direct long-term cost-saving effects, including by raising potential growth, and therefore a verifiable positive impact on the long-term sustainability of public finances, will be taken into account,' and a safety margin with respect to the 3% reference value must be preserved at all times.

With regard to the corrective arm, the changes introduced go in the direction of introducing more flexibility into the EDP, in particular by relaxing, adding specificity to or clarifying the availability of various escape clauses. The changes include:

- *The definition of a 'severe economic downturn'*: The benchmark for a severe economic downturn is now a negative annual real GDP growth rate or an accumulated loss of output during a protracted period of very low annual real GDP growth relative to potential growth.
- *Specification of the 'other relevant factors'*: The Treaty specifies that, in its report that constitutes the first step of an EDP, the Commission should take into account '*all other relevant factors, including the medium-term economic and budgetary position of the Member State*'. However, neither the Treaty nor the original SGP further elaborated what these other relevant factors might be. The reformed SGP now more explicitly spells out the relevant factors that should be taken into account. Regarding the medium-term economic position, these include in particular potential growth, the prevailing cyclical conditions, the implementation of the Lisbon Agenda, and policies to foster research and

development and innovation. Relevant developments in the medium-term budgetary position include fiscal consolidation efforts in 'good times', debt sustainability, public investment, and the overall quality of public finances. Attention should also be given to any other factors which, in the opinion of the Member State concerned, are relevant to a comprehensive assessment of the excess over the reference value in qualitative terms. Special consideration will be given to budgetary efforts towards increasing or maintaining a high level of financial contributions with the aim of fostering international solidarity and achieving European policy goals, notably the unification of Europe, if they have a detrimental effect on growth and the fiscal burden of the Member State. However, when assessing whether or not a deficit above 3% of GDP is to be considered excessive, the other relevant factors are only taken into account if the general government deficit remains 'close to' the reference value, and if the excess over the reference value is 'temporary'. If the Council has decided that an excessive deficit exists, the other relevant factors will be considered when issuing recommendations or notices to the Member State concerned.

- *Extension of procedural deadlines*: A number of procedural deadlines have been extended. These include the deadline for the Council to issue its recommendation to the Member State in excessive deficit (extended from three to four months after the date on which the excessive deficit was first reported), the deadline for effective action in response to a Council recommendation (extended from four to six months), the deadline for the Council to issue a notice if it has established that no effective action has been taken in response to its recommendation (extended from one month to two months), and the deadline for taking effective action in response to a notice (extended from two to four months).
- *Extension of the deadlines for the correction of excessive deficits*: The standard deadline for correcting an excessive deficit remains the 'year following its identification unless there are special circumstances'. However, the consideration of whether there are special circumstances justifying an extension by one year should take into account a balanced overall assessment of the 'other relevant factors' mentioned above. Moreover, the initial deadline for correction should be set such that the Member State with an excessive deficit will have to achieve a minimum annual improvement in its cyclically adjusted balance of 0.5% of GDP as a benchmark, net of one-off and temporary measures.
- *Unexpected adverse events and repeated recommendations or notices*: The original SGP did not explicitly provide for the reissuance of Council recommendations or for the extension of deadlines for the correction of excessive deficits, and these issues were at the heart of the procedural deadlock in the EDPs for Germany and France. The SGP reform has now clarified such matters by explicitly stating that if effective action has been taken in compliance with a recommendation under Article 104(7) of the Treaty or a notice under Article 104(9) of the Treaty, and if '*unexpected adverse economic events with major unfavourable consequences for government finances*' occur after the adoption of the recommendation or notice, the Council may decide to issue

a revised recommendation or notice, which may also extend the deadline for the correction of the excessive deficit by one year.

- *Increasing the focus on debt and sustainability*: The ECOFIN Council report of March 2005 also called for a strengthening of debt surveillance, for example by applying the Treaty concept of a debt ratio that is 'sufficiently diminishing and approaching the reference value at a satisfactory pace'. However, no agreement could be reached on a quantitative definition of the satisfactory pace of debt reduction, as had been proposed by the Commission, and no changes to the Pact regulations were introduced.

Finally, concerning governance, the reform of the SGP did not, in itself, introduce major changes in the area of governance. In particular, it did not change the basic procedures and voting rules, which in any case would require changes to the Treaty. However, the ECOFIN Council report of March 2005 did make a number of proposals and suggestions for improving governance and strengthening national ownership of the rules. In this context, it called for closer co-operation between Member States, the Commission and the Council, as well as for improved peer support and peer pressure. It called for the development of complementary national budgetary rules, the continuity of budgetary targets when a new government takes office and greater involvement of national parliaments. It also stressed the importance of reliable macroeconomic forecasts and budgetary statistics.

2.4 The implementation of the reformed SGP: initial experiences and challenges

Reactions to the reform of the SGP were quite diverse. The proliferation of escape clauses under the EDP led some to conclude that the reform represented a significant watering-down of the rules while not having addressed the essential problem of weak enforcement provisions (e.g. Calmfors, 2005; Feldstein, 2005). Others, by contrast, emphasized positive elements. The Commission considers that the reform has increased the economic rationale of the SGP and should therefore lead to increased ownership on the part of Member States, although it also points out that the Council deviated from its initial reform proposals in certain respects (European Commission, 2005).

More important than the precise wording of the revised EU fiscal rules is their effective implementation. Even if the new rules may, on the whole, be more flexible and less stringent than the old ones, they can, presumably, still enhance fiscal discipline if they are implemented in a rigorous manner. But this will depend on whether the reform achieves the objective of renewing ownership and strengthening political commitment to the rules on the part of Member States. Alternatively the reform may merely serve as a green light for opportunistic behaviour, minimalist efforts, and an implementation of the rules that is determined by political pressure and horse-trading (Coeuré and Pisani-Ferry, 2005; Buti, 2006). Bearing this in mind, this section examines the first experiences with the implementation of the new framework in the first year and a half or so after the reform. It should be stressed, however, that at this stage any assessment of the implementation of the reformed Pact has to focus primarily on *ex ante* fiscal plans and decisions and in this sense has to be seen as preliminary. Ultimately, the success or failure of the reformed SGP will be judged on *ex post* fiscal outcomes, in particular on whether it actually delivers a timely correction of excessive deficits and the achievement of sound public finances in the euro area notably in the context of the next cyclical downswing.

2.4.1 The implementation of the reformed preventive arm

Between December 2005 and February 2006, all euro area Member States submitted their first updated stability programmes under the revised framework. The content of these programmes and the assessment and opinions of the Commission and the ECOFIN Council provided the first indications as to the impact of the changes to the preventive arm on Member States' medium-term fiscal plans.[19]

MTOs in the updated stability programmes

According to the revised SGP, MTOs should ensure rapid progress towards fiscal sustainability. As soon as an appropriate methodology has been agreed, MTOs should take into account implicit liabilities stemming from future age-related spending. In the meantime, however, and in accordance with the ECOFIN Council report of March 2005, MTOs are differentiated primarily in the light of countries' debt/GDP ratios and potential growth. Moreover, in this context, it has been decided to give more weight to the debt ratio in determining country-specific MTOs (see Commission, 2006). Bearing these clarifications in mind and given the predefined range for euro area MTOs of between −1% of GDP to 'in balance or surplus', the following three reasonable working assumptions concerning the MTOs can be made. First, only countries with debt/GDP ratios below the 60% reference value should be allowed to target deficits of up to 1% of GDP. Second, countries with debt ratios above the 60% of GDP reference value should aim for budgets that are at least 'close to balance' (i.e. a deficit of no more than 0.5% of GDP) in order to bring their debt ratios towards the reference value at a satisfactory pace. Third, countries with very high debt ratios should be more ambitious and target budgetary positions that are 'in balance or surplus'.

Adopting these working assumptions, the MTOs presented by euro area Member States in their stability programmes all seem to be at least consistent with the requirements of the reformed Pact. The countries targeting deficits of up to 1% of GDP (Luxembourg and the Netherlands) have debt ratios below the 60% reference value. Portugal is targeting a deficit of up to 0.5% of GDP, which is consistent with the fact that its debt ratio currently lies within a medium range of 60–80% of GDP. All the other countries are targeting either balanced or in-surplus budgetary positions.

The picture that emerges from the stability programmes in terms of actual and planned compliance with MTOs is less satisfactory, however. In 2005 only four out of 12 euro area Member States (Spain, Ireland, the Netherlands and Finland) reported outcomes that were in line with their MTOs. Three out of the remaining eight Member States (Belgium, Austria and Luxembourg) plan to achieve their MTOs by the end of the period covered in their stability programmes. Extrapolating planned consolidation progress towards the end of the programme periods into the future suggests that all countries that are currently in excessive deficit at the time (Germany, Greece, France, Italy and Portugal) do not intend to achieve their MTOs until (in some cases well into) the next decade. This horizon clearly calls into question the relevance of these targets for policymaking (which typically looks at most at the next three to four years as the medium-term horizon) and, hence, for assessing medium-term fiscal positions.

It is also important to bear in mind that the MTOs presented in the updated stability programmes do not yet take into account implicit liabilities related to future ageing-related expenditures. At present, the Council opinions on the stability programmes provide an assessment of the sustainability of public finances in the light of such liabilities, and categorize their positions as being either low, medium or high risk. As can be seen from Table 2.3, however, there is no obvious link between this assessment and the MTOs.

The adjustment path towards the MTO

The benchmark adjustment path introduced by the new Pact represents a development of previous commitments rather than an entirely new initiative. Responding to proposals by the Commission, in October 2002 the Eurogroup agreed that euro area Member States with budgetary imbalances should improve their underlying fiscal positions by at least 0.5% of GDP per annum. At the time, it was hoped that expressing consolidation requirements in terms of an annual adjustment effort, rather than setting a date for achieving a close-to-balance budget, would prevent any undue

Table 2.3 Main elements of updated stability programmes and Council opinions

	MTO	*Year in which MTO achieved*	*Sustainability risk*	*Recommendation on national institutions*
Belgium	0.5% Surplus	2007	Medium	No
Germany	Budget balance	~2011–12	Medium	Yes
Greece	Budget balance	~2013	High	Yes
Spain	Budget balance	Already	Medium	No
France	Budget balance	2010	Medium	Yes
Ireland	Budget balance	Already	Medium	No
Italy	Budget balance	~2011–2012	Medium	Yes
Luxembourg	0.8% deficit	2007	Medium	No
Netherlands	−1% to −0.5% deficit	Already	Medium	No
Austria	Budget balance	2008	Low	No
Portugal	−0.5% deficit or better	~2011	High	Yes
Finland	1.5% surplus	Already	Low	No

Source: Updated stability programmes December 2005-February 2006, and Council opinions.

back-loading of fiscal adjustment. Moreover, expressing the adjustment effort in structural terms was intended to ensure that consolidation would not compromise the stabilization function of fiscal policy, since the automatic fiscal stabilizers can be allowed to operate around a predefined structural adjustment path (provided that there is a sufficient safety margin to prevent breaches of the 3% deficit threshold).

The provisions introduced by the SGP reform differ slightly from the earlier Eurogroup agreement. It has now been made more explicit that the adjustment effort should be measured net of one-off and temporary measures. This can be seen as a strengthening of the adjustment requirement with the welcome intention of reducing, if not excluding, the recourse to measures that do not contribute to sustainable consolidation. At the same time, there is more flexibility in that the 0.5% annual adjustment path is now described as a benchmark around which efforts can vary in good times and bad times. A reasonable interpretation of the reformed SGP provisions is that the overall adjustment effort should be the same over the medium term as in the case of a constant annual adjustment of 0.5%. However, fluctuations in the nominal balance could be greater, with more scope for differentiating consolidation efforts in response to the cyclical position of the economy. Figure 2.3 illustrates two scenarios with identical starting and end points, but with very different adjustment paths for the nominal and structural balance.

Examining the adjustment path towards MTOs presented in the first set of post reform stability programmes, it appears that planned compliance with the new adjustment path benchmark is only partially satisfactory (see Table 2.4). All of the seven euro area countries with budgetary imbalances at least plan to adhere to the 0.5% annual adjustment benchmark on average over the course of the programme period. In the cases of Greece, Italy and Portugal, planned consolidation is somewhat more ambitious than the benchmark adjustment path, reflecting the setting of fiscal targets to comply with Council recommendations and notices under the EDP. For the remaining four countries with budgetary imbalances (Germany, France,

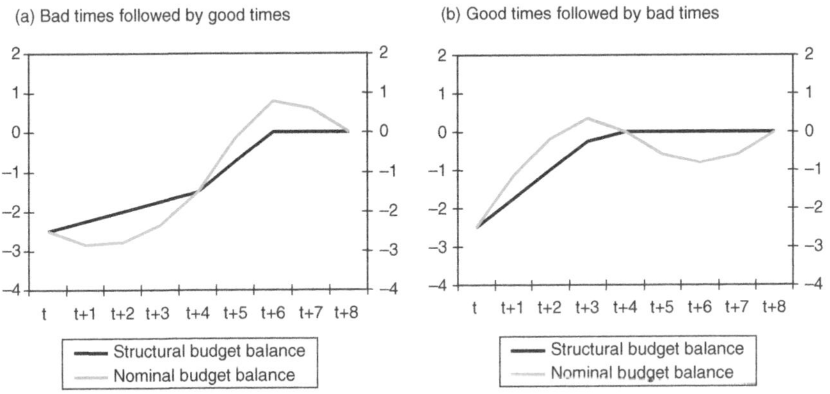

Figure 2.3 Stylised representation of the adjustment path towards the MTO (as a % of GDP).

Table 2.4 Fiscal developments under the revised SGP (as a % of GDP)

	Outcomes		*Plans in 2005–6 stability programmes*			
	2005	*2006*	*2005*	*2006*	*2007*	*2008*
General government budget balance						
Belgium	−2.3	0.2	0.0	0.0	0.3	0.5
Germany	−3.2	−1.7	−3.3	−3.3	−2.5	−2.0
Greece	−5.5	−2.6	−4.3	−2.6	−2.3	−1.7
Spain	1.1	1.8	1.0	0.9	0.7	0.6
France	−3.0	−2.5	−3.0	−2.9	−2.6	−1.9
Ireland	1.0	2.9	0.3	−0.6	−0.8	−0.8
Italy	−4.2	−4.4	−4.3	−3.5	−2.8	−2.1
Luxembourg	−0.3	0.1	−2.3	−1.8	−1.0	−0.2
Netherlands	−0.3	0.6	−1.2	−1.5	−1.2	−1.1
Austria	−1.6	−1.1	−1.9	−1.7	−0.8	0.0
Portugal	−6.1	−3.9	−6.0	−4.6	−3.7	−2.6
Finland	2.7	3.9	1.8	1.6	1.6	1.5
Euro area	**−2.5**	**−1.6**	**−2.5**	**−2.3**	**−1.8**	**−1.4**
Structural budget balance						
Belgium	0.0	−0.4	0.0	−0.3	0.4	0.7
Germany	−2.4	−1.5	−3.0	−2.9	−1.8	−1.5
Greece	−6.1	−3.9	−4.8	−3.7	−2.8	−2.4
Spain	1.6	2.3	1.2	1.2	1.2	0.9
France	−3.2	−2.3	−3.3	−2.9	−2.3	−1.5
Ireland	1.0	2.9	1.1	0.1	0.1	0.1
Italy	−3.9	−2.6	−4.1	−3.2	−2.3	−1.7
Luxembourg	1.0	0.5	−1.5	−1.2	−0.6	0.1
Netherlands	0.7	1.1	0.1	−0.7	−0.6	−0.6
Austria	−1.1	−1.0	−1.6	−1.2	−0.4	0.2
Portugal	−5.0	−2.9	−5.0	−3.4	−2.6	−1.8
Finland	3.6	3.7	2.1	1.7	1.7	1.8
General government debt						
Euro area	**70.5**	**69.0**	**71.0**	**70.8**	**69.6**	**64.7**

Sources: European Commission. Member States' updated stability programmes.

Luxembourg and Austria), planned consolidation is in line with (but does not go far beyond) the 0.5% annual adjustment on average. What is much less satisfactory, however, is an apparent back-loading of consolidation efforts, with these four countries targeting adjustments of less than 0.5% of GDP in 2006.

Interpreting fiscal plans under the new preventive arm

One way of assessing the impact of the SGP reform on fiscal plans under the preventive arm is to compare the implications for the euro area of the fiscal plans presented in the stability programmes prior to and after the reform. Figure 2.4 compares how euro area real GDP growth and the main euro area fiscal aggregates

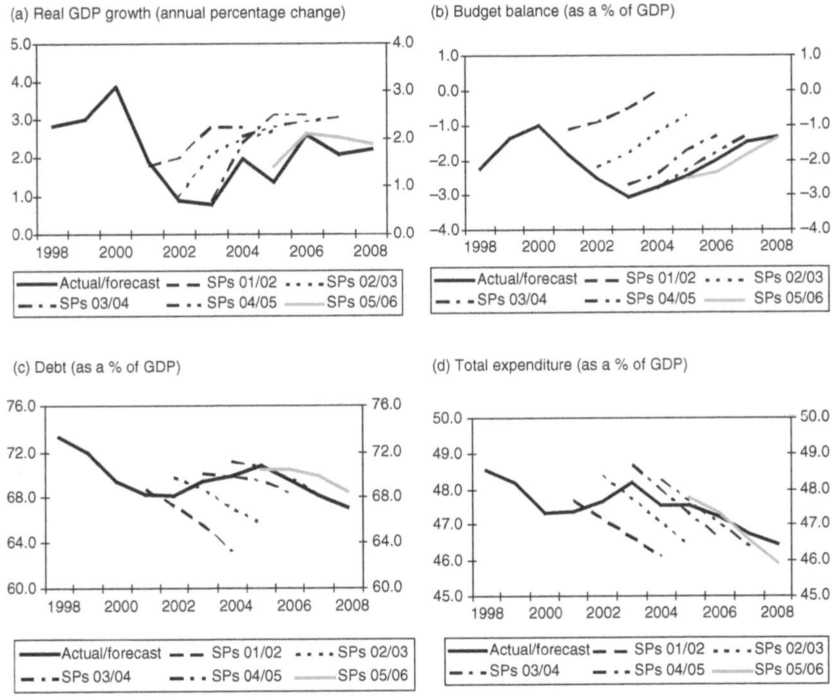

Figure 2.4 Euro area fiscal outlook: new versus old stability programmes.

Sources: Member States' updated stability programmes 2001–6 and own calculations, European Commission Autumn 2006 economic forecasts (AMECO database).

are assumed to evolve in the first post-reform round of stability programme updates compared to pre-reform programme updates, as well as vis-à-vis actual developments (up until 2005) and the European Commission's autumn 2006 forecasts (for the period 2006–8).

According to the post-reform programmes, real GDP growth is assumed to pick up to around its potential rate and then remain close to that level in the coming years (see Panel *a* of Figure 2.4). This is broadly in line with the Commission's forecast, although the stability programmes are slightly more optimistic with respect to 2007 and 2008. These growth assumptions are similar to those presented in pre-reform programmes, although they appear to have become slightly more moderate and more realistic, especially with respect to the later years of the programme horizon. Indeed, according to the Commission assessments of the post-reform programmes, most Member States did base their fiscal plans on realistic or plausible macroeconomic assumptions.

As for the euro area budget balance (Panel *b* of Figure 2.4), the envisaged adjustment in the post-reform stability programme updates is smaller than in previous programme updates, amounting to around 1% of GDP over three years (2006–8), compared to around 1.5% of GDP in previous programmes. Moreover, Figure 2.4 illustrates the above-mentioned very limited planned improvement in the budget balance in 2006 and an increase in the degree of back-loading of consolidation efforts. The slower decline in the planned deficit is also reflected in a more gradual decline in the debt/GDP ratio, which is planned to fall by only around 1% of GDP between 2005 and 2008.[20] Finally, in terms of the composition of planned fiscal consolidation, there is little change compared with previous years, with most Member States focusing on expenditure restraint, as can be seen from the projected reduction in the expenditure/GDP ratio (see Panel *d*).

One way of interpreting these numbers is that, having missed targets in previous years, Member States have decided to use the additional flexibility provided by the reformed SGP to present more realistic (i.e. achievable) deficit and debt targets. If such targets were actually achieved, this would constitute a strengthening of the preventive arm. However, the reduced ambition of the programmes also implies that unless compliance with fiscal plans genuinely improves, actual fiscal outcomes may develop less favourably (or at least not better) than before the SGP reform, which would imply that the preventive arm has been adjusted to accommodate existing policies rather than the other way around.

In fact the reform of the SGP has coincided with a much-improved economic outlook. In 2005 and even more so in 2006, most euro area governments benefited from significant revenue windfalls loading to budget outcomes that were significantly better than planned. This stands in stark contrast to the distinctly less favourable environment in 2001–3 that culminated in the breakdown of the 'original' SGP. Indeed, since the first stability programmes were submitted in 1998, there now appears to have been more or less a full economic and budgetary cycle so that the conditions facing the revised SGP are akin to those faced in the first years by its predecessor. This should perhaps serve as a warning not to draw premature conclusions regarding the success of the revised SGP on the basis of just fiscal plans and one or two years of fiscal outcomes. Rather, the revised Pact will ultimately need to be judged on how it performs in good and bad times. For now, the challenge for implementing the revised preventive arm is to avoid repeating past mistakes and to ensure that significant consolidation progress is actually made to reach safe budgetary positions before 'good times' come to an end.

Since the SGP reform five euro area countries (Germany, Greece, France, Italy and Portugal) have been the subject of ongoing EDPs. Among these, Germany and France first exceeded the 3% of GDP reference value in 2002 and, in the following year, received recommendations from the Council to correct the situation by 2004 at the latest. Following the procedural deadlock of November 2003, this deadline was *de facto* extended to 2005.[21]

France's deficit was marginally below 3% of GDP in 2005 (and the EDP for France was abrogated in January 2007). Germany's deficit remained above 3% of GDP in 2005 and towards the end of that year the German government announced a package of fiscal measures which effectively targeted the correction of its excessive deficit only in 2007. In the light of the continued breach of the reference value, the Council decided to move to the next step of the EDP by issuing a notice to

Germany under Article 104(9) of the Treaty.[22] Flexibility was shown, however, by granting an extension until 2007 to correct the excessive deficit, in line with the German government's announced fiscal plans. The reasons stated for this extension included the fact that Germany's budgetary adjustment was embedded in a comprehensive strategy, that measures were well advanced in the legislative process and that some measures already implemented would only produce results with a lag. It was also deemed sufficient that Germany would comply with the 0.5% annual adjustment path on average in 2006 and 2007 rather than in each individual year. Following the Council's decision, however, the budgetary situation in Germany evolved more favourably and the deficit was brought well below 3% of GDP already in 2006.

The EDP against Greece was launched in 2004 (following an initial breach of the reference value in 2003), and the Greek government was given until 2005 to correct the excessive deficit. By early 2005 it became clear that Greece was facing severe difficulties in complying with this deadline, in particular given that statistical revisions had pushed Greece's deficit well above the 3% threshold (and also confirmed breaches of the reference value in earlier years). The Council therefore issued a notice to Greece to take measures to correct its excessive deficit by 2006, which on the basis of fiscal data available in early 2007 appears to have been achieved.

EDPs against Italy and Portugal were launched shortly after the SGP reform. In the case of Italy, this was due to a breach of the 3% reference value being confirmed for 2004. Moreover, due to low growth and a phasing-out of temporary measures, the government announced that it planned an even higher deficit of around 4% of GDP in 2005. Portugal, meanwhile, announced that it would no longer take temporary measures to keep its deficit below 3% of GDP as it had done in the previous three years and that, as a result, its deficit in 2005 would rise to around 6% of GDP.

In July and September 2005 respectively, the Council decided that Italy and Portugal had excessive deficits and issued recommendations for their correction.[23] Since neither Italy nor Portugal could be considered to have deficits that were close to and only temporarily above 3% of GDP, the revised exceptional circumstances clause was not applicable, and the Commission's assessment of the other relevant factors was not taken into account when deciding whether or not the deficits were excessive.

When setting the deadlines for the correction of the excessive deficits, however, in both cases 'special circumstances' were found to warrant extensions. In the case of Italy, the cyclical weakness of the economy and the size of the required adjustment were deemed sufficient grounds to grant a one-year extension of the deadline to 2007. After realizing the deterioration of Italy's budgetary position in 2005, the Council recommended that Italy undertake a structural consolidation effort amounting to 1.6% of GDP by 2007, with at least half of this adjustment occurring in 2006. In the case of Portugal, the same reasons as well as the intention to no longer rely on temporary measures were considered as warranting an extension by two years to 2008.

Interpreting the implementation of the new corrective arm

The initial experience outlined above suggests that the changes introduced by the SGP reform have facilitated decision-making under the corrective arm. Procedural deadlocks such as the one that occurred in the context of the EDPs for Germany and France in November 2003 have not been repeated. All deficits above 3% of GDP have been considered excessive. In the case of Germany, a decision to issue a Council notice under Article 104(9) of the Treaty (which was the main stumbling block in November 2003) was taken without any controversy. Fiscal targets in the affected countries are mostly in line with minimum requirements under the respective EDPs. Moreover, recourse to temporary measures appears to be significantly reduced, which is encouraging given that the extended use of one-off measures and creative accounting was a factor that undermined the implementation of the original SGP.

With regard to the use of the additional flexibility and broader escape clauses, it may be premature to draw any firm conclusions, particularly since initial experiences may reflect a transition from the old to a new steady state. However, in all three countries for which important decisions have been taken, the invoking of special circumstances (in the case of Portugal and Italy) and *ad hoc* justifications (in the case of Germany) to extend deadlines could be viewed as a lenient implementation of the new rules.

Another conclusion that can be drawn from the experience so far is that the new rules introduced by the reform are themselves malleable. For example, while the reformed Pact refers to the possibility of extending deadlines 'by one year', deadlines have been extended by two years in the cases of Portugal and Germany. In the case of Germany, the 'annual' 0.5% of GDP adjustment benchmark was applied in cumulative terms over a two-year period (hence becoming a 'biennial' benchmark) in order to accommodate a longer deadline. Even if one rationale behind the SGP reform was to clarify and codify the flexibility or judgement that had previously been exercised under the EDP, room for (additional) discretion remains.

From the perspective of governance, it is notable that all recommendations issued so far under the reformed corrective arm have effectively endorsed the budget plans of the Member States concerned, although in some cases the latter may already have reflected the interests and concerns of the Commission and the other Member States. The emphasis has thus been on peer support for previously announced policies (with the Member State in question acting as leader, and the Council as a follower). Moreover, the call for 'closer co-operation between the Member States, the Commission and the Council' seems to be implemented by the Commission trying to strike a balance between issuing recommendations that boost consolidation in line with the revised Pact while also achieving qualified majority support in the Council. In this way the Commission acts as a 'consensus builder', which not only has the advantage of facilitating a smooth implementation of the EDP, but also limits the Commission's ability to act as an independent arbiter.

2.5 Conclusions

In the run-up to EMU, fiscal positions in euro area Member States improved significantly as Member States sought to comply with the 3% of GDP reference value of the Maastricht Treaty for participation in the single currency. The SGP, adopted shortly prior to the introduction of the euro, was intended to promote fiscal discipline once the incentive of EMU membership had disappeared by subjecting Member States' fiscal policies to clear rules and surveillance procedures.

Experience with the implementation of the SGP has been mixed, however. While some countries managed to achieve and maintain sound budgetary positions, in accordance with the rules, six euro area Member States (including the largest three, Germany, France and Italy) have incurred excessive deficits. Moreover, as fiscal positions deteriorated, the implementation of the SGP procedures became beset with difficulties and criticisms of the rules themselves also became louder.

The 2005 reform of the SGP did not fundamentally change the Pact's original two-armed (i.e. its preventive/corrective) structure, but it did respond to criticisms by making the rules and procedures more flexible. While the changes to the preventive arm could essentially be considered as a shift in favour of sophisticated as opposed to simple rules, in the context of the corrective arm the increased flexibility is associated with less stringent rules and procedures. Compared to the original framework, there are now more grounds for permitting deficits above 3% and extending deadlines for their correction. For this reason, the reform has been criticized as a weakening of the EU fiscal framework and there is a risk that it will result in more frequent and more persistent deficits above 3% of GDP and less favourable debt developments.

Ultimately, what matters, however, is how effectively the revised SGP will be implemented. Notwithstanding some additional flexibility of the rules, a rigorous implementation of the revised framework would be conducive to fiscal discipline and sound public finances in EMU. So far, the implementation of the new rules has been smooth, but there are also worrying signs of consolidation efforts in some countries again tending to be back-loaded. A full and proper assessment of the revised SGP will only be possible when its implementation can be assessed over a full economic cycle. The agreement on the SGP reform appears to have coincided with the re-emergence of economic good times and significant revenue windfalls, which has not only contributed to improving fiscal balances but also risks giving rise to complacency in the short-term. In order for the revised SGP to be deemed a success in the longer term, the revised preventive arm needs to deliver more in 'good times' while the increased room for judgement under the corrective arm needs to be backed by appropriate, credible and timely enforcement. In short, much depends on whether the reform gives rise to enhanced ownership of the rules on the part of the Member States, the Council and the Commission and to an intelligent but 'strict' and 'symmetric' use of the additional flexibility that they imply.

Notes

1 This chapter partly draws on and updates (until spring 2007) previous work, in particular Morris *et al.* (2006). The views expressed in this paper are those of the authors and do not necessarily reflect those of the ECB. JEL classification: E61, E62, H6. Key words: Stability and Growth Pact, Fiscal policy, Fiscal rules, EMU.
2 See ECB (2001).
3 For a more detailed overview of fiscal developments since the early 1990s, see Briotti (2004).
4 For an inside account of the negotiations leading to the agreement on the SGP, see Stark (2001). For an analysis of the economic and political factors that led to the SGP, see Heipertz and Verdun (2004).
5 The two Council Regulations are Council Regulation 1466/97 'on the strengthening of the surveillance of budgetary positions and the surveillance and coordination of economic policies' (the preventive arm), and Council Regulation 1467/97 'on speeding up and clarifying the implementation of the excessive deficit procedure' (the corrective arm). These are supplemented by a European Council Resolution on the SGP and a Code of Conduct, although these are not legally binding.
6 Resolution of the European Council on the SGP, Amsterdam, June 1997.
7 Non-euro area Member States submit convergence programmes.
8 On the role of budgetary policy in responding to cyclical developments in the context of the SGP see Stark and Manzke (2002).
9 In this sense, recent experience in the euro area appears to support the findings of a growing body of literature on fiscal consolidation which argues that revenue-based fiscal adjustments tend to be less successful (i.e. less sustainable) than consolidations based primarily on expenditure restraint (Alesina and Perotti, 1995; von Hagen *et al.*, 2001). See also Briotti (2004) for an overview.
10 Regarding one-off measures and creative accounting see Koen and van den Noord (2005).
11 ECOFIN Council conclusions of 12 February 2002.
12 In the case of Portugal, a public finances audit in spring 2002 showed that the deficit had already exceeded 3% of GDP by a considerable margin back in 2001. Hence, the Commission's recommendation for an 'early' warning actually followed the breaching of the reference value.
13 Commission recommendations of 18 November 2003 for Council decisions giving notice to Germany and France to take measures to correct their excessive deficits.
14 ECOFIN Council conclusions of 25 November 2003.
15 Ruling of the ECJ of 13 July 2004 on the affair C-27/04 by the Commission of the European Communities against the Council of the European Union.
16 See the Commission Communication to the Council and the European Parliament of November 2002 on strengthening the co-ordination of budgetary policies, and the ECOFIN Council report of March 2003 on strengthening the implementation of the SGP.
17 See the Commission Communication to the Council and the European Parliament of September 2004 on strengthening economic governance and clarifying the implementation of the SGP. See also Deroose and Langedijk (2005) for an overview of the European Commission's motivations for and approach to reforming the SGP.
18 The changes are laid down in two new Council Regulations, No 1055/2005 and No 1056/2005 amending Regulations 1466/97 and 1467/97 respectively.
19 As far as actual fiscal outcomes are concerned, 2005 budget balances turned out to be somewhat better than expected in the autumn of 2005 while falling marginally short of the target implied by the 2004/5 vintage of stability programmes (see panel b of Figure 2.4). It seems premature to attribute this development to the reform of the SGP, however, since the relevant fiscal policy decisions and plans were adopted prior to the reform,

while fiscal balances in some countries were boosted by unexplained, non-discretionary increases in tax revenues.

20 The comparison of previous stability programme targets and actual fiscal outcomes in Figure 2.4 is affected by recent changes to national accounts. The latter have resulted in upward revisions of GDP and corresponding downward revisions in government revenue, expenditure and debt when expressed as a percentage of GDP. This explains why debt/GDP ratios and expenditure/GDP ratios were initially observed to be at higher levels in the 01/02 to 04/05 programme vintages than currently recorded by actual data.

21 Following the annulment by the ECJ of the ECOFIN Council conclusions of 25 November 2003, the Commission issued a Communication in December 2004 setting out its approach in the context of the EDPs against Germany and France. In its Communications the Commission concluded that the Council's initial recommendation under Article 104(7) remained in force. However, in the light of subsequent events, it argued that the 2004 deadline should be extended to 2005. The ECOFIN Council endorsed this approach at its meeting on 18 January 2005.

22 Council Decision of 14 March 2006 giving notice to Germany to take measures to correct its excessive deficit.

23 Council Recommendation of 28 July 2005 with a view to bringing to an end the situation of an excessive deficit in Italy; Council Recommendation of 20 September 2005 with a view to bringing to an end the situation of an excessive deficit in Portugal.

References

Alesina, A. and Drazen, A. (1991), 'Why are stabilisations delayed?', *American Economic Review*, 82: 1170–88.

Alesina, A. and Perotti, R. (1995), 'Fiscal expansions and adjustments in OECD countries', *Economic Policy*, 14(2): 210–48.

Bini Smaghi, L. (2004), 'What went wrong with the Stability and Growth Pact?' Paper presented at the conference on Monetary Union in Europe: Historical Perspectives and Prospects for the Future, Copenhagen.

Blanchard, O. J. and Giavazzi, F. (2004), 'Improving the SGP through a proper accounting of public investment', CEPR Discussion Paper no. 4220.

Briotti, M. G. (2004), 'Fiscal adjustment between 1991 and 2002: stylised facts and policy implications', ECB Occasional Paper no. 9.

—— (2005), 'Economic reactions to public finance consolidations: a survey of the literature', ECB Occasional Paper no. 38.

Buiter, W. and Grafe, C. (2002), 'Patching up the Pact: some suggestions for enhancing fiscal sustainability and macroeconomic stability in an enlarged European Union', CEPR Discussion Paper no. 3496.

Buti, M. (2006), 'Will the new Stability and Growth Pact succeed? An economic and political perspective', European Commission Economic Paper no. 241.

Buti, M. and van den Noord, P. (2003), 'Discretionary fiscal policies and elections: the experience of the early years of EMU', OECD Economic Department Working Paper no. 351.

Buti, M. Eijffinger, S. and Franco, D. (2003), 'Revisiting the Stability and Growth Pact: grand design or internal adjustment?', CEPR Discussion Paper no. 3692.

—— (2005), 'The Stability Pact pains: a forward-looking assessment of the reform debate', CEPR Discussion Paper no. 5216.

Buti, M., Franco, D. and Ongena, H. (1998), 'Fiscal discipline and flexibility in EMU: the implementation of the Stability and Growth Pact', *Oxford Review of Economic Policy*, 14: 81–97.

Calmfors, L. (2005), 'What remains of the Stability Pact and what next?', Swedish Institute for European Policy Studies, 2005:8.

Coeuré, B. and Pisani-Ferry, J. (2005), 'Fiscal policy in EMU: towards a Sustainability and Growth Pact', Bruegel Working Paper no. 2005/01.

Creel, R. and Fitoussi, J.-P. (2002), 'How to reform the European Central Bank', Centre for European Reform.

Deroose, S. and van Langedijk, S. (2005), 'Improving the Stability and Growth Pact: the Commission's three pillar approach', European Economy Occasional Paper no. 15.

European Central Bank Monthly Bulletin (2001), 'The economic policy framework in EMU', Frankfurt, November.

—— (2002), 'The operation of automatic stabilisers in the euro area', Frankfurt, April.

—— (2005), 'The reform of the Stability and Growth Pact', Frankfurt, August.

—— (2006), 'Fiscal policies and financial markets', Frankfurt, February.

European Commission (2005), 'Public finances in EMU', *European Economy*, 3/2005.

—— (2006a), 'Economic forecasts – spring 2006', *European Economy*, 2/2006.

—— (2006b), 'Public Finances in EMU', *European Economy*, 3/2006.

Fatás, A., von Hagen, J., Hughes-Hallet, A., Sibert, A. and Strauch, R. (2003), 'Stability and growth in Europe: Towards a better pact', CEPR – ZEI Monitoring European Integration, 13.

Feldstein, M. (2005), 'The euro and the Stability Pact', NBER Working Paper no. 11249.

Gros, D., Mayer, T. and Ubide, A. (2004), 'The nine lives of the Stability and Growth Pact: a special report of the CEPS Macroeconomic Policy Group', Centre for European Policy Studies, Brussels.

von Hagen, J., Hughes-Hallet, A. and Strauch, R. (2001), 'Budgetary consolidation in EMU', European Commission Economic Paper no. 148.

von Hagen, J., Halleberg, M. and Strauch, R. (2004), 'Budgetary forecasts in Europe – the track record of stability and convergence programmes', ECB Working Paper no. 307.

Heipertz, M. and Verdun, A. (2004), 'The dog that would never bite? What we can learn from the origins of the Stability and Growth Pact', *Journal of European Public Policy*, 11: 765–80.

Koen, V. and van den Noord, P. (2005), 'Fiscal gimmickry in Europe: one-off measures and creative accounting', OECD Economics Department Working Paper no. 417.

Marín, J. (2002), 'Sustainability of public finances and automatic stabilisation under a rule of budgetary discipline', ECB Working Paper no. 193.

Morris, R., Ongena, H. and Schuknecht, L. (2006), 'The reform and implementation of the Stability and Growth Pact', ECB Occasional Paper no. 47.

Pisani-Ferry, J. (2002), 'Fiscal discipline and policy coordination in the Eurozone: Assessment and proposals', Paper for the European Commission President's Group for Economic Analysis.

Schuknecht, L. (2004), 'Stability and Growth Pact: issues and lessons from political economy', *International Economics and Economic Policy*, 2: 65–89.

Stark, J. (2001), 'Genesis of a Pact', in A. Brunila, M. Buti and D. Franco (eds), *The Stability and Growth Pact: The Architecture of Fiscal Policy in EMU*, New York Palgrave.

Stark, J. and Manzke, B. (2002), 'Which role should budgetary policy play in response to cyclical developments?', Paper presented at the seminar of the Netherlands' ministry of finances on 'Budgetary policy in E(M)U: design and challenges', Mimeo.

Wyplosz, C. (2005), 'Fiscal policy: institutions versus rules', *National Institute Economic Review*, 191: 64–78.

3 Macroeconomic adjustment in the euro area

The role of fiscal policy

A. Muscatelli, T. Ropele and P. Tirelli

3.1 Introduction

There is a general consensus that national fiscal policies should play an enhanced role in adjusting to macroeconomic shocks within EMU. The absence of national monetary policies and the potentially destabilizing impact of inflation differentials on national real interest rates only leave fiscal policy as a tool to offset asymmetric shocks. Some economists have gone as far as advocating a greater emphasis on fiscal policy as a key policy instrument in macroeconomic adjustment (see Ball, 1997; Wren-Lewis, 2000, 2002). In the context of EMU, this has also led to calls to radically reform the Stability and Growth Pact and render fiscal policy-making more transparent. Calmfors (2003) argues for a more transparent institutional framework for national (discretionary) fiscal policies within EMU, with clear objectives and a solution based on national fiscal committees. Other economists have challenged this perspective and see automatic stabilizers, within the constraints of a reformed SGP, as the key to macroeconomic adjustment within EMU (Buti *et al.*, 1997, 2001; European Commission, 2001). This 'Brussels consensus' is based on the view that the ECB alone should stabilize the union-wide economy (Buti *et al.*, 2001). The key question which we ask is whether fiscal policy, modelled as feedback rules on output, that is, automatic stabilizers, adds value to the stabilization role played by monetary policy in the euro area.

In this chapter we examine the validity of this proposition and assess the performance of fiscal stabilizers within EMU. We do this using a small two-country DSGE model of EMU, estimated using the synthetic euro-data collected over the period 1970–98. While the structural model used in this chapter has many elements in common with other New Keynesian DSGE models, our analysis differs in a number of respects. First, relative to similar New Keynesian models, we include a wider range of fiscal policy transmission channels, including 'non-Ricardian' effects on consumption due to rule-of-thumb (RoT, henceforth) consumers (as in Galì *et al.*, 2007; Amato and Laubach, 2003; and Muscatelli *et al.*, 2003) and supply-side distortions. Second, our model is estimated, whereas others use calibration or numerical simulations (see Andres and Domenech, 2003). Third, our two-country model features a home bias in consumption which, as we shall demonstrate, impacts on how automatic fiscal stabilizers interact with monetary policy in a monetary union.

Earlier contributions (Andres and Domenech, 2006; Gordon and Leeper, 2003; Muscatelli *et al.*, 2004) found that counter-cyclical fiscal policy can be welfare-reducing in the presence of optimizing consumers. Muscatelli *et al.* (2003) estimate the proportion of RoT consumers in the United States and show that automatic stabilizers based on taxation improve the performance of the economy. Here we find that the proportion of RoT consumers is far larger in the euro area, possibly due to financial market imperfections. This result is in line with a relatively large body of empirical evidence. Asdrubali and Kim (2004) find that, following an output shock, EU capital markets enable a very limited degree of consumption smoothing relative to the United States. Fair (2001) finds that, unlike the United States, in most EU countries there is little evidence of real interest rate effects on aggregate consumption. This is easily reconciled with our result about the large share of RoT consumers who do not directly react to interest rate shocks. Finally, our estimate is consistent with the cross-country evidence about the share of current income consumers presented in Sarantis and Stewart (2003).

We use our estimates to simulate a two-country version of the model with a single central bank and independent fiscal authorities. We find that the stabilizing effects of fiscal policy in response to EMU-wide shocks carry over to the case of asymmetric disturbances only if a significant home bias characterizes national consumption bundles. Thus, our results suggest a novel approach to the philosophy of EMU macroeconomic policy-making. At the euro area level, the action of automatic stabilizers should be regarded as a useful complement to the ECB actions. On the other hand, the usual case for fiscal stabilization of within-EMU asymmetric shocks is confirmed only if the composition of national aggregate demand functions is sufficiently biased towards domestic production. This is in sharp contrast with the 'Brussels consensus' based on the view that the ECB alone should stabilize the union-wide economy (Buti *et al.*, 2001).

In the next section we outline our model and the empirical methodology. In Section 3.3 we report our econometric results and illustrate the properties of the model by looking at its impulse responses. In Section 3.4 we consider the value-added of having national fiscal stabilizers in EMU using our two-country monetary union model. Section 3.5 concludes.

3.2 A two-country New Keynesian model with home-biased consumer preferences

3.2.1 General approach

Early vintages of New Keynesian DSGE models involved a limited role for fiscal policy, by assuming lump-sum taxation and representative agents with infinite planning horizon. Another strand of literature has modelled more complex supply-side effects for fiscal stabilization policies by allowing distortionary taxation (see Andres and Domenech, 2003 and the references therein).

Studies of the business cycle using VAR-type models do not provide empirical support for this simple description of demand-side effects in the New Keynesian model. Giavazzi *et al.* (2000) show that both Keynesian and neoclassical (Ricardian) effects are present. Fatas and Mihov (2001), Blanchard and Perotti (2002) and Muscatelli *et al.* (2004) show that fiscal shocks have conventional Keynesian effects, in that an increase in government spending causes a persistent rise in output[1] and consumption. Galí *et al.* (2007) demonstrate that this problem can be addressed by adding non-optimizing behaviour to the conventional New Keynesian model. They assume that a proportion of consumers are constrained to consume out of current income and show that, under plausible parameterizations, this provides an explanation for the positive response of consumption to a temporary government spending shock. The increase in government spending generates an increase in real wage (providing the substitution effect between consumption and leisure dominates the wealth effect), and causes an increase in aggregate consumption because RoT consumers spend out of current income.[2] Introducing non-optimizing consumers also potentially allows for other transmission channels for fiscal policy. Even if taxes are lump sum, they will impact on aggregate consumption behaviour through their effect on the current nominal income of RoT consumers. Furthermore, payroll taxes affect marginal costs and inflation. This, in turn, has an obvious impact on aggregate consumption if wages are sticky.

There are other ways, however, to model non-Ricardian consumers. Debt-financed fiscal deficits will have an impact on aggregate demand in versions of the New Keynesian model which depart from Ricardian equivalence because of the presence of finite horizons, as in the classic Blanchard–Yaari model (Leith and Wren-Lewis, 2000). Other effects of government debt on consumer behaviour can also be considered, such as the impact that financial wealth has on household transaction costs, which can explain the observed positive correlation between public expenditure shocks and consumption (see Schabert, 2004).

Unfortunately, there is a trade-off between estimating New Keynesian models which contain all these channels of fiscal policy transmission and maintaining the model sufficiently parsimonious in terms of structural parameters to allow the use of classical econometric techniques. A complex model will typically be under-identified with respect to the structural parameters of interest or will result in poorly defined (in a statistical sense) estimated parameters. In modelling the transmission of fiscal policies, we have therefore chosen to restrict the demand side to the inclusion of non-optimizing (RoT) consumers. On the supply side, we allow for taxation effects on firms' marginal costs (through payroll taxes). This allows for a richer range of transmission channels for fiscal policy than with early attempts to estimate structural New Keynesian models.[3]

3.2.2 The model

The global economy (monetary union) consists of two countries of equal size: Home country (H) and Foreign country (F). We ignore third-country effects. The two economies are totally symmetric. The structural model will then reduce to a small forward-looking New Keynesian DSGE model, comprising, for each country, a dynamic "IS" equation for output and a 'New Keynesian Phillips Curve' specification for inflation. In addition to the channels for fiscal policy transmission outlined above, we allow for habit formation in consumption, which is necessary to capture the observed persistence in the output-gap response to shocks (see Leith and Malley, 2005). We model a hybrid Phillips curve, allowing for partly backward-looking inflation expectations (see Galí *et al.* 2001, 2003).

Consumers

We follow Galí *et al.* (2007) in assuming two types of households: those in the first group, denoted by i, benefit from full access to national and international capital markets and as such are free to optimize. The proportion of optimizing consumers in each country is given by $(1-\vartheta)$. The representative Home optimizing households have the following instantaneous separable utility function:

$$U_t(C^{oi}, N^{oi}) = \frac{(C_t^{oi}/H_t^i)^{1-\sigma_c}}{1-\sigma_c} - \frac{(N_t^{oi})^{1+\sigma_n}}{1+\sigma_n} \tag{3.1}$$

where C_t^o represents consumption of a basket of goods (to be defined below), H_t is an index of external habits and N_t^o is the level of employment. $\beta \in (0, 1)$ represents the subjective rate of time preference, σ_c the coefficient of relative risk aversion, σ_n the inverse of the elasticity of labour supply with respect to real wage. Following Smets and Wouters (2003), we assume that habits depend on past aggregate consumption, C^T:

$$H_t = \left(C_{t-1}^T\right)^{\lambda}, \tag{3.2}$$

with $\lambda > 0$.

Optimizing consumers maximize (3.1) subject to their intertemporal budget constraint, which in real terms reads as

$$\frac{a_{t+1}^i}{r_t} = a_t^i - C_t^{oi} + \frac{W_t}{P_t} N_t^{oi} + D_t^i - T_t^i . \tag{3.3}$$

Their financial wealth (a_t) is held in the form of one-period state-contingent securities, which yield a return of r_t. Home households can hold their wealth in bonds issued in country H, $B_{H,t}$, and bonds issued in country F, B_F, which offer the same return ($a_t = B_{H,t} + B_{F,t}$). The optimizing consumer's disposable income is defined as consisting of labour income $W_t/P_t N_t^{oi}$ plus the dividends from the profits of the imperfectly competitive firms D_t^i, minus personal taxes T_t^i, which are lump-sum by assumption.

The second group of households, a proportion ϑ of the total, follows a RoT behaviour. RoT households consume out of current disposable income, and supply a constant amount of labour,[4] N^{RoT}. This admittedly *ad hoc* assumption may be justified assuming myopia or limited participation to capital markets. Thus, the consumption function of the representative Home RoT consumer is simply

$$C_t^{RoTj} = N^{RoT} \frac{W_t}{P_t} - T_t^j. \tag{3.4}$$

The Home country household's optimization problem

Rearranging the first-order conditions associated to the optimizing consumers' problem and aggregating across consumers over $i \in (\frac{\vartheta}{2}, \frac{1}{2}]$ yields the consumption intertemporal Euler equation:

$$\frac{\left(C_t^o / C_{t-1}^\lambda\right)^{-\sigma_c}}{C_{t-1}^\lambda} = E_t \left\{ \beta \frac{\left(C_{t+1}^o / C_t^\lambda\right)^{-\sigma_c}}{C_t^\lambda} (1+i_t) \frac{P_t}{P_{t+1}} \right\}. \tag{3.5}$$

Given the symmetry of the model, equations (3.5) and (3.4) hold true also for country F, that is

$$\frac{\left(C_t^{*o} / C_{t-1}^{*\lambda}\right)^{-\sigma_c}}{C_{t-1}^{*\lambda}} = E_t \left\{ \beta \frac{\left(C_{t+1}^{*o} / C_t^{*\lambda}\right)^{-\sigma_c}}{C_t^{*\lambda}} (1+i_t) \frac{P_t^*}{P_{t+1}^*} \right\} \tag{3.6}$$

and

$$C_t^{*RoT} = N^{*RoT} \frac{W_t^*}{P_t^*} - T_t^*$$

where $C_t^{*o} \equiv \int_{(1+\vartheta)/2}^1 C_t^{*oi} di$ and $C_t^{*RoT} \equiv \int_{1/2}^{(1+\vartheta)/2} C_t^{*RoTi} di$.

At a given time, t, each household is called to solve an intratemporal allocation problem for the optimal choice of consumption bundles and differentiated consumption goods, indexed by $z \in [0, 1]$. We let goods indexed by $z \in \left[0, \frac{1}{2}\right]$ and by $z \in \left[\frac{1}{2}, 1\right]$ be produced in country H and F respectively.[5] Preferences over consumption bundles are modelled according to a constant elasticity of substitution (CES) specification with parameter $\chi \in (0.5, 1)$ capturing idiosyncratic taste or *home bias*:

$$C_t = \left[\chi^{\frac{1}{\eta}} C_{H,t}^{\frac{\eta-1}{\eta}} + (1-\chi)^{\frac{1}{\eta}} C_{F,t}^{\frac{\eta-1}{\eta}} \right]^{\frac{\eta}{\eta-1}} \tag{3.7}$$

Subindexes $C_{H,t}$ and $C_{F,t}$ are themselves constructed as CES aggregators, that is $C_{H,t} = \left[\int_0^{1/2} C_{H,t}(z)^{(\theta-1)/\theta} dz\right]^{\theta/(\theta-1)}$ and $C_{F,t} = \left[\int_{1/2}^1 C_{F,t}(z)^{(\theta-1)/\theta} dz\right]^{\theta/(\theta-1)}$. Parameters η and θ, both assumed greater than one, respectively measure the elasticity of substitution between consumption bundles $C_{H,t}$ and $C_{F,t}$ and the elasticity of substitution among each of the differentiated goods being produced in either country H or F.

Solving the cost minimization problem for the purchase of one unit of the composite consumption C_t gives the Home household's demand schedules for $C_{H,t}$ and $C_{F,t}$:

$$C_{H,t} = \chi \left(\frac{p_{H,t}}{P_t}\right)^{-\eta} C_t \quad \text{and} \quad C_{F,t} = (1-\chi)\left(\frac{p_{F,t}}{P_t}\right)^{-\eta} C_t. \tag{3.8}$$

In the same vein, Home household's demand schedules for good z produced in country H and F are given by

$$c_{H,t}(z) = \left(\frac{p_{H,t}(z)}{P_{H,t}}\right)^{-\theta} C_{H,t} \quad \text{and} \quad c_{F,t}(z) = \left(\frac{p_{F,t}(z)}{P_{F,t}}\right)^{-\theta} C_{F,t}. \tag{3.9}$$

Two things are noteworthy. First, demand functions for consumption bundles $C_{H,t}$ and $C_{F,t}$ are affected by the home bias parameter χ. Even in the instance of $p_{H,t} = p_{F,t}$ the ratio of H-produced goods to F-produced goods is higher in the Home country. Second, in the case $\eta = \theta$, demand functions for $c_{H,t}(z)$ and $c_{F,t}(z)$ reduce to

$$c_{H,t}(z) = \chi \left(\frac{p_{H,t}(z)}{P_t}\right)^{-\theta} C_t \quad \text{and} \quad c_{F,t}(z) = (1-\chi)\left(\frac{p_{F,t}(z)}{P_t}\right)^{-\theta} C_t. \tag{3.10}$$

In the rest of the analysis we continue to assume that $\eta = \theta$.

By symmetry, in country F the following relations hold true:

$$C^*_{H,t} = (1-\chi)\left(\frac{p^*_{H,t}}{P^*_t}\right)^{-\eta} C^*_t; \quad C^*_{F,t} = \chi \left(\frac{p^*_{F,t}}{P^*_t}\right)^{-\eta} C^*_t; \tag{3.11}$$

$$c^*_{H,t}(z) = (1-\chi)\left(\frac{p^*_{H,t}(z)}{P^*_t}\right)^{-\theta} C^*_t \quad \text{and} \quad c^*_{F,t}(z) = \chi \left(\frac{p^*_{F,t}(z)}{P^*_t}\right)^{-\theta} C^*_t. \tag{3.12}$$

Consumption-based price indices

Consumption price indices, which minimize the cost of purchasing one unit of C_t and C^*_t, are given by

$$P_t = \left[\chi P_{H,t}^{1-\eta} + (1-\chi)P_{F,t}^{1-\eta}\right]^{1/(1-\eta)} \quad \text{and} \quad P^*_t = \left[\chi P_{F,t}^{1-\eta} + (1-\chi)P_{H,t}^{1-\eta}\right]^{1/(1-\eta)},$$

where

$$P_{H,t} = \left[\int_0^{1/2} p_{H,t}(z)^{1-\theta} dz\right]^{1/(1-\theta)} \quad \text{and} \quad P_{F,t} = \left[\int_{1/2}^{1} p_{F,t}(z)^{1-\theta} dz\right]^{1/(1-\theta)}.$$

Because there are no impediments to trade and the two countries share the same currency, the price of each differentiated good is the same in both countries, that is, $p_{H,t}(z) = p^*_{H,t}(z)$ and $p_{F,t}(z) = p^*_{F,t}(z)$ for each variety z. Thus, it also follows that $P^*_{H,t} = P_{H,t}$ and $P^*_{F,t} = P_{F,t}$. However, due to the idiosyncratic taste introduced in the preferences over consumption bundles, purchasing power parity does not hold in general. Hence: $P_t \neq P^*_t$.

Firms

In both economies there is a continuum of firms producing varieties of goods. Firms act as monopolistic competitors and use a Cobb–Douglas production technology which depends on employment, N, and a technology parameter A_t:

$$Y_t(z) = [N_t(z)]^{1-\alpha}. \tag{3.13}$$

We introduce a channel for fiscal policy by assuming that taxes on labour take the form of a uniform payroll tax.[6] Firms' demand for labour in each country for each good variety is therefore defined as

$$p_{j,t}(z)\left\{(1-\alpha)A_t\,[N_t(z)]^{-\alpha} - t_t^{PR}\right\} = W_t,\ \text{with}\ j = F,\ H, \tag{3.14}$$

where t_t^{PR} is the tax rate per unit of employed labour, that is, $t_t^{PR} = \frac{T_t^{PR}}{N_t}$, where T_t^{PR} are the total revenues from the payroll tax.

Turning next to firms' pricing behaviour, we consider a standard model of monopolistic competition with sticky prices, as in Galí *et al.* (2001) and Leith and Malley (2005).[7] More precisely, sticky prices are incorporated into this model by assuming a Calvo pricing mechanism. At any given time, only a fraction $1-\xi$ of firms can adjust prices, whereas the remainder supplies output on demand at a constant price. A share γ of the adjusting firms is assumed to follow a RoT,[8] while the remainder $1-\gamma$ set prices optimally to maximize expected discounted real profits.[9] The profit maximization problem can be formulated as

$$p_t^f(z) \max E_t \sum_{\infty}^{j=0} \alpha^j \Delta_{t,t+j}\left[\frac{p_t^f(z)}{P_{H,t+j}} Y_{t+j}(z) - TC_{t+j}^r(Y_{t+j}(z))\right] \tag{3.15}$$

$$\text{s.t.} \qquad Y_{t+j}(z) = \left[\frac{p_t^*(z)}{P_{H,t+j}}\right]^{-\theta} Y_{t+j}$$

where $p_t^f(z)$ denotes the new optimal price of producer z, $TC_{t+j}^r(Y_{t+j}(z))$ the real total cost function and $\Delta_{t,t+j}$ is the stochastic discount factor. The solution to this problem yields the familiar formula for the optimal reset price in a Calvo's setup:

$$p_t^f(z) = \frac{\theta}{\theta-1}\frac{E_t\sum_{j=0}^{\infty}\alpha_j\Delta_{t,t+j}\left[P_{H,t+j}^{\theta}Y_{t+j}MC_{t+j}^r(i)\right]}{E_t\sum_{j=0}^{\infty}\alpha_j\Delta_{t,t+j}\left[P_{H,t+j}^{\theta-1}Y_{t+j}\right]} \tag{3.16}$$

where $MC_t^r(i)$ denotes the real marginal costs function. Moreover, it is possible to show that

$$P_{H,t} = \left[\xi P_{H,t-1}^{1-\theta} + (1-\xi)(1-\gamma)\left(p_t^f\right)^{1-\theta} + (1-\xi)\gamma\left(p_t^b\right)^{1-\theta}\right]^{\frac{1}{1-\theta}} \tag{3.17}$$

where $p_t^b = \overline{p}_{t-1}(P_{H,t}/P_{H,t-1})$ and $\overline{p}_{t-1}$ is the index of prices set at time $t-1$. Similar expressions apply for country F.

Fiscal authority

In modelling the fiscal authorities' behaviour in each country there are two possible alternatives. On the one hand, we can consider fiscal authorities as having the same households' preferences (with the bias parameter as well). In this case, total demand for the generic good z stems from domestic and foreign households' consumption and from domestic *and* foreign governments' consumption. In this case

$$g_{H,t}(z) = \chi\left(\frac{p_{H,t}(z)}{p_{H,t}}\right)^{-\theta}\left(\frac{p_{H,t}}{P_t}\right)^{-\eta} G_t.$$

On the other hand, we can model domestic fiscal authority's preferences as defined only on domestically produced goods and similarly for the foreign fiscal authority. In this case

$$g_{H,t}(z) = \left(\frac{p_{H,t}(z)}{P_{H,t}}\right)^{-\theta} G_t.$$

For the sake of simplicity we shall model public expenditures according to the latter specification.

The global economy

The solution method first requires to derive expressions for the world weighted averages: $X_t^W = \frac{1}{2}\left[X_t + X_t^*\right]$. Country-specific variables are thus given by the simple transformation: $X_t = X_t^W + \frac{1}{2}\left[X_t - X_t^*\right]$. Let us define two other variables that will be useful throughout the analysis: the CPI-based real exchange rate $Q_t = P_t^*/P_t$ and the terms of trade $S_t = P_{F,t}/P_{H,t}$. At the world economy level, the resource constraint implies that

$$Y_t^W = C_t^W + G_t^W$$
$$Y_t + Y_t^* = C_t + C_t^* + G_t + G_t^*$$

where, according to our notation: $Y_t^W = \frac{1}{2}\left[Y_t + Y_t^*\right]$, $G_t^W = \frac{1}{2}\left[G_t + G_t^*\right]$.

World demand schedules for Home and Foreign differentiated good

World demand schedules for the generic z Home-produced differentiated good is given by $y_t(z) = c_{H,t}(z) + c^*_{H,t}(z) + g_{H,t}(z) + g^*_{H,t}(z)$, which can be rewritten as

$$y_t(z) = \chi \left(\frac{p_{H,t}(z)}{P_t}\right)^{-\eta} (C_t + G_t) + (1-\chi)\left(\frac{p^*_{H,t}(z)}{P^*_t}\right)^{-\eta} (C^*_t + G^*_t). \tag{3.18}$$

Integrating the above expression over $z \in [0, 1/2]$ and log-linearizing around the deterministic zero inflation steady state leads to

$$\hat{Y}_t = \chi\eta \left[\frac{C+G}{Y}\right](\hat{P}_t - \hat{P}_{H,t}) + \chi\left(\frac{C}{Y}\right)\hat{C}_t + \frac{G}{Y}\hat{G}_t$$
$$+ (1-\chi)\eta\left[\frac{C^*+G^*}{Y}\right](\hat{P}^*_t - \hat{P}_{H,t}) + (1-\chi)\left(\frac{C^*}{Y}\right)\hat{C}^*_t. \tag{3.19}$$

Hatted variables are defined as $\widehat{x} = \log(x_t/x)$, where x is the steady state value.

As the quantities $(\hat{P}_t - \hat{P}_{H,t})$ and $(\hat{P}^*_t - \hat{P}_{H,t})$ can compactly be written in terms of $\hat{S}_t$ as $\hat{P}_t - \hat{P}_{H,t} = (1-\chi)\hat{S}_t$ and $\hat{P}^*_t - \hat{P}_{H,t} = \chi\hat{S}_t$, expression (3.19) becomes

$$\hat{Y}_t = \Gamma\hat{S}_t + \chi\left(\frac{C}{Y}\right)\hat{C}_t + \frac{G}{Y}\hat{G}_t + (1-\chi)\left(\frac{C^*}{Y}\right)\hat{C}^*_t + \frac{G^*}{Y}\hat{G}^*_t \tag{3.20}$$

where $\Gamma = (C + G + C^* + G^*)\chi(1-\chi)\eta/Y$.

The IS and the Phillips curves

Derivation of the approximated IS curves requires a number of steps. Consider country H. First, log-linearize equations (3.4) and (3.5) to obtain

$$\hat{c}^{RoT}_t = \left[\frac{N^{RoT}\left(\frac{W}{P}\right)}{C^{RoT}}\right]\widehat{w}_t - \vartheta\left(\frac{T}{C^{RoT}}\right)\hat{T}_t, \tag{3.21}$$

$$\hat{C}^o_t = E_t\hat{C}^o_{t+1} - \lambda\left(\frac{1-\rho}{\rho}\right)\left[\hat{C}_{t-1} - \hat{C}_t\right] - \frac{1}{\rho}(\widehat{i}_t - E_t\widehat{\pi}_{t+1}), \tag{3.22}$$

where $\widehat{w}_t$ denotes the log-linearized real wage and $\widehat{i}_t = \log\left([1+i_t]/[1+\bar{i}]\right)$. Then, approximate the definition of aggregate consumption:

$$\hat{C}_t = \left[\frac{C^o}{C}\right]\hat{C}^o_t + \left[\frac{C^{RoT}}{C}\right]\hat{C}^{RoT}_t. \tag{3.23}$$

Note that imposing no habit, that is, $\lambda = 0$, and no RoT consumers, that is, $N^{RoT}/N = \vartheta = 0$, our specification would collapse to a purely forward-looking IS curve (see Carroll, 2000). More importantly, note also that the presence of non-optimizing consumers establishes a link between the demand for goods, net personal taxes, $\widehat{T}$, and the real wage. Analogously, in country F we have

$$\hat{C}_t^* = \left[\frac{C^{o*}}{C^*}\right]\hat{C}_t^{o*} + \left[\frac{C^{RoT*}}{C^*}\right]\hat{C}_t^{RoT*} \tag{3.24}$$

$$\hat{C}_t^{RoT*} = \left[\frac{N^{RoT*}(\frac{W^*}{P^*})}{C^{RoT*}}\right] w_t^* - \vartheta\left(\frac{T^*}{C^{RoT*}}\right)\hat{T}_t^* \tag{3.25}$$

$$\hat{C}_t^{o*} = E_t\hat{C}_{t+1}^{o*} - \lambda\left(\frac{1-\rho}{\rho}\right)\left[\hat{C}_{t-1}^* - \hat{C}_t^*\right] - \frac{1}{\rho}(\widehat{i}_t - E_t\widehat{\pi}_{t+1}^*). \tag{3.26}$$

Consolidating equations (3.21), (3.22) and (3.23) and making use of (3.20), we obtain the IS curve for country H (in what follows, Δ denotes the first difference operator):

$$\begin{aligned} E_t\Delta\hat{Y}_{t+1} &= \kappa_1(\widehat{i}_t - E_t\widehat{\pi}_{t+1}) + \kappa_2 E_t\Delta\hat{S}_{t+1} - \kappa_3 E_t\Delta\hat{S}_t + k_4 E_t\Delta\hat{C}_t^{RoT} + \\ &+ \kappa_5 E_t\Delta\hat{G}_{t+1} + k_6 E_t\Delta\hat{Y}_{t+1}^* - k_6\frac{G}{Y}\Delta E_t\hat{G}_{t+1}^* + \chi\kappa_3 E_t\Delta\hat{Y}_t + \\ &- (1-\chi)\kappa_3\Delta\hat{Y}_t^* - \chi\frac{G}{Y}\kappa_3 E_t\Delta\hat{G}_t + (1-\chi)\frac{G}{Y}\kappa_3 E_t\Delta\hat{G}_t^* \end{aligned} \tag{3.27}$$

and similarly for country F:

$$\begin{aligned} E_t\Delta\hat{Y}_{t+1}^* &= \kappa_1(\widehat{i}_t - E_t\widehat{\pi}_{t+1}^*) - \kappa_2 E_t\Delta\hat{S}_{t+1} + \kappa_3 E_t\Delta\hat{S}_t + k_4 E_t\Delta\hat{C}_t^{RoT*} + \\ &+ \kappa_5\Delta\hat{G}_{t+1}^* + k_6 E_t\Delta\hat{Y}_{t+1} - k_6\frac{G}{Y}E_t\Delta\hat{G}_{t+1} + \chi\kappa_3 E_t\Delta\hat{Y}_t^* + \\ &- (1-\chi)\kappa_3 E_t\Delta\hat{Y}_t - \chi\frac{G}{Y}\kappa_3 E_t\Delta\hat{G}_t^* + (1-\chi)\frac{G}{Y}\kappa_3 E_t\Delta\hat{G}_t \end{aligned} \tag{3.28}$$

where $\kappa_1 = (C^O/C)\rho^{-1}(2\chi - 1)/\chi$, $\kappa_2 = (\Gamma/\chi)$, $\kappa_3 = [\lambda C^O/C(\rho - 1)/\rho]1/\chi^2$, $k_4 = (2\chi - 1)/\chi$, $k_5 = G/Y$, $k_6 = ([1-\chi]/\chi)$. The variables $\widehat{\pi}_t$ and $\widehat{\pi}_t^*$ respectively define domestic and foreign consumer price inflation rates in terms of the inflation rates of domestically- and foreign-produced goods, that is,

$$\widehat{\pi}_t = \chi\widehat{\pi}_{H,t} + (1-\chi)\widehat{\pi}_{F,t} \tag{3.29}$$

$$\widehat{\pi^*}_t = (1-\chi)\widehat{\pi}_{F,t} + \chi\widehat{\pi}_{H,t} \tag{3.30}$$

and, moreover, $\Delta\hat{S}_t = \widehat{\pi}_{F,t} - \widehat{\pi}_{H,t}$.

Fiscal policy directly impacts on output in this model through three channels. First, through the usual resource withdrawal effect of government consumption, $\widehat{g}_t$. Second, through the impact of net personal taxes, $\widehat{T}$, on the current disposable income of RoT consumers. Third, through the impact of payroll taxes, T^{PR}, on the real wage of RoT consumers.[10] Finally, RoT consumers weaken the impact of interest rate policy on aggregate demand. As shown in Galí *et al.* (2007), this may have important implications for the conduct of monetary policy. Indeed, our estimates confirm that RoT consumers weaken the output response to interest rate changes. It is important to note that whilst government spending impacts on the consumption behaviour of optimizing consumers via the resource-withdrawal effect, taxation impacts through its effect on disposable income for RoT consumers, and hence via the external habit (total consumption) variable. As we shall see below, this drives some of the results of the model.

Turning to the Phillips curve, the log-linearization of the firms' optimal pricing decision together with the dynamic equation for the price index under the Calvo mechanism with indexation, leads to a New Keynesian Phillips Curve (NKPC). See Galí *et al.*, 2001 and Muscatelli *et al.*, 2003 for details. For each country, the Phillips curves are defined for the bundle of domestically produced goods:

$$\widehat{\pi}_{H,t} = \frac{\gamma\widehat{\pi}_{H,t-1} + \beta\xi E_t\widehat{\pi}_{H,t+1}}{\xi + \gamma(1-\xi(1-\beta))} + \frac{(1-\gamma)(1-\xi)(1-\beta\xi)}{[\xi+\gamma(1-\xi(1-\beta))]\left(1+\frac{\alpha\theta}{1-\alpha}\right)}\widehat{s}_{H,t} \tag{3.31}$$

$$\widehat{\pi}_{F,t} = \frac{\gamma\widehat{\pi}_{F,t-1} + \beta\xi E_t\widehat{\pi}_{F,t+1}}{\xi + \gamma(1-\xi(1-\beta))} + \frac{(1-\gamma)(1-\xi)(1-\beta\xi)}{[\xi+\gamma(1-\xi(1-\beta))]\left(1+\frac{\alpha\theta}{1-\alpha}\right)}\widehat{s}_{F,t} \tag{3.32}$$

$$\widehat{s}_{H,t} = \frac{N\left(\frac{W}{P}\right)}{N\left(\frac{W}{P}\right)+T^*}\left(\widehat{W}_t - \widehat{p}_{H,t}\right) + \frac{T^*}{N\left(\frac{W}{P}\right)+T^*}(\widehat{t^*_{H,t}} - \widehat{n}_{H,t}) + \widehat{n}_{H,t} - \widehat{y}_{H,t} \tag{3.33}$$

$$\widehat{s}_{F,t} = \frac{N\left(\frac{W}{P}\right)}{N\left(\frac{W}{P}\right)+T^*}\left(\widehat{W}^*_t - \widehat{p}_{F,t}\right) + \frac{T^*}{N\left(\frac{W}{P}\right)+T^*}(\widehat{t^*_{F,t}} - \widehat{n}_{F,t}) + \widehat{n}_{F,t} - \widehat{y}_{F,t} \tag{3.34}$$

where $\widehat{s}_{H,t}$ and $\widehat{s}_{F,t}$ are the percentage deviations from steady state of the labour cost share in country H and F respectively.

It is important to note that in estimating the parameters of the Phillips Curves, we do not explicitly model wage-setting behaviour, and the determination of employment is given by the static production function. Other recent contributions (Leith and Malley, 2005; Smets and Wouters, 2003) estimate wage equations, and adding a wage equation would have enabled us to consider the possibility of sticky wage dynamics with some forward-lookingness in wage-setting. However, this would have also added to the complexity of the model. In simulating our model, as we shall see below, we introduce an element of adjustment in nominal wages.

This amplifies the inertia generated by RoT consumers as the flexible wage introduces an immediate change in RoT consumption.

3.3 Estimates

3.3.1 Data

In order to simulate our model, we need to estimate or calibrate the parameter values. As we intend to employ a symmetric model of the EMU area, the best approach is to estimate the values of the parameters using aggregate euro-area data, and use these parameters for our two representative countries (H and F). The data employed is the aggregated euro-area data produced by the European Central Bank (see Fagan *et al.*, 2001). The time series are quarterly over the sample period 1970(3.1)–98(3.2). While we obtain new estimates of the structural parameters present for the global IS curve, for the NKPC we use the estimates reported in Galí *et al.* (2001, 2003), as these were obtained using the same data set.[11]

To capture the spirit of the New Keynesian models as log-linearizations, the data are transformed so that the variables are expressed in deviations from the 'steady state'.[12] Both real and nominal variables are de-trended using the Hodrick–Prescott filter with smoothing parameter set to 1600. Note that, as the inflation rate and interest rate always enter the model together, all the equations are 'balanced' in terms of the levels of integration of the dependent and explanatory variables.[13]

3.3.2 Estimation methods

The New Keynesian model consists of equations that are non-linear in parameters. Following Hansen (1982), a model with rational expectations suggests some natural orthogonality restrictions that can be used in the generalized methods of moments (GMM) framework. Each equation estimated using GMM is of the form:

$$\mathbf{y}_{it} = \mathbf{f}_i(\theta_i, \mathbf{z}_{it}) + \mathbf{u}_{it} \tag{3.35}$$

where, for each equation i, $\mathbf{y}_{it}$ is the vector of dependent variables, θ_i is the $(a_i \times 1)$ vector of unknown parameters to be estimated, and $\mathbf{z}_{it}$ is the $(k_i \times 1)$ vector of explanatory variables. The GMM approach is based on the fact that $\widetilde{\theta}_i$, the true value of θ_i, has the property $E[\mathbf{h}_i(\widetilde{\theta}_i, \mathbf{w}_{it})] = 0$, where $\mathbf{w}_{it} \equiv (\mathbf{y}'_{it}, \mathbf{z}'_{it}, \mathbf{x}'_{it})$, and $\mathbf{x}_{it}$ is an $(r_i \times 1)$ vector of instruments that are correlated with $\mathbf{z}_{it}$. GMM then chooses the estimate θ_i so as to make the sample moment as close as possible to the population moment of zero. The validity of these instruments can be tested for each equation by using Hansen's J-test, which is distributed as a $\chi^2(r_i - a_i)$ statistic under the null of valid orthogonality conditions.

GMM or IV estimation has been used by a number of authors to estimate NK models.[14] One problem is that the estimated IS and NKPC equations are highly non-linear in parameters, and the rank condition for identification is not met unless a number of parameters in these two equations are fixed. To begin with, in estimating the IS equation we impose that steady-state ratios for the global economy are

Table 3.1 Steady state ratios [sample period 1990(1)–1998(2)]

$\frac{C^W}{Y^W}$	$\frac{G^W}{Y^W}$	$\frac{(T^{PR})^W}{N^W(W/P)}$	$\frac{T^W}{Y^W}$	$\frac{(T^{PR})^W/N^W}{(W/P)+(T^{PR})^W/N^W}$
0.8	0.2	0.353	0.121	0.260

Table 3.2 Structural parameters estimates

Parameter	*Estimate*	*Description*
ϑ	0.508* (0.036)	Share of rule of thumb consumers
$(N^{Rot})^W/N^W$	0.617 (0.310)	Rule of thumb employment over total employment
$(C^O)^W/C^W$	0.658 (0.156)	Optimising consumption over total consumption
β	0.923+ (0.071)	Subjective discount factor
ξ	0.843+ (0.066)	Calvo parameter
γ	0.307+ (0.128)	Share of rule of thumb firms

Notes
Standard errors are reported in brackets.
* estimated in the first step of our procedure.
+ estimates taken from Gali *et al.* (2001, 2003).

given by their average values computed over the sub-sample period 1990(3.1)–98(3.2).[15] Results are reported in Table 3.1 (superscript W refers to the global economy).

Furthermore, in order to increase the accuracy of the estimation we calibrate some structural parameters at values taken from other empirical studies. We impose the habit formation parameter on aggregate consumption to be equal to unity, that is, $\lambda = 1$, the coefficient of relative risk aversion to be equal to two, that is, $\sigma_c = 2$.

3.3.3 Model estimates

Table 3.2 reports our results obtained using GMM over the full sample period for the model expressed in world variables terms. Our vector of instruments include a constant plus de-trended output, government spending excluding government transfers, direct taxes per worker, nominal exchange rate, wage rate, inflation rate and nominal interest rate. Our results are obtained imposing six lags on the instruments.

In estimating the NK output equation we employ a two-step procedure. Initially, we estimate a reduced form of IS curve for the global economy rewritten as

$$\widehat{Y}_t^W = b_1 E_t(\Delta\widehat{w}_{t+1}) + b_2 E_t \Delta \widehat{T}_{t+1}^W + b_3 \widehat{G}_t^W + b_4 \left(\widehat{Y}_{t-1}^W \quad \frac{G}{Y} \widehat{G}_{t-1}^W \right) + b_5 \left(\widehat{i}_t - E_t \widehat{\pi}_{t+1}^W \right) + b_6 \left(E_t \widehat{Y}_{t+1}^W - \frac{G}{Y} E_t \widehat{G}_{t+1}^W \right) \tag{3.36}$$

where

$$b_1 = -\frac{k_4 (N^{RoT})^W (W/P)}{(1+\chi\kappa_3)(C^{RoT})^W}; \quad b_2 = \vartheta \frac{k_4 T^W}{(1+\chi\kappa_3)(C^{RoT})^W};$$

$$b_3 = \frac{\kappa_5 + \chi G^W / Y^W \kappa_3}{1+\chi\kappa_3}; \quad b_4 = \frac{\chi\kappa_3}{1+\chi\kappa_3};$$

$$b_5 = -\frac{\kappa_1}{1+\chi\kappa_3}; \quad b_6 = 1/(1+\chi\kappa_3).$$

In (3.36) we thus restrict the coefficients on $\widehat{Y}^W_{t-1}$ and $E_t\widehat{Y}^W_{t+1}$ to be respectively equal to negative the coefficients on $(G^W/Y^W)\widehat{G}^W_{t-1}$ and $(G^W/Y^W)E_t\widehat{G}^W_{t+1}$. Dividing the estimated coefficient on $\Delta\widehat{T}^W_{t+1}$, that is, $\hat{b}_2$, by the coefficient on $E_t\widehat{Y}^W_{t+1} - (G^W/Y^W)E_t\widehat{G}^W_{t+1}$ multiplied by $-(T^W/Y^W)$, that is, $-\hat{b}_6(T^W/Y^W)^{-1}$, one retrieves a point estimate for the share of RoT consumers. In particular, it turns out that $\hat{\vartheta}$ is 0.508 with asymptotic standard error of 0.036.[16] In the second step we re-estimate (3.36) imposing the values of σ_c, λ and $\hat{\vartheta}$ and the steady state ratios and obtain structural estimates for the parameters $(N^{RoT})^W/N^W$ and $(C^o)^W/C^W$.

We find that 65% of total consumption in steady state is generated by optimizing consumers. RoT consumers account for about 61% of total employment. The overall fit for the estimated equation is good: the R^2 statistic for (3.36) is 0.83. The Hansen statistic for over-identifying restrictions test is 59.39, which is distributed as a $\chi^2(41)$ under the null hypothesis of valid instruments. The null hypothesis of valid instruments is not rejected at the 5% significance level. In the following table we report parameter estimates for the NKPC. Point estimates of the Calvo parameter suggest that about 84% of firms do not adjust their prices every period and of those who adjust prices, about 30% simply index prices.

In addition to the estimated parameters, we set χ, the proportion of home-produced goods in the consumption of each country, as equal to 0.7, which reflects a bias towards home-produced goods in most large Euroland countries and the parameter θ, the elasticity of demand for consumption goods, as equal to 4. In order to close the model we need to describe the behaviour of the monetary and fiscal authorities. As noted above, we do not consider strategic interactions between the ECB and the two countries' fiscal authorities. Instead, we examine the interaction between a central bank which operates a forward-looking inflation targeting framework, and fiscal authorities which rely on fiscal rules based on automatic stabilizers. In this model, monetary policy has a relatively weak effect due to the relatively large proportion of RoT consumers, who only indirectly react to the interest rate rule.[17] In addition, fiscal policy operates through a wider number of channels: taxation effects on consumption through liquidity-constrained consumers, taxation wedge effects on inflation, and interaction effects due to the presence of RoT consumers.

3.3.4 Monetary rule

In contrast to the numerous papers on the behaviour of the Federal Reserve and other central banks, the empirical literature on the behaviour of the ECB is limited, mainly due to its short history. We assume that the ECB's monetary policy rule for the nominal interest rate $\widehat{i}_t$ is similar to the standard forward-looking Taylor rule specification which has become commonplace in the literature[18] (see Clarida *et al.*, 1998, 2000; Muscatelli *et al.*, 2002; Giannoni and Woodford, 2002a,b):

$$\widehat{i}_t = \phi_1 E_t \widehat{\pi}_{t+q} + \phi_2 E_t \widehat{y}_{t+s} + \phi_3 \widehat{i}_{t-1} \tag{3.37}$$

where we also allow for inertia, due to interest-rate smoothing, if $\phi_3 \neq 0$. As shown by Sauer and Sturm (2003), this forward-looking inertial Taylor rule fits the Euroland data reasonably well for the post-EMU period. We use their estimates of the ϕ_i parameters to simulate our model. This provides a benchmark to assess the performance of different designs for automatic fiscal stabilizers in our structural model.

3.3.5 Fiscal rules

Unlike Muscatelli *et al.* (2003a), we consider a simple format for our fiscal policy rules and let automatic stabilizers depend on current real activity condition and lagged debt accumulation (relative to output). Thus

$$\widehat{g}_t = -\delta_1 \widehat{y}_t - \delta_2 (\widehat{b}_{t-1} - \widehat{y}_{t-1}) \tag{3.38}$$

$$\widehat{g}_t^* = -\delta_1 \widehat{y}_t^* - \delta_2 (\widehat{b}_{t-1}^* - \widehat{y}_{t-1}^*) \tag{3.39}$$

and

$$\widehat{\tau}_t = \varphi_1 \widehat{y}_t + \varphi_2 (\widehat{b}_{t-1} - \widehat{y}_{t-1}) \tag{3.40}$$

$$\widehat{\tau}_t^* = \varphi_1 \widehat{y}_t^* + \varphi_2 (\widehat{b}_{t-1}^* - \widehat{y}_{t-1}^*) \tag{3.41}$$

where $\widehat{\tau}_t$ is the vector of our two tax measures, personal taxes $\widehat{t}_t$ and payroll taxes $\widehat{t}_t^{TR}$. Our taxation rule therefore imposes the same adjustment pattern on both taxes, and does not look at how a mix of tax measures might improve the design of policy.[19] The importance of the fiscal policy mix is considered further below. We have a limited feedback to the debt accumulation, through a debt/GDP term which approximates to a response to the debt/GDP ratio. For our baseline case, we set $\delta_1 = \varphi_1 = 0.5$ and $\delta_2 = \varphi_2 = 0.05$. A coefficient of 0.5 on output is consistent with the empirical evidence in Van den Noord (2000) and adopted in studies on fiscal stabilization (e.g. Westaway, 2003). The coefficient on debt ensures stability but ensures that this does not swamp the impact of fiscal stabilizers given the configuration of the temporary shocks.

3.4 Dynamic simulations

Having obtained the structural parameter estimates, we can perform dynamic simulations of our two-country New Keynesian model[20] and examine the transmission mechanism of fiscal and monetary policies. We focus on the dynamic model solution under rational expectations and examine impulse response functions to a number of shocks. As we do not have an estimated wage equation, we assume a minimum amount of nominal inertia in the model by stipulating that nominal wages adjust gradually towards the initial real wage equilibrium with an autoregressive parameter of 0.5 per quarter. Employment is determined by the log-linearization of the production technology (3.13).

We examine the extent to which national fiscal policies can assist with macroeconomic adjustment in EMU. The key issues we consider are: do automatic stabilizers actually assist the ECB's function of stabilizing output and inflation in the union, that is, do the fiscal authorities assist or impede the efforts of the ECB? Which fiscal instruments are more effective in stabilizing the union and the individual economies? How do the stabilization properties of fiscal policy vary in response to symmetric and asymmetric shocks?

3.4.1 Government spending rules versus taxation rules in the global economy

We first perform some dynamic simulations for the global economy. In each simulation we consider four different policy scenarios:

1 where fiscal policy is kept exogenously fixed, that is, the automatic stabilizers (3.38), (3.39), (3.40) and (3.41) are switched off (labelled 'M');
2 where only the government spending rule is switched on (labelled 'M+G');
3 where only the taxation feedback rule is switched on (labelled 'M+T');
4 where both rules are switched on (labelled 'M+G+T').

Figure 3.1 displays the impulse response functions for output gap, inflation, nominal and real interest rate following a unit negative supply shock, modelled as a disturbance appended to the aggregate Phillips curve, with 0.5 autoregressive parameter. Consider first the case 'M'. A negative supply shock on impact increases inflation (about 6% relative to steady state) and calls for a restrictive monetary policy. The rise in both nominal and real interest rate engineers a series of negative output gaps which gradually take the economy back to long-run equilibrium. As shown in the Figure 3.1, the role of automatic stabilizers is clear. When the government spending rule operates alone (M + G), there is initially a more pronounced recession for the first three quarters, but then it tends to mildly stabilize output. Inflation dynamics is essentially unaffected. Fiscal rules based on taxation (M + T) instead achieve a sizeable stabilization of output and inflation. This is obtained both through the direct effect of lump-sum taxes on disposable income, and through the impact of the payroll tax on inflation. By contrast, government expenditure only

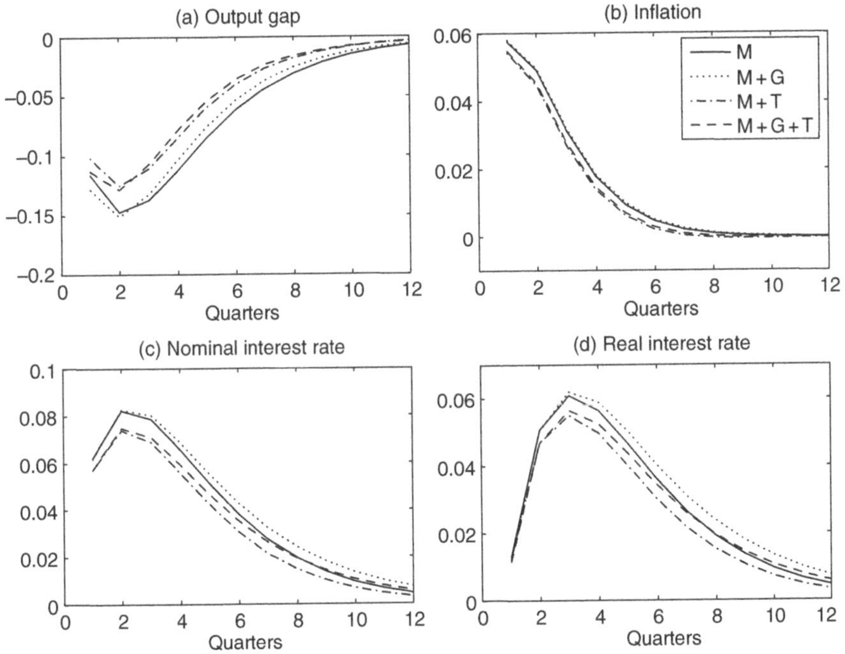

Figure 3.1 Impulse response function to a unit negative supply shock $\rho^a = 0.5$.

has an indirect effect on RoT consumption, by marginally stabilizing output. The performance is relatively good when the three rules operate contemporaneously, (M + G + T), although again government spending has initially adverse effects on output and inflation.

Figure 3.2 displays the impulse response functions for output gap, inflation, nominal and real interest rate following a positive preference shock modelled as a disturbance appended to the aggregate IS curve, with 0.5 autoregressive parameter. In this case the fiscal rules have very different effects on output and inflation. In general, spending rules and taxation rules do guarantee output stabilization (and it turns out that having all the three rules active is better) but might have distorting effects on inflation. In particular, this is true for taxation rules.

Rather than assuming a particular form of welfare loss function, in what follows we consider how the introduction of a fiscal policy rule impacts on output and inflation variability (variance frontiers) when it is combined with a monetary policy rule such as (3.37). Conducting welfare analysis is complex in this model, due to the presence of heterogeneous consumers (optimizers and RoT consumers),[21] but computing variance frontiers allows a certain ranking of policy rules, where it is apparent that one rule dominates the other in terms of reducing both output and inflation variability. To construct the variance frontiers we apply a monetary policy rule where we keep fixed parameters ϕ_2 and ϕ_3 and we allow ϕ_1 to vary.[22] We

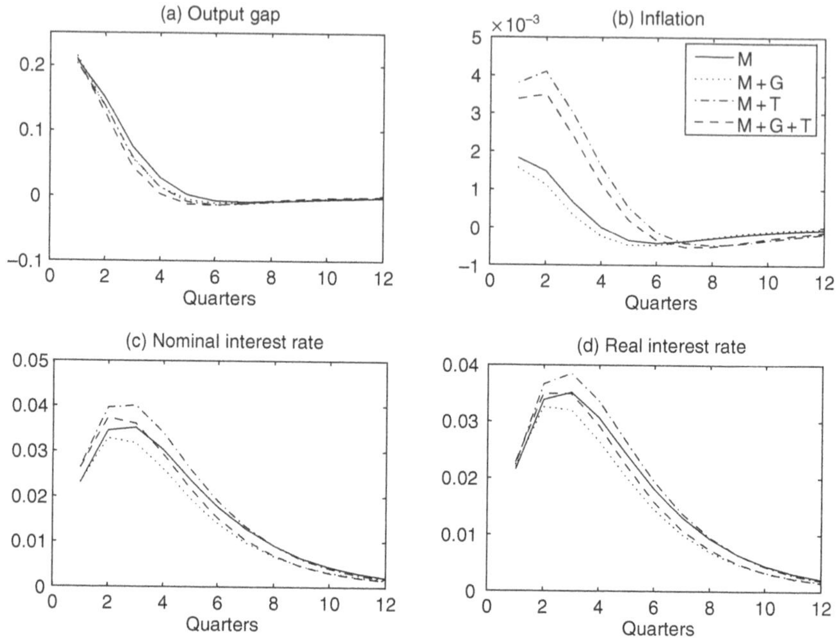

Figure 3.2 Impulse response function to a unit preference shock $\rho^c = 0.5$.

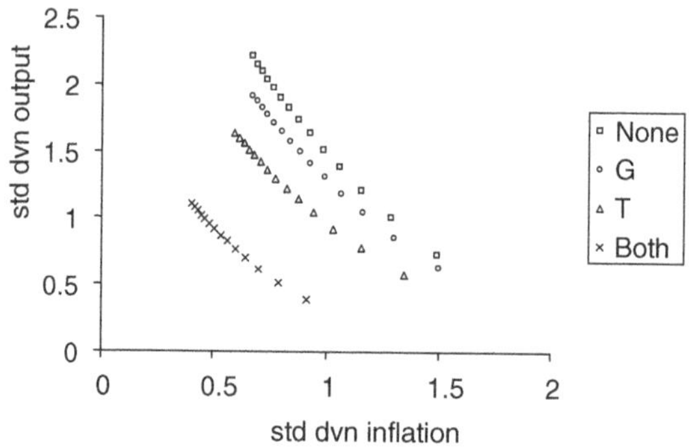

Figure 3.3 Variance frontiers and monetary-fiscal interaction.

then compute the standard deviation of output and inflation in dynamic simulations following a shock to the Phillips Curve, and report these 'variance frontiers' in the figure which follows.

Figure 3.3 shows the variance frontiers when the model is simulated following a temporary negative technology combining the forward-looking monetary policy rule with the four fiscal regimes outlined above (M, M + G, M + T, M + G + T). There are three points to note about these results. The first is that, in contrast with

Muscatelli *et al.* (2003), automatic stabilizers are no longer welfare-reducing. In particular, counter-cyclical taxation policy seems able to reduce the variance of both output and inflation. The second point to note is that also government spending does not have an unambiguous welfare-enhancing effect: introducing a feedback rule for government spending tends to shift the variance frontier, although less than in the previous case, towards the origin lowering the variability of both output inflation. The explanation for this result lies in the different ways in which government spending and taxation operate in the model: government spending varies the profile of output but its impact is ultimately reversed, as the distributed lag effect sums to zero. In contrast, taxation has an impact through the wedge (a level effect) and through the IS curve (in difference terms), and this is not reversed because of its impact on external habits. The third point is that introducing both automatic stabilizers is still preferable to having none. In this case the westwards shift in the variance frontier is even more visible, suggesting that a combination of both automatic stabilizers can have a much greater impact on the variance frontier.

To investigate the importance of personal taxes relative to payroll taxes in stabilizing output and inflation, we repeated the above experiment using only personal taxes and then using only payroll taxes. In general, we found that most of the stabilization effect comes from payroll taxes through their impact on the wedge, especially for cases where ϕ_1 is high. The intuition for this is straightforward: following an adverse shock to the Phillips curve, payroll taxes fall, stabilize both inflation (through the wedge effect) and output (through the disposable income of RoT consumers). In contrast, personal taxes act only through the IS curve and hence stabilize output at the expense of inflation stability. Only when ϕ_1 is low, so that the monetary authority reacts less forcefully to the inflation shock, personal taxes help to stabilize output and inflation. In other words, payroll taxes are generally more complementary to monetary policy in this model.

3.4.2 *What is the value added from fiscal automatic stabilizers in individual countries?*

We now simulate the model in response to a temporary demand (to the IS curve) and a temporary supply (to the NKPC curve) shock to one of the two countries. We consider a shock of 1% in the first period which then decays over time with an autoregressive parameter of 0.5. The reason for not considering pure asymmetric shocks (shocks of equal and opposite sign on each EMU country) is that, given the identical structure of the two countries, and that the ECB is assumed to target EMU average outcomes, monetary policy will not react to such shocks. Following the asymmetric demand and supply shocks considered here, the union's inflation and output levels will change, thus triggering a response from the ECB. This will allow us to compute the value added in terms of the impact on output and inflation variability. We report the results in Tables 3.3 and 3.4 for both asymmetric demand and supply shocks (modelled respectively as transitory shocks to the IS and the Phillips curve in country H), and symmetric demand and supply shocks (transitory shocks to IS curves in both countries and Phillips curves in both

Table 3.3 Relative variances to asymmetric shocks

	Asy. demand shock			*Asy. supply shock*		
	$T+G/M$	T/M	G/M	$T+G/M$	T/M	G/M
Var(Y)	0.216	0.960	0.885	0.834	0.955	0.868
Var(Y*)	0.191	0.913	0.768	0.809	0.942	0.845
Var(Y-Y*)	0.211	0.951	0.863	0.824	0.949	0.858
Var(π)	0.204	0.922	0.889	0.982	0.992	1.001
Var(π*)	0.181	0.853	0.426	1.150	1.217	0.970
Var(πc)	0.214	0.949	0.659	0.995	0.992	1.001
Var(πc*)	0.141	0.728	0.187	1.009	1.014	0.998

Table 3.4 Relative variances to symmetric shocks

	Sym. demand shock			*Sym. supply shock*		
	$T+G/M$	T/M	G/M	$T+G/M$	T/M	G/M
Var(Y) = Var(Y*)	0.894	0.973	0.920	0.894	0.984	0.922
Var(π) = Var(π*)	1.005	1.059	0.964	0.999	0.999	1.000
Var(πc) = Var(πc*)	1.005	1.058	0.964	0.999	0.999	1.000

countries respectively). The results in Tables 3.3 and 3.4 are reported as the ratio of the variances of output (for each country and for the output differential) and inflation (for both product prices π and consumer prices π^c) and in the scenarios 2–4 relative to scenario 1. Thus, for instance G/M gives the relative variance of output and inflation under policy scenario 2 relative to scenario 1, and $(T+G)/M$ reports the relative variances for scenario 4 relative to scenario 1. A value of the variance ratio in excess of unity suggests that adding the fiscal instrument(s) is destabilizing relative to using ECB policy alone, and vice versa.[23] In the case of the symmetric shocks, the variability of output and inflation is obviously identical across countries because of model symmetry.

Turning first to Table 3.3, we immediately see that both fiscal instruments stabilize output and that simultaneous activation enhances their role. The latter result is particularly strong in the case of asymmetric demand shock, where the variability of domestic output is reduced by approximately 80%. To a much lesser extent, this conclusion also holds for asymmetric supply shocks. Turning to Table 3.4, 3.5, 3.6, the results for symmetric shocks also suggest a complementarity between the two fiscal policy instruments. This is in sharp contrast with the 'Brussels consensus' based on the view that the ECB alone should stabilize the union-wide economy (Buti *et al.*, 2001).[24]

3.5 Conclusions

This chapter has used a two-country New Keynesian DSGE model to examine the extent to which national fiscal policies can assist macroeconomic adjustment

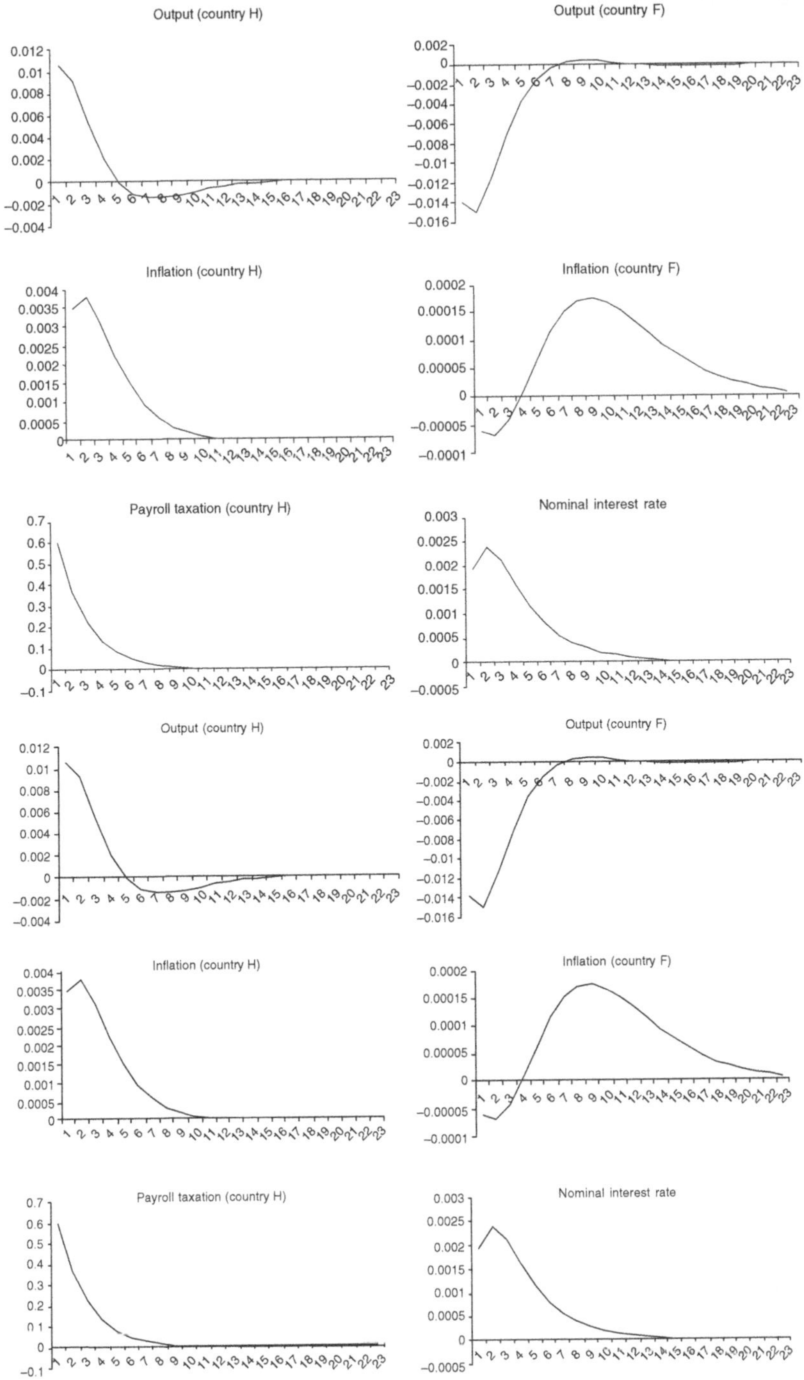

Figure 3.4 Impulse response functions to a 1% payroll taxation shock.

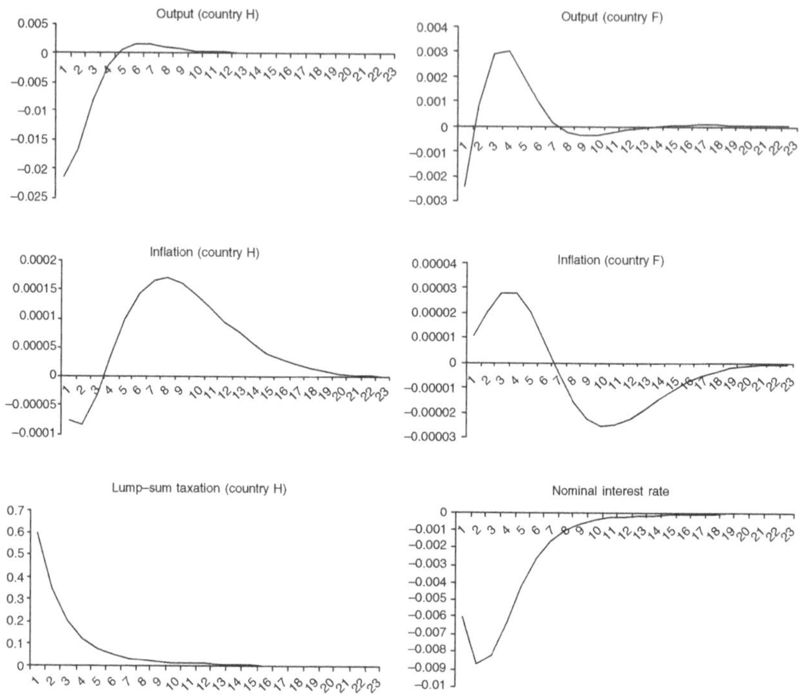

Figure 3.5 Impulse response functions to a 1% lump-sum taxation shock.

within EMU, in response to a variety of shocks. We use a model which embodies liquidity-constrained (RoT) consumers and home bias in consumption, and use some recent estimates of the structural model on euro area data to calibrate our model. The key conclusion which emerges from our analysis is that automatic stabilizers based on both government spending and taxation policy seem to combine efficiently with forward-looking (inertial) Taylor rules on the part of the ECB in the case of symmetric shocks. In contrast with the popular view that takes for granted the effectiveness of automatic stabilizers in the face of asymmetric shocks, we find that national stabilizers play a role only if private consumption and/or government spending exhibit a significant home bias. Further research should consider the possibility that progressive income tax rates could help to stabilize inflation through the well-known fiscal drag mechanism.

Notes

1 The implied fiscal multiplier is close to or greater than unity.
2 Whether consumption actually increases in such models depends crucially on the assumptions made about labour supply and price-stickiness, given the linkage between consumption and leisure (and hence the real wage) via the consumer's optimization problem.

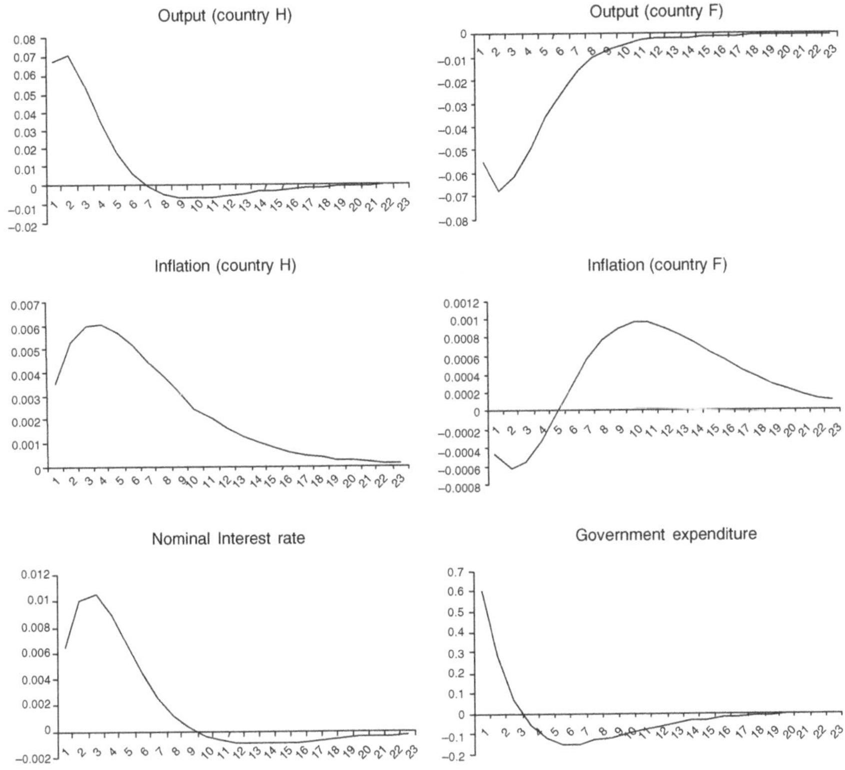

Figure 3.6 Impulse response functions to a 1% government expenditure shock.

3 See Galí *et al.* (2001); Smets and Wouters (2003); Leith and Malley (2005).

4 Galí *et al.* (2007) show that supplying a constant amount of labour is optimal when personal taxes, T_t, levied on RoT consumers are always nil. This result would never obtain in our model, where taxes and transfers are explicitly modelled. Thus, for the sake of simplicity we assume a constant labour supply. Since consumption cannot be negative, this implies that we impose a lower bound on T_t for any given level of the real wage.

5 In what follows, subscript H or F denote the country where differentiated consumption goods are produced.

6 This implies that the optimizing consumer's choice between leisure and consumption is not affected.

7 See also Erceg *et al.* (2000) and Sbordone (2002).

8 This was pioneered by Galí and Gertler (1999). Similar backward-looking elements can be introduced to the NKPC equation by introducing indexation of all non-re-optimized prices (Woodford, 2002, chapter 3; and Christiano *et al.*, 2005).

9 A similar specification for the NKPC can be obtained by making the indexation process part of the optimization process (see Smets and Wouters, 2003).

10 From equations (3.4) and (3.14) it should be clear that, in each period, the equilibrium real wage is inversely related to employment and the payroll tax.

11 The estimation was carried out using RATS, version 5.
12 Which is commonplace in this literature (see Smets and Wouters, 2003; Leith and Malley, 2005).
13 The government spending data (G) is total government spending excluding transfers and interest payments, whilst we use employers' social security contributions as payroll taxes (T^{PR}), and personal taxes as (T).
14 For instance, Galí *et al.* (2001); Kara and Nelson (2002); Muscatelli *et al.* (2003) and Leith and Malley (2005).
15 $N(W/P)/Y$ is simply equal to the labour share in equilibrium, which we set equal to $(1-\alpha) = 0.6$.
16 The standard error has been computed using the delta method.
17 As shown in Galí *et al.* (2007), RoT consumers are affected by interest rate changes only to the extent that the real wage adjusts following the new labour conditions determined by the optimizing consumers' reaction to such interest rate changes.
18 The main difference is that we use a contemporaneous value of the output gap (see Muscatelli *et al.* (2002)) as opposed to expected future values, as in Clarida *et al.* (1998, 2000). For a detailed discussion of these issues, see Giannoni and Woodford (2002a,b). For an alternative approach to modelling interest rate responses involving non-linearities in reaction functions, see Cukierman and Muscatelli (2001).
19 Andres and Domenech (2003) provide an analysis of how different tax measures might impact on output and inflation variability.
20 The model is solved using Winsolve version 3.0 (see Pierse (2000)), which provides numerical solutions for linear and non-linear rational expectations models. We solve our model using the Stacked Newton method in Winsolve. In solving the models with structural shocks (and further below with policy shocks) these are treated as unanticipated by economic agents.
21 See for instance Benigno and Woodford (2004). We are currently considering the extension of our modelling framework to include some welfare analysis.
22 The variance frontiers are plotted for values of ϕ_1 which vary between 0.2 and 1.5. The reason for focusing on higher values of ϕ_1 compared to the estimated value is that it is often argued that estimated monetary policy rules tend to underestimate the response of the central bank to shifts in expected inflation (and conversely overestimate the degree of inertia) because central banks do not continuously change their monetary stance.
23 To facilitate the understanding of how fiscal policy tools affect individual economies, in Figures 3.4, 3.5, 3.6 at the end of the chapter we show the impulse response functions to fiscal variables in the home economy.
24 Following Van den Noord (2000); Andres and Domenech (2003) and Westaway (2003), in our simulation exercises we also experimented backward-looking specification, where fiscal instruments depend on y_{t-1}. Our results are robust to this modification. However, some important differences arise when the fiscal rules include an autoregressive term with coefficient 0.5. In this case, the stabilizing properties of automatic stabilizers are significantly weakened.

References

Amato, J. D. and Laubach, T. (2003), 'Rule-of-thumb behavior and monetary policy', *European Economic Review*, 47: 791–831.

Andres, J. and Domenech, R. (2006), 'Automatic stabilisers, fiscal rules and macroeconomic stability', *European Economic Review,* 50: 1487–1506.

Asdrubali, P. and Soyoung Kim (2004), 'Dynamic risksharing in the United States and Europe', *Journal of Monetary Economics*, 51: 809–36.

Ball, L. (1997), 'A proposal for the next macroeconomic reform', *Victoria Economic Commentaries*, March, 1–7.

Benigno, P. and Woodford, M. (2004), 'Optimal monetary and fiscal policy: a linear-quadratic approach', in NBER Macroeconomics Annual 2003, 18: 271–333 Cambridge (US).

Blanchard, O. J. (1985), 'Debt, deficit and finite horizons', *Journal of Political Economy*, 93: 223–47.

Blanchard, O. J. and Perotti, R. (2001), 'An empirical characterization of the dynamic effects of changes in government spending and taxes on output', *Quarterly Journal of Economics*, 117: 1329–68.

Buti, M., Franco, D. and Ongena, H. (1997), 'Budgetary Policies during Recessions – Retrospective Application of the "Stability and Growth Pact" to the Post-War Period', European Commission, Economic Paper no. 121.

Buti, M., Roeger, W. and in't Veld, J. (2001), 'Stabilizing output and inflation in EMU: policy conflicts and cooperation under the Stability Pact', *Journal of Common Market Studies*, 39: 801–28.

Calmfors, L. (2003), 'Fiscal policy to stabilise the domestic economy in the EMU: what can we learn from monetary policy?', *CESifo Economic Studies*, 3: 3–25.

Christiano, L. J., Eichenbaum, M. and Evans, C. (2005), 'Nominal rigidities and the dynamic effects of a shock to monetary policy', *Journal of Political Economy*, 113: 1–45.

Clarida, R., Galí, J. and Gertler. M. (1998), 'Monetary policy rules in practice: some international evidence', *European Economic Review*, 42: 1033–67.

—— (2000), 'Monetary policy rules and macroeconomic stability: evidence and some theory', *Quarterly Journal of Economics*, vol. CXV, issue 1, 147–80.

Cukierman, A. and Muscatelli, V. A. (2001), 'Do central banks have precautionary demands for expansions and for price stability? – theory and evidence', CESifo Discussion Paper no. 764.

Erceg, C. J., Henderson, D. W. and Levin, A. T. (2000), 'Optimal monetary policy with staggered wage and price contracts', *Journal of Monetary Economics*, 46: 281–313.

Fagan, G., Henry, J. and Mestre, R. (2001), 'An area-wide model (AWM) for the Euro area', ECB Working Paper no. 42.

Fair, R. (2001), 'Estimates of the effectiveness of monetary policy', Cowles Foundation and International Center of Finance, Yale University. Discussion Paper no. 1298.

Fatás, A. and Mihov, I. (2001), 'Government size and automatic stabilizers: international and intranational evidence', *Journal of International Economics*, 55: 3–28.

Favero, C. A. and Monacelli, T. (2003), 'Monetary-fiscal mix and inflation performance: evidence from the US', CEPR Discussion Paper no. 3887.

Galí, J. (2003), 'New perspectives on monetary policy, inflation, and the business cycle', in M. Dewatripont, L. Hansen and S. Turnovsky (eds), *Advances in Economic Theory*, vol. III, 151–97, Cambridge: Cambridge University Press.

Galí, J. and Gertler, M. (1999), 'Inflation dynamics: a structural econometric analysis', *Journal of Monetary Economics*, 44: 195–222.

Galí, J., Gertler, M. and López-Salido, D. (2001), 'European inflation dynamics', *European Economic Review*, 45: 1237–70.

—— (2003), 'Erratum to "European inflation dynamics"', *European Economic Review*, 47: 759–60.

Galí, J., López-Salido, D. and Valles, J. (2007), 'Understanding the effects of government spending on consumption', *Journal of the European Economic Association*, 5(1): 227–70.

Giannoni, M. P. and Woodford, M. (2002a), 'Optimal interest-rate rules: I. general theory', NBER Working Paper no. 9419.

Giannoni, M. P. and Woodford, M. (2002b), 'Optimal interest-rate rules: I. applications', NBER Working Paper no. 9420.

Giavazzi, F., Jappelli, T. and Pagano, M. (2000), 'Searching for non-linear effects of fiscal policy: evidence from industrial and developing countries', *European Economic Review*, 44: 1259–89.

Gordon, D. B. and Leeper, E. M. (2003), 'Are countercyclical fiscal policies counterproductive?', Paper presented at 5th Bundesbank Spring Conference, May.

Hansen, L. P. (1982), 'Large sample properties of generalized method of moments estimators', *Econometrica*, 50: 1029–54.

Kara, A. and Nelson, E. (2002), 'The exchange rate and inflation in the UK', Bank of England, External MPC Unit, Discussion Paper no. 11.

Leith, C. and Malley, J. (2005), 'Estimated general equilibrium models for the evaluation of monetary policy in the US and Europe', *European Economic Review*, 49: 2137–59.

Leith, C. and Wren-Lewis, S. (2000), 'Interactions between monetary and fiscal policy rules', *The Economic Journal*, 110: C93–C108.

Linnemann, L. and Schabert, A. (2003), 'Fiscal policy in the new neoclassical synthesis', *Journal of Money Credit and Banking*, 35: 911–29.

Muscatelli, V. A., Tirelli, P. and Trecroci, C. (2002), 'Does institutional change really matter? Inflation targets, central bank reform and interest rate policy in the OECD countries', The Manchester School, 70: 487–527.

—— (2003), 'Can fiscal policy help macroeconomic stabilization? evidence from a New Keynesian model with liquidity constraints', CESifo Working Paper no. 1171.

—— (2004a), 'The interaction of fiscal and monetary policies: some evidence using structural models', *Journal of Macroeconomics*, 2: 257–280.

—— (2004b), 'Monetary and fiscal policy interactions over the cycle: some empirical evidence', in R. Beetsma, C. Favero, A. Missale, V. A. Muscatelli, P. Natale and P. Tirelli (eds), *Fiscal Policies, Monetary Policies and Labour Markets. Key Aspects of European Macroeconomic Policies after Monetary Unification*, Cambridge: Cambridge University Press: 256–296.

Pierse, R. (2000), Winsolve, version 3.5. University of Surrey.

Sarantis, N. and Stewart, C. (2003), 'Liquidity constraints, precautionary saving and aggregate consumption: an international comparison', *Economic Modelling*, 20: 1151–73.

Sauer, S. and Sturm, J. E. (2003), 'ECB monetary policy: how well does the Taylor Rule describe it?', Mimeo, University of Munich.

Sbordone, A. G. (2002), 'Prices and unit labor costs: a new test of price stickiness', *Journal of Monetary Economics*, 49: 265–92.

Smets, F. and Wouters, R. (2003), 'An estimated dynamic stochastic general equilibrium model of the euro area', *Journal of the European Economic Association*, 1: 1123–75.

Van den Noord, P. (2000), 'The size and role of automatic fiscal stabilizers in the 1990s and beyond', OECD Working Paper no. ECO/WKP 2000.

Westaway, P. (2003), 'Modelling shocks and adjustment mechanisms in EMU', HM Treasury, EMU Studies.

Woodford, M. (2002), *Interest and Prices: Foundations of a Theory of Monetary Policy*, Princeton: Princeton University Press.

Wren-Lewis, S. (2000a), 'The limits to discretionary fiscal stabilization policy', *Oxford Review of Economic Policy*, 16: 92–105.

—— (2002b), 'Fiscal policy, inflation and stabilisation in EMU', Working Paper, University of Exeter.

Part II

Empirical analyses of national fiscal stances

4 Measuring and assessing fiscal automatic stabilizers*

J. Mélitz

4.1 Introduction

Studies of discretionary fiscal policy often centre on the 'cyclically-adjusted budget balance', or the budget balance following an adjustment for the part that depends on an automatic response to events. It is also often assumed that all of the adjustments to the cycle come from taxes and unemployment compensation. In addition, following cyclical adjustment, the analysis of discretionary fiscal policy frequently concerns the ratio of the cyclically adjusted government balance to output or potential output rather than the level. I shall put forward two criticisms of this procedure. First, many of the automatic responses to events result from other transfer payments besides unemployment compensation, including payments for pensions, sickness, subsistence, invalidity, childcare and subsidies of all sorts to firms. Second, if the issue is the ratio of the cyclically adjusted budget balance, the cyclical adjustment should be for the ratio rather than the level. Otherwise, the estimates of the cyclical adjustment are inefficient. According to both arguments, the usual estimates of the series for discretionary fiscal policy are often incorrect. The first criticism always applies when there is recourse to official sources for figures for the 'cyclically-adjusted budget balances' since those figures are constructed on the assumption that taxes and unemployment compensation are the sole elements of the budget that respond to the cycle. The second criticism follows whenever the subsequent analysis focuses on ratios.

If the analysis relates to the ratio of the budget balance to output, then the problem of estimation is not the only issue. Some important conceptual differences also arise. Interestingly, the recent report of the European Commission on Public Finances in EMU for 2004 (European Commission, 2004) recognizes these differences (Part II, chapter 3 and Annexe II). As the report observes, if the ratio of the government balance to output is the issue, then only progressive taxes can contribute much to stabilization over the cycle. Proportional taxes will do little, if anything, to stabilize. Any stabilizing response of the budget to the cycle probably will come mostly from the spending side and will arise because of inertia in government expenditures on goods and services. During a recession, the ratio of government spending on goods and services to output will automatically rise if the spending is unaffected while output falls. Not only are these observations in the recent report correct, but it is also difficult to know how well they are understood since they are rarely acknowledged.

A further conceptual issue must be raised right at the start. The part of the budget balance that responds without delay to the cycle independently of any fresh political decision-making might not be entirely beyond potential discretionary control and therefore might not be 'automatic' in the full sense of the word. This applies especially to government spending on goods and services, which we usually consider to be under potential discretionary control. For this reason, I will refer to 'non-discretionary fiscal policy' as a more general term than 'automatic fiscal policy' or 'automatic stabilization'. On the other hand, within the same calendar year the cyclical responses of transfer payments for health, retirement, subsidies to firms, or anything else, result predominantly from the application of existing laws apart from any discretionary behaviour by government officials. By and large, whatever is automatic about the immediate responses of taxes and unemployment compensation to the cycle is also automatic about the immediate responses of the rest of transfer payments. Thus, I will treat all responses of transfer payments to the cycle as automatic.

The tests in this study rest on the annual data in the OECD CD-Rom for 2003 containing the *Economic Outlook* databank. The official estimates of automatic stabilization generally distinguish five different elements of the government budget balance and then study each of them separately: household direct taxes, business direct taxes, social security contributions, indirect taxes and unemployment compensation (see Giorno *et al.*, 1995). It is also official practice to estimate the cyclical response of the five respective bases on which these five tax and spending items rest, and then to apply the national tax code or else to assume a unitary elasticity of response to the base in order to derive the five items, whichever seems more appropriate. Van den Noord (2000) offers an up-to-date, clear and detailed review of the method (in the OECD version, used by the EC as well).[1] I will deviate from this official procedure in three ways. First, I will abandon the preconception that unemployment compensation is the only type of transfer payment that responds automatically to the cycle. Second, I will examine the non-discretionary responses of government balances in levels and as ratios of output separately. Both of these deviations follow from my opening remarks. As a third deviation, I will also rely entirely on simultaneous-equation methods of estimation. This next departure deserves a separate word.

Simultaneous-equation estimation methods have several advantages. The four relevant classes of taxes depend on distinct tax schedules of varying complexity that change over time and have different collection periods and delays. From this standpoint alone, there is something to be said in favour of estimating tax responses directly rather than inferring them from some preset figures after studying the responses of the tax bases, however well founded those preset figures may be. In addition, the cyclical responses of different tax bases and unemployment (the relevant base concerning unemployment compensation) will tend to be correlated. Hence, the residuals in the separate estimates of these bases will be correlated too. On this ground, seemingly unrelated regression would appear to be fitting. Finally, taxes and government spending could have a reciprocal effect on the cycle, even within a year. Thus, simultaneous-equation estimation may be proper.

4.2 The framework

At issue then is the response of government revenues and expenditures to environmental factors independently of discretionary policy. Therefore, we want a specification that does not reflect the aims of the authorities. Nothing concerning official expected values and official objectives, as such, should enter. In addition, the focus should be on reactions to changes in a short enough period to preclude discretionary policy. Changes in tax regulations take significant time. So do fresh spending decisions. As regards spending, the European Commission (2004) underlines the delays:

> Taking into account relatively long recognition lags, the complexity and slowness of budgetary processes and the political economy of political inaction, a viable working hypothesis over the short term, for instance one year, is to assume full inertia or full adherence to spending plans, i.e. to assume that spending is not adjusted for unexpected short- [*sic*] or windfalls of growth
>
> (Annexe II.2)

Canzoneri *et al.* (2002) take the same view. There are three variables that are likely to affect government revenues and expenditures even within a year and to do so fairly automatically: output, inflation and the nominal rate of interest. Deviations of output (Y) from potential output (Y^*) are of particular interest, since the ultimate aim is to distinguish between discretionary and non-discretionary fiscal policy.

On these general principles, I decided to study the current yearly impact of *first differences* in $Y - Y^*$ (as present in the OECD database), or the output gap, on *first differences* in government receipts and expenditures. Especially because of the first-difference form, this focuses on short-run responses. I also admitted non-discretionary effects of inflation and the interest rate into the analysis. But while using first differences for inflation, I kept the interest rate in levels, on the ground that any automatic influence of this variable on the government budget would depend largely on initial debt and therefore could be cumulative. If the interest rate does have a cumulative effect on the interest payments on the debt, its level could affect the first difference of the budget balance just as well as the level. While I stuck to these initial choices throughout, it turns out that the use of levels or first differences for inflation and the rate of interest makes almost no difference. In addition, better estimates of current responses may result from the presence of lagged influences. Thus, I also included the lagged level and the lagged first difference of the dependent variable in the estimates. Further, I added a trend and dummies for six-year intervals (1973–8, 1979–84, 1985–90, 1991–6, 1997–2002). Since the data concerns a panel of different countries, I included country-fixed effects too.

All of the country data entering into the statistical analysis goes up through 2002. Most of it begins in the early seventies. But though some of the series in the database begin in 1960, only a scattering of observations dating prior to 1970 enters in the econometric tests (because of lack of other required series starting as early). The results concern 20 OECD countries, and include 14 of the 15 members of the EU. The missing EU member is Luxembourg, and the 6 OECD countries outside the EU are Australia, Canada, Japan, New Zealand, Norway and the United States.

4.3 The estimates in levels and ratios

In general, the lagged level and first difference of the dependent variable as well as the time trend are almost always insignificant and do not affect the results. Therefore, even though the analysis allows for some delays in responses, the dynamics are totally negligible. No lagged effects occur. On the other hand, the six-year intervals often matter and the country-fixed effects generally do. Table 4.1 contains the most aggregative results. Table 4.1 does so for the 20 OECD countries, as well as for the 14 members of the European Union. The top half shows the results in levels; the bottom half in percentages. The notes to Table 4.1 recapitulate the entire specification from start to finish. Let us examine the levels first.

4.3.1 Levels

In the case of levels, the dependent variable on the left and the output gap on the right are in identical units; namely, home currency at current prices. Thus, the coefficient of the output gap gives a meaningful figure. For example, for the members of EMU, it states by how many cents the budget will respond to a movement of the output gap of one euro. But the coefficients of the change in inflation ($\Delta\pi$) and the interest rate (r_L) do not have any clear meaning and are not reported. The measure of the inflation rate is the implicit price of GDP; that of the interest rate r_L is the long-term interest rate. I experimented with both the short-term and the long-term interest rate in the OECD database, and the long-term one is much more important. The Table omits the coefficients of all the explanatory variables besides the output gap, inflation and the rate of interest. The parenthetical figures concern statistical significance: t statistics in case of single-equation estimates, z ones in the 3SLS analysis.

In row 1, the dependent variable is the net public surplus. The results are simple least squares. As seen, according to the estimate, a one-euro rise in output above potential output increases the net surplus by 55 cents in the OECD 20 and by 35 cents in the EU 14 alone. Both coefficients are highly significant. Both estimates are also comforting, since they are in the general vicinity of the typical figures. These typical figures are remarkably close to 0.5 for either grouping, at least in previous applications of the OECD method (see Giorno *et al.*, 1995; Buti and Sapir (eds), 1998: 132; and van den Noord, 2000). However, the estimates in row 1 ignore any reciprocal influence. The next ones, in row 2, correct for this neglect by introducing instruments for $\Delta(Y - Y^*)$, $\Delta\pi$ and r_L. The chosen instruments are listed in the notes to Table 4.1. They include, among others, the lagged values of aggregate taxes and spending – the two variables whose reciprocal effect on $\Delta(Y - Y^*)$, $\Delta\pi$ and r_L is our main concern. The instruments designed to take account of the output gap require a special word, since this variable is particularly difficult to forecast by construction. With regard to the gap, I made two special choices. First, I assumed that fiscal policy does not affect unemployment within the current year. Accordingly, I included current unemployment among the instruments. Second, in line with Galí and Perotti (2003), I used the current output gap in the United States as an instrument for the other 19 countries in the study and the current output gap in the EU (as reported by the OECD) as an instrument in the case of the United States. These particular two instruments, which relate to contemporary values (unlike the rest), notably improve the fit. In their presence, the R^2s for $\Delta(Y - Y^*)$ approximately double, going up to around 50–60%. The R^2s for $\Delta\pi$ that result from the instruments are always a bit worse, closer to 40%, and those for r_L notably higher, around 90%.

As seen from rows 2, after introducing the instruments, the estimates of the influence of the output gap on the net public surplus rise from 0.55–0.64 for the OECD 20 and from 0.35–0.44 for the EU 14. This is not a satisfactory result. The failure to consider the reciprocal influence of fiscal policy on current performance in row 1 should have led to overestimates, not underestimates, of non-discretionary fiscal policy. To explain, suppose that a cyclical rise in output raises net government receipts. In principle, the rise in the government surplus should limit the increase in output. If it does, then the correction for the reciprocal influence means raising the swings in $\Delta(Y - Y^*)$ above observed levels: that is, substituting higher positive values of $\Delta(Y - Y^*)$ in expansions and higher negative values of it in contractions. On the other hand, following the cyclical corrections, the series for the net government surplus stay the same. Thus, regressing the latter series on the corrected (larger absolute) values for $\Delta(Y - Y^*)$ should yield lower coefficients. The opposite happens. Notwithstanding, I consider the estimates with the instruments preferable on general statistical grounds.

The next four equations relate to the elementary decomposition of the net government surplus between taxes and spending. In rows 3 and 4, taxes and spending are estimated separately with the same instruments as before for $\Delta(Y - Y^*)$, $\Delta\pi$ and r_L. The decomposition yields precisely the same estimate as before for the impact of the output gap on the net public surplus for the OECD 20 (0.47 in row 3 minus −0.17 in row 4 gives 0.64) and a somewhat higher estimate of this impact for the EU 14 (0.54 instead of 0.44).

The trouble with these last estimates, however, as indicated earlier, is that the equations for taxes and spending should be estimated simultaneously. Rows 5 and 6 provide the correction. The results rest on three-stage-least-squares for a five-equation system containing equations for $\Delta(Y - Y^*)$, $\Delta\pi$ and r_L in addition to taxes and spending. These three additional equations depend on the earlier instruments. Following the use of 3SLS, we can see that the separate effects of $\Delta(Y - Y^*)$ on taxes and expenditures in the OECD 20 (Table 4.1) appear exactly as before in rows 3 and 4, but the precision of the estimates shoots up. In the case of the EU 14, the precision of the estimates also goes up, though not as spectacularly. But things are more complicated in the case of EU 14. The impact of the cycle on taxes stays the same while that on expenditures rises (in absolute terms, from −0.22 to −0.3). Taking stock of both the estimates as a whole, the basic outcome of using 3SLS is to improve precision and to narrow the differences between the estimates of the impact of the output gap on the net public surplus in the EU 14 and the OECD 20. After introducing 3SLS, the impact on the public surplus approximates 0.6 in both cases. Still, in the strictly European part of the sample, taxes respond notably less and expenditures notably more than in the full sample.

It is interesting to compare these last results in rows 5 and 6, for taxes and expenditures, with received ideas. Automatic stabilization is currently supposed to come essentially through taxes. Unemployment compensation – the only relevant spending item – makes up less than 10% of tax receipts in most countries (often much less), and therefore cannot compare in importance with taxes under proportional taxation (or anything resembling it). Thus, the results conform better to standard views on automatic stabilization on the tax than the spending side. The coefficient of the output gap of 0.47 for taxes in the OECD 20 (line 5) is particularly close to what we would anticipate from earlier work on automatic stabilization (though the 0.3 estimate for the EU 14 is on the low side). However, the −0.17 estimate for expenditures in the OECD 20 looks high, to say nothing of the −0.3 estimate in the EU 14 (lines 6) (compare Giorno *et al.*, 1995; and van den Noord, 2000). We shall come back to this issue below, but for the moment let us turn our attention to the revised estimates if we simply substitute ratios of output as the dependent variables and correspondingly substitute Y/Y^* as the output gap.

4.3.2 Ratios

Ratios often serve in the analysis of fiscal policy. Quite apart, the case for using them is strong. Stabilization policy relates to smoothing economic performance or keeping output close to potential. It does not essentially concern long-run production and growth in the level of output. Accordingly, analysis of fiscal policy often focuses on keeping the ratio of output to potential output close to one. As a result, even in cases where study focuses on a single country (and there is therefore no interest in using ratios simply to promote international comparison), the critical fiscal policy variable is often the ratio of the net budget balance to output, and the critical problem is to determine this ratio in the absence of non-discretionary responses to the environment. In line with these remarks, the European Commission centres on the ratio of the budget balance to output in its surveillance of country members' adherence to the Stability and Growth Pact (European Commission, 2004, Part II, chapter 3).

Notwithstanding, in analysing discretionary fiscal policy, studies often correct the budget balance in levels for non-discretionary responses and subsequently merely divide by output in order to obtain the ratios of cyclically adjusted figures to output or potential output. The European Commission is not the only one to do so. Two leading recent academic examples are Taylor (2000) and Galí and Perotti (2003). Both explicitly proceed from cyclically adjusted figures in levels based on official numbers (from the US Congressional Budget Office in one case, the OECD in the other) to subsequent division by potential output in order to analyse discretionary fiscal policy.

If potential output were perfectly deterministic and not subject to any shocks, there would be nothing wrong with this last practice (i.e. because of the division by *potential* instead of observed output). The division would then not call for any difference in estimation procedure at all, and the choice of dividing by potential output would be a critical one indeed. However, potential output is subject to supply shocks. Thus, if ratios of output are the matter of interest, direct estimates of the correction of this ratio for the cycle will yield more efficient estimates, regardless of whether we divide by observed or potential output. A further benefit will be to clarify the stabilizing forces at work. In the absence of a separate estimate of the ratios, as such, these forces acting on the ratios remain in the background, even in the dark.[2] As for the choice of observed or potential output, I shall centre on ratios of observed output here, since in any shift of focus on ratios, estimates of automatic effects of Y/Y^* on the original data deserve priority, in my opinion.

Row 7 of Table 4.1 repeats the OLS estimates of row 1. As evident, a cyclical expansion notably raises the ratio of the net public surplus to output. A 1% rise in Y/Y^* increases this ratio by over one-third of a per cent (0.36). So far, so good: the impact of the cycle on the government balance is stabilizing, just as it was before. Moreover, the impact of the cycle is now identical for the EU 14 and the full sample. All the better. Once again, if we introduce instrumental variables for $\Delta(Y/Y^*)$, $\Delta\pi$ and r_L (row 8), the cyclical influence goes up. It rises to 0.46 (or 0.45); that is, by a greater percentage (10/36 or 9/36) than it did previously. There is no need to pause once more on the separate IV estimates of taxes and spending (rows 9 and 10). If we go directly to the preferable simultaneous-equation estimates of the two in rows 11 and 12, we find that the impact of the cycle on the net public surplus is around 0.42 for the OECD 20 and the EU 14$(-0.07 - (-0.49)$ or $-0.11 - (-0.53))$ or close to the corresponding separate estimates (of 0.45–0.46) in rows 8. However, as was also true before in levels, the response of taxes is somewhat lower in the EU 14 than it is for the OECD 20, while the opposite is true for spending (though the difference is now more muted than before).

But the most striking result of all relates to the size of the respective responses of taxes and expenditures. Taxes move moderately less than output in response to the cycle. Thus, they move in a destabilizing direction. They do so to the tune of 0.07–0.11.[3] By contrast, government spending moves in the stabilizing direction. This too is largely the outcome of a smaller percentage movement in the numerator than the denominator, but in this case the difference in movement is stabilizing. The stabilizing change of the ratio of government spending to output is also marked: on the order of 0.49–0.53.[4] This is basically in conformity with expectations, as observed near the start in connection with the Commission. Once we reason in terms of ratios, we can no longer expect much non-discretionary stabilization, if any, to come from taxation, but must expect it to come largely

Table 4.1 Taxes, spending and government deficits: the aggregates

Dependent variable: 1st differences	*Test method*	$\Delta(Y - Y^*)$	$\Delta\pi$	r_L	R^2	N
OECD 20						
(1) Net public surplus	OLS	0.55	+n.r.	−n.r.	0.58	553
		(4.3)	(1.83)	(−0.66)		
(2) Net public surplus	IV	0.64	+n.r.	+n.r.	0.58	513
	2SLS	(3.8)	(1.08)	(0.44)		
(3) Taxes	IV	0.47	+n.r.	−n.r.	0.82	513
	2SLS	(4.2)	(0.85)	(−0.61)		
(4) Expenditures	IV	−0.17	−n.r.	−n.r.	0.89	514
	2SLS	(1.89)	(−0.26)	(−1.43)		
(5) Taxes	3SLS	0.47	+n.r.	−n.r.	0.82	513
		(17)	(1.06)	(−0.69)		
(6) Expenditures	3SLS	−0.17	+n.r.	−n.r.	0.89	513
		(7.5)	(0.89)	(−0.47)		
(7) Net public surplus ÷Y	OLS	0.36	0.16	~ 0	0.35	553
		(9.5)	(4.6)	(0.08)		
(8) Net public surplus ÷Y	IV	0.45	0.09	0.03	0.35	513
	2SLS	(8)	(1.95)	(0.61)		
(9) Taxes ÷Y	IV	−0.07	0.08	0.06	0.19	513
	2SLS	(−1.87)	(2.6)	(1.73)		
(10) Expenditures ÷Y	IV	−0.5	0.02	0.04	0.52	514
	2SLS	(−10.9)	(0.58)	(1.19)		
(11) Taxes ÷Y	3SLS	−0.07	0.07	0.04	0.19	513
		(−2.15)	(2.63)	(1.74)		
(12) Expenditures ÷Y	3SLS	−0.49	−0.1	0.04	0.54	513
		(−13.9)	(−0.23)	(1.24)		
EU 14						
(1) Net public surplus	OLS	0.35	+n.r.	−n.r.	0.49	364
		(2.9)	(1.02)	(−0.43)		
(2) Net public surplus	IV	0.44	+n.r.	−n.r.	0.49	341
	2SLS	(3.2)	(0.84)	(−0.66)		
(3) Taxes	IV	0.32	+n.r.	+n.r.	0.66	341
	2SLS	(2.2)	(2.44)	(2.7)		
(4) Expenditures	IV	−0.22	+n.r.	+n.r.	0.74	341
	2SLS	(−1.94)	(2.3)	(2.27)		
(5) Taxes	3SLS	0.3	+n.r.	+n.r.	0.65	341
		(3.9)	(2.2)	(2.4)		
(6) Expenditures	3SLS	−0.3	+n.r.	+n.r.	0.72	341
		(−3.9)	(2.1)	(1.9)		
(7) Net public surplus ÷Y	OLS	0.36	0.14	~ 0	0.35	364
		(7.3)	(4)	(0.05)		
(8) Net public surplus ÷Y	IV	0.46	0.16	0.06	0.37	341
	2SLS	(6)	(2.2)	(1.13)		
(9) Taxes ÷Y	IV	−0.12	0.13	0.04	0.17	341
	2SLS	(−2.45)	(2.96)	(1.93)		
(10) Expenditures ÷Y	IV	−0.53	0.04	0.05	0.54	341
	2SLS	(−8.2)	(0.81)	(1.16)		

Table 4.1 Continued

Dependent variable: 1st differences	*Test method*	$\Delta(Y - Y^*)$	$\Delta\pi$	r_L	R^2	N
(11) Taxes $\div Y$	3SLS	−0.11 (−2.73)	0.12 (3.2)	0.07 (2.19)	0.18	341
(12) Expenditures $\div Y$	3SLS	−0.53 (−11.5)	−0.01 (−0.31)	0.03 (0.97)	0.57	341

Source: OECD *Economic Outlook* CD-ROM.

Notes

Y = output (GDP) in current prices Y^* = potential output in current prices
π = rate of inflation of price of GDP (percentage) r_L = long term rate of interest (percentage)
N = number of observations n.r. = not reported

All the dependent variables are in current prices. t or z statistics in parentheses (z in case of 3SLS estimates). In case of 3SLS, the R^2s are also adapted.

The general estimation form for all 12 equations is:

$$\Delta A = a_o + a_1 \Delta B + a_2 \Delta\pi + a_3 r_L + a_4 t + \mathbf{a_5 C} + \mathbf{a_6 D} + a_7(\Delta A)_{-1} + a_8 \Delta_{-1}(\Delta A) + u$$

where ΔA is the first difference of the dependent variable A: either net public surplus, taxes, expenditures as such or these three divided by Y

- ΔB is either the first difference of $Y - Y$ or Y/Y^*
- $\Delta\pi$ is the first difference of π
- t is a time trend
- **C** is a matrix of country fixed effects
- **D** is matrix of dummies for the 6-year intervals: 1973–78, 1979–84, 1985–90, 1991–96, and 1997–2002
- $(\Delta A)_{-1}$ is the lagged level of ΔA (in notation with usual time subscripts, it is $A_{t-1} - A_{t-2}$)
- $\Delta_{-1}(\Delta A)$ is the lagged first-difference of ΔA (in notation with usual time subscripts, it is $(A_{t-1} - A_{t-2}) - (A_{t-2} - A_{t-3})$)
- u is a disturbance term with the usual properties

In the case of equations (2), (3), (4), (8), (9) and (10), ΔB, $\Delta\pi$ and r_L are replaced by estimates based on instruments. The instruments for ΔB are

- t, the time trend
- **C**, the country fixed effects
- **D**, the dummies for the six-year time intervals
- B_{-1} and $(\Delta B)_{-1}$ and $\Delta_{-1}(\Delta B)$, the lagged level, the lagged first difference and the twice-lagged first difference of B (either $Y - Y$ or Y/Y^*)
- g_{-1} and g_{-2}, the one-period and two-period lagged growth rate of Y
- π_{-1} and $(\Delta\pi)_{-1}$, the lagged level and the lagged first difference of inflation
- G_{-1} and $(\Delta G)_{-1}$, the lagged level and the lagged first difference of public expenditures
- T_{-1} and $(\Delta T)_{-1}$, the lagged level and the lagged first difference of taxes
- U, U_{-1} and $(\Delta U)_{-1}$, the level, lagged level and lagged first difference of the rate of unemployment
- either $(Y - Y^*)_{\mathrm{US}}$, $((Y - Y^*_{\mathrm{US}}))_{-1}$ and $(\Delta(Y - Y^*)_{\mathrm{US}})_{-1}$ or $(Y/Y^*)_{\mathrm{US}}$, $((Y/Y^*)_{\mathrm{US}})_{-1}$ and $(\Delta((Y/Y^*)_{\mathrm{US}}))_{-1}$, regarding the level, lagged level and lagged first difference of the US GAP (except for the US, where the EU GAP serves instead)

The instruments for $\Delta\pi$ and r_L are identical except that the lagged level, the lagged first difference and the twice-lagged first difference of either $\Delta\pi$ or r_L replace B_{-1}, $(\Delta B)_{-1}$ and $\Delta_{-1}(\Delta B)$.

In the case of equations (5) and (6) and equations (11) and (12), both equations belong to a 5-equation system with extra equations for ΔB, $\Delta\pi$ and r_L. In these cases, the equations for ΔB, $\Delta\pi$ and r_L include all of the same instruments as before as the explanatory variables. The only difference is that the lagged levels, lagged first differences and twice-lagged first differences of all 3 dependent variables enter in all three equations.

from spending instead. However, major questions remain outstanding. How much of the relevant stabilization results from inertia in government consumption and investment? How much is instead the work of transfer payments and is therefore automatic in the usual sense? To answer, we must distinguish between the contribution of government spending on goods and services and the rest.

4.4 Further decomposition of government receipts and expenditures

As long as any further decomposition of government spending between goods and services and transfers is essential, why not exploit all of the information available in the OECD CD-Rom? On the tax side, the OECD provides separate figures for household direct taxes, business direct taxes, social security tax receipts, transfers received, and indirect taxes. On the spending side, it offers figures for public wages, non-wage consumption, investment, social benefits paid, subsidies, other transfer payments, and net interest payments. There is also a residual category of spending, which includes capital transfers and payments, and government consumption of fixed capital. This makes 13 rubrics in all.

The division of transfer payments between social benefits paid, subsidies and other transfer payments requires further elucidation. 'Social benefits paid' includes payments to individuals for sickness, retirement benefits, subsistence, childcare and invalidity. It also contains unemployment compensation. The 'subsidies' are payments to firms. The 'other transfer payments' are then a residual category collecting all the transfers that have not been filed into the other two and better-defined rubrics.[5]

Once again, Table 4.2 shows separate results in levels and ratios. The ones in levels correspond exactly to those in rows 5 and 6 of the preceding table and those in ratios correspond exactly to those in rows 11 and 12 of that table. More precisely, the estimates in Table 4.2 are joint estimates with further equations for $\Delta(Y - Y^*)$ or $\Delta(Y/Y^*)$, $\Delta\pi$ and r_L based on the same instruments as before. The new estimates rest on 3SLS. Thus, these estimates concern a 16-equation system, including separate equations for the 13 different tax and spending items, and three more for the sources of non-discretionary effects. For the sake of legibility, I omit the results for r_L from Table 4.2 (these are almost always insignificant except for the effects on net interest payments). The results on the left side of the table concern levels (and the impact of $\Delta(Y - Y^*)$), while those on the right side concern ratios (and the impact of $\Delta(Y/Y^*)$).

With respect to levels, all of the tax items have the expected positive signs. They are also all significant for the OECD 20 but only household and business direct taxes are so for the EU 14. On the spending side, wages are highly significant with a positive sign and non-wage consumption is highly significant with a negative sign for the OECD 20. But both influences are small and cancel each other out. As regards the EU 14, the corresponding two effects are smaller and statistically insignificant. With respect to transfer payments, social benefits paid enter very significantly with a negative sign both for the OECD 20 and EU 14. The other two categories of transfer payments also bear significant signs (marginally so in

Table 4.2 Taxes, spending: the decomposition: 3SLS estimates

Dependent variable:	*Dependent variables in levels: first differences*			*Dependent variables as a percentage of Y: first differences*		
	$\Delta(Y - Y^*)$	$\Delta\pi$	R^2	$\Delta(Y/Y^*)$	$\Delta\pi$	R^2
OEC 20						
Household Direct Taxes	0.21	+n.r	0.73	−0.04	0.015	0.14
	(21)	(2.4)		(−1.8)	(2.75)	
Business Direct Taxes	0.17	+n.r.	0.52	0.04	−0.01	0.13
	(17)	(5.2)		(2.3)	(−0.59)	
Social Security Tax Receipts	0.07	−n.r.	0.75	−0.08	~ 0	0.24
	(7.9)	(−1.08)		(−5.1)	(0.39)	
Transfers Received By Government	0.001	+n.r.	0.27	−0.02	−0.01	0.09
	(3.6)	(0.86)		(−1.64)	(−1.3)	
Indirect Taxes	0.07	+n.r.	0.61	0.03	−0.02	0.12
	(7.2)	(0.34)		(1.7)	(−1.86)	
Wages	0.014	+n.r.	0.93	−0.12	0.01	0.39
	(5.3)	(3.3)		(−9.4)	(0.81)	
Non-Wage Consumption	−0.013	+n.r.	0.94	−0.06	~ 0	0.21
	(−3.5)	(1.66)		(−6.2)	(0.45)	
Investment	−0.09	−n.r.	0.29	−0.02	~ 0	0.14
	(−7)	(−2.03)		(−1.94)	(0.35)	
Social Benefits Paid	−0.066	−n.r.	0.94	−0.21	−0.03	0.55
	(−17.5)	(−1.92)		(−13.9)	(−2.84)	
Subsidies	0.012	+n.r.	0.34	−0.05	~ 0	0.21
	(5.1)	(0.92)		(−5.5)	(0.65)	
Other Transfer Payments	0.006	+n.r.	0.24	−0.04	−0.01	0.20
	(1.89)	(~ 0)		(−3.8)	(−0.98)	
Net Interest Payments	0.03	−n.r.	0.13	−0.01	−0.01	0.26
	(1.66)	(−0.42)		(−0.81)	(0.01)	
Residual Spending	−0.09	−n.r.	0.21	0.04	−0.01	0.33
	(−5.6)	(−1.2)		(1.26)	(0.25)	
EU 14						
Household Direct Taxes	0.19	+n.r	0.50	−0.04	0.04	0.15
	(5.9)	(2)		(−1.87)	(1.97)	
Business Direct Taxes	0.08	+n.r.	0.12	0.05	0.01	0.10
	(3.2)	(0.75)		(3.38)	(1.28)	
Social Security Tax Receipts	0.05	+n.r.	0.43	−0.09	0.01	0.27
	(1.3)	(−1.9)		(−4.7)	(0.49)	
Transfers Received By Government	−0.007	+n.r.	0.16	−0.01	~ 0	0.15
	(−1.2)	(0.79)		(−1.2)	(−.5)	
Indirect Taxes	0.05	+n.r.	0.33	0.02	−0.03	0.10
	(1.3)	(0.47)		(.95)	(−1.78)	
Wages	0.009	+n.r.	0.68	−0.13	0.2	0.43
	(0.44)	(3.8)		(−9.33)	(1.74)	
Non-Wage Consumption	−0.005	+n.r.	0.54	−0.05	~ 0	0.23
	(−0.25)	(1.92)		(−4.9)	(0.32)	
Investment	−0.003	+n.r.	0.29	−0.01	.01	0.16
	(0.35)	(−2.85)		(−1.27)	(1.37)	
Social Benefits Paid	−0.2	+n.r.	0.64	−0.23	−0.05	0.56
	(−7.2)	(−1.44)		(−13.5)	(−3.9)	
Subsidies	−0.054	−n.r.	0.24	−0.05	−0.01	0.23
	(−5.4)	(−0.96)		(−4.8)	(0.66)	
Other Transfer Payments	0.05	−n.r.	0.07	−0.05	−0.03	0.23
	(−3.12)	(−3.06)		(−3.8)	(−2.7)	
Net Interest Payments	0.03	+n.r.	0.31	−0.01	~ 0	0.29
	(0.79)	(1.42)		(−0.63)	(−0.29)	
Residual Spending	−0.19	−n.r.	0.35	0.05	−0.03	0.34
	(−5.35)	(−0.17)		(1.26)	(−1.06)	

Notes

Both sets of 3SLS estimates include additional equations for $\Delta(Y - Y^*)$ or $\Delta(Y/Y^*)$ and $\Delta\pi$ and r_L. There are other regressors for the 13 dependent variables shown, and for $\Delta(Y - Y^*)$ or $\Delta(Y/Y^*)$, $\Delta\pi$ and r_L. These are the same as in Table 4.1. z statistics in parentheses. The R^2s are adapted. Number of observations: OEC 20, 415; EU 14, 335.

the case of 'other transfer payments' for the OECD 20 at conventional confidence levels). But the signs are opposed between the OECD 20 and EU 14, only those for the OECD 20 (positive) going in the destabilizing direction. These last signs are also much smaller than the corresponding ones for the EU 14, which go the 'right' way.

As an important consideration, the residual category ('residual spending') is significant both for the OECD 20 and the EU 14. Importantly, this category covers government injections of capital into enterprises and can hide many things. To make matters worse, the variable enters with opposite signs in Table 4.2, and with large coefficients to boot. In the case of the EU 14, the coefficient is enormous: 0.19. These opposite signs could well explain the conflicting signs for subsidies and other transfer payments in the two samples (those signs being much lower – that is, more negative – in the case of the EU 14, where the coefficient for residual spending is positive). Some doubt consequently surrounds the estimates of the individual spending items. Notwithstanding, it should be noted that the stabilizing movement of 'social benefits paid' on the left-hand side would be difficult to contest, since the signs of influence of $\Delta(Y - Y^*)$ on this variable are negative in the table, despite the opposite signs of the residual spending in the two. In addition, both coefficients are large, and both of them have exceedingly high statistical significance – especially the one closer to zero (−0.066) concerning the OECD 20 (and which, judging from the associated estimate of residual spending, is probably an underestimate and should be even more negative). Whatever the doubts about exact magnitudes, a stabilizing movement of 'social benefits paid' of at least 0.066 in levels can be accepted. The estimates for wage and non-wage consumption in the OECD 20 and the EU 14 are also consistent with one another and merit confidence. On the other hand, the estimates for investment are wide apart and they do not.

The results on the right-hand sides, concerning the ratios, are far more satisfactory. There the residual spending items are totally insignificant. Thus, though those items move with the cycle, they evidently do so approximately in step with output, so that when calculated as percentages of output, their importance vanishes. Very significantly too, there is a remarkable conformity all down the line between the estimates of the impact of $\Delta(Y/Y^*)$ in Table 4.2. If we add up the coefficients for taxes on the right-hand side in Table 4.2, we get the identical figure, −0.07, in both cases. The discrepancy with Table 4.1 is negligible too. Looking back at line 11 of that table, the estimates of the impact of Y/Y^* on total taxes there were respectively −0.007 and −0.11. If we repeat the same operation for the seven itemized elements of spending besides the residual element, the respective totals of the coefficients in Table 4.2 are −0.51 or −0.53. This then compares with estimates of −0.49 and −0.53 in line 12 of Table 4.1. In sum, the decomposition on the right-hand side in Table 4.2 merits confidence.

What story do those estimates tell us? First, household direct taxes move in a destabilizing way. They do not keep up with the cycle. Social security taxes do so even less. However, indirect taxes keep up, while business direct taxes do better than just keep up. These results may carry conviction. We would expect profits to move more than wages with the cycle, and therefore business direct taxes to be more stabilizing (less destabilizing) than household direct taxes. Turning to the spending side, the results for transfer payments are the most striking. Social benefit payments fall markedly as a percentage of income during cyclical upswings. Further, subsidies and other transfer payments also both move significantly in the stabilizing direction. But though they matter, the contributions of these last two rubrics to stabilization taken together are less than half as large as the contribution of social benefits paid alone. The results regarding wages and non-wage consumption also merit notice. Neither class of government expenditures keeps up with the cycle, but wages do so less than non-wage consumption – by far.[6]

With these results in hand, we may return to the question of the extent to which the aggregate stabilizing response of the budget in ratios depends on the contribution of government spending on goods and services. The overall stabilizing response of the budget as a ratio of output does indeed owe a great deal to government spending on goods and services. If we sum over all the five tax and the seven spending items other than residual spending, the stabilizing response of the budget balance is of the order of 0.42–0.45. But even when we ignore this inertia, the figure for automatic stabilization is still around 0.25. Thus, though government consumption and investment is important in explaining the stabilizing movement, transfer payments are even more so. A 1% rise in the ratio of output to potential output leads to a fall in transfer payments of 30–33% of the rise, enough by itself (apart from the inertia in government current expenditures) to overcome the associated fall in the ratio of taxes to output (7% of the rise) by around 25%.

How shall we interpret the greater stabilizing role of transfers than government consumption and investment? To answer, let us go back first to Table 4.1 concerning levels. There we see that spending adds about 17% to stabilization in levels. Next, Table 4.2 tells us that this stabilization comes essentially from transfers rather than government consumption and investment (despite some ambiguities stemming from the unreliability of the results associated with residual spending). The left-hand sides of both tables clearly indicate that government consumption adds little to the 17% while a single class of transfers alone, 'social benefits paid', adds a lot. Suppose we interpret all of the 17% as coming from transfers, as it is easy to do, then everything falls into place. Government spending on goods and services plays a stabilizing role in terms of ratios strictly because of initial size. But government transfers do so both on account of initial size and a stabilizing movement in level. While transfer payments are effectively smaller than government consumption and investment in most countries, they still amount to nearly 0.8 of this spending on average. Hence, the stabilizing response of transfer payments stemming from the combination of movement and initial size trumps the stabilizing response of government spending on goods and services coming from initial size alone.[7]

4.5 Some individual country analysis

The study would also suggest the importance of national distinctions. Such distinctions obviously matter greatly in case of the usual conception of automatic stabilization (which excludes most transfer payments), since tax structures and systems of unemployment compensation differ by country. But national distinctions are still more important if a central element in non-discretionary fiscal policy is aggregate transfer payments. Programmes of government financing of retirement, health, unemployment, poverty, childcare, regional assistance and subsidies to firms not only differ by countries but there are also cases of big programmes that do not even exist in other countries.

Unfortunately, however, it is impossible to replicate the analysis for individual countries. The national data series are too short. The previous 3SLS analysis proves impracticable. The most comparable tests by country I was able to perform depend on seemingly unrelated regressions (SUR) with instruments for the environmental factors $\Delta(Y - Y^*)$ or $\Delta(Y/Y^*)$, $\Delta\pi$ and r_L. Even then, five of the countries in the previous work needed to be dropped because of insufficiently long time series (Denmark, Greece, Ireland, New Zealand and Spain). Table 4.3 displays a few of the results for the other 15 countries in turn. These results pertain to four separate estimates per country: two in levels, two in ratios. One of the estimates in levels and one of them in ratios relate to the net government surplus. These two correspond exactly to lines 2 and 7 of Table 4.1. The other pair relates to the 13 dependent variables in Table 4.2, and rest on SUR with IV instead of 3SLS. With respect to those SUR estimates, I only display the results for 5 of the 13 variables, and I only report them for the impact of $\Delta(Y - Y)$ or $\Delta(Y/Y^*)$. This selectiveness in reporting avoids reams of pages that would be difficult to digest and to comment on seriously. The five chosen variables for display focus on the spending rubrics that may be of special interest are: wages, non-wage consumption, social benefits, subsidies and other transfer payments. Even limited in this way, the table still contains a large number of figures. Therefore, I highlight the significant *z* values at the 10% confidence level with the use of bold letters and the significant *z* values above the 5% confidence level with bold letters for the coefficients as well as the *z* values.

All these estimates obviously deserve much less confidence than those in Table 4.2. There are too few degrees of freedom. Each equation contains estimates of 10 or 11 separate coefficients (for ($\Delta(Y - Y^*)$ or $\Delta(Y/Y^*)$, $\Delta\pi$, r_L, the lagged level and first difference of the dependent variable, the trend, and four or five six-year dummies). But there are only around 28 observations altogether (the Table reports the exact number of observations per country (N)). As a result, the typical number of degrees of freedom is around 16. Notwithstanding, a few points can be made. The stabilizing response of the net public surplus to the cycle emerges – in levels or ratios, one or the other – for 12 of the 15 countries (all but Australia, Norway and Sweden). In eight of the countries, it emerges in both forms. Wages and non-wage consumption often appear as moving in the stabilizing direction. In addition, the stabilizing influence of at least one of the three classes of transfer payments always emerges – that is, if we go down to the 10% level of significance. In ten of the countries, the significance of one or more classes of transfer payments is clearly above the 95% confidence level.

I propose to take a closer look at the estimates for the United States. As in many other instances of closed-economy macroeconomics, the United States has been the

Table 4.3 Selected individual-country responses to $y - y^*$ or y/y^*. Levels in columns 1; percentages of y in columns 2

Dependent variable: first differences	*AUS*		*AUT*		*BEL*		*CAN*		*FIN*		*FRA*		*GER*		*ITA*	
	(1)	*(2)*	*(1)*	*(2)*	*(1)*	*(2)*	*(1)*	*(2)*	*(1)*	*(2)*	*(1)*	*(2)*	*(1)*	*(2)*	*(1)*	*(2)*
Net Public	0.036	0.01	0.105	0.30	**0.29**	**0.45**	**0.40**	**0.45**	**0.94**	**0.43**	**0.39**	0.26	**0.26**	**0.46**	**0.49**	**0.50**
Surplus	(0.23)	(0.18)	(0.58)	**(1.69)**	**(2.52)**	**(2.15)**	**(2.94)**	**(1.97)**	**(2.59)**	**(1.97)**	**(2.84)**	(1.53)	**(2.53)**	**(1.98)**	**(2.1)**	**(3.85)**
Wages	0.024	**−0.046**	0.027	−0.053	−0.015	**−0.042**	0.029	**−0.09**	**−0.045**	**−0.054**	−0.016	**−0.058**	0.007	**−0.032**	−0.077	−0.021
	(1.4)	**(−4)**	(0.60)	**(−1.85)**	(−0.84)	**(−2.64)**	(1.42)	**(−4.41)**	**(−2.43)**	**(−2.18)**	(−1.03)	**(−3.77)**	(0.57)	**(−2.7)**	(−1.44)	(−0.77)
Non-Wage	**−0.13**	−0.014	−0.03	0.006	**−0.056**	**−0.058**	**−0.034**	−0.034	**−0.036**	−0.20	−0.042	−0.005	−0.018	−0.024	**−0.78**	−0.021
Consumption	**(−3.1)**	(−0.03)	(−1.07)	(0.32)	**(2.68)**	**(−2.8)**	**(−2.11)**	**(−1.58)**	**(−3.2)**	(−1.38)	(−1.17)	(−0.17)	(−0.84)	(−1.17)	**(−2.14)**	(−0.90)
Social Benefits	**−0.08**	**−0.64**	**−0.11**	**−0.14**	**−0.04**	**−0.145**	—	−0.48	−0.048	**−0.065**	**−0.101**	−0.053	**−0.091**	−0.065	0.064	
Paid	**(−3)**	**(−2.54)**	**(−3.48)**	**(−4.19)**	**(−2.51)**	**(−6.78)**	—	**(−1.69)**	(−1.23)	**(−3.36)**	**(−3.25)**	**(−1.85)**	**(−2.01)**	(−1.55)	**(1.79)**	
Subsidies	0.005	**−0.02**	**−0.05**	**−0.05**	−0.01	0.006	**−0.051**	−0.016	−0.004	0.017	**−0.024**	−0.224	**0.036**	**0.025**	**−0.045**	−0.066
	(0.63)	**(−2.9)**	**(−2.42)**	**(−3.28)**	(−1.22)	(0.81)	**(−3.06)**	(−0.99)	(−0.46)	(1.49)	**(−1.97)**	**(−1.71)**	**(3.8)**	**(2.66)**	**(−2.59)**	(−0.28)
Other Transfer	**−0.026**	−0.01	−0.04	**−0.03**	0.001	0.001	−0.028	**−0.128**	0.025	0.001	−0.001	0.01	0.007	0.002	**−0.049**	−0.005
Payments	**(−2.17)**	(−1.12)	**(−1.66)**	**(−2.15)**	(1.20)	(0.18)	(−1.54)	**(−3.63)**	(1.44)	(0.03)	(−0.16)	**(1.63)**	(0.22)	(0.93)	**(−3.48)**	(−0.49)

Continued

Table 4.3 Continued

	JAP		*NETH*		*NOR*		*POR*		*SWE*		*UK*		*US*		*N*
	(1)	*(2)*	*(1)*	*(2)*	*(1)*	*(2)*	*(1)*	*(2)*	*(1)*	*(2)*	*(1)*	*(2)*	*(1)*	*(2)*	
Net Public	**0.47**	0.175	**0.51**	**0.41**	−0.075	0.56	0.17	0.09	0.11	0.22	**0.50**	0.28	**0.42**	**0.48**	AUS 24
Surplus	**(4.5)**	**(1.73)**	**(2.65)**	**(1.94)**	(−0.12)	(1.4)	**(1.59)**	(0.55)	(0.35)	(0.74)	**(2.54)**	(0.99)	**(2.80)**	**(3.07)**	AUT 27
Wages	−0.003	**−0.029**	**−0.058**	**−0.085**	−0.042	−0.051	**0.091**	**−0.048**	−0.052	**−0.149**	**−0.112**	−0.069	**−0.015**	**−0.093**	BEL 28
	(−0.44)	**(−4.35)**	**(−2.2)**	**(−2.93)**	(−1.04)	(−0.95)	**(2.16)**	**(−3.33)**	(−1.42)	**(−3.47)**	**(−3.04)**	**(−1.89)**	**(−2.26)**	**(−10)**	CAN 28
Non-Wage	−0.008	**−0.035**	**−0.107**	−0.054	0.019	0.005	**0.156**	0.013	0.042	−0.002	−0.019	−0.047	−0.021	**−0.061**	FIN 24
Consumption	(−0.70)	**(−2.77)**	**(−2.63)**	(−1.52)	(0.57)	(0.17)	**(3.87)**	(0.58)	(1.1)	(−0.07)	(−0.36)	**(−1.83)**	(−1.54)	**(−5.48)**	FRA 28
Social Benefits	**−0.031**	**−0.047**	**−0.127**	**−0.10**	−0.048	−0.013	0.007	−0.01	0.018	0.05	**−0.083**	−0.044	0.019	−0.041	GER 33
Paid	**(−2.71)**	**(−2.78)**	**(−2.36)**	**(−2.02)**	**(−1.74)**	(−0.18)	(0.21)	(−0.60)	(0.42)	(0.71)	**(−2.08)**	(−1.1)	(0.49)	**(−1.71)**	ITA 36
Subsidies	0.002	**−0.018**	**−0.044**	−0.004	0.022	−0.01	~0	0.02	0.033	−0.007	0.008	**−0.05**	−0.01	0.002	JAP 29
	(0.28)	**(−2.22)**	**(−1.94)**	(−0.18)	(1.14)	(−0.39)	(~0)	(0.80)	**(1.60)**	(−0.41)	(0.65)	**(−3.25)**	(−1.04)	(0.38)	NETH 27
Other Transfer	0.001	0.001	−0.009	−0.001	−0.058	**−0.058**	**−0.254**	−0.056	0.041	0.06	**0.048**	0.01	—	—	NOR 26
Payments	(0.09)	(0.14)	(−0.52)	(−0.07)	**(−1.72)**	**(−1.98)**	**(−6.71)**	**(−1.67)**	(1.24)	**(1.58)**	**(3.48)**	(0.87)			POR 28
															SWE 31
															UK 29
															US 30

Notes

The coefficients in columns 1 are responses to $\Delta(Y - Y^*)$; those in columns 2 are responses to $\Delta(Y/Y^*)$. All dependent variables are in first-difference form. z statistics in parentheses. Denmark, Greece, Ireland, New Zealand and Spain figure in the previous estimates but not here because the time series for them are too short. In the case of net public surplus, the specifications correspond exactly to those in rows 2 and 8 of Table 4.1. They are 2SLS with the same instruments as before for $\Delta(Y - Y^*)$, $\Delta(Y/Y^*)$, $\Delta\pi$ and r_L. The estimates of the other 5 dependent variables are obtained simultaneously, together with estimates of the other 8 dependent variables in Table 4.2. But these estimates are based on SUR (seemingly unrelated regressions) with instruments for $\Delta(Y - Y^*)$ or $\Delta(Y/Y^*)$, $\Delta\pi$ and r_L. The regressors and the instruments are the same as those in Table 4.2 (to which the details are given in the notes to Table 4.1) except for the omission of all the twice-lagged variables as instruments in order to preserve degrees of freedom.

outstanding individual-country laboratory for studies of automatic stabilization. Some especially careful estimates are available for this country, even at the microeconomic level (see, especially, Auerbach and Feenberg, 2000). It is reassuring, therefore, that the stabilizing response of the net public surplus to the output gap comes out plainly both in levels and in ratios for the United States. The country is thus a good laboratory in this regard. However, the United States happens to be highly untypical in another respect. It is one of the few countries in the sample where the impact of transfer payments emerges faintly if at all. Measured in levels, transfer payments are totally insignificant for the United States, and in ratios the significance of these payments appears for only one of the three relevant rubrics, 'social benefits paid', and then only near the 10% confidence level.[8] Thus, the tendency to focus on the United States could have something to do with the usual failure to give proper attention to transfer payments. On the other hand, principal focus on this country will obviously not explain the typical disregard of the issue of levels or ratios. Quite apart from the matter of principle, the difference in the sources of stabilization in levels and ratios emerges clearly in the United States. When judged in terms of ratios, the government spending on goods and services in the country contributes greatly to the stabilizing movement of the budget balance. Indeed, nowhere does the significance of public wages and non-wage consumption in stabilization come out more plainly.

4.6 Conclusions

I have rejected the mere guess that 'among primary expenditures [or apart from interest payments], only unemployment benefits probably have a non-negligible built-in response to output fluctuations' (Galí and Perotti, 2003: 542–3). I have also stressed that if, for whatever reason, the interest lies in the cyclically adjusted ratio of government budget balance to observed or potential output, then the right way to proceed is to correct for the automatic impact of the cycle on the ratio itself. Basing the cyclically adjusted figures on estimates of the numerator alone is inefficient. When the proper estimates in the case of ratios take place, transfer payments appear as especially prominent in automatic stabilization. But the main point, as regards ratios as such, is the issue of estimation.

Two sorts of questions remain wide open. One relates to the specific transfer programmes that contribute to stabilization. Some programmes may not contribute at all, some may do so more than others, and some may even work in a pro-cyclical direction. The OECD classification of social benefits paid, subsidies, and other transfer payments is far from adequate. Social benefits paid embrace too many things: payments for pensions, sickness benefits, invalidity, unemployment, subsistence and childcare. We would clearly expect pensions, for example, to respond to the cycle in a stabilizing manner. Cyclical upswings are likely to induce people to work longer and to delay pension receipts. Pensions are also very expensive. In addition, unemployment compensation probably also responds counter-cyclically, though only with a lag (unless there is a rise in the number of people who qualify for benefits within a year during a contraction among those who are already unemployed, which is possible). However, it is not clear that payments for childcare should move counter-cyclically. The stabilizing influence of subsidies to firms poses similar interrogations. Subsidies can cover many diverse programmes, going from agricultural price supports to help for firms in difficulty. What are the subsidy programmes at work? Finally, it would be nice to know too where the stabilizing impact of 'other transfer payments' comes from.

The second sort of questions that demand investigation relate to discretionary fiscal policy. If the series for the cyclically adjusted budget balances should be constructed differently, measures of fiscal policy stances need to be re-estimated. In addition, so do many estimates of the impact of discretionary fiscal policy on the economy. This is true regardless of estimation in levels or ratios. But in the case of ratios, the problems go further since they relate to the estimation procedure as well as the failure to consider any transfer payments besides unemployment compensation.

A big final question is that of the policy implications. As regards the size of automatic stabilization, the answer is easy: the estimates are larger. They go up in levels from usual figures of 0.5 to around 0.6. This is only reasonable since the sources of automatic stabilization are wider and cover all transfer payments. In the case of ratios, there is still the issue whether to use the 0.42 figure inclusive of government spending on goods and services or the 0.25 one exclusive of this spending. I believe the larger estimate to be better. It is the only one consistent with the 0.6 figure in levels, which clearly depends on the response of all government spending as well as taxes to the cycle. We might be tempted to exclude the contribution of government consumption and investment in levels in order to resolve the problem. But this would be unwise. The point of no contribution of government spending on goods and services in levels is precisely the one where inertia in government spending, as such, exerts a maximum effect in the corresponding calculation in ratios. Thus, the only way to maintain coherence in the analysis in levels and ratios is to admit inertia in government spending on goods and services when reasoning in ratios. Unless we do so and thus admit all non-discretionary responses to the cycle in the case of ratios, we generate a discrepancy mainly based on terminology alone.

The 0.42 figure in ratios and the 0.6 one in levels are also easy to fit together. Taxes and government spending, individually, are mostly of the order of 0.3–0.5 of output in the OECD. Let us take 0.4 as our basis for reasoning and, only to facilitate the calculation, let us translate the entire response of the budget balance to the cycle into a change in taxes (thereby putting aside the opposite signs of taxes and expenditures in the budget balance). Consider then the case of a cyclical doubling of output. The earlier 0.42 estimate for the influence on the ratio of the budget balance to output means that the government's income share would go up from 0.4 by 0.42 or to about 0.57, close to 0.60. This then fits well with the estimate of the change in the budget balance of around 0.60 of the rise in output.

But there are other policy implications. Consider the popular advice 'let the automatic stabilizers work.' In the case of taxes and government spending on goods and services, the injunction has essentially the same interpretation as before.

When reasoning in levels, it advises not to interfere with the stabilizing effect of taxes through discretionary government spending. When reasoning in ratios, it gives similar advice, though this may not be transparent. We see it most easily by referring to the case of lump-sum taxation. In that case, the ratio of taxes to output would automatically fall in a cyclical expansion, which would then be destabilizing. But since, in fact, taxes rise with income, this does not happen (or less so). Income-related taxes thus avert a destabilizing outcome. It follows that, when reasoning in ratios, the earlier injunction to let the automatic stabilizers work can be interpreted to advise, nearly identically, not to interfere with the reduction in destabilization coming from income-related taxes through discretionary government spending. The real *policy* difference in the injunction to let everything alone regards transfer payments. Now the injunction also says 'do not interfere with the automatic stabilizing effects of transfer payments and subsidies.'

As observed many times in the past, the automatic stabilization coming from taxes is not the product of any deliberate design. Ratios of taxes to output rose greatly following World War II in the richer section of the world for reasons mostly having nothing to do with desired macroeconomic stabilization. Smoothing of business cycles resulted. However, by and large, this fortuitous outcome meets approval.[9] In contradistinction, in the case of unemployment compensation, automatic stabilization was indeed part of the design. The same cannot be said for transfer payments as a group. Some of them, like agricultural price supports, are even the subjects of political opposition. Transfer payments typically concern programmes that are intended for their redistributive effects and that carry some controversial features – if only in their detailed configuration. There is little doubt that the motto 'let the automatic stabilizers work' assumes a different political colour if it says, as the data suggests, 'let more people go into retirement or on the poverty rolls and let public aid to currently subsidized firms increase during recessions.' Already the principle of letting the automatic stabilizers work encounters some opposition because of the international differences in the sizes of stabilizers and the lack of any bearing of these different sizes on optimal stabilization (see, for example, Farina and Tamborini, 2004). Any call for unqualified reliance on transfer programmes could only stir more controversy. Yet, according to the data, that is precisely what the motto calls for.

Notes

* I would like to thank Marco Buti; the editors, Peter Wierts, Servaas Deroose, Elena Flores and Alessandro Turrini; and Julia Darby, Paul van den Noord and Charles Wyplosz for valuable comments. Paul van den Noord was of special help.

1 To quote from van den Noord's summary:

> First, the elasticities of the relevant tax bases and unemployment with respect to (cyclical) economic activity, *i.e.* the output gap, are estimated through regression analysis. Next, the elasticities of tax proceeds or expenditure [unemployment compensation] with respect to the relevant bases are extracted from the tax code

or simply set to unity in cases where proportionality may be assumed. These two sets of elasticities are subsequently combined into reduced-form elasticities that link the cyclical components of taxes and expenditure to the output gap.

2 The most recent report on public finances in EMU of the European Commission (2004) edges toward this position. First, the report recognizes major conceptual differences when study concerns the ratio of cyclically adjusted budget balances to output, as mentioned at the start. Next, the report also recognizes an issue of estimation if ratios to output serve because the predicted ratio to output then depends not only on the predicted value of cyclically adjusted budget balances, but also the predicted ratio of output to potential output Y/Y^* (section 3.3 of Part II and Annex II). In other words, based on the report, forecast errors in Y/Y^* affect both the numerator and the denominator in the ratio. But according to my reasoning, the difficulty lies deeper: it is inefficient to estimate the numerator separately.
3 Note, though, that this destabilizing movement in the ratio of taxes to output is true at a constant rate of inflation. Suppose instead a percentage-point rise (fall) in Y/Y^* that is associated with an equal percentage-point acceleration (deceleration) of inflation. Then, according to the estimates, taxes move in perfect step with output (since the –0.07 and -0.11 estimates for $\Delta(Y/Y^*)$ in line 11 of Table 4.1 are perfectly matched by (more significant) 0.07 and 0.12 respective estimates for $\Delta\pi$ on these lines).
4 Arreaza *et al.* (1999) probably deserve credit as the first to bring attention to the issue. Reasoning in ratios, they obtain similar results to those in the text and conclude that taxes are destabilizing and government spending is stabilizing in the OECD and the EU. Mélitz (2000) notes the seeming unorthodoxy of their stand (without siding with them, as might have been right).
5 More specifically, 'Other current transfers' include payments by the central government for damages resulting from natural causes, such as fires and floods (which may be associated with insurance (net of income receipts for the insurance) or with emergency relief). Another element is 'annual or other regular contributions paid by member governments to international organizations (excluding taxes payable to supra-national organizations)'. Still another element is 'fines and penalties'. Somewhat mysteriously (since the figures concern general government), the numbers include some 'transfers between different levels of government, such as frequently occur between central and state or local government units'. I quote from a text from the Statistics Division of the UN, to which the services of the OECD refer me.
6 These last results, regarding spending, compare well with Lane (2002), who concentrates on the cyclical sensitivity of government activity on the spending side.
7 The math helps to see. Let spending be x, output y, normal output y^* and suppose $x = f(y)$. Then $d(x/y)/d(y/y^*) = (1/y^*)[(dx/dy) - (1/y)(x/y)]$. The negative value of the second term varies with x/y while dx/dy is just the same regardless of x/y. Thus, if dx/dy is -0.17 and $x/y = 0.22$ (0.22 being about the right figure for government consumption plus investment relative to output in the period on average), the first term may easily dominate the second. This is the decisive consideration (even though the reasoning abstracts from differences between the estimates of $dx/d(y-y^*)$ – or dx/dy, supposedly the same – and $d(x/y)/d(y/y^*)$ stemming from the separate estimation of the two in a stochastic environment).
8 Why there is no data for the United States for 'other transfers paid' is not clear.
9 Not always. Some people worry that automatic stabilization owes much to big government. True, the size of government can be reduced without cutting down automatic stabilization by lowering taxes and spending concurrently while increasing the progressiveness of taxation. However, progressive taxes can have serious disincentive effects on supply. For an emphasis on this conundrum and related discussion, see Buti *et al.* (2003).

References

Arreaza, A., Sørensen, B. and Oved, Y. (1999), 'Consumption smoothing through fiscal policy in OECD and EU countries', in James Poterba and Jürgen von Hagen (eds), *Fiscal Institutions and Fiscal Performance*, Chicago: University of Chicago Press.

Auerbach, A. and Feenberg, D. (2000), 'The significance of federal taxes as automatic stabilizers', *Journal of Economic Perspectives*, 22: 37–56.

Buti, M. and Sapir, A. (eds) (1998), *Economic Policy in EMU: A Study by the European Commission Services*, Oxford: Oxford University Press.

Buti, M., Martinez-Mongay, C., Sekkat, K. and van den Noord, P. (2003), 'Macroeconomic policy and structural reform: a conflict between stabilisation and flexibility?', in M. Buti (ed.), *Monetary and Fiscal Policies in EMU – Interactions and Coordination*, Cambridge: Cambridge University Press.

Canzoneri, M., Cumby, R. and Diba, B. (2002), 'Should the European central bank and the Federal Reserve be concerned about fiscal policy?', Rethinking Stabilization Policy, A symposium sponsored by the Federal Reserve Bank of Kansas City, August.

European Commission (2004), 'Public Finance in EMU 2004', *European Economy*, Reports and Studies, 3.

Farina, F. and Tamborini, R. (2004), ' "Set a Sufficiently Ambitious Budget Target and Let Automatic Stabilizers Work". Will it really work in the European Monetary Union?', *Open Economies Review*, 15: 143–68.

Galí, J. and Perotti, R. (2003), 'Fiscal policy and monetary integration in Europe', *Economic Policy*, 37: 533–72.

Giorno, C., Richardson, P., Roseveare, D. and Van den Noord, P. (1995), 'Potential output, budget gaps, and structural budget balances', *OECD Economic Studies*, 24: 167–209.

Lane, P. (2003), 'The cyclical behaviour of fiscal policy: evidence from the OECD', *Journal of Public Economics*, 87: 2661–75.

Mélitz, J. (2000), 'Some cross-country evidence about fiscal policy behaviour and consequences for EMU', *European Economy Reports and Studies*, 2.

Taylor, J. (2000), 'Reassessing discretionary fiscal policy', *Journal of Economic Perspectives*, 25: 21–36.

Van den Noord, P. (2000), 'The size and role of automatic stabilizers in the 1990s and beyond', *OECD Economics Department Working Paper no. 230*, revised and abridged in L. Buti, J. von Hagen and C. Martinez-Mongay, *The Behaviour of Fiscal Authorities*, Houndmills, Basingstoke, Hampshire, UK: Palgrave, 2002, chapter 8.

5 Getting measures of fiscal stance right for the new SGP*

E. Gaffeo, G. Passamani and R. Tamborini

[. . .] since the second half of 2004, growth in the Euro area has been modest, below the area's potential growth rate

Jean-Claude Trichet (30 May 2005)

[. . .] the delivery of the new, refocused Lisbon agenda could boost Europe's natural rate of growth to around 3 percent per year and bring our goal of full employment within reach by the end of the decade

José-Manuel Barroso (2 April 2005)

5.1 Introduction

In November 2004, France and Germany obtained from the Council of the Finance Ministers (Ecofin) suspension of the 'excessive deficits procedure' recommended by the European Commission in application of the norms established by the Maastricht Treaty and the Stability and Growth Pact (SGP). The decision was unanimously viewed as the political end of the SGP in its then current form. In March 2005, the Ecofin approved a revision of the rules on the excessive deficit procedure. Was the breakdown of the SGP in 2004 due to brute political pressure applied by the major stakeholders? Was it merely by chance that it occurred after three years of stagnation, if not recession, in the euro area, and that the drive for reform was led by the two early guardians of the SGP orthodoxy? Will the new SGP be more successful in combining 'rigour and flexibility'?

The revision of the SGP in March 2005 confirmed the 3% deficit/GDP ratio as the pillar of the excessive deficits procedure. On the other hand, some of the many criticisms levelled against the original version of the SGP were recognized insofar as

- some more 'flexibility' has been injected into the procedure by allowing the deduction of a list of long-run growth-promoting expenses;
- a longer time span for the correction of excess deficits has been granted;
- a less stringent definition of 'recession' has been introduced for a country to qualify for exemption from the excess deficit procedure.[1]

The previous exemption clauses were based on the increasing 'gravity of recessions'. All of them included *negative* GDP growth rates (from less than −0.75%

('mild') to more than −2% ('exceptional')). To the negative growth rate criterion the new exemption clauses add that of '*growth gap*', this being a growth rate that, albeit positive, *falls short of the potential rate*:

> a breach of the threshold [of 3% deficit] will now be considered exceptional if it results from a negative growth rate or *an accumulated loss of output during a protracted period of very low growth relative to potential growth*
>
> (Buti and Franco, 2005: 15, italics added).

However, since the deficit/GDP ceiling of 3% is still in place, research on its implications for fiscal discipline and macroeconomic stabilization in the frame of the new SGP should be taken further. We argue that the agenda largely involves empirical matters. In particular, the issues involved require careful examination and control of complex dynamic interactions between the fiscal variables and the other macro-variables. This task can be accomplished better by quantitative simulations. Hence, this chapter presents a simulation of the evolution of fiscal aggregates after a negative growth gap in two representative euro-countries: Italy and Germany. Our study addresses the following issues:

First, analyses and prescriptions concerning fiscal and monetary policy in a monetary union should be framed in a fully specified macroeconomic scenario in which the interactions between the two policies are clearly understood and identified. Favero (2002) reviews the theoretical reasons behind this claim and shows the empirical mistakes that may be generated by piece-wise analyses of monetary and fiscal policies. Developments in this direction, however, are only recent (e.g. Melitz, 2002; Muscatelli *et al.*, 2004; and this volume). By contrast, most of the empirical work on the SGP produced to date does not meet this requirement. This remark applies to studies intended to show the tendency of pre-Maastricht European governments towards 'fiscal indiscipline' (e.g. Buti and Sapir, 1998, chapter VII), to those concerned with the adequacy of domestic stabilizers within the SGP limits (e.g. Buti *et al.*, 1998; Artis and Buti, 2000; Brunila *et al.*, 2002),[2] as well as to assessments of the sufficient flexibility for stabilization purposes granted by the 3% deficit/GDP constraint based on past cyclical performances of the euro-economies (e.g. Buti and Sapir, 1998, chapter VII; Eichengreen and Wyplosz, 1998; Artis and Buti, 2000).

Second, it is well known that the deficit/GDP ratio is a variable highly sensitive to the business cycle, if anything because the numerator and the denominator are mutually correlated. Nonetheless, most applied research still uses the deficit/GDP ratio as a single variable. Moreover, the official methods employed to identify the cyclical component of the total budget are far from satisfactory. As shown by Melitz (this volume), the current practice that starts from the total deficit and proceeds by correcting for selected cyclical stabilizers is likely to miss the target. Selection of candidate items based on *ex ante* institutional information (see, for example, Perotti, 2002) soon enters a tangle of norms and practices that differ hugely from country to country.[3] The textbook distinction between 'cyclical budget/automatic stabilizers' on the one hand, and 'structural budget/discretionary interventions' on the other, is misleading in practice. Stabilization policy may be implemented by means of discretionary measures, and these measures may also have structural effects: by way of example, consider a cut of distortionary taxes during a recession (Galí and Perotti, 2003). We argue that renewed effort should be made to trace the cyclical behaviour of the deficit/GDP ratio back to its two components, especially because 'excessive deficits' measures and procedures should be based on a clear identification (and delimitation) of governments' responsibilities.

In this perspective, a third issue is budget analysis by components. Decomposition between primary and total budget is a minimal requirement, given that over the typical time horizon of the business cycle interest payments are largely predetermined by the stock of outstanding debt and by the effect of monetary policy on interest rates. Hence, a reasonable approximation to the actual fiscal stance of the government would at least require a good measure of the cyclically adjusted primary budget. In this regard it should be borne in mind that the existing evidence suggests that primary expenditure on the one hand, and total tax revenue on the other, may have different cyclical properties (see, for example, Favero, 2002; Galí and Perotti, 2003; Melitz, this volume; Muscatelli *et al.*, this volume).

Finally, the correct measurement of a country's cyclical position and the response of its fiscal variables should be carefully reconsidered. Indeed, the words of the Presidents of the European Central Bank and of the European Commission quoted above[4] provide anecdotal evidence for what seems to be an uncontroversial fact. When policy-makers consider macroeconomic performance and how it can be influenced by policy actions, they reason in terms of differences between actual and potential GDP growth rates. The stability and growth programmes they are required to submit to the Commission are based on projections of future growth rates. Thus, in the policy-makers' view, a downturn starts whenever the observed growth rate is *negative relative to the trend (potential) rate*, even though it may be *positive in absolute terms*. This requirement has to some extent been recognized, and has at the same time been made compelling, by the reformulation of exemption clauses in the new SGP in terms of growth gaps. Given that the focus of the new normative macroeconomics (Taylor, 1999) is on how policy-makers do and should behave in practice, why is it that the bias of central bankers and prime ministers towards percentage points is seldom considered by theoretical and empirical models which continue to deal with billions of euros?

Our treatment is organized as follows: Sections 5.2 and 5.3 introduce a New Keynesian macroeconomic model with monetary and fiscal policy rules suitable for econometric estimation. The model includes aggregate demand and supply for GDP and the inflation rate, a Taylor rule for the nominal interest rate, and two fiscal rules for primary expenditure and total tax revenue. The main features of the model are intended to remedy the deficiencies in the empirics of SGP pointed out above.

1 The model is specified so as to capture cycles in terms of gaps in growth rates rather than in levels of GDP. We consequently have a system of linear dynamic equations whereby we can study the evolution of the endogenous

variables over the cycle in terms of rates of deviation from their steady-state *growth paths* or target values.

2 The monetary and fiscal rules are interdependent in that each rule includes a variable determined by the other.

3 The government budget is split into its main components (primary expenditure, total tax revenue, interest payments) and each is treated separately. Primary expenditure and tax revenue are treated as the dependent variables of specific fiscal rules; interest payments are treated as an exogenous variable conditioned by monetary policy.

4 All fiscal policy variables are treated in real terms and absolute values (not as GDP ratios).

Section 5.4 reports on the econometric results for Italy and Germany with yearly data from 1962 to 2004.[5] It should be understood that the model has not been estimated in order to test hypotheses or to make forecasts, but in order to provide an empirical quantitative basis for the core part of our study, which consists of simulations. We have therefore chosen these two countries not only because they are major euro-economies but also, and especially, because they differ markedly as to their monetary and fiscal histories and may represent two different ideal types whose comparison may convey rich information on the various issues at stake. The estimation has confirmed that, while the two countries show similar structures in the determinants of their non-policy variables (GDP and inflation), they differ as far as their policy variables (interest rate, primary expenditure and tax revenue) and monetary–fiscal interactions are concerned. On the other hand, we are aware of the number of economic and institutional events that, in the period of time covered by our dataset, may qualify as sources of structural breaks for policy rules. Last but not least, the advent of the EMU, with its indisputable consequence that the national monetary authorities have been replaced by the European Central Bank (ECB). As a first step, we have not performed formal controls for structural breaks (also for the lack of sufficient observations), but we have instead resorted to dummy variables for the pre-EMU major events. Also, we have stretched the specification of independent national Taylor rules into the EMU period; first, because the available data do not allow reliable inferences about the ECB policy conduct,[6] and second, because major central banks in Europe had long pursued converging frames and practices of policy conduct in view of the creation of the single central bank, so that the institutional changeover has probably been less dramatic than it may appear (see, for example, Dornbush *et al.*, 1998; Begg *et al.*, 1999; and, for the Bank of Italy, Angeloni, 1994).

Section 5.5 presents simulations for Italy and Germany, based on the respective estimated models, of a temporary negative shock to the GDP growth rate with respect to potential growth. The simulations concern the five endogenous variables, as well as two additional variables derived from the previous ones; namely, the primary and the total budget. As explained above, the system yields the sequence of *deviations* of the variables from their baseline growth rates or target values until a new steady-state is reached. This provides information on the different dynamics of the various budget components over the cycle. These simulated data can also be used to examine the evolution of the deficit/GDP ratio, shedding light on the much-debated question of the actual control of governments over its cyclical behaviour.

The evidence can be read in two ways. Counterfactually, the simulations indicate how each economy and its public finances would perform, given its inherited macroeconomic structural relationships and policy rules. Our main findings are that (1) relatively small, and hence frequent, negative growth gaps may suffice to deteriorate the government budget up to 3% of GDP even in the absence of discretionary fiscal profligacy; (2) governments have little control over the cyclical evolution of the deficit/GDP ratio, and current methods of correction of the budget for the cycle are misconceived and deceitful; (3) the extent of the two previous results crucially depends on fiscal–monetary policy interactions, and they are more pronounced in a country like Italy, where fast-growing public debt appears among the determinants of the central bank's interest-rate policy. These findings suggest that the aforementioned studies that tested the feasibility of the old SGP against the past cyclical performances of the euro-economies were overly simplistic in their foundations and reached overly optimistic verdicts that were in fact overturned at the first serious growth slowdown in Europe. From a normative perspective, our findings also suggest that the new SGP moves in the right direction in that it re-focuses on growth gaps as a basis for exemption clauses and introduces a longer-term horizon for stability programmes centred on debt stabilization and control. Thus, maintenance of the 3% deficit/GDP ceiling as a sort of *taboo* imposed on governments appears even less justifiable and more questionable than in the old SGP. An important caveat to be borne in mind is that attention should be paid to the role of monetary–fiscal interactions, and how they will develop in the new institutional setup of the EMU with respect to the picture emerged from the past on which we have based our simulations.

The chapter closes with Section 5.6, which presents a summary of the results and makes some concluding remarks.

5.2 The core model of practical macroeconomic policy[7]

Our analysis is based on a theoretical framework rooted in the so-called New Keynesian approach. It typically consists of three main components:

- an IS curve relating current real spending with the real interest rate;
- an AS curve which relates prices and output, so that the relationship is vertical in the long-run and positively sloped in the short-run;
- one (or more) policy reaction function(s) or 'rules' showing how policy-makers react to shocks.

In this section we shall illustrate how this general framework has been extended to highlight monetary–fiscal policy interactions, and then how it has been specified with a view to empirical analysis.

5.2.1 The fundamental equations

The basic relationships in the approach under consideration can be represented in log–linear terms as follows (e.g. Allsopp and Vines, 2000),[8] where we omit time indexes that will be introduced later in the context of the testable versions of the model:

$$\text{(IS)} \quad y = y^* + \alpha r + \beta f + u_y \tag{5.1}$$

$$\text{(AS)} \quad \pi = \pi^* + \gamma(y - y^*) + u_\pi \tag{5.2}$$

$$\text{(TR)} \quad i = i^* + \delta(\pi - \pi^*) + \phi(y - y^*) + u_i \tag{5.3}$$

$$\text{(FR)} \quad f = f^* + \eta(y - y^*) + u_f \tag{5.4}$$

Equation (5.1) represents the goods-market equilibrium (IS) and it states that the actual GDP y is determined by its potential value y^*,[9] the real interest rate r (where $\alpha < 0$), a variable measuring the fiscal stance f, and possible real shocks u_y. Note that the real interest rate is a derived variable, since it is given by $r = i + \pi^e$. Under the rational expectations hypothesis, the expected inflation rate π^e is a function of other variables present in the model, and consequently r results to be entirely determined. The variable f may be a measure of expenditure, of taxation or of the overall government budget, depending on different specifications and microfoundations of the model, whereas the parameter β may be positive or negative. Equation (5.2) represents the determination of the inflation rate by the supply side of the economy (AS), according to which the actual inflation rate coincides with the official target π^* up to deviations of the level of output from its potential, and to inflationary shocks u_π. The parameter $\gamma > 0$ is usually interpreted as a measure of the flexibility of prices: the higher γ is, the more rapidly prices adjust to their market-clearing level. Temporary deviations of output from its potential imply a positively sloped relation between inflation and output, while non-zero realizations of the inflation shock when output is at its potential cause the inflation rate to shift along a vertical (long-run) relation. Note that this specification is consistent with an expectations-augmented AS, where the expected inflation rate is assumed equal to the central-bank target π^*.[10]

The next two equations constitute the policy block of the model. Equation (5.3) is a basic parameterization of a monetary rule in the form of the well known Taylor rule (TR), with the term u_i representing a monetary shock. The main idea here is that the central bank sets the nominal interest rate i in relation to a given target value i^*, while positive (negative) *deviations* of actual inflation from its target level, and of actual output from its potential, are associated with positive (negative) deviations of the interest rate from its target (i.e. $\delta, \phi > 0$). As discussed in Allsopp and Vines (2000), and more extensively in Woodford (2003, chapter 4), a monetary authority endowed with a rule like (5.3) can successfully deal with the two main functions usually assigned to monetary policy: that is, provide a nominal anchor for the economy, and stabilize output fluctuations. Finally, equation (5.4) is the fiscal authority's policy rule, and represents a more recent extension of this framework into fiscal policy analysis (e.g. Taylor, 2000a). Typically, normative as well as descriptive fiscal rules, like the monetary ones, are considered from the macro-stabilization viewpoint, and consist of a 'systematic' and an 'unsystematic' (or 'discretionary') part. In the systematic part, the government sets a target (or a 'structural') value f^* of the variable, which is then allowed to be sensitive to *deviations* of output from its potential level in a predictable way (e.g. by means of 'automatic stabilizers'); the sign of the parameter η can then be positive or negative depending on the fiscal variable chosen. The unsystematic part u_f captures discretionary and non-anticipated fiscal decisions by the government. These, in turn, may be aimed at stabilization as well as at other fiscal ends.[11] Note that the systematic relationship of the policy variables with the deviations of output and inflation from the respective targets, rather than with their levels, is regarded as a major innovation of the New Keynesian approach not only with respect to the Old one of the Sixties and Seventies, but also with respect to the New Classical Revolution of the Eighties which confined effective policy interventions only to their unsystematic part.[12]

The key to the New Keynesian interpretation of model (5.1)–(5.4) is that there exists a steady state of the economy where

$$y = y^*, \quad \pi_t = \pi^*, \quad i = i^*, \quad f = f^*.$$

In this framework, the business cycle is viewed as the transitory deviation of output and inflation from their steady-state values (i.e. a sequence of 'output gaps' and 'inflation gaps', respectively) which may be triggered by non-policy (u_y, u_π) as well as policy shocks (u_i, u_f). Under suitable conditions (which will be discussed later), the system is considered globally stable; that is, all variables tend to converge to the steady state after a shock. Among these suitable conditions are well-behaved policy rules such as (5.3) and (5.4), where it is crucial that the policy authorities set the relevant target values consistently with the steady state of the economy. In this respect, note that by imposing the steady-state condition $y = y^*$, we obtain from (5.1) the so-called neutral real interest rate:[13]

$$r* = -\frac{\beta}{\alpha} f^*. \tag{5.5}$$

Hence, the neutral real interest rate, associated with potential GDP and a constant inflation rate, is a function of the steady-state fiscal variable. As a result, given f^*, r^* and π^*, there is only one possible steady-state value of the nominal interest rate too, that is, $i^* = r^* + \pi^*$.

The system (5.1)–(5.4) can be expressed in a more compact manner that highlights this interpretation of the business cycle and of the role of policy rules. Let $\hat{x} \equiv x - x^*$ denote a 'gap' variable; that is, the deviation of the level of a variable from its target or steady-state value. Then, making use of (5.5), and considering that $r = r^* + \hat{r}, f = f^* + \hat{f}$, system (5.1)–(5.4) may be rewritten as

$$\hat{y} = \alpha\hat{r} + \beta\hat{f} + u_y \tag{5.6}$$

$$\hat{\pi} = \gamma\hat{y} + u_\pi \tag{5.7}$$

$$\hat{i} = \delta\hat{\pi} + \phi\hat{y} + u_i \tag{5.8}$$

$$\hat{f} = \eta\hat{y} + u_f. \tag{5.9}$$

The foregoing theoretical framework can be employed for empirical policy analysis by means of a general specification like the following:

$$\mathbf{A}(L)\mathbf{x}_t = \mathbf{B}(L)\mathbf{z}_t + \mathbf{v}_t \tag{5.10}$$

where $\mathbf{x}_t$ is the vector of the endogenous variables, $\mathbf{z}_t$ is the vector of the exogenous variables, $\mathbf{v}_t$ is a vector of structural errors on the equations, with $E(\mathbf{v}_t) = \mathbf{0}$ and $Var(\mathbf{v}_t) = \Omega$, L is the lag operator, and $\mathbf{A}(L)$ and $\mathbf{B}(L)$ are polynomials in L of order p, q. The elements in $\mathbf{A}(L)$ capture the interactions between the endogenous variables as well as their time structure; the elements in $\mathbf{B}(L)$ represent the impact of exogenous variables with their time structure. The conditions for dynamic stability of the model are that all the roots of the determinant polynomial lie within the unit circle. Theoretical as well as empirical elaborations may then impose *a priori* restrictions on the elements in $\mathbf{A}(L)$ and $\mathbf{B}(L)$ and add other exogenous variables.

5.2.2 Refining the Taylor rule

The policy rules embedded in the basic framework put forward above are highly stylized representations of the policy processes. When they are applied to specific countries, attention should be paid to historical periods and institutional settings. We are aware of the considerable structural and institutional differences between the two countries of interest, Italy and Germany, as well as of the number of institutional events that occurred in the time period covered by our dataset. The most important of these were the end of the Bretton Woods exchange-rates system (1971), participation in the European Monetary System (1979–1998 for Germany; 1980–1992, 1996–1998 for Italy), national reunification of Germany (1989), endorsement of the Maastricht Treaty's criteria for admission to EMU (1992) and subsequently of the SGP (1996), and inception of EMU (1999). All these events qualify as causes of structural changes in the data-generating process, especially as regards policy variables.

Owing mainly to a lack of sufficient observations, we have not performed formal tests for structural breaks. As a first step, we have introduced *a priori* information on institutional events by means of dummy variables. Those that proved to be significant or which significantly altered the quality of the estimates are reported in the next section. Of course, we do not conclude that events not associated with these selected dummies are irrelevant; simply, we leave the matter for further and more rigorous investigation. As to the advent of EMU, we have imposed no *a priori* change in the specification of national TR equations for two main reasons: First, the very small number of yearly observations available prevents reliable statistical analysis of a structural break in the TR equations of the two countries as well as estimation of an independent equation. Faced with the trade-off between curtailing the sample period at 1998 and losing observations and degrees of freedom on the one hand, and including the EMU sub-period with a structural break on the other, we have taken the second option. Hopefully, the small number of observations may also restrict the statistical importance of this break. Second, several studies point out that the convergence and harmonization process across the main central banks largely took place well before the creation of the ECB, so that the impact of the institutional changeover may have been milder than expected. This is most likely the case, as is well known, for one of our sample countries, that is, Germany (see, for example, Dornbush *et al.*, 1998; Begg *et al.*, 1999; and, for the Bank of Italy, Angeloni, 1994).

As said above, not only historical events, but also institutional specificities, should be taken into account. To begin with, the TR has been conceived with reference to a 'large', independent, almost 'closed' economy where the central bank can freely set and pursue its own targets. As regards Italy, none of these preconditions has ever existed. First, over a considerable part of the sample period (1962–1971, 1980–1992, 1996–1998), Italy was part of exchange-rate agreements (Bretton Woods and the European Monetary System, respectively) which limited her central bank's ability to manage an independent monetary policy. Second, the Bank of Italy did not adopt explicit inflation targeting policy until the second half of the 1980s, although it can be argued that an exchange-rate target implies a target on domestic inflation vis-à-vis major trading partners (Visco, 1995). Thus, we have sought a specification of equation (5.3) in consideration of the interest-rate parity constraint to which an open economy like Italy was probably subject.[14] Admittedly, this constraint was not always equally tight. In the Bretton Woods era, low and controlled capital mobility left substantial room for domestic monetary policy. By contrast, according to well-established interpretations, the monetary policies of non-German member countries in the EMS were severely constrained by interest-rate parity vis–à-vis Germany, while the anti-inflationary goal was pursued, not by choosing the domestic inflation target, but by anchoring the domestic nominal interest rate to the German one (Visco, 1995; Giavazzi and Pagano, 1988). Accordingly, the TR should in principle be replaced by the interest-rate parity (IRP) constraint with Germany. In the simplest possible form we have

$$i^{ITA} = i^{GER} + \mathrm{E}(\Delta e) + [\text{risk premium}]$$

where E is the expectation operator, e is the log of the nominal lira–DM exchange rate and $\Delta e > 0$ is the lira depreciation rate. The IRP equation may also include a risk premium on domestic bonds, to which we shall return below. Assuming that the depreciation rate is determined by the inflation differential, and leaving the risk premium aside for a moment, the IRP appears as a special TR with $i^* = i^{GER}$, $\pi^* = \pi^{GER}$, and $\delta = 1$, $\phi = 0$. On the other hand, the IRP constraint may come closer to the traditional TR to the extent that the presence of relaxing factors (e.g. capital controls, fluctuation bands of the exchange rate, realignments, etc.) allows (at least in the short run) for a limited reaction to inflation differentials, that is, $\delta < 1$, as well as for domestic GDP targeting, that is, $\phi > 0$. Therefore, the monetary rule (5.3) might be rewritten as

$$i^{ITA} = i^{GER} + \delta\hat{\pi}^{ITA} + \phi\hat{y}^{ITA} + u_i^{ITA} \qquad (5.3a)$$

with $\hat{\pi}^{ITA} = \pi^{ITA} - \pi^{GER}$.

As regards Germany, her role as monetary-policy leader for the pre-EMU period admits of the use of the unconstrained TR. However, there are at least two possible regimes for the inflation target. The first includes a time-varying target; this hypothesis has required a historical reconstruction of the official inflation target of the Bundesbank (as provided, for example, by Geberding *et al.*, 2004). The second follows the widely held belief that the ECB has substantially reproduced the monetary policy framework of the Bundesbank, which amounts to assuming that the inflation target for Germany has been constantly equal to 2%. It should be noted, however, that according to the available reconstruction, although the official inflation target of the Bundesbank was not always equal to 2% until 1987, it was rarely changed. Therefore, the two specifications produce two almost coincident time series, and for the sake of simplicity we have assumed a constant $\pi^{*GER} = 2\%$, obtaining a monetary rule like the following:

$$i^{GER} = i^{*GER} + \delta\hat{\pi}^{GER} + \phi\hat{y}^{GER} + u_i^{GER} \qquad (5.3b)$$

with $\hat{\pi}^{GER} = \pi^{GER} - 2\%$.

5.2.3 Refining the fiscal rules

As recalled above, investigation into fiscal rules has started more recently, and is less developed, with respect to monetary rules (e.g. Taylor, 2000a,b). On the other hand, the SGP has represented a major historical and institutional innovation that has prompted lively research on fiscal rules (e.g. Buti *et al.*, 1998; Beetsma and Uhlig, 1999; Artis and Winkler, 1999; Artis and Onorante, 2006). As a result of the (almost exclusive) focus on governments' budget deficits in the practical implementation of the SGP, empirical research initially concentrated on this variable. However, more recent developments present disaggregations of the budget into at least the two main determinants, namely total expenditure and total taxation (e.g. Favero, 2002; Perotti, 2002; Galí and Perotti, 2003; Melitz, this volume). That is to say, the FR equation (5.4) can be split into $f = g, \tau$. The main rationale for this disaggregation is that the systematic and unsystematic parts of the components of the budget may respond unequally to the cyclical position of the economy as well as to other fiscal aims. Likewise, each component may have a different impact on aggregate demand and GDP in the IS equation.

From another point of view, the government's actual fiscal stance and choices may be more precisely identified by observing expenditure and taxation separately.

A related issue is that if the aim is to establish the extent to which a government is complying with a given target or rule (as is typically the case with the SGP), it is crucial to identify the fiscal variables that can actually be traced back to direct government control. In this regard, we have also found it useful to narrow the measure of g to the sole primary expenditure, with the exclusion of interest payments (e.g. Favero, 2002). As we shall see, this is also propaedeutic to analysis of the feedback from monetary to fiscal policy.

Moreover, contrary to the common practice in both theoretical and empirical models, we have measured fiscal policy variables in absolute real terms instead of ratios to GDP. As stressed by Melitz (this volume), the two specifications yield different empirical results and lead to different policy implications. In particular, fiscal policy equations in real absolute values allow estimation of the exact elasticity of each real fiscal variable with respect to GDP gaps, whereas the cyclical elasticity of total budget can be correctly derived by compounding the partial elasticities of each component. Thanks to this estimation of the elasticities of primitive fiscal variables, also the notorious pitfall of fiscal ratios to GDP, which stir the cyclical components of the numerator and of the denominator, can easily be avoided. This yields important information, as will be shown by means of our simulations.

A final critical issue regards the targets associated with the fiscal policy variables, in our case real expenditure and taxation. The SGP targets, which naturally come to mind, are of little help for our study. First, because they were not in place for a large part of the time-span of our database, even allowing for anticipation of the new rules as early as 1992; second, because they are aggregate targets, whereas we wish to study the disaggregate components of the government budget. Further, available empirical results on fiscal target variables are less developed and more controversial than those on monetary ones. The official statistics closest to our theoretical variables are the so-called structural or cyclically adjusted fiscal items and balances released by national and international institutions. These, however, are far from satisfactory because they are fraught with arbitrariness in their *a priori* distinction between 'structural' and 'cyclical' components, as well as in the econometric methodologies employed.[15] The foregoing considerations have led us to proxy the fiscal targets by means of the least prejudged strategy that will be explained in the context of our 'growth-gap' version of the model.

5.2.4 Fiscal–monetary policy interactions

In a model like (5.6)–(5.9) there are two-way relationships between the macro and the policy variables, but no direct relationship between the latter. The direct spillovers between monetary and fiscal policy have been a matter of increasing theoretical interest, especially in relation to the inception of the euro system with its peculiar institutional setup consisting of a single supernational monetary authority vis-à-vis a number of national fiscal authorities (e.g. Beetsma and Bovenberg, 1998; Beetsma and Uhlig, 1999; Buti *et al.*, 2001; Dixit, 2001; Dixit and Lambertini, 2001; Tamborini, 2004a,b). However, empirical investigations are still relatively less developed. Among recent studies on monetary–policy interactions in the euro area, Favero (2002) and Melitz (2002) make use of macro-structural models, Muscatelli *et al.* (2004, and this volume) rely on microfounded models, all of which consist of specifications and refinements of the basic New Keynesian framework. Taking stock of these contributions, we have sought to enrich the specifications of policy rules by paying particular attention to the channels through which fiscal–monetary interactions operate.

Considering first the monetary policy rule, it should be noted that, as far as we know, no empirical model includes a fiscal term in it. Yet the basic TR includes the neutral real interest rate $r*$ as the 'real anchor' of the nominal interest rate. The direct measurement of this variable is highly problematic, and its estimates, whether as a constant or on a time-varying basis, are regarded as unsatisfactory and unreliable (see Caresma *et al.*, 2005, for a recent survey). However, theory does relate r^* to fiscal variables (see Woodford, 2003, chapter 4, and above, equation (5.5)). Hence, we have considered the hypothesis that when the national central banks were in existence, they tracked the dynamics of r^* with reference to a measure of the fiscal stance impinging upon the private sector's asset holdings which are supposed to underpin the determination of r^*. According to Woodford's model, there exists an equilibrium *stock* of public debt which, together with all other asset stocks, is associated with r^*. Following this theoretical indication, we have opted for a stock measure such as the (log) of real public debt d.[16] An additional merit of this variable is that it fits both the TR equation for a monetary independent country like Germany and that of a constrained open economy like Italy. In fact, in the case of Germany, d can be used to proxy a time-varying r^*, so that

$$i^{*GER} = \mu d^{GER} + \pi^{*GER}.$$

In the case of Italy, d can be introduced as a proxy for the risk premium that can be added to the IRP, so that

$$i^{*ITA} = i^{GER} + \mu d^{ITA}.$$

Turning to the fiscal policy rules, the main interaction channel with monetary policy is generally considered to be interest payments (Favero, 2002). In fact, given outstanding debt, changes in interest rates determined by monetary policy may affect the government budget substantially. This channel should be particularly important in countries where the government operates under a *total* budget target or constraint, since the fiscal authority should respond to changes in interest payments by adjusting their primary balance. That is to say, a monetary restriction is likely to induce a fiscal restriction as well. In the fiscal case, we found no compelling reasons to distinguish between Italy and Germany in the specification of the relevant rules. Therefore, we have limited ourselves to introducing the variable *IP*, measuring real interest payments, into the equations of expenditure and taxation for both countries.[17] Non-null estimates of the relevant coefficients would provide evidence both of a direct feedback from monetary to fiscal policy and of the government compliance with a given (implicit) budget target or constraint.

5.2.5 Other exogenous variables

The refinements of the basic model put forward above amount to including d_t and IP_t into the vector of exogenous variables $\mathbf{z}_t$. In view of empirical analysis, other exogenous variables can be added. Following Favero (2002), we have corrected the IS equation of both countries for the world business cycle represented by the US output gap, $\hat{y}_t^{US}$.

5.3 The 'growth-gaps' model

The change of perspective required to account for the attitude of policy-makers as well as of the new SGP to reason in terms of gaps in growth rates rather than of gaps in levels, may be accomplished straightforwardly within the foregoing framework.

By construction, the model (5.6)–(5.9) is fully consistent with a balanced-growth solution such that at every point in time the output level Y_t equals its potential, Y_t^*, which in turn is assumed to grow over time by the constant potential growth rate q^*, that is, $Y_t^*/Y_{t-1}^* = 1 + q^*$, all t. Hence, along this growth path:

- the inflation rate is constant and equal to the target value set by the central bank, π^*;
- the nominal and real interest rates are constant and fulfil the Fisher equation, $i^* = r^* + \pi^*$;
- for a constant real interest rate to be possible, all real asset stocks should be on a balanced growth path with GDP, which for public debt, in real terms, implies $D_t^*/D_{t-1}^* = 1 + q^*$, all t (i.e. a constant real debt/GDP ratio, $D_t^*/Y_t^* = \delta^*$, all t);
- consequently, real interest payments, $IP_t = r^* D_{t-1}$, also grow at the GDP rate, $IP_t^*/IP_{t-1}^* = 1 + q^*$ (i.e. they are constant as a ratio to GDP, $IP_t^*/Y_t^* = r^*\delta^*$);
- the government budget, in real terms, must satisfy the condition $B_t^* = -q^* D_{t-1}^*$, which implies a target value for the primary balance such that $PB_t^* = -q^* D_{t-1}^* + IP_t^*$; as a consequence, $PB_t^*/PB_{t-1}^* = 1 + q^*$ (i.e. both the total and the primary balance/GDP ratios are constant, $B_t^*/Y_t^* = -\delta^*[q^*/(1+q^*)]$, $PB_t^*/Y_t^* = \delta^*[(r^* - q^*)/(1+q^*)]$);
- a sufficient condition for targets on primary expenditure G_t^* and total tax revenue T_t^* to satisfy the primary balance constraint is that $G_t^*/G_{t-1}^* = T_t^*/T_{t-1}^* = 1 + q^*$ (i.e. constant ratios to GDP).

It is well known that the SGP arithmetic is consistent with this reference state as long as $q^* = 3\%$, $\pi^* = 2\%$, and $\delta^* = 60\%$, which yield a target deficit/GDP ratio of 3% in nominal terms. The target primary budget/GDP ratio can be close to balance on the 'classical' assumption that $r^* = q^*$. The recommendation that the target *total* budget be 'close to balance or in surplus' implies a *positive* target primary balance, and a *reduction* of any non-zero debt/GDP ratio, along the GDP potential path.

Now let q_t be the actual growth rate of a variable x_t in logs, that is, $q_t = x_t - x_{t-1}$, and $q_t^* = x_t^* - x_{t-1}^*$ its target growth rate. Clearly, the growth gap of x_t is given by $q_t - q_t^* = \Delta x_t - \Delta x_t^* = \hat{x}_t - \hat{x}_{t-1} = \Delta\hat{x}_t$. Thus, our growth-gap model can simply be obtained as the time first-difference of the basic gap model (5.6)–(5.9). With reference to the general formulation for estimation (5.10), the growth-gap model can be viewed as the result of particular constraints on the first-order elements in the coefficient matrices $\mathbf{A}(L)$ and $\mathbf{B}(L)$ or, more directly, as a respecification of the endogenous (and possibly exogenous) variables; namely, for $j = \text{ITA, GER}$

$$
\begin{aligned}
&\mathbf{C}(L)\Delta\mathbf{x}_t^j = \mathbf{D}(L)\Delta\mathbf{z}_t^j + \varepsilon_t^j \\
&\Delta\mathbf{x}_t^j = [\Delta\hat{y}_t^j, \Delta\hat{\pi}_t^j, \Delta\hat{i}_t^j, \Delta\hat{g}_t^j, \Delta\hat{\tau}_t^j]' \\
&\Delta\mathbf{z}_t^j = [\Delta\hat{y}_t US, \Delta\hat{d}_t^j \Delta\hat{I}P_t^j]'
\end{aligned}
\tag{5.11}
$$

Accordingly, the IS equation now gives the GDP growth gap $\Delta\hat{y}_t$ that measures the difference between the actual and the potential growth rate, while the AS equation yields the associated inflation growth gap $\Delta\hat{\pi}_t$: that is, the extent to which inflation accelerates or decelerates relative to the target. Hence, the TR equation is just the 'accelerationist' version of the basic TR: that is, $\Delta\hat{i}_t$ measures by how much the nominal interest rate increases or decreases in relation to its target. Likewise, the FR equations measure by how much the relevant fiscal variable deviates from its balanced path in response to output growth gaps and interest-payments gaps.

Before proceeding, let us draw attention to the correct interpretation of this model. It represents an economy in which all real variables and prices grow over time. In steady state, each variable grows along its balanced growth path, while the nominal interest rate is constant at its target value, as explained above. The reader can easily check that this state occurs as the vectors of shocks and of exogenous variables are null. The problem of interest is the system's dynamic response when one or more variables are shocked and display positive or negative growth gaps. A crucial part of the problem is how the policy variables react in the presence of undesired growth gaps in the relevant variables, and how changes in policy variables react back onto growth gaps.

As said above, the 'starred' variables in the model are difficult to observe and measure. Though not free from faults, the only generally accepted and officially certified variable in this category is the year potential GDP, which we have used to compute the GDP potential growth rate Δy_t^*. Our treatment of the remaining variables was already discussed in the previous section. It is worth recalling that, as a result, Italy and Germany had different specifications of some target-variables in the TR equation. In the growth-gap context these are

$$\Delta i_t^{*GER} = \mu \Delta \hat{d}_t^{GER}{}_t, \quad \Delta i_t^{*ITA} = \Delta i_t^{GER} + \mu \Delta \hat{d}_t^{ITA}{}_t,$$
$$\Delta \pi_t^{*GER} = 0, \quad \Delta \pi_t^{*ITA} = \Delta \pi_t^{GER}$$

where $\Delta \hat{d}^j_t = \Delta d^j_t - \Delta d^{*j}_t$. Germany, being a monetary independent country, follows an independent 'accelerationist' TR. The *changes* in the interest-rate target for Germany are given by changes in the neutral real interest rate and in the domestic inflation rate. The latter are zero under the assumption of a constant target at 2%. The former are proxied by the growth gap of real public debt: in fact, as explained above, as long as the public debt grows at a rate consistent with the balanced growth path of the country, Δd_t^{*GER}, the neutral interest rate does not change, while it increases or decreases as the public debt accelerates or decelerates. In the case of Italy, an IRP-constrained country, the changes in the interest-rate target are driven by changes in the German interest rate and in the risk premium on the domestic debt, according to its acceleration/deceleration relative to the balanced growth rate $\Delta d_t^{*\mathrm{ITA}}$, whereas the changes in the inflation target are dictated by accelerations/decelerations of the actual inflation rate in Germany.

As to the target values of fiscal variables, the growth-gap model provides a consistent indication. In fact, assuming that the year before our sample started (i.e. in 1961) primary expenditure, fiscal revenue, public debt and interest payments were exactly at their target, the implication of the model is that from the following year onwards all these fiscal variables, if undisturbed, would grow along their balanced growth path, that is, at a rate equal to the potential GDP growth rate:

$$\Delta g_t^* = \Delta \tau_t^* = \Delta d_t^* = \Delta IP_t^* = \Delta y_t^*.$$

Furthermore, to account for major institutional events in the sample period, the following dummy variables were also added:

- Italy, TR equation, 1992 (breakdown of the EMS parity); FR equations, 1996 (readmission procedure to the EMS and EMU process);
- Germany, all equations, 1991 (post-reunification shock).

Finally comes specification of the dynamic structure of the estimation model (5.11). The basic theoretical relationships presented in the previous paragraph are too simple to give guidance. Yet, economic theory in general does not deliver univocal results concerning the time structure of dynamic models. Dynamic stochastic general equilibrium models stress the role of rational *forward-looking* behaviour such that expected future variables determine current ones. However, they deny the relevance of, or ignore, the role of lagged variables, which by contrast are widely used in econometric practice. Agnostically, one might conceive of a general dynamic structure like (5.11) whereby all endogenous and exogenous variables enter with current and lagged values, and 'let the data say' what the best time structure is. However, unconstrained estimation of system (5.11), and a full-blown 'general-to-specific' procedure, would have been too demanding in our case, given the insufficient amount of observations relative to the number of coefficients to be estimated. We have therefore proceeded by imposing structure regarding the endogenous variables, the exogenous variables as well as the model's time profile embedded in the matrices **C** and **D**, based on *a priori* theoretical or empirical information gathered from existing studies.[18]

The two main issues in the relevant literature concern the imposition of 'leads and lags' for (1) identification of systematic policy interventions with respect to unsystematic policy innovations (the errors in the relevant equations) and (2) identification of the effects of policy on non-policy variables with respect to the reverse feed-back effects. This latter issue is particularly relevant in our case because of the simultaneous presence of fiscal and monetary variables. Among the works dealing with this problem, we have followed Favero (2002), who posits that non-policy variables and policy shocks have contemporaneous effects on policy variables, while the latter have delayed effects on non-policy variables. In other words, policy variables react quickly to their own determinants, but they take time to develop their effects on non-policy variables. A consistent endorsement of this hypothesis should exclude that policy variables have a significant autoregressive structure, which typically indicates that policy-makers adjust slowly to incoming information. By contrast, we have included a first-order autoregressive structure of the non-policy variables, since if policy variables have delayed effects, these are likely to induce dependence of non-policy variables on their own lagged values.

The resulting estimation model is reproduced below. The superscript j = ITA, GER indicates specifications that are common to both countries, whereas specifications valid for a single country are indicated by the relevant country superscript.

$$
\begin{aligned}
\Delta\hat{y}^j_t &= c_{10} + c_{11}\Delta\hat{y}^j_{t-1} + c_{12}\Delta\hat{r}^j_{t-1} + c_{13}\Delta\hat{g}^j_{t-1} + c_{14}\Delta\hat{\tau}^j_{t-1} \\
&\quad + c_{15}\Delta\hat{y}_t{}^{USA} + c_{16}dummy91^{GER} + v^j_{1t}
\end{aligned}
$$

$$
\Delta\hat{\pi}^j_t = c_{20} + c_{21}\Delta\hat{\pi}^j_{t-1} + c_{22}\Delta\hat{y}^j_t + c_{23}dummy91^{GER} + v^j_{2t}
$$

$$
\Delta\hat{i}^j_t \begin{cases} ITA = c_{30} + c_{31}\Delta i_t{}^{GER} + c_{32}\Delta\hat{\pi}^{ITA}_t + c_{33}\Delta\hat{y}^{ITA}_t + c_{34}\Delta\hat{d}^{ITA}_t \\ \qquad + c_{35}dummy92^{ITA} + v^{ITA}_{3t} \\ GER = c_{30} + c_{31}\Delta\pi^{GER}_t + c_{32}\Delta\hat{y}^{GER}_t + c_{33}\Delta\hat{d}^{GER}_t \\ \qquad + c_{34}dummy91^{GER} + v^{GER}_{3t} \end{cases}
$$

$$
\Delta\hat{g}^j_t = c_{40} + c_{41}\Delta\hat{y}^j_t + c_{42}\Delta\hat{I}P^j_t + \begin{cases} ITA = c_{43}dummy96^{ITA} \\ GER = c_{43}dummy91^{GER} \end{cases} + v^j_{5t}
$$

$$
\Delta\hat{\tau}^j_t = c_{50} + c_{51}\Delta\hat{y}^j_t + c_{52}\Delta\hat{I}P^j_t + \begin{cases} ITA = c_{53}dummy96^{ITA} \\ GER = c_{53}dummy91^{GER} \end{cases} + v^j_{5t}
$$

where $\Delta\hat{r}_{t-1} = \Delta i_{t-1} - \mathrm{E}_{t-1}(\Delta\hat{\pi}_t)$.

5.4 Econometric estimations

The source for the data are yearly observations for each primitive variable in the OECD CD-Rom Database over the period 1962–2004.[19] Elaborations on primitive variables to obtain estimation variables are those described in the previous sections. The time series of selected estimation variables are reproduced in Figure 5.1.

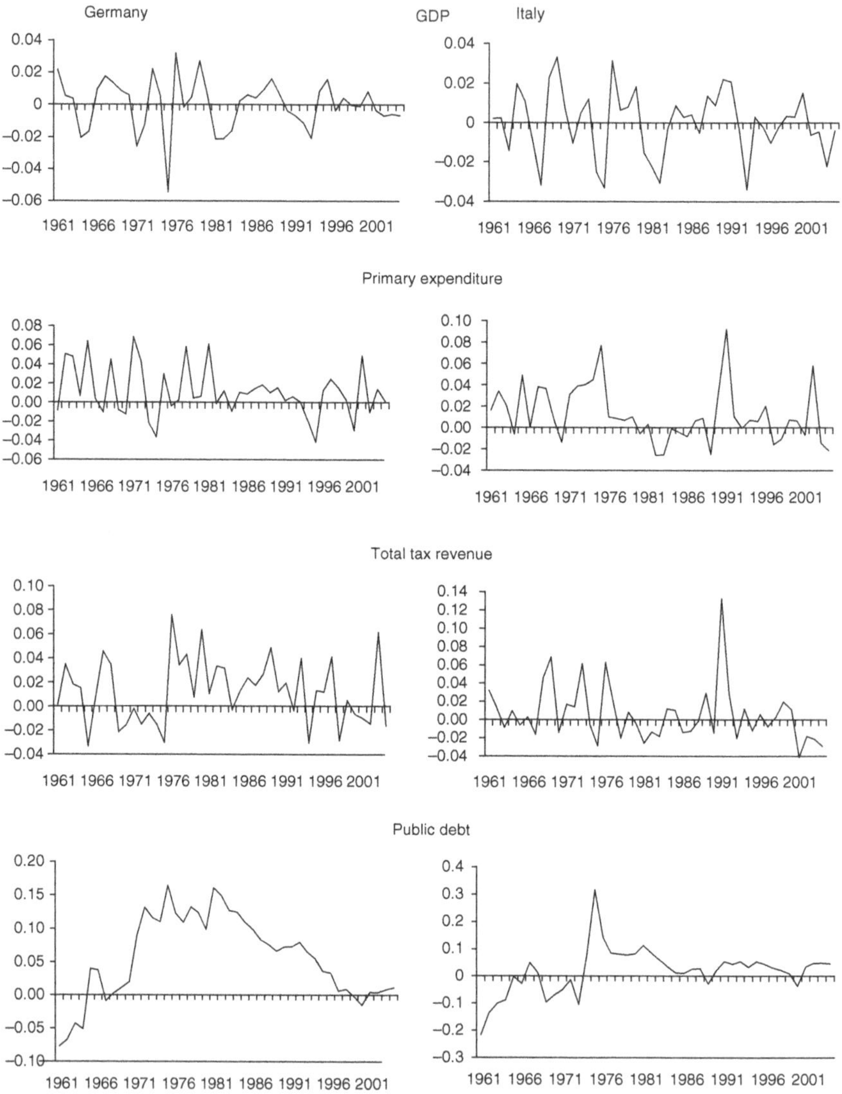

Figure 5.1 Selected estimation variables, growth gaps, 1961–2004.

We have used the 3SLS method with instrumental variables to correct for simultaneity. In the system's unrestricted reduced form (URF) for both countries, no test revealed any major problem: no evidence of significant first-order residual autocorrelation, and normality seemed a good approximation to the residuals' distributional shape. We therefore considered the system specification and its lag structure to be a congruent representation of the data. The results, with the instrumental variables employed, are presented in Table 5.1.

Equation for $\Delta\hat{y}_t$. One variable is strongly significant (p-value $< 5\%$) with the expected (negative) sign for both countries: the change in the real interest rate anticipated one year earlier (which should trigger a deviation of private expenditure from its growth path one year earlier). The US GDP growth gaps, which we interpret as world business cycles, turn out to be strongly significant for Germany, but very weakly significant or rejectable for Italy (p-value $> 10\%$). For both countries, the 1-year lagged values of the GDP growth gap itself, and of the fiscal variables, present the expected sign, but are definitely non-significant.

Though there is extensive world-wide evidence that GDP displays autocorrelation, it does not come as a surprise that GDP *growth gaps* fail to obey this empirical regularity. In fact, it is also well known that first-order differenced variables generally display low order or no autoregressive structures. As to the relationship between GDP growth gaps and fiscal variables, this is notoriously open to debate. Not only is the evidence inconclusive, but different views are deeply rooted in unresolved theoretical issues. To say the least, the international evidence allows no firmer conclusion than that the effects of fiscal variables on GDP may differ substantially across countries, being in some countries apparently weak and/or shrinking over time (see, for example, Favero, 2002; and works by Perotti, 2002; Galí and Perotti, 2003). However, as explained above, our estimation differs from most of the reference literature because it yields the exact elasticity of GDP *growth gaps* to real fiscal variables *growth gaps*. Hence, our results may have a statistical origin in that GDP growth gaps show low variability vis-à-vis remarkably high variability of rates of change in real fiscal variables. Also to be considered is that GDP growth gaps may be due to a combined deviation of observed GDP growth from the potential path and a shock to the path itself. A paradox is possible here. Suppose that both observed and potential GDP depend on real fiscal variables (see, for example, Barro, 1990); then if, say, during a downturn the government spends more and/or taxes less, the result may be that the observed GDP rises while the potential GDP is also revised upwards, with the effect that the gap is not closed.

Equation for $\Delta\pi_t$. The estimated equation supports the 'accelerationist' version of the AS curve for both countries, though Germany displays negligible persistence of changes in the inflation rate, whereas Italy shows a remarkably large effect of GDP growth gaps.

Equation for Δi_t. No component of our 'accelerationist' monetary policy equations is to be rejected statistically, with the theoretical sign and with high confidence (p-values $< 5\%$). As to Italy, our interpretation is that the central bank substantially tracked interest-rate parity with Germany, corrected for the risk

Table 5.1 Estimation results by 3SLS

Italy			*Germany*		
$\Delta\hat{y}_t$	Constant	0.002 (0.002)	$\Delta\hat{y}_t$	Constant	−0.004 (0.002)
	$\Delta\hat{r}_{t-1}$	−0.357** (0.048)		$\Delta\hat{r}_{t-1}$	−0.205** (0.089)
	$\Delta\hat{g}_{t-1}$	0.006 (0.048)		$\Delta\hat{g}_{t-1}$	0.108 (0.126)
	$\Delta\hat{\tau}_{t-1}$	−0.153 (0.136)		$\Delta\hat{\tau}_{t-1}$	−0.024 (0.062)
	$\Delta\hat{y}_t^{USA}$	0.115 (0.078)		$\Delta\hat{y}_t^{USA}$	0.261** (0.091)
				Dummy91	0.081** (0.013)
$\Delta\hat{\pi}_t$	Constant	−0.000 (0.003)	$\Delta\hat{\pi}_t$	Constant	0.000 (0.002)
	$\Delta\hat{\pi}_{t-1}$	0.807** (0.224)		$\Delta\hat{\pi}_{t-1}$	0.245 (0.161)
	$\Delta\hat{y}_t$	1.405** (0.259)		$\Delta\hat{y}_t$	0.377* (0.166)
				Dummy91	−0.020 (0.017)
Δi_t	Constant	−0.000 (0.002)	Δi_t	Constant	0.001 (0.003)
	Δi_t^{GER}	0.599** (0.209)		$\Delta\pi_t$	0.619** (0.245)
	$\Delta\hat{\pi}_t$	0.461** (0.122)		$\Delta\hat{y}_t$	0.149** (0.418)
	$\Delta\hat{y}_t$	0.682** (0.284)		$\Delta\hat{d}_t$	−0.040 (0.069)
	$\Delta\hat{d}_t$	0.223** (0.123)		Dummy91	−0.007 (0.036)
	Dummy92	0.040** (0.017)			
$\Delta\hat{g}_t$	Constant	0.010 (0.004)	$\Delta\hat{g}_t$	Constant	0.006 (0.004)
	$\Delta\hat{y}_t$	−1.018** (0.261)		$\Delta\hat{y}_t$	−1.185** (0.348)
	$\Delta\hat{IP}_t$	0.008 (0.032)		$\Delta\hat{IP}_t$	−0.009 (0.059)
	Dummy96	−0.033 (0.022)		Dummy91	0.170 (0.040)
$\Delta\hat{\tau}_t$	Constant	0.012 (0.004)	$\Delta\hat{\tau}_t$	Constant	0.003 (0.004)
	$\Delta\hat{y}_t$	0.520* (0.292)		$\Delta\hat{y}_t$	1.854** (0.297)
	$\Delta\hat{IP}_t$	0.016 (0.038)		$\Delta\hat{IP}_t$	0.091 (0.051)
	Dummy96	−0.007 (0.026)		Dummy91	−0.025 (0.034)
Instrumental variables: $\Delta\hat{r}_{t-1}$, $\Delta\hat{y}_t^{USA}$, $\Delta\hat{d}_t$, $\Delta\hat{IP}_t$, Dummy96			Instrumental variables: $\Delta\hat{r}_{t-1}$, $\Delta\hat{y}_t^{USA}$, $\Delta\hat{d}_t$, $\Delta\hat{IP}_t$, Dummy91		

Notes
Standard errors in brackets. (**), (*) indicate significance at 5% and 10% level, respectively.

premium proxied by the excess growth rate of public debt, while trading-off GDP growth gaps. As to be expected, our estimated TR equations show that in Italy more weight was given to growth-targeting than to inflation-targeting, whereas the opposite was the case in Germany. On the other hand, the so-called Taylor principle did not operate in either country: that is to say, the estimated coefficient of the inflation gap is less than one. Notably, the fiscal variable turns out to be significant only for Italy. We believe that this is an informative result: in two countries with sharp differences in the speed of public-debt growth, the monetary policy rules differ. The central bank facing slow-growing debt (Germany) has given no weight to the fiscal variable, whereas the one facing fast-growing debt (Italy) has given substantial weight to it.

Equations for Δg_t *and* $\Delta \tau_t$. First of all, both countries display sizeable anti-cyclical contemporaneous components of the rate of change of real fiscal variables. In fact, the parameters of GDP growth gaps are strongly significant and with the theoretical sign (p-values $< 5\%$). The conventional wisdom on the 'long and variable lags' of fiscal policy does not seem confirmed, or else the importance and extent of in-built stabilizers is vindicated (see also Melitz, this volume). As regards the elasticities of fiscal variables to contemporaneous growth gaps,

- expenditure elasticity is about -1.0 in both countries;
- taxation elasticity is about 0.5 in Italy and 1.8 in Germany.

At first sight, both elasticities in the two countries are much larger than in other empirical studies, where they are around 0.3 in absolute value, and where 0.5 is regarded as the typical elasticity of the *total budget* (see, for example, Giorno *et al.*, 1995; Artis and Buti, 2000; Van den Noord, 2000; Brunila *et al.*, 2002). Italy is also at variance with the received wisdom that taxation is the more elastic stabilizer. Yet, as already discussed, our results are not directly comparable with standard practice, which typically a) estimates fiscal rules *in isolation*, and b) measures the elasticity of fiscal–GDP *ratios* to output gaps, both in *levels*. A measurement (partially) comparable to ours has been proposed by Melitz (this volume, Table 4.1) who, in a panel of euro-countries, finds slightly larger values of the elasticities of first differences of both public expenditure and taxation to first differences in output gaps. It should also be considered that the difference between our estimated values and the others may simply be due to the algebra of respecification (empirically, estimates may be roughly equivalent).[20] Whatever the case may be, our aim here is not so much to dispute the magnitude of the cycle elasticities of fiscal variables as to focus on the implications of our proposed change of approach with regard to assessment of the government budget over the cycle, one implication being that knowing these elasticities, if it is ever possible, *per se* conveys little information. These implications will be clarified with the help of the simulations.

Neither Italy nor Germany pass the 'budget-target' hypothesis that implies the adjustment of the primary fiscal variables to compensate for interest payments. The respective parameters are negligible in size and non-significant. If taken at face value, only Italy displays the correct sign.[21] However, another interpretation is possible, which is consistent with the difference between the two countries' monetary rules detected above: namely, that a virtuous fiscal–monetary circle was in place in the slow-growing-debt country (Germany) and a vicious one in the fast-growing-debt country (Italy). In the former country, the mutual sensitivity between fiscal and monetary policy is negligible as slow-growing debt, low and stable interest rate and sustainable interest payments are mutually consistent. The opposite occurs in the latter country, where the fast-growing debt compels mutual sensitivity between fiscal and monetary policy.

5.5 Simulations

By means of the estimated system, it has been possible to simulate the responses of the endogenous variables to exogenous shocks.[22] Here we only report as an example the results of a -1% temporary shock to the GDP growth below potential at time 0 (1963), with no other shock thereon. The simulation has yielded, for each endogenous variable, the per cent rate of deviation from the correspondent baseline value (which, for analogy with the theoretical model, we still denote with $\Delta(\hat{\ })$).[23] Recall that in our model the baseline value is a growth rate for all real variables and the price level, and a constant for the nominal interest rate.

In order to gather information on the government budget, we also used the simulated dynamics of the endogenous variables to compute relevant compound budget variables such as

real primary balance: $\Delta\hat{PB}_t = \Delta\hat{\tau} - \Delta\hat{g}$
real interest payments: $\Delta\hat{IP}_t = \Delta i_t - \Delta\hat{\pi}_t$
total budget: $\Delta\hat{B}_t = \Delta\hat{PB}_t - \Delta\hat{IP}_t.$

Thus, in the simulation, the primary balance deviates from its baseline value by the difference between the deviations of the tax revenue and of the primary expenditure. The deviation rate of real interest payments is approximated by the change of the real interest rate on outstanding debt. As to total budget, this deviates from its baseline value by the difference between the deviations of interest payments and of the primary balance.

The graphs (Figures 5.2 and 5.3) show the post-shock dynamics of the five primitive endogenous variables ($\Delta\hat{y}_t, \Delta\hat{\pi}_t, \Delta\hat{i}_t, \Delta\hat{g}_t, \Delta\hat{\tau}_t$) and of the two generated variables ($\Delta\hat{PB}_t, \Delta\hat{B}_t$) for the two countries. The following comments are in order.

5.5.1 Stability and transitory dynamics

All variables are dynamically stable with low persistence in both countries. In fact, deviations in all variables shrink to zero in a relatively small number of rounds. In other words, each variable returns to its baseline value. Transitory dynamics is almost monotonic for all variables in both countries, except inflation in Italy. As regards Italy, on impact we see a typical pattern of demand shock: the negative growth gap triggers a deceleration in the inflation rate and anti-cyclical policy adjustments. The nominal interest rate is reduced, though less than the

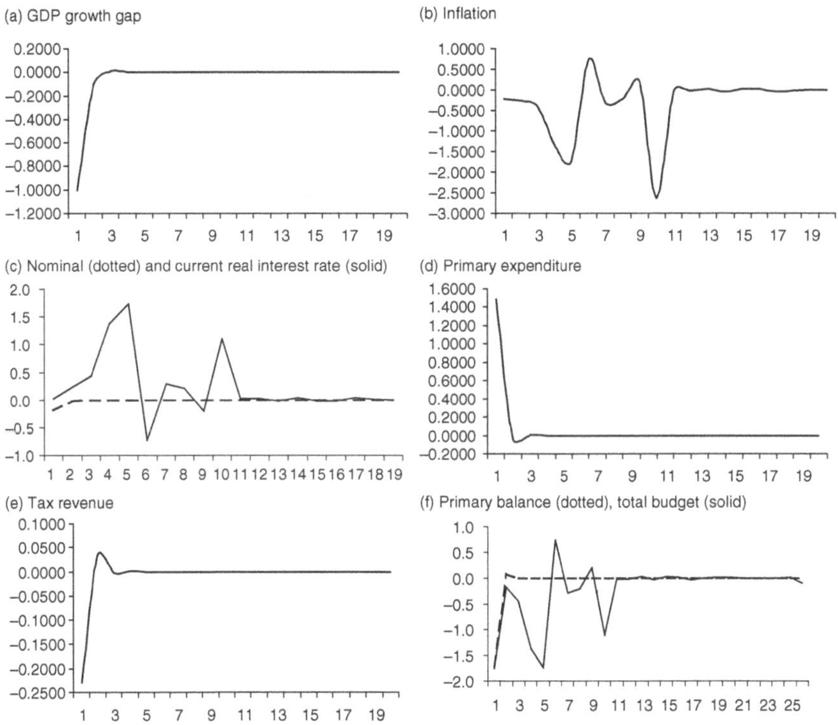

Figure 5.2 Italy. Responses (per cent deviations from baseline values) to a temporary negative 1% multiplicative shock to the GDP growth gap.

deceleration of inflation: the real interest rate deviates above the neutral rate most of the time. Fiscal stabilization consists of a sequence of impulses accelerating primary expenditure and decelerating tax revenue with respect to baseline growth rates. Consequently, the economy is set on a path of negative growth gaps of decreasing magnitude up to zero. Germany instead shows a typical pattern of supply shock: on impact of the negative growth gap, the simulation yields an acceleration of inflation. The policy variables now react in opposite directions. The nominal interest rate immediately rises, though not as much as the acceleration of inflation; yet subsequent adjustments bring the real interest rate above the neutral rate. Fiscal variables react to the negative GDP growth gap as expected, until the gap is progressively reduced to zero.

5.5.2 Elasticities and stabilization capacity: measurement puzzles

How should we measure stabilization capacity and the ensuing budget requirements correctly? Are estimated elasticities of fiscal variables to a cyclical measure of GDP really informative? If fiscal variables do respond 'automatically' to growth

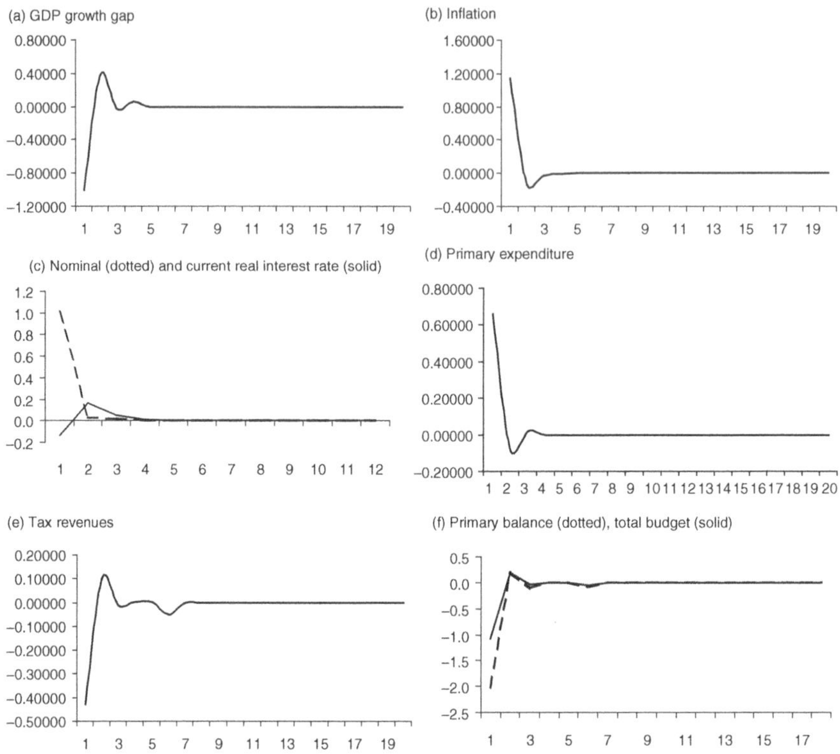

Figure 5.3 Germany. Responses (per cent deviations from baseline values) to a temporary negative 1% multiplicative shock to the GDP growth gap.

shocks, these shocks – as they are usually understood in models – are unobservable, while estimates are based on observed data which probably already embody at least some of the stabilization effects of fiscal variables on GDP and vice versa. Our simulation exercise has enabled us to disentangle this matter. First, we had a well-defined shock, and secondly we could track the response of fiscal variables precisely up to the new steady state. We could thus distinguish (at least) two measures of elasticities with respect to the shock, (1) on impact of the shock, and (2) in the new steady state, that is, the *cumulated* rates of deviation of fiscal variables from target necessary to nullify the initial GDP growth gap (the 'integrals' of the graphs in Figures 5.2 and 5.3). The respective values are reported in Table 5.2.

As can be seen, steady-state elasticities are smaller than impact ones, with one important exception. Consider the primary versus total budget. In Italy as well as in Germany, on impact both variables deteriorate relative to their baseline value by roughly the same amount (about 1.7% in Italy and 1.0% in Germany). However, the paths of the primary and total budgets differ markedly in Italy with respect to Germany (see Figures 5.2 and 5.3, panel (f)). In the latter country the

Table 5.2 Measures of elasticities to −1% GDP growth gap

	Simulated elasticities	
	Impact	*Steady-state*
	Italy	
Primary expenditure	−1.48	−1.45
Total tax revenue	0.23	0.20
Primary balance	1.71	1.65
Total balance	1.74	6.22
	Germany	
Primary expenditure	−0.66	−0.59
Total tax revenue	0.43	0.39
Primary balance	1.09	0.98
Total balance	0.95	1.06

two measures of fiscal stance roughly follow the same monotonic path. In Italy, by contrast, the total budget worsens at higher (absolute) rates and for a longer time than does the primary budget. Hence, the steady-state elasticity of the total budget is strikingly higher in Italy than in Germany, although the underlying fiscal rules are quite similar in the two countries. The difference is due to real interest payments. As we know, although in Italy the nominal interest rate is reduced, the inflation rate decelerates even more, imposing a sequence of inflation-tax cuts. Thus, real interest payments rise most of the time, whereas the opposite occurs in Germany.

This exercise substantiates the idea that the total budget is not under the government's full control over the cycle, even when the government does 'let the automatic stabilizers work' and does not engage in discretionary activism. Even if an almighty econometrician could tell us the exact elasticities of primary fiscal variables to growth shocks, we would still be unable to infer the evolution of the government budget unless we also knew all the details of the underlying macroeconomic process. A major 'detail' is that the actual cyclical evolution of total budget is closely dependent on the concomitant monetary–fiscal interactions.

5.5.3 Monetary–fiscal interactions

Since more weight is given in Italy to growth-targeting than to inflation-targeting, whereas the opposite occurs in Germany, this may explain the handbook reactions of monetary policy both in the deflationary case of Italy and in the stagflationary case of Germany. On the other hand, the nominal interest rate does *not* over-react to deviations of inflation from target, causing, at first sight, unintended movements in the real interest rate: it *rises* in Italy and *falls* in Germany (at least initially). One reason may be that in both countries the estimated coefficient of the inflation gap is, in fact, less than one. Another reason may be that our TR equations also respond to public debt dynamics as a determinant of the neutral real interest rate.

As remarked above, the coefficient of this variable is significant and positive for Italy, whereas it is not for Germany. Since this variable in the sample period of the simulation is rapidly increasing in Italy, the ensuing 'fiscal spillover' may reduce the responsiveness of monetary policy and sustain the rise in the real interest rate. We now consider the other side of the monetary–fiscal interactions; namely, interest payments. The estimation results reject this hypothesis for both countries. Nonetheless, interest payments also exert direct influence on the evolution of the total budget, as seen above.

One is tempted to conclude from our exercise that in a slow-growing-debt country not only are fiscal and monetary policy *complements*[24] but they may also be (virtually) *independent.* By contrast, in a fast-growing-debt country the two policies may still be complements but not independent. As a consequence, in the first type of country both policies can be more aggressive with less overall impact on the total budget, whereas in the second type of country one policy checks the other, but they nonetheless have an overall negative effect on the total budget.

5.5.4 Growth gaps, levels and the SGP rules

Let us finally examine the much-debated question of the cyclical evolution of the deficit/GDP ratio. For this purpose, we have to go back from rates of deviation to levels, which also facilitates comparison between our results and existing ones. The interpretation of the foregoing results within our theoretical model is that the *growth rates* of output, tax revenue, primary expenditure and prices return to their respective initial values. This, however, does not imply that the *levels* of those variables will thereafter be equal to those that would have obtained along the growth path of the economy in the absence of the shock. To verify this property, the simulation data in rates of deviations from baseline values can easily be converted into data in levels (index numbers).[25] This exercise shows that, for instance, a *temporary* negative gap in the *growth rate* of output determines a *permanent* output gap *in levels*. Likewise, a temporary positive growth gap in public expenditure will end up with a permanent positive gap in level and so on. In this respect, important information is given by the cumulative deviations of the variables discussed above, which determine the respective gaps in levels in the new steady state. The latter are reported in Table 5.3 both for absolute fiscal variables and for their GDP ratios.

Let us first consider final output gaps, which are −1.04% for Italy and −0.57% for Germany. This means that in Italy the initial growth shock leaves behind a permanent output gap of the same magnitude, whereas in Germany it is almost halved. In both countries the bulk of stabilization is borne by primary expenditure (particularly in Italy) rather than by taxation as presumed by most studies on automatic stabilizers (on this point see also Melitz (this volume)). Remarkably, however, Germany's stronger stabilization capacity is obtained with less fiscal effort as measured by the cumulative deterioration of the primary balance, which reaches −1.57% of baseline value in Italy but stops at −0.94% in Germany. Notice that the figures are somewhat different if measured in ratios to GDP: in particular, the expenditure/GDP and taxation/GDP ratios *are larger* than the gaps in

Table 5.3 Steady-state gaps in levels after the shock (per cent)

	Italy	*Germany*
Output	−1.04	−0.57
Primary expenditure	+1.38	+0.57
Ratio to GDP	+2.45	+1.14
Total tax revenue	−0.19	−0.37
Ratio to GDP	+0.86	+0.20
Primary balance	−1.57	−0.94
Ratio to GDP	−1.59	−0.94

absolute terms (overestimating the increase in expenditure and underestimating the reduction in taxation – which even appears to have been increased). The well known reason for this is that GDP ratios embody the lower level of the denominator.[26]

In any case, these figures deliver an important message concerning the new exemption clauses introduced by the SGP reform. As reported in the Introduction, these clauses correctly recognize that not only negative growth rates, but also 'prolonged' negative growth gaps (while the absolute growth rate may remain positive) may account for 'exceptional' fiscal deficits. They also give the right emphasis to the related concept of 'cumulated loss of output'. These are welcome amendments, which, however, will require careful re-examination of the criteria used to assess the fiscal stances of member countries.

First of all, unlike the sparse occurrences of the former definitions of 'exceptional conditions' found by Buti and Sapir (1998) from 1961 to 1997,[27] one should expect statistics – if not interested governments – to report negative growth gaps roughly half of the time, owing to the sheer statistical artifact that these are stationary variables around the trend (see Figure 5.1). And we have seen that econometric analysis supports the hypothesis that fiscal variables are highly sensitive to *this* measure of the business cycle. Further, cycles are typically characterized by strings of negative and positive growth gaps. Consequently, strings of negative years impinging upon fiscal balances are frequent events rather than exceptional ones. Our simulated steady-state elasticities suggest that in a country like Italy, even starting from balance, the 3% deficit/GDP ratio may be reached after two years of negative growth gaps in the order of 1%, not an infrequent occurrence in the sample. These findings raise doubts concerning the early assessments on the substantial safety margin guaranteed by the 3% deficit ceiling.

Second, we have seen that 'cumulated losses of output' have far-reaching consequences. Temporary growth gaps leave long-lasting traces in public finances, even in well-managed (simulated) ones. On looking at the statistics of our simulated economies, the SGP guardians might be tempted to conclude that, as the GDP is driven back to its potential growth rate, there is no longer justification for a deficit. However, the extant primary deficit – not to mention the total deficit – though created by 'legitimate' cyclical factors, becomes, in a sense, structural.

It is bound to last until a new positive impulse to growth overcomes the previous cumulative output loss. Admittedly, as we argued above, at each point in time there is about a 50% chance that this will happen. But what is, then, an 'excessive deficit'? And how is the return to normality ascertained? At the moment it is unclear whether the SGP institutions are ready to address these crucial questions, and how.

5.6 Conclusions

In this chapter we have sought to reframe the questions of assessment and measurement of fiscal variables in view of the Maastricht Treaty's prescriptions within a consistent macroeconomic model whereby the cyclical dynamics of GDP, inflation, monetary and fiscal variables are jointly determined. The model has been specified in terms of growth gaps, rather than level gaps, consistently with the common perception and measurement of business cycles as well as with the new exemption clauses introduced by the reformed SGP. The results from estimation of the model for Italy and Germany have been used for simulations of the effects of a negative growth gap shock on policy and non-policy variables, tracking the sequence of deviations of the variables from their baseline growth rates or target values until a new steady-state is reached. In particular, the simulated data have been used to examine the evolution of the deficit/GDP ratio as a result of the two components of the ratio, shedding light on the much-debated question of the actual control exerted by governments over its cyclical behaviour.

To begin with, the results can be read counterfactually: that is to say, how each economy and its public finances would perform after a growth gap shock, given its inherited macroeconomic structural relationships and policy rules. Our main findings can be summarized as follows:

1 Our estimations provide evidence of 'well-behaved' fiscal rules for both Germany and Italy, at least in the sense that a good number of the observed deviations of primary expenditure and total tax revenue from the respective balanced growth paths are explained by the growth cycle. Contrary to the widespread belief of unfettered fiscal indiscipline, this conforms with the Commission's popular view that the EMU governments should simply 'let the automatic stabilizers work'. As also indicated by Melitz, and by Muscatelli *et al.* (this volume), we have seen that *broad* measures of public expenditure and taxation do respond to the business cycle contributing to stabilization; hence we cannot but agree with these authors that the larger these items the better. The other side of the coin shown by our simulations is that small negative growth gaps may easily deteriorate the government budget up to the 3% of GDP even in the absence of discretionary fiscal profligacy. Moreover, growth gaps of this kind are statistically much more frequent than the *negative* growth rates that would qualify a country for exemption from the excessive deficit procedure in the old SGP.

2 Governments have little control over the cyclical evolution of the deficit/GDP ratio, while the current methods of correction of the budget for the cycle are misconceived and deceitful. On the one hand, the implication of the previous point is that not many of the observed changes in fiscal variables can indisputably be subtracted from anti-cyclical stabilization. In other words, the body of evidence required to open excessive deficits procedures may be very limited if excessive means beyond legitimate anti-cyclical deficits. We have also shown that attempts to measure the cyclical components of fiscal variables by means of estimated elasticities encounter several pitfalls. With the help of our simulations, we have obtained what we think is the theoretically correct measure of these elasticities: the steady-state rates of deviations in absolute fiscal measures in response to the initial GDP growth gap (last column, Table 5.2). True, this measure can hardly be obtained in practice; yet researchers should be aware that measures obtained on observable data, which probably contain at least part of the stabilization effect of fiscal variables on GDP, tend to overestimate the magnitude of elasticities (especially if measured as GDP ratios), and all the more so the more effective the fiscal variables are.
3 The extent of the two previous results crucially depends on fiscal–monetary policy interactions. We have seen that they are more pronounced in a country like Italy, where public debt appears among the determinants of the interest-rate policy of the central bank, and the interest rate has considerable impact on payments by the government. If it may be wise for an independent central bank to operate in this way, it is disputable that the ensuing loss of budget control of the government vis-à-vis the 3% ceiling is the best way to achieve fiscal discipline.

These findings suggest that the crisis of the old SGP was, at least in part, boosted by some internal flaws on the 'flexibility' side that had been underestimated and that became manifest at the first serious growth slowdown in Europe.

Our study can also be read, with some 'out-of-sample' caution, in the normative perspective of the new SGP. Caution is necessary because the above-mentioned role of monetary–fiscal interactions in our exercise are based on the past institutional setup of the two sample economies. If there are good reasons and some evidence to believe that the ECB will not operate in a way dramatically different from the one parametrized by our national TR equations, at present the attitude of the ECB towards specific national positions, the impact of national fiscal variables on the ECB policy and the common bonds market, and the future evolution of monetary–fiscal interactions in the EMU are largely hidden from view. Bearing this caveat in mind, the new SGP is moving in the right direction in that it re-focuses on growth gaps as a basis for exemption clauses, and introduces a longer-term horizon for stability programmes centred on debt stabilization or reduction. On the other hand, the long-standing criticisms about the total deficit/GDP ratio as the pillar of the SGP rules are still valid. The relative frequency of negative strings of growth gaps, combined with the responsiveness of large fiscal aggregates to these gaps, shed doubts on the view that the 3% deficit ceiling allows a sufficient safety margin for cyclical manoeuvres. More importantly, we have shown that these episodes, even though triggered by temporary shocks, determine *permanent* output losses to which there correspond *permanent* primary deficits. These will not be reabsorbed by a mere return to 'normal' growth. Hence, it is not clear how the Commission will assess these situations. Overall, the maintenance of the 3% deficit/GDP ceiling as a sort of *taboo* imposed on governments seems at variance with the prescription set out in the recent developments of the theory of policy rules, according to which rules should make reference to, and policy-makers should be examined on, *instruments* that they can control, not on *outcomes* they do not control (Woodford, 2003, chapter 1).

Notes

* We wish to thank the participants in the conferences organized by the Jean Monnet Chair in 'European Macroeconomics' at the University of Siena, and Chris Gilbert for their comments. We remain fully responsible for this paper.

1 See Buti *et al.* (2003); Galí and Perotti (2003); Buti and Franco (2005) for brief accounts of these progressive adjustments.
2 Preliminary works that address this issue are Farina and Tamborini (2002, 2004); Tamborini (2004b).
3 And the estimates of 'fiscal shocks' obtained by Perotti are, on his own admission, not very plausible in several instances.
4 Respectively available at http:/www.bis.org/review/r050602d.pdf and at http://www.eua.be/eua/jsp/en/upload/Barroso_speech.1112693429657.pdf.
5 The year frequency of the observations has been dictated by the well known unreliability of higher-frequency data on fiscal variables.
6 Hopefully, the small number of observations may also restrict the statistical importance of this institutional change.
7 The terminology is from AEA (1997).
8 Similar equations can be derived from a microfounded dynamic general equilibrium model (e.g. Clarida *et al.*, 1999; McCallum and Nelson, 1999; Woodford, 2003; among many others), where the relations corresponding to our equations (5.1) and (5.2) are derived from households choosing optimal intertemporal paths for their consumption and firms setting prices optimally according to a Calvo-type mechanism. The main difference from the specification which we employ is that explicit microfoundations allow expectations on future output and inflation to explicitly appear in the IS and the Phillips curves, respectively.
9 There are various possible specifications of potential output (e.g. Woodford, 2003, chapters 4 and 5). Generally, it is interpreted as the level of output that would prevail with full use of resources up to the natural rate of unemployment, and it is computed as the non-cyclical component of actual GDP.
10 On the other hand, if the central bank consistently pursues its inflation target, then π^* is also the rational expectation of the inflation rate.
11 There is a tendency in the literature to identify the systematic fiscal policy with stabilization and the discretionary one with other ends. But this identification is clearly unwarranted since governments may well opt for anti-cyclical discretionary interventions (e.g. a temporary cut in taxation).
12 See Woodford (2003, chapters 1, 2) for a thorough discussion of this point.
13 Although r^* very closely resembles the Wicksellian notion of the natural real rate of interest (Woodford, 2003), it is directly influenced by fiscal policy, so that the term

'neutral' is more suitable (Allsopp and Vines, 2000). In fact, standard economic theory implies that the neutral rate of interest is a function of consumers' preferences and of the trend growth rate of output. If an endogenous growth mechanism is added to the model, fiscal policy may affect the neutral rate of interest, even in a Wicksellian world via its impact on the steady-state growth rate. Note, however, that the channel involved here is quite different.

14 An example of a New Keynesian model of a small open economy is provided by Galí and Monacelli (2005); an open-economy model applied to Italy has been employed by Chiades and Gambacorta (2004).

15 See Perotti (2002); Galí and Perotti (2003); Melitz (this volume) for recent discussions of these problems.

16 Unfortunately, the existing empirical studies do not give clear guidance in this respect; in particular, it is not yet clear whether a stock or a flow measure of government borrowing is appropriate (e.g. Schiavo, this volume).

17 Unlike Favero (2002), however, for simplicity we have taken the whole value of interest payments as a single variable without disaggregating the interest component from the debt component.

18 See, for example, Chiarella *et al.* (2005) for extended treatment of, and variations on, the New Keynesian basic framework.

19 Primitive variables are: Gross domestic product at current market prices (ITA, GER, US), Potential output at current market prices (ITA, GER, US), GDP deflator (1995 = 100) (ITA, GER, US), Government non-interest expenditure at current market prices (ITA, GER), Government interest payments (ITA, GER), Total tax revenue at current market prices (ITA, GER), Government net borrowing and lending (ITA, GER), Public debt (ITA, GER), Short-term interest rate (ITA, GER).

20 Consider any fiscal variable in isolation f_t, in relation to a cyclical measure of GDP only. Our 'growth-gaps' specification is

$$\Delta\hat{f}_t = \alpha + \beta\Delta\hat{y}_t + u_t.$$

On expanding this expression according to our definition of growth gap, and rearranging, it is possible to obtain a respecification in the following form:

$$(f_t - y_t) = \alpha + (f_{t-1} - y_{t-1}) + (1-\beta)(y_t - y_t^*) + (1-\beta)(y_{t-1} - y_{t-1}^*) + u_t.$$

This is the standard specification of an estimation equation for the fiscal variable/GDP ratio $(f_t - y_t)$ in level, regressed on its own lagged value and on the current and lagged value of the output gap in level (see, for example, Melitz, 2002; and Favero, 2002). Clearly, the cyclical coefficents estimated in the standard specification are complements to those estimated by means of the 'growth-gaps' specification; if the former are smaller than 0.5, the latter will be larger than 0.5.

21 On the other hand, Favero (2002) has found that both Germany and Italy display sensitivity to interest payments to some extent.

22 The simulation software was Winsolve.

23 It should be borne in mind that the simulator creates the baseline value of each endogenous variable for each point in time by means of an initial simulation of the estimated system whereby the system is fed with the 'true' times series of the exogenous variables used in the econometric estimation. These same time series are also used in the simulation. Hence, the simulation results should be understood as deviations of the endogenous variables from their 'historical' estimated values in the absence of shocks. This procedure also implies that simulation results are 'history sensitive' in that they depend on the shock date chosen and on the true historical values of the exogenous variables.

24 It should be stressed that complementarity emerged in our simulation of a GDP shock. Preliminary inspections of different shocks, such as inflationary or fiscal shocks, indicated that the two policies are used as substitutes. A similar result can be found in Muscatelli *et al.* (2004).

25 Let $X_0 = 100$ be the initial absolute value of any variable. Then for any $t = 1, \ldots,$ the new level along the steady-state growth path of the economy is given by $X_t^* = X_{t-1}^*(1+q_t^*)$, whereas the new level after the shock is given by $X_t = X_{t-1}(1+q_t^*+\Delta\hat{x}_t)$. We have taken q_t^* to be the potential growth rate of GDP in the data set for each country, and, according to the theoretical model, we have used it also for fiscal variables.

26 The figures in Table 5.3 further exemplify the above-mentioned pitfalls of estimating ex-post elasticities. These figures in fact closely resemble the typical statistical information available; that is, realized output gaps on the one hand, and changes in absolute fiscal variables or in their GDP ratios on the other. Yet Table 5.3 highlights that, whereas the data have been generated by the same growth shock in the two countries, ex-post elasticities in Germany would be grossly overestimated merely because stabilization has been more effective.

27 They detected just 84 observations for all EU countries (5 for Italy, 8 for Germany).

References

AEA (1997), 'Is there a core of practical macroeconomics that we should all believe?', Panel at the American Economic Association, New Orleans, LA, 4–6 January 1997, Papers and Proceedings of the American Economic Association, *American Economic Review*, 87: 230–46.

Allsopp, C. and Vines, D. (2000), 'The assessment: macroeconomic policy', *Oxford Review of Economic Policy*, 16: 1–32.

Angeloni, I. (1994), 'Strumenti e obiettivi operativi della Banca d'Italia: verso un modello europeo', *Note Economiche*, 14: 128–61.

Artis, M. J. and Buti, F. (2000), 'Close to balance or in surplus. a policy maker's guide to the implementation of the Stability and Growth Pact', *Journal of Common Market Studies*, 38: 563–92.

Artis, M. J. and Onorante, L. (2006), 'The economic importance of fiscal rules', CEPR Discussion Paper no. 5684.

Artis, M. J. and Winkler, B. (1999), 'The Stability and Growth Pact: trading off flexibility for credibility', in A. J. Hughes Hallett, M. M. Hutchinson, S. E. Hougaard Jensen (eds), *Fiscal Aspects of European Monetary Integration*, Cambridge: Cambridge University Press.

Barro, R. J. (1990), 'Government spending in a simple model of endogenous growth', *Journal of Political Economy*, 98: 103–25.

Beetsma, R. M. and Bovenberg, A. L. (1998), 'Monetary union without fiscal coordination may discipline policymakers', *Journal of International Economics*, 45: 239–58.

Beetsma, R. M. and Uhlig, H. (1999), 'An analysis of the Stability and Growth Pact', *Economic Journal*, 109: 546–71.

Begg, D., De Grauwe, P., Giavazzi, F., Uhlig, H. and Wyplosz, C. (1999), *The ECB: Safe at Any Speed?, Monitoring the European Central Bank*, 1, London: CEPR.

Brunila, A., Buti, M. and in't Veld, J. (2002), 'Fiscal policy in Europe: how effective are automatic stabilizers?', *European Economy*, Economic Paper no. 177.

Buti, M. and Franco, D. (2005), 'The Stability Pact's pains: a forward-looking assesment of the reform debate', CEPR Discussion Paper no. 5216.

Buti, M. and Sapir, A. (1998), *Economic Policy in EMU*, Oxford: Clarendon Press.

Buti, M., Eijffinger, S. and Franco, D. (2003), 'Revisiting the Stability and Growth Pact: grand design or internal adjustment?', *European Economy*, Economic Paper no. 180.

Buti, M., Franco, D. and Ongena, H. (1998), 'Fiscal discipline and flexibility in EMU: the implementation of the Stability and Growth Pact', *Oxford Review of Economic Policy*, 14: 81–97.

Buti, M., Roeger, W. and in't Veld, J. (2001), 'Stabilizing output and inflation in the EMU: policy conflicts and co-operation under the Stability Pact', *Journal of Common Market Studies*, 39: 801–28.

Caresma, J. C., Gnan, E. and Ritzberger-Gruenwald, D. (2005), 'The natural rate of interest. concepts and appraisal for the Euro area', *Monetary Policy and the Economy*, Austrian National Bank, Q4.

Chiades, P. and Gambacorta, L. (2004), 'The Bernanke and Blinder Model in an open economy: the case of Italy', *The German Economic Review*, 5: 1–34.

Chiarella, C., Flaschel, P. and Franke, R. (2005), *Foundations for a Disequilibrium Theory of the Business Cycle*, Cambridge: Cambridge University Press.

Clarida, R., Galí, J. and Gertler, M. (1999), 'The science of monetary policy: a new Keynesian perspective', *Journal of Economic Literature*, 37: 1661–707.

Dixit, A. (2001), 'Games of monetary and fiscal interactions in the EMU', Papers and Proceedings of the European Economic Association, *European Economic Review*, 45: 589–613.

Dixit, A. and Lambertini, L. (2001), 'Monetary–fiscal interaction and commitment versus discretion in a monetary union', Papers and Proceedings of the European Economic Association, *European Economic Review*, 45: 977–87.

Dornbush, R., Favero, C. A. and Giavazzi, F. (1998), 'Immediate challenges for the European Central Bank', *Economic Policy*, 26: 15–64.

Eichengreen, B. and Wyplosz, C. (1998), 'Stability Pact: more than a minor nuisance?', *Economic Policy*, 26: 67–112.

Farina, F. and Tamborini, R. (2002), 'Le politiche macroeconomiche di stabilizzazione in Europa nel nuovo regime di unione monetaria', in F. Farina and R. Tamborini (eds), *Da Nazioni a Regioni. Mutamenti strutturali e istituzionali dopo l'ingresso nella Unione Monetaria Europea*, Bologna: Il Mulino.

—— (2004), ' "Set a sufficiently ambitious budget target and let the automatic stabilizers work". Can it really work in the European Monetary Union?', *Open Economies Review*, 15: 143–68.

Favero, C. (2002), 'How do European monetary and fiscal authorities behave?', CEPR Discussion Paper no. 214.

Galí, J. and Monacelli, T. (2005), 'Monetary policy and exchange rate volatility in an open economy', *Review of Economic Studies*, 72: 707–34.

Galí, J. and Perotti, R. (2003), 'Fiscal policy and monetary integration in Europe', *Economic Policy*, 31: 533–72.

Geberding, C., Worms, A. and Sietz, F. (2004), 'How the Bundesbank really conducted monetary policy: an analysis based on real-time data', Deutsche Bundesbank, Discussion Paper no. 25.

Giavazzi, F. and Pagano, M. (1988), 'The advantage of tying one's hands: EMS discipline and central bank credibility', *European Economic Review*, 32: 371–90.

McCallum, B. T. and Nelson, E. (1999), 'An optimizing IS-LM specification for monetary policy and business cycle analysis', *Journal of Money, Credit and Banking*, 31: 296–316.

Melitz, J. (2002), 'Some cross-country evidence about fiscal policy behaviour and consequences for EMU', in M. Buti, J. Von Hagen and C. Martinez-Mongay, *The Behaviour of Fiscal Authorities*, London: Palgrave.

—— (2007 – this volume), 'Non-discretionary and automatic fiscal policy in the EU and the OECD', in F. Farina and R. Tamborini, *Macroeconomic Policy in the European Monetary Union*, London and New York: Routledge.

Muscatelli, V. A., Ropele, T. and Tirelli, P. (2007 – this volume), 'Macroeconomic adjustment in the euro area: the role of fiscal policy', in F. Farina and R. Tamborini, *Macroeconomic Policy in the European Monetary Union*, London and New York: Routledge.

Muscatelli, V. A., Tirelli, P. and Trecroci, C. (2004), 'Monetary and fiscal policy interactions over the cycle: some empirical evidence', in R. Beetsma, C. Favero, A. Missale, V. A. Muscatelli, P. Natale and P. Tirelli (eds), *Fiscal Policies, Monetary Policies and Labour Markets. Key Aspects of European Macroeconomic Policies after Monetary Unification*, Cambridge: Cambridge University Press.

Perotti, R. (2002), 'Estimating the effects of fiscal policy in OECD countries', ECB Working Paper no. 168.

Schiavo, S. (2007 – this volume), 'Euro bonds: in search of financial spillovers', in F. Farina and R. Tamborini, *Macroeconomic Policy in the European Monetary Union*, London and New York: Routledge.

Tamborini, R. (2004a), 'One monetary giant with many fiscal dwarfs: the efficiency of macroeconomic stabilization policies in the European Monetary Union', in A. V. Deardorff (ed.), *The Past, Present and Future of the European Union*, London: Palgrave Macmillan.

—— (2004b), 'The "Brussels consensus" on macroeconomic stabilization policies in the EMU. A critical assessment', in F. Torres, A. Verdun, C. Zilioli and H. Zimmermann (eds), *Governing EMU: Political, Economic, Historical and Legal Aspects*, Florence: European University Press.

Taylor, J. B. (1993), 'Discretion versus policy rules in practice', *Carnegie-Rochester Conference Series on Public Policy*, 39: 195–214.

—— (ed.) (1999), *Monetary Policy Rules*, Chicago: Chicago University Press.

—— (2000a), 'Reassessing discretionary fiscal policy', *Journal of Economic Perspectives*, 14: 21–36.

—— (2000b), 'The policy rule mix: a macroeconomic policy evaluation', in G. Calvo, M. Obstfeld and R. Dornbusch (eds), *Robert Mundell Festschrif*, Cambridge, MA: MIT Press.

Visco, I. (1995), 'Inflation, inflation targeting and monetary policy: notes for discussion on the Italian experience', in L. Leiderman, and L. E. O. Svensson (eds), *Inflation Targets*, London: CEPR.

Woodford, M. (2003), *Interest and Prices*, Princeton: Princeton University Press.

6 Testing the fiscal theory of the price level for European countries

A cointegrated VAR approach*

F. Farina and R. Ricciuti

6.1 Introduction

In their celebrated article, Sargent and Wallace (1981) argued that Monetary Dominance takes place when the central bank rigorously pursues monetary stability. In the Chicken Game between the monetary and the fiscal authorities, the Nash equilibrium prevails in which monetary policy is 'active' and the fiscal policy is 'passive' as the government abides by the restrictive monetary stance (Leeper, 1991). In contrast, under Fiscal Dominance, fiscal authorities do not impede the dynamics of nominal variables to be affected by changes in the public budget, so that fiscal policy is 'active'. However, the price level remains a monetary phenomenon. Since fiscal laxity requires to make recourse to seignorage, the central bank keeps influencing the nominal variables.

The so-called Fiscal Theory of the Price Level (FTPL) contends this view. Although following different research lines, many contributions argue that the relationships between money, debt and prices is more complex than assessed by the quantitative theory of money (Woodford, 1995, 1996, 2001, 2003; Cochrane, 1998, 2001; Christiano and Fitzgerald, 2000; Chadha and Nolan, 2003). In fact, the FTPL claims that the intertemporal public budget constraint (IPBC) can alternatively be generated by a Ricardian (R) Regime or a Non-Ricardian (NR) Regime.

In an R Regime, the central bank acts as the Stackelberg leader. Once monetary policy is set by the monetary authorities, the price level is determined through a money demand equation, based on the quantitative theory of money. The fiscal authorities' compliance with the monetary stance implies that they cannot violate their budget constraint, on the same ground as private agents. To fulfil the IPBC, the pattern of future expected surpluses must match the present value of the budget constraint for any possible values of the price level and the interest rate. This amounts to saying that in each period of time the government determines a fiscal stance consistent with the price level resulting from the money demand equation (Leith and Wren-Lewis, 2000: C97–C98). After any exogenous shock, such as a rise in the real interest rate impinging on the total (primary plus secondary) public deficit, or a slowdown in the GDP growth rate causing a lower potential output, fiscal authorities should adjust tax revenues and/or expenditures. If this does not happen, the financial market will react to the violation of the fiscal sustainability condition, and a risk premium will increase the interest rate on the public debt (Buiter, 2001 and 2005).

In a Non-Ricardian Regime, the government acts as the Stackelberg leader. By drawing upon the volatility of the money demand function, and the consequent switch of central banks to manoeuvre the monetary stance by setting the interest rate (e.g. in the Taylor rule the real interest rate is increased, according to a coefficient bigger than one, as a response to a rise in the inflation rate), the FTPL claims that the price level is left indeterminate.

Can fiscal policy get in and provide the nominal anchor for the economy? The traditional approach stemming from the Sargent–Wallace analysis opposes the FTPL view that the IPBC is an equilibrium condition. Since 'prices clear markets, not budget constraints' (Buiter, 2005: C19), there is no alternative to the Ricardian Regime and the IPBC is always satisfied as an identity. The FTPL rejoinder emphasizes that the renege from the commitment to meet the IPBC puts fiscal authorities in the position to take hold of the determination of the price level. Whenever the government does not fulfil its intertemporal budget constraint, a Non-Ricardian Regime is established. A jump in the price level will do the business of reducing the real value of government debt, making it possible to rebalance the present value of taxes with future spending obligations.

In this chapter we evaluate the FTPL tenet of an alternative between following a Ricardian or a Non-Ricardian Regime by conducting econometric estimates for European countries which cover the four decades from 1962 to 2000. In the first two decades, central banks of most countries deviated from the anti-inflationary behaviour, so that the strategy mix put forward by the interaction between the monetary and the fiscal authorities proved to be highly inefficient. In the subsequent two decades, European countries have experienced a smooth – albeit slow – downward trend of the inflation rate. We will test whether European governments have been adjusting period-by-period their fiscal stances, so as to establish a Ricardian Regime, or their fiscal stances failed to comply with the monetary stance implied by a credible monetary policy committed to low inflation, thus establishing a Non-Ricardian Regime.

The chapter is organized as follows: Section 6.2 casts the Ricardian and Non-Ricardian regimes in the IPBC equation; Section 6.3 analyses the institutional boundaries within which the behaviour of fiscal authorities was framed during the monetary integration process and provides the link between the FTPL and fiscal policy under Monetary Dominance; Section 6.4 introduces the empirical methodology; Section 6.5 presents the results, and Section 6.6 concludes.

6.2 Ricardian and Non-Ricardian Regimes

Let us write the flow government budget constraint as

$$B_t = B_{t-1}(1 + i_t) + P_t(G_t - T_t) - (M_t - M_{t-1}), \text{ for any } t \tag{6.1}$$

where B is the stock of public debt, i is the nominal interest rate, G are the public expenditures, T are the tax revenues, M is the money supply. In a steady state, $M_t/M_{t-1} = P_t/P_{t+1} = \mu = \Pi_{t+1} + 1$. Under a zero-inflation monetary rule $\mu = 1$, seignorage is ruled out $\Pi = \mu - 1$ and $\Pi = 0$ for any t. Therefore, the flow budget constraint becomes

$$b_t = b_{t-1}(i + r_t) + (\gamma_t - \tau_t) \tag{6.2}$$

where the real interest rate (r) is equal to the nominal, and lower case letters denote values of the income level normalized to the steady state. If fiscal authorities behave according to Monetary Dominance, the year-by-year equilibrium of this equation is sufficient for the IPBC to be satisfied.

Suppose now that expected inflation turns to be positive, the nominal interest rate lifts up, and new public bonds will then be issued in order to fund the increased amount of interest payments. To cope with this increase in public debt, fiscal sustainability asks fiscal authorities to set up the appropriate amount of current and future primary surpluses. In the case the government does not comply with this obligation, the discounted value of current and future primary surpluses will not match the stock of public debt, and seignorage will be endogenously determined. The price level change which is needed to satisfy the IPBC can be rationalized by assuming that the increase in the bond issuing determines a wealth effect. The consequent excess demand creates the appropriate increase of the price level, such that the real value of public debt is reduced and fiscal solvency is achieved.

In the scenario sketched above, in order to impose monetary stability in front of soaring inflationary expectations, a restrictive monetary stance will raise the nominal interest rate. Due to the permanent lift in the funding of the debt service, the stock of public debt will be posited on a rising dynamic path. The higher the accumulated stock of public debt, the more an increase in the interest rate engineered by monetary authorities will endanger Monetary Dominance, which in turn will affect fiscal sustainability (Chadha and Nolan, 2003). Since fiscal authorities are required to take responsibility for any exogenous change in the real interest rate impinging on the debt service, equation (6.2) does not adequately reflect the intertemporal constraint a government is facing after the upward lift of interest rates. Indeed, to verify whether or not fiscal sustainability will be preserved, the secondary deficit must be incorporated in the analysis of fiscal sustainability (McCallum, 1984).

Let us then define the total deficit (d_t) as

$$d_t = (\gamma_t - \tau_t) + r_{bt-1}/(1 + r). \tag{6.3}$$

To fulfil fiscal sustainability, in the case of a positive stock of public debt the future series of d_t must present a negative value. Let us then express the IPBC as

$$b_t = b_{t-1}(i + r) - v_t \tag{6.4}$$

where the surplus $v_t = \tau_t - \gamma_t - \text{rb}_{t-1}/(1+r)$. By solving equation (6.4) for b_{t-1} and iterating for the subsequent periods, after k iterations we get

$$b_t = \sum_{i=0}^{k} (1+r)^{-i}(v_{t+i}) + (1+r)^{-k} b_{b+k} \tag{6.5}$$

where the first term on the right side is the present value of the planned future surpluses and the second term is the so-called transversality condition, which controls for the variation in the debt/GDP ratio not to exceed the difference between the interest rate and the GDP growth rate. In the case of a positive difference, fiscal solvency is still warranted, as the debt explosion could only happen under the inconsistent condition of tax revenues greater than the GDP (Bohn, 1998). When the 'transversality condition' is met, the second term converges to zero ($k \to \infty$):

$$\lim_{k \to \infty} (1+r)^{-k} b_{t+k} = 0. \tag{6.6}$$

The IPBC requires the public debt (b_t) to be equalized by the present value of future surpluses:

$$b_t \sum_{i=0}^{k} (1+r)^{-i}(v_{t+i}). \tag{6.7}$$

To assess whether equation 6.7 was satisfied by European governments as an identity according to the Ricardian Regime, or as an equilibrium condition according to the Non-Ricardian Regime, we have to tune the two regimes on the specific enforcement devices for Monetary Dominance which have been in place during the decades during which monetary integration has taken place.

6.3 The FTPL and the enforcement of Monetary Dominance

A largely shared view on the European monetary integration process holds that in many countries the monetary and fiscal policy interactions have been characterized by a lack of co-ordination between the two authorities. However, monetary authorities have resisted fiscal prodigality by not showing any disposition to co-ordinate with fiscal authorities and conduct an expansionary monetary policy. Neither during the years in which the Bundesbank's tight monetary policy was providing the nominal anchor of the fixed exchange rate regime (EMS), nor while accomplishing the tough task of complying with the Maastricht criteria and afterwards with the constraint put on public finances by the Stability and Growth Pact (SGP),[1] the European central banks have appeared to give in to fiscal authorities. By acting as Stackelberg leaders vis-à-vis their governments, the central banks of European countries were successful in obtaining low inflation, which was instrumental in eventually launching the monetary union.

The evolution of the European monetary integration amounts to a series of steps characterized by the fiscal authorities' obligation to comply with the monetary stability pursued by monetary policy. The degree of enforcement has progressively strengthened. The European governments' fiscal stances increasing coherence with the restrictive monetary policy was due to the commitment to defend the EMS bilateral parities, on which the success of the domestic disinflationary process was relying. The Maastricht criteria stated that a rapid process of public deficit and debt reduction was the inescapable condition for the prize of participation in the monetary union. In approaching the EMU, however, the enforcement device represented by the need to comply with the Maastricht criteria for public finances and be admitted in the eurozone was bound to the end. The concern that the commitment to fiscal restraint would have been jeopardized by the launch of the euro led to the decision to introduce a more stringent institutional straitjacket for fiscal authorities. The SGP constraints can be considered the enforcement device for the fiscal stances to comply with Monetary Dominance.[2]

Let us analytically describe the main requirement to obtain the fiscal restraint needed for Monetary Dominance; that is, to keep the public budget 'close to balance or in surplus' in structural terms (net of the operation of the automatic stabilizers) in the medium-term:[3]

$$d_s = d + \hat{s}(\hat{y}) \tag{6.8}$$

where (d_s) is the 'structural' (cyclically adjusted) total deficit/GDP ratio, ($\hat{s}$) is the cyclical sensitivity of the budget depending on the automatic stabilizers, and ($\hat{y}$) is the output gap. In the medium-term equilibrium, with the output gap equal to zero, the second term is nil, the total (d) equalizes the 'structural' total deficit/GDP ratio (d_s). Considering this medium-term equilibrium, tax revenues as a percentage of GDP (τ_t) could be devoted to discretionary fiscal policy – aimed at allowing the public expenditures not to be cut after a disturbance to the potential output (y_t^*); that is, $y_t^* < y_{t-1^*}$ – and/or to debt decumulation, respectively:

$$\tau_t = \alpha(y_t^*) + \beta(b_{t-1}/p_t). \tag{6.9}$$

Under a R Regime, fiscal authorities abstain from discretionary interventions ($\alpha = 0$) as the Ricardian equivalence applies. The appropriate series of future surpluses are set, such that the public debt could be fastly paid back ($\beta = 1$). The IPBC of equation 6.7 is then met as an equilibrium condition.

The SGP requirement to bring the 'structural' total deficit/GDP ratio d_s down to zero is an attempt to avoid a deviation of the total deficit from its zero medium-term value which could hamper the fulfilment of the debt consolidation target. Suppose now an upward tendency of the total deficit, caused by a slowdown in the formation of tax revenues after a lowering of the GDP growth rate, or by an exogenous rise of the interest rate which increases the interest payments. In order for fiscal sustainability to be preserved, this exogenous shock to the medium-term zero total deficit should be counteracted by a correspondent fiscal restriction (granted that the tax rate is kept constant, according to the Tax Smoothing doctrine). Yet, in the case that fiscal authorities do not upwardly correct the stream of current and future surpluses, the R Regime does not establish, and the transversality condition is not met. This is just the case highlighted by the FTPL. Considering that in equation (6.5) $b_t = B/py$, the IPBC will be satisfied by a rise in the price level, such that the reduction in the real value of the public debt on the left side could offset the lack of zero convergence of the second term on the right side.

Therefore, the econometric assessment of the existence of a Ricardian or a Non-Ricardian Regime corresponds to verifying what happens when fiscal authorities are unwilling and/or unable to equalize the present value of current and future surpluses to the stock of public debt. Econometric tests of the FTPL often present ambiguous results (Afonso, 2002; Ballabriga and Martinez-Mongay, 2003; Favero and Monacelli, 2005; see also Wren-Lewis, 2003). Indeed, testing the FTPL is often doubted (Woodford, 1995), as the public sector budget constraint is a relationship consisting of equilibrium data in which no causality can be detected. The difficulty to assess the right causality link between surpluses and the debt dynamics requests not to interpret a correlation connecting the reduction of public liabilities to a positive innovation in the surplus (Canzoneri *et al.*, 2001) as an unambiguous proof of a 'passive' fiscal policy in a Ricardian Regime. This finding might also signal a Non-Ricardian Regime, whereby expectations of a future reduction in primary surpluses caused by an 'active' fiscal policy, such as expansionary discretionary interventions or an overturn in the trend of debt consolidation, brings about an increase in the price level downward adjusting the real value of government liabilities (see Cochrane, 1998).

Our investigation attempts to overcome this indeterminacy. Firstly we estimate the liabilities' response to an innovation in the primary surplus, and secondly the series of surpluses in the periods subsequent to an innovation in the primary surplus. A positive sign in the first correlation shall not be straightforwardly taken as a confirmation of the hypothesis of a Non-Ricardian Regime. One might also think of reverse causation; that is, a positive primary surplus responding to an increase in the real value of the public debt, which is a proof of an R Regime. In the literature, the label of Ricardian Regime has been assigned both to a negative response of public debt to the primary surplus (Canzoneri *et al.*, 2001) and to a fiscal surplus counteracting an increase in public debt (Bohn, 1998). Any negative relationship between fiscal surpluses and public liabilities is then exposed to the presence of reverse causation. Therefore, we control for the sequence of current and future surpluses in order to understand whether a government implementing an innovation in surplus, which was meant to ensure fiscal sustainability, was persistently maintained. When the series of future surpluses follow a stable path, we conclude in favour of an R Regime. When the sequence turns out to be stochastic – for instance, a rise in the primary surplus at time t is followed by a reduction in the surplus at time $t + 1$ – we think of a Non-Ricardian Regime. In this latter case, contrary to the presumption that a negative correlation between an innovation in surplus and public liabilities unambiguously designates a Ricardian Regime, the IPBC is met just because a positive innovation in surplus is followed by a hike in the price level, causing the real value of the public debt to fall down.

6.4 Model and data

We apply the methodology devised by Canzoneri *et al.* (2001). In an R Regime, the surplus at time t pays off some of the debt, and liabilities at $t+1$ fall. In an NR Regime, there are three possibilities. First, an innovation in surplus is not correlated with the subsequent surpluses. In the case we are considering, liabilities at time $t+1$ should not be affected by the innovation in surplus at time t. Second, an innovation in surplus at time t is positively correlated with future surpluses and discount factors. In this case, liabilities at time $t+1$ should rise. In either of these cases, it should in principle be possible to differentiate between R and NR Regimes. For example, the impulse response function from a VAR in surplus and liabilities would tell us how liabilities respond to an innovation in surplus. If liabilities fall, we have an R Regime; if it does not, we have an NR Regime.

The first step of the analysis is the characterization of the stochastic properties of the series. As shown in the next section, the series involved in our analysis contain unit-roots, therefore we need to modify the empirical strategy undertaken by Canzoneri *et al.* (2001), who find that their series were stationary. The second step of our analysis involves cointegration between the variables included. Having assessed that the series are cointegrated, we can move to the impulse response analysis. In the I(0) case the effect of a shock can be seen in its moving average representation:

$$y_t = \Phi_0 \mathrm{u}_t + \Phi_1 \mathrm{u}_{t-1} + \Phi_2 \mathrm{u}_{t-2}, \tag{6.10}$$

where $\Phi_0 = I_K$, and the

$$\Phi_s = \sum_{j=1}^{s} \Phi_{s-j} A_j, \quad s = 1, 2, \ldots \tag{6.11}$$

are computed recursively from the reduced-for of the VAR in levels. The coefficients of this representation may be interpreted as the responses to impulses hitting the system. In this case $\Phi_s \to 0$ as $s \to \infty$, and the effect of an impulse vanishes over time.

In the I(1) case, that our preliminary tests show being relevant to the variables involved in the analysis, although the Wold representation does not exist for non-stationary cointegrated processes, the Φ_s matrices can be computed in the same way as in standard VAR with in I(0) variables. In this case, the Φ_s may not converge to zero as $s \to \infty$, therefore some shocks may have permanent effects (Breitung *et al.*, 2004). From Johansen (1995) we know that if y_t is generated by a reduced-form VECM, it has the following moving average representation:

$$y_t = \Xi \sum_{i=1}^{t} u_i + \Xi^*(L) u_t + y_0^*, \tag{6.12}$$

where $\Xi = \beta_\perp (\alpha'_\perp (I_K - \sum_{i=1}^{p-1} \Gamma_i) \beta_\perp)^{-1} \alpha'_\perp$, $\Xi^*(L) = \sum_{j=0}^{\infty} \Xi_j^* L^j$ is an infinite-order polynomial in the lag operator with coefficients matrix Ξ_j^* that goes to zero as $j \rightarrow \infty$. y_0^* contains the initial values. The matrix Ξ_j^* has rank $K - r$ if the cointegrating rank of the system is r. It represents the long-run effects of the forecast impulse responses, whereas the Ξ_j^* contains the transitory effects.

To identify the shocks we can replace u_t by $\mathrm{A}^{-1}\mathrm{B}\varepsilon_t$, the orthogonalized short-run impulse response is obtained as $\Xi_j^*\mathrm{A}^{-1}\mathrm{B}$ as in the stationary VAR. The long-run effects of a shock are given by $\Xi\mathrm{A}^{-1}\mathrm{B}$. This matrix has rank $K - r$, and therefore can have at most r columns of zeros. Hence, there can be at most r shocks with no long-run impact, and at least $k^* = K - r$ shocks with permanent effects. Assuming $\mathrm{A} = I_\mathrm{K}$, we have just enough restrictions to identify B.

We consider eight European countries that have been involved in the process of monetary integration, though not all of them participate in the EMU. Two variables are considered: *LIAB* (defined as the sum of government outstanding debt and monetary base over GDP), and *SPL*, government surplus over GDP. Data are taken from the International Financial Statistics database of the International Monetary Fund. They cover the period ranging from 1960 to 2000, with the exception of Spain (1962–2000).[4]

6.5 Results

6.5.1 Unit-roots tests

The first step of the analysis is to study the stochastic properties of the series. To do so, we run two unit-roots tests: ADF1 and ADF2 (Fuller, 1976; Dickey and Fuller 1979; Said, 1991). For the former the null hypothesis is unit-root and the alternative is stationarity, for the latter the null is unit-root with drift and the alternative is trend stationarity. ADF1 specification includes a constant and ADF2 includes constant and trend. The lag-length is determined using the Schwarz Information Criterion. For all the countries and for both series we cannot reject the null hypothesis of a unit-root (Table 6.1).

6.5.2 Cointegration tests

Having established that our series are all characterized by unit-roots, the second step is to see whether they are cointegrated; that is, there exists a linear combination of the two series that is stationary. We employ the Johansen procedure (1988, 1991) by calculating two statistics: the λmax and the λtrace tests. Models include intercept and trend, with cointegrating restrictions on the time trend imposed. Again, the lag-length is determined by using the Schwarz Information Criterion.

In the Johansen tests we first test the null hypothesis that there are zero cointegrating vectors, and second we test the null that there is one cointegrating vector. For all countries but Germany (Table 6.2), we can reject the first null hypothesis, but we can never reject the second one.[5] Therefore, we proceed with the impulse response analysis for all countries with the exception of Germany.

Table 6.1 ADF tests results, 1960–2000

	LIAB		*SPL*	
	ADF1	*ADF2*	*ADF1*	*ADF2*
Belgium	−0.617 (1)	−2.270 (8.4)	−1.279 (1)	−0.699 (1)
Finland	−0.801 (6)	−0.172 (6)	−2.539 (1)	−3.179 (1)
France	−0.824 (1)	−2.017 (1)	−0.110 (1)	−3.002 (1)
Germany	−1.436 (1)	−1.725 (1)	−2.799 (1)	−3.101 (1)
Italy	−0.191 (1)	−1.663 (1)	−1.394 (1)	−0.896 (1)
Netherlands	−1.693 (1)	−2.283 (1)	−2.018 (1)	−1.646 (1)
Spain[1]	−0.726 (1)	−2.195 (1)	−2.248 (1)	−2.031 (1)
Sweden	−2.308 (1)	−3.392 (1)	−2.726 (1)	−2.209 (1)

Notes
Critical values at 5% and 1% are equal to −3.58 and −3.22, respectively for the ADF1 test, and −4.15 and −3.80 respectively for the ADF2 test for a sample size equal to 50. Number in parentheses indicate the lag-length determined using the Schwarz Information Criterion. ADF1 specification includes a constant and ADF2 includes constant and trend.[1] The time-span is 1962–2000.

Table 6.2 Cointegration results

Country	*Lag length*	*r*	λ_{max}	λ_{trace}
Belgium	1	0	28.3	38.4
		1	10.1	10.1
Finland	1	0	88.7	6.1
		1	6.1	94.8
France	1	0	45.5	55.0
		1	9.4	9.4
Germany	1	0	13.0	20.6
		1	7.6	7.6
Italy	1	0	23.4	31.4
		1	8.0	8.0
Netherlands	1	0	70.3	73.8
		1	3.5	3.5
Spain	1	0	32.8	40.0
		1	7.2	7.2
Sweden	2	0	24.2	40.3
		1	6.9	4.2

Notes
Critical values at 10 and 5% are equal to 16.9 and 19.2, respectively for 0 cointegrating vectors to 10.6 and 23.5, respectively for 1 cointegrating vector in the λ_{max} test, and 23.0 and 25.4 respectively for 0 cointegrating vectors and 10.6 and 12.5, respectively for 1 cointegrating vector for the λ_{trace} test. Models include intercept and trend, with cointegrating restrictions on the time trend imposed.

6.5.3 Impulse response functions in a non-stationary VAR

In Section 6.3 we have presented the framework of the impulse response analysis in the case of a non-stationary VAR. In small samples more reliable statistical inference can be obtained by constructing confidence intervals through bootstrapping than using asymptotic theory. Moreover, the analytical expressions of the asymptotic variances of the impulse response coefficients are rather complicated, and the use of bootstrapping avoids calculating these expressions explicitly (Kilian, 1998). Denote with $\phi, \hat{\phi}$, and $\hat{\phi}^*$ some impulse response coefficient, its estimator implied by the estimators of the model coefficients, and the corresponding bootstrap estimator, respectively. Hall (1992) states that the distribution of $(\hat{\phi} - \phi)$ is approximately equal to that of $(\hat{\phi}^* - \hat{\phi})$ in large samples. Therefore, the confidence interval

$$CI_H = \left[\hat{\phi} - t^*_{(1-\gamma/2)}, \hat{\phi} - t_{\gamma/2}\right] \tag{6.13}$$

can be derived. We constructed bootstrapping confidence intervals by using 2000 replications.

In Figures 6.1–6.7, we present the results of the analysis. In each graph, in the upper panels the order of causality is *LIAB* → *SPL*, in the lower panels the VAR is based on the opposite order of causality. In each figure we report the lag-length of the VAR, obtained applying the Schwarz Information Criterion. In the figures bands represent 95% confidence levels of each response.

The general picture emerging from Figures 6.1–6.7 is not completely in line with the results found by Canzoneri *et al.* (2001), though it does not support an NR regime. In particular, we can summarize our findings along these lines:

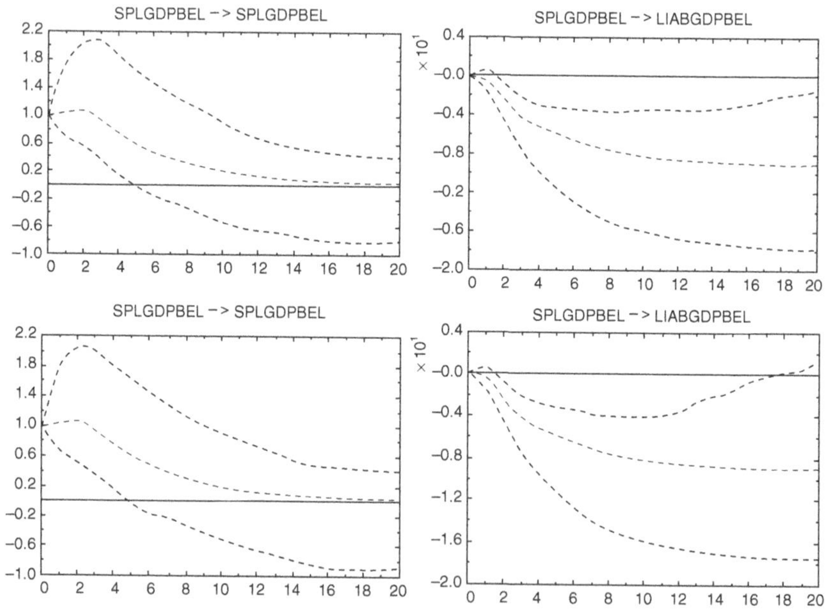

Figure 6.1 Belgium (p = 1).

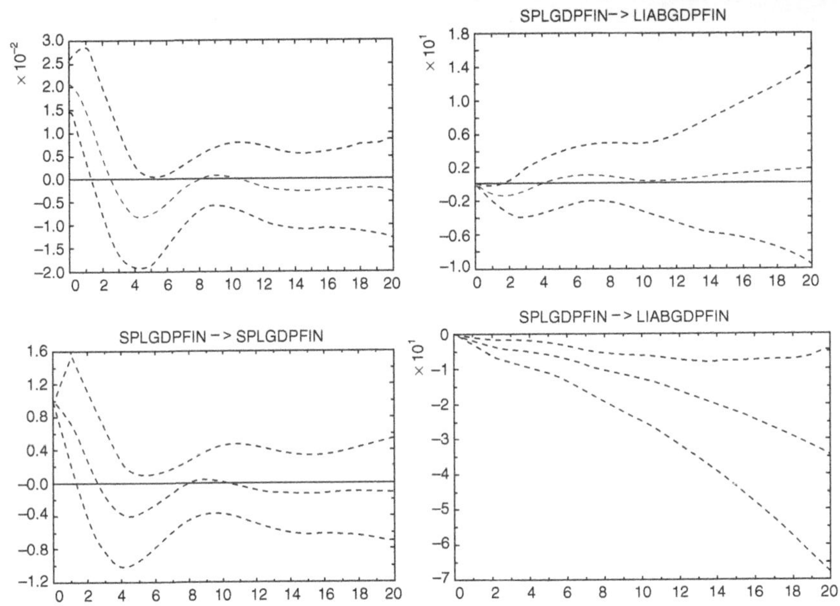

Figure 6.2 Finland (p = 2).

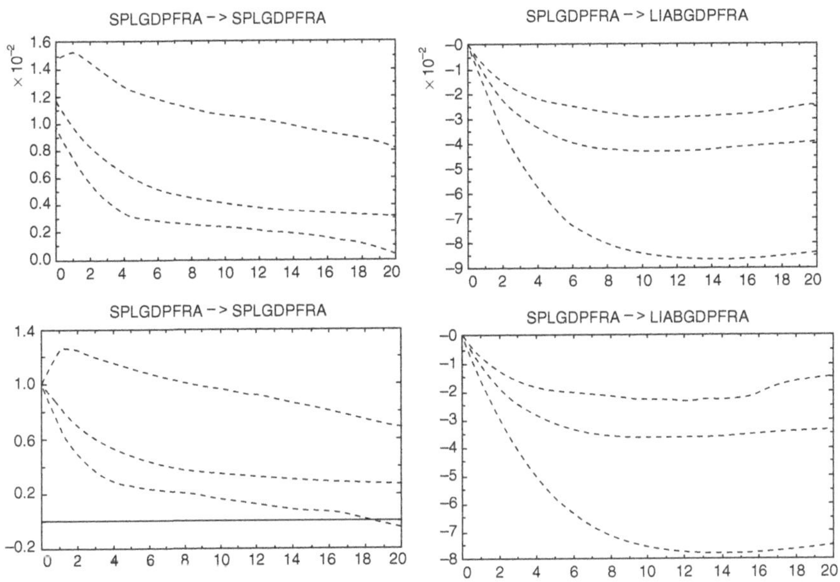

Figure 6.3 France (p = 1).

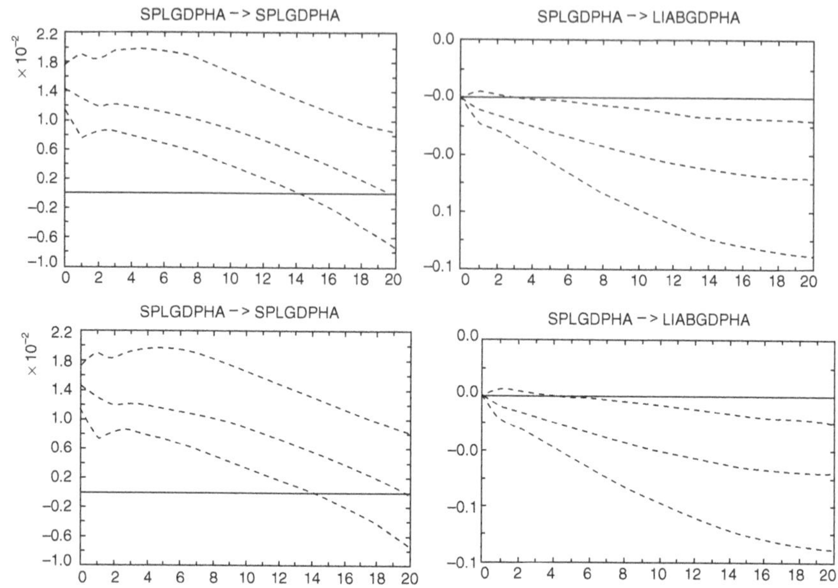

Figure 6.4 Italy (p = 2).

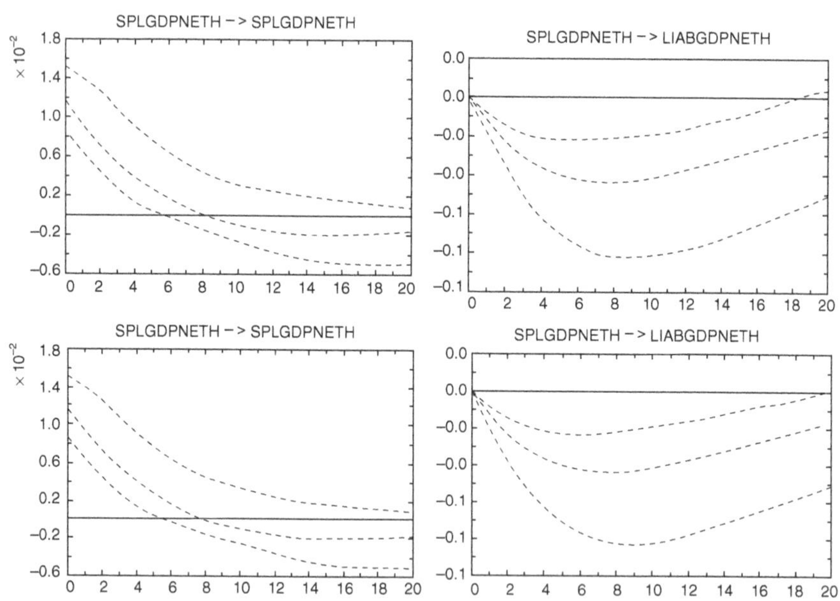

Figure 6.5 Netherlands (p = 1).

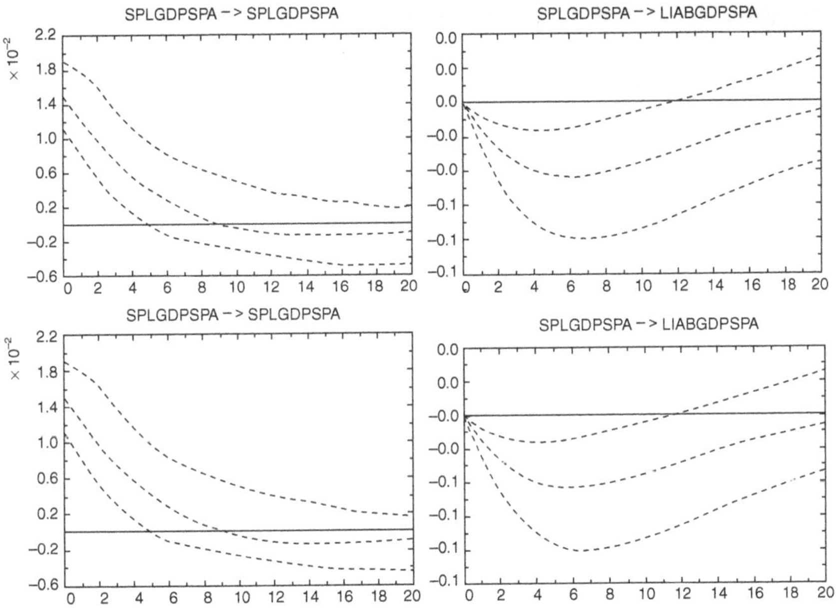

Figure 6.6 Spain (p = 1).

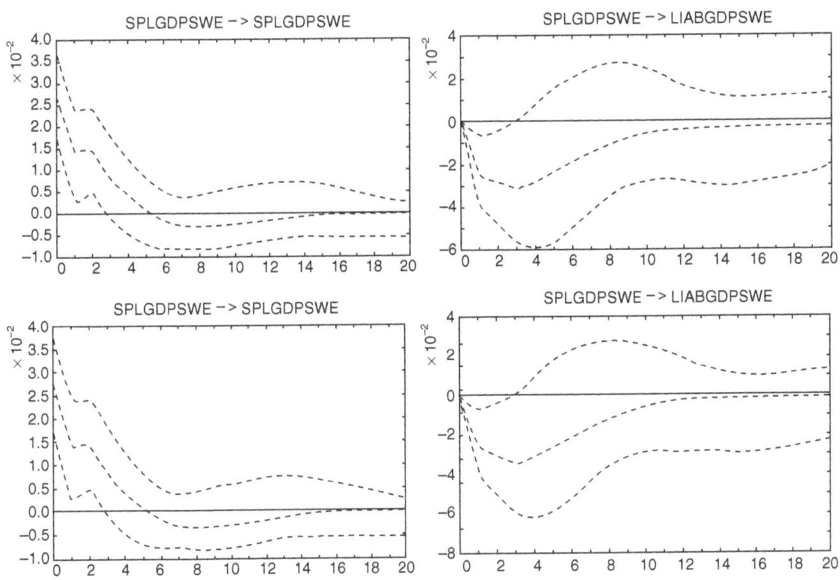

Figure 6.7 Sweden (p = 1).

1. a 1% shock on the surplus/GDP ratio has a temporary positive effect on the same variable, and eventually the ratio returns to its starting level within ten years. This can be interpreted as evidence of an R Regime;
2. a 1% shock on the surplus/GDP ratio has typically a negative effect on the liabilities/GDP ratio in the first few years, but it does not bring the liabilities/GDP ratio – as it instead happens in the case of the United States – to a level lower than the starting one in the majority of the countries. Indeed, this is the most important case to distinguish between an R and an NR Regime.

Results are similar for both orders of causality.

The contrast between finding 1 and finding 2, pointing to the presence of an R Regime and of an NR Regime, respectively, is difficult to solve. We might interpret it as a confirmation of exogenous shocks weakening the fiscal authorities' determination to comply with Monetary Dominance. A restrictive fiscal stance may have created a surplus in the primary budget, which has been lasting for several years. Yet, according to our hypothesis, this fiscal restraint proved insufficient whenever an exogenous shock made more severe the fiscal restriction which would have been required by fulfilment of the IPBC.

Looking more closely to individual countries, we can distinguish two groups. First, there are three countries that strictly behave as the R Regime predicts: Belgium, France and Italy (Figures 6.1, 6.3 and 6.4). However, France has a Ricardian behaviour more in the case of a shock of surplus on liabilities, than in the case of a shock of surplus on itself. Second, countries like Finland, The Netherlands, Spain and Sweden (Figures 6.2, 6.5, 6.6 and 6.7) bring the surplus/GDP ratio to its initial level, but fail to significantly reduce the liabilities/GDP ratio. In particular, The Netherlands and Spain experience an uprising trend in the liabilities/GDP ratio after an initial period in which this ratio is lowered. In the 20 years period this increase is significant for the former and insignificant for the latter. The difference between these groups of countries possibly lies in the fact that Belgium and Italy have the highest debt/GDP ratio in the European Union, whereas debt is not a significant issue for other countries. Belgium and Italy, therefore, needed to respond by reducing their debt because of their unsound financial stance. However, this explanation leaves aside France.[6]

6.6 Concluding remarks

In this chapter we analysed the fiscal theory of the price level in a number of European countries, applying the methodology devised by Canzoneri *et al.* (2001). Having assessed that the series involved in the analysis are cointegrated, we use a cointegrated VAR approach to test for the theory. We find that only Belgium and Italy show that a shock on the surplus/GDP ratio has a temporary positive effect on the same variable, and eventually the ratio returns to its starting level, and a shock on the surplus/GDP ratio has typically a negative effect on the liabilities/GDP ratio in the first few years, bringing the liabilities/GDP ratio – as in the case of the United States – to a level lower than the initial one. For most countries the second circumstance is not fulfilled, while France is closer to the two high-debt countries than the others.

What can we learn from these results on the debate over the SGP? Too expansionary fiscal stances are not the only threat to sound public budgets. Fiscal sustainability is constantly threatened by the need to cope with a worsening in the deficit/GDP ratio, after a rise in interest payments and/or a slowdown in the GDP growth rate. It is then striking that Belgium and Italy – the two countries which for the most of the 1980–2004 period experienced the highest figures for the stock of public debt – strictly fulfil the criteria for an R Regime. We may speculate that for the governments of these high-debt countries to leave the monetary authority to deal with monetary stability was not a solution. Accordingly, once an innovation in surplus had been implemented, these fiscal authorities did not let the fiscal stance revert from restriction, but a stable path of future surpluses was continuously followed. In other words, the proximity to an ultimate loss of fiscal sustainability forced these governments to set $\alpha = 0$ and $\beta = 1$ in equation 4. On the other hand, fiscal authorities that were not burdened by a high public debt do not appear to follow the prescription of an R Regime and to behave consistently with Monetary Dominance.

Our investigation has highlighted the absence of a common behaviour shared across European fiscal authorities. This finding suggests that heterogeneity across European countries has probably been the most important missing element in the enforcement mechanism for fiscal solvency. Yet, it should not be left unnoticed that the progressive strengthening in the enforcement of restrictive public stances has found most EMU countries – also those with an accumulation of public debt much lower than Belgium and Italy – unable to bring the liabilities/GDP ratio to a level lower than the starting one. The new design of the SGP, pointing to a lessening of obligations just for these countries, may then be doubted. It is likely that the whole philosophy of the SGP is worth being revised.

Notes

* We wish to thank Sebastian Rovira for useful research assistance. A previous version was presented at the First International Conference on 'Small Open Economies in a Globalized World' organised by the University of Bologna at Rimini in 2006. We wish to thank the audience for useful comments. Funding provided by MIUR under the research programme 'The European Economic Institutions and the new Keynesian dynamics with unionised labour markets' are gratefully acknowledged.

1 The SGP guidelines for the implementation of Art. 104 of the Maastricht Treaty have been integrated many times. The most important clarifications are the Resolution of the European Council and the two ECOFIN Council Regulations of 1997, that introduced the concept of 'close to balance or in surplus' and the Excess Deficit Procedure, and the 2002 Council Opinion whereby the 'cyclically adjusted' (structural) deficit has to be used to assess the budgetary position of a country. In March 2005, the so-called New GDP has opened to a discretionary evaluation the evolution of public finances, also lessening the constraints on fiscal stances. In particular, countries with a 'low' public debt are allowed a higher deficit/GDP ratio (3.5%) limit, a longer time spam within which an excessive

deficit is to be reversed with no sanctions, and growth-friendly public expenses are excluded from the computation of the 3.5% limit.

2 Some authors have found confirmation of this hypothesis in the upward trend experienced the public deficit and debt over GDP in many EMU countries at the inception of the EMU. They claim that, by the time in which the euro has provided the shield for public finances, fiscal authorities have been taken by a 'consolidation fatigue' (Huges-Hallett *et al.*, 2003).

3 The link between Monetary Dominance and the fiscal stances under the SGP constraints have been extensively analysed. See Buti *et al.* (2001); Farina and Tamborini (2001) and (2004); Andrés *et al.* (2002); Allsopp and Artis (2003); Hughes-Hallett *et al.* (2003).

4 The United Kingdom was excluded because data were available only for a shorter period (1970–2000).

5 For Germany the results are similar if we add a break in 1989 for the reunification.

6 These results are quite in line with Creel and Le Bihan (2006), which consider France, Germany, Italy and the United Kingdom. They use structural balance data to overcome the Cochrane (1998) critique but still along the Canzoneri *et al.* (2001) methodology, and do not find support for the FTPL.

References

Afonso, A. (2002), 'Disturbing the fiscal theory of the price level: can it fit the Eu-15?', Department of Economics, Lisbon University, Working Paper no. 2002/01.

Allsopp, C. and Azhs, M. (2003), "The assessment: Emu, four years old, in Oxford Review of Economic Policy, 19: 1–29.

Andrès, J., Ballabriga F., Vallès, J. (2002), 'Hou-Ricaronian fiscal policies is an Olzeu Woultary Union', European Commission, Economic Papers, no. 169.

Ballabriga, F. C. and Martinez-Mongay, C. (2003), 'Has EMU shifted fiscal policy?', in M. Buti (ed.), *Monetary and Fiscal Policies in EMU*, Cambridge: Cambridge University Press, 246–272.

Bohn, H. (1998), 'The behaviour of U.S. Public Debt and Deficits', *Quarterly Journal of Economics*, 113: 949–63.

Breitung, J., Brüggeman, R. and Lütkepohl, H. (2004), 'Structural vector autoregressive modeling and impulse response', in H. Lütkepohl and M. Krätzig (eds), *Applied Time Series Econometrics*, Cambridge: Cambridge University Press, 159–196.

Buiter, W. H. (2002), 'The fiscal theory of the price level: a critique', *Economic Journal*, 112: 459–80.

—— (2005), 'New developments in monetary economics: two ghosts, two eccentricities, a fallacy, a mirage and a mythos', *Economic Journal*, 115: C1–C31.

Buti, M., Roeger, W. and In't Veld, J. (2001), 'Monetary and fiscal policy interactions under a stability pact', *Journal of Common Market Studies*, 39: 801–24.

Canzoneri, M., Cumby, R. and Diba, B. (2001), 'Is the price level determined by the needs of fiscal solvency?', *American Economic Review*, 91: 1221–38.

Chadha, J. S. and Nolan, C. (2003), 'On the interaction of monetary and fiscal policy', in S. Altug, J. S. Chadha and C. Nolan (eds), *Dynamic Macroeconomic Analysis*, Cambridge: Cambridge University Press, 243–307.

Christiano, L. J. and Fitzgerald, T. J. (2000), 'Understanding the fiscal theory of the price level', *Economic Review*, 36: 2–38.

Cochrane, J. H. (1998), 'A frictionless view of U.S. inflation', in B. S. Bernanke and J. Rotemberg (eds), *NBER Macroeconomics Annual Cambridge*, Cambridge, MA: MIT Press, 323–384.

—— (2001), 'Long term debt and optimal policy in the fiscal theory of the price level', *Econometrica*, 69: 69–116.

Creel, J. and Le Bihan, H. (2006), 'Using structural balance data to test the fiscal theory of the price level: some international Evidence', *Journal of Macroeconomics*, 28: 338–60.

Dickey, D. A. and Fuller, W. A. (1979), 'Estimators for autoregressive time series with a unit root', *Journal of the American Statistical Association*, 74: 427–31.

Farina F. and Ricciuti, R. (2006), 'L'évaluation des politiques budgétaires en Europe: règles budgétaires et marges de manoeuvre des gouvernements', *Revue de l'OFCE*, 99: 275–301.

Farina F. and Tamborini, R. (2001), 'Macroeconomic stabilization policies in Europe under the new regime of monetary union', *Quaderni del Dipartimento di Economia Politica*, Università di Siena, no. 317.

—— (2004), '"Set a sufficiently ambitious budget target and let automatic stabilizers work." Will it really work in the European Monetary Union?', *Open Economies Review*, 15: 143–68.

Favero, C. and Monacelli, T. (2005), 'Fiscal policy rules and regime (in)stability: evidence from the U.S.', IGIER Working Paper no. 282.

Fuller, W. A. (1976), *Introduction to Statistical Time Series*, New York: John Wiley.

Hall, P. (1992), *The Bootstrap and Edgeworth Expansion*, New York: Springer-Verlag.

Hughes Hallett, A., Lewis, J. and von Hagen, J. (2003), *Fiscal Policy in Europe, 1991–2003. An Evidence-based Analysis*, London: CEPR.

Johansen, S. (1988), 'Statistical analysis of cointegrating vectors', *Journal of Economic Dynamics and Control*, 12: 231–54.

—— (1991), 'Estimation and hypothesis testing of cointegrating vectors in Gaussian vector autoregressive models', *Econometrica*, 59: 1551–80.

Kilian, L. (1998), 'Small-sample confidence intervals for impulse response functions', *Review of Economics and Statistics*, 80: 218–30.

Leeper, E. (1991), 'Equilibria under active and passive monetary and fiscal policies', *Journal of Monetary Economics*, 27: 129–47.

Leith, C. and Wren-Lewis, S. (2000), 'Interactions between monetary and fiscal policy rules', *Economic Journal*, 110: C93–C108.

Said, S. E. (1991), 'Unit root test for time series data with a linear time trend', *Journal of Econometrics*, 47: 285–303.

Sargent, T. J. and Wallace, N. (1981), 'Some unpleasant monetarist arithmetic', Federal Reserve Bank of Minneapolis, *Quarterly Review*, 5: 1–17.

Woodford, M. (1995), 'Price level determinacy without control of a monetary aggregate', *Carnegie-Rochester Series on Public Policy*, 43: 1–46.

—— (1996), 'Control of the public debt: a requirement for price stability?', NBER Working Paper no. 5684.

—— (2001), 'Fiscal requirements for price stability', *Journal of Money, Credit and Banking*, 33: 669–728.

—— (2003), *Interest and Prices: Foundations of a Theory of Monetary Policy*, Princeton: Princeton University Press.

Wren-Lewis, S. (2003), 'The compatibility between monetary and fiscal policies in EMU: a perspective from the fiscal theory of the price level', in M. Buti (ed.), *Monetary and Fiscal Policies in EMU*, Cambridge: Cambridge University Press.

Part III

Fiscal policy and the EMU countries

Heterogeneity, Interdependence and Divergence

7 One size does not fit all

Country size and fiscal policy in a monetary union[1]

J. Le Cacheux and F. Saraceno

7.1 Introduction

After the decision of the Ecofin Council, in November 2003, to waive the sanctions recommended against France and Germany by the European Commission, and then the decision by the Commission to take the Ecofin Council to court for not respecting the letter of the treaties with regard to fiscal policy rules in the euro zone, there has been widespread feelings that 'large' countries were somehow taking advantage of their size and power to violate the rules they themselves had imposed on others. This resentment was aired again by several governments of 'small' countries on the eve of the 23 March 2005 Council meeting when a somewhat reformed Stability and Growth Pact eventually emerged from the discussions and gained unanimous support. Coming after several years of skirmishes between the Commission and a number of governments from fiscally 'virtuous' countries, on the one hand, and the governments of a small number of countries, mostly large ones, who were finding it difficult, if not impossible, to meet the stringent requirements of the SGP as interpreted by the Commission, on the other, these episodes point to a number of difficulties and misunderstandings concerning the purpose and precise design of fiscal policy rules in a monetary union with decentralized fiscal authorities.

Newspaper and layman explanations of why violations of the SGP by large countries have tended to be more frequent and more protracted than those committed by small countries have mostly been variations over the 'arrogance' argument: national governments of large countries tend to be more spiteful of rules, including the ones they have advocated and imposed on others. A related argument is sometimes added; namely, the hypothesis that interest groups may be powerful, and may therefore be in a better position to get their way in large countries, effectively blocking politically painful fiscal consolidation policies.

These explanations do not really explain anything. Couldn't it be the case that country size matters for the choice of macroeconomic strategies in a monetary union? Shouldn't we pay more attention to the standard textbook arguments: (i) that multipliers are larger in less open economies; (ii) that spillovers are weighted by size? Even refurbished with proper micro-foundations in the spirit of the recent literature on fiscal–monetary policy interaction, these arguments appear still valid, and we contend that such an explanation is more appealing than the standard argument in terms of intrinsic differences in policy-makers' preferences or attitudes, that is, what we have termed earlier the 'arrogance factor'.

In order to support the argument that 'size matters', we explore a simple two-country model of a monetary union in the spirit of this recent literature in order to demonstrate that country size has an effect on the optimal level of public spending or public deficit in response to fiscal or demand shocks.

Sections 7.2 and 7.3 document the very significant degree of heterogeneity of national fiscal policies and macroeconomic performances and, more generally, the differences in responses of national economies to common shocks and policies. In Section 7.4, we propose a simple, two-country model showing that country size is a relevant dimension to consider when analysing the incentives facing national governments in a monetary union. Finally, Section 7.5 offers some tentative conclusions about the design of rules and institutions.

7.2 Heterogeneity in the euro zone

In spite of efforts during the transition phase to economic and monetary union, especially through the imposition of convergence criteria – the so-called Maastricht criteria – the economies of the euro zone have proven much more heterogeneous than what had been expected. In particular, they have tended to pursue divergent fiscal policies, with on average larger budget deficits in large countries (Table 7.1).

There has also been a great deal of heterogeneity in the standard macroeconomic performance indicators of economic growth (Table 7.2), price stability (Table 7.3), and hence – because nominal interest rates have tended to be very close within the monetary union – in short- and long-term real interest rates (Tables 7.4 and 7.5).[2] These persistent differences make macroeconomic policy-making in the euro zone more difficult, especially to the extent that national indicators are still published and widely regarded as more relevant than euro zone averages.

For monetary policy, the heterogeneity of monetary conditions and transmission mechanisms raises a number of serious problems: the better known ones relate to the decision-making rules in the ECB council, with the excessive weight of small countries, many of which happen to have inflation rates higher than average (see below). With regard to fiscal policies, the 'one-size-fits-all' character of the rules may also prove harmful in a number of contexts.

7.3 Small and large states: coping with differences in incentives

Although the equal treatment principle is deeply entrenched in the democratic ideals and widely regarded as the only fair organization rule in a democracy, the recent crises with the implementation of the SGP and the failed adoption of the constitutional treaty project have revealed a profound cleavage between small and large countries in the EU, a distinction that had never been that apparent before. For scholars of the history of federal states and institutions, especially of the United

Table 7.1 Fiscal deficit and public debt ratios, Euro zone countries, 1999–2005 (as percentages of GDP)

	1999	*2000*	*2001*	*2002*	*2003*	*2004**	*2005**
Belgium	−0.4	0.2	0.6	0.1	0.4	−0.1	−0.3
	114.8	109.1	108.0	105.4	100.0	95.8	94.4
Germany	−1.5	1.3	−2.8	−3.7	−3.8	−3.9	−3.4
	61.2	60.2	59.4	60.9	64.2	65.9	67.2
Greece	−4.0	−4.1	−3.7	−3.7	−4.6	−5.5	−3.6
	105.2	114.0	114.7	112.5	109.9	112.2	111.9
Spain	−1.2	−0.9	−0.4	0.1	0.4	−0.6	−0.1
	63.1	61.1	57.5	54.4	50.7	48.2	45.5
France	−1.8	−1.4	−1.5	−3.2	−4.1	−3.7	−3.0
	58.5	56.8	56.5	58.8	63.7	64.9	65.5
Ireland	2.4	4.4	0.9	−0.2	0.1	−0.2	−0.6
	48.6	38.3	35.9	32.7	32.1	30.4	30.7
Italy	−1.7	−0.6	−2.6	−2.3	−2.4	−3.0	−3.0
	115.5	111.2	110.6	107.9	106.2	106.0	104.6
Luxembourg	3.6	6.0	6.4	2.8	0.8	−0.8	−1.6
	6.0	5.5	5.5	5.7	5.3	4.9	4.8
Netherlands	0.7	2.2	−0.1	−1.9	−3.2	−2.9	−2.4
	63.1	55.9	52.9	52.6	54.1	55.7	58.6
Austria	−2.3	−1.5	0.3	−0.2	−1.1	−1.3	−2.0
	67.5	65.8	66.1	65.7	64.5	64.0	63.9
Portugal	−2.8	−2.8	−4.4	−2.7	−2.8	−2.9	−3.7
	54.3	53.3	55.8	58.4	60.3	60.8	62.0
Finland	2.2	7.1	5.2	4.3	2.3	2.3	2.1
	47.0	44.6	43.8	42.6	45.6	44.8	43.4
Euro area	−1.3	0.1	−1.7	−2.4	−2.7	−2.9	−2.5
	72.8	70.4	69.4	69.4	70.7	71.1	71.1

Source: European Commission, Autumn forecasts, November 2004.

Note
* Forecasts.

States of America, this should not come as a surprise (see Laurent and Le Cacheux, 2004).

Nor it is a surprise for economists, as it may easily be shown that the incentives facing a small open economy (e.g. Ireland) are not at all the same as the ones facing a medium-sized one, such as Germany or France, which may help explain the differences in performances and strategies that seem so systematic in the recent history of the euro zone (Le Cacheux, 2005).

In economic terms, the differences between large and small countries are real and far-reaching: they correspond, in a monetary union, to a strategic asymmetry that triggers distinct incentives for each group of countries and allow 'small' ones to make choices that large ones can not afford without negative consequences and costs for themselves as well as for the whole monetary zone.

No wonder then that their respective macroeconomic situations differ sharply and systematically, most of the 'small' member states displaying relatively higher inflation, less unemployment and sounder public finances.

Table 7.2 GDP annual growth rates, 2000–5

	2000	*2001*	*2002*	*2003*	*2004**	*2005***
Belgium	3.9	0.7	0.9	1.3	2.5	2.5
Germany	2.9	0.8	0.1	−0.1	1.9	1.5
Greece	4.5	4.3	3.6	4.5	3.8	3.3
Spain	4.4	2.8	2.2	2.5	2.6	2.6
France	3.8	2.1	1.2	0.5	2.4	2.2
Ireland	9.9	6.0	6.1	3.7	5.2	4.8
Italy	3.0	1.8	0.4	0.3	1.3	1.8
Luxembourg	9.0	1.5	2.5	2.9	4.0	3.5
Netherlands	3.5	1.4	0.6	−0.9	1.4	1.7
Austria	3.4	0.7	1.2	0.8	1.9	2.4
Portugal	3.4	1.6	0.4	−1.2	1.3	2.2
Finland	5.1	1.1	2.3	1.9	3.0	3.1
Euro Zone	3.5	1.6	0.9	0.6	2.1	2.0
EU 15	3.6	1.7	1.1	0.9	2.3	2.2
US	3.7	0.8	1.9	3.1	4.4	3.0

Source: EU Commission, Autumn forecasts, November 2004.

Notes
* Estimate, October 2004.
**Forecasts, October 2004.

Table 7.3 Annual inflation rates, 1999–2004 (harmonized consumer price index)

	1999	*2000*	*2001*	*2002*	*2003*	*2004**
Belgium	1.1	2.7	2.4	1.6	1.5	2
Germany	0.6	1.4	1.9	1.3	1.0	1.7
Greece	2.1	2.9	3.7	3.9	3.4	3.0
Spain	2.2	3.5	2.8	3.6	3.1	3.1
France	0.6	1.8	1.8	1.9	2.2	2.3
Ireland	2.5	5.3	4.0	4.7	4.0	2.3
Italy	1.7	2.6	2.3	2.6	2.8	2.3
Luxembourg	1.0	3.8	2.4	2.1	2.5	3.0
The Netherlands	2.0	2.3	5.1	3.9	2.2	1.2
Austria	0.5	2.0	2.3	1.7	1.3	2.1
Portugal	2.2	2.8	4.4	3.7	3.3	2.4
Finland	1.3	3.0	2.7	2.0	1.3	0.2
Euro Zone	1.1	2.1	2.4	2.3	2.1	2.1
Denmark	2.1	2.7	2.3	2.4	2.0	1.1
Sweden	0.6	1.3	2.7	2.0	2.3	1.1
United Kingdom	1.3	0.8	1.2	1.3	1.4	1.4
United States	2.2	3.4	2.8	1.6	2.3	2.6

Source: EU Commission, Autumn forecasts, November 2004.

Note
*Forecasts, October 2004.

Table 7.4 Short-term real interest rates, 1999–2004

	1999	*2000*	*2001*	*2002*	*2003*	*2004**
Belgium	1.9	1.7	1.9	1.7	0.8	0.1
Germany	2.4	3	2.4	2	1.3	0.4
Greece	8	4.8	0.6	−0.9	−1.1	−0.9
Spain	0.8	0.9	1.5	−0.3	−0.8	−1
France	2.4	2.6	2.5	1.4	0.1	−0.2
Ireland	0.5	−0.9	0.3	−1.4	−1.7	−0.2
Italy	1.3	1.8	2	0.7	−0.5	−0.2
The Netherlands	1	2.1	−0.8	−0.6	0.1	0.9
Austria	2.5	2.4	2	1.6	1	0
Portugal	0.8	1.6	−0.1	−0.4	−1	−0.3
Finland	1.7	1.4	1.6	1.3	1	1.9
Euro Zone	2	2.4	1.9	1	0.2	0
Denmark	1.3	2.3	2.4	1.1	0.4	1.1
Sweden	2.7	2.8	1.4	2.2	1	1.2
United Kingdom	4.2	5.4	3.8	2.8	2.4	3.2
United States	3.2	3.1	1	0.2	−1.1	−1

Source: EU Commission, Autumn forecasts, November 2004.

Table 7.5 Long-term real interest rates, 1999–2003

	1999	*2000*	*2001*	*2002*	*2003*	*2004*
Belgium	3.7	2.9	2.7	3.4	2.7	2.3
Germany	3.9	3.9	2.9	3.5	3.1	2.5
Greece	4.2	3.2	2.2	1.2	0.9	1.4
Spain	2.5	2.0	2.3	1.4	1.0	1.2
France	4.0	3.6	3.2	3.0	1.9	2.0
Ireland	2.2	0.2	0.9	0.2	0.1	2.0
Italy	3.0	3.0	2.9	2.4	1.5	2.1
The Netherlands	2.6	3.1	−0.1	1.0	1.9	3.1
Austria	4.2	3.6	2.8	3.3	2.9	2.3
Portugal	2.6	2.8	0.8	1.4	0.9	1.9
Finland	3.4	2.5	2.3	2.9	2.8	4.1
Euro zone	3.6	3.3	2.6	2.6	2.0	2.1
Denmark	2.8	2.9	2.8	2.6	2.3	3.4
Sweden	4.4	4.1	2.4	3.3	2.3	3.5
United Kingdom	3.7	4.5	3.7	3.6	3.2	3.7
United States	3.4	2.6	2.2	3.0	1.7	1.7

Source: EU Commission, Autumn forecasts, November 2004.

Indeed, for a small country, tools available to adjust to a negative macroeconomic shock (recession and rise of unemployment) are not of the same essence, and thus of the same effects, than for a large one. Because its economy is largely open, regarding goods and services as well as foreign direct investments and other capital flows fiscal policy will have little effect on domestic demand, since most of its impact will be absorbed through imports.

Hence, for a small open economy, traditional fiscal policy of the Keynesian kind will usually be of little efficiency, whereas all policies that improve the competitiveness of the national economy by lowering production costs of firms located in the domestic economy are relatively more powerful: this may explain why fiscal consolidations in small countries have been found to have 'non-Keynesian' effects (see Giavazzi and Pagano, 1996); it also suggests that tax competition, 'structural reforms' and wage moderation policies will all have very powerful, positive effects for a small open economy, both because exports represent a major fraction of demand to domestic firms and because the elasticity of the supply of external capital – in particular, foreign direct investments – is higher, the smaller and the more open the economy is. In addition, policies that lower production costs in a small economy do not harm domestic demand very much, and they have little incidence on domestic inflation, so that they do not raise real interest rates, as nominal rates in a monetary union tend to be uniform across countries and to be relatively little influenced by the policies of a single, small country.[3]

For large countries, on the contrary, free riding is impossible, and the various policy choices reviewed above tend to be more costly, or even counterproductive. Traditional, Keynesian-style demand-management policies, especially fiscal policies, are more efficient than for a small open economy, because demand spillovers are relatively less. On the other hand, all policies tending to lower production costs are less effective, and they all tend to lead to a lower domestic inflation, which then results in a higher real interest rate, so that they tend to be costly in terms of economic activity and growth. The fate of Germany over the past few years seems to be a perfect illustration of this difficulty of large countries in an economic and monetary union.

This helps explain why small countries may be tempted to free ride on large ones in the face of a common macroeconomic shock. Benefiting from the latter's expansionary policies, they do not bear the costs of them, not in fiscal nor in real interest terms. Furthermore, one should not be surprised that small countries undertake 'virtuous' fiscal consolidations and 'structural reforms' strongly advocated by the European Commission, while the large countries are apparently inherently 'vicious'. The debates, at times polemics, over the SGP reveal just this inescapable divide.

In the rapidly growing literature on international political economy, country size has indeed been emphasized as a major dimension of national strategic choices (Alesina and Spolaore, 2003; Alesina, Spolaore and Warcziac, 2005), though the rationale has often been in terms of optimal country size in the presence of both decentralization (centrifugal) forces – such as the necessity to better adhere to citizens' preferences in the provision of public goods – and centripetal forces – such as economies of scale in administration and fixed costs of governments. In the EU context, this distinction has also been shown to generate a genuine cleavage in terms of strategies for reforms and economic policies, as well as economic performance (Duval and Esmelkov, 2005; Creel and Le Cacheux, 2006; Laurent and Le Cacheux, 2006): in this strand of analyses, the rationale is closer to our analytical framework, the reasoning being squarely in terms of macroeconomic adjustments and policies.

7.4 The model

7.4.1 The economy

Our model is similar in spirit to Uhlig (2002). We have a monetary union with two countries and one central bank, which sets the unions' interest rate. The IS curve, for each of the two countries ($j = 1, 2$), is

$$x_j = -\phi\left(\bar{i} - \pi_j^e\right) + g_j + \gamma \frac{\psi_{-j}}{\psi_j} x_{-j}$$

where x_j is the output gap, π_j^e is expected inflation, and $\bar{i}$ is the union-wide interest rate. g_i is the government's decision variable, and represents government deficit. Our innovation with respect to the standard literature is the term $\gamma \frac{\psi_{-j}}{\psi_j} x_{-j}$, that captures the correlation of output gaps across the union ($-j$ denotes the country other than j), that depends on relative size ($\psi_1 + \psi_2 = 1$ are the weights). We assume that $0 \leq \gamma < 1$.

The supply side is modelled by a standard Phillips curve:

$$\pi_j = \lambda x_j + u_j$$

where u_j is a cost-push supply shock ($E(u_j) = 0$). The IS and the Phillips curve can be derived by a standard sticky-prices model, in the spirit of the Neo-Keynesian literature (Woodford, 2003). Uhlig (2002) shows how to derive this reduced form.

We have two fiscal authorities and a central bank; the objective function of the latter is

$$\max_{\bar{i}} \mathcal{L}_{CB} = -\frac{1}{2}(\alpha \bar{x}^2 + \bar{\pi}^2)$$

where union-wide values are weighted averages: $\bar{x} = \psi_1 x_1 + \psi_2 x_2$ and $\bar{\pi} = \psi_1 \pi_1 + \psi_2 \pi_2$.

The objective function of fiscal authorities

$$\max_{g_j} \mathcal{L}_j = -\frac{1}{2}\left[x_j^2 + \theta(g_j - \varepsilon_j)^2\right]$$

that assumes national authorities to care about the output gap, but also about deviations of public expenditure from a random target value ε_j, that are weighted by θ. In fact, on average ($E(\varepsilon_j) = 0$), the government values a balanced budget, $g_j = 0$. A positive shock ε_j represents the additional slack that may be given by unexpected revenues, or unforeseen spending needs; conversely, a negative value of ε_j captures the *ex ante* unexpected need to tighten fiscal policy.

The sequence of events is standard:

- the public forms inflation expectations π_j^e, that are set rationally;
- shocks ε_j and u_j are drawn;

- fiscal authorities choose g_j;
- the monetary authority chooses $\bar{i}$.

7.4.2 *The central bank's problem*

The model is solved backwards, starting from the central bank problem. If we take union-wide averages, the output gap equation becomes

$$\bar{x} = \psi_1 x_1 + \psi_2 x_2 = -\phi(\bar{i} - \bar{\pi}^e) + \bar{g} + \gamma\bar{x}$$
$$\Rightarrow \bar{x} = \frac{\bar{g} - \phi(\bar{i} - \bar{\pi}^e)}{1 - \gamma}$$

The programme of the central bank is

$$\max_{\bar{i}} \mathscr{L}_{CB} = -\frac{1}{2}(\alpha\bar{x}^2 + \bar{\pi}^2)$$
$$s.t.$$
$$\bar{x} = \frac{\bar{g} - \phi(\bar{i} - \bar{\pi}^e)}{1 - \gamma}$$
$$\bar{\pi} = \lambda\bar{x} + \bar{u}$$

Maximizing with respect to $\bar{i}$ gives

$$\bar{i} = \frac{(\phi\bar{\pi}^e + \bar{g})}{\phi} + \frac{(1 - \gamma)\bar{u}\lambda}{\phi\left(\alpha + \lambda^2\right)};$$

substituting back into the equation for the output gap, we obtain

$$\bar{x} = -\frac{\bar{u}\lambda}{\left(\alpha + \lambda^2\right)} = -\lambda q\bar{u}$$

where $q \equiv (\lambda^2 + \alpha)^{-1}$. Then, it is straightforward to compute

$$\bar{\pi} = \lambda\bar{x} + \bar{u} = -\frac{\bar{u}\lambda}{\left(\alpha + \lambda^2\right)}\lambda + \bar{u}$$
$$= \alpha q\bar{u}$$

The interest rate rule is derived by substituting the value for inflation, and by noticing that $\bar{\pi}^e = E(\bar{\pi}) = \alpha q E(\bar{u}) = 0$. We can then obtain

$$\bar{i} = \frac{\bar{g}}{\phi} + \frac{(1 - \gamma)q\lambda}{\phi}\bar{u}.$$

Notice that, by moving after the governments, the central bank can adjust to their policies, and use the interest rate to attain its preferred inflation and output gap objective. As a consequence, the equilibrium output gap and inflation rates only depend on the cost-push shock; the interest rate is the only variable that depends on average deficit, precisely because it is set in order to undo the behaviour of fiscal authorities. In this model there is no role for fiscal policy in the union as a whole. We chose this setting to better emphasize our results.

7.4.3 The fiscal authorities

Proceeding backwards, we can analyse the fiscal authorities problem. The two governments have to solve the following programme:

$$\max_{g_j} \mathcal{L}_j = -\frac{1}{2}\left[x_j^2 + \theta(g_j - \varepsilon_j)^2\right]$$

$$s.t.$$

$$x_j = -\phi\left(\bar{i} - \pi_j^e\right) + g_j + \gamma\frac{\psi_{-j}}{\psi_j}x_{-j} +$$

$$\phi\bar{i} = \psi_1 g_1 + \psi_2 g_2 + (1-\gamma)q\lambda\bar{u}$$

Take country one (country two is symmetric). The unconstrained maximization problem can be written as

$$\mathcal{L}_1 = -\frac{1}{2}(A_1 + \psi_2 g_1)^2 - \frac{1}{2}\theta(g_1 - \varepsilon_1)^2$$

where $A_1 \equiv -\psi_2 g_2 - (1-\gamma)q\lambda\bar{u} + \phi\pi_1^e + \frac{\gamma\psi_2}{\psi_1}x_2$ collects all terms not depending on g_1. The First order condition (FOC) is

$$\frac{\partial L_1}{\partial g_1} = \theta\varepsilon_1 - \psi_2 A_1 - g_1(\psi_2^2 + \theta) = 0$$

that yields

$$g_1 = \frac{\theta\varepsilon_1 - \psi_2 A_1}{(\psi_2^2 + \theta)} = \frac{\theta\varepsilon_1 + \psi_2\left(\psi_2 g_2 + (1-\gamma)q\lambda\bar{u} - \phi\pi_1^e - \gamma\frac{\psi_2}{\psi_1}x_2\right)}{(\psi_2^2 + \theta)}.$$

Thus, fiscal policy is positively correlated with own fiscal shocks, as well as with supply shocks; this sensitivity increases with the size of the country (a lower weight of the other member, ψ_2). Reactivity to the fiscal policy of the other members of the union, though positive, is positively related to $\psi_2 = 1 - \psi_1$, thus negatively correlated to own size.

Both fiscal policy and the interest rate are linear in the shocks, and thus inflation rates in individual countries will be given by (zero mean) deviations from the union average. As a consequence,

$$\pi_j^e = \bar{\pi}^e = 0.$$

Repeating the same steps for country 2, we obtain the following system:

$$g_1 = \frac{\theta\varepsilon_1 - (1-\psi_1)\left(-(1-\psi_1)g_2 - (1-\gamma)q\lambda\bar{u} + \gamma\frac{1-\psi_1}{\psi_1}x_2\right)}{(1-\psi_1)^2+\theta}$$

$$g_2 = \frac{\theta\varepsilon_2 - \psi_1\left(-\psi_1 g_1 - (1-\gamma)q\lambda\bar{u} + \gamma\frac{\psi_1}{1-\psi_1}x_1\right)}{\psi_1^2+\theta} \tag{7.1}$$

$$x_1 = (1-\psi_1)(g_1-g_2) - (1-\gamma)q\lambda\bar{u} + \gamma\frac{1-\psi_1}{\psi_1}x_2$$

$$x_2 = \psi_1(g_2-g_1) - (1-\gamma)q\lambda\bar{u} + \gamma\frac{\psi_1}{1-\psi_1}x_1$$

The solution to this system gives the equilibrium values of public expenditure (g_1 and g_2) and output gap (x_1 and x_2) as linear functions of demand and supply shocks. We focus on one country, the other being symmetrical, and we obtain the following expression for g_1:

$$\begin{aligned} g_1 &= \frac{\psi_1^2+\theta(\gamma+1)}{1+\theta(\gamma+1)-2\psi_1(1-\psi_1)}\varepsilon_1 \\ &+ \frac{(1-\psi_1)^2}{1+\theta(\gamma+1)-2\psi_1(1-\psi_1)}\varepsilon_2 \\ &+ \frac{(1-\psi_1)\left((\psi_1(1-\gamma)+\gamma)\theta+\psi_1^2\right)}{\psi_1\theta\left(1+\theta(\gamma+1)-2\psi_1(1-\psi_1)\right)}q\lambda\bar{u} \\ &= A_{\varepsilon_1}\varepsilon_1 + A_{\varepsilon_2}\varepsilon_2 + A_u\bar{u} \end{aligned}$$

The sign of the reaction coefficients is unambiguous:

$$A_{\varepsilon_1} = \frac{\psi_1^2+\theta(\gamma+1)}{1+\theta(\gamma+1)-2\psi_1(1-\psi_1)} > 0$$

$$A_{\varepsilon_2} = \frac{(1-\psi_1)^2}{1+\theta(\gamma+1)-2\psi_1(1-\psi_1)} > 0$$

$$A_u = \frac{(1-\psi_1)\left((\psi_1(1-\gamma)+\gamma)\theta+\psi_1^2\right)}{\psi_1\theta\left(1+\theta(\gamma+1)-2\psi_1(1-\psi_1)\right)}q\lambda > 0$$

This is intuitive in what concerns fiscal disturbances: fiscal policy reacts positively to the additional slack given by ε. Interestingly,

$$A_{\varepsilon_2} > A_{\varepsilon_1} \quad \Leftrightarrow \quad 1 > 2\psi_1 + \theta(\gamma+1),$$

which means that for ψ_1 (i.e. country size) small enough, the country may react more to the shock hitting the partner than to its own. The spillover effects (γ) mitigate this feature of the model.

It is, on the other hand, interesting to notice that $A_u > 0$. The reason is that fiscal authorities rationally forecast a tightening of monetary policy in response to cost-push shocks, and hence react by increasing their deficit in order to compensate for the restrictive effect of $\bar{i}$ on the output gap (a result already found by Alesina and Tabellini, 1987). In fact, each country attempts to free ride on the others (Uhlig, 2002), and to increase its own level of activity.

7.4.4 Country size and optimal fiscal policy

We are now in a position to look into the main question of this chapter. The relationship between country size and fiscal policy is captured by $\frac{\partial A_{\varepsilon j}}{\partial \psi_1}$ $(j = 1, 2)$, that we can easily sign as follows:

$$\begin{aligned} \frac{\partial A_{\varepsilon 1}}{\partial \psi_1} &= \frac{2\,(1-\psi_1)\,(\psi_1+\theta(\gamma+1))}{(1+\theta(\gamma+1)-2\psi_1(1-\psi_1))^2} > 0 \\ \frac{\partial A_{\varepsilon 2}}{\partial \psi_1} &= -\frac{2\,(1-\psi_1)\,(\theta(\gamma+1)+\psi_1)}{(1+\theta(\gamma+1)-2\psi_1(1-\psi_1))^2} < 0 \end{aligned} \tag{7.2}$$

Thus, the simple model we presented delivers the result we argued for: the reaction of fiscal policy to shocks depends positively on country size: the optimal response to fiscal shocks of larger countries relies more on fiscal policy. Intuitively, the weight of external factors in the determination of the output gap is lower for larger countries that, as a consequence, have to rely more heavily on their own policy in order to deal with shocks. The same logic explains why large countries react less to shocks hitting their partners.

Notice furthermore that $\lim_{\psi_1 \to 1} A_u = \lim_{\psi_1 \to 1} A_{\varepsilon 2} = 0$, and $\lim_{\psi_1 \to 1} g_1 = \varepsilon_1$. When the union tends to a single country (and a single fiscal authority), we converge to a perfect division of labour, with the central bank that takes care of supply shocks u, while fiscal policy takes care of fiscal shocks ε. In fact, if there is only one country, the reaction of monetary policy to the deficit will be fully internalized by the fiscal authority, and there will be no incentive for attempting to free ride.

Finally, we need to analyse the role of the parameter γ, that captures the importance of spillovers in the output gap equation. In fact, the existence of spillovers is not necessary to establish our main result, as in equation (7.2) we have $\frac{\partial A_{\varepsilon 1}}{\partial \psi_1} > 0$ even when $\gamma = 0$. Thus, it is not spillovers *per se*, but rather the complementarity between fiscal policies in the union that yields our results. Nevertheless, the spillover amplifies this effect, as

$$\begin{aligned} \frac{\partial A_{\varepsilon 1}}{\partial \gamma} &= \theta \frac{1-\psi_1(2-\psi_1)}{(1+\theta(\gamma+1)-2\psi_1(1-\psi_1))^2} > 0 \\ \frac{\partial A_{\varepsilon 2}}{\partial \gamma} &= -\frac{(1-\psi_1)^2\,\theta}{(1+\theta(\gamma+1)-2\psi_1(1-\psi_1))^2} < 0 \end{aligned}$$

We can derive the output gap, using the system (7.1) and some algebraic manipulation:

$$x_1 = \frac{(1-\psi_1)\theta}{(1+\theta(\gamma+1)-2\psi_1(1-\psi_1))}(\varepsilon_1-\varepsilon_2) - \frac{\psi_1\theta(1-\gamma)+\psi_1^2+\gamma\theta}{\psi_1\,(1+\theta(\gamma+1)-2\psi_1(1-\psi_1))}q\lambda\bar{u}$$

The first term is positive if $\varepsilon_1 > \varepsilon_2$, as it is to be expected (more slack for fiscal policy yields higher deficit and higher positive output gap). What is interesting is that, as long as $\theta(\gamma+1) > 1$, this positive effect is decreasing with country size:

$$\theta\,(\gamma+1) > 1 \Rightarrow \frac{\partial\left(\frac{(1-\psi_1)\theta}{(1+\theta(\gamma+1)-2\psi_1(1-\psi_1))}\right)}{\partial\psi_1} = \theta\frac{2\psi_1\,(\psi_1-2)-\theta\,(\gamma+1)+1}{(1+\theta(\gamma+1)-2\psi_1(1-\psi_1))^2} < 0.$$

This result is in line with our previous finding: small countries are more able to exploit the slack given by fiscal shocks than large countries; this happens if sufficient weight is given to budget discipline (high θ) and/or if the externality γ is large enough. For large ψ_1 the effect is even more evident.

The effect of country size on the supply shock 'multiplier' is instead impossible to sign. In this respect, the effect of γ becomes crucial. Assuming $\theta = 1$, we can plot (Figure 7.1) the value of the multiplier for different values of γ. Except for the solid line that corresponds to $\gamma = 0$, the shape of the lines is similar:

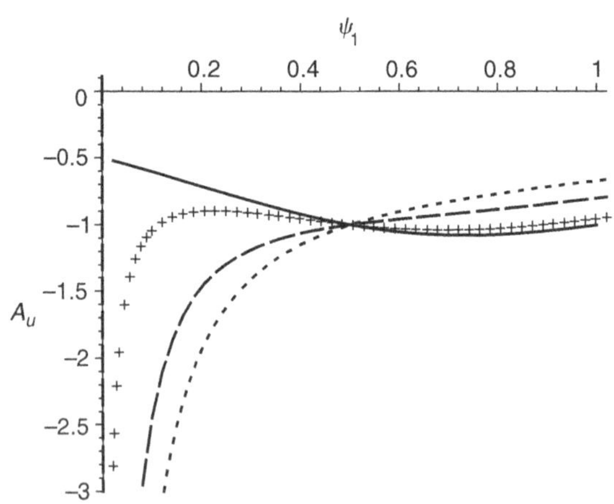

Figure 7.1 Supply shock multiplier for $\theta = 1$ and different values of γ ($\gamma = 0$, solid line; $\gamma = 0.1$, crosses; $\gamma = 0.5$; dashes; $\gamma = 0.99$, dots).

an increase in country size reduces the absolute value of the supply shock multiplier. Furthermore, the larger γ, the larger the change of the multiplier.

This admittedly simple model, in which countries interact strategically in deciding their deficit level, shows how country size and the type of shock hitting the economy affect the reaction of fiscal authorities. Demand shocks require a more important reaction of larger countries, and the existence of demand spillovers emphasizes this result.

7.5 Conclusion and policy implications

This chapter suggests that the present institutional design of the EU regarding macroeconomic policies might not be suited to allow for high levels of growth and foster integration and solidarity between member states involved in the EMU. The major reason for this unfitness could be that the criterion of size (determining economic constraints and incentives) of the different yet interdependent countries, while prominent in the new context created by the Eastward enlargement of May 2004, has never been taken into account by European officials and national governments while implementing and enforcing the 'rules of the game' of the EU. The provisions regarding economic governance contained in Part III of the project of Constitutional Treaty submitted to the approval of the member states is unfortunately no exception to this failure. Time should thus come to thoroughly discuss the EMU rules on the basis of the size criteria, starting with the SGP. Unfortunately, also, the re-interpretation of the Pact decided upon at the Brussels Council meeting of 23 March 2005, although it may end up introducing more judgement and hence more 'political' reasoning in the implementation of fiscal rules, has not taken this criterion explicitly into account.

Notes

1 Research collaboration with economists of OFCE, especially Jean-Paul Fitoussi, Jérôme Creel and Eloi Laurent, as well as long-standing exchanges with members of the GOVECOR research network have been important in feeding our reflection. We also thank Anton Granik for comments and suggestions.
2 See also Creel and Le Cacheux in this volume.
3 The notion of 'small, open economy' also refers to the idea that it has no influence on its environment, therefore is a 'price taker' and, in game theory terms, chooses strategies without caring about possible reactions or retaliation from partners. Our arguments are also somewhat reminiscent of, though different from the well known result of trade theory, namely that small countries gain from a unilateral tariff reduction, whereas larger countries are likely to lose.

References

Alesina, A. and Spolaore, E. (2003), *The Size of Nations*, Cambridge, MA: MIT Press.
Alesina, A. and Tabellini, G. (1987), 'Rules and discretion with non-coordinated monetary and fiscal policies', *Economic Inquiry*, 25: 619–30.

Alesina, A., Spolaore, E. and Warcziarg, R. (2005), 'Trade, growth and the size of countries', in P. Aghion and S. Durlauf (eds), *Handbook of Economic Growth*, Amsterdam: North Holland, pp. 1499–542.

Creel, J., Latreille, T. and Le Cacheux, J. (2002), 'Le Pacte de stabilité et les politiques budgétaires dans l'Union européenne', *Revue de l'OFCE*, Hors série, mars.

Duval, R. and Elmeskov, J. (2005), 'The effects of EMU on structural reforms in labour and product markets', OECD Economics Department Working Paper no. 438.

Fitoussi, J.-P. (2002), *La règle et le choix – De la souveraineté économique en Europe, Coll. La République des idées*, Paris: Seuil.

Fitoussi, J.-P. and Le Cacheux, J. (eds) (2003), *Rapport sur l'état de l'Union européenne 2004*, Paris: Fayard and Presses de Sciences Po.

—— (eds) (2005), *L'état de l'Union européenne 2005*, Paris: Fayard and Presses de Sciences Po.

Giavazzi, F. and Pagano, M. (1996), 'Non-Keynesian effects of fiscal policy changes: international evidence and the Swedish experience', NBER Working Paper no. 2082.

Laurent, E. and Le Cacheux, J. (2004), 'L'Europe boucles d'or: trois maximes pour sortir d'une impasse', *Lettre de l'OFCE*, 246.

—— (2006), 'Integrity and efficiency in the EU: the case against the European Economic Constitution', Center for European Studies, Harvard University, CES Working Paper no. 130

Le Cacheux, J. (2000), 'Les dangers de la concurrence fiscale et sociale en Europe', in Questions européennes, *Les Rapports du CAE*, 27.

—— (2005), 'Politiques de croissance en Europe: un problème d'action collective', *Revue Économique*, May 2005, 56(3): 705–13.

Lucas, R. E. Jr (2003), 'Macroeconomic priorities', *American Economic Review*, 93(1): 1–14.

OECD (1998), *Harmful Tax Competition: An Emerging Global Issue*, Paris: Organization for Economic Cooperation and Development.

OFCE (1999), 'Etude sur la concurrence fiscale en Europe', in Marini (Rapp.) 'La concurrence fiscale en Europe: une contribution au débat', *Les Rapport du Sénat*, no. 483, Paris. http://www.senat.fr/rap/r98-483/r98-483.html

Olson, M. (1965), *The Logic of Collective Action*, Cambridge, MA: Harvard University Press.

Sapir, A., Aghion, P., Bertola, G., Hellwig, M., Pisani-Ferry, J., Rosati, D., Vinals J. and Wallace H. (2004), *An agenda for a growing Europe -The Sapir Report*, Oxford: Oxford University Press.

Uhlig, H. (2002), 'One money, but many fiscal policies in Europe: what are the consequences?', CEPR Discussion Paper no. 3296.

8 Euro bonds

In search of financial spillovers[1]

S. Schiavo

8.1 Introduction

This paper investigates the empirical relevance of *negative financial spillovers* among EMU member countries. The integration of national bond markets that resulted from the inception of the euro and the consequent elimination of exchange rate risk has rendered securities issued by different EMU governments closer substitute. In a recent survey on financial integration in the euro area, Baele *et al.* (2004) show that in the last few years movements in government bond yields are increasingly explained by the behaviour of the benchmark asset. Out of finance jargon, one can interpret this as evidence that security returns are now driven more by international factors and less by purely domestic news. Building on this notion, the financial spillovers hypothesis questions the ability of financial markets to correctly price risk and to discriminate among different issuers. More in detail, this hypothesis postulates a link between the fiscal imbalances run by each government in the euro zone and the borrowing costs faced by all other countries participating in the currency area. Such an externality in turn entails a redistribution of costs through the common monetary policy and results in crowding out of productive investments in economies where the interest rate would otherwise be lower.

The negative financial spillover hypothesis is often regarded as one of the (few) theoretical foundations of the SGP: yet, as it will become apparent below, economic theory does not establish a clear-cut link between fiscal variables and the rate of interest.

Beside the relevance for European economic policy – the recent debate about the opportunity and costs of having binding fiscal rules witnesses for that – the topic is also interesting on purely academic grounds, as it rests on two broader unresolved issues in modern macroeconomics: the impact of the fiscal stance on interest rates, and whether the latter are determined by stock or by flow variables. The first contribution to the existing literature therefore consists on an analysis of different classes of models that reach opposite conclusions on both the aforementioned issues. Hence, we show that – contrary to what is usually claimed – theory offers only limited support to the negative financial spillover hypothesis.

Despite the fact that the issue remains an empirical question, the phenomenon has never been tested explicitly so far. This represents the second contribution of the paper. In particular, the presence and relevance of spillover effects is investigated from different angles and using a wide array of techniques.

The paper is organized as follows: Section 8.2 contextualizes the financial spillover hypothesis in the recent debate over fiscal rules and the SGP. Section 8.3 shows that economic theory offers little guidance as not only different models present different implications, but the same model may lead to opposite conclusions when a single assumption is modified. The paper then takes a step backwards and Section 8.4 analyses German unification as an episode where spillovers from fiscal variables to bond yields may have occurred. Moving to more formal empirical analysis, Section 8.5 investigates the impact of a European-wide fiscal indicator on the average yield on government bonds, while Section 8.6 narrows the focus on a subset of EMU member countries and estimates the effect of fiscal variables on domestic and foreign interest rates. Section 8.7 concludes.

8.2 Negative financial spillovers and the SGP

The whole process of European integration is based not only on the belief that fiscal discipline is necessary for the correct functioning of a monetary union, but also on the conviction that such discipline must be imposed onto member states from above (i.e. from European institutions). By joining a monetary union, in fact, countries are thought to incur a bias towards excessive deficit since the common monetary policy -tailored to serve the 'representative country' – redistributes costs onto all economies, thus generating an incentive to free ride (Afonso and Strauch, 2004: 6). Moreover, easier access to international markets (granted by the EMU) reduces the financial constraint on national governments and thus spurs fiscal laxity.

Three sets of mechanisms have been devised to limit this perverse outcome: the first aims at furnishing the ECB with the highest degree of independence and credibility, the second limits the ability of governments to run fiscal deficits, the third explicitly states that no co-responsibility exists among member states with respect to national debts (no-bail-out clause). To gain some insight, assess the relevance of the hypotheses formulated to support and rationalize the Pact, and weight pros and cons of such an institutional framework, it is useful to analyse the reasons that lead to the creation of the SGP.

In the road towards the single currency, at the beginning of the 1990s, European countries decided to give themselves a set of conditions to fulfil before joining the monetary union. This was done in order to make the monetary reform as smooth as possible. As is well known, the famous Maastricht criteria required a certain degree of convergence in terms of inflation and interest rates; moreover, candidate countries were committed to adopt measures of fiscal consolidation apt to assure low-budget deficits and decreasing debt burdens. On the basis of the conditions contained in the Maastricht Treaty, in May 1998 the European Council admitted 11 countries to join the EMU.

The rationale behind these rules was to give a solid fiscal backing to the newly established single currency, limit pressures to monetize fiscal imbalances on the ECB, and give the latter a jump start in terms of anti-inflationary credibility. The Maastricht Treaty, however, only served to judge potential entrants at one moment in time while having no power to restrain future fiscal stances. Arguably, once admitted, a government could start cumulating fiscal deficits, piling up public debt and so on and so forth.

The subsequent debate generated the SGP, which basically gives a permanent status to the fiscal rules contained in the Maastricht Treaty. This agreement (much more concerned with stability than with growth) establishes an institutional framework whereby member countries are required to achieve balanced or surplus budgets on average over the business cycle, while imposing an upper limit to deficits (no larger than 3% of GDP) in bad years. This ceiling to the deficit/GDP ratio is not binding in the (rather unlikely) event of a downturn in real GDP larger than 2%. All the criticisms of the SGP directly or indirectly question its foundations and the reasons that lead to its creation. Many of the contributions to the debate, however, fail to distinguish between two separate issues: the need for *a pact* and the rationale behind *this Pact*.

In one of the contributions contained in the famous Delors Report, Lamfalussy (1989) suggests that default in one country may force other members to intervene since part of the defaulted debt would be held by their citizens. However, even when no default occurs, in a deeply integrated market negative financial spillovers can take place. In this case, crowding out of more useful/profitable investments results in countries where the interest rate would otherwise be lower.

The basic question is then whether markets are able to discriminate among different issuers. Evidence from US states and Canadian provinces suggests this is indeed the case (see, among others, Bayoumi *et al.*, 1993; Cheung, 1996).[2] On the other hand, Thygesen (1999) reports that, in the mid-1990s, the premium paid by Italian 10-year government bonds over German *Bunds* narrowed to 30 basis points well ahead of debt reduction.

Restoy (1996) claims that three conditions have to hold for markets to be efficient in pricing risk: (i) free capital mobility, (ii) availability of complete and up-to-date information about member countries' public finance, (iii) credibility of the no-bail-out clause. Bayoumi *et al.* (1993) add a fourth condition, that is, (iv) resiliency of the financial system to potential failure of a large borrower.

Tamborini (2002) correctly points out that for fiscal rules to be sensible one needs to assume fiscal stimuli to be expansionary in the home country and contractionary abroad. Otherwise, there is incentive neither to run a budget deficit nor to limit this ability. In his paper, there exist two separate channels through which public spending in one country spills over: a trade channel linking domestic to foreign aggregate demand and production, and a financial channel working via the impact of budget deficits on the common interest and exchange rate. The strength of this latter channel depends crucially on the elasticity of aggregate demand to changes in the interest rate and on money/bond substitutability, that is, the elasticity of money demand to changes in the interest rate. When the latter is low, a larger movement in the interest rate is required to accommodate the excess demand of money generated by increased production (in turn due to the fiscal expansion). Deeper financial markets integration spurred by the introduction of the single currency should favour money/bond substitutability and hence reduce the strength of this financial channel.

Artis and Winkler (1999) as well identify three ways through which an increase in the interest rate can affect the real economy: crowding out of private investments, appreciation of the exchange rate and consequent decrease of exports, contagion in presence of a crisis. Buiter *et al.* (1993) elaborate on this contagion effect, suggesting that to avoid a credit crunch the ECB would need to inject liquidity into the system, thus raising inflation expectations. This in turn would severely damage the goal of price stability. From an empirical point of view, this kind of spillovers working through money demand and the common monetary policy of the ECB should have an impact mainly on short-term rates, that is, on monetary policy instruments.

Kenen (1995) stresses an absorption effect that is more relevant to our work: by issuing more debt, each country runs the risk of saturating the market by absorbing a large share of European saving.[3] Such demand/supply imbalances would result in a lower price (higher interest rate) for bonds. Again, this channel rests on the assumption that markets do not fully discriminate among different issuers, that is, that a monetary union makes bonds of different countries (almost) perfect substitutes. If this is not the case, this supply effect would be limited by the fact that securities issued by different countries span separate segments of the bond market; increased supply of one bond, then, would only raise the interest rate paid in that particular segment, with low or no repercussions on other 'goods'. For this 'loanable funds' hypothesis to work we need an additional condition to hold; namely, that after the introduction of a single currency (and the subsequent elimination of exchange rate risk) European financial markets have become so integrated that they represent a single pool of saving. At this point it is worth noting that according to Hartman *et al.* (2003) quantity based indicators show that a significant home bias still remains in European portfolios. The resulting segmentation in asset markets makes Kenen's hypothesis about financial spillovers less likely.

Fiscal events in one country should affect bond yields at the maturity for which the new issue has occurred. Hence, if Italian deficit is financed by means of 10-year bonds, yields on long-term bonds for all other countries should go up. If fiscal imbalances are covered by a mixture of debt instruments spanning the entire maturity spectrum, then the entire yield curve should shift upwards.

The present discussion has placed the issue of negative financial spillovers within the broader frame of the SGP and has shown that it represents one of the main justifications for having binding fiscal rules. In the next section we will go beyond this policy-oriented approach with the aim of investigating whether economic theory offers any support to the idea that a loose fiscal stance in one country may push upwards the world rate of interest.

8.3 The theoretical background

The debate about the existence and the relevance of negative financial spillovers rests on two broader theoretical issues in modern macroeconomics: whether fiscal policy has any impact on interest rates and whether the latter are determined by stock or flow variables. This section presents an overview of selected contributions that – far from constituting a comprehensive review of the endless literature on the topic – serves the purpose of providing us with a theoretical framework for subsequent analysis and with a context for our discussion.

All models presented here (with the exception of Branson, 1988) assume solvency is not at stake: therefore, changes in bond yields do not affect debt sustainability. The reason for so doing is multifaceted: first of all, default should be taken care of by the no-bail-out clause and has in principle little to do with the SGP. On a more practical ground, given current credit ratings the likelihood of default is extremely limited for all EMU member countries. Therefore, we will not cover the part of the literature that deals with debt repudiation and default and focus our attention on negative financial spillovers in their narrow meaning, that is, public spending resulting in crowding out of private expenditure via its effect on the common interest rate.

This section presents a taxonomy based on the distinction between models where the stock of government debt matters and models emphasizing the role of flow variables (budget deficits). We have chosen to concentrate on works that address the role of fiscal policy in an open economy with a fixed exchange rate regime, as this is the natural benchmark for EMU member countries. As will become apparent, not always clear-cut results emerge and different model specifications lead to different results. Thus, we will see under which conditions the theory predicts fiscal policy to have international spillover effects, in particular by affecting the world interest rate.

8.3.1 Flow models

We open our review with the classic Mundell–Fleming (MF) framework that has for long constituted the main workhorse of open economy macroeconomics.[4] Despite its limitations, among which there are the lack of microfoundations and its failure to distinguish among government consumption and investment (which makes it ill-suited to study the effects of fiscal policy (Obstfeld and Rogoff, 1996: 700)), the MF model is still regarded as a benchmark reference among professionals and academics. The MF framework postulates a simple income–expenditure Keynesian model with interest-bearing public bonds, fixed prices and demand-determined output. One consequence of the lack of any forward-looking behaviour is that no attention is given to intertemporal budget constraints and therefore to sustainability issues: hence, there is no role for stock variables.

As is often the case for open economy macroeconomic models, a distinction is drawn between the small country case and the fully-fledged two-country model.

The former assumes an economic system too small to affect world markets, so that prices and the interest rates are taken as given: fiscal policy then has no chance to impact on the these variables. This feature is not peculiar to the MF framework but rather spans the whole literature, irrespective of other basic assumptions: in the rest of the section therefore we will focus only on two-country versions of all models presented.

In the MF model, a debt-financed increase in public spending bids the interest rate up independently of the direction of output changes (which can be positive or negative depending on the effect of the interest rate on world demand for domestic and foreign products).

The second class of models consists of the neoclassical (intertemporal) ones:[5] here, a representative agent with infinite horizon and perfect foresight maximizes utility subject to a budget constraint. Perfect credit markets allow households to borrow and lend at the same interest rate as the government, which in turn levies lump-sum taxes and engages in public expenditures whose path is exogenously given. Under this set of strict conditions the interest rate, investment and consumption are invariant with respect to the way the government finances its expenditures: all that matters is the present value of government spending.[6] This result easily translates into an open economy framework: yet, while the irrelevance of the timing of taxes does not depend on size, size does matter for the timing of public expenditure G_t. Since the world economy cannot offset shifts of G_t towards, say, the present by borrowing and lending (even though the present value of the infinite stream of government spending does not change), such a shift will put upward pressure on the interest rate as in the traditional Keynesian model.

So far the government has not played any active role: by explicitly introducing government spending as a choice variable subject to an intertemporal budget constraint, one can actually study the effect of fiscal policy. Frenkel and Razin (1992) stress that there are two channels though which G_t influences the equilibrium of the model: the absorption of resources that affects consumption and wealth, and the consumption tilting that depends on the intra- and intertemporal complementarity/substitutability between public and private consumption. Assuming that G_t enters the utility function separately, one gets an intertemporal marginal rate of substitution independent of government spending and therefore shuts the second channel.

The absorption effect may produce different results according to the model setup: in case of a temporary increase in government spending the interest rate goes up as there is an excess demand for current goods; on the other hand, a permanent shift in G_t may lead to lower or higher interest rates depending on the marginal saving propensities of domestic versus foreign agents.

When we incorporate into the picture the distinction between tradeable and non-tradeable goods, we get that the effects of government spending depend on two aspects: the intertemporal allocation of public versus private consumption and their commodity composition. In particular, if public expenditures are biased towards non-tradeables (as one would expect), the effects on the interest rate depend on the marginal saving propensities of the government and households, plus on the intertemporal elasticity of substitution of the latter.

Another way to break Ricardian equivalence is introduced by the third 'family' presented here: overlapping generation (OG) models *à la* Diamond (1965) and Blanchard (1985). The presence of individuals characterized by a finite horizon together with an infinitely lived society results in households using a different interest rate than the government to discount future events: therefore, budget deficits do have a wealth effect. Frenkel and Razin (1992, chapter 11) present a two-period, two-country OG model where a budget deficit results from a decrease in taxes, holding the path of G_t given. As anticipated, in this setup the timing of taxes does have an effect on the world interest rate, but while current deficits undoubtedly push it up, the impact of current and future deficits is less clear-cut and depends on the comparison between the public and private saving propensities.

By introducing a third period into the model it is possible to study the impact of a budget deficit on the term structure of interest rates. Frenkel and Razin show that as long as the present value of government spending is held constant, expected future tax cuts increase the interest rate in the period of the deficit, while the short-term (current) rate of interest will be affected only if domestic and foreign marginal saving propensities are different. Shifting now to the effect of changes in government spending, transitory variations in current G_t bid up the interest rate along the entire maturity spectrum, while in the case of both transitory and permanent expected future changes, the direction of the interest rate shift depends once again on marginal saving propensities.

The last part of this section is dedicated to the new standard model in open economy macroeconomics, namely the Obstfeld and Rogoff (1996) (OR) framework. This is basically a sticky-price intertemporal model that combines Keynesian features into a fully microfounded framework based on utility maximization. In the simplest case, government expenditure is considered pure waste (it affects neither productivity nor private utility) and displays no home-bias. While a temporary rise in G_t has no effect on the interest rate, a permanent rise in world government spending actually reduces the short-term interest rates, thus reaching the opposite conclusion to the older MF model.[7] The authors, however, warn that different ways to model public expenditure would lead to different predictions about the interest rate. Corsetti and Pesenti (2001), for instance, assume that government spending enters households' utility function and obtains the standard MF result whereby a fiscal expansion (domestic or foreign) bids up the world interest rate.

8.3.2 Stock models

There are a number of models predicting an active role for the stock of government debt: the first and foremost example that comes to mind is portfolio models, where asset demand for bonds results from the maximization of a utility function subject to a wealth constraint. Tamborini (1997) provides an example referred to EMU member countries: investors allocate their wealth among two bonds issued by different countries in order to maximize an exponential utility function with constant absolute risk aversion. Despite securities having symmetric statistical properties, Tamborini (1997) shows that in presence of different stocks of outstanding debt, an interest rate differential may develop as a result of the *relative supply effect* typical of portfolio analysis. This kind of model, however, determines interest-rate differentials, not their absolute values and therefore is ill-suited to guide our empirical analysis.

Branson (1988) addresses the shift in the external position that characterized the United States in the 1980s (and then Germany after unification): in so doing, the author presents a two-country 'fundamental' model in the Keynesian tradition where the domestic interest rate is determined via uncovered interest parity, adjusted by a risk premium. The latter depends on the relative size of domestic to foreign debt and so any fiscal deficit, by adding to the outstanding stock of debt, modifies the risk premium and hence the interest rate. Branson (1988) considers a floating exchange-rate regime and the impact of foreign deficits on the domestic interest rate depends on the sensitivity of the current account to the exchange rate. As this would be zero in the case of a monetary union, it is not clear whether the specification would produce the same outcome with a different exchange-rate regime.

Branson (1988) introduces for the first time default risk into the picture: when that is taken into consideration, it is clear that the stock of debt matters. As we have anticipated above, however, credit risk will not be considered here on the ground that it is extremely unlikely that any European country defaults on its debt. Moreover, unless a country nosedives into debt, markets will not impose severe restrictions on its borrowing ability (including risk premia on bond yields).[8] As will become apparent by the rest of this brief literature review, however, there exists models in which default is not taken into consideration, yet the stock of debt does play a role of some sort.

First of all, Barro (1989) notes that, in open economy, invariance of equilibrium with respect to initial debt B_0 vanishes if foreigners hold part of it. This is because they are not subject to future taxes levied to pay back initial debt, which therefore represents a free lunch for them. A related issue is the so-called *transfer problem*: in a neoclassic intertemporal model, initial debt positions (stocks) may affect the equilibrium world interest rate if the two countries display different marginal saving propensities. Yet this example holds the stock of initial world debt fixed and deals just with a redistribution of shares, so there is no role for an active policy.

In the two-country OG model presented in Frenkel and Razin (1992, chapter 11), higher levels of past public expenditure means a larger stock of initial debt for the current generation. The result is reminiscent of the transfer problem and the effect on the interest rate depends on the comparison between domestic and foreign marginal propensity to save.

Within the OG framework, Obstfeld and Rogoff (1996, chapter 3) describe a government that, starting from a zero net asset position, issues a given amount of debt and distributes it to the current old. Current and future young are then subject to taxes in order to keep the ratio of debt to the labour force constant. Savers must now acquire government debt as well as productive capital, with the result that the steady state capital stock will be lower (and the interest rate higher) than without debt.

Leith and Wren-Lewis (2001) introduce an OG structure in a new Keynesian open economy model *à la* Obstfeld and Rogoff (1996). Since consumers are not infinitely lived, the rate of interest is different from their rate of time preference and it will be affected by the outstanding stock of government debt, which produces wealth effects.

In a recent contribution, Beetsma and Vermeylen (2005) present another OG model where – after monetary unification – countries exert interest-rate externalities on each other. The paper concentrates on the supply side of the public debt and makes the assumption that debt of all members in a monetary union is perfectly substitutable and the bond yields become perfectly correlated. This in turn increases the risk of the investors' portfolio, who therefore require a higher return. Two main results are of interest for us: first, the relative importance of interest-rate externalities depends on relative debt levels; second, while the average expected real return increases as a result of monetary unification, individual countries may experience a fall in the cost of finance.

Our review of flow models ended by noting that different ways to model government expenditure may lead to very different results. An interesting example is the paper by Aoki and Leijonhufvud (1987), where the authors present a characterization of investment whereby the return on capital (defined as the present value of the income stream resulting from the investment) depends on the stock of capital inherited from the past as well as on the rate of accumulation of new machinery. This is because a higher rate of investment and a larger stock of capital generate an increase of future production, which in turn implies an increase in future supply that is likely to drive down prices and revenues with them. Of course, to adapt this model to government consumption one needs to assume it (at least partly) to be constituted of investment goods and that such goods are substitutes rather than complements to private investment. This represents a further example of how much modelling choices can affect final results and hence the policy implications of economic theory.

We conclude this section by discussing one last channel through which stocks may influence bond yields, namely liquidity. The marketability of a security in the secondary market may in fact be an important determinant of bond yields and one expects diffusion to be closely related to the amount of outstanding assets. In a more sophisticated fashion, Gravelle (1999) calls this the 'effective supply hypothesis'. Effective supply represents the amount of bonds in the hands of active market participants, that is, investors that do not buy securities to hold them to maturity (the so-called buy-and-hold investors). The author assumes a link between the stock of outstanding securities and liquidity via effective supply and trading activity. Empirical evidence presented in the paper supports this intuition: in the case of US government T-bills, in fact, turnover appears to be correlated with the outstanding stock of assets. The paper goes on claiming that when liquidity is proxied by the bond turnover ratio, there is evidence supporting the idea that 'an increase in the size of the benchmark issue increases its liquidity' (Gravelle, 1999:29).

To reconcile the opposed forces of absorption and liquidity we have to assume that while the negative impact on interest rates dominates in the case of the issuer country (i.e. the interest rate fall due to a larger issue more than compensates its increase due to the excess supply effect), the opposite holds for the foreign country. In other words, while the saturation effect spills over to all economies drawing from the same pool of saving (and so generates a generalized rise in interest rates), the liquidity effect is a local phenomenon.[9]

8.4 Historical perspective: German unification

In our quest for financial spillovers it is useful to turn back to the past and analyse instances in recent European history when fiscal variables in one country moved in a significant way. By focusing on such large swings, and by observing the concurrent movement in European bond yields, we can establish a sort of benchmark episode to which subsequent, more ordinary dynamics can be compared.

Here we will analyse German unification: the magnitude and persistence of the shock is such that strong negative financial spillovers are expected to emerge and hit all European countries. In other words, if externalities exist, this is one place where we trust them to show up.

At the end of the 1980s, Germany represented the third economy in the world and played a pivotal role in the process of European integration. The European Monetary System had been established a decade before (1979), was basically centred on the DM, and was used by many countries as a device to import monetary credibility from the Bundesbank (Giavazzi and Pagano, 1988). Sound macroeconomic fundamentals made the yield on German long-term government bond the benchmark 'safe' asset for European investors.

For what concerns possible spillover effects, uncover interest parity (UIP) tells us that an interest-rate differential is explained by expectations about future exchange-rate movements (or by country-specific risk): in short, we can write

$$i_t - i_t^* = E_t\left[\dot{e}_{t+1}\right] + \rho \tag{8.1a}$$

where i_t and i_t^* are the domestic and foreign interest rates, $E_t\left[\dot{e}_{t+1}\right]$ the expectation about future movements in the exchange rate (price of foreign currency in terms of domestic currency) and ρ is a country-specific risk factor. Let us now take the vantage point of Italian investors and observe some of the consequences of German unification. Assuming that capital is freely mobile and that an increase in German deficit and debt puts upward pressure to the domestic interest rate, one should witness capital flows from Italy to Germany, as Italian investors are attracted by the higher interest rate paid on German bonds. We can further imagine that a risk coefficient is attached to Italian government bonds, so that ρ is larger than zero. Starting from an equilibrium characterized by a balanced Current account (CA), such financial flows will put upward pressure on the exchange rate, calling for an appreciation of the mark (and a consequent depreciation of the lira). Had this to actually occur, Italian investors holding German securities would experience a capital gain generated by the increased price of the foreign currency. To restore the equilibrium, the Italian interest rate not only has to reach German levels, but has to climb even further in order to compensate the expected devaluation:

$$i_t^{ita} = i_t^{ger} + E_t\left[\dot{e}_{t+1}\right] + \rho. \tag{8.1b}$$

This latter mechanism based on exchange-rate expectation is obviously eliminated by a currency union: hence, on purely theoretical ground, once a single currency circulates in a different economic system, the chances for financial spillovers should be – *ceteris paribus* – lower.

In the second part of the section we will describe the developments in German public finances, external position and interest rates, while at the same time investigating the impact on interest rates of other European countries. The discussion is based on data from the IMF *International Financial Statistics* and the Deutsche Bundesbank *Time Series Database*.

There is little doubt that German unification required a massive disbursement on part of the Federal Government: although part of the required funds were collected by rising taxes and cutting expenditures in other sectors, integration of new Länder into market economy resulted in a surge of public deficit and debt. The Bundesbank (1997: 18) claims that this was partly due to the fact that 'not only was the fiscal policy challenge associated with this [the unification process] unforeseen, its magnitude was also underestimated at first.'

From the same source we learn that the ratio of debt/GDP jumped from under 42% in 1989 to over 60% in 1996, despite the positive impulse to production generated by unification itself;[10] in fact, while between 1991 and 1993 nominal GDP grew at an average rate of 4.94%, in the following three years growth was 'only' 2.78%. The same applies to the deficit/GDP ratio that, thanks to robust production growth, never overcame 3%.

To get a feeling of the magnitude of the amount of resources drained by unification we can look at a few summary statistics: between 1985 and 1989, the average growth rate of public debt was 5.88%, while the average deficit of the public sector amounted to less then 20 DM billion. Over the years 1990–94, the stock of debt grew at an average rate above 15% and excessive spending amounted to almost 60 DM billion on average. Table 8.1 displays information about some key macroeconomic variables before and after 1990: one important aspect that emerges clearly from the data is not only the magnitude, but also the length of the fiscal effort required by unification.

As we can infer from columns (4) and (5) of Table 8.1, financing needs were met quite easily since foreign capital flew heavily into the country and kept coming for a long time after unification. This was facilitated by the increase in bond yields and by expectations about exchange-rate dynamics (which would in fact be fulfilled in September 1992 with the EMS crisis). A glance at Figure 8.1 gives an immediate idea of the dramatic turnaround in the external position of Germany: in the five

Table 8.1 German fiscal position: summary statistics

	Period averages			
	Debt growth rate	*Deficit*	*Current account*	*Financial account*
1985–9	5.88%	19.66	40.16	−41.73
1986–90	8.46%	23.56	46.08	−48.97
1989–94	15.07%	59.77	−7.92	9.46
1991–5	16.57%	64.23	−22.25	29.19

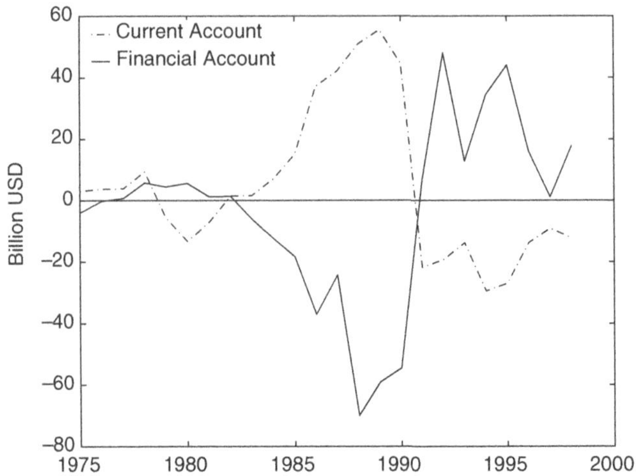

Figure 8.1 Current and financial account for Germany 1971–98.

Source: International Financial Statistics (IFS).

Note

Figures in billion USD.

years following unification, the country imported capital at an average rate of almost 30 billion dollars per year, for a cumulated financial inflow of roughly 150 billion. This stands in sharp contrast with what happened in the previous decade when German investors had exported an average of 48 USD billion each year.

So far, we have repeatedly claimed that the process of integrating East Germany implied an impressive and prolonged injection of resources on the part of the public sector. Moreover, BoP data suggest that Germany absorbed resources from abroad and in particular from European countries that constituted Germany's main trading partners. Table 8.2 reports the ratios of the German deficit to European GDP and to a European-wide stock of debt. These figures provide us with some information on the incidence of the German fiscal shock on continental asset markets.

While the deficit/GDP ratio has become a sort of benchmark measure of fiscal imbalances, the outstanding stock of debt proxies for market depth should therefore indicate the ability of the market to absorb a given amount of bonds. Of course,

Table 8.2 Impact of German unification on European-wide variables

	$deficit_{Ger}/debt_{EU}$ †	$deficit_{Ger}/GDP_{EU}$ ‡
1989	0.35%	0.05%
1990	4.03%	0.47%
1991	4.22%	0.67%
1992	4.05%	0.76%
1993	3.68%	0.84%
1994	2.03%	0.46%
1995	2.47%	0.62%
	notional limits implied by Maastricht criteria	
	1.00%	1.00%

Note
†EMU 11 save for Ireland and Portugal; ‡EMU 11.

we expect a larger impact to cause a larger movement in European interest rates and, hence, a larger negative financial spillover. To get a clearer picture we can use the Maastricht criteria to compute the notional limits on the ratios displayed in Table 8.2. Using some elementary algebra, we can write

$$\frac{deficit_{Ger}}{debt_{Ger}} = \frac{deficit_{Ger}}{GDP_{Ger}} \cdot \frac{GDP_{Ger}}{debt_{Ger}} \cdot \frac{debt_{Ger}}{debt_{EU}}$$

and

$$\frac{deficit_{Ger}}{GDP_{EU}} = \frac{deficit_{Ger}}{GDP_{Ger}} \cdot \frac{GDP_{Ger}}{GDP_{EU}}$$

where the first term on the right-hand side of both equations is the deficit ceiling of 3%, and $GDP_{Ger}/debt_{Ger}$ is the inverse of the debt limit of 60%. For $debt_{Ger}/debt_{EU}$ and GDP_{Ger}/GDP_{EU} we use long-term averages of the German to European debt and GDP, which for the period 1970–1995 are 19.41% and 31.67%, respectively. In both cases we obtain threshold values that are just below 1%.[11]

Let us now focus on the behaviour of long-term interest rates in Germany and in the other European countries. We expect the yield on German bonds to go up under the pressure of the fiscal shock determined by unification. The first rows of Table 8.3 show the monthly yield on long-term German bonds between 1 and 36 months before and after unification: we take June 1990 – when the DM was formally introduced in the former GDR as the legal tender – as the origin of our imaginary time line. One thing to notice is that unification came at the end of an expansionary period and hence it contributed to overheating the economy: the Bundesbank raised interest rates sharply in order to control domestic inflation (Dornbusch and Wolf, 1992), and high demand resulted in full capacity utilization and spurred new investment. From Table 8.3 it emerges that German rates did not react immediately to the shock (one month after unification the yield on long-term bond is 30bp lower than one month before), but then the upswing is rather persistent: the average yield

Table 8.3 Yields on German and European bonds

		Months before and after unification						
		1	*3*	*6*	*12*	*18*	*24*	*36*
Germany	before	8.96	8.73	7.60	6.90	6.35	6.21	5.60
	after	8.64	9.21	8.95	8.50	8.51	8.28	6.62
Europe†: GDP weighted	before	11.18	11.35	10.53	9.98	9.44	9.38	9.47
	after	10.96	11.47	11.07	10.71	10.37	10.22	8.77
Europe†: trade weighted	before	10.67	10.82	10.01	9.37	8.83	8.82	8.86
	after	10.46	10.99	10.61	10.23	9.96	9.79	8.25

Note
†Austria, Belgium, Denmark, France, Ireland, Italy, Luxembourg, Netherlands, Portugal, Spain, Sweden, UK.

in the 18 months that followed unification is 124bp higher than the average yield prevailing in the 18 months that preceded June 1990. These two facts suggest the presence of rigidities that may have hindered the adjustment and that unification was perceived as a permanent rather than a transitory shock.

Turning now to the other European countries, the bottom part of Table 8.3 reports the yield on a weighted average of government bonds of European countries. Due to data availability, the basket of countries that constitute our European sample is slightly different from previous analysis, where we used the first 11 countries to join EMU, and takes into consideration also non-EMU countries like Denmark and the United Kingdom. Yields of different governments are weighted according to two different criteria: nominal GDP and a measure of trade linkages with Germany (imports on the part of Germany). While the former represents a natural choice to determine the importance of different economic systems in a European-wide context (Sinn, 1996, uses weights based on 1980 GDP figures), the latter method – giving more weight to countries more closely linked to Germany – should produce a European rate more prone to financial spillovers.

What emerges from Table 8.3 is that the European rate as well reacted with a lag to the shock of unification, but this time the upward pressure fades rapidly as the yield is back to pre-unification levels within six months of the event. Different weighting methods do not result in any difference in the behaviour of the European rate. Figure 8.2 plots the difference between the German and the European yields over the years 1988–92 and gives therefore a pictorial description of the phenomena analysed so far. Between June 1990 and September 1992, when speculators drove the lira and the pound out of the EMS, the spread shows a small tendency to decline and only on the verge of the crisis does it jump back to the levels of the beginning of the 1990s.

To better understand the issue of spillovers from Germany to other European countries we analyse spreads vis-à-vis the German bond yield. As anticipated above, the latter have long since been playing a pivotal role in the market for

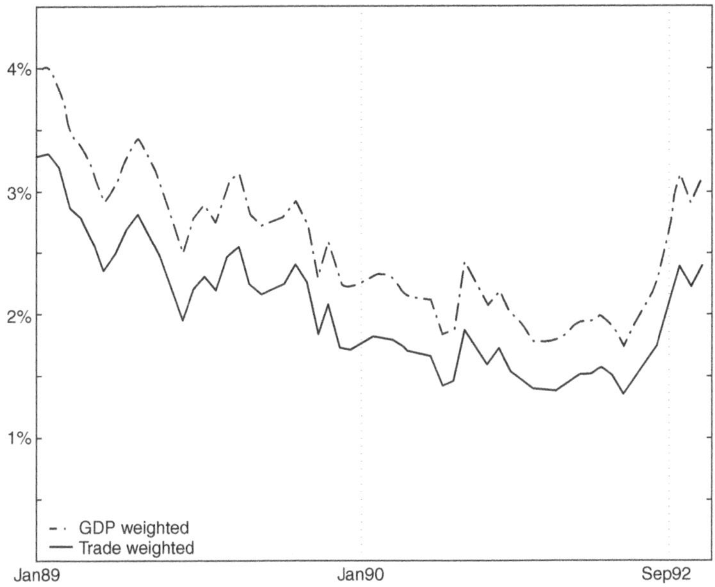

Figure 8.2 EU†– Germany long-term interest rate differential.

Note:

†Austria, Belgium, Denmark, France, Ireland, Italy, Luxembourg, Netherlands, Portugal, Spain, Sweden, UK. Dot-dashed line represents the difference between the German rate and an average European rate obtained weighting countries' yield by relative GDP shares; solid line repeats the exercise weighting yields by German import shares.

government securities and most debt instruments issued by other European countries pay a premium over it. Table 8.4 presents average-yield spreads of selected European countries: we consider not only future EMU members, but also the United Kingdom (one of the EU members that opted out of EMU) and Switzerland (which is neither member of the EMU nor of the EU). We expect that looser linkages with Germany result in smaller spillover effects. These in turn should provoke the spread to change only slightly as an increase in the German rate is closely followed by an analogous movement in foreign interest rates. In the limit, with a one-to-one spillover effect, the spread should not change at all. On the contrary, if national economies are insulated from external fiscal shocks, then the spread should decline (or increase, depending on whether it is a positive or a negative spread) in response to the increase in German rates caused by unification.

The picture that emerges from Table 8.4 is not homogeneous for all the countries examined. Grouping them according to the behaviour of their spread, we can say that Belgium, Ireland, Spain and, to a lesser extent, France display a marked decline of the premium paid over German rates. The same applies to Italy in the early aftermath of unification, while later on the Italian spread moves up again in response to the particularly weak fiscal position of the country, the latent fiscal crisis that was mounting, and the speculative attack that hit the lira in September 1992.

Table 8.4 Spread vis-à-vis German yields

		Months before and after unification						
		1	*3*	*6*	*12*	*18*	*24*	*36*
Austria	before	−0.15	0.02	0.25	0.27	0.18	0.41	1.02
	after	0.07	−0.23	−0.15	0.03	0.14	0.32	0.28
Belgium	before	0.89	1.18	2.07	1.50	1.70	1.63	2.22
	after	0.96	1.34	1.03	0.87	0.51	0.62	0.37
France	before	0.66	1.24	1.54	1.79	2.27	2.73	3.72
	after	0.97	1.31	0.98	0.65	0.28	0.46	0.50
Ireland	before	0.98	1.70	1.68	2.06	2.06	3.40	5.33
	after	0.88	1.35	0.94	0.74	0.34	0.59	0.87
Italy	before	2.57	2.82	3.84	3.94	3.67	3.91	3.89
	after	2.69	2.22	2.86	4.59	4.45	4.83	5.26
Luxembourg	before	−0.45	−0.24	0.74	0.38	−0.21	0.23	2.54
	after	−0.22	−0.64	−0.42	−0.28	−0.41	−0.36	0.37
Netherlands	before	−0.01	0.25	0.15	0.30	0.15	0.31	0.68
	after	0.10	−0.05	0.11	0.14	0.21	0.02	−0.03
Portugal	before	9.51	9.65	10.23	8.27	7.60	7.53	9.64
	after	9.90	9.65	9.83	9.87	8.62	6.82	7.90
Spain	before	5.67	6.13	6.89	6.88	6.47	4.65	7.60
	after	5.81	5.93	5.59	3.42	3.36	3.42	3.72
				non EMU members				
Switzerland	before	−2.64	−2.15	−1.85	−1.78	−2.12	−2.07	−1.49
	after	−2.56	−2.67	−2.27	−2.52	−2.16	−1.30	−2.08
UK	before	2.53	2.73	2.36	2.98	3.10	3.11	3.30
	after	2.39	2.11	1.47	1.84	1.05	0.74	1.77

Note
Data for Finland not available.

Luxembourg increased its margin over the German rate and 2 years after unification its (negative) spread was still larger than the value of March 1990. This date is taken as reference in order to shield from the possibility that markets had somehow anticipated unification and therefore bond yields prevailing one month before the formal introduction of the DM into former GDR were already uncommonly high.

The Austrian spread became negative after unification, then it climbed back to the values prevailing three months before unification. Dutch figures as well underwent only minor shifts: yet two years after unification the German-Dutch spread is nil, while two years before it amounted to 30bp. Portugal exhibits a puzzling dynamic that pushed up the interest rate spread vis-à-vis Germany; this tendency is only reversed at longer horizons, but it is nevertheless difficult to reconcile it with our analysis.

Turning now to the United Kingdom, we again observe that the spread is sensibly reduced, both in absolute terms (along the time line) and in comparison to average values before German unification; the oddity here is represented by the fact that, while the pound underwent in September 1992 a speculative attack that forced its exit from the EMS, no sign of upward pressure on the British rates emerges from the data. This behaviour can be rationalized by observing that having followed a policy of high interest rates for more than two years (in order to comply with the narrow fluctuation bands imposed by the EMS), the Bank of England cut its discount rate in half as soon as it was driven out of the EMS. The marked difference with respect to Italy may be justified by the stronger macroeconomic fundamentals that characterized the British economy at that time and that resulted in the currency crises not to impact on long-term interest rates.

The last country, Switzerland, constitutes a sort of 'control group': given its historical neutrality and its peculiar role in international capital markets, we expect German unification to have no effects on Swiss yields. In fact, the negative spread between the latter and German ones became even larger and it takes 18 months for it to go back to the levels observed three months before unification. Hence, the increase in German rates did not produce any comparable movement in Swiss yields.

All in all, there seems not to be much evidence in support of the negative financial spillovers hypothesis. While it is rather clear that the German rates were shifted up by the fiscal shock due to unification, yield on long-term securities issued by other European countries do not display any marked tendency towards an increase. Spreads vis-à-vis German rates declined for most countries considered. To support this interpretation one can integrate exchange-rate expectations into the picture and note that, in presence of an expected appreciation of the DM, not only should European rates have moved upwards, but they should have jumped higher than German ones as predicted by the UIP condition (1b). Hence, in presence of an expected appreciation of the DM, financial spillovers would not be the only determinant of any upward movement in other European interest rates. Despite a generalized consensus existing on the fact that the EMS crisis of 1992 was not anticipated by the market,[12] the realignment proposed by Germany as early as 1989 and the flexibility (albeit very limited) granted by EMS fluctuation bands suggest that the expected change in exchange rates could not realistically be set at zero and thereafter the limited upward movement of European rates is at least partially to be ascribed to exchange-rate movements, thus giving even less support to the spillover hypothesis.

Moreover, many authors (see, for instance, Rose and Svensson, 1994; Sinn, 1996, and the references therein) claim that the EMS crisis of September 1992 was caused by German unification itself: in particular, the upward swing in German rates and the consequent flow of financial resources into the central European country called for a revaluation of the DM. Once France, the United Kingdom and Italy opposed to the realignment in fear of undermining the anti-inflationary credibility they were importing through the pegged rate, real appreciation of the DM had to arrive through price changes. The liberalization of capital flows mandated by the Single European Act and implemented in most countries by the beginning of 1990 made it impossible to reconcile fixed exchange rates and independent monetary policies. Thus, a conflict emerged between the Bundesbank commitment to control domestic inflationary pressures, the sluggish economic performance of partner countries and their unwillingness to realign. This tension opened the door to a speculative attack and hence to the crisis with the resulting redefinition of central parities. This chain of events excludes any strong role for spillover effects on European interest rates: had they occurred, in fact, the flow of capital to Germany would have been limited, the need for revaluation not emerged and EMS band would have likely granted the system enough flexibility to face the shock.

It is probably fair to say that German unification is not the only culprit for the EMS crisis. In a classic contribution of the topic, Eichengreen and Wyplosz (1993) review four different explanations, do not find a great deal of support for the view that unification played a leading role, but nonetheless present some evidence in this direction. Their conclusion privileges the explanation based on self-fulfilling expectations but still acknowledges that several other factors contributed in building-up favourable conditions for speculators to succeed.[13]

8.5 Empirical analysis: aggregate behaviour in the euro area

Turning now to more formal empirical analysis, the search for potential spillovers of fiscal policies on the European interest rate crosses with tests of the 'Ricardian equivalence' hypothesis. One of the traditional means used for the purpose addresses the relation between fiscal deficits and interest rates.[14] The amount of research devoted to the issue is extremely vast, though empirical evidence is confused and gives mixed results.[15]

Recently, some authors have taken a slightly different route and have investigated the impact of world fiscal variables on interest rates. The parallelism with the issue of financial spillovers is straightforward. Indeed, Ford and Laxton (1999: 77–8) explicitly claim that with globally integrated capital markets it is world debt that matters for the determination of country-specific interest rates. Hence, they continue, 'countries with high levels of government debt may be imposing negative externalities on others.' The fundamental hypothesis at work here is that a euro cent of debt has the same impact on world markets regardless of the issuer. The conclusion of the two authors is that the ratio of OECD public debt to world GDP has had a substantial effect on the interest rates of nine industrial countries over the period 1977–97. Local developments, on the other hand, are only relevant to explain persistent *spreads*, though their effect is not significant on interest rate *levels*.

Breedon *et al.* (1999), who study G-3 economies over period 1975–88 using *ex-post* 10-year real interest rates, present similar results, even if they find a more relevant role for domestic factors that – they claim – are at least as important as international ones. The three authors interpret their result as evidence against financial markets integration.

Chinn and Frankel (2003) repeat the exercise, investigating the impact of G7 debt on the interest rates of Germany, France, Italy and Spain over the period 1988–2002, but find no significant effect.

Ardagna *et al.* (2004) investigate the relation between fiscal variables and long-term interest rates using a panel of 16 OECD countries over the last 40 years. Their findings support the idea international factors are relevant (so that negative financial spillovers do occur), yet to a much lesser extent than domestic ones. Again, this evidence points towards a lack of integration in capital markets. Closely related to our work is the finding by the authors that EMU does not constitute a breakpoint for European countries: the introduction of the single currency in fact seems not to have resulted in international variables to be more relevant and/or domestic ones to lose importance in the determination of bond yields. In sum, this work suggests that while there is an effect of international fiscal variables on interest rates, the inception of EMU has not provoked any structural change in the relation between deficit, debt and bond yields.

Following Chinn and Frankel (2003), we test the hypothesis that European capital market can be considered as a single pool of funds from which all countries draw and for which they all compete. Once confirmed by the data, this theory would back the idea that by absorbing a significant share of European saving, the fiscal imbalances in one country can affect the common interest rate and thus impose negative externalities on economic partners. Yet, the budget limits incorporated into the SGP are not aimed at limiting European-wide fiscal expansions, but rather the behaviour of single states. The relevant hypothesis is therefore more stringent than the one tested here. In other words, a failure to reject our null hypothesis does not immediately lend support to the existence of negative financial spillovers as postulated in the SGP.

In this first empirical exercise we consider the euro area as a single economic entity and look for a relation among aggregate measures of the fiscal stance and a weighted average of different bond yields. We exploit two sets of data, both of which report figures for the 12 EMU countries as a whole: first, we use quarterly data on the EMU published in the OECD *Economic Outlook* for the period 1980Q1 to 2004Q2, then – in order to isolate the effect of EMU – we turn to monthly data taken from the ECB *Monthly Bulletin* that range from January 1999 to April 2004.[16]

8.5.1 Quarterly data

In this first part of the analysis we exploit quarterly data for the EMU area as a whole published by the OECD. We have opted for the simplest possible specification, and therefore the basic estimating equation takes the form:

$$YLD_t = \varphi_0 + \varphi_1 t + \varphi_2 \frac{surplus_t}{GDP_t} + \varphi_3 \frac{debt_t}{GDP_t} + \varepsilon_t \tag{8.2}$$

where *YLD* is an average real yield on long-term bonds issued by EMU area governments, *t* is a time trend and *surplus* the primary balance.[17] As a robustness check, we introduce a second measure of the fiscal position specifically aimed at capturing the non-anticipated part of the fiscal stance. This variable, which appears as *fiscal* in the tables, is constructed following Blanchard (1990); Brunila *et al.* (1999);

and Farina and Tamborini (2002), and basically reports the fiscal stance net of cyclical effects: it is therefore an indicator of discretionary fiscal policy. Its construction is fairly easy: the first step is running a regression of the primary balance/GDP ratio (*PB*) on a constant, a time trend and GDP growth ($G\dot{D}P$)

$$PB_t = \lambda_0 + \lambda_2 t + \lambda_3 G\dot{D}P_t \; ; \qquad (8.3)$$

then estimated coefficients are used to build a *growth-adjusted primary balance* (*GAPB*), which is obtained by inserting the previous period GDP growth rate into the estimated equation. This variable represents the primary balance that would have prevailed in period t, had the GDP grown at the same rate as in period $t-1$. This is computed as

$$GAPB_t = \hat{\lambda}_0 + \hat{\lambda}_1 t + \hat{\lambda}_2 G\dot{D}P_{t-1} \qquad (8.4)$$

while our fiscal stance indicator is simply given by the difference between the growth-adjusted measure and the observed value of the primary balance

$$fiscal_t = GAPB_t - PB_{t-1} \, . \qquad (8.5)$$

As it is for *surplus*, a positive value of *fiscal* implies a fiscal restriction.

Columns (1)–(3) of Table 8.5 present results for estimation of equation (8.2) in levels. We find that fiscal imbalances do not have any impact on real bond yields, regardless of the variable used (either the primary surplus or the measure of discretionary policy *à la* Blanchard), whilst the stock of outstanding debt has a significant effect on the cost of borrowing, most probably via risk premia (columns (1) and (2)). Column (3) reports results for a new specification whereby a dummy for the EMU is included and interacted with fiscal variables, to check the hypothesis that the introduction of the single currency marks a break in the data so that after 1999 deeper integration of European capital market results in EMU fiscal variables having a larger impact on bond yields. Interaction terms are significant at 8% and 1% and suggest that monetary integration may in fact have increased the importance of euro-area variables in determining interest rates. In particular, the primary balance/GDP ratio (interacted with the EMU dummy) is positive, contrary to what theory suggests, while the stock of debt is negative. The latter interesting result tells that after 1999 liquidity effects dominate default risk consideration: financial markets cease to discriminate among EMU members' sovereign issuers and as the amount of outstanding debt increases, bond yields are pushed down by the increased liquidity of the securities.

One major caveat applies to these estimates: as unit-root tests cannot reject a null of non-stationarity for most of the variables involved in the regression, results may be spurious. This suspicion is confirmed by residual-based tests for cointegration:[18] regression residuals from equation (8.2) – considered as the cointegrating relation – are not stationary and therefore point towards the lack of any long-run equilibrium relation.

Table 8.5 Impact of fiscal variables on real long-term yields: quarterly data

	Levels			*Differences*		
	(1)	*(2)*	*(3)*	*(4)*	*(5)*	*(6)*
Surplus/GDP	−0.051		−0.229	−0.149		−0.380
	(0.20)		(0.39)	(0.49)		(0.75)
Fiscal/GDP		−0.094			−0.267	
		(0.36)			(0.74)	
Debt/GDP	0.153	0.134	−0.068	−0.203	−0.208	−0.268
	(2.50)*	(2.29)*	(0.58)	(1.43)	(1.55)	(1.34)
EMU • surplus/GDP			1.136			0.582
			(1.78)			(1.08)
EMU • debt/GDP			−0.079			0.303
			(−2.79)**			(1.14)
Observations	98	97	98	97	96	97
Adjusted R^2	0.26	0.28	0.39	0.06	0.07	0.06

Notes
Absolute value of HAC robust t-statistics in parentheses; * significant at 5%; ** significant at 1%; constant and time trend not included.

We therefore run the same regression in first differences and display the results in columns (4)–(6). Estimated coefficients lose significance and, more importantly, the ratio of debt/GDP now changes sign and becomes negative; albeit it is not significant at 10%. Again, the situation does not improve if we substitute *fiscal* for *surplus*. Interacting fiscal variables with the EMU dummy does not change the overall picture: coefficients are positive, but not significant, so the inception of the monetary union seems not to have had any strong impact. Table 8.5 tells that bond yields are not determined by fiscal variables.[19]

8.5.2 Monthly data

In order to focus on the impact of EMU, we now restrict our attention to the period that followed the introduction of the single currency: to cope with this short time span we have to resort to monthly observations compiled by the ECB and therefore, instead of analysing the impact of public deficits on bond yields, we concentrate on the issuing activity on part of the public sector (data on fiscal variables only exist at lower frequencies). This 'restriction' has the additional benefit of allowing for a direct test of the hypothesis that the absorption of saving by the pubic sector – rather than fiscal variables *per se* – is what really matters for the determination of bond yields.

Our baseline specification for the real interest rate is

$$\Delta YLD_t = \gamma_0 + \gamma_1 t + \gamma_2 \frac{issue_t^g}{GDP_t} + \gamma_3 \frac{issue_t^p}{GDP_t} + \gamma_4 \Delta \frac{stock_t^g}{GDP_t} + \gamma_5 \Delta \frac{stock_t^p}{GDP_t} + \varepsilon_t \tag{8.6}$$

where *YLD* is the real yield on government benchmark bonds and the superscripts g and p identify the public and private sector, respectively.

Many variables are non-stationary and thus enter the estimating equation in first differences. Euro-area yields are calculated on the basis of weights corresponding to nominal outstanding amounts of bonds in each maturity, and are deflated *ex post* using the harmonized consumer price index. Our dataset consists of monthly observations from January 1999 to April 2004 for a total of 64 observations.[20] We do not focus on a single maturity but use both 3- and 10-year bonds in order to span the yield curve. This is intended to give some information on the nature of spillovers: while in fact, according to the absorption hypothesis, bonds of all maturities should be affected by an increase in the issuing activity of the public sector, the spillover would occur only at longer time horizons were the driving force credit risk.

Interpretation of equation (8.6) is straightforward: under the 'standard' view the real rate should be affected by the absorption of resources by the public and the private sector. In addition, the basic equation is augmented with the introduction of GDP growth, which should capture responses of the interest rate to the business cycle.

Table 8.6 reports results for real yields on 3- and 10-year benchmark government bonds. Durbin–Watson statistics suggest the presence of autocorrelation among the residuals: this is confirmed by Ljung-Box Q test and leads us to compute Newey–West heteroskedasticy and autocorrelation consistent (HAC) standard errors from which t-statistics are computed. As one would expect, the short-term yield is more sensitive to business cycle fluctuations represented by GDP growth; interestingly, something similar occurs to the stock of private debt which also has a positive impact on bond yields once GDP growth is included. During economic upturns, interest rates go up and as the private sector increases its stock of debt, corporate bonds will bear a higher risk premium that pushes up returns. This, combined with return-seeking behaviour on the part of investors (typical of economic growth phases) may explain why a higher stock of private debt spills over to government benchmark bonds: in order to attract savers, public securities have to offer a higher return. In sum, Table 8.6 suggests that at shorter maturities it is as if private and public debt are less segmented due to the risk-seeking behaviour of investors. This effect is much less pronounced at longer horizons: columns (3) and (4) in fact show that neither GDP growth nor the stock of private debt are significant at 5%. Bond issue to GDP as well is not significantly different from zero at all maturities.

Overall, the empirical analysis does not provide much credit to the hypothesis that the fiscal position of the euro area as a whole affects either bond yields or the current account. This is consistent with recent evidence put forward by Breedon *et al.* (1999); Chinn and Frankel (2003); Ardagna *et al.* (2004); and Kormendi and Protopapadakis (2004). On the other hand, the results obtained in the case of 10-year bonds (and shown in Table 8.6) may be read as a sign that at longer maturities some sort of linkage exists between public finances and real interest rates: in this case, the relevant transmission channel would be credit risk.

Table 8.6 Impact of fiscal variables on real yields: monthly data

	3-year rate		*10-year rate*	
	(1)	*(2)*	*(3)*	*(4)*
Δ (issue/GDP)$_{gov}$	0.039	0.018	0.059	0.048
	(0.82)	(0.38)	(1.16)	(0.91)
Δ (issue/GDP)$_{pvt}$	0.024	0.014	0.033	0.028
	(0.38)	(0.26)	(0.60)	(0.57)
Δ (stock/GDP)$_{gov}$	−0.041	−0.024	−0.038	−0.028
	(0.67)	(0.48)	(0.59)	(0.48)
Δ (stock/GDP)$_{pvt}$	0.054	0.079	0.034	0.048
	(1.46)	(2.47)*	(0.97)	(1.73)
GDP growth		0.051		0.029
		(2.78)**		(1.38)
Observations	63	63	63	63
Adjusted R^2	0.01	0.08	0.02	0.03

Notes
1st difference of dependent variable; absolute value of HAC robust t-statistics in parentheses; * significant at 5%; ** significant at 1%; constant and time trend not shown.

8.6 Linkages among EMU member states

This section goes deeper in the empirical analysis by narrowing the focus on the linkages among government bonds issued by EMU members. Recently, there has been a surge of interest on European government bonds market.[21] The latter is often regarded as the most important financial market, as government securities represent the dominant financial instrument in European portfolios (Perée and Steinherr, 2001). Moreover, different authors agree in identifying the bond market as the segment that has more promptly reacted to the inception of the EMU and that has most remarkably integrated to form a single pan-European market.

Most studies focus on spreads among securities issued by different European states, trying to detect their main determinants now that, with the elimination of exchange-rate risk, segmentation should decline and assets become closer substitutes. In presence of spillovers, however, it is not possible to assess whether spreads reflect correctly priced risks and so the strategy has to be adjusted.[22]

Codogno *et al.* (2003) investigate the behaviour of relative asset swap spreads (RAS) with respect to Germany; RAS – the difference between the bond yield spread and the spread on swap rates of the same maturity – represent the component of the yield differential not related to exchange-rate factors and thus allow the authors to pool together data collected before and after 1999. Empirical evidence suggests that international risk factors dominate liquidity, while no role is played by different debt/GDP ratios.

Hartman *et al.* (2003) agree on the point that remaining spreads cannot be explained by credit risk differentials and judge the fact that prices of bonds with identical ratings have not fully converged as a legacy of market segmentation.

According to their view, this hypothesis is backed up by the fact that quantity-based indicators still show a significant home-bias in European portfolios (though it has diminished after the introduction of the single currency).

Afonso and Strauch (2004) study the impact of 2002 fiscal policy events on default risk (measured by the spread between the swap rate and the yield on bonds of the same maturity). They use daily data for the same year and their findings witness to the lack of a strong reaction. This is consistent with the interpretation that with current credit ratings default risk is negligible for almost all EMU member countries.

Dunne *et al.* (2003) analyse interactions among German, French and Italian bonds in order to find the benchmark asset. Using cointegration analysis, they find that German bonds are the financial instrument to which the price of other securities react (the benchmark).

8.6.1 Linkages across bond yields

Figure 8.3 plots the yields on 10-year government bonds for the 11 countries that joined EMU in 1999: the graph spans the period between January 1990 and June 2004 and displays monthly averages of long-term bond yields. Two facts emerge: first, a dramatic convergence process took place between 1995 and 1997 and was almost completed before the actual introduction of the single currency; second, it is clear that yields on bonds issued by different European countries move together. This is striking since 1999, but even at the beginning of the sample there was a marked tendency to co-move.

Does this imply the existence of financial spillovers? Not necessarily: according to Dunne *et al.* (2003) and their definition of the benchmark asset, we need to distinguish financial spillovers from long-term equilibrium relations that link different

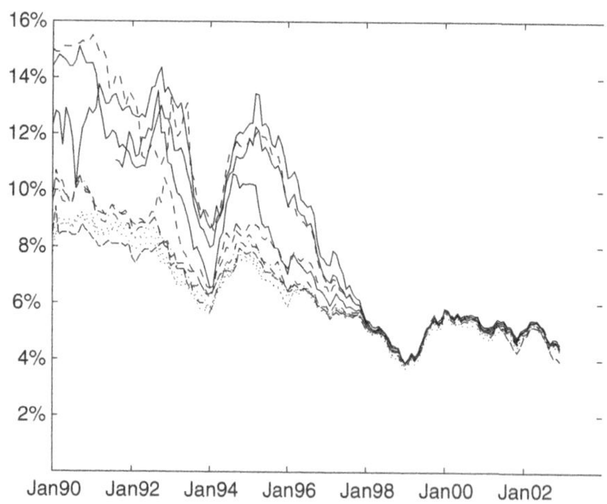

Figure 8.3 Yield on 10-year government bonds: EMU 11 countries.

financial instruments in the same market. Empirically, this entails addressing short-term dynamics rather than long-term analysis, that is, taking the opposite route from Dunne *et al.* (2003). This is consistent with what was suggested by Favero (2001), who notes that in recent research VARs in levels rather than Vector Error Correction Models are used when the focus is on short-run dynamics, regardless of the presence of non-stationary variables and cointegrating relations.

The first halt in our search for financial spillovers is then a VAR in levels with subsequent Granger-causality tests. We concentrate on the period that followed the introduction of the euro as spillovers should emerge more clearly once exchange-rate risk is eliminated; we exploit a dataset comprising daily observations on 10-year bond yields from January 2001 to June 2004. Results (not presented and available upon request) show that Granger-causality is never rejected for all variables and all equations and suggest that there is in fact co-determination of bond yields.

This being established, we are left with the main part of the problem yet unsolved: we need to determine the source of such interactions among government securities. The negative financial spillover hypothesis suggests that at least part of the co-movements is due to externalities stemming from the fiscal position of EMU member states. Theory therefore provides us with some guidance and directs our analysis towards the potential impact of domestic fiscal imbalances on foreign interest rates.

8.6.2 The role of fiscal policy

In order to analyse the impact of fiscal variables on bond yields, it is necessary to move to lower frequencies. In what follows we will once again exploit both quarterly and monthly data. These are still rather high frequencies in terms of fiscal indicators and we are going to pay a cost in terms of available series (and may be their reliability). On the other hand, the time span on which we can concentrate is not very large and these data allow us to maximize the number of observations.

Our empirical specification draws from recent works on the topic, especially Afonso and Strauch (2004); Ardagna *et al.* (2004); and Bernoth *et al.* (2004). The latter is especially interesting as it develops a very simple framework for analysing the relation between fiscal variables and bond yields. We have explored a number of different specifications, but decided to concentrate here on one similar to that used in section 8.5 in order to be consistent throughout the exposition. The estimating equation thus reads:

$$
\begin{aligned}
ras_t^i = {} & \beta_0 + \beta_1 t + \beta_2 int3m_t + \beta_3 infl_t + \beta_4 \left[\frac{surplus_t}{GDP_t}\right]^i \\
& + \beta_5 \left[\frac{debt_t}{GDP_t}\right]^i + \beta_6 \left[\frac{surplus_t}{GDP_t}\right]^{EMU-i} + \beta_7 \left[\frac{debt_t}{GDP_t}\right]^{EMU-i} + \varepsilon_t .
\end{aligned}
\tag{8.7}
$$

On the left-hand side we have the 10-year relative asset swap with respect to Switzerland. Investigating the presence of financial spillovers among EMU member countries, we are forced to look for a reference country that is not part of the monetary union: we have opted for Switzerland as it is small enough not to exert particular influences on the international bond market, and its historical record is one of remarkable stability and sound fiscal position (the return on Swiss bonds is always lower than that paid on other European securities). In addition, Switzerland has not experienced any significant change in its budgetary position (contrary, for instance, to the United States, which would represent another natural point of reference) and this is another reason that makes it an excellent benchmark country. Moreover, we can feel sufficiently safe in assuming that the fiscal position of any EMU member state will not influence the yield on Swiss bond as the traditional neutrality of the latter country results in looser linkages with neighbouring nations.

The list of controls included in equation (8.7) comprises the three-month interest rate, inflation, domestic and foreign primary surplus and debt/GDP ratios.[23] The superscript *i* stands for the object countries of our study, namely France, Germany, Italy and the Netherlands, while the label *EMU-i* indicates the aggregated fiscal position of the other 11 EMU member countries. We have chosen to aggregate foreign fiscal variables in order to avoid potential collinearity problems. All variables are measured as deviation from the relevant Swiss figure. Data are taken from the OECD *Economic Outlook* except for swap rates which come from *Datastream*. Given that available fiscal indicators are at quarterly frequency, we are left with less than 60 observations.[24]

All variables (apart from the three-month interest rate) display a unit root, so we cannot simply proceed with estimation of the SUR in levels. We first tackle the problem by differencing all non-stationary variables: odd columns in Table 8.7 display results for such specification for each country. Unfortunately, none of the controls is significant, nor does the inclusion of the squares of the fiscal variables help to improve the situation much. Even columns present the results for an augmented specification in which the foreign fiscal variables are interacted with a dummy for EMU: in this way we can directly test the hypothesis that with the introduction of the single currency the fiscal position of other EMU member countries has gained importance. Relevant coefficients are significant in some cases (above all Italy), though the surplus coefficients display the wrong sign (so that a larger primary balance would result in a higher interest rate).

Alternatively, we test the hypothesis that equation (8.7) represents a long-run equilibrium relation and therefore test I(1) variables for cointegration. Residual-based tests on the four equations of the SUR give conflicting results: it is possible to reject the null of unit root (equivalent to no cointegration) for Italy, France and the Netherlands at 5%, 10% and 12.5% respectively, while this hypothesis cannot be rejected in the case of Germany. Nonetheless, we have decided to keep the four equations together and estimate the whole SUR by dynamic GLS (DGLS), as suggested by Stock and Watson (1993). Results are reported in Table 8.7: many coefficients are now significantly different from zero, but signs often change when

Table 8.7 Impact of domestic and foreign fiscal variables on yields

	France		*Germany*		*Italy*		*Netherlands*	
	(1)	*(2)*	*(3)*	*(4)*	*(5)*	*(6)*	*(7)*	*(8)*
3-month rate	−0.034	−0.039	−0.024	−0.040	−0.006	−0.020	−0.047	−0.054
	(2.57)*	(2.86)**	(1.33)	(2.02)*	(0.33)	(1.15)	(2.33)*	(2.59)*
Δ inflation	0.013	0.008	0.017	0.010	−0.107	−0.091	−0.005	−0.009
	(0.55)	(0.31)	(1.46)	(0.85)	(1.62)	(1.40)	(0.37)	(0.62)
Δ $(surplus/GDP)_{dom}$	−0.011	0.014	0.013	0.080	0.009	0.118	−0.004	−0.011
	(0.36)	(0.37)	(0.47)	(1.91)	(0.28)	(2.51)*	(0.19)	(0.51)
Δ $(debt/GDP)_{dom}$	−0.012	−0.009	0.010	0.019	−0.009	−0.017	−0.004	−0.005
	(0.38)	(0.27)	(0.61)	(1.06)	(0.43)	(0.88)	(0.32)	(0.35)
Δ $(surplus/GDP)_{for}$	−0.002	−0.032	0.005	−0.061	−0.098	−0.331	0.016	0.008
	(0.04)	(0.61)	(0.16)	(1.19)	(1.13)	(2.99)**	(0.37)	(0.18)
Δ $(debt/GDP)_{for}$	0.028	0.023	−0.018	−0.020	−0.079	−0.080	−0.019	−0.022
	(0.94)	(0.78)	(0.86)	(0.94)	(1.59)	(1.74)	(0.70)	(0.85)
Δ $(surplus/GDP)_{for}$ •EMU		0.157		0.250		0.813		0.216
		(1.27)		(1.94)		(3.12)**		(1.72)
Δ $(debt/GDP)_{for}$ •EMU		−0.003		−0.007		−0.019		−0.004
		(0.73)		(1.36)		(2.89)**		(0.89)
Observations	50	50	55	55	52	52	51	51
Adjusted R^2	−0.08	−0.05	−0.12	−0.06	0.03	0.11	−0.11	−0.06

Notes
SUR on 1st difference of dependent variable; monthly data; absolute value of HAC robust t-statistics in parenthesis; * significant at 5%; ** significant at 1%; constant and time trend not shown.

Table 8.8 DGLS estimates of the cointegrating relation

	France	*Germany*	*Italy*	Netherlands
	(1)	*(2)*	*(3)*	*(4)*
3-month rate	−0.051	−0.077	0.011	−0.121
	(4.70)**	(3.21)**	(0.43)	(3.53)**
inflation	0.044	−0.098	0.038	−0.096
	(2.28)*	(5.21)**	(0.48)	(5.33)**
$(\text{surplus/GDP})_{\text{dom}}$	0.037	−0.138	0.111	−0.145
	(1.05)	(6.28)**	(1.41)	(4.14)**
$(\text{debt/GDP})_{\text{dom}}$	0.209	0.016	−0.066	−0.130
	(5.36)**	(1.14)	(3.51)**	(8.28)**
$(\text{surplus/GDP})_{\text{for}}$	−0.083	0.171	−0.249	0.119
	(1.97)*	(7.51)**	(1.64)	(3.05)**
$(\text{debt/GDP})_{\text{for}}$	−0.178	−0.034	−0.046	0.081
	(4.71)**	(3.90)**	(3.16)**	(6.43)**
Observations	49	52	51	49
Adjusted R^2	0.76	0.94	0.92	0.82

Notes
1st difference of dependent variable; monthly data; absolute value of HAC robust t-statistics in parentheses; * significant at 5%; ** significant at 1%; constant and time trend not shown.

we move from one country to another and it is frankly difficult to tell a clear pattern in the results.

The fact that every country reacts differently to changes in its own fiscal position and in that of other countries may be read as a clue that financial markets can efficiently discriminate among different borrowers. This implies that each country faces a cost of borrowing that depends on the status it enjoys on financial markets and on other characteristics of its economic system and that financial spillovers are not particularly relevant.

In order to test for the absorption effect mentioned by Kenen (1995), we shift our attention to bond issues rather than primary balance/GDP ratios. Stock variables continue to appear in our analysis as they proxy for market depth and hence for liquidity.

In what follows we restrict our attention to Italy and Germany, as their Central Banks publish monthly series for the amount of securities issued by the central government and their total outstanding stock. Data are taken from the statistical annexes of the monthly publications of the Banca d'Italia and the Bundesbank. The estimating equation is not very different from the previous one, although it is now refined and adapted to the new dataset:

$$\Delta ras_t^i = \alpha_0 + \alpha_1 t + \alpha_2 \Delta ras_{t-1}^i + \alpha_3 \left[\frac{issue_t}{GDP_t}\right]^i + \alpha_4 \Delta \left[\frac{debt_t}{GDP_t}\right]^i + \alpha_5 \left[\frac{issue_t}{GDP_t}\right]^j + \alpha_6 \Delta \left[\frac{debt_t}{GDP_t}\right]^j + \varepsilon_t \qquad (8.8)$$

We continue to use the RAS with respect to Switzerland as our dependent variable in order to be able to clean our data from exchange-rate risk. Superscripts i and j represent Italy or Germany: now we have a bidimensional system, which we again estimate by means of a SUR. Despite the fact that we have to focus on only two countries, we believe that they represent a significant sample in our search for financial spillovers. Germany is the leading economy in the euro area and its securities have long served as a benchmark in the bond market; Italy, on the other hand, is a large country (with respect to EMU), is characterized by a very large stock of debt and is traditionally viewed as a 'non-virtuous' country. The RAS and the total stock of debt to GDP are non-stationary and therefore enter equation (8.8) in first differences. Columns (1) and (3) of Table 8.9 report results derived from estimation using both 10-year (top panel) and 3-year bonds (bottom panel), in order to see whether different maturities display different behaviours.

Once again, coefficients on bond issues and outstanding stocks are barely significant, so that data offer not much support to the idea that, by absorbing a larger share of European saving, each government can raise the overall cost of borrowing.

The signs of the coefficients suggest that while Germany may suffer a limited degree of spillover stemming from the Italian issuing activity, the opposite does not hold. On the contrary, an increase in the stock of Italian debt has a negative impact on both the Italian and the German yield, signalling the presence of liquidity effects.

The finding that only Italian variables appear to matter (albeit marginally) lends credit to the view that financial markets are indeed able to discriminate among different issuers, so that the same action has dissimilar results depending on the identity of the debtor. Hence, the privileged status enjoyed by its securities would grant less stringent limits to the public finances of Germany, while the fact that Italy has one of the world's largest public debts implies closer surveillance by market participants.

This is reminiscent of the results by Flandreau *et al.* (1998), according to whom financial markets behave in non-linear ways and only beyond a given threshold do borrowers start feeling the bite of market discipline.[25]

Another attempt to improve the fit of the equation (and the results) consists of augmenting equation (8.8) along the line of Afonso and Strauch (2004). Table 8.9 displays on even columns the outcome of the empirical analysis when we include among the regressors the slope of the yield curve and a measure of stock market volatility. The former, which is measured by the difference between the yield on 10-year government bonds and the 3-month Euribor, captures future growth expectations: a steeper slope reduces the risk of private relative to government securities, and therefore pushes up the cost of borrowing for the government. On the contrary, the standard deviation of daily return on the S&P500 index proxies for stock market risk and is supposed to reduce the return required to hold safer assets (government bonds). Both panels of Table 8.9 highlight that such modifications do not produce any alteration in the results and give us some confidence in the fact that our findings are not driven by the particular specification chosen.

Table 8.9 Impact of bond issues on yields

	Italy		*Germany*	
	(1)	*(2)*	*(3)*	*(4)*
	panel A: 10-year rate			
Δ ras_{t-1}	−0.131	−0.140	−0.187	−0.184
	(1.93)	(2.06)*	(2.98)**	(2.94)**
Δ slp_t		0.024		0.053
		(0.39)		(1.25)
S&P500 volatility		4.922		0.989
		(1.40)		(0.41)
$(issue/GDP)_{ita}$	0.02	0.02	0.016	0.016
	(1.55)	(1.58)	(1.79)	(1.75)
Δ $(stock/GDP)_{ita}$	−0.008	−0.008	−0.011	−0.011
	(0.90)	(0.92)	(1.76)	(1.70)
$(issue/GDP)_{ger}$	−0.015	−0.015	−0.011	−0.01
	(0.67)	(0.67)	(0.74)	(0.64)
Δ $(stock/GDP)_{ger}$	0.015	0.016	0.017	0.016
	(0.82)	(0.89)	(1.43)	(1.26)
Observations	159	159	170	170
Adjusted R^2	0.01	0.05	0.16	0.16
	panel B: 3-year rate			
Δ ras_{t-1}	−0.311	−0.314	−0.352	−0.354
	(4.13)**	(4.14)**	(5.52)**	(5.56)**
Δ slp_t		0.008		0.085
		(0.11)		(1.50)
S&P500 volatility		1.892		0.869
		(0.48)		(0.26)
$(issue/GDP)_{ita}$	0.024	0.024	0.018	0.017
	(1.54)	(1.52)	(1.49)	(1.41)
Δ $(stock/GDP)_{ita}$	−0.016	−0.015	−0.017	−0.016
	(1.43)	(1.41)	(1.98)*	(1.89)
$(issue/GDP)_{ger}$	−0.003	−0.002	−0.004	−0.002
	(0.10)	(0.07)	(0.21)	(0.09)
Δ $(stock/GDP)_{ger}$	−0.002	−0.002	0.009	0.006
	(0.11)	(0.10)	(0.53)	(0.34)
Observations	136	136	170	170
Adjusted R^2	0.06	0.05	0.16	0.16

Notes
1st difference of dependent variable; monthly data; absolute value of HAC robust t-statistics in parentheses; * significant at 5%; ** significant at 1%; constant and time trend not shown.

8.7 Conclusions

The paper has investigated the presence of negative financial spillovers among euro area government bond yields and their relations with fiscal imbalances. While returns on assets issued by different European governments do show a large degree of co-movements, little evidence emerges to relate this common dynamics to the fiscal positions of EMU members.

We have reviewed a number of open economy models, focusing in particular on the predictions about the effect of a fiscal expansion on the international rate of interest. Theory does not provide clear-cut indications: different models give different outcomes; hence, the issue of fiscal spillovers remains an empirical question.

We have analysed the impact of German unification on European interest rates. Since this represented a large shift in the fiscal and external position of the leading European economy, one would expect it to result in a sensible movement in the cost of borrowing faced by other countries as capital started flowing into Germany to finance unification. Contrary to these predictions, evidence offers little support to the spillover hypothesis and shows that the fiscal deterioration affected only domestic interest rates.

The negative financial spillover hypothesis takes for granted that a relation exists linking domestic fiscal variables and interest rates. To gather some evidence on the topic, we have investigated whether the fiscal position of the euro area as a whole has any impact on the average yield of European government bonds. Econometric analysis does not highlight any significant relation between the two variables and therefore adds to the number of studies that postulates the neutrality of fiscal variables with respect to the cost of borrowing.

In the last part of the paper we have directly examined the behaviour of bonds issued by some EMU member governments. We have used a number of different specifications and considered both fiscal variables and bond issues in order to directly test the absorption hypothesis. Results are less clear-cut, but overall it appears that neither fiscal imbalances nor issuance activity have the direct negative impact on interest rates postulated in the SGP.

Notes

1 I am grateful to Roberto Tamborini, Axel Leijonhufvud, Gabriella Berloffa, Christopher Gilbert, Giuliana Passamani, seminar participants at Università di Trento and at the workshops Lectures on Macroeconomic Governance in the EMU, and The Architecture of Financial System Stability: from Market Micro Structure to Monetary Policy for helpful comments. Flavio Bazzana, Giorgio Cipriani, Gabriella Mazzalai and Enrico Salvetta helped me with the data. All remaining mistakes are only mine.

2 The experience of New York State default in 1975 may have made American financial markets efficient in controlling public borrowers.

3 In practice only large enough countries are likely to produce this result.

4 See Mundell (1963), Mundell (1964) and Fleming (1962).

5 For a comprehensive analysis of the role of fiscal policy in the neoclassical model see Barro (1989).

6 Relaxing any of the basic assumptions, the predictions of the model change: 'Ricardian equivalence' between debt and taxes ceases to hold and 'Keynesian' outcomes on the interest rate emerge. For instance, by assuming finite horizons for households, one obtains that higher future taxes will be levied partly after the death of currently living agents, so that government spending has a wealth effect that increases present consumption, reduces saving and bids up the interest rate (the Ricardian result continues to hold in presence of intergenerational altruism: hence, more than finite horizons themselves, what matters is the degree of linkage across generations). Other extensions

account for imperfect credit markets where different groups face different interest rates, uncertainty about future taxes and income streams and the presence of distortionary taxation.

7 The reason is that output is demand determined: therefore an unanticipated temporary rise in G_t results in a temporary rise in world output, with no effect on the amount of resource available to the private sector (see Obstfeld and Rogoff, 1996, chapter 10 for details).

8 See for instance Flandreau *et al.* (1998).

9 Empirically, Cottarelli and Mecagni (1991) find that, during the 1970s and 1980s, supply factors seem more relevant than risk indicators in pushing up the interest rate on Italian public debt. On the other hand, Codogno *et al.* (2003) conclude that international risk factors dominate liquidity in determining the yield spreads among EMU bonds.

10 In terms of debt/GDP ratio Germany is not the worst performer among European countries: in the same period, in fact, France and Italy display an even faster growth of debt relative to GDP. The economic expansion triggered by unification, together with the poor economic performances suffered by many European countries in the beginning of the 1990s can explain this apparent oddity.

11 A different measures of the flow impact of German unification can be found in Tamborini (1997, table 8.3). It is given by the ratio of government net borrowing (GNB) to the sum of gross private saving in the EU12 countries (GPS12) and measures the absorption of EU saving due to each national borrowing needs. German figures jump from 1.8% (1986–90) to 4.2% (1991–95).

12 Rose and Svensson (1994) quote the behavior of interest rates –which did not jump up until the onset of the crisis – to corroborate this view.

13 An alternative explanation for the lack of financial spillovers is that the latter were 'compressed' by accommodating monetary policies in European countries, unsustainable in light of the anti-inflationary stance pursued by the Bundesbank. While it is certainly true that a conflict between Germany and other countries emerged as the former economy was heating up under the stimulus of unification while Europe was sliding towards a recession, there is little evidence supporting the view that the British and Italian authorities pursued a particularly loose monetary policy in the period between German unification and the EMS crisis.

14 Yet one has to recognize that it is possible to observe no correlation between fiscal variables and interest rates for reasons that have little to do with Ricardian equivalence.

15 Seater (1993) is often regarded as the main reference on the topic, though it is somehow dated.

16 Preliminary analysis has been conducted also on nominal yields and, following Kormendi and Protopapadakis (2004), on the impact of fiscal imbalances on the current account: results gave a similar qualitative picture but were of a lesser statistical quality and are therefore not reported.

17 Hence we expect the coefficient on this variable to be negative as an increase in the primary balance should lower the borrowing cost faced by the government.

18 ADF, Phillips-Perron and KPSS tests.

19 Coefficients remains not statistically different from zero also when (8.2) is augmented with the squares of fiscal variables (primary balance and debt to GDP) to capture non-linear effects. Also, using the difference between long- and short-term yields as the dependent variable does not alter the results.

20 Data are taken from the ECB *Monthly Bulletin*, which is the reference for more information on the data.

21 See among others Lemmen and Goodhart (1999); Lønning (2000); Camarero *et al.* (2003); Codogno *et al.* (2003); Dunne *et al.* (2003); Hartman *et al.* (2003); Afonso and Strauch (2004); Bernoth *et al.* (2004); Piga and Valente (2004).

22 If the interest rate faced by a country depends on all other EMU countries' behaviour it is not possible to assess whether a lower yield spread between, say Italian and German

bonds depends on the strengthening of the Italian fiscal fundamentals, or rather on the effect of a weak Italian position on German yields (or on a mixture of the two effects).

23 We have chosen not to use the indicator of discretionary fiscal stance à la Blanchard (1990) because the first stage fit needed to compute the sensitivity of the primary balance to GDP growth (from which the Blanchard indicator is then constructed) is extremely poor and therefore our estimates very imprecise.

24 Previous versions of the work used both disaggregated fiscal variables for the four countries and monthly series obtained by interpolation. Results were dominated by noise and very poor and therefore are not reported.

25 To explore this intuition in more detail we have added the squares of bond issues and debt stocks to the estimating equation, but the picture does not change. Also, we have interacted them with a dummy for EMU, but again these new controls were not significant and results are not shown.

References

Afonso, A. and Strauch, R. (2004), 'Fiscal policy events and interest rate swap spreads: evidence from the EU', Working Paper 303, European Central Bank.

Aoki, M. and Leijonhufvud, A. (1987), 'The stock-flow analysis of investment', Working Paper 445, UCLA.

Ardagna, S., Caselli, F. and Lane, T. (2004), 'Fiscal discipline and the cost of public debt service: some estimates for OECD countries', Working Paper 10788, NBER.

Artis, M. and Winkler, B. (1999), 'The Stability Pact: trading off flexibility for credibility?', in M. Hughes Hallett, M. Hutchinson and S. Hougaard Jensen (eds), *Fiscal Aspects of European Monetary Integration*, Cambridge: Cambridge University Press. 157–88.

Baele, L., Ferrando, A., Hördahl, P., Krylova, E. and Monnet, C. (2004), 'Measuring financial integration in the euro area', Occasional Paper 14, ECB.

Barro, R. (1989), 'The neoclassical approach to fiscal policy', in R. Barro (ed.), *Modern Business Cycle Theory*, Cambridge: Harvard University Press. 178–235.

Bayoumi, T., Goldstein, M. and Woglom, G. (1993), 'Do credit markets discipline sovereign borrowers? Evidence from U.S. states', *Journal of Money Credit and Banking*, 27: 1045–59.

Beetsma, R. and Vermeylen, K. (2005), 'The effect of monetary unification on public debt and its real return', Working Paper 1400, CESifo.

Bernoth, K., von Hagen, J. and Schuknecht, L. (2004), 'Sovereign risk premia in the European bond market', Discussion Paper 4465, CEPR.

Blanchard, O. (1985), 'Debt, deficits and finite horizons', *Journal of Political Economy*, 93: 223–47.

—— (1990), 'Suggestions for a new set of fiscal indicators', Working Paper 79, OECD Economics Department.

Branson, W. (1988), 'International adjustment and the dollar: policy illusions and economic constraints', in W. Guth (ed.), *Economic Policy Coordination*, IMF. 44–84.

Breedon, F., Henry, B. and Williams, G. (1999), 'Long–term interest rates: evidence on the global capital market', *Oxford Review of Economic Policy*, 15: 128–42.

Brunila, A., Hukkinen, J. and Tujula, M. (1999), 'Indicators of the cyclically adjusted budget balance: the Bank of Finland's experience', Discussion Paper 1, Bank of Finland.

Buiter, W., Corsetti, G. and Roubini, N. (1993), 'Disavanzo eccessivo, ragionevolezza e nonsenso nel Trattato di Maastricht', *Rivista di Politica Economica*, VI: 3–82.

Bundesbank (1997), 'Trends in public sector debt since German unification', *Deutsche Bundesbank Monthly Report*, March: 17–31.

Camarero, M., Ordoñez, J. and Tamarit, C. (2003), 'Tests for interest rate convergence and structural break in the EMS: further analysis', *Applied Financial Economics*, 12: 447–56.

Cheung, S. (1996), 'Provincial credit ratings in Canada: an ordered probit analysis', Working Paper 96-6, Bank of Canada.

Chinn, M. and Frankel, J. (2003), 'The euro area and world interest rates', Working Paper 03-17, Santa Cruz Center for International Economics.

Codogno, L., Favero, C. and Missale, A. (2003), 'Governement bond spreads', *Economic Policy*, 18: 503–32.

Corsetti, G. and Pesenti, P. (2001), 'Welfare and macroeconomic interdependence', *Quarterly Journal of Economics*, 116: 421–45.

Cottarelli, C. and Mecagni, M. (1991), 'The risk premium over Italian government debt, 1976–88', in T. Mayer and F. Spinelli (eds), *Macroeconomics and Macroeconomic Policy Issues*, Vol. 11/91 of *Quaderni di Economia e Banca*, Trento: Banca di Trento e Bolzano. 33–72.

Diamond, P. (1965), 'National debt in a neoclassic growth model', *American Economic Review*, 55: 1126–50.

Dornbusch, R. and Wolf, H. (1992), 'Economic transition in Eastern Germany', *Brookings Papers on Economic Activity*, 1: 235–72.

Dunne, P., Moore, M. and Portes, R. (2003), 'Defining benchmark status: an application using euro-area bonds', Working Paper 9087, NBER.

Eichengreen, B. and Wyplosz, C. (1993), 'The unstable EMS', *Brookings Papers on Economic Activity*, 1: 51–143.

Farina, F. and Tamborini, R. (2002), 'Le politiche di stabilizzazione in Europa nel nuovo regime di unione monetaria', in F. Farina and R. Tamborini (eds), *Da Nazioni a Regioni. Mutamenti Strutturali e Istituzionali dopo l'Ingresso nella Unione Monetaria Europea*, Bologna: Il Mulino. 15–126.

Favero, C. (2001), *Applied Macroeconometrics*, Oxford: Oxford University Press.

Flandreau, M., Le Cacheaux, J. and Zumer, F. (1998), 'Stability without a pact? Lessons form the European gold standard, 1880–1914', *Economic Policy*, 13: 115–62.

Fleming, M. (1962), 'Domestic financial policies under fixed and under floating exchange rates', IMF Staff Papers, 9: 369–79.

Ford, R. and Laxton, D. (1999), 'World public debt and real interest rates', *Oxford Review of Economic Policy*, 15: 77–94.

Frenkel, J. and Razin, A. (1992), *Fiscal Policies and the World Economy*, 2nd edn, Cambridge: The MIT Press.

Giavazzi, F. and Pagano, M. (1988), 'The advantage of tying one's hands: EMS discipline and central bank credibility', *European Economic Review*, 32: 1055–82.

Gravelle, T. (1999), 'Liquidity of the government of Canada securities market: stylized facts and some market microstructure comparisons to the United States treasury market', Working Paper 11, Bank of Canada.

Hartman, P., Maddaloni, A. and Manganelli, S. (2003), 'The euro area financial system: structure, integration and policy initiatives', Working Paper 230, ECB.

Kenen, P. (1995), *Economic and Monetary Union in Europe*, Cambridge: Cambridge University Press.

Kormendi, R. and Protopapadakis, A. (2004), 'Budget deficits, current account deficits and interest rates: the systematic evidence on Ricardian equivalence', Macroeconomics

0403010, EconWPA. Online. Available HTTP: <http://ideas.repec.org/p/wpa/wuwpma/0403010.html> (accessed 18 October 2006).

Lamfalussy, A. (1989), 'Macro-coordination of fiscal policies in an economic and monetary union in Europe', in Committee for the Study of Economic and Monetary Union (ed.), *Report on Economic and Monetary Union in the European Community*, Office for the Official Publications of the European Communities. 91–125.

Leith, C. and Wren-Lewis, S. (2001), 'Compatibility between monetary and fiscal policy under EMU', Discussion paper in Economics 01-15, University of Glasgow.

Lemmen, J. and Goodhart, C. (1999), 'Credit risk and European government bond markets: a panel data econometric analysis', *Eastern Economic Journal*, 25: 77–107.

Lønning, I. (2000), 'Default premia on European government debt', *Weltwirtschaftliches Archiv*, 136: 259–83.

Mundell, R. (1963), 'Capital mobility and stabilization policy under fixed and flexible exchange rates', *Canadian Journal of Economics and Political Science*, 29: 475–85.

—— (1964), 'A reply: capital mobility and size', *Canadian Journal of Economics and Political Science*, 30: 421–31.

Obstfeld, M. and Rogoff, K. (1996), *Foundations of International Macroeconomics*, Cambridge: The MIT Press.

Perée, E. and Steinherr, A. (2001), 'The euro and capital markets: a new era', *World Economy*, 24: 1295–308.

Piga, G. and Valente, G. (2004), 'The term structure of interest rates and the public debt issuance policy: a note', *Finance Letters*, 2.

Restoy, F. (1996), 'Interest rates and fiscal discipline in monetary unions', *European Economic Review*, 40: 1629–46.

Rose, A. and Svensson, L. (1994), 'European exchange rate credibility before the fall', *European Economic Review*, 38: 1185–216.

Seater, J. (1993), 'Ricardian equivalence', *Journal of Economic Literature*, 31: 142–90.

Sinn, H.-W. (1996), 'International implication of German unification', Working Paper 5839, NBER.

Stock, J. and Watson, M. (1993), 'A simple estimator of cointegrating vectors in higher order integrated systems', *Econometrica*, 61: 783–820.

Tamborini, R. (1997), 'Living in the EMU. The dynamics of the Maastricht Treaty's fiscal rules', *Rivista Italiana degli Economisti*, II: 335–59.

—— (2002), 'One monetary giant with many fiscal dwarfs: the efficiency of macroeconomic stabilization policies in the EMU', Discussion paper 4.02, Dipartimento di Economia, Università di Trento.

Thygesen, N. (1999), 'Fiscal institutions in EMU and the Stability Pact', in A. Hughes Hallett, M. Hutchinson and S. Hougaard Jensen (eds), *Fiscal Aspects of European Monetary Integration*, Cambridge: Cambridge University Press. 15–36.

9 Inflation divergence and public deficits in a monetary union*

J. Creel and J. Le Cacheux

9.1 Introduction

The relationship between public deficits (or fiscal policy), inflation and interest rates has long given rise to an abundant literature. Two distinct seminal works can be emphasized. On the one hand, the Hicksian IS-LM model (see Hicks, 1937) reveals the positive short-term effect of public deficits on nominal interest rate. The ensuing 'crowding-out' effect would be detrimental to GDP. On the other hand, Diamond (1965)[1] showed that, in the long run, higher public deficits and debt may enhance social welfare when the capital stock exceeds the golden rule level (e.g. when the interest rate is below its natural level). In both cases, higher deficits and debts push interest rates up and private investment down.

This line of reasoning has been used as an argument for restricting fiscal policies in a monetary union: an expansionary fiscal policy would produce 'beggar-thy-neighbour' effects, since higher interest rates would be undergone not only by the country implementing the policy but also by the other monetary union member states. Although not the single argument,[2] it had strong influence on the adoption of fiscal convergence criteria in the Maastricht Treaty and on the enactment of the Stability and Growth Pact.

Despite strong theoretical support, the crowding-out effect remains disputable (see the seminal paper of B. Friedman, 1978, and a recent survey by Ducoudré, 2005). In a monetary union, for instance, wider financial markets after the monetary union was constituted reduce the sensitiveness of long-term interest rates to a domestic deficit.

The controversy between those arguing about crowding-out effects and those arguing about crowding-in effects remains important in the euro area. According to the former, higher deficits would produce higher interest rates, whereas, for the others, the reverse could be true. In empirical terms, since 1999, the discrepancy in fiscal deficits among euro area's member states has been large, while divergent inflation rates and divergent real interest rates have persisted. Is one responsible for the other? In this paper, we wish to analyse precisely the interrelationships between these variables and wish to study the determinants of inflation divergence and fiscal policies' divergence.

To do so, we take as a point of departure a recent model elaborated by R. Beetsma and K. Vermeylen (2005). Their model is an elegant framework which links real rates of return, public debts and inflation rates in a monetary union made up of a multiplicity of countries. They concluded that within a monetary union, 'the expected real interest rate paid on public debt exceeds its pre-unification level'. This result is explained as follows: 'a (public) debt increase in one country exerts a direct positive effect on the required rate of return on other countries' (public) debt when these countries all form a monetary union, while this effect is absent when the countries do not form a union.' They conclude that: 'monetary unification may cause worries in low-debt countries about the fiscal discipline of highly-indebted countries'.

This would suggest that crowding-out effects are larger after unification than before. However, their model is unable to fit the evidence on the two above-mentioned divergent patterns in the euro area: Beetsma and Vermeylen assume that inflation is perfectly correlated across countries participating in a monetary union and, by construction, real interest rates are also perfectly correlated.

We decided to use their model, but to relax the assumption of perfectly correlated inflation and real interest rates in a monetary union and to introduce inflation divergence instead. This led us to an inconsistency in the conclusion of the model. To solve the inconsistency, we introduce a distinction between two categories of public expenditures, productive and unproductive ones. The resulting model is admittedly rather different in spirit from Beetsma and Vermeylen's, but it seems more in line with reality in the euro area; and also to produce new results.

With this new framework, we demonstrate that the causation between inflation rates (and interest rates) and public deficits is reversed in comparison with Beetsma and Vermeylen's earlier statement. Our model then explains public deficits' divergence within the euro area by inflation divergence. Finally, an empirical investigation gives some support to this theoretical conclusion.

9.2 The stylized facts

The relationship between public deficits and long-term interest rates has a long history which goes beyond the scope of this paper.[3] Simple statistics may be used to shed light on this relationship within the euro area.

The early years of the Stability and Growth Pact have been rather turbulent: despite general improvements of public finances in 1999 and 2000, public deficits have started increasing in 2001 in all euro area countries, except Belgium and France, where the starting point was 2002, and Spain, whose starting point was 2004 (see Figure 9.1). Four countries among the ten euro area member states[4] have even exceeded the deficit threshold: France and Germany since 2002, Portugal in 2001 and the Netherlands in 2003.

Although the Stability and Growth Pact was meant as a mechanism fostering fiscal discipline, it has been poorly enforced. The rationale behind the discipline embedded in the Pact is to prevent inflationary pressures that the independent

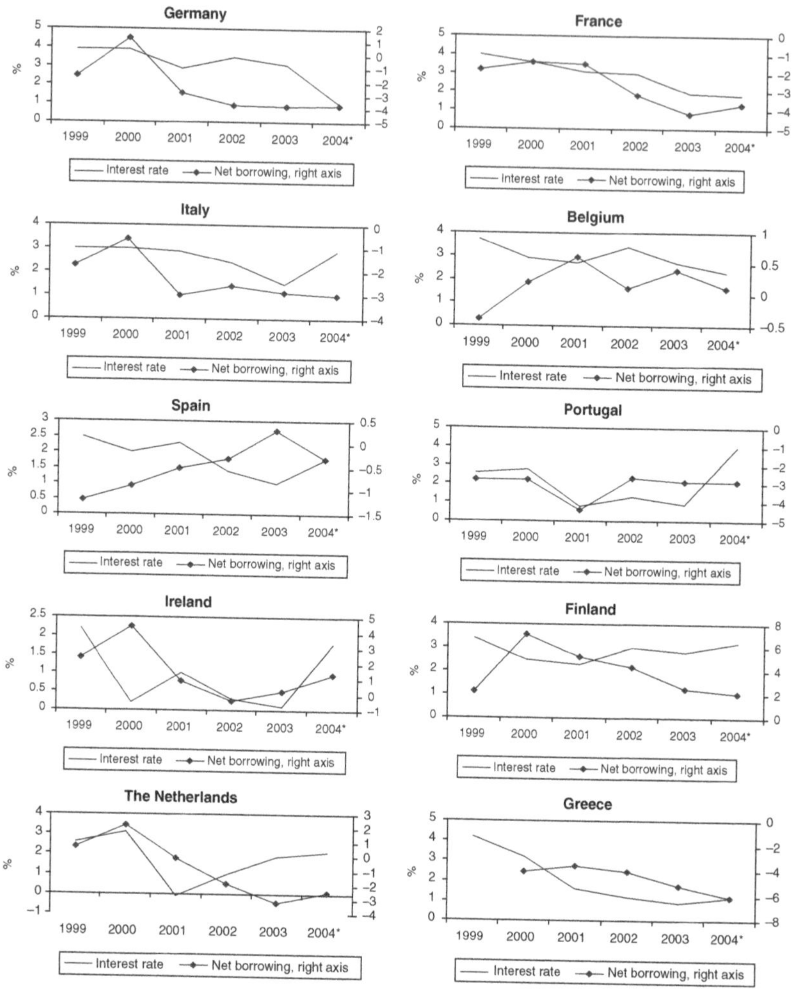

Figure 9.1 Public deficits and interest rates in Euro area countries.

Source: European Commission, Spring Forecasts 2005.

Notes

Interest rate means "real long-term interest rate", i.e. nominal long-term interest rate deflated by the yearly variation of the harmonized index of consumer prices. *Net borrowing* is net borrowing of general government expressed in percent of GDP.

European Central Bank would have to curb ultimately. With binding fiscal constraints, the ECB was meant to be able to focus on private inflation determinants and to improve the overall price competitiveness of the euro area.[5]

So, has the indiscipline of some major euro area countries led to higher inflation or to higher real interest rates on public bonds?

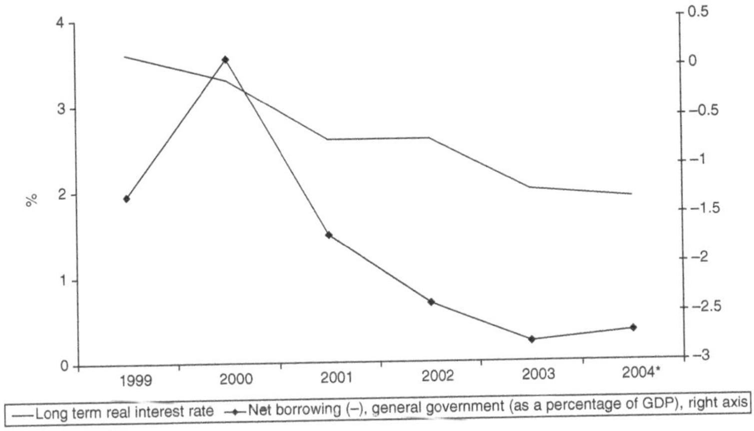

Figure 9.2 Public deficit and the real long-term interest rate in the Euro area.

Source: European Commission, Spring Forecasts 2005.

Figure 9.2 displays the evolution of public finances and that of real long-term interest rates in the euro area; it appears that a sensible decrease in the long-term real interest rate has occurred despite a sharp increase in public deficits.

Except in Belgium, Spain and Finland, a positive relationship between public surpluses and real interest rates is also found in most of the euro area countries (*cf.* Figure 9.1).

9.3 The euro area's puzzle

Of course, basic empirical evidence that poorly disciplined fiscal policies do not seem to have increased real interest rates is not a necessary or sufficient proof for rejection of the theory of crowding-out effects. The above-presented data do not permit discrimination between different determinants of long-term interest rates. Indeed, the fiscal part of these determinants may have been compensated by an appropriate monetary policy, a dramatic change in the liquidity preference of households and so on.

If macroeconomic data are useless in this respect, we propose to turn towards a micro-founded theoretical model to investigate the real long-term interest rates' determinants. Beetsma and Vermeylen (2005) have developed a nice micro-founded framework in which they model the link between public debt and the interest rate in a general equilibrium setting. They make use of two strong assumptions: the correlations among inflation rates and among real long-term interest rates are increasing and finally perfect when countries form a monetary union, to be compared with the pre-union situation. These two assumptions are crucial for their final conclusion, according to which an extended union-wide crowding-out effect is expected when one country in the monetary union increases its public debt.

Nevertheless, diverging monetary conditions within the euro area can be identified in the covariance matrices, respectively for the real long-term interest rates (Table 9.1) and for the inflation rates (Table 9.2) between 1999 and 2004. In these tables, we have set in bold the values of the covariance which were at least superior to 0.5. In the first case, only Greece and to a lesser extent Germany seem to have converging long-run real interest rates vis-à-vis their euro area partners. In the second case, only the Netherlands seems to generate a covariance of their inflation rate with that of other countries superior to 0.5. Convergent inflation rates occur among 'small countries' (Austria, Greece and Portugal vis-à-vis the Netherlands), but still remain a scarce situation.

Data in Figure 9.3 also show that the convergence of long-term real interest rates within the euro area is far from complete. The same applies to the inflation rates

Table 9.1 Covariance matrix for the long term real interest rates in the Euro area, 1999–2004

	Bel	*Dnk*	*Grc*	*Spa*	*Fra*	*Ire*	*Ita*	*Nld*	*Aus*	*Por*
Bel										
Dnk	0.4									
Grc	0.4	0.6								
Spa	0.1	0.1	0.5							
Fra	0.4	0.6	0.8	0.3						
Ire	0.1	−0.2	0.7	0.4	0.3					
Ita	0.0	−0.1	0.4	0.3	0.2	0.4				
Nld	0.1	−0.1	0.5	0.0	0.0	0.4	0.0			
Aus	0.4	0.8	0.7	0.1	0.6	0.1	0.0	0.1		
Por	−0.1	−0.8	0.4	0.2	−0.2	0.8	0.4	0.7	−0.3	
Fin	0.1	0.0	0.2	0.0	0.0	0.2	0.0	0.3	0.1	0.3

Sources: European Commission, authors' computations.

Table 9.2 Covariance matrix for the inflation rates in the Euro area, 1999–2004

	Bel	*Dnk*	*Grc*	*Spa*	*Fra*	*Ire*	*Ita*	*Nld*	*Aus*	*Por*
Bel										
Dnk	0.2									
Grc	0.1	0.2								
Spa	0.1	0.1	0.2							
Fra	0.1	0.1	0.3	0.2						
Ire	0.4	0.2	0.4	0.5	0.4					
Ita	0.1	0.1	0.2	0.2	0.2	0.3				
Nld	0.3	0.4	0.6	0.1	0.2	0.2	0.0			
Aus	0.3	0.3	0.3	0.2	0.2	0.5	0.1	0.5		
Por	0.2	0.3	0.4	0.1	0.3	0.3	0.1	0.8	0.4	
Fin	0.4	0.2	0.1	0.2	0.1	0.5	0.1	0.4	0.4	0.2

Source: European Commission, authors' computations.

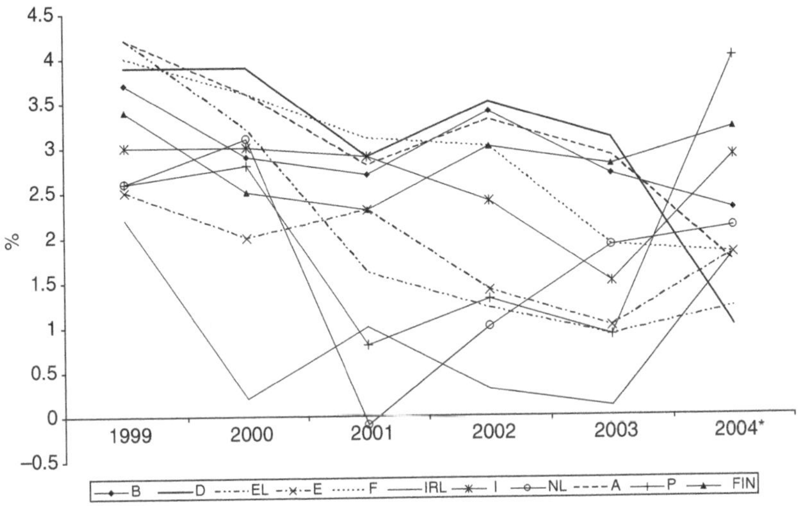

Figure 9.3 Domestic real long term interest rates in the Euro area.

Source: European Commission, Spring Forecasts 2005.

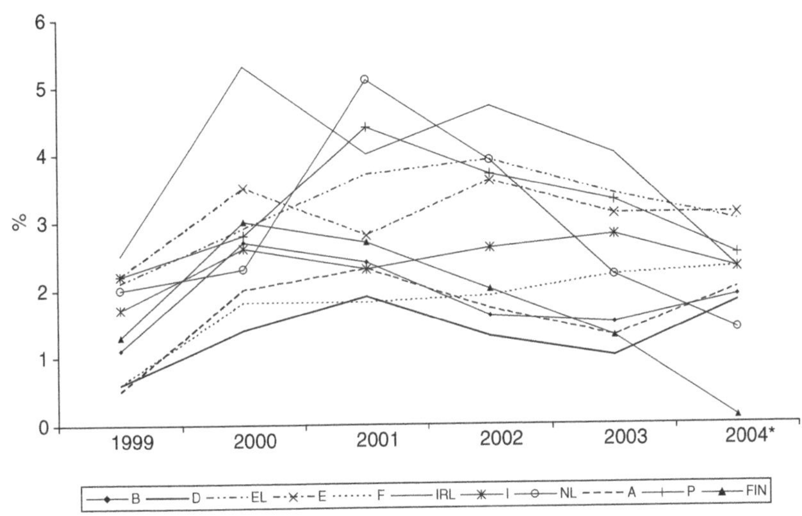

Figure 9.4 Domestic HICP-based inflation rates in the Euro area.

Source: European Commission, Spring Forecasts 2005.

(*cf.* Figure 9.4); although convergence has improved since 1999, except the recent experiences of the Netherlands and Finland, the range of domestic inflation rates is still large and explains the discrepancy of real interest rates: nominal interest rates have already converged, but insofar as inflation divergence within the euro area persists, so does real interest rate spreads. Identifying the sources of inflation divergence is crucial in this respect.

The convergence of nominal long-term interest rates reveals that financial markets do not discriminate among euro area's governments despite the *no-bail-out* clause. For those who argue that inflation trends impinge on long-run nominal interest rates along the Fisher equation, for instance, the present situation in the euro area, with divergent inflation rates and highly convergent nominal interest rates, is a *puzzle*.

In fact, the usual links between inflation and long-run nominal interest rates can be at least twofold. First, present inflation may fuel expectations of future inflation and, hence, may have a direct positive impact on nominal interest rates (the Fisher effect). Second, nominal interest rates and inflation rates may have a common determinant: fiscal policy. Via the goods and the capital markets, public deficits may produce inflationary pressures and may increase the nominal interest rates, hence provoking the so-called crowding-out effect. Basing upon the stylized fact that the nominal interest rate in the euro area has generally been higher the higher net [? SENSE ?] *lending* by general governments (see Figure 9.2), the crowding-out effect does not seem to be validated, and we have to turn towards the direct link between inflation and public deficits to gather the pieces of the European puzzle.

9.4 The model by Beetsma and Vermeylen

Thanks to the convergence criteria established in the Maastricht Treaty, and in a context of full liberalization of markets for goods and services (European capital markets had already been liberalized since 1990), inflation convergence in the euro area has indeed occurred in the pre-unification period; it was therefore considered likely to go on after the launching of the single currency in January 1999. Since 1999, however, inflation divergence within the euro area has been a major and early concern for the ECB[6] and has been precisely documented (Duarte, 2003; Honohan and Lane, 2003; Angeloni and Ehrmann, 2004). Most contributions endeavour to characterize the determinants of inflation divergence and they fail to conclude that public deficits have had an impact. Since Beetsma and Vermeylen's normative conclusion is exactly the opposite, it has been appealing to extend their model to make it fit the empirical literature.

Most of the assumptions that will be introduced in the model hinge extensively on the modelling choices made by Beetsma and Vermeylen. Although some are quite strong and are related to a monetarist framework, which empirical reliability is, at best, questionable, we have decided to take Beetsma and Vermeylen's model as our theoretical point of departure; their model is the most recent one trying to link public debt, inflation and real interest rates in a monetary union.

9.4.1 The model

In a world made up of N countries, where countries $1, \ldots, N^U$ form a monetary union ($N > 1$ and $1 < N^U \leq N$), countries are constituted of two-period overlapping generations of a constant size (normalized to one). The representative agent in each country i maximizes an expected lifetime quadratic utility subject to the budget constraint:

$$U_t^i = C_{1,t}^i - \frac{1}{2}\gamma\left(C_{1,t}^i\right)^2 + \frac{1}{1+\rho}E_t\left[C_{2,t+1}^i - \frac{1}{2}\gamma\left(C_{2,t+1}^i\right)^2\right] \tag{9.1}$$

$$C_{2,t+1}^i = (Y - T_{i,t} - C_{1,t}^i)\left[\sum_{j=1}^{N}\omega_{j,t}^i(1+r_{j,t+1}) + \left(1 - \sum_{j=1}^{N}\omega_{j,t}^i\right)(1+r^*)\right], \tag{9.2}$$

where $C_{1,t}^i$ *and* $C_{2,t+1}^i$ are the representative agent's consumption in periods t and $t+1$, respectively, ρ is the agent's discount rate, E_t is the expectations operator conditional on the available information, γ a positive parameter, Y the agent's endowment, $T_{i,t}$ the taxes paid by the representative agent, $\omega_{j,t}^i$ the share of this agent's savings in period t invested in public debt (or bonds) of country j, $r_{j,t+1}$ is the real interest rate paid in period $t+1$ on public debt and r^* the real, risk-free, interest rate on private savings.

Each government is able to spend an amount $G_{i,t}$ at period t and finance it by raising taxes $T_{i,t}$ and/or by issuing public debt $B_{i,t}$, following the usual dynamic budget constraint:

$$B_{i,t} = G_{i,t} + B_{i,t-1}(1+r_{i,t}) - T_{i,t}. \tag{9.3}$$

Beetsma and Vermeylen argue that fiscal policy is described as a trade-off faced by governments between the cost of raising taxes and the cost of deferring them, hence

$$L_{i,t}^{gov} = T_{i,t} + \frac{1}{1+\beta_i}E_t\left[B_{i,t}(1+r_{i,t+1})\right], \tag{9.4}$$

where parameter β_i 'captures the relative importance that government i attaches to the interests of the taxpayers'.

As for central banks, Beetsma and Vermeylen assume that: first, the central bank determines at period t the growth rate of the money supply $m_{i,t}$ from period t to $t+1$; second, the inflation rate is closely, although stochastically, related to the growth rate of the money supply:

$$\pi_{i,t} = m_{i,t}(1+\varepsilon_{i,t}), \tag{9.5}$$

with $\pi_{i,t}$ the inflation rate in country i between periods t and $t+1$, and the stochastic term $\varepsilon_{i,t} \sim N(0,\sigma^2)$ is *i.i.d.* over time and across countries; and, third, central banks' loss function incorporates two objectives: maintaining price stability and stabilizing public debt. The parameter λ in equation (9.6) below, in the case of monetary union, can be interpreted as the degree of central bank's dependence on the government:

$$L_t^{cb,u} = \frac{1}{2} E_t \left(\pi_{t+1}^u\right)^2 + \lambda^u E_t \left[\frac{1}{N^u} \sum_{i=1}^{N^u} B_{i,t}(1 + r_{i,t+1}) \right], \tag{9.6}$$

with $\lambda^u > 0$ and N^U is the number of countries (out of N) forming a monetary union.

Under perfect foresight, the expected *nominal* interest rate is equal to the actual future *nominal* interest rate, hence

$$r_{i,t+1} = r_{i,t+1}^e + \pi_{i,t}^e - \pi_{i,t}, \tag{9.5b}$$

and as uncertainty in the model only stems from the inflation rate (equation (9.5)), the variance of the domestic real debt return follows:

$$Var_t(r_{i,t+1}) = Var_t(\pi_{i,t+1}) = m_{i,t+1}^2 \sigma^2. \tag{9.7}$$

Unlike Beetsma and Vermeylen, we disregard the assumption that inflation rates and, thus here, real debt returns would be perfectly correlated across countries in the monetary union. On the contrary, and as discussed in the preceding section, these correlations are low and we assume in the following that they are very close to zero, hence

$$\begin{aligned} \text{cov}_t(r_{i,t+1}; r_{j,t+1}) &= 0 \quad \forall i \neq j \\ \text{cov}_t(\pi_{i,t}; \pi_{j,t}) &= 0 \quad \forall i \neq j. \end{aligned} \tag{9.8}$$

These assumptions do introduce inflation divergence in the framework. Note that they will have a strong consequence on the inconsistency we have found in Beetsma and Vermeylen's conclusions. This we interpret as a weakness of their framework: they can demonstrate a close relationship between public debt, inflation rate and real interest rates, but only insofar as inflation divergence is understated.

9.4.2 An inconsistent result under EMU

Incorporating the budget constraint of the representative young agent of country i in her first-order conditions with respect to her decisions to hold country j's public debt and to invest in the risk-free technology, and aggregating across the representative agents of the different countries, taking into account the equilibrium conditions and assuming that $r^* = \rho$, where ρ is the agent's discount rate, the 'mean-variance'-expression for the demand for country i's debt as a function of the expected real interest rate is

$$r_{i,t+1}^e = r^* + \mu_t \left[B_{i,t} Var_t(r_{i,t+1}) \right] \tag{9.9}$$

with $\mu_t = \frac{\gamma}{N(1-\gamma \bar{C}_{1,t})}$; and $\bar{C}_{1,t} = \frac{C_{1,t}}{N}$.

The intuition is as follows: representative agents demand public debt until its real return equals the real return on private assets plus a risk premium proportional to public debt's holdings and the variability of the real interest rate. Thanks to diversification opportunities, the risk premium is lower, the higher the number of the countries in the world. Moreover, a growing debt might reduce the real rate of return but only insofar as the variance of this rate is also sharply reduced.

In a Nash situation, each government minimizes its loss function (9.4) subject to its budget constraint (9.3). Full information incorporated in (9.9) is given, so that

$$r^{e}_{i,t+1} = \beta_i - \mu_t \left[B_{i,t} Var_t(r_{i,t+1})\right]. \tag{9.10}$$

For countries participating in a monetary union, the common central bank sets m^u_t to minimize equation (9.6) subject to

$$\pi_{u,t} = m_{u,t}(1 + \varepsilon_{u,t}), \tag{9.5b}$$

taking domestic debts, expected real rates of return and expected inflation rates as given, yielding

$$m^u_{t+1} = \pi^{e,u}_{t+1} = \frac{\lambda^u \bar{B}^u_t}{1+\sigma^2}, \tag{9.11}$$

with $\bar{B}^u_t = \frac{1}{N^u} \sum_{i=1}^{N^u} B^u_{i,t}$, the average level of public debt in the monetary union.

Substituting equation (9.11) into equation (9.7) gives

$$Var_t(r_{u,t+1}) = \left(\frac{\lambda^u \bar{B}^u_t}{1+\sigma^2}\right)^2 \sigma^2 \equiv \hat{\sigma}^2 \quad \forall i \in [1, N^u]. \tag{9.12}$$

The variability of the average public debt real return depends on the uncertainty of the relationship between money and average inflation, and on the average level of public debt in the monetary union.

At equilibrium eqns. (9.9) and (9.10) give the steady state level of public debt for country i:

$$B^*_{i,t} = \frac{\beta_i - r^*}{2\mu_t Var(r_{i,t+1})}. \tag{9.13}$$

Substituting (9.12) into (9.13) yields

$$B^*_{i,t} = \frac{(\beta_i - r^*)(1+\sigma^2)^2}{2\mu_t \left(\lambda^u \bar{B}^u_t\right)^2 \sigma^2}. \tag{9.14}$$

Eqn (9.14) states that the steady state level of debt in country i is lower the higher the average of public debts in the monetary union. Unfortunately, this statement is supposed to hold for any country participating in the union, hence for all countries of the union, and, of course, if all countries decrease their respective debt level, the monetary union average will also decrease, not increase!

This specification of the model incorporating inflation divergence thus leads to an inconsistency. The model by Beetsma and Vermeylen without inflation divergence is therefore highly specific. No general conclusion on the relationship between public debt and real returns can be drawn from their framework.

9.5 A variant to the model by Beetsma and Vermeylen

9.5.1 Doing without inflation divergence

Disregarding inflation divergence, a very typical situation within a monetary union arises: any country that's debt is growing, all else equal in the other countries of the monetary union, will provoke higher uncertainty in the whole union that will feed inflationary pressures. Average inflation in the monetary union can be rewritten as a function of the average public debt level, substituting equation (9.11) into equation (9.5b):

$$\pi_{u,t} = \frac{1}{N^u}\sum_{i=1}^{N^u} \pi_{i,t}^u = \frac{\lambda^u(1+\varepsilon_{u,t})}{(1+\sigma^2)}\bar{B}_t^u. \tag{9.15}$$

Average inflation rate in the monetary union also depends on the average level of public debt, so that a country implementing a *lax* fiscal policy will make its partner countries suffer from a higher average inflation rate which will trigger a restrictive monetary policy by the common central bank. This kind of argument is very usual in the macroeconomic literature. The story that one poorly behaving country can adversely affect the entire union is exactly the argument that led the governments of future EMU to legislate, in the Maastricht Treaty, that each country was responsible for its own debt and that other countries would not be bound by solidarity.

9.5.2 Taking inflation divergence seriously

However, acknowledging the presence of inflation divergence in the monetary union, the conclusion of the model is no longer satisfactory. The inconsistency has to be solved. To succeed in this task, we modified the fiscal policy part of the model. In Beetsma and Vermeylen, fiscal policy is described as a trade-off faced by governments between the cost of raising taxes and the cost of deferring them (their equation (4)). In a rational expectations framework and since public expenditures are not productive, Ricardian equivalence must hold, so that private agents are indifferent between higher taxes today and higher taxes in the future. However, the trade-off as it stands in

Beetsma and Vermeylen's model is not the only choice facing fiscal policy in contemporary economies; rather, we assume that the trade-off may be between the cost of raising taxes and the cost of deferring them *only insofar as* public expenditures *are not* productive. Ricardian equivalence does not hold in this setting.

On the one hand, our assumption entails that governments have their loss *lowered* if they are able to finance *productive* expenditures via public debt issuance. On the other hand, financing such expenditures via taxation is costly. Higher taxes in period t thus reduce the lifetime welfare of the present generation, which has to pay the taxes in period t but does not benefit from the productive expenditures whose positive externalities will occur only in the future.

Public expenditures hence split in two main categories: some are productive ($G^{p}_{i,t}$) and can be associated with high-productivity (investment) expenditures; while others are not ($G^{np}_{i,t}$) and can be associated with low-productivity (consumption) expenditures. Of course, $G_{i,t} = G^{p}_{i,t} + G^{np}_{i,t}$. If public expenditures are productive, issuing public debt is beneficial to the governments (as it is presumably for the whole domestic economy), that is, the government's loss is reduced, all else equal.

Because the general model does not incorporate economic growth, the distinction between productive and unproductive expenditures has to rely on a specific mechanism. This mechanism is related to the 'crowding-in vs. crowding-out effects' debate (Friedman, 1978): productive expenditures have an *ex post* rate of return superior to that of unproductive expenditures; within a perfect foresight framework, they hence reduce the present financial cost of public debt, here represented by $r_{i,t+1}$, in comparison with the financing of unproductive expenditures. Productive expenditures impinge positively on welfare in that they provoke a crowding-in effect, while unproductive expenditures produce a crowding-out effect.

On theoretical grounds, we thus depart from Beetsma and Vermeylen in terms of the specification of governments' loss functions: the government of country i minimizes a loss function of the form:

$$L^{gov}_{i,t} = T_{i,t} + \frac{1}{1+\beta_i} E_t \left[B_{i,t}(r_{i,t+1} - r^*) \right], \tag{9.4b}$$

where β_i is now the rate at which government of country i discounts the real debt burden for the future generations.

We also interpret the presence of public debt in central banks' loss functions differently from Beetsma and Vermeylen: public debt may be inflationary in the future if it *does not* finance a productive public investment. Hence, we assume that central banks can possibly accept a higher current inflation rate insofar as it eases the financing process of a *productive* capital asset. However, this monetary policy is inefficient (or costly) if this real public debt finances unproductive public consumption. The central bank hence faces an uncertainty as regards the productive or unproductive nature of public expenditures, a reason why the inflation rate is stochastic. The parameter λ in eqn (9.8) can be interpreted as the degree of *indirect* participation of the central bank in the implementation of public investment.

In this new setting, the government's problem is somewhat different from what it was in Beetsma and Vermeylen's framework. If public investment (or *productive* public spending) becomes the key variable of the government, the latter will control the financing of this spending. In the logic of the Golden Rule of Public Finance, which is implicit in our fiscal framework, taxes pay for current expenditures, and public debt 'pays' for public investment: the government will hence choose public debt so that it maximizes its welfare.

In a Nash situation, each government minimizes its loss function (9.4b) subject to its budget constraint (9.3):

$$-\left(\frac{1}{1+\beta_i}\right)\left[E_t\left(r_{i,t+1}-r^*\right)-E_{t+1}\left(r_{i,t+2}-r^*\right)\left(1+r_{i,t+1}\right)\right]=0. \quad (9.16)$$

Under the assumptions that $r_{i,t}^2 \to 0$ and $r_{i,t}.r^* \to 0$, one obtains

$$E_t(r_{i,t+1}) = E_t(r_{i,t+2}). \quad (9.17)$$

Proposition 1

In equilibrium, under perfect foresight, the path of the real return on public debt is constant over time; thus, an optimal level of public debt exists in each economy and it is designed by this steady state rate of return.

Proof

(directly ensuing from equation (9.17)).

Applying equation (9.5b) forward, substituting into (9.9), also stated forward, and using equation (9.17), the general solution for the real return on public debt is

$$Var_t(r_{i,t+1}) = \frac{E_t\pi_{i,t+1}^e - \pi_{i,t}^e - (E_t\pi_{i,t+1} - \pi_{i,t})}{\mu_t B_{i,t} - \mu_{t+1}E_t B_{i,t+1}}. \quad (9.18)$$

Uncertainty on public debt's return depends on three distinct, though related, dynamics: first, the dynamics of expectations for the inflation path; second, the dynamics of future effective inflation; and the prospective evolution of public debt. The higher expected acceleration of inflation or the lower effective acceleration of inflation, the higher uncertainty; and the higher future fiscal surplus, the lower uncertainty.

As, in this framework, it is assumed that uncertainty only stems from the monetary aggregate which is set by the ECB, the variance of average inflation is the same as the variance of domestic inflation rates,[7] so that

$$Var_t(r_{u,t+1}) = Var_t(r_{i,t+1}) = (m_t^u)^2\sigma^2. \quad (9.19)$$

Substituting equations (9.12) and (9.19) in equation (9.18) yields the average public debt level:

$$(\bar{B}_t^u)^2 = \frac{(1+\sigma^2)^2}{\sigma^2(\lambda^u)^2}\left[\frac{E_t\pi^e_{i,t+1} - \pi^e_{i,t} - (E_t\pi_{i,t+1} - \pi_{i,t})}{-E_t d_{gov_i,t+1}}\right] \quad \forall i \in [1, N^U] \tag{9.20}$$

with $d_{gov,t+1} = E_t G_{i,t+1} + B_{i,t}E_t r_{i,t+1} - E_t T_{i,t+1}$, the fiscal deficit inclusive of net interest payments.

Equation (9.20) holds for every country in the monetary union and there is actually a close relationship between domestic inflation dynamics, future domestic fiscal policies and the *average* public debt level. Moreover, the inconsistency has disappeared: all else equal, eqn (9.20) states that the average level of debt in the monetary union decreases if the public surplus increases in one member state. QED.

Now, rewriting equation (9.20) for two countries i and j which are member states of the monetary union gives

$$\frac{E_t\left[\pi_{i,t+1} - \pi^e_{i,t+1}\right]}{E_t d_{gov_i,t+1}} = \frac{E_t\left[\pi_{j,t+1} - \pi^e_{j,t+1}\right]}{E_t d_{gov_j,t+1}} \quad \forall i \neq j \text{ with } (i,j) \in [1, N^u]^2. \tag{9.21}$$

Proposition 2

The general solution of the model implies that monetary uncertainty in a monetary union may necessitate the implementation of heterogeneous domestic fiscal policies by the member states.

Proof

If, for any reason, both countries do expect the same future inflation rate, but the realized inflation rates differ, future fiscal policies *must* be different according to equation (9.21).

The intuition is as follows. In equilibrium, each domestic market for public debt in the monetary union must be balanced and the optimal level of real public debt is given by equation (9.17) and is fixed. Since monetary policy is common to all member states, the variances of the domestic inflation rates and real interest rates must converge, that is, their divergence is stabilized (equation (9.19)), so that, *in fine*, the divergence among domestic public debts is also stabilized. This also means that the levels of public debts in the monetary union (*can*) *differ*. Moreover, if one country in the monetary union has a higher inflation rate than expected, in comparison with its other partners, this country has to implement a more expansionary fiscal policy than its partners', in order for its *real* public debt not to diverge too much from its optimal initial level. Thus, *overall* public debt in the monetary union does not diverge from its initial level. Equilibrium is satisfied on all markets, domestic and union-wide.

Stated shortly, as inflation tends to reduce *real* public debt, a country can satisfy its present value budget constraint with a growing fiscal deficit. This mechanism can be related to the 'real-balance-Pigouvian effect' of the FTPL (Woodford, 2001): if one can demonstrate the existence of a given optimal level of public debt, economic behaviours as expressed in equations (9.18), (9.12) and (9.19) should always tend to make actual debt converge to this optimum. QED.

9.5.3 Discussing inflation determinants

Of course, the model does not say much on the determinants of inflation; within this modified Beetsma and Vermeylen's framework, inflation remains a pure monetary phenomenon. Although this is a very disputable issue, the current framework for the ECB monetary policy strategy still hinges extensively on the Quantity theory: reliance of the first pillar on M3 growth rate is one important example. The conclusion of our model is thus that, even if one were to believe in the Quantity theory, fiscal policy would matter, but not in the usual sense: the causality does not go from deficits to inflation like in Sargent and Wallace (1981), but from inflation to deficits.

In light of proposition 2, the relevance of the SGP adopted in 1997 can be questioned. The SGP – that is, the adoption of an homogeneous limit on public deficit among countries in the EU[8] and an homogenous mid-term target for the cyclically adjusted deficit – leads automatically to some standardization of the European economies as they should have the same actual and expected inflation rates, according to equations (9.20) and (9.21). This, however, seems quite at odds with the present situation in the EU. Though nominal convergence has been largely increased, in part due to the Maastricht Treaty criteria which were the prerequisites to the adoption of the euro, discrepancies between European countries still provoke persistent real divergence.

Real divergence is not only related to the usual 'GDP-per-capita' divergence – it has been following a converging path between EU countries well before the transition process towards adopting the euro – but also to some important domestic economic structures. Different international specialization and different trade partners, with Germany and Austria relatively more open towards the Central and Eastern European countries (CEECs) and Russia than France, for instance; different situations as regards the labour market, with France and Germany still facing mass unemployment while the Netherlands had almost reached full employment a few years ago and Spain has steeply decreased its unemployment rate; different situations as regards labour productivity, hence a different pace for supply-driven inflation; all these elements may continue to provoke some de-synchronization of European business cycles and different paths for domestic inflation rates. Though this de-synchronization has been reduced in the years preceding the adoption of the euro (see Bentoglio *et al.*, 2001 and Fidrmuc and Korhonen, 2001), the occurrence of asymmetric shocks as well as different economic structures still remain a prominent issue in the euro area (seminal work on this topic is due to Bayoumi and Eichengreen, 1993). Real and inflation divergence must be taken seriously.

9.6 An application to Euro area member states

9.6.1 The empirical model

From the above theoretical model, inflation divergence can be an explaining variable in the equation of public deficits divergence, whereas inflation may not be determined by public finances.

Public deficits, exclusive of interest payments, are usually explained by the output gap and the level of public debt (see Barro, 1986; Bohn, 1998). In the following, we use the public deficit inclusive of interest payments as the dependent variable accordingly with the theoretical model.

We also compute the whole data set in difference vis-à-vis the average-weighted value in the euro area. All data come from the OECD dataset. Descriptive statistics are given in Table 9.3 below. The standard deviation of public deficits' difference is quite high, amounting to 3.7% of GDP, while inflation divergence has a standard deviation of 4.5%. Not reported in Table 9.3, the mean of inflation divergence in the euro area has decreased over the transition period towards euro's adoption, but it has increased again since its adoption: over the 1992–2003 period, the mean of inflation divergence was 0.4%, but was slightly above at 0.5% between 1999 and 2004.

The general specification for public deficits' divergence can be written as

$$\mathrm{ps_t} = \mathrm{c} + \alpha_{\mathrm{gap}}\,\mathrm{gap}_t + \alpha_{\mathrm{debt}}\,\mathrm{debt}_t + \alpha_{inf}\,inf_t + \varepsilon_t,$$

where ps_t is public surplus, gap_t is the output gap, debt_t is the net public debt and inf_t is the inflation rate based upon the Harmonized Index of Consumer Prices (HICP). Surpluses and debts are expressed in per cent of GDP; output gaps and inflation rates are expressed in per cent.

To correct for endogeneity between explained and explanatory variables, we have performed multivariate panel regressions using the general method of moments (GMM). One-lag explaining variables have been used as instruments.

Table 9.3 Descriptive statistics, pooled series, 1980–2004

	CPI (%)	*Public debt (% of GDP)*	*Output gap (%)*	*Public deficit (% of GDP)*
Mean	1.1	7.6	−0.2	−0.2
Median	0.1	−1.5	−0.1	0.1
Maximum	23.2	82.0	7.2	10.6
Minimum	−7.7	−115.4	−9.5	−11.1
Std. Dev.	4.50	38.82	2.21	3.72
Observations	264	264	264	264
Cross sections	11	11	11	11

Source: OECD.

9.6.2 Estimation results

Estimation results are reported in Table 9.4. Results for multivariate panel regressions establish the relative contributions of the output gap, net public debt and the inflation rate, all stated in difference vis-à-vis the euro area average, in driving euro area public surplus' differentials, also stated in difference vis-à-vis the euro area average.

The pooled GMM estimate for the inflation differential is not significant over the 1999–2004 sample (equations (9.1) and (9.4) in Table 9.4). The public debt differential is the only explanatory variable of the discrepancy in public surpluses within the constituted euro area, although not with fixed effects: a higher-than-average level of public debt is logically correlated with a higher-than-average public *deficit*. The GMM estimate testifies for causation from debts to deficits: high debt levels reduce fiscal margins for manoeuvre.

Increasing the sample to the period beginning with the Maastricht Treaty (1992–2004), hence taking into account the convergence process,[9] the inflation differential has a statistically significant impact on public deficits' differentials: a higher-than-average inflation rate provokes a higher-than-average public *deficit*. This result is robust to the introduction of fixed effects and to sample change provided the full sample is chosen. This confirms the theoretical result.

This may seem at odds with the specific situation of Germany since 2000, where inflation has been dramatically reduced whereas public deficits were set above the SGP threshold. On a longer time-horizon, however, the result is no longer surprising: higher deficit countries, like Italy, have long had higher inflation rates than the EU average; whereas low deficit countries, like Germany, have long had lower inflation rates than the EU average. We interpret the situation of Germany since 2000 as a transitory change in its own history (see also Creel and Le Cacheux, 2006).

Table 9.4 Panel public surplus regressions, pooled GMM estimates

	Without fixed effects			*With fixed effects*		
	(1) *1999–2004*	*(2)* *1992–2004*	*(3)* *1980–2004*	*(4)* *1999–2004*	*(5)* *1992–2004*	*(6)* *1980–2004*
gap	0.42	0.44	0.29	0.23	0.03	0.26
	(1.3)	(5.5)***	(3.4)***	(0.4)	(0.1)	(2.5)**
debt	−0.03	−0.03	−0.06	−0.23	−0.12	−0.07
	(4.3)***	(6.1)***	(14.6)***	(1.4)	(3.6)***	(4.7)***
inf	−0.21	−0.47	−0.27	0.39	−0.82	−0.35
	(0.2)	(4.9)***	(6.3)***	(0.4)	(5.2)***	(4.3)***
R^2	0.35	0.45	0.54	0.54	0.62	0.59
see	1.96	1.84	2.57	1.91	1.59	2.53
Obs.	66	143	275	66	143	275

Notes

Standard errors are White-corrected for heteroscedasticity. *, **, *** denote significance at the 10, 5 and 1% levels respectively.

Moreover, although public deficits cannot reasonably be attributed exclusively to inflation rates – they are not in our regressions which incorporate other explanatory variables like the output gap and public debt – we have argued in the theoretical framework and we argue in the empirical part of the paper that the convergence towards, and the constitution of, a monetary union in Europe have exacerbated the incidental power of inflation divergence on public deficits' divergence.

Also noteworthy in our estimation results, the explanatory power of public debts' differential is high on the two longer samples, with or without fixed effects. Finally, a higher-than-average output gap tends to induce a higher-than-euro-area-average fiscal surplus. This latter statement is true without fixed effects over the two following periods: 1992–2004 and 1980–2004, and true on the larger one provided fixed effects are introduced. In this respect, reliance on cyclically adjusted deficits in the SGP seems reasonable.[10]

9.7 Conclusions

This chapter analysed a possible explanation for the interrelationships between inflation divergence and public deficits' divergence in a monetary union. Although inflation convergence was expected, thanks to higher competition and higher transparency, inflation divergence has remained an important issue. As such, it has incidence on trade balances among euro area member states – highly competitive countries gain trade market shares at the expense of their low-competitive EU partners – it has also had incidence on the efficiency of the ECB monetary policy: a single short-run interest rate like the repo rate cannot handle heterogeneity of situations.

In this context, it has sometimes been argued that diverging situations of public finances were responsible for diverging inflation trends: higher inflation and higher long-term interest rates were supposed to occur in those countries implementing expansionary or lax fiscal policies. The existence of crowding-out effects was considered crucial in this respect.

Data from the first years of existence of the euro do not confirm the argument. Despite high deficits in some euro area member states, long-term interest rates in Europe have continued to decrease, and then to remain at low levels, since the beginning of the new millennium.

Reversing the causation between inflation, long-term interest rates, and public deficits may be considered as an option. In a theoretical model including some monetarist properties, which should have given some strength to the crowding-out effect argument, but also including a mechanism discriminating between productive and unproductive public expenditures, which has given some realism to the overall setting, we have demonstrated that inflation divergence, resulting from shocks unrelated to public finances, can explain public deficits' divergence in a monetary union. To ensure fiscal solvency at their country level, but also at the monetary union level for which a shadow market for public debts does exist, countries with higher-than-average inflation rates, hence lower-than-average real public debt, have to implement higher-than-average public deficits. The latter are a stabilizing device in a general equilibrium framework like the one described in the theoretical part of the paper.

To escape general equilibrium issues, empirical tests have been performed: public deficits' divergence has been explained not only by inflation divergence, but also by divergence in the output gap and in ratios of public debts on GDP. Empirical tests do not invalidate our main theoretical result, though they may suggest that other forces have also been at work since the launching of the euro.

We conclude that inflation divergence in Europe may have been responsible for the diverging patterns of public finances in the same area, some countries having had to let their public deficits go adrift to cope with high inflation pressures. Despite the constitution of the euro area, the issue remains and must be accommodated by different fiscal strategies. Homogeneous fiscal rules, like in the SGP, are not optimal in this respect, at least insofar as inflation convergence has not been achieved.

Notes

* Helpful comments by Michele Fratianni, Henri Sterdyniak and Koen Vermeylen on a preliminary draft are gratefully acknowledged. We do also thank participants at Journées AFSE 2003 in Lille, at Third Journées internationales d'études Jean Monnet 2003 in Bordeaux, and Third Lectures on macroeconomic governance in the EMU 2006 in Siena for their remarks on this draft. The usual disclaimer applies.

1 Other important contributions are Modigliani (1961) and Tobin (1965). See also Elmendorf and Mankiw (1999) for a survey.

2 See Fitoussi and Padoa-Schioppa (2005) for a comprehensive investigation on why European countries adopted fiscal rules with a ceiling on public deficits and why they urged fiscal consolidations. See also Le Cacheux (2006).

3 See Laubach (2004) for a recent review of the literature.

4 Luxemburg is not documented here. The case of Greece is specific: Eurostat has discovered rather late (in 2004!) that public finances data for this country were heavily biased. In 2001, when Greece joined the euro area, her public deficit was in fact well above the 3%-of-GDP limit.

5 See Fitoussi and Padoa-Schioppa (2005) for a comprehensive analysis.

6 See former ECB President W. Duisenberg's 6 September 2000 speech 'Are Different Price Developments in the Euro Area a Cause for Concern?', or 'Inflation Differentials in a Monetary Union', in the Monthly Bulletin of the ECB, October 1999.

7 Note that it does not mean that inflation rates *per se* do not differ among countries forming a monetary union.

8 The SGP applies to all EU members. Nevertheless, only euro area members may incur fines if they do not fulfil the dispositions of the Pact.

9 At that time, most future euro area members had already begun mimicking the German monetary policy, thus reducing the discrepancy of nominal short-run interest rates to levels that made these countries behave somewhat on the monetary side, as if they were already in a monetary union.

10 The critical appraisal of cyclically adjusted deficits is beyond the scope of this chapter. See Farina and Ricciuti (2006) for a comprehensive discussion and the elaboration of an alternative computation method.

References

Angeloni, I. and Ehrmann, M. (2004), 'Euro area inflation differentials', ECB Working Paper no. 388.

Barro, R. J. (1986), 'US deficits since WW I', *Scandinavian Journal of Economics*, 88: 195–222.

Barro, R. J. and Gordon, D. B. (1983), 'A positive theory of monetary policy in a natural-rate model', *Journal of Political Economy*, 91: 589–610.

Bayoumi, T. and Eichengreen, B. (1993), 'Shocking aspects of European unification', in F. Torres and F. Giavazzi (eds), *Adjustment and Growth in the EMU*, Cambridge: Cambridge University Press.

Beetsma, R. and Vermeylen, K. (2005), 'The effect of monetary unification on public debt and its real return', CESifo Working Paper no. 1400 (also CEPR Discussion Paper no. 3491, 2002).

Bentoglio, G., Fayolle, J. and Lemoine, M. (2002), 'Unity and plurality of the European cycle', OFCE Working Paper, 2002–03.

Bergin, P. R. (2000), 'Fiscal solvency and price level determination in a monetary union', *Journal of Monetary Economics*, 45: 37–53.

Bohn, H. (1998), 'The behavior of US public debt and deficits', *Quarterly Journal of Economics*, 113: 949–63.

Creel, J. and Le Cacheux, J. (2006), 'La nouvelle désinflation compétitive européenne', *Revue de l'OFCE*, 98: 9–36.

Diamond, P. A. (1965), 'National debt in a neoclassical growth model', *American Economic Review*, 55: 1126–50.

Duarte, M. (2003), 'The Euro and inflation divergence in Europe', *FRB of Richmond Economic Quarterly*, 89: 53–70.

Ducoudré, B. (2005), 'Fiscal policy and interest rates', OFCE Working Paper no. 7, July.

Elmendorf, D. W. and Mankiw, N. G. (1999), 'Government debt', in J. B. Taylor and M. Woodford (eds), *Handbook of Macroeconomics*, Volume IC, chapter 25, Amsterdam: Elsevier.

Farina, F. and Ricciuti, R. (2006), 'L'évaluation des politiques budgétaires en Europe: règles budgétaires et marges de manoeuvre des gouvernements', *Revue de l'OFCE*, 99: 275–301.

Fidrmuc, J. and Korhonen, I. (2001), 'Similarity of supply and demand shocks between the euro area and the CEECs', Bank of Finland, BOFIT Discussion Paper, no. 14.

Fitoussi, J.-P. and Padoa-Schioppa, F. (eds) (2005), *Report on the State of the European Union*, Basingstoke: Palgrave MacMillan.

Friedman, B. M (1978), 'Crowding out or crowding in? the economic consequences of financing government deficits', *Brookings Papers on Economic Activity*, 3: 593–641.

Gros, D. and Thygesen, N. (1992), *European Monetary Integration*, London and NY: Longman and St Martin's Press.

Hicks, J. R. (1937), 'Mr Keynes and the "Classics": a suggested interpretation', *Econometrica*, 5: 147–59.

Honohan, P. and Lane, P. R. (2003), 'Divergent inflation rates in EMU', *Economic Policy*, 37: 357–94.

Laubach, T. (2004), 'The effects of budget deficits on interest rates: a review of empirical results', Paper presented at the Sixth Banca d'Italia Workshop on Public Finances, Perugia, Italy, April.

Le Cacheux, J. (2006), 'To co-ordinate or not to co-ordinate', in I. Linsenmann, C. O. Meyer and W. Wessels (eds), *Economic Government of the EU, a Balance Sheet of New Modes of Policy Coordination*, Basingstoke: Palgrave MacMillan.

Leeper, E. (1991), 'Equilibria under "Active" and "Passive" monetary policies', *Journal of Monetary Economics*, 27: 129–47.

Modigliani, F. (1961), 'Long-run implications of alternative fiscal policies and the burden of the national debt', *Economic Journal*, 71: 730–55.

Modigliani, F. and Sutch, R. (1966), 'Innovations in interest rate policy', *American Economic Review*, 56: 178–97.

Sargent, T. J. and Wallace, N. (1981), 'Some unpleasant monetarist arithmetic', Federal Reserve Bank of Minneapolis, *Quarterly Review*, 5: 1–17.

Tobin, J. (1965), 'The burden of the public debt: a review article', *Journal of Finance*, 20: 679–82.

Woodford, M. (1996), 'Control of the public debt: a requirement for price stability?', NBER Working Paper no. 5684.

—— (2001) 'Fiscal requirement for price stability', *Journal of Money, Credit, and Banking*, 33: 669–728.

Index

Routledge Revivals

The International Distribution of Raw Materials

First published in 1938, *The International Distribution of Raw Materials* by Herman Kranold offers a comprehensive analysis of the global distribution and management of raw materials. This seminal work examines the natural conditions of production, the existing distribution of resources, and the challenges of rationalizing their allocation. Kranold also delves into the political complexities of raw material supplies and their role in international planning. Rich with statistical tables and graphs, this book remains a vital resource for understanding the economic and political dimensions of global resource management.

The International Distribution of Raw Materials

Herman Kranold

Routledge
Taylor & Francis Group

First published in 1938
by George Routledge & Sons Ltd.

This edition first published in 2026 by Routledge
4 Park Square, Milton Park, Abingdon, Oxon, OX14 4RN

and by Routledge
605 Third Avenue, New York, NY 10158

Routledge is an imprint of the Taylor & Francis Group, an informa business

Publisher's Note
The publisher has gone to great lengths to ensure the quality of this reprint but points out that some imperfections in the original copies may be apparent.

Disclaimer
The publisher has made every effort to trace copyright holders and welcomes correspondence from those they have been unable to contact.

For Product Safety Concerns and Information please contact our EU representative GPSR@taylorandfrancis.com. Taylor & Francis Verlag GmbH, Kaufingerstraße 24, 80331 München, Germany

A Library of Congress record exists under LCCN: 43032870

ISBN: 978-1-041-31092-1 (hbk)
ISBN: 978-1-003-77751-9 (ebk)
ISBN: 978-1-041-31093-8 (pbk)

Book DOI 10.4324/9781003777519

THE INTERNATIONAL DISTRIBUTION OF RAW MATERIALS

BY

HERMAN KRANOLD

Associate Professor of Economics,
Talladega College.

LONDON:
GEORGE ROUTLEDGE & SONS LTD.,
BROADWAY HOUSE, 68-74, CARTER LANE, E.C.

First published 1938.

PRINTED IN GREAT BRITAIN BY
MACKAYS LIMITED, CHATHAM

" That resources for war are to be obtained by abstention from ordinary consumption is an old doctrine."

—F. Y. EDGEWORTH,

Papers Relating to Political Economy, III, 218.

TABLE OF CONTENTS

LIST OF STATISTICAL TABLES

A.—TABLES CONTAINED IN THE TEXT

(*Note*.—All these tables have the sign T before their number.)

PAGE

B.—TABLES CONTAINED IN APPENDIX

LIST OF GRAPHS

REFERENCES AND SOURCES

1. ANGELL, N. *This Have and Have-Not Business;* London, 1936.
2. ANGELL, N. *The Great Illusion,* 1933; New York, 1933.
3. ANSTEY, V. *The Economic Development of India;* 3rd edition; London, 1936.
4. BARNES, L. *The Future of Colonies;* London, 1936.
5. BASTABLE, C. F. (Ed. T. E. *Gregory*). *The Commerce of Nations;* 10th edition; London, 1927.
6. BEER, G. L. *The Old Colonial System,* 1660–1754 (Part I; 2 vols.); New York, 1914.
7. BIRCH, L. *The Demand for Colonies;* London, 1936.
8. BRADLEY, Ph. *Can We Stay Out of War?* New York, 1936.

8a. CROWTHER, S. (editor). *A Basis for Stability;* Boston, 1932.

9. DAS, R. K. *The Industrial Efficiency of India;* London, 1930.

9a. DAVENPORT, E. H., and COOKE, S. R. *The Oil-Trusts and Anglo-American Relations;* New York, 1924.

10. *Der Welthandel in wichtigen Nahrungsmitteln und Rohstoffen vor und nach dem Kriege;* Berlin, 1926.
11. *Die Wirtschaft des Auslandes* 1900–1927; Berlin, 1928.
12. EDGEWORTH, F. Y. *Papers Relating to Political Economy,* Vol. III; London, 1925.
13. EMENY, B. *The Strategy of Raw Materials;* New York, 1936.
14. *Encyclopedia Britannica;* 14th edition; 24 vols.; London, 1936.
15. *Encyclopedia of the Social Sciences* (Ed. E. R. SELIGMAN and A. JOHNSON); 15 vols.; New York, 1930–1935.
16. GREAVES, H. R. G. *Raw Materials and International Control;* London, 1936.
17. *Handwörterbuch der Naturwissenschaften;* 10 vols.; Jena, 1912–1915.
18. *Handwörterbuch der Staatswissenschaften;* 4th edition; 9 vols.; Jena, 1923–1929.
19. HOGBEN, L. *The Retreat from Reason;* London, 1936.
20. JOHNSON, C. S., EMBREE, E.R., and ALEXANDER, W. W. *The Collapse of Cotton Tenancy;* Chapel Hill, N.C., 1935.
21. KILLOUGH, H. W., and KILLOUGH, L. B. *Raw Materials of Industrialism;* New York, 1929.
22. KUCZYNSKI, R. R. *Population Movements;* Oxford, 1936.
23. *Landlexikon* (Ed. K. ZU PUTLITZ and L. MEYER); 6 vols.; Stuttgart, 1911–1914.

23a. LAWRENCE, J. C. *The World's Struggle with Rubber;* London, 1931.

24. *League of Nations:* " Statistical Year Book "; Geneva, 1926–1936.
25. *League of Nations:* " World Economic Survey "; Geneva, 1933, 1934.
26. LIPPINCOTT, I. *Economic Resources and Industries of the World;* New York, 1929.
27. McDOUGALL, F. L. *Sheltered Markets;* London, 1925.

27a. MOHR, A. *The Oil War;* New York, 1926.

28. PALGRAVE. *Dictionary of Political Economy;* new edition, ed. H. HIGGS; 3 vols.; London, 1926.

29. PHILLIPS, P. D. and WOOD, G. L. (editors). *The Peopling of Australia;* Melbourne, 1928.

29a. PLUMMER, A. *Raw Materials or War Materials?* London, 1937.

30. *Raw Materials and Colonies* (The Royal Institute of International Affairs); London, 1936.

31. REICHWEIN, A. *Die Rohstoffwirtschaft der Erde;* Jena, 1928.

32. RICHARDSON, J. H. *British Economic Foreign Policy;* New York, 1936.

33. ROBBINS, L. *An Essay on the Nature and Significance of Economic Science;* 2nd edition; London, 1935.

34. ROWE, J. W. F. *Markets and Men;* Cambridge, 1936.

34a. SARGENT, A. J. *Coal in International Trade;* London, 1922.

35. *Statistical Abstract for the Several British Overseas Dominions* (later: " . . . for the British Empire"); London, 1927 *et seq.*

36. *Statistical Abstract for British India;* London, 1926 *et seq.*

37. *Statistical Abstract for the United Kingdom;* London, 1926 *et seq.*

38. *Statistical Abstract of the United States;* Washington, D.C.; 1926 *et seq.*

39. *Statistisches Handbuch der Weltwirtschaft;* Berlin, 1936.

40. *Statistisches Jahrbuch für das Deutsche Reich;* Berlin, 1915–1936.

41. *The Cotton Yearbook;* Bradford and London, 1935.

42. *The Mineral Industries of the British Empire and Foreign Countries;* London, 1931 *et seq.*

43. *The Wheat Situation,* 1931 (20th Report of the Imperial Economic Committee); London, 1932.

44. *Vierteljahrshefte zur Konjunkturforschung;* Berlin, 1926 *et seq.*

45. WALLACE, B. B., and EDMINSTER, L. R. *International Control of Raw Materials;* Washington, D.C., 1930.

46. WOOFTER, Jr., T. J. *Landlord and Tenant on the Cotton Plantation;* Washington, D.C., 1936.

47. ZIMMERMANN, E. W. *World Resources and Industries;* New York, 1929.

PREFACE

THE purpose of this study is to clear up the facts of an economic problem which are intricate and numerous, though they do not offer particular intellectual difficulties, and to marshal the practical implications of the incongruity of facts with interests and ambitions.

In the course of this study a number of red herrings was found to have been drawn across the trail of truth; these were followed and shown up for what they are; then the hunt returned to the genuine trail.

Opinions on the subject are widely at variance. Authors have written many books on the subject, and the number of articles and speeches reported in the daily and periodical Press, etc., is very large. The books have been mentioned, as far as they seem to me to deserve serious study, in the list of references and sources; but that does not mean that I consider all of them, indiscriminately, as apt reading matter.

I did not find it propitious, after having explained what seems to me to be the truth, to refute other authors who think differently.

The need for brevity forced me to neglect some aspects of the subject. For instance, the position of the Small Powers is scarcely discussed in this essay. But the most sympathetic treatment would have been unable to change the sad truth that they will be victims, not masters, of future developments. There are, it is true, some minor problems in regard to raw materials which they might be able to solve by activities of their own: perhaps only provisionally, but with some alleviation of their present situation. By such action they might give a useful example of what can be done in international matters by good-will and readiness to act with sweet reasonableness; but as I cannot see the slightest traces of such a spirit in them (any more than in the Great Powers) I thought it useless to give much space to a detailed discussion of their positions.

To save space I have left out raw materials which may not be without importance. I have excluded, *e.g.*, leather (a material whose production is widespread and which has many substitutes), tanning materials (now largely superseded by chromium compounds, which are included in my treatment of chromium), iodine (which can be produced, at a pinch, nearly everywhere in the small quantities that are of vital importance), and camphor (for which a satisfactory substitute from coal-tar exists). The only commodity that I should have liked to include, but which I have omitted, is castor oil. It is important not because it was used on a large scale in the civil war in Italy to torture the " enemy," but because it is the best lubricant of quickly-rotating machinery, particularly aeroplane motors; but I was unable to find any reliable source for the facts necessary for a discussion of this commodity.

The figures, although they are not equalled in existing literature in completeness and up-to-dateness, are sadly inadequate. That is not my fault; the sources do not give us all that we need. I have tried to avoid lengthy discussions on points of statistical method; the few exceptions will, I hope, find their explanation in the importance of the conclusions which could be reached only in this way. Part of this study, particularly the first chapter and the Appendix of statistical tables, were finished in manuscript before most of the figures for 1934 and 1935 appeared. I have included those which seemed important when they recently became available, and have modified the text where the new figures seemed to require it. But as I did not intend to make a statistical handbook, and as in any case the figures will no longer be quite up to date a year or so hence, I have left it at that. The chief object was to get the figures as complete as possible for the particular period under consideration, *i.e.*, the business cycle 1928/1929 to 1934/1935/1936. That time is a potent factor in changing facts has been shown in the text explicitly and clearly.

What is the possible use of such a study? To influence politicians and statesmen? I hope they read books, though I sometimes think that they do not read many. The impact of reason has become very small nowadays. To show, *e.g.*, the objective futility of the endeavours to get access to more raw materials by conquest is one thing; to show that, though this is an irrational thing, it is a potent factor in modern politics, is a second thing; to recommend better means of attaining the same end is a third thing; and to estimate the chances of the reasonable thing being done, against advice inspired by jealousy and the desire for prestige, or by the hankering of orators for spectacular formulas and a gushing phraseology, is a fourth, and again a quite different, thing.

So I fear that this study will have to look for its public elsewhere: to the few politicians who want to know what they and the others are speaking about, to the educated layman and journalist, and to those many people in the middle and the working class who seriously want to instruct themselves in a matter which is attracting the spotlights in so spectacular a way. I think particularly of my many friends in the Workers' Educational Association, in the Fabian Society, in some Trade Unions and Co-operative Guilds with whom for nearly three years I had the pleasure of studying the economic questions of the day.

In the meantime the enquiry of the League of Nations, proposed in the autumn of 1935 by the then Foreign Minister of Great Britain, Sir Samuel HOARE, has begun. The League has appointed a committee for the study of the raw materials problem. The first meeting was on March 8th, 1937, Mr. W. STUCKI (Switzerland) being in the chair. Non-members of the League were represented by Mr. Y. SHUDO for Japan and Mr. H. F. GRADY for the U.S. Germany and, among the members of the League, Italy were not represented. The British delegate, Sir Frederick LEITH-ROSS, declared that the raw materials problem cannot be solved by the transfer of territory (so far, so good), that the open-door policy would sometimes be harmful to the colonies themselves (but the open-door policy and preference for the Mother Country are not the only possibilities!), etc., etc. In short, he seems in a particularly encouraging way to have said that nothing can be done. Similarly with others. A not very hopeful beginning. But perhaps this only meant that the speakers were clearing their throats, and that sweet advice will come later. Let us hope that the future meetings of the committee will endeavour more seriously to find out what can be done, why and how it can be done, and to show that it should be done!

The book by Mr. Plummer, I am sorry to say, came too late into my hands to be taken into consideration; the only thing I could do was to include its title in the list of references and sources.

April 5th, 1937.

Now I am reading the proofs I cannot find that the result of the deliberations of the committee of the League of Nations has contributed anything new to the subject. But I have seen what Mrs. Vera Anstey, D.Sc. (Econ.), our dear friend, has done for the book when she undertook to supervise the smoothing-out of the numerous germanisms of my manuscript. I hope she feels the deep gratitude which I feel for this, as for so many acts of friendship and kindness of hers.

HERMAN KRANOLD.

Talladega College,
Talladega, Ala., U.S.A.

November 5th, 1937.

THE
INTERNATIONAL DISTRIBUTION
OF RAW MATERIALS

CHAPTER I

REVIEW OF INTERNATIONALLY INTERESTING RAW MATERIALS

RAW materials are all things which are either consumed in the form in which nature offers them to us, or are processed into a shape and size which enables them to serve the purposes of consumption. Not only material things are raw materials in an economic sense. The economic term comprises services also: the services which the inorganic forces of nature are able to offer us: heat, electricity, the energy of falling water or of moving air, and the services of living things.

These services are multiple. Leguminous plants (peas, beans, etc.), *e.g.*, offer them by accumulating nitrogenous compounds in the soil. Some trees protect the soil on which they grow against erosion and drought. Animals offer them when they are domesticated, like horses, cattle, donkeys, mules; sometimes even if not domesticated, like those useful beasts of prey introduced into a district to get rid of an invasion of rabbits, or like insects parasitic on destructive insects, which serve merely by living. The most useful economic service is, of course, given to mankind by its own labour.

But not all these materials and services are interesting from the viewpoint of the international distribution of productive resources. We need not compile an encyclopedia of them; we may pick out those which interest us in connection with our subject. We will treat them directly, case by case, and discuss later the important question whether we have chosen all those which are relevant to our inquiry.

Our work has to be done with the help of statistical figures, as accurate and complete as can be obtained. Again we do not endeavour to have a whole and complete encyclopedia of statistical data as to these goods and services, but only to give what is useful for the purposes of our study. As to dates, we limit ourselves to pertinent data, generally those covering the last full business cycle (roughly 1928 to 1936), in so far as they are available, and add figures for earlier years only where it seems relevant for our conclusions.[1]

A.—Metals.

1.—*Iron.*

Iron is the most important of the metals. We are probably living in an age in which the use of iron in its pure form becomes rarer and rarer. The Stone Age, the Age of Brass and the Iron Age will, in all probability, be followed by a period which may be called AAAC, the Age of Alloys and Artificial Compounds, and the young members of the present generation may expect to live into a period when the use of a bar of iron will be just as obsolete, technically, as the use of stone is now for making a knife. The transformation of some vegetable materials (such as the protein of milk, the cellulose substance of wood, the components of that complicated compound which we call "coal," and the basic substances of the soya bean and many others) into new chemical compounds, and the admixture of the light metals, especially aluminium, and of some of the other metals, like vanadium, with iron will complete a development which, with the production of artificial stone from cement and of artificial fibre from wood, has already made enormous headway during the last two score of years. But even then iron will remain what it is now: the backbone of all uses of metal. An increasing variety of iron alloys and steels may well mean not a decrease, but a further vast increase of the technical, and therefore economic, significance of iron.

The quantities of iron and steel produced at the top of the last boom, in 1929, viz., 99 million tons of pig iron and 111 million tons of steel, show increases of 68 and 175 per cent. over 1913. There are some other raw materials the production and consumption of which grew still more rapidly, but even if we take into account that the year 1929 was wholly exceptional, the increase remains large, particularly if compared with the much slower increase of mankind during the same period.

[1] For similar reasons we do not attempt to give numbers complete to the last unit, but content ourselves with "round figures".

From a table printed by Mr. H. W. *Killough* and Mrs. L. B. *Killough* (p. 231) I quote the following figures for the production of iron and steel :

TABLE T1.

PRODUCTION OF IRON AND STEEL, 1800–1921.

	In thousands of Metric Tons. Pig Iron.	Steel.
1800	825	?
1870	11,900	692
1900	38,973	28,273
1914	59,337	59,800
1921	35,415	40,491

Further figures can be found in the Appendix. The deep drop of 1921 soon gave way to a new tremendous increase, and so did the slump of 1932. Steel[1a] overtook iron in 1914, and never again declined to second place, even during the post-war slump.

The sources from which iron is obtained for the production of pig iron are ores and, to a small extent, scrap metal. The sources from which iron is obtained for steel-making are iron

[1a] For steel the corresponding figures were, for four significant years, as follows, in million metric tons :

1880	1900	1926	1935
4·27	28·34	91·23	99

If we disregard the abnormal peak of 1928/29 and the equally abnormal low figure of 51 million in 1932, we get, by assuming a further increase of 8 million tons every 9 years, the following forecast :

1926	1935	1944	1953
91	99	107	115

An extrapolation according to the curve of the actual increase from 1880 to 1935 would lead almost to a standstill in production.

TABLE T1a.—ANNUAL AVERAGE INCREASE OF STEEL PRODUCTION.

Years.	Mill. Tons.	Increase or Decrease Compared with Previous Period (in per cent.)
1880/1900	1·2	
1900/1926	2·4	+100
1926/1935	·9	− 63
And hypothetically for 1935/53	·333	− 63

or a production in 1953 of $99 + 18 \times \cdot 333 = 105$ million tons only. But I think that this is entirely improbable, and that the other forecast approaches more nearly to what will happen.—At the moment of reading the proofs (September, 1937) reports seem even to show that the present production of steel has by far overtaken the larger estimate.

ores, pig iron, iron alloys and scrap metals, the last to a rather important extent. The actual ultimate consumption of iron comprises the whole quantity of steel produced; but it is difficult to discover how much iron metal is ultimately consumed in other forms than steel. We would have to deduct from the pig iron produced that part which is processed into steel. We know the quantity of steel, and how much metal it contains (viz., about 98 per cent.); but we do not know how much non-iron metal is contained in it,[2] nor do we know even approximately how much of the iron in the steel comes from scrap, because this information is supplied by very few countries.

The increase in the world's production from 1913 to 1929 was: in iron ore 15 per cent. (the increase or decrease of iron metal content being unknown); increase in pig iron produced 25 per cent., in steel produced 40 per cent. But what about the quantities of scrap metal used?

Mr. E. W. *Zimmermann* mentions in his book (p. 775, *note*) that for every pound obtained from ores of the following metals marketed (presumably in the U.S.), the following fractions of a pound produced from scrap material ("secondary metal," "salvaged material," etc.) were marketed also:

TABLE T2.

SCRAP METAL MARKETED IN THE U.S.[2a]

	Pound Scrap.
Aluminium	·41
Antimony	·44
Copper	·53
Lead	·30
Nickel	·12
Tin	·38
Zinc	·23

[2] The admixtures with manganese vary from 5 to 40 per cent., with chromium from 2 to 15 per cent., whilst other, much smaller, percentages apply to vanadium and molybden, and others again to aluminium in aluminium steels.

[2a] Another collection of facts as to the recovery ("salvage") of metals in the U.S. is given in the following table:

TABLE T2a.—METALS RECOVERED IN THE U.S.

	Unit.	1928	1929.	1930.	1933.	1934.	1935.
Aluminium	1,000 long tons				29·9	41·4	45·9
Antimony	,, ,, ,,				6·6	6·7	8·6
Nickel	,, ,, ,,				1·5	1·7	1·8
Platinum	1,000 troy ounces				35·1	35·5	47·1
Palladium	,, ,, ,,	59	48	43·5	4·8	5·6	7·9
Iridium	,, ,, ,,				·7	1·3	2·2
Other platinum metals	,, ,, ,,				·8	1·3	2
Tin	1,000 long tons	32	30·6	23·4	19·7	22·2	24·9

The percentage of scrap metal among the whole quantity produced varies, then, in these cases between 11 and 35 per cent. As to iron, Mr. Zimmermann quotes for the U.S. that in 1929, at the top of the boom, 22·6 million tons of scrap entered into the production of 54·9 million tons of steel, which works out at a proportion of 41 per cent. of the steel produced, or probably nearly 50 per cent. of the iron metal contained in it.

Mr. Zimmermann adopts the following ingenious method of estimating the world increase in the use of scrap iron. He compares:

1913:	World production of pig iron ...	78 million tons
	,, ,, ,, steel ...	75 ,, ,,
	(Surplus of iron over steel 3 million tons.)	
1929:	World production of pig iron ...	96·4 million tons
	,, ,, ,, steel ...	118 ,, ,,
	(Surplus of steel over iron 21·6 million tons.)	

In the U.S. 25 per cent. of the pig iron produced is not transformed into steel. If this percentage is applied to the world figures, we get:

Steel produced	118 million tons
From pig iron (75% of 96·4)	72·3 ,, ,,
From other sources	45·7 ,, ,,

On this basis Mr. Zimmermann assumes a scrap contribution to the world's requirements of iron in 1929 of no less than 37 million tons or about one-third of the steel produced. There are some weak points in this argument, such as the application of the percentage of pig iron not entering into steel production in the U.S. to the whole world. But there are reasons to assume that, even if many countries use less scrap in relation to pig iron than the U.S., the large steel-making countries in Europe (Germany, France, Great Britain) probably use the last bit of scrap available. Hence it is likely that Mr. Zimmermann has understated rather than overstated the importance of scrap iron.

As a further illustration I give a few figures on Germany In making pig iron Germany:

TABLE T3.

CONSUMPTION OF SCRAP IRON IN GERMANY, 1929–1934.

	Produced Million Tons.	Consumed Scrap Iron. Million Tons.	Consumed Scrap Iron. Per Cent.
A. Production of pig iron:			
1929	13·2	·7	5·3
1932	3·9	·17	4·4
1933	5·2	·26	5
1934	8·7	·47	5·4
B. Steel production: ...			
1929	16·1	7·84	48·7
1932	5·7	3·32	58·2
1933	7·5	4·16	55·5
1934	11·7	6·16	52·7

Unfortunately figures for 1935 have not yet been published. A comparison of prices gives us (in RM. per metric ton):

TABLE T4.

PRICES FOR STEEL AND SCRAP, 1913–1936.

	1913.	1929.	1932.	1936, July.
Heavy steel scrap, N. England ...	55·12	64·57	26·24	35·36
Steel bars, round, ⅝-in.	163·43	160·03	96·30	115·0
Scrap price in % of steel price ...	33·6	40·3	28·3	30·8

This shows the following features:

(1) With the slump the percentage of scrap used in making pig iron decreased, that used in making steel increased; recovery reversed that process.

(2) The boom increased the fraction characterizing the proportion of the scrap iron price to steel price, the slump decreased it, recovery made it increase again.

(3) The use of record quantities of scrap at the top of the boom came about in spite of the fact that scrap material was very expensive at that time in terms of steel.

For the U.S. one more addition seems worth while, *i.e.*, more than 50 per cent. of the exports of heavy iron and steel products consists, in recent years, of scrap, as the following figures show:

TABLE T5.

SCRAP IRON IN EXPORTS FROM U.S., 1923–1934.

	1923.	1926.	1931.	1932.	1933.	1934.
Quantity in 1,000 long tons:						
All sorts	2,010	2,167	969	595	1,341	2,813
Scrap	66	105	136	227	773	1,835
Value in million $:						
All sorts	167	174	63	29	46	89
Scrap	1	2	2	2	7	19
Value in $ per ton of scrap ...	15·15	19·05	14·71	8·81	9·06	10·35

It is very interesting to observe this sudden increase of the exportation of scrap iron and steel during the second half of the depression and during the recovery period.

The German Statistical Abstract for 1936 gives the following figures:

TABLE T6.

WORLD EXPORTS OF SCRAP IRON, 1929–1935.

	1929.	1930.	1931.	1932.	1933.	1934.	1935.
Quantity—							
in 1,000 tons ...	2,976	2,178	1,741	1,632	2,721	3,986	4,285
value, in million RM.	180	117	69	45	75	109	121
price, RM. per ton	61	54	40	28	28	27	28

These figures again show that the slump was very deep, and there was no recovery at all in prices. This makes the enormous increase in quantity during the first three years of the recovery period only the more striking.

Thus we may say, without danger of making a serious mistake, that the use of scrap iron as a source of iron metal in making steel is increasing with great speed, that the rate of increase of scrap consumed is greater than that of iron ores, and that in the not remote future the total quantity of iron produced from scrap is likely to exceed that produced from ores year by year. This much increased use of the scrap materials is a distinct sign of the increased technicality of our metallurgical methods.

All this brings us immediately to an important conclusion: as technique develops, less and less of the iron and steel produced originates from newly-mined ore. Iron is a relatively non-perishable material,[3] and the situation with iron, therefore, approaches similarity with the situation as to gold. There the quantity disappearing "for good" year by year is a very small proportion of the whole annual production,[4] so that the world's stock of available gold increases every year by something like 90 per cent. of the gold actually mined. As to our present subject, iron, this means: as technique develops every country depends, for its requirements of new iron and steel, less and less on newly-mined iron ores and can rely more and more on the scrap iron originating from its obsolescent former investments.

The obvious outcome of this is: (1) the production of iron ores within the home country becomes quickly less vital for a nation; (2) the future of the "national" character of a country's iron production comes to depend more and more on the rate of its present investment in iron and on the velocity of obsolescence of these investments.

It was necessary to establish this truth first of all and to drive it home. All the forthcoming statements and reflexions on the inequality of the nations in regard to the distribution of the world's resources of iron ores must be looked at in the light of this truth. It shows us that all the inequalities which we shall presumably find are bound to become less important during the next twenty years or so.

This is the more significant since Table A1 (2) (a) shows us that nature has indeed treated the several parts of the world

[3] I venture to ask the reader to remember this in connection with quite a number of other metals also. Things must be analogous with many of them, though we do not always know enough to show this statistically, as we are fortunately able to do with iron.

[4] The industrial use of gold is sometimes estimated to absorb something like a third of the annual production. But this does not mean that this gold disappears. Most ornamental gold is "frozen down" for a time, but may reappear. Much of the gold exported from India during the slump was melted "scrap" gold from jewels. Even the dead are not always buried with their golden teeth. . . . If we assume that 10 per cent. of the annual production disappears "for good", this is probably too generous an estimate.

in a very unequal way as regards providing them with resources of iron ores. If we disregard the rather uncertain figures of the last column of this table we find, with the help of column three, that of the total quantity of iron believed to have been found with practical certainty by the experts of 1913,[5] the following percentages give us a picture of its distribution in the earth :

TABLE T7.

PERCENTAGE DISTRIBUTION OF WORLD SUPPLIES OF IRON LODES.

	Per cent. of the World's Lodes.	
Europe		33
Great Britain	7	
France	11	
Germany	2	
U.S.S.R.	3·5	
Asia		10
Africa		2
America		50
U.S.	17	
Oceania		5
		100

Now many of these deposits are entirely, or almost entirely, unworked to-day : India and Brazil have old iron mines, just as some parts of Africa have, but nothing of great importance has been mined there so far,[6] and Cuba, Newfoundland and Oceania, with a seventh part of the total supplies, have practically remained untouched. The quantity of iron extracted from world resources by current mining is not important quantitatively when compared with the size of the lodes known with certainty to exist. If we assume that mining were to continue at the rate averaged for the years 1925 to 1933, viz., 147 million metric tons annually, the known lodes of ores

[5] To do justice to the uncertainty and subjectivity of such estimates we give in Table A1 (2) (b) another estimate which, however, differs in no very important way from the table discussed in the text. The most remarkable differences are those relating to France and the United States. More important seems to me the way in which the rather speculative character of such estimates emerges from these tables.

[6] Even iron-ore mining in India is, as yet, carried on on a very small scale, though the future holds more important possibilities.

would allow this rate to be maintained for another 393 years.[6a] But if only half the mined iron were to survive, to be used over and over again through the melting down of scrap, the world would, by that time, be incredibly full of iron. Even if a further big increase of mining takes place, there is, therefore, no prospect of a future shortage of iron—at least for the world as a whole.

Table A1 (3) shows that the existing production of iron ores and of iron and steel is very unequally distributed over the world, the dispersion, however, being very different from that of the wealth in iron ores present in the soil. The following

[6a] We come to a similar conclusion when we inquire critically into the foundations of some pessimistic forecasts of an imminent world scarcity of iron. Mr. *Lippincott* discusses the question as to whether a comparative shortage of iron may threaten the world and develops what seems to me an undue pessimism. It is quite true that the appearance of, *e.g.*, China and India as buyers on the iron market on a large scale might mean a great increase in world consumption. It is doubtful whether the present per-head figure for annual iron consumption in the U.S. will ever be reached by countries much more densely populated and beginning their full " development " only in an age when railways will be already old-fashioned. A rise in the consumption of iron in China and India to half the per-head level of the U.S. would, therefore, mean a very great rise over two-score years or more. If we put the per-head annual consumption of steel in China and India for the future at two-tenths of a ton this would mean an increase of ·15 tons per head or annually 760,000,000 × ·15 = 114 million tons. Assuming an iron content of 50 per cent. in these ores, the annual consumption would need to be 228 million tons. This would bring future world consumption, allowing for other increases, up to something like 500 million tons per year, so that the " certain " lodes of ore in our Table A1 (2) (a) would be sufficient for a century if consumption were to continue at such a rate and if no corrections had to be made in this computation.

But we may safely assume that investment at such a rate over a whole century or longer is very improbable and that it is not over-sanguine to expect that after a certain time 40 per cent. of the iron contained in new steel will come from scrap material. If we then assume 80 per cent. of the above figure to be the maximum probable permanent annual consumption (400 million tons of ore) and a saving of 40 per cent. of that by the use of scrap iron (Mr. Lippincott assumes that only 25 per cent. of the annual production of iron does not ultimately reappear ; if I put 40 per cent. instead of 75 per cent. I am certainly extremely conservative), we arrive at a figure for permanent annual consumption of only 240 million tons ; if we deduct a further 20 per cent. of this to allow for other metals admixed with iron in the steel alloys to be used in future (stainless steel contains 17 per cent. chromium, 2 per cent. carbon, etc.), we have to divide the " certain " lodes of 57,812 million tons by 192 million. This gives the result that world stores of iron ore should last for 301 years. As the peak in consumption will be reached only very gradually, we should be safe for 350 or 360 years—certainly a more reassuring outlook than for quite a lot of other raw materials.

I hope the reader will excuse this web of entirely hypothetical figures and calculations. I only wanted to show in an example how utterly shaky the foundations are on which some optimistic and pessimistic forecasts are based.

table shows the existing unequal dispersions under these three headings in a very striking manner:

TABLE T8.

DISPERSION OF RESOURCES AND PRODUCTION OF IRON IN PERCENTAGES.

Percentages.	Lodes of Iron Ores.		Proportion of the World's Production of Ores, 1933.		Proportion of the World's Production of Pig Iron and Raw Steel, 1934.	
EUROPE		33		72		60·8
Great Britain ...	7		8·5		10·5	
France	11		34		8·5	
Germany ...	2		3		17	
U.S.S.R. ...	3·5		16		14	
AMERICA		50		20·2		30·5
U.S.	17		20		29·5	

The inevitable drawback of this table is that since the proportion of pig iron reappearing in steel cannot be eliminated there is some double counting of uncertain size. Though the figures used for making the totals for Europe and America in the second and third columns of this table are not quite complete the discrepancy between them is enormous. Even countries like Italy and Japan are comparatively well off as regards the production of iron and steel, though certainly not as regards resources of iron ore.

TABLE T9.

THE WEALTH OF ITALY AND JAPAN IN IRON.

Percentages of World Totals.	Proportion of the World's Population, 1931–1932.	Proportion of the World's Production of Pig Iron and Raw Steel, 1934.
Italy	2	1·7
Japan, including Manchuria and Korea	5·5	4·2

The disadvantages of these two countries are, however, slight and bound to lose much of their significance in the light of what we found concerning the increasingly important part played by scrap iron in the provision of raw material for the heavy industries.

Another result of the inspection of our Tables A1 (2) and (3) is that the importance of the colonial territories[7] in the provision of iron for the world's consumption is quite subordinate

[7] We do not treat the Dominions of Newfoundland, Canada, etc., as colonies for reasons explained later in the text. The same applies to India.

(only French and Spanish North Africa are exceptions to this rule which deserve to be mentioned). This is, in all probability, bound to remain so, unless quite unexpected new discoveries of iron ores in colonial territories change the whole picture fundamentally.

The production of pig iron and raw steel has varied very much from year to year, as our tables show. It has ranged after the war between the very low figures of 76 million metric tons in 1921 and 91 million in 1932 and a peak of no less than 223 million tons in 1929 (with some double counting in all of these cases, see above).

The order of precedence in the production of pig iron and raw steel among the first-class powers (the " Big Seven ") is shown by Table A1 (4) to have changed in the following ways :

TABLE T10.

ORDER OF RANK IN PRODUCTION OF IRON AND STEEL, 1913–1934.

Relative Importance.	1913.	1929.	1934.
France	4	3	5
Great Britain	3	4	4
Germany	2	2	2
Italy	6	7	7
Japan	7	6	6
U.S.	1	1	1
U.S.S.R.	5[1]	5	3

[1] Including Poland and Baltic Provinces.

The changes, in spite of all the 1919 adjustments of political territories, are on the whole not very significant. Italy and Japan, and again France and Great Britain, have exchanged places ; the U.S. and Germany still lead, though in 1934 in a less overwhelming way than in former years. Only Russia has been advancing rapidly since her great programme of industrialization. Another leap like that from 1929 to 1934 would bring her, without doubt, up to second place—a fact which has obvious military and political implications. So far the " dissatisfied " and the " satisfied " countries (if we exclude the U.S. from the comparison) have developed their aggregate production of pig iron and raw steel in the following way :

TABLE T11.

IRON INDUSTRY IN "SATISFIED" AND "DISSATISFIED" COUNTRIES, 1913–1934.

Nations.	In millions of Metric Tons.		
	1913.	1929.	1934.
"Satisfied"	39·3	46·4	47·5
"Dissatisfied" ...	43·3	40·4	32·9

This shows us a steady and total reversal of the former situation. The balance of production of the "dissatisfied" over the "satisfied" nations in 1913 was one of 4 million tons; their negative balance was one of 6 million tons in 1929, and in the midst of the new boom, in 1934, it had reached as much as 14·6 million tons! Here again the political and military implications are equally clear.[7a]

Comprehensive, reliable figures for international commerce in iron ores, pig iron, raw steel and semi-processed goods, like tinplate, wire and rails, are—just as is the case with most other raw materials which interest us in this study—unfortunately available only for the years of the last business cycle. They show, from a very high peak in 1929, an enormous drop which reached its deepest point in almost all cases in 1932. Nineteen thirty-three brought a distinct, though in most cases modest, recovery, except for iron in bars and the mixed group "other sheet iron". Recovery was hastened in 1934 and 1935, and as far as we can judge from the figures for some countries quoted in Table A1 (6), and from other sources which need not be quoted here, this speeding-up of the international movement of iron in 1934 had a lot to do with building and armaments. This is illustrated by the figures for the importation of iron ores into Germany, Great Britain and Japan, although only Japan had regained by 1934 the level of her 1929 imports. Unfortunately, the figures in the Tables A1 (5) and (6) do not cover the same field and are therefore not strictly comparable, though the figures in Table A1 (6), column six, show that the total of world exports of iron ores in 1934 must

[7a] The figures for 1935 have come to hand during the revision of the manuscript. The total production of the "satisfied" nations was 53·7, that of the "dissatisfied" nations 39·6 million tons, a surplus in favour of the first group of 14·1 million tons.

have been at least 32 million tons, so that this gauge of industrial recovery would read:

TABLE T12.

WORLD EXPORTS OF IRON ORE, 1932–1934.

In million Metric Tons.		
1932.	1933.	1934.
20·5	24·6	32

Table A1 (7) shows, in gold marks,[8] that the decrease in prices of iron ore went on, even during the period of recovery, and even up to July, 1936, the date at which our table ends, on a rather impressive scale. At this latter date, though, a standstill seemed to be near at last. The same price trend is apparent up to 1935 for products of the processing of ores

[8] One of the great difficulties in an inquiry like ours is that statistics are so much more often given in money units than in units of weight, etc. Where we could not avoid taking money figures because quantitative data in units of weight or volume were not available, we have done so generally by using, over a period of time, prices reduced to quantities of gold. The RM., a rather fictitious unit with its official rate of exchange on the old (theoretical) gold standard, as fixed after the Dawes Agreement, may quite well serve as such a defined unit of gold. The £, the $, etc., are " off gold " now and data given in terms of them would require after 1931 and 1933 respectively to be reduced to gold pounds and gold dollars. The purchasing power of gold has, of course, changed also in the course of time, as is shown by the following example. In the official German publication, *Der Welthandel in wichtigen Nahrungsmitteln und Rohstoffen vor und nach dem Kriege*, the volume of world commerce is measured on the basis of prices, reduced to the same level of purchasing power in relation to equal quantities of gold. The several goods are weighted. So the authors arrive at a table which gives, in terms of the pre-war purchasing power of gold, the value of world trade in the following figures:

TABLE T12a.—VALUE OF WORLD TRADE IN GOLD MARKS, 1913–1924.

	1913.	1922.	1923.	1924.
" Gold marks," 1,000 million	170	132	140	161
1913 = 100	100	78	82	95

Moreover, in this inquiry, we generally measure world trade in any commodity in the quantities and values appearing in the statistics of exporting, not importing, countries. The quantities, it is true, should be identical in both cases, if there were not differences in the completeness with which imports and exports are registered; but the values must be different. The best detailed statistics are available for exports, but the figures for imports and exports cannot be mixed, because import money figures have a tendency to be determinately greater than export figures. Hence they cannot be used together as a measure of quantities, even if due allowance is made for price changes. Import values include, as even J. B. Say knew, transport costs, commercial profits, import duties, handling costs in ports, etc., in their

which were not protected by duties in England, like pig iron and sheet iron; but for these goods the drop in prices from 1932 to 1935 was much smaller than that for iron ores in the U.S., and in 1936 recovery of prices was distinct. The same is

estimated values at the moment of importation. We find, *e.g.*, in the German Statistical Year Book for 1936, two series of figures (from which we have calculated the third and fourth series):

TABLE T12b.—VALUE OF WORLD TRADE, 1929–1935, IN 1,000 MILLION RM.

	1929.	1930.	1931.	1932.	1933.	1934.	1935.
I.—Value of all imports in world commerce:							
a. Living animals	1·4	1·5	1·1	·6	·4	·4	·4
b. Foodstuffs and beverages	35·9	29·5	23·2	16·8	13·8	12·3	12·3
c. Raw materials and semi-processed goods ...	54·7	42·8	29	19·6	19	18·8	19·3
d. Finished goods	55·9	46·3	33·3	20·8	18·8	18·3	18·5
II.—Value of all exports, do.:							
a.	1·4	1·4	·9	·5	·4	·3	·4
b.	21·6	25·7	19·5	14·2	11·8	10·8	10·9
c.	47·4	35·8	24·3	16·5	16·7	16·5	17
d.	55·8	45·8	32·8	20·8	18·8	18·4	18·4
I. *a–d*, Totals	147·9	120·1	86·6	57·8	52	49·8	50·5
II. *a–d*, Totals	136·2	108·7	77·5	52	47·7	46	46·7
III.—Surplus of import or export (—) values, do:							
a.	0	·1	·2	·1	0	·1	0
b.	4·3	3·8	3·7	2·6	2	1·5	1·4
c.	7·3	7	4·7	3·1	2·3	2·3	2·3
d.	·1	·5	·5	0	0	—·1	·1
IV.—The same, in per cent., of exports:							
a.	0	7·1	22·2	20	0	33·3	0
b.	13·6	14·8	18·9	18·4	16·9	13·9	12·9
c.	15·4	19·5	19·3	18·8	13·7	13·9	13·5
d.	·2	1·1	1·2	0	0	—·5	·5
III. Totals	11·7	11·4	9·1	5·8	4·3	3·8	3·8
IV. Totals	8·6	10·5	11·7	11·1	9·1	8·3	8·1

If we look through the columns of group IV we find an extremely wide range of values, from −·5 to +19·5 (even if we disregard the less important and rather unreliable figures for living animals with their extreme percentage of 33·3). We further find a maximum in 1930 or 1931 with the wide range from +1·1 to +19·5 in the first of these years, and we get then in general a decrease and a convergence, so that the series for 1929 and 1935 are not so very dissimilar, being as follows:

TABLE T12c.—DIVERGENCES IN IMPORT SURPLUSES IN WORLD TRADE, 1929–1935.

	a	*b*	*c*	*d*	Totals.
1929 ...	0	13·6	15·4	·2	8·6
1935 ...	0	12·9	13·5	·5	8·1

Though we may assume that further approach to the peak of the coming boom may tend towards full restoration of the series which we found for 1929, the whole inquiry makes it clear that, in the intermediate period, the "natural" differences in import and export valuations were so wide that we cannot mix import and export values in attempting to measure quantities.

true for some other items in our table. The increase in prices is shown in the following table:

TABLE T13.

INCREASES IN CERTAIN IRON PRICES, 1932 TO 1936.

	Per cent. 1932 to July, 1936.
Belgium, girders	28
Belgium, iron bars	25
Great Britain, scrap iron	35

Conclusions can be based on Table A1 (8) only with great caution, for during the same period the consumption of steel has, in all probability, not decreased like that of pig iron, but increased, though unfortunately comparable figures are not available for 1913 and 1929.

Table A1 (9) shows in rather more detail the rapid increase of production in Russia. The increase from the low point of 1931 is indeed impressive, and no end may be expected of this development during the next few years, unless the Russian government, contrary to their present policy, should deliberately want to stop it—which, in view of the international political situation, is not very probable.

Tables A1 (10) (a) and (b) show the development of the heavy industries in Western Europe since 1913. In regard to Table (a) we must not forget that coal provides now much more energy per unit burnt than it did in 1913. If we increase the figures for 1929 by 10 per cent. to make up for this difference, our comparison for coal looks like this:

TABLE T14.

COAL PRODUCTION IN CERTAIN EUROPEAN COUNTRIES, 1913 AND 1929.

	1913.	1929.	In million Metric Tons. + or —	in per cent. + or —
Germany (excl. Saar) ...	141	179	+38	+27
Belgium	23	30	+ 7	+34
France	40	59	+19	+37·5
Great Britain	292	288	− 4	− 1·4
Holland	2	13	+11	+550
Total area	498	569	+71	+14

The position of Great Britain has, comparatively, greatly deteriorated. The explanation of this is to be found, as Table (b) shows, not only in the collapse of the export of coal for navigation purposes, but also in the very hesitating recovery in the production of pig iron. The increase in the making of steel could give to coal mining only a very imperfect compensation for this.

We shall learn the implications of the above facts only at a later stage, when we begin the discussion of our problems. But even the short exposition of the facts as shown by the statistical tables is already pregnant with rather suggestive hints.

2.—*Aluminium.*

Aluminium is one of the metals which are only just beginning to transform our life. Shortly before the war its use was quite limited; the excellent and, at that time, absolutely up-to-date, six-volume *Landlexikon*, says in Vol. I (published 1911) that this metal was used for the following purposes: domestic and kitchen apparatus, art and craft work (*Kunstgewerbe*), scientific instruments, for inducing chemical reactions, as a substitute for lithographic slabs in the cheap multiplication of graphs and typescripts, and for fireworks. In view of these extremely limited uses (the principal one being for pots and pans) a world production of 65,000 metric tons in 1913 was already quite a remarkable thing.

The use of aluminium in modern technique is based on its high electric conductivity, its very low specific weight (2·7) and its aptness for alloy with other metals. The resulting compounds (chiefly made with copper, silicium, magnesium, iron) unite the low specific weight of aluminium with the mechanical and electrical virtues of the other metals (strength in case of iron, electric conductivity in the case of copper, ductility, brittleness, etc.). Aluminium is malleable at as low a temperature as +100°C. It, therefore, serves as an increasingly important raw material for cables, for the building of aeroplanes, motor-cars, railway coaches, and will, in all probability, continue to be used in wider and wider fields. Its present uses make it very important for military purposes. It is employed, for instance, in the building of torpedo boats and U-boats, and in the manufacture of thermit for bombing. Thermit is a powder consisting of a mixture of metallic aluminium and iron oxide (Fe_3O_4) ; when lighted, this mixture burns and develops a blazing heat (3,000°C.). Thermit powder is, therefore, used as a filling for incendiary bombs to be thrown from aeroplanes, and seems to have a great future. . . .

Aluminium is not found at all in its pure elementary form, but is quite common as a component of all clayey substances. It can be produced from clay, but only at a pinch and with the help of an enormous quantity of electric power. So the fact that it can be made from clay is unimportant in peace-time, but in war-time no country that has clay in its soil and can afford the consumption of the necessary electric power need be really short of it. That is why all who look at the military side of the problem of raw materials discount a great scarcity of it anywhere under such conditions, and even bring aluminium into their plans as the one great, nearly inexhaustible, source of substitutes for other metals. Maybe they are right ; we shall discuss these questions later. But in peace-time, when cost is not a *quantité négligeable*, only a raw material which is rich in metal and gives it up with comparative ease and only cheap electric power in the smallest quantities possible are used.

The highest content of aluminium (in the form of the compound Na_3AlFl_6) is present in cryolite, an ore which is found and mined only near the western coast of Greenland. The mines there are the property of the Greenland government, the number of lodes known to exist is rather limited, and the quantity mined annually is, therefore, limited by the government according to how much money they need to balance the budget. The quantities exported from Greenland have been :

TABLE T15.

EXPORTS OF CRYOLITE FROM GREENLAND, 1928–1935.

In 1,000 Metric Tons.

1928.	1929.	1930.	1931.	1932.	1933.	1934.	1935.
25·9	29·8	36·2	17·7	17·9	10·4	15·2	25·2

Cryolite is rarely used as the only raw material in making aluminium in the electrolytic way. It is too expensive for that. But one of its useful qualities is that other aluminium ores are soluble in cryolite when this is made molten by heating; so cryolite is added to these other ores when they are subjected to electrolysis. The most important among these ores is bauxite, a mineral originally found only in France, but now produced in large quantities in some other countries as well. Table A2 (1) shows the distribution of the production of these ores. By far the largest volume is still produced in France. For the other countries given in the table the order, according to size of production, was:

TABLE T16.

ORDER OF RANK OF BAUXITE-PRODUCING COUNTRIES, 1929 AND 1934.

	1929.	1934.
Italy	5	2
Jugoslavia	6	5
Hungary	1	3
U.S.	2	1
British Guiana	3	6
Dutch Guiana	4	4

The comparatively comfortable situation of Italy and the diminishing importance of British Guiana deserve particular note.

The production of the metal from bauxite and cryolite is centred round the sources of cheap electrical energy produced from falling water. In Europe Germany, Switzerland, France and Norway are the chief producing countries, and in North America Canada appears as an important producer side by side with the U.S. Germany easily held first place in Europe in 1934 and second place in the world, though she scarcely produces any ore. Technological, industrial and military interests depend on aluminium, and the production of the metal is a state monopoly (for military reasons), a fact which removes all difficulties of capitalization from the way of the industry.

The table showing the volume of international trade reveals a steep decline (about 60 per cent.) in the quantities of aluminium crossing international frontiers from 1929 to 1932, but a far from equal drop in the shipments of bauxite (only about 30·5 per cent.). German exportation had almost entirely stopped in 1934, while her imports were very large. The following table gives an idea of the situation :

TABLE T17.

GERMANY : CONSUMPTION OF ALUMINIUM, 1929–1935.

	In 10,000 Metric Tons.		
	1929.	1934.	1935.
Production	33	32	70·8
Imports	14·2	6·4	18·1
Totals	47·2	38·4	88·9
Exports	4·1	·7	·2
Consumption	43·1	37·7	88·7

Consumption had then, in 1934, already nearly reached the enormously high peak of 1929 ; in 1935, under the pressure of rearmament, it had more than doubled it. This quick recovery in the industry was attained, as Table A2 (4) shows, in spite of the fact that prices in Germany went on decreasing till 1935, and did not recover before July, 1936, where our table ends. In the U.S. the gold price of aluminium continued to fall right up to the end of our table. But on the whole the aluminium price drop in Germany with her monopoly had been small during the slump. The percentage decrease in its price from 1929 to July, 1936, was

in the U.S.	50·6
in Germany	24·4

or less than half as much in Germany as in the U.S. with her competitive production of aluminium. But the systematic use of aluminium in Germany as a substitute particularly for copper, forced on industry more or less directly by the government, had some importance on the level of its price also. In other countries such substitution could not be very attractive at a time when copper, as a consequence of the slump, was " dirt cheap ". In Germany substitution was enforced by the limitations put by the government on the importation and use of metals of foreign origin ; so its comparative expensiveness could have no bearing on the problem.

Though the government of Greenland restricts the production

of cryolite according to budget requirements, it has never shown the least sign of differentiating between foreign customers.

3.—*Chromium.*

Chromium is a metal used for making several important alloys and coatings. The coatings protect the underlying material against the oxygen of the atmosphere. The alloys are very hard and resistant to rust (" stainless steel ") and organic acids. An alloy of chromium and nickel is very much used for electrical heating apparatus, as the electrical resistance of chromium is very high. The age of electric heating and cooking opens a great future for it. Some of the chromium compounds provide important dyes and pigments. The metal is used for photomechanical processes, and as a rapidly-acting tanning material its use is now widely spread.

As our table shows, the distribution of chromium in the world is very " haphazard " (in a politico-economic sense). Its use is quickly increasing, as is that of all metals which are used in the making of the long range of new alloys, particularly iron alloys, which are so characteristic of new technique. The rapid development of production in Turkey is worth noting. Two important producing countries, viz., New Caledonia (French) and Southern Rhodesia (British), are colonial.

Chromium alloys with steel often contain as much as 17 per cent. chromium metal ; this high percentage is bound to lead to a further quick increase in consumption. As it is doubtful how far the existing mines may be able to keep pace with this demand the situation may end in a strangling of further use by very high prices and in the partial diversion of demand to other substitutes.

4.—*Copper.*

Copper is so well known a metal that it is scarcely necessary to say much about its world-wide and vital importance for our economic life and about its technical achievements. Its enormous importance for the age of electricity is a truism. Copper is a widely-spread metal. It is found, in small quantities, in so many parts of the world that mankind could use it as the basic metal of civilization on a comparatively large scale, at a period when populations were still very thinly scattered everywhere, even though transport from country to country was very limited. We find " bronze ages " all the world over in the more remote or recent past.

The total production of copper ores has increased in an imposing way. Table A4 (1) shows for the period 1913 to 1929 an increase of something like 100 per cent. The drop during the slump was very severe, nearly 54 per cent. from 1929 to 1932, which brought production down again into the neighbourhood of the 1913 level and even slightly below it for one year. Only for that one year; the recovery was immediate and very quick.

If we take for our guidance the figures for 1929, when presumably all producing areas, at the top of the boom, did their best to produce whatever they then could, we find that if we compare the total area of Europe (excluding the U.S.S.R.) with overseas territories of something like a similar size which are important producers of copper ores, we get

TABLE T18.

COPPER PRODUCTION IN SOME COUNTRIES, 1929.

	In 1,000 Metric Tons. Production of Copper Ores.
Europe	132·6
Canada	112·5
U.S.	905

Among these European countries there was at least one, Jugoslavia, which was able to increase her production of copper ores considerably through slump and recovery. The European production as a whole fell comparatively little during the slump (by only about 15 per cent.), whereas the U.S. production fell by 76 per cent.

The production of copper ores has pursued an astonishingly meandering course round the globe during the last quarter of a century. The following table of the changes in the relative positions of the chief producing countries shows this. To get a correct picture, however, we must add to the Table A4 (1) the production of copper in the smelting works of Katanga (Belgian Congo), as this country does not publish statistics of the quantities of copper ores mined, and smelts and refines practically all its ores before exportation. We disregard Japan, as she is a minor producer. So we find :

TABLE T19.

RELATIVE IMPORTANCE OF COUNTRIES PRODUCING COPPER, 1913-1934.

	In 1,000 Metric Tons.							
	1913.		1929.		1932.		1934.	
World production	990·4		1,947·6		900·8		1,287·3	
U.S.	555·4	/1/	905	/1/	216	/1/	217·1	/2/
Chile	42·3	/3/	320·6	/2/	103·2	/3/	256·7	/1/
Canada	34·9	/4/	112·5	/4/	112·3	/2/	166·5	/3/
Northern Rhodesia	—	/7/	5·6	/7/	88·6	/4/	140	/4/
Mexico	52·6	/2/	86·6	/5/	35·2	/6/	44·3	/6/
Peru	27·8	/5/	54·4	/6/	21·5	/7/	27·6	/7/
Katanga	7·5	/6/	137	/3/	54·1	/5/	110·1	/5/

Figures between / / indicate the relative positions of the several countries ranked according to volume of production. If we arrange the countries in order of importance as producers we see the following developments :

TABLE T20.

CHANGES IN RELATIVE IMPORTANCE OF SOME COUNTRIES IN THE PRODUCTION OF COPPER ORES, 1913–1934.

1913.	1929.	1932.	1934.
1. U.S.	1. U.S.	1. U.S.	1. Chile
2. Mexico	2. Chile	2. Chile	2. U.S.
3. Chile	3. Katanga	3. Chile	3. Canada
4. Canada	4. Canada	4. N. Rhodesia	4. N. Rhodesia
5. Peru	5. Mexico	5. Katanga	5. Katanga
6. Katanga	6. Peru	6. Mexico	6. Mexico
7. N. Rhodesia (nothing)	7. N. Rhodesia	7. Peru	7. Peru

We must not forget that during these years many countries which we have not included in our tables, as they were not of real importance as copper producers, would have come before No. 6. For a country to have dropped to one of the two last places in our list means, therefore, at least after the war, that it has fallen into comparative insignificance. To discuss the reasons for the repeated dramatic changes which we find in our table would lead us too far away from our subject. But the peripeties of this development are themselves memorable enough and will turn up again in our later discussion of the problems.

But copper is not the only case where changes of this kind occur. Mr. Lippincott says on p. 114 of his book:

> "A very common phenomenon in the extraction of minerals is the abandonment of sources which were formerly worked, upon the development of other areas which reveal a lower cost."

He goes on to mention that this has occurred with gold, silver, iron, coal, petroleum, and proceeds:

> "This process of abandonment is always a serious matter for property-owners and for capitalists who have invested funds in works, but it also at times is a matter of considerable national interest. To abandon a partially exploited resource involves the loss of a portion of the mineral remaining in the ground, for this remaining material can only be reclaimed at a later date at great cost."

Though this seems some overstatement of the case, as the careful comparison of the two halves of the last sentence shows, we have no objection to the author's conclusion, because the fate of the working population of the abandoned mining district, of the trades catering for them, etc. (which Mr. Lippincott does not mention), is in jeopardy also. Again, he says:

> "The question of competitive exploitation of resources involves the matter of conservation of national resources."

We would add: and of the international resources also.

So this shifting of the centre of gravity of production within a comparatively short time, and in spite of international endeavours to stop it, is not a feature of copper alone, but is a more or less general problem. As such it will be treated later in its impact on some of the most interesting questions of international commercial policy.

Table A4 (2) again shows us that the processing of the ores, at least in a number of important cases, is quite differently distributed, internationally, from the mining of the ores. The general tendency for the world as a whole is, however, similar to that of the production of ores.

TABLE T21.

PRODUCTION OF COPPER IN ORES AND OF COPPER METAL, 1913–1934.

	In 1,000 Metric Tons. Copper Content of Ores Mined.	Copper Produced.
1913	990·4	1,018·5
1929	1,947·6	1,894·7
1932	900·8	929·1
1934	1,287·3	1,280·9

The following changes in world production can be calculated from these figures :

TABLE T22.

CHANGES IN PRODUCTION OF COPPER IN ORES AND OF COPPER METAL, 1913–1934.

	In per cent. Ores Mined.	Metal Produced.
1913/1929 ...	+97	+86
1929/1932 ...	−54	−51
1932/1934 ...	+30	+38

So here, in these statistics, we find no sign of a widely spread use of scrap metal in copper production.[8a]

The degree of discrepancy between the production of copper ores and of metallic copper in the different countries is best shown by a table showing changes in relative importance. If

[8a] But this is not so certain as this table might seem to prove. For Germany, at least, the figures for copper production available for 1913 to 1925 allow us to calculate the proportion of copper produced from scrap, as shown by the following table :

TABLE T22a.—PROPORTION OF COPPER PRODUCED FROM SCRAP IN GERMANY, 1913–1925.

	In 1,000 Metric Tons. 1913	1920	1921	1922	1923	1924	1925
From ores, etc.	41·5	20·5	25	32	26·2	34·6	39·1
From scrap	8	28	39	46·5	47·9	36·5	41·1
Totals	49·6	48·5	64	78·5	74·1	71·1	80·2
Per cent. from scrap ...	16	58	61	59	65	59	51

we limit ourselves to the eight first places and to the year 1934 we get the following:

TABLE T23.

COUNTRIES PRODUCING COPPER ORE AND COPPER, NUMBERED ACCORDING TO RELATIVE IMPORTANCE.

	Rank among Producers of Ore.	Rank among Producers of Metal.
Germany	below 8	7
U.S.S.R.	8	below 8
Chile	1	1
Canada	3	3
N. Rhodesia	4	5
Katanga	5	6
Jugoslavia	6	below 8
Mexico	7	below 8
U.S.	2	2
Belgium	nothing	4
Japan	nothing	8

Of some significance politically is the fact that among the producers of ore, France with her colonies, Great Britain, Germany, Italy with her colonies, and Japan with hers, play a rather insignificant part, and that among the British colonies only Northern Rhodesia saves the situation. In this respect at least four of the seven Great Powers might be called "dissatisfied" nations.[9] As to the distribution of the actual production of copper, things are rather different; we find the "satisfied" and the "dissatisfied" nations to be:

"satisfied"	"dissatisfied"
Germany.	Russia.
Japan.	Italy.
Great Britain (thanks to N. Rhodesia only).	France.
U.S.	

[9] But there is a qualification to be added to this statement. The following table describes the aggregate balance sheet of the three so-called "Have-Not" nations (Germany, Italy, Japan) in regard to copper for the years 1933, 1934 and 1935:

TABLE T23a.—BALANCE-SHEET OF "DISSATISFIED NATIONS" IN REGARD TO COPPER

	in 1,000 long tons of Copper 1933	1934	1935
Imports	495.5	622	730.7
— Exports	97.5	87.4	68.1
	397.9	535.5	662.6
+ Home production	119.2	122.3	128.3
Balance	517.1	657.8	790.9

These balances were, then, available for consumption or the laying-in of stocks: certainly not particularly poor results.

Table A4 (3) shows the steady and considerable decrease of international trade in copper and copper ores. The third line of this table is given in money terms, as it is obviously impossible to add up copper cables and copper buttons by means of any other common denominator. But money figures may be misleading. The particularly large fall, and the continuation of the decrease beyond 1932, are to be explained partly by the fact that this line expresses the result of the multiplication of decreasing quantities by decreasing prices.

The figures in the next Table A4 (4) concern chiefly countries of minor interest. A preponderance of home consumption over exports is of interest in the following particular cases:

TABLE T24.

COPPER CONSUMPTION OF THREE COUNTRIES, 1934.

In 1,000 Metric Tons.

(1) Germany: production 105; imports 180; exports 12; *consumption* 283.
(2) Belgium: production 106; imports 74; exports 61; *consumption* 119.
(3) U.S.: production 407·1; imports 175; exports 238; *consumption* 344·1.

But as these figures exclude for Germany "copper refined from foreign raw copper and copper salvaged in factories making semi-finished copper goods," and as it is unknown how far recovered copper is included in the Belgian figures, whereas the figures for the U.S. include all "secondary" copper, the value of these figures is not great; the consumption in Germany was certainly much more, and that in Belgium may or may not have been larger.

But even so, it is very interesting to see how near Germany has come to the level of the U.S. in her consumption of copper, while there is even a distinct possibility that she actually consumed more.

Table A4 (5) shows in its first line that the international convention for limiting the output of copper has been successful. Though production was increased after 1932 it was kept within such limits that world stocks of copper, which had attained a tremendously high figure in that year, decreased considerably during the following years. This could be done only, as the two other lines of this table show, by allowing prices to decrease still more. The minimum was only reached as late as about the middle of 1935, and the rise since then up to the end of our table is very modest; only 1937 brought a real recovery in prices.

5.—*Gold and Silver.*

The tables under this head do not require much explanation. Statistics of the production and movement of precious metals are particularly reliable and detailed. Though quite an amount of gold and silver is used for industrial purposes the field of its employment here does not seem to widen very much ; use for monetary purposes and the making of jewellery and of silver plate are entirely in the foreground. Silver plate, it is true, has come to be used much more widely all the world over during the last two-score of years or so, during which time the production of the metal has increased enormously. Silver, therefore, lost much of its value in terms of gold (53·8 per cent.) between 1928 and 1933. It recovered only a very small piece of ground when the American Treasury began to buy silver on a large scale, as China got rid of great quantities of silver currency at about the same time by changing to a kind of gold currency.

So much has been said about the unequal distribution of the world's gold mines that it is scarcely necessary to go at any length into that matter. Table A5 (5) shows with what enormous speed the known stocks of gold in the currency banks and in monetary circulation have increased during the last ten years. The increase in the purchasing power of gold, a consequence of the universal drop in the prices of commodities and in wage rates since the breakdown of 1929, has given a new fillip to production. The latter rose by 28·4 per cent. from 1929 to 1934. But this table requires some explanation. The temporary decrease of " visible " gold stocks which apparently occurred in 1930 is only a consequence of the fact that, beginning with that year, our table no longer includes gold in monetary circulation (in itself nowadays no longer an important amount). The decrease in 1933 is explained by the disappearance of large quantities of gold into hoards, particularly in France. The increase of visible stocks in 1934—1·3 million kg.—is in excess of that year's production by no less than half a million kg. This hints at the element of uncertainty which is introduced into the figures of our table as well as into the situation in the world markets by the hoarding and de-hoarding of gold. The gold output of every year is supposed to flow into central banks to the tune of about 60 per cent.

If this assumption is correct, the production of the year 1934 would have meant an increase of (statistically) "visible" stocks by 510,000 kg. or less than 3 per cent. In view of these facts it would seem that the considerable inequalities in production are of less actual importance than the still greater inequalities in possession and in resources for acquisition in other ways than by production.

These inequalities are indeed important. As to production: if we take the year 1933, we find that, of the whole world production, 15 per cent. came from the U.S.S.R., 11·8 per cent. from Canada, 9·2 per cent. from the U.S., and 44·1 per cent. from South Africa; the rest of the world together produced only 19·9 per cent.

As to the possession of gold, we find the following interesting data for the year 1934 (for simplicity's sake I give the figures in million RM.):

TABLE T25.

DISTRIBUTION OF GOLD STOCKS, 1934, IN MILLION RM.

The world	54,880	British Empire	1,927
Europe	29,537	Other colonies	273
Non-colonial America ...	22,048	Other countries	1,095

But we have to re-group these figures for the sake of greater clarity:

TABLE T26.

DISTRIBUTION OF GOLD STOCKS, 1934, BY COUNTRIES.

	In million RM.		Relative Importance
British group:			
Great Britain	3,928		
Dominions[1] and India	1,887		
Colonies, protectorates, mandated territories	40		
		5,855	/3/
France:			
Mother Country	13,745		
Colonies, protectorates, etc. ...	62		
		13,807	/2/
Belgium and colonies		1,469	/8/
Germany		152	
Italy		1,284	
U.S.S.R.		1,845	/4/
U.S.		20,425	/1/
Japan, including Manchuria		981	
Netherlands and colonies		1,676	/6/
Switzerland		1,593	/7/
Spain		1,837	/5/

[1] Excluding Southern Rhodesia.

The U.S.S.R. stocks have shown a remarkably steady increase throughout recent years, whereas those of other countries have been subject to wild fluctuations, and Germany has lost her gold with constant obstinacy. The figures for 1934 are quite obsolete now as I write this (January, 1937), because in the meantime France has lost much gold and Italy the best part of what gold she had got before her Ethiopian war. Whereas other countries, particularly England and the U.S., have got so much more of it that they are now in serious difficulties as to what to do with it all. There is an increasing tendency to "sterilize" gold; but that sometimes the possession of large stocks of gold, in the banks, in monetary circulation, or in private hoards, may be of help in times of scarcity and of breakdown of important exports during a slump, can be seen from the recent experience of India. Up to the end of 1930 India had been, on balance, an importer of gold for many years, and had been able to build up an important reserve in the hands of her government, as the succeeding figures show:

TABLE T27.

GOLD IN POSSESSION OF GOVERNMENT OF INDIA, 1913–1934.

In million RM.

1913	1926	1927	1928	1929	1930	1931	1932	1933	1934
520	456	506	527	544	538	679	680	681	681

In 1931 India began to export gold on a large scale; she lost gold to the following extent:

TABLE T28.

LOSSES OF GOLD FROM INDIA, 1931–1934.

To	For million RM.			
	1931	1932	1933	1934
Great Britain	265	895	499	513
France	9	4	5	–
The U.S.	34	112	108	188
Totals	304	1,011	612	701
And produced	28	29	29	28
NET LOSS	276	982	583	673

Over the whole period this meant a loss of no less than 2,514 million RM. or about five times the reserve of the government. It must be added that this gold had been acquired and saved by the Indian population at times of high prices and was spent again in times of low prices, so that a distinct gain on the purchasing power of at least 40 per cent. ought to have been made, covering the loss in interest over quite a number of years of hoarding.

These changes are so frequent that there is not much point in bringing the figures up to the most recent date—they become obsolete again while the ink of the manuscript dries. In any case we have seen that the international inequality in the distribution of gold stocks is of a more serious character than the quite different international inequality in the distribution of production.

Silver is scarcely a raw material of much political importance at the present moment. We might say of it, stealing another author's *bon mot*, that it has a great future behind it. Its great loss of value during the slump and its hesitating recovery (as long as purchases for monetary purposes do not enhance its price artificially for a time) show that it is, to a certain extent, more a source of embarrassment than of advantage for a country nowadays to have a large silver production. Only the richest deposits are still mined for the silver itself. But its production is, to a certain extent, an automatically functioning side-line in the production of other, more important metals, like gold, lead, copper and zinc. This maintains large-scale production even at extremely low prices and, as long as gold monometallism sweeps the field, makes hopeless all endeavours to bring the price of silver back again to the neighbourhood of the old, famous, but now long-lost gold-silver ratio of 16 : 1.

6.—*Lead.*

Lead serves many important purposes, from gunshot and water-pipes to accumulators, soldering media, flint glass, pigments and letterpress. Most of the figures in our tables explain themselves, but a few comments may be made; for instance, that Great Britain and Jugoslavia increased their production right through the last depression; and that the recovery in some countries was quite rapid. Nineteen thirty-four showed a level of output nearly as high, or even higher, than in 1929 in the following countries:

Producers of lead ore.	*Producers of lead.*
Germany.	Germany.
Great Britain.	Australia.
Jugoslavia.	
India.	
Canada.	
Australia.	

The brunt of the losses was, and still is, borne chiefly by the U.S., Mexico and Spain. The drop in the quantities passing through the channels of international trade was not particularly deep during the slump: only about 26 per cent.—much less than the drop in production. On the other hand, visible stocks on the world market did not decrease, but went on increasing during the first two years of recovery, in spite of a particularly steep and progressive fall in prices, which changed into an increase only in the early months of 1935.

The production of lead ore in small quantities is widely spread. Large-scale production is, so far, concentrated in North America and Australia.

7.—*Manganese.*

Manganese is chiefly used to make steel tough and hard; for that purpose alloys with iron containing 6 to 12 per cent. of manganese are widely used. There are four countries with a large-scale production of the ore: the U.S.S.R., the U.S., India and the Gold Coast. The metal is nowhere produced as a pure metal on a large scale, as it is not used in that form for any quantitatively important purpose; alloy steels for special uses are made with the help of manganese compounds.

The slump had an enormous effect on the production of the ore. The percentage decrease from 1929 to 1932 was: in Germany 88, in the U.S. 97, in Egypt 99·8 per cent. Relatively the best resistance was shown by the manganese ore production of Russia, where the drop in production was only one of 30 per cent. But the fact that there was a drop in that country at all, as opposed to the developments in most branches of mining in Russia during this time, is worth noting. Recovery was quick in Germany and in the Gold Coast, particularly slow in India and the U.S., and of moderate speed in the other countries.

International trade did not show quite the same deep wounds, though the losses were certainly big enough. The deepest point of the depression was again reached in 1932, when shipments were below those of 1929 by 71 per cent. Recovery began quickly, on the whole, in 1933.

As the Gold Coast is one of the important producers of manganese this is one of the few cases in which colonial countries have some importance as sources of mineral wealth.

8.—*Nickel.*

Statistics of nickel production are very incomplete. But in comparison with Canada all other countries are unimportant as producers of this ore.

The U.S. since 1921 imported and exported nickel in the following quantities :

TABLE T29.

NICKEL IN FOREIGN TRADE OF THE U.S., 1921–1934.

	1921/25.	1926/30.	1931.	1932.	1933.	1934.
	Annual Averages.		In 1,000 lbs.			
Exports of metal and alloys ...	3,203	2,353	1,777	2,059	1,509	4,576
Imports :						
Ore	8,195	18,709	11,630	5,918	19,220	11,846
Nickel oxide...		1,772	305	688	2,019	950
Nickel in pigs		42,068	23,862	14,923	31,621	45,800

The production of metallic nickel shows the following changes for the U.S. :

TABLE T30.

PRODUCTION OF NICKEL IN THE U.S., 1915–1934.

In Short Tons of ·907 Metric Tons.

1915	1920	1925	1930	1933	1934
822	365	272	308	126	157

For the years 1928–1930 the following figures are interesting :

TABLE T31.

WORLD TRADE IN NICKEL, 1928–1930.

	In Long Tons of 2,240 lbs. 1928.	1929.	1930.
A. Exports :			
(1) Ores and matte[1,2] :			
(a)	20,526	18,345	21,707
(b)	2,570	7,096	8,122
(2) Metal and alloys	41,421	48,889	34,291
B. Imports :[3]			
(1) Ores and matte	13,669	32,215	27,059
(2) Metal and alloys	45,890	54,419	38,279

[1] Partially processed ore. [2] Including nickel oxide. [3] Less re-exports.

The table cannot unfortunately be added up, as line (*a*) gives figures for the nickel content of ores and matte, whereas line (*b*) gives the weight of the minerals.

It can be seen from these figures that most of the ores mined in Canada and New Caledonia (the only other producer country of any importance) are smelted and refined, or at least partially processed, in the country of origin. It is probably a high estimate if we assume that the nickel ores contain as much as 10 per cent. of nickel.

On the whole the statistics are thoroughly unsatisfactory if inspected with a methodical eye. But they allow us to draw the following conclusion : Canada enjoys a quasi-monopoly of the production of the ore, and its only, though quite subordinate, partner is a French colony.

Nickel-mining in Canada is organized on the basis of a private capitalistic monopoly. That this has not worked worse than free competition in other branches of ore-mining has done can be seen from the fact that the drop in prices from 1929 to 1932 was not particularly large, though certainly deep enough, showing that the crisis could be stood with a remarkably moderate and slow decrease of the price. The deepest point in our Table A8 (b) was only reached in 1934.

Nickel is of great importance. It has many convenient uses, *e.g.*, in the manufacture of coatings protecting other metals against tarnishing, and in the making of " German silver ", which contains two-ninths of nickel, etc. But its chief importance is technical and nautical; the iron-plates of battleships and armoured cruisers consist of a steel alloy containing about 5 per cent. of nickel.

9.—*Quicksilver (Mercury)*.

The world depends for its provision of quicksilver chiefly on three countries: Spain, Italy and the U.S. These three countries among them produced in 1929 no less than 94·8 per cent. of the total quantity produced on the globe.

Among the countries producing small quantities some are perhaps worth mentioning. The production in Japan in 1929, including Korea, was 3,903 lbs., in Algeria 10,415 lbs. For the world market both quantities were, of course, negligible.

10.—*Tin*.

Old-established European tin-mining has never been on a large scale, and the mines have been worked over such long periods that the lodes give nowadays only poor results. At the same time tin has become more and more important of late years owing to the larger scale on which tinplate is used for "tinning" or "canning" all kinds of eatable and drinkable things. Beer in tins instead of in bottles or casks—an idea rather terrifying still to an average Chestertonian European—is, after all, becoming a quite ordinary thing in American life since the dawn of the New Deal. No wonder, then, that the production of tin ore and metal has increased very quickly in recent times. Scrap material is not used in the production of tin to a large extent, as yet. To recover the very thin layers of tin from tinplate is technically quite possible, but expensive and, therefore, not economically attractive.

The chief producing countries now are, as Table A10 (1) shows, two British colonial territories (British Malaya and Nigeria), the Dutch East Indies, Belgian Africa and two independent states, Siam and Bolivia, both of which are distinctly on the up-grade in producing tin. In 1929 British Malaya, the Dutch Indies, Siam and Nigeria, producing between them no less than 65 per cent. of the world output, measured in tin content of the ores, became the chief partners in an international private organization for the limitation of the production of tin ores. On February 27th, 1931, the governments of Bolivia, the Dutch East Indies, Malaya and Nigeria concluded an agreement on restriction of output, which the government of Siam joined in September of that year, and the governments of the Belgian Congo, French Indo-China, Great Britain (for Cornwall), Portugal and Ruanda-Urundi joined in the course of 1934. By this year the distribution of production within the organized group had changed distinctly—at the cost of British Malaya, which delivered 36 per cent. of the world production in 1929, but only 30½ per cent. in 1934. The chief gainer was Siam, with the Dutch Indies coming second.

The development of production and consumption is shown for the years after 1924 by the following table :

TABLE T32.

PRODUCTION AND CONSUMPTION OF TIN, 1925–1935.

		1925.	1926.	1927.	1928.	1929.	1930.	1931.	1932.	1933.	1934.	1935.
Production	1,000	148·1	145·2	159·3	178·8	195·1	177·5	149·6	98	89·4	118·1	149·8
Increase (−), decrease (+) of stocks	metric	+8[1]	+6·6	+1·4	−3·7	−8·4	−15·5	−13·4	−1·9	+15·4	+21·9	+4·4
Actual consumption	tons	156·1	151·8	160·7	175·1	186·7	162	136·2	96·1	104·8	140	154·2
Price (per 100 kg., London, blocks)	RM.	522	582	577	456	412	286	222	197	265	286	272

This shows that consumption shrank between 1929 and 1932 by 49 per cent., production by nearly 50 per cent., and price by 52 per cent., *i.e.*, slightly more than the two other items.

The largely colonial character of the production of tin ores and tin metal is worth noting. We find that the percentage of colonial production was as follows in the years 1929 and 1934 :

TABLE T33.

COLONIAL PRODUCTION OF TIN, 1929 AND 1934.

	Per cent. of Total Production. 1929.	1934.
Output of ores (tin content)	58	53
Output of metal	62	49

[1] This figure from J. K. *Eastham*, Review of Economic Studies, October, 1936, p. 18 ; the others from German Statistical Abstracts.

This high proportion of colonial smelting is particularly remarkable. Recently, however, the most important colonial smelting place, Singapore, has lost much of its former large share.

The Tables A10 (5) and (6) indicate the results of the policy of limitation of output. The drop in prices during the slump was rather marked (52 and 51 per cent. from 1929 to 1932 in both columns of Table A10 (6)). The movement of gold prices of tin for the last ten years before the war and for the time after 1923 is shown by the following table :

TABLE T33a.

PRICES FOR BANCA TIN AT HAMBURG, 1905–1914 AND 1924–1935.

In RM. per 100 kg.

1905	1906	1907	1908	1909	1910	1911	1912	1913	1914		
304	383	366	285	285	324	400	441	427	348		
1924	1925	1926	1927	1928	1929	1930	1931	1932	1933	1934	1935
481	542	601	610	470	430	295	233	213	279	306	302

I quote this series, though it shows a gap (for obvious reasons) of nine years after the beginning of the war, because the prices in RM. may be used as gold prices without further conversion. They give us the following averages for longer periods :

	(1) 1909–1914	(2) 1930–1935	(2) in % of (1)
For a period of 6 years ...	371	271	73
	1905–1914	1926–1935	(2) in % of (1)
For a period of 10 years ...	356	374	105

The movement of prices before the war was certainly less hectic than after 1923 (range of prices 1905–1914 = 35 per cent., 1924–1935 = 65 per cent. of the highest price). But that is characteristic of nearly all price movements during these two periods and is chiefly caused, in the case of tin, by the deep drop in 1931 and 1932 which the " monopoly " did not (perhaps could not) prevent.

The drop in tin prices began already years before the general slump (they reached their peak between August, 1926, and March, 1927). Recovery in prices was at first quick, then distinctly slow, and showed later a tendency upwards, though with temporary variations. The movement up to June, 1936, is shown by the following table:

TABLE T33b.

MONTHLY PRICE MOVEMENTS OF BANCA TIN AT HAMBURG, 1934–1936.

In RM. per 100 kg.

Year.	January.	February.	March.	April.	May.	June.	July.
1934 ...	306	295	301	319	316	300	304
1935 ...	305	305	297	294	298	305	306
1936 ...	290	286	292	286	280	260	

Year.	August.	September.	October.	November.	December.
1934 ...	303	304	305	305	306
1935 ...	301	302	305	309	302

For later months comparable data are not yet available, though it is known that a considerable rise in prices again took place between the summer of 1936 and the spring of 1937, only to be followed by a new slight, but distinct setback with a period of hesitating recovery in the second quarter of 1937.

The tendency towards recovery in prices since 1933 is a general one for all raw materials, with or without monopolistic control of output, and is not a particular feature of tin, and the fluctuations in the price of tin (which varied over a period of 30 months by RM. 59 = 18 per cent. of the highest price) are not exceptionally large but fairly normal. The large stocks which had developed during the slump were unloaded at moderate prices; in July, 1936, stocks had diminished to 15,700 metric tons, *i.e.*, below the figure for any year in our Table A10 (5). Restriction, during the last two years, of production has been moderate in extent. Prices were excessive for years (1924–1929) before the "monopoly" was organized, but have gradually become very moderate since; the average prices were (in RM. per 100 kg.) for 1924–1929: 522; for 1930–1935: 271. Of course, one may argue that prices might have fallen much deeper still during the slump had it not been for the intervention of the syndicate. But does that amount to much more than to the rather trite argument that anything for which you have to pay at all is too expensive? In any case, we should not expect figures like the series with which tin provides us to be taken as a striking proof of intolerable monopolistic exploitation.

The Federated Malay States introduced in 1903 a practically prohibitive export duty of $11.50 per picul (133 lbs. or 60 kg.) on exports of all tin ores not to be smelted in the Straits Settlements; this was the work of Sir Frank Swettenham who was at that time both High Commissioner for British Malaya and Governor-General of the Straits Settlements. In 1904 the exemption from duty was extended to ore exported to the United Kingdom and in 1916 to that exported to Australia. Smelting of tin stopped for a time in the U.S. as a consequence of this policy; when it later re-established itself, it processed Bolivian ores. After the war the same policy was introduced in Nigeria. The importance of this discrimination by export duties was never so much that it influenced the ultimate availability of tin metal to the several nations as that it shifted smelting and refining. As the example is unique in character it is worthy of mention.

11.—*Zinc (Spelter).*

As our tables show, zinc is a metal produced in many countries. Europe is quite a large producer, and some colonial territories come into prominence as producers, such, for instance, as Northern Rhodesia, French Indo-China and Algeria. Our Table A11 (4) shows that only a slight decrease of stocks has taken place since 1932; and the renewed drop in prices, in the midst of recovery, proves that there is a particularly strong tendency towards overproduction. It should be noted that at least one colonial country, viz., Northern Rhodesia, is a producer not only of the ore but of the metal also.

12 *and* 13.—*Metals of the Platinum Group and Minor Metals.*

Only a few notes are necessary to show why we include these metals in our tables; in a few cases, to tell the truth, we do so simply to be on the safe side.

Antimony.—Alloys used as type metal; compounds in the vulcanization of rubber. There exists an interesting explosive form of the elemental metal which may be one of the nice surprises held in store for us for the next war.

Cadmium.—The ores contain only 1 to 5 per cent. of the metal. Provides alloys for quick soldering. Compounds serve as pigments.

Cobalt.—Serves chiefly for the making of pigments and paints.

Iridium.—In alloys with platinum is used to make implements for chemical laboratories; in alloy with osmium provides a material for the threads of electric bulbs.

Molybdene.—In a fifty-fifty alloy with iron makes an extremely hard steel, from which important implements used in the heavy industries are made.

Osmium.—See iridium.

Palladium.—Protects, when applied as a thin coating, the silver surface of the reflectors of large-scale flashlights in military use against tarnishing; serves to make non-magnetic watches to be used in laboratories, etc.

Strontium.—Interesting only for two reasons: it burns with a strong, deep-red flame, and the nitrate is therefore used for military purposes, as it serves for signal rockets; in this regard strontium is rather a key material. The hydroxide is used in the sugar refining industry.

Thorium.—The chief raw material for incandescent gas mantles, etc., and an important one for threads in electric bulbs.

Titanium.—Its tetrachloride, when evaporated, is the basic substance of artificial fog; it is very important for the production of smoke screens; it should be important in the next war and, by rights, popular with politicians all round.

Tungsten (*Wolfram*).—Gives very hard steels in alloy with iron and 30 per cent. chromium. Serves also as a material for the threads in electric bulbs. About 90 per cent. of the production goes into steel alloys.

Vanadium.—Very important, in alloy with iron, as a material providing extremely hard steel for quick-working, mechanical cutting implements, chisels, gears, piston rods, transmission shafts, gun barrels. Is also used in combination with chromium as a steel alloy.

B.—Non-Metallic Minerals.

1.—*Coal.*

Coal is the most important source of mechanical and chemical energy to-day, though it has found strong competitors in oil, and in electricity produced with the help of water-power, during the last two-score of years. Other combustible substances which in former times were more important as sources of heat, viz., wood and peat, have lost much of their customary use for these purposes, though locally they may still be important enough here and there. Both are very voluminous and therefore inconvenient for transport. Both contain a high proportion of water and non-burning mineral substance, so that their burning and heating value is seriously handicapped. Peat has become exhausted in many places where it existed in big quantities forty or fifty years ago. Wood generally can be used for more profitable purposes than for the production of mere warmth.

Coal, on the other hand, is being processed now in many ways, so as to provide combustible substances adapted to the requirements of modern technique; it is totally or partly coked; is ground into a powder. Coal dust is briquetted, brown coal is freed of water, and coal dust is liquefied or suspended in oil. Its great advantages in competition with oil are:

(*a*) It is found in a much bigger variety of places, and is generally closer to the centres of large-scale industries than oil.

(*b*) As far as we know it exists, within easy reach, in quantities immensely superior to those of oil.

Signs of the depletion of natural stocks of oil are distinct and even disquieting in many places. With coal this is true only to an incomparably smaller extent. The technique of extracting oil from the earth seems hardly open to much further improvement. The technique of coal-mining is still just as primitive in many a country, as it ever was. Large future reductions in costs and improvements in economic organization are therefore possible.

Let us first take a look at the Table B1 (1) which gives us estimates of the coal seams which are supposed to exist on this planet. "Supposed," for the data are of very unequal and uncertain degrees of probability. But we may take it that the columns which give us the so-called "certain" seams are fairly safe as extremely cautious estimates. If we take the first estimate we find that the chief known deposits exist in the U.S. and in Canada, with Britain as a third and Germany as a fourth favourite of nature. Of the total known world supplies of 992 thousand million metric tons, these four countries are reasonably sure to contain respectively 511+185+141+89= 926 thousand millions.

But some other countries appear in the list with comparatively low figures only because they have been explored very perfunctorily. So far the quantity of coal coming on to the world market has been generally so plentiful that the inclination to invest on a large scale in the development of other seams has been limited to a few cases where large local consumption is found in the comparatively close vicinity of particularly easily-mined seams, as, *e.g.*, in India.[10] Prospecting is expensive, the development of new mines very risky; and if we ignore the acute and short-lived scarcity of coal during and immediately after the Great War the problem has always been, during the last hundred years or so, how to sell all the coal which could be mined in the developed fields, not how to exploit new sources of this valuable mineral.

The comparatively wide distribution of coal is shown by Table B1 (2) which gives details of present production. The fact that the figures for 1934 are generally lower than they were during the last year before the war is explained by three facts.[11]

(*a*) 1934 was only the second year of the upward trend of the trade cycle after a particularly deep slump;

(*b*) During the last twenty years the progress made in the use of water-power and oil in the generation of electricity,

[10] For details see the latest (third) edition of *V. Anstey's, The Economic Development of India, passim*, particularly the last chapter

[11] The discrepancy between the figures for world production in the Tables B1 (2) and B1 (3) is remarkable, though the trend shown by both tables is identical. I was unable to trace the causes of this discrepancy. The recovery from 1934 to 1935 was rapid.

in the movement of goods at sea, in the navies, and even by land traffic has been steadily developing ;

(*c*) Technical progress in engine-building and in domestic heating has meant that the same quantity of coal burnt provides a much larger quantity of heat and energy now than before.

The slump brought all these factors to full development.

The most characteristic features of the above-mentioned table are : nearly all countries having important industrial activities are well provided with coal, the one glaring (and politically important) exception being Italy ; and in spite of their particularly rich seams of coal the proportion of the aggregate coal production of the world, of the combined shares of the United States, Canada, Great Britain and Germany, decreased from 84 per cent. of the whole quantity produced in 1913 to only 69·6 per cent. in 1935.

The concentration of the production of coal becomes clearly apparent if we look at the figures of production in 1935 :

TABLE 33c.

PERCENTAGE DISTRIBUTION OF PRODUCTION OF COAL BY REGIONS, 1935.

	In million Metric Tons.	In per cent. of World Production.	
North American Centre[1]	387·7	30	83
Countries round English Channel[2] ...	594·2	45	
U.S.S.R.	102·2	8	
Split up	205·9	17	
TOTALS	1,290		

[1] U.S. and Canada. [2] Great Britain, France, Holland, Belgium, Luxemburg, Germany.

Production seems very small still in India, in comparison with the size of her industries and population. The same is true of the Dutch Indies and of China. Another estimate, compiled differently and obtained from a different source (nearly all figures for China are more or less clever or lucky guesses), tells us that the production of coal there was 13·4 million metric tons in 1913 and as much as 26 million metric tons in 1933. This example shows well with what caution all statistics of this kind ought to be used. The two figures for the production of coal in China which are so widely at variance come, the one from the German Statistical Year Book, published at the end of 1935, the other from the *Statistical Handbook of World Economics*, published a few months later, at the beginning of 1936, both by the same German authority, the *Statistisches Reichsamt*.

Since 1914 the purchasing power of gold has generally decreased, and Germany has introduced high protective duties on imported coal. But in spite of that the price of coal is still comparatively low. The Reichsmark prices quoted in Table B1 (4) are practically gold prices. During the various years of the last business cycle these were 10 to 25 per cent. higher in Germany, thanks to monopolistic and customs protection, than in countries which do not protect coal by fiscal measures. The true situation becomes obvious in the second line of that table, where we see that the value of British coal, in terms of gold, scarcely reached the pre-war level at the peak of the last boom and later dropped almost 44 per cent. below it. The recovery of 1932 to 1935 could not prevent a further drop and even the first half of 1936 brought only a tiny increase. This shows clearly that coal producers try to sell wherever they can and at whatever price they can get. The problem of the international distribution of coal has been, so far, chiefly one of finding markets for an almost permanent glut.

The quantities of coal entering into international trade are shown in Table B1 (5). Here again we look in vain for the recovery which might have been expected from the changed phase of the business cycle. The list of exporting and importing countries (which excludes all those whose foreign coal trade is only small) not only shows, as we might expect, the importance of importation of coal to Italy, but further that two countries well provided with coal seams and with a large coal output of their own are heavy net importers, viz., Poland and France —the latter even to a larger extent than Italy. The net imports of Canada are equally remarkable in view of that country's rich coal seams. Her coal imports are practically identical with the exports from the U.S., and these latter appear, by their smallness, rather disproportionate to the enormous quantities waiting unused in the soil of that large country.

2.—*Oil.*

Our statistical review of the stocks of natural oil in the various countries of the world is given in the form of alternative tables, only slightly different in age though rather dissimilar in their figures. The mere fact that several of them are presented here is meant to show clearly that they must be taken with the necessary scepticism. Large parts of the world have not yet been reliably prospected, though the stimulus for doing this—high profitability of a lucky *trouvaille*—is certainly not missing in this case.

But howsoever the tables differ, they have this in common, that they show to the consumers of oil the proximate danger of a quick exhaustion of existing known resources (and thereby open a distinct hope to the holders of coal-mining shares).

From 1928 to 1935 all the world over the production of oil increased from 184 to 226 million metric tons ; this was an increase of 42 million tons or 22·8 per cent. in seven years, or roughly 3·2 per cent. per annum. We are, I think, on the safe side if we make the following two assumptions :

1. That this rate of increase during a period which included the deepest slump so far known in the economic history of mankind will be the minimum rate of increase which we must expect for quite a time to come.
2. That the stocks in the soil have remained undiminished between the time when the above several estimates were made and the end of 1935, an assumption which allows for quite a number of new discoveries without our results becoming particularly questionable.

If we work out the effects of such a rate of increase in the consumption of oil from such a starting point and apply it, with the further assumption that it will work on the principle of compound interest, we come to the following conclusions as to the expected dates when the existing estimated stocks will be exhausted, according to the several estimates:

TABLE T34.

PROBABLE DATE OF EXHAUSTION OF NATURAL RESOURCES OF OIL

	According to the Estimate of		
	Garfia (3,495 million tons).	American Petroleum Institute (5,774 million tons).	D. White (8,000 million tons).
Number of years after 1935	12 (1947)	18 (1953)	23 (1958)

Here, then, is one of the raw materials for which not only is economical international organization all-important, but for which a strong case can also be made out for a thorough international organization of prospecting.[12]

Equally remarkable is the existing distribution of production over the continents and countries of the world. Five countries (U.S., U.S.S.R., Irak, Iran and Venezuela) possess 21,700 million barrels or seven-eighths of the geological stocks according to Mr. Garfia's estimate. Between them, in 1934, these

[12] Mr. W. C. *Teagle* gives a good description of the nature of competition in the production of oil (and natural gas) in a contribution to Mr. *Crowther's* book (p. 110–111) from which I quote the following details: "Oil is unlike other minerals because it does not remain just where nature stored it until the time it is brought to the surface of the earth. . . . It flows towards the wells, wherever they may be, and that is why one producer may recover oil that really belongs to another producer. . . . When land above a pool is owned by many people, many wells are drilled. The oil is brought to the surface . . . regardless of whether every producer has a market for it, and regardless of dissipation of gas pressures and accelerated intrusion of water which will result, sooner or later, in placing enormous quantities of the oil beyond hope of recovery. . . . As the oil is produced in greater quantities than are required by the market, it is stored at heavy cost above ground. The producer offers it for sale for whatever he can get. . . . Refiners are tempted by bargain prices to buy oil in excess of their needs and to make more gasoline than the market demands. . . . The ills of the oil industry are peculiar to that industry" (?) "and require peculiar remedies. These are modification of anti-trust laws, co-operation among producers, *and the exercize of the policing powers of the States.*" (Italics mine.) *Voilà* a high-pressure capitalist calling for international planning concerning his raw material! Mr. *Mohr* fills 30 pages of his book with an attempt to pooh-pooh the forecasts of an early shortage of oil in the world. But he only shows that the actual consumption of oil has increased very quickly, without going into the question of the size of the natural resources at all, so that we may safely discard his opinion as not dealing with the crux of the question at all.

countries produced 175 million metric tons, or about the same proportion of total production as their share in total geological stocks. This was in spite of the fact that production in Irak had scarcely begun and that in Iran output was distinctly low in comparison with all other countries where oil is known to exist. For the production of 1934 (in million metric tons) we find the following distribution amongst geographical units:

TABLE T35.

PERCENTAGE DISTRIBUTION OF OIL PRODUCTION BY CONTINENTS, 1934.

Colonial America	2
Independent America	155
TOTAL AMERICA	157
Colonial Asia	6·6
India	1
TOTAL ASIA	15·8
U.S.S.R.	24
Europe	8·8

This one-sided geographical distribution means that, of the existing production (and, as far as we know, of the geological stocks, too), the chief part lies in the U.S. and the U.S.S.R., and only a very small part in " colonial " areas. A not unimportant output is maintained, however, in non-imperialist sovereign overseas countries like the South American republics, Iran and Irak. The relationship between quantities of oil produced and the numbers of motor-cars and ships driven by oil or its derivatives is favourable (in the sense that there is a plentiful home supply) in the United States and in Soviet Russia. In all other countries which use these vehicles, for peaceful or " defence " purposes, on a large scale this relationship is thoroughly and unequally unfavourable. Italy, Germany and Japan are just as badly off as France, Belgium, Switzerland, Czechoslovakia, etc., though not worse off. And in this connection the quickly-growing importance of the consumption of oil and its derivatives by aeroplanes and dirigible balloons should not be forgotten.

Table B2 (3) gives world exports during the last business cycle. The effects of the cycle are reflected distinctly, though not with overwhelming strength, in the volume of traffic in raw petroleum, light fuel oil and lubricating oil. The table also illustrates in the large-scale decrease of the importation of lighting oil the very deep fall in the consumption of all imported goods which took place in some " backward " countries. But the technical revolution in transport due to the Diesel engine has continued unchecked even during the slump. So we see the international trade in heavy fuel oils steadily increasing right throughout the business cycle.

The stocks of petroleum and processed products held by producers, which had increased in a dangerous way during the last boom, were diminished during the latter half of the depression and particularly during the recovery from 1933 to 1936. But prices for light oils, in terms of gold, continued to fall all the same. Price statistics for heavy fuel oils and for lubricating oils are not available in a comparable form. If we try to get a price index by dividing values by quantities as given in Table B2 (3) we obtain the following result :

TABLE T36.

PRICES OF HEAVY OILS, 1929–1935, IN RM. PER TON.

	1929	1932	1933	1934	1935
Heavy fuel oil	35·2	21·3	21·3	20·5	
Lubricating oil	271	194	154		125

Thus not only did lubricating oil fall in gold value, but even in the case of heavy fuel oil the increase of consumption during the general slump could not check the ruinous fall of prices due to unbridled competition, nor could it improve prices in the first two years after recovery had set in. It is true that these figures refer only to those quantities which crossed frontiers in the form of heavy fuel oil, and not to heavy fuel oil made from raw oil in the country of consumption. But we have no reason to assume that the part we have taken is not a fair sample of the whole trade in fuel for Diesel and other heavy oil engines.

3.—*Asbestos.*

This material is important for some technical purposes. Like stone it is non-combustible, but it is flexible, consists of short fibres and may, in virtue of these qualities, be spun and woven or worked into a coarse kind of felt. Asbestos products provide materials destined to insulate against heat.

Our table is a combination of two tables taken from different sources, but the figures are fairly comparable. The enormous drop in production in Canada was a consequence of the slump, since this latter brought about an extensive decrease in the installation of new factory plant, ships' machinery, locomotives and domestic central heating all the world over. The big increase of production in Russia is significant as showing

(*a*) The rapid industrialization of that country;

(*b*) The large extent to which the Russian home market is independent of the business cycle experienced in the capitalist and pre-capitalist ("backward") areas of the world.

As asbestos is useful for military purposes also, it is a distinct advantage in war-time if a country has its own supply. The distribution of existing production is extremely unequal. Only the small output of Cyprus comes clearly under the heading of "colonial" production, and, of course, Rhodesia is, according to our definition of colonies, a marginal case (see discussion of this point later on). No asbestos is found in Europe. Technically satisfactory substitutes can be found and produced artificially, though at a high cost only.

4.—*Salt.*

The table shows that production is fairly equally spread over the world. The three sources from which salt can be obtained are:

(*a*) Salt mined from the subsoil;

(*b*) Salt gained from the water of salty inland lakes;

(*c*) Salt gained from sea water.

The number of countries where one at least of these three sources is inaccessible is extremely small. The fact that salt is not actually produced in all countries where such production would be possible is explained if we look at the price factor. Though salt is vital for human food and necessary for the feeding of fully domesticated live-stock and for many chemical purposes, the quantities used are not big and transport and production are cheap. As a result the price is low. There is, therefore, not much attraction towards the investment of large sums in salt production as long as this commodity can be bought at the prevailing low international price.

The retail price is raised in many countries because of excise duties, or because of monopoly profits in connection with embargoes on importation or protective duties. The salt monopolies are nearly everywhere State monopolies.

5.—*Mineral Fertilizers.*

The importance of mineral fertilizers in maintaining the fertility of cultivated land and in making it more productive is becoming increasingly known throughout the world. The application of these substances has grown enormously since the end of the Great War, though at very different rates for the several minerals in question. The present level of agricultural production depends to a large extent on the regular and reasoned use of these substances. The non-organic materials at present added, by way of artificial manuring, to land under crops consist chiefly of lime, potash, phosphorus and/or nitrogen ; whereas the development of agricultural research is now showing that small quantities of other substances, like iodine, manganese, etc., seem to be in a key position as regards the fertility of some widely-found soils and should, accordingly, be also systematically used. But the latter research is only beginning to give definite and practicable results, while the importance of the other substances has been firmly established by research and practice during scores of years.

Now the value and the natural distribution of these substances vary enormously. The most important is probably lime. But the occurrence of lime is so widespread throughout the world that international trade in it for the purpose of artificial fertilizing has scarcely developed. We may disregard it completely in our study, and the table which we give of mineral fertilizers contains no figures concerning it.

Next in importance as a fertilizing substance comes probably nitrogen. It is provided by nature in two forms, viz., in guano and in sodium nitrate compounds. Guano is an animal, semi-fossilized product, sodium nitrate is genuinely non-organic. These two substances are found only within a very limited area, viz., in the extremely dry border districts between Chile and Peru and on the islands opposite the Chilean and Peruvian coast. The production of sodium nitrate was up to the last slump an extremely important one. In former centuries it was sought not so much for its value in agriculture, but as one of the basic substances of gunpowder—up to two score of years ago the most important explosive for civilian and military purposes. But gunpowder has passed its heyday since Nobel invented dynamite, and as a source of nitrogen for chemical and agricultural purposes sodium nitrate has found strong competitors, *e.g.*, guano, which became important seventy years ago, and a lot of artificial nitrate and ammonia compounds. These may be either by-products of chemical processes like the generation of gas from coal, or may be specially derived from processing the nitrogen content of the atmosphere, with the help of electricity, heat and high pressure. At the same time agriculture has learned, to a large extent, to achieve the nitrogen fertilization of the soil by more organic methods like cultivating and ploughing-under leguminous plants, etc. So we find a very distinct decrease, nearly a disappearance, of sodium nitrate from Chilean exports, particularly during the depression; while the exportation of nitrogenous manure in the form of guano has increased remarkably.

On the whole the importance of both these substances as sources of nitrogen for industrial and agricultural purposes is on the wane. Ammonia compounds, compounds of nitric acid, cyanides and organic manures take their places proportionally more and more. As these are not all raw materials in the strcit sense, the nitrogen problem is disappearing quickly from the ranks of the raw material problems.

A similar position exists in regard to phosphorus. There is the same competition between natural phosphorus compounds and those which are the by-product of iron production. Many iron ores, particularly those with a low content of metal, contain admixtures of phosphoric compounds which are obtained as "basic slag" when the ores are melted down with limestone and coke. But here we have a different type of distribution of production if we look at it geographically. It is widely spread and divided among countries producing basic slag and countries mining natural lodes of phosphates. The first group coincides with the few European countries where we have a large iron industry and the U.S.; the second consists of some regions in Europe, Africa and Oceania, many of these being colonial regions.

In Table B5 (1) we have, in addition, a column "superphosphates". These are not raw materials in a strict sense and are not a net addition to the other forms in which phosphates turn up in that table. They are the results of processing "raw" phosphates so as to make them best suitable for agricultural and gardening purposes.

The situation as to phosphorus is that there does not now exist any international control of total production. And in the case of war a quantity sufficient to maintain the existing rate of fertility of the soil, as far as phosphorus is concerned, seems assured only to a very few important countries like Germany (provided she can go on importing iron ores from French Lorraine), France, the U.S., the U.S.S.R., Belgium, Luxemburg and, to a certain extent, Great Britain. For other countries (particularly Italy, Poland, Japan) supply in case of war depends entirely on uninterrupted importation either of the raw materials or of the processed superphosphates.

The last type of geographical distribution is given by potash. Here we have a semi-monopolistic type of supply. Nature supplies potash compounds which can be used commercially only in comparatively few places. Up to the Great War Germany had practically a monopoly of the production. Even in 1934, after the havoc the slump brought about in the German potash-mining industry, Germany produced about 1,200 of the 1,900 units of potash produced throughout the world. Of the rest more than half came from the Alsatian potash mines which Germany lost to France in 1919. So it seems that between them these two countries possess practically a world monopoly. They behave absolutely like monopolists, show a high degree of concentration in their capital and have shared out world consumption between them.

But they behave like cautious and prudent monopolists; in fixing their scale of prices they do not exploit to the full the possibilities of their present position. In the background loom not only the minor existing outputs in Spain, Poland and the U.S., which might be stimulated to violent (though for a time expensive) expansion; new productions might also arise in many places at any moment should the price policy of the monopolists make it profitable for entrepreneurs to invest in such enterprises for producing potash and to put money into propaganda for protective duties in favour of such new enterprises. The figures of our table show us that the existing countries outside the monopoly did not suffer (as France and Germany did) as producers of potash, from the slump, but were able either to hold their own (Poland) or to increase production at the expense of the monopolists.

In the case of interruption of supplies by war it would probably be only a question of time and money before quite a number of new producing countries would appear on the world's markets. We know already for certain that Palestine (with the waters of the Dead Sea) and Russia are potential large-scale producers, and if the economic spurs of high prices or Government subventions are strongly applied in case of a political catastrophe, it might become profitable even to use that ubiquitous potential source of potash compounds, the sea. So far the latter has not been exploited because it is so hopelessly more expensive to undertake extraction from this source than to buy potash from Germany or France, both of which have, so far, offered the potash compounds rather cheaply all over the world.[13]

6.—*Sulphur.*

Sulphur and several sulphurous compounds are vitally necessary basic substances for the chemical industries; they rank in this respect with coal and nitrogen. Sulphur as a raw material is produced in two forms chiefly: brimstone, and sulphur as a constituent of iron pyrites.[13a] The production of brimstone accounts for a quarter to a third of world production. It is practically all produced in Italy, Japan and (chiefly) the U.S.

The production of sulphur compounds from pyrites and other ores is more widespread, the pyrites and other ores being laıgely imported into the processing countries. We have, therefore,

[13] Some widely-found rocks contain potash in quantities worth mentioning. They have not been used for the production of potash because such production is very expensive. But again price may become a minor consideration in case of war.

[13a] Some copper ores, when heated, also yield sulphuric compounds as by-products.

limited our statistical table to those quantities of sulphur which are produced from ores mined in the several sulphur-producing countries themselves. This gives us a picture of a fairly widely distributed production, the United Kingdom, Poland, India and China only, among the great powers, being missing from our list (though the very primitive state of the chemical industries in the two last-named countries makes the fact unimportant to them for the time being). The three big so-called " Have-Nots", viz., Germany, Italy and Japan, are particularly well off, as Table B6 (2) shows.

The figures of Table B6 (1) reflect a deep fall of production during the slump and a prompt recovery the moment the favourable phase of the business cycle began.

7.—*Minor Non-Metallic Minerals.*

Graphite is important as a material for some chemical and metallurgical processes. Chief producers are two " Have-Not " nations, viz., Germany and Japan.

Mica comes chiefly from the other group of countries, the " Haves ": Russia, the U.S., India, and Canada.

Silicious earth (*diatomeæ earth*) is a necessary raw material for the fabrication of some explosives (dynamite is silicious earth soaked with nitro-glycerine). Among the " Haves", France (with Algeria) and Great Britain, and among the " Have-Nots " Japan are conspicuous as producers.

C.—Vegetable and Animal Raw Materials.

1.—*Cereals, including Wheat Flour and Rice.*

I.—The Production of Cereals in Important Countries (Tables (a) to (d)).

Statistics of wheat production lack completeness, and figures published from authoritative sources for the year n in the year $n+1$ or $n+2$ may be any number of times altered again in the years $n+x$, x being >2, not to speak of the differences in the figures gleaned from different, though equally " authoritative ", sources. The estimates by many countries of the size of the harvest are often made by the following method :

(*a*) In spring the area sown is estimated by local experts in their local districts, and these estimates are added up centrally.

(*b*) Round about harvest time or shortly afterwards (taking into regard results of " sample threshing ") the same or another set of experts report their estimates of the average yields per unit of area harvested. These are multiplied by the area formerly reported to have been sown, and the results added up centrally into an estimated total for the country.

This is, obviously, an extremely hazardous procedure. The only reliable method would be to introduce a double legal obligation on every producer of an agricultural product, the results to be calculated centrally, namely :

(*a*) The obligation to report to a definite authority at a definite time the size of the area sown or planted, and

(*b*) The obligation to report in the same way the quantity of the harvest, with a further legal obligation

(*c*) To report all important later changes.

But very few countries provide for anything of that sort. Some control of the results of the slipshod methods now generally used is possible, in a number of important cases, from figures supplied by co-operative organizations, by mills or other processing factories, by port authorities, etc. These checks are the sources of the later corrections in official records of which we have already spoken. These are probably necessary, but are, all the same, a great source of confusion.

So we find that in most cases it is difficult to know with any accuracy what the harvest in any country of a certain crop in a certain year has been. But to add up these figures, as they are published year by year, for all the countries of the world is another extremely hazardous procedure. Harvests occur at very different times of the calendar year. Some governments report quickly, some extremely slowly, some always, and others in some years do not report at all. Some statistics are at least not wilfully and deliberately faked, other governments are highly suspected of " beautifying " or otherwise manipulating their figures so as to adapt them to their political or propaganda purposes. War-time figures are particularly unreliable.

It is, therefore, not astonishing that our Table C1 I(a), in spite of its size, leaves numerous questions of high importance unanswered.

The year 1933 gives us the following percentages as the shares of the five traditional continents in the world harvest of wheat of that year:

TABLE T37.

PERCENTAGE DISTRIBUTION OF WHEAT PRODUCTION BY CONTINENTS, 1933.

In per cent. of World Harvest

Europe	57·4	America	24·3
Asia	11·8	Australia ...	3·8[14]
Africa	2·5		

[14] ·2 per cent. has, I am afraid, got lost while I was calculating the percentages.

This shows Europe in a very strong position. But is it actually true? And is it a passing phase, or a permanent feature? If one looks through the figures for Russia, Italy, France, Germany and some of the minor countries not appearing separately in our table, if one thinks of all the endeavours we have heard of to achieve national self-sufficiency, the *battaglia del grano*, etc., it seems that wheat might indeed become less and less a commodity in the production of which some countries specialize. The same development which bred strains of wheat able to ripen farther to the north than formerly in Canada and farther to the south in the Argentine is bound to overcome difficulties of the length of the season of growth, of excessive heat, of lack of rains, etc., in other countries also. But the harvests in Europe of 1932 and 1933 were particularly and abnormally high; the harvests of 1934 to 1936 have been much smaller, and, quite contrary to the expectations of most authors, politicians, business people, agriculturists and economists two years ago, we find at the time of writing (January, 1937) that the Canadian Wheat Pool is able to unload all its stocks carried over from former years at more than reasonable prices. A dollar a bushel seemed a beautiful dream to many a farmer in Saskatchewan in 1935; one and a half dollars a bushel is the price now actually within immediate reach for all the old stuff remaining from former years on which he and his "co-op."

and his government just avoided going bankrupt. It was a hair-breadth escape, but escape they did.[14a]

The table for rye is really more complete than it looks, since the rye production of Russian Asia is included in that of Europe, and countries in America other than the U.S. are not great producers.

For barley and oats the following table for 1933 can be given :

TABLE T38.

DISTRIBUTION OF PRODUCTION OF BARLEY AND OATS BY CONTINENTS, 1933.

	In 1,000 Metric Tons.	
	Barley.	Oats.
Europe (including the whole of the U.S.S.R.) ...	24,755	43,548
Asia	7,190	435
Africa	2,350	264
America	5,890	16,370
Australia	16	60
WORLD TOTALS	40,380	61,030

This enables us to give a comprehensive table of the production of grains, by continents, again in 1,000 metric tons, for the year of the European bumper crop of 1933. This is Table C1 I (e) of the Appendix. In this world table we have simply added up the figures for the several sorts of grains, though it is certainly going rather far to assume that wheat, rye, rice, etc., have a common caloric denominator. But we do not usually bother about the fact that all of these grains serve partly as human food, partly for fodder, partly for making alcohol, etc., and that " wheat " covers, in the same year and from year to year, things very different in quality. So we may perhaps be allowed for a moment to sin again in this manner. The result, as with most deliberate and conscious sinning, is very interesting and shows us things quite beyond the limits of possible error, if we take the liberty of increasing the figures for Asia and for the world by something like 20 million tons. This we must do because the figures for rice in Asia are certainly much too low (see Table C1 I (d), which gives the world rice harvest in 1933

[14a] While reading the proofs (September, 1937) I find that even the wave of war danger could not prevent a serious new slump in the wheat price. Spot wheat is quoted at Chicago now at something like $1.25 per bushel. This shows how awkward a business forecasting on this field is !

as 90,087 units, though this neglects the U.S.S.R., Iran, Irak and as important a country as China). We get then :

TABLE T39.

COMPARISON OF GRAIN HARVESTS AND POPULATIONS, BY CONTINENTS, 1933.

	Population in Millions.	Harvest of grains in mill. tons.	Percentage of world totals.	
			Population.	Grains.
Europe	516	215	25	43
Asia	1,135	131	55	26·5
Africa	147	14	7	2·8
America	261	132	12·5	26·6
Australia	10	5	·5	1
WORLD TOTALS	2,069	496	100	99·9

Even if we think of the unreckoned primitive[15] starchy foods and fodders consumed in large parts of Asia, Africa and America, such as millet, sweet potatoes and manioc, these omissions from our table will certainly be more than compensated by the consumption, for satisfying the basic human requirements of starch, of such a primitive food as the ordinary or "Irish" potato.

Potatoes are mostly consumed in the countries where they are grown. In 1933 Europe harvested 187 million metric tons of potatoes, America 13 million, the rest of the world together only 3·3 million ! It is very remarkable that Europe, in spite of its enormously favourable proportion of starchy food to population (·41 tons per head, without potatoes, etc.) is an importer of grain, whereas America, with little more than the same proportion (·51 tons per head) is a large-scale exporter.[15a]

[15] And do not let us forget that they are, after all, primitive.

[15a] That this tendency on the part of some countries on the European Continent towards self-sufficiency in foodstuffs and fodders is not of purely recent date is shown by the following table :

TABLE T39a.—SHARE OF SOME COUNTRIES IN WORLD TRADE IN CERTAIN FOODSTUFFS AND FODDERS.

(In Per Cent. of World Totals, 1913 and 1924.)

	Grains for				Animal Products.		Sugar.	
	Bread.		Fodder.					
	1913.	1924.	1913.	1924.	1913.	1924.	1913.	1924.
Great Britain ...	11·8	13·8	11·8	15·4	33·6	30·6	17·9	12·2
U.S.	8	14·6	4·5	5	8·6	8·7	18·3	25·8
Germany	8·6	4	14·6	5·6	7·3	7·2	9·9	2·8
France...	3·1	3·2	3·4	3·1	2·9	3·2	3	4

II.—International Trade in Grain (Tables II (a) to (c))

The tendency in a number of European countries towards self-sufficiency in cereals, which we have already seen at work in their growing grain production, finds expression even more clearly in the statistics of international trade in cereals. If we add these up, as they appear in Table (a) for the period 1929 to 1935, including this time for the sake of completeness wheat flour (the only flour for which international trade is of any importance) we find:

TABLE T40.

WORLD EXPORTS OF CEREALS, 1929–1935.

In million metric tons	1929	1930	1931	1932	1933	1934	1935
Total exports of grains and flour	44	41·8	49·5	43·2	39·9	38·3	31·1[1]

[1] Without rice; average 1929-1934; 7·1; this would bring the figure for 1935 to 38·2

The impression given by this table is deepened and further clarified when we study Table (b). Here we see that the tendency towards much smaller imports of grains and flour shows itself distinctly in countries like Germany, Italy and, to a lesser extent, France; while Great Britain shows a slight movement in the opposite direction. A very remarkable thing is the tendency towards a shrinkage of the exports of the U.S.

Our Table (d) for rice demonstrates conclusively that the Japanese Empire was well on the road to self-sufficiency in this fundamental food before it undertook the conquest of Manchuria and before it found itself under the necessity of providing food for the population of its conquest. The fact that in 1934 (Table (c)) British Malaya was able to export more rice than she imported was probably due only to temporary factors, though a general tendency towards self-sufficiency is here, too, clear enough.

III.—Prices (Tables (a) to (d))

Some of the price-falls during the last slump were remarkably large. The recovery which has taken place in agriculture in England and the U.S. since these countries went off gold is not revealed by a study of prices when these are quoted in *Reichsmark* (*i.e.*, in terms of gold) ; I have therefore quoted the prices for wheat per bushel in cents and per hundredweight in shillings and pence in footnotes. Despite the introduction of protective measures after the Ottawa Conference, prices in shillings continued to fall in London throughout 1934. Now, however, (January, 1937) wheat is on the up-grade all the world over.[15b] The prices for wheat, rye and oats in Berlin show the remarkably steadying influence of German protectionism on agriculture. The relative price-falls down to 1934 were, in per cent., of the highest prices for the different countries in the several commodity series :

TABLE T41.

FALLS IN GRAIN PRICES IN GERMANY, POLAND AND THE ARGENTINE.

In per cent. of the Highest Price: Rye.		Oats.	
Germany.	Poland.	Germany.	Buenos Aires.
38	64	28	75

The fall in the price of rice was particularly great and must have injured the cultivators of rice in India terribly. The slump deprived them of half their exports of rice and of more than half the value of these exports. Let us compare the following figures :

TABLE T42.

DECLINE IN INDIAN RICE EXPORTS, 1929–34.

	1929	1932	1934
Net quantity exported, million tons	2·4	2·2	1·1
Price per ton, RM.	218	103·90	62·30
Money yield of exports, RM. millions	523	229	69
Loss against 1929 RM. millions		294	454

Whoever looks for an explanation as to why India had to export so much gold from the hoards of her small cultivators will find it in these four lines !

15b On March 9th, 1937, the following prices were quoted on the New York Commodity Exchanges (figures in brackets are those of the previous year) :—Wheat No. 2, red, per bushel $1·54 7/8 ; corn No. 2, yellow, per bushel $1·26 ; copper, electrolytic, per lb. $·1625 (·0925) ; lead, per lb. $·0725 (·0460) ; tin, Straits Settlements, per lb. $·60 (·4835) ; rubber, smoked sheets, per lb. $·2263 (·1581). The boom is in full swing ! How long will it be before it will pay to use regenerated rubber ?—But see note 14a.

IV.—Visible Stocks

The imperfection of this table, as explained in the appropriate footnote, is so grave that it is scarcely possible to draw any important conclusions from the figures. No statistics of world stocks of rice are, unfortunately, available.

The daily and periodical press is full of so-called statistics of the fluctuations in grain stocks, but the figures are generally more or less clever guesses and subject to much, and mostly well-founded, criticism. This is the reason why I have not drawn on these sources for the purpose of filling the gaps left by the table I am giving here. In recent years the reliable material has shown a very welcome tendency towards a greater degree of completeness.

2.—*Sugar.*

We are excluding a number of foodstuffs from this review, but we have to include sugar, as the most important representative of the group of sweetening substances.

Sugar is only rarely offered to mankind freely by the kindness of nature requiring no more than the pains of collecting it, as, *e.g.*, in honey, in the juice of the American maple tree, etc. Honey was for a long time the only source of sweetening in Europe, and the inhabitants of that continent managed with sugar from this source for a long time. In the same way maple sugar was more important than cane sugar in colonial times in the North American territories though here the production of cane sugar was going on in the West Indies right under their noses. The old Colonial System of Great Britain looked to that.

A new phase in the indulgence of the human race's " sweet tooth " came with the growing cultivation of particular plants for the sake of their sugar content. This development coincided with the time when the experience that " sugar feeds " found theoretical approval in the scientific discovery that sugar is only one of a large group of carbohydrate nourishing materials among which starch is the most important. Sugar is as good as starch (in cereals, maize, potatoes, manioc, rice, etc.) in providing the human and animal body with physical energy. It is similar to these starch foods in being one of the sources for the production of alcohol by fermentation. Sugar has only to be extracted from the vegetable substance in which it is harvested and purified (" refined ") in order to be fit for human and animal consumption. In this second phase, which still obtains, sugar is chiefly produced from either sugar cane or sugar beet.

A third phase in the history of sugar production seems to be just now beginning; namely, the manufacture of sugar by chemical processes from vegetable materials in which it does not appear as sugar, particularly from wood pulp. But though it is quite possible that this development may suddenly change the whole aspect of the situation, it is not as yet important for the existing problems of the international distribution of this raw material.

The consumption of sugar for the production of alcohol is probably slightly on the decrease. The consumption of sugar for feeding animals and for the nourishment and enjoyment of human beings has increased enormously during the last fifty years or so, but it is still increasing very quickly. Not only is *per capita* consumption in the industrialized countries of the world rising, but a rapid intrusion is also being made into the daily consumption of the four large-scale population centres which have had, so far, a rather low *per capita* consumption, viz., China, India, Indonesia and Negro Africa.[16]

We give in Table (10) some figures relating to the domestic consumption of sugar which show us the effects of the slump on this " semi-luxury " or " mass-luxury " food. The decrease in consumption was remarkably small. The figures for France and Germany show that the period of decrease was very quickly followed by a new increase directly the upward trend of the business cycle began. Great Britain with her enormous *per capita* consumption proved more sensitive. But on the other side of the ocean the United States, with an even higher *per capita* consumption, showed a positive increase. So we cannot say much more, on the strength of the scanty statistical materials available, than that the chief brunt of the slump in the sugar industry must have been borne by the industry itself

[16] The following figures and explanations are obsolete in regard to India where, with the recent introduction of a high protective duty on sugar, the growing of sugar-cane and the production and refining of sugar has begun on a large scale. The development is so recent that figures are not yet available.

in the form of decreasing prices and disappearing profits and not by the consumer by way of restricting his use of this commodity.

This, however, is not quite borne out by our Table (6) which shows the decline in the volume of sugar transported across international borders continuing even into the new upward phase of the business cycle. And this in spite of the fact that the drop in sugar prices has been absolutely catastrophic. It has been large even in the United States with their protective duty. But though prices were cut down by nearly three-quarters in Czechoslovakia, this could not prevent a decrease of about three-fifths in the quantity exported. In the United Kingdom the protection of home-grown sugar was not calculated to improve the price of imported Java sugar, though the cheapness of this latter did help to keep the quantity imported on the rather high pre-slump level.

Vigorous international limitation of production (of which we will say more later) set in during the slump and brought the total world production from its peak of 28·3 million metric tons in 1930–31 down to as little as 22·9 in 1932–33, allowing only for a small increase again in the following two post-slump years. The ensuing decrease of stocks was distinctly beneficial to the producer by preventing an even deeper fall in prices. But the restriction of production did not enhance prices, and so we may safely conclude that limitation of production in this case has, so far, not been paid for by the consumer. He got, during the slump, his sugar " dirt cheap "—at least in so far as the tax-collector did not charge him with heavy duties and excises, as was done, in fact, in many countries.

Sugar statistics are somewhat confusing because the production of sugar cane and of sugar beet is mostly carried on in two separate regions which communicate only in a few consuming areas. The U.S. is, I think, the only country where sugar cane and sugar beet are produced within the same political frontiers, and there most of the cane produced is not used for making sugar. Also the two regions of production in the U.S. are small and remote from one another. The last few decades have seen far-reaching changes in the relative importance of beet sugar and cane sugar. There were times when early rationalization and, in the cases of Russia and Czechoslovakia, extremely low wages, gave beet sugar a fillip.[17] But since that time the cheap wages have disappeared from Europe and rationalization has begun to make strong headway in the tropics, too ; and so cane sugar is again clearly advancing. If we pick out four years for comparison, we find :

TABLE T43.

PERCENTAGE SHARES OF BEET AND CANE IN TOTAL SUGAR PRODUCTION.

	Beet Sugar.	Cane Sugar.
	Per cent.	
1912/13	43	57
1930/31	42	58
1934/35	41	59
1935/36	39	61

Politically three of the great powers (Germany, Russia, France) are at least self-sufficient, and do not depend on international traffic in war-time, but not so Great Britain, the U.S., Italy (which allowed her production of sugar beet to disappear during the slump) and Japan. Germany, Russia, Poland and France are well provided for. The chief problem in peace-time is (and has been for the last fifty years) not how to secure sugar for the customer countries but how to organize such an international policy of production that a marketing crisis like the last one becomes impossible.

3.—*Rubber.*

Rubber is one of the new substances the large-scale use of which is characteristic of the technology of everyday life in modern countries. The tyre revolutionized road transport, and experience with internal combustion motors in motor-cars opened the way to flying. In other directions the use of rubber on a large scale seems likely in the future : for making paper which is water-resistant, for laying pavements and floors, etc. One of the uses of enormous economic importance, which should not be forgotten in even so sketchy a review as this, is that of providing important and efficient means for birth control. Though in this respect rubber is probably already becoming obsolescent, the change of mentality of a wide public towards birth control is due to the use of rubber, not of chemicals, and

[17] We refer later to the system of sugar export subsidies and its partial stopping by the Brussels sugar convention.

birth control may well be considered as a revolutionary feature of our time. The aggregate quantity of rubber going into this use is, of course, very small. On the whole we may say: though the use of rubber was increased manifold during the first 37 years of this century, we may be sure that its use will go on increasing at an enormous rate in the near future.

Rubber is produced by tapping the bark of certain tropical plants which used to be found growing wild in the forests of Brazil, the Congo and other more or less unexplored parts of the tropical world. The collection of the rubber from these wild trees was a powerful factor in tropical colonization up to about 1900. But the present century found enterprising capitalists and planters trying to cultivate some of the most productive species. Cultivation in many parts of colonial Africa was tried but did not prove particularly successful. In the long run the best combination of soil, humidity, heat, labour and reliability of climate was found in the Malayan Peninsula, in the Dutch East Indian Islands, in Ceylon and in parts of India.

It seems, furthermore, that hopeful experiments, with the help of sufficient capital to undertake them on a large scale, are going on in Liberia (West Africa, Firestone concession) and in Brazil (Ford concession), though results of positive value have not so far become known.[17a] This does not mean, however, that success there is impossible. The whole thing must be treated as an open question. If one or both of these enterprises should prove successful, the political aspect of the existing distribution of the production of rubber would change with about the same completeness with which it changed between 1910 and 1920 when the collection of wild African and South American rubber died out and the plantations and peasant farms of South-eastern Asia took their place.

[17a] Mr. J. C. *Lawrence*, in his book (see Bibliography, No. 23a), gives a short history of the American quest for countries outside those in the Stevenson plan in which to grow rubber cheaply for the needs of the American tyre industry. It was pursued in Brazil and in Liberia, though the drop in prices after the breakdown of the Stevenson scheme has, so far, prevented things from developing very far in both countries. Mr. Lawrence prints also the relevant documents referring to the Stevenson scheme. From these it is clear that Sir James Stevenson saw quite well at the beginning that it would be dangerous if the rubber producers, actual and potential, of the Dutch Indies remained outsiders, so that he at first advised that the plan should be dropped. Why he later reversed his position and thought a slight and not very significant revision of the planned sliding scale of export duties on rubber a sufficient safeguard is not clear from perusing these documents.

World production increased in the period 1913 to 1934 by about 800 per cent. The price dropped, at the same time, measured in terms of gold, by more than 90 per cent. The stocks held in April, 1935, were equal to more than six times the total production of 1913. The productivity of the existing plantations has grown at such a rate that even the fantastic increase of consumption has been unable to keep pace with it. The plantations are either large-scale enterprises, owned mostly by European capitalist joint-stock companies, or small-scale native holdings of a peasant character. The first employ brigades of wage-workers, often recruited over long distances; the second tap their trees chiefly with the labour available (and mostly otherwise useless) in the peasant owners' families. Bad prices damage the interests of the companies more than those of the peasants.

Two recent periods of high prices have led to a rush of capital into the cultivation of rubber trees; first the high prices brought about by the war with its unexpectedly high consumption of rubber, later the first plan for "stabilizing" rubber prices on a "reasonable" level, the Stevenson Scheme. The former rubber boom brought a violent extension of capitalist plantations, the second a scarcely less violent extension of peasant cultivation.

The Stevenson Scheme did not include the Dutch East Indies. It will ever be one of the great enigmas of economic history how any official or semi-official authority could have taken on the responsibility for such a rash and, as the slightest acquaintance with economic theory should have taught, hopeless undertaking. However, we are obliged to those responsible for one of the most clear and instructive experiments modern economic history can boast of and can use. The plan limited production in the British South-eastern Asiatic territories so efficiently that prices rocketed sky-high instead of climbing to a moderate level profitable to entrepreneurs but not intolerably extortionate, and therefore not provocative to large-scale consumers. High prices, as so often happened in colonial history, proved a mighty incentive to native cultivation and the natives of the Dutch East Indies went increasingly into rubber. When their rubber-tree gardens began to produce rubber, world production, in spite of its thoroughgoing limitation in the areas covered by the

Stevenson Scheme, began to increase, prices to fall, and stocks to accumulate.

The Stevenson Scheme was brought to an abrupt end in 1928. For a time the drop in prices was able to check a further increase of production. The slump, therefore, found its corollary in a fairly stable production of rubber between 1929 and 1933. But the disappearance of the Stevenson Scheme had provoked new planting in many plantations ; in 1934 these trees began to bear, production suddenly jumped upward, stocks rose further, and a new scheme of limitation of output was introduced, this time (a) covering the whole South-eastern Asiatic area, and (b) limiting production only cautiously, so as to avoid sudden sensational jumps in prices which might favour the intrusion of outsiders elsewhere and annoy the consuming industries.

Prices, in terms of gold, showed an increase of 75 per cent. from the average of 1933 to that of 1934 ; but measured absolutely rubber is still extremely cheap, and even in the near future a further high increase in prices seems unlikely. The managers of the new scheme have learned the bald truth of the saying that you may kill the goose if you induce it to lay too many golden eggs.

In 1913, when the cultivation of rubber trees was in its infancy, the proportionate quantities produced in British Malaya and in the Dutch Indies respectively were something like 33 to 5. The limitation of production in the British areas under the first Stevenson plan brought the production of both territories to equality in 1924, though the production capacity was much higher in the British areas, where output was restricted, than in the Dutch area, where it was unrestricted. The next figures in our Table (3) signify, up to 1929, increased tapping of existing trees in the British area and the tapping of increasing numbers of maturing trees in the Dutch area. Though production in the British area is still superior the ratio was in 1934 much less in its favour than in 1913, viz., only 6⅛ to 5.

Control of production led, in the first Stevenson scheme, to the suicide of the controlling organization by provoking the growth of a formidable group of outsiders ; it deeply angered the consumers by causing a period of absolutely exploitative prices. The leaders of the second scheme seem to have learned the wisdom necessary for the successful handling of even the most convenient monopoly.

It must be stressed here that there was no differentiation in prices against any country or group of countries. But since, with the high concentration of the world's motor-cars in the U.S. and the use of rubber in the motor-car industry, the U.S. was the chief importer, the high prices were severely felt there and were used for propaganda of a typical " Have-Not " character. The poor little man in the U.S. exploited by the powerful and ruthless British and Dutch plantation capitalist ! This is a glaring example of such complaints. The U.S., one of the richest and easily the most many-sided producer of raw materials in this world, complaining passionately because it had to bear in a small way what it imposes on others in so many cases !

For the whole production of rubber, as shown in Table (1a), we find the following distribution :

TABLE T44.

DISTRIBUTION OF RUBBER PRODUCTION BY CONTINENTS, 1925 TO 1934.

	In 1,000 Metric Tons.	
	1925	1934
Africa	8	3
America	35	9
Areas of collection of wild rubber	43	12
Asia and Oceania	491	1,019
Colonial	483	992
Non-colonial	51	39
TOTALS	534	1,031

This table requires some explanations and slight qualifications. " Colonial " includes Ceylon and the whole of Africa ; " non-colonial " includes India and the whole of America. There is some small cultivation of rubber in Africa and America (*e.g.*, Liberia, Tanganyika Territory), and a certain, though inconsiderable, amount of wild rubber is collected in Asia and Oceania. The colonies in question belong chiefly to the British and Dutch Empire, with the French coming in as a rather subordinate third.

4.—*Timber.*

Our series of tables requires a number of explanations. The source from which they are taken is the German *Statistisches Jahrbuch für das Deutsche Reich.* This does not distinguish between " hard " and " soft " woods, but between *Laubholz* (wood-bearing leaves) and *Nadelholz* (conifers) ; the divisions are not quite identical. For practical reasons I have translated in the following way :

Laubrundholz—hard wood, unsawn.
Nadelrundholz—soft wood, unsawn.
Laubschnittholz—hard wood, sawn.
Nadelschnittholz—soft wood, sawn.

To avoid unnecessary length in the tables I have excluded (with a few exceptions which seem to me appropriate) all those countries the figures for which were so small over the period treated that no one entry would have been as big as 100,000 tons. The table gives us a clear idea of the widespread distribution of timber production for export, and of the use of imported timber. International statistics of forests and of total production and consumption of timber are scarcely available, at least not of a quality which gives us a right to rely on them. In some cases we are sure that exports can be only a small proportion of production (*e.g.*, the U.S.) or that they must be a very large proportion of it (*e.g.*, Finland) ; in others we know that imports can supply only a small part of total consumption ; in the cases of other countries which are, as we know, very poor in forests, imports are bound to cover a comparatively large part of total consumption, *e.g.*, in the United Kingdom. But there is no purpose to be served by covering pages and pages with further statistics for sundry countries, as the gaps in these statistics would be so wide and the differences in unit measurement (the measuring being done here by weight, here by volume, here by square measure, here by running units of length like board-feet) are so fundamental that we should only get an enormous heap of scarcely comparable data.

Some countries depend for their supply or sales of timber in war-time very much on the freedom of international transport ; this is obvious. In some cases this dependence may become vital in a future war, as it was during the Great War, when

Great Britain experienced difficulty in regard to supplies of pitprops and pulpwood and Germany as to pulpwood for newsprint. But technical progress may provide substitutes made from other materials for pitprops (steel, concrete) or even newsprint (milk).

5.—*Wood Pulp.*

As we have seen already, the production of wood pulp depends, in many cases, on the importation of wood. We may combine, *e.g.*, for the year 1933 the following table :

TABLE T45.

IMPORTATION OF PULP WOOD INTO CERTAIN COUNTRIES, 1933.

	In 1,000 Metric Tons.		
	Imports of Wood for Pulp and Paper.	Exports	Production of Wood Pulp.
Germany...	2,472	—	2,703
Sweden	23	19	2,563
Finland	—	475	1,479
Canada	33	1,416	2,703
U.S.	1,571	23	3,898

This table shows the various degrees to which the production of wood pulp is dependent on importation of the raw material, the extremes being for independence of imports Finland in Europe and Canada in America and for dependence on imports for their supplies of raw material Germany in Europe and the U.S. in America.

Wood pulp is the raw material not only for paper and cardboard, but also for the production of many kinds of artificial silk (rayon). In war-time it is important as raw material for some explosives (nitro-cellulose), which in peace-time are produced from waste cotton fibres.

6.—*Oil Seeds.*

Among all the raw foodstuffs there are very few instances where a large number of countries are vitally dependent upon supply from foreign producers, although many countries are interested in producing these foods totally or partly for exportation. Wheat, *e.g.*, is only imported in quantities large in proportion to domestic production in a few cases, though in quite a number even of these countries importation has shown a rapid tendency to decrease in proportion to home production. In peace-time, with the long-term glut of production, there is scarcely any problem at all, and in war-time the problem is much more one of transport than one of production; and this we shall discuss later.

Other "foodstuffs" playing an important part in international commerce are things like coffee, tea and cocoa, and we should do well to include tobacco with this group. The commodities of this sort are definitely "mass luxuries". Their consumption has become a highly-cherished part of the usual standard of life of the consuming masses in industrialized countries, and even in some others, but experience has shown that demand is very elastic and adapts itself easily to increasing or decreasing prices by comparatively large variations in aggregate (and, therefore, individual) consumption.

There are two important exceptions: sugar and fats. We have treated sugar above. As to edible fats (and fats for industrial use) we cannot cover the whole field, if we limit ourselves to fats in the strict sense. Fats are bought and sold internationally only partly in the form of foodstuffs ready for consumption, like butter or lard. A not unimportant part of the international exchange consists of raw fats which require further processing before they can be consumed, as, *e.g.*, whale-oil. Another important, probably the most important, group of fats entering international commerce is bought and sold in the form of vegetable raw materials. We more or less neglect animal fats in our tables with the exception of whale-oil, because no comparable international statistics are available. The international range of the commerce in fats is shown by the following table:

TABLE T46.

WORLD EXPORTS OF FATS.

	In 1,000 Metric tons. 1929	1933
1. Butter	515	568
2. Pig's lard, goose-fat, and similar fats	434	320
3. Raw tallow, molten tallow, refined tallow ...	185	175
4. Olive oil	190	208
5. Palm oil	238	339
6. Cocoa butter	19	18
7. Margarine and similar edible fats	87	23
8. Fats and oils from sea animals	198	180

In butter no less than approximately four-fifths of the world's total exports went to Great Britain in 1933. The importation of all other countries taken together does not amount to very much. A scarcity of butter is often created locally by the endeavours of certain governments to keep the price low without their being able or willing to increase the supply by importation. But as long as other fats are plentiful such a shortage is rather of political than of economic importance. This is not so when the scarcity of butter is only the expression of a general shortage of fats in a country's provision of food. In such cases a shortage of this sort should be taken as a very serious sign ; it is then only the most spectacular case of a general shortage of one of the most important foodstuffs and shows that something is seriously wrong.

Palm oil, palm-kernel oil and margarine are chiefly produced from oil seeds, to which we will now turn our attention. For the purpose of producing oil from oil seeds the seeds are mostly crushed and pressed, hot or cold, with or without the addition of water or under the effect of steam. There remains the non-fatty and non-watery substance of the fruit, and in all cases vegetative fibres (cellulose) and proteins, salts, etc. Most of these proteins are not yet used for human food,[18] but are valuable for feeding livestock. Much of the feeding of cattle and pigs depends on the use of these substances, which are generally called oil cake. Oil seeds are, therefore, economically joint-supply raw materials, producing both fat and protein fodders.

Unfortunately, it is impossible to strike a statistical balance of the whole international trade in oil seeds, as these differ considerably in fat and protein content, and are, accordingly, quite incommensurable. So we must limit ourselves to giving separate statistical tables for each of the most important.

As to the importance of the colonial and non-colonial areas our tables may be combined into the following one :

[18] The exception is the soya bean, the protein content of which is already widely used for human food. Some oil seeds or oil cakes, like, *e.g.*, those of cotton, are used in some parts of the world as manure ; but they scarcely enter into international trade if destined for such a use. Palm oil and palm-kernel oil are important in the tin-plate industry.

TABLE T47.

COLONIAL AND NON-COLONIAL PRODUCTION OF OIL SEEDS.

Percentages of Weight of Oil Seeds Entering International Trade.

Year.	1933/4	1933	1933	1933	1932/3	1933–1934			1933	1933/4
	cotton seed	copra	ground nuts	soya beans	sesa-mum	hemp seed	rape seed	lin-seed	palm oil	olive oil
Colonial... ...	21	100	86	12	20			13	99	12
Non-colonial ...	79		14	88	80	100	100	87	1	8

The qualifications as to the completeness of our figures given in the notes accompanying our tables must not be forgotten. They largely concern the lack of complete figures for China, which makes the non-colonial part of our figures come out much too low in some important cases (cotton seed, ground nuts, soya beans, etc.). The table above is therefore an over-statement of the importance of the present share of the colonial territories in the whole production of oil seeds. The production of butter, whale-oil and lard is practically all non-colonial, as far as these goods enter into international commerce.

It may be interesting to note the following example of the unreliability of all statistics in such international comparisons. The figures concerning oil seeds have been compiled from the various volumes of the *International Statistical Year Book* published by the League of Nations. They, again, rely chiefly on publications and communications of the International Institute for Agriculture in Rome. If one goes into the figures more closely one finds that data for the same year for the same country vary considerably from volume to volume of the year book. The figures, *e.g.*, for the production of cotton seed for the U.S.S.R., show the following amounts :

TABLE T48.

PRODUCTION OF COTTON SEED IN RUSSIA.

In 1,000 q.

For the year	1925	1926	1927	1928	1929	1930	1931	1932	1933
Year Book 1931/32	3,955	3,787	4,813	5,500	5,998	6,812			
Year Book 1933/34	3,560	3,560	4,750	5,420	5,700	7,350	8,500	8,400	9,500
Year Book 1934/35	*id.*	*id.*	*id.*	5,410	5,670	7,330	8,510	8,380	8,910

This engenders an entirely wholesome scepticism in regard to these figures. The differences are, of course, not the fault of the League of Nations or of the Rome Institute. It *is* difficult to reach fairly complete and ascertained figures for the whole world. In the tables of the Appendix I have always taken the latest figure printed in the League of Nations' Year Book.

In 1916 an export duty on palm kernels of £2 per ton was enacted to cover only kernels not exported to any part of the British Empire. It was put into force in 1919 and repealed in 1922. As the case is of comparatively recent date and very exceptional in kind it is worth mentioning. The experience was obviously unsatisfactory, which explains the early repeal of the measure.

7.—*Cotton.*

The types of cotton grown and used are very numerous. We have distinguished in our tables only the American, Indian and Egyptian types, grouping all the rest under " others ". The reader should pay attention to whether the text uses the expression " American cotton " or " cotton from America ". The first expression is a definition of quality, the second one of geographical provenance. Not all cotton from America is " American cotton " according to our terminology, nor does all " American cotton " come from America. This is a little confusing, it is true ; but I did not think it my task, or even right, to discard the internationally accepted terminology and to build up one of my own.

Of the three large groups Egyptian cotton is generally considered to be the finest, Indian the least valuable, and American to come between the two. Among " others " we find the quite superior " Sea Island " as well as the very coarse and short-fibred " native " cottons of the interior of Africa, etc., so that as to quality the " others " are not a uniform group.

The second half of the Table (1b) gives us the proportion of the shares in total production of the four chief producing countries. The sudden increase of the share of " others " has been chiefly due to the rapid growth of Brazilian production and of that of China and the Anglo-Egyptian Sudan. The figures for China are :

TABLE T49.

COTTON PRODUCTION IN CHINA, 1927–1934.

In 1,000 q.

1927–1931, annual average	4,638
1932	4,900
1933	5,909
1934	6,754

The order of importance of producing countries according to quantity produced was in 1934:

TABLE T50.

ORDER OF IMPORTANCE OF CHIEF COTTON-PRODUCING COUNTRIES, 1934.

United States of America.
India.
China.
Russia.
Egypt.
Brazil.

It is quite possible that Brazil will overtake Egypt in the near future.

The drop in the absolute amount and in the proportion of world production supplied by the U.S. is chiefly the consequence of the government policy of limitation of production for the purpose of buttressing prices. Pressure as well as subvention was brought into play to ensure this feature of the New Deal. How long this state of things will hold depends on political developments on the U.S. as well as on the future price level of cotton. At the low prices prevailing during the last few years a revival of cotton cultivation to former production level in the south of the U.S. with its exhausted and eroded soils seems scarcely probable, except through the occasional occurrence of a bumper crop.[18a]

The figures mentioned in the second part of Table (3) are found by conversion of bales into metric weight. The figures are, however, only roughly correct, as the actual weight

[18a] While correcting the proofs I find that such a bumper crop has occurred this year. The official estimate of the U.S. harvest of cotton runs now (September, 1937) at 16½ million bales, and in spite of a Government guarantee of 12c. per lb. the spot price oscillates now around 9·5c. per lb. only. Crop control does not exist at the moment; it was destroyed by a decision of the Supreme Court of the U.S. Government plans to re-introduce it for the year 1938, but it is more than doubtful whether a form will be found which enables such federal legislation to withstand the tests of constitutionality applied by the Supreme Court.

per bale is far from being uniform ; the figure for " others " is a poor makeshift. It is quite possible that the totals for 1913 and 1934 (4,856 and 5,082) may be too small or too large by something like 10 per cent. This qualification concerns all quantities of cotton given by us in metric weight.

Table (4) shows that the policy of limiting production (which has been applied only in a few producing countries, the most important being the U.S.) has not been unsuccessful. The peak in stocks was reached in 1932 with 2,087,000 tons, and at the end of June, 1935, they were at the level of only 1,134,000, the decrease being 953,000 tons. The decrease of stocks of American cotton, during the same time, was 950,000 tons, so that the improvement of the situation was almost entirely an achievement of the U.S. policy. The misery created in the cotton belt of the U.S. by this policy has been terrible.[18b]

Table (5) shows the incongruity of the geographical distributions of consumption and production—a fact which has always characterized the cotton industry and which was even more marked in former times. The fact that this incongruity is of very old standing is rather significant. Many of the spindles in the " old " spinning countries, it may be remarked, lead, entirely or partly, only a statistical existence. Fifteen per cent. would be a very conservative estimate of these superfluous spindles for Germany and the United Kingdom. This would bring Germany down from fourth to seventh place or so and Great Britain much nearer to the U.S. The U.S. have written off and resolutely thrown onto the scrap-heap most of their obsolete spindles ; Germany and Great Britain have scarcely begun to do so.

Table (6) shows that the policy of improving prices by means of limitation of production of raw cotton has been successful, to some extent, in the U.S. The rest of the world shows nothing of the kind.[19]

In a separate table we sketch the development in Russia. It shows many interesting details and foretells a great future

[18b] Stocks were slightly higher again in June, 1936, because the governmental control of production in the U.S. began to lose its efficiency.

[19] The figures would have shown, of course, a different tendency if we had quoted them in paper currency units. But though gold, as a measure of value, is certainly not very stable, its " elasticity " is much less than that of paper currencies.

for the production of raw cotton and the exportation of cotton goods from that country.

Table (8) allows us to compute the proportion of colonial in the total production as being only 1·2 per cent. Though the table applies to the annual average of the pre-slump period, this percentage should be fairly correct still, as the decrease of production in the U.S. will have been made up for by increases in other non-colonial countries like Russia, Brazil and China.[20] This figure shows that the international distribution of raw cotton, whatever other considerations it may involve, is, in any case, not a colonial problem.

8.—*Minor Textile Fibres : Flax, Hemp, Silk, Jute.*

The importance of these fibres for the consuming countries consists chiefly in the fact that employment (and profits) in certain large industries depend on their being supplied freely. Like cotton (and even wool) these fibres suffer from the competition of yarns made from artificially-manufactured fibres. With the exception of silk their production is very highly concentrated geographically, the most remarkable case being that of jute, where only a part of the Indian province of Bengal supplies the whole world. There is a distinct tendency for more and more of the Bengal-grown jute to be processed on the spot.

9.—*Wool.*

Wool is one of the most important textile raw materials. It serves not only for clothes, underclothes and swimming suits, but for carpets and rugs, etc. In the form of felt it is widely used in industry.

The chief source of wool is the hair of sheep. The distribution of sheep over the world is very unequal. The following are the most notable sheep-rearing countries ; the figures are those of the last census taken in 1930 or later ; the years are not exactly the same for all countries.

[20] The increase of production in China shown by our tables may be in part only the result of more complete data having been collected in recent years ; this is quite probable ; but it is quite impossible to measure the inaccuracy on this account.

TABLE T51.

SHEEP POPULATION IN RELATION TO HUMAN POPULATION, BY COUNTRIES.

	Human population in million.	Sheep population in million.	Sheep per head of human population.
Germany	66·6	3·5	·05
Bulgaria	6·1	8·7	1·4
France	41·9	9·6	·2
Greece	6·6	7·4	1·1
Great Britain	46·7	26·7	·6
Irish Free State	3	3·4	1·1
Italy	42·6	10·3	·2
Jugoslavia	14·2	8·9	·6
Portugal	7·1	3·7	·5
Rumania	18·8	12·3	·7
U.S.S.R. (including goats) ...	165·7	50·6	·3
Spain	24·2	16·5	·7
Canada	10·7	3·4	·3
U.S.	126·4	49·8	·4
Mexico	16·6	3·7	·2
Argentine	11·8	44·4	3·8
Brazil	45·3	10·7	·2
Chile	4·4	6·3	1·4
Peru	6·1	11·2	1·8
Uruguay	1·9	15·4	8·1
India	360	43·5	·1
Turkey	13·6	10·7	·8
Union of S. Africa	8·5	48·4	5·7
Algeria	6·6	5·8	·9
French Morocco	5·4	8·6	1·6
Tunisia	2·4	3·1	1·3
Australia	6·6	112·9	17
New Zealand	1·6	29	18

In absolute figures we find the following countries leading:

In Europe:

The U.S.S.R. with	50·6	million.
The U.K. with	26·7	,,
Spain with	16·5	,,
Rumania with	12·3	,,
Italy with	10·3	,,

Outside of Europe:

Australia with	112·9	million.
The U.S. with	49·8	,,
The Union of S. Africa	48·4	,,
Argentine with	44·4	,,
India with	43·5	,,

whereas the incidence of sheep per head of the human population shows the following ranges:

In Europe:

Highest	Bulgaria	1·4
.	Greece, Irish Free State	1·1
.	.	
.	.	
.	.	
.	U.S.S.R.	·3
.	France, Italy ...	·2
Lowest	Germany	·05

Outside of Europe:

Highest	New Zealand ...	18
.	Australia	17
.	.	
.	.	
.	.	
.	.	
.	.	
.	Mexico, Brazil ...	·2
Lowest	India	·1

Table (1) shows the fairly wide distribution of the production of wool, but if taken in conjunction with Table (6) shows also the incongruity of the production of raw wool and of its use in the textile industries in the several countries. Wool spinning and weaving still scarcely exists in colonial territories on an industrial scale, and of the whole supply of wool only 7·4 per cent. is provided by colonial countries. So this again is not a colonial problem at all.

The glut of wool was considerable during the slump up to 1932, but although stocks continued to increase for two years prices recovered to a remarkable extent, and 1935 brought a sudden and dramatic drop in stocks. Probably the universal putting of official and party armies into uniforms had much to do with this. It is quite possible that a distinct shortage of wool may develop. This would favour the further development of substitutes, which has, so far, given only poor results (chiefly in Germany and Italy).

10.—*Artificial Silk* (*Rayon*).

This section is given as a supplement to the tables on "natural" fibres. It shows that artificial silk production developed with fantastic speed all through the slump, though at the cost of very low prices, which enabled rayon to make considerable inroads into the former markets for cotton, linen, silk and recently even wool (Germany !). The chief raw materials for the production of artificial silk are wood and, far behind as the second in the race, raw cotton.[21] The development of good qualities in artificial yarns, chiefly durability and resistance to hot soapy water, is probably only in its infancy If we compare the world production of the chief competitors, cotton and rayon, we find :

TABLE T52.

COMPARISON OF TOTAL PRODUCTION OF COTTON AND RAYON, 1912-1934.

In Metric Tons.

Cotton, 1913/4 :	5·7 mill.	1934 :	5 mill.
Rayon, 1912 :	9,000.	1934 :	414,000.

So we shall see, in all probability, in the near future the raw material problem of the textile industry gradually ceasing to

[21] To a large extent inferior grades of cotton and cotton waste, though as to the latter rayon has now found a strong competitor in the production of nitro-cellulose for explosives.

be a problem of cotton and becoming, to a large extent, one of pulp wood, shavings and even sawdust.

D.—Appendix.

11.—*Electrical Energy.*

Our table does the best we can do in the way of affording statistical data which are better than nothing, though they are not strictly comparable from country to country nor always even from year to year within the same country.

It is impossible to give an estimate of a really valuable character of the possibilities, in the various countries, of developing the generation of electrical power. The electrical "Have-Nots" of to-day may quickly become the "Haves", by some fortunate stroke of technical invention, provided they have strong sunshine or a high oceanic tide or strong steady winds; and most of them have one or more of these vast potential power resources of the perhaps quite near future. In the case of electricity we can reason from what is, to what may be very soon, with less assurance than in the case of anything else we are discussing. After all the whole age of electricity, though it has existed scarcely half a century, has been technically as well as economically and politically one huge chain of fundamental surprises. It is not probable that it will lose this, its only steady characteristic, in the near future.

The state of development of water-power a short time ago is illustrated by Table (2), which is probably incomplete. Its greatest defect is that it gives the developed water-powers of Russia as only a few hundred thousand horse-power. This is certainly much too small an estimate.

It will readily be seen from the table that the "Have-Not" nations are far in advance of many others in the development of their water-power. Their territory (including colonies, Ethiopia and Manchuria) comprises 5·2 million square kilometres as against 9·4 million square kilometres of the U.S. (including Alaska), their population is 243 millions against 129 millions of the U.S. As their water-power resources are 69 per cent. of those developed in the U.S., their area 56 per cent. of the size of the U.S. and their population 188 per cent. of that of the U.S., the first at least of these two gauges shows their position in a very favourable light.

CHAPTER II

THE FIELD OF OUR STUDY

§ 1

RAW materials form a group of commodities containing hundreds of different things ; and if we take into account quality, *e.g.*, the proportion and accessibility of useful substance in the raw materials offered by nature, we have to extend the list still further. From the economic point of view what interests us most about iron ores, for instance, is, in most cases, the proportion of iron they contain. Now this proportion varies considerably according to the particular kind of iron ores. Within certain limits we may safely assume that the price of iron ore is proportional to its metallic content. For instance we find that in 1935 Germany imported 5·51 million metric tons of iron ore from Sweden and 5·83 million tons from France and Algeria ; for the former she paid 66·35 million RM., but for the latter only 31·20 million RM. The average prices per ton were, then, for the Swedish ore (with its high iron content) RM. 12·04 a ton and for the French ore (which has a rather low iron content) only RM. 5·35 a ton. Only by a liberal interpretation of the term " iron ore " is it possible to treat two sorts of ores of such different quality as one and the same commodity in our statistical researches.

We shall take this liberty, in order to keep our study within the limits necessarily imposed by space and readability. We can do so with a good conscience, for these differences are not always of really great relevance when looked at from the viewpoint of our study. However, they must certainly be taken into account in some cases. If, for instance, we speak of the satisfaction of the demand for rubber by either natural rubber, or by regenerated scrap rubber, or by synthetic rubber, we have, in certain discussions, to lay stress on the fact that the average duration of life for goods made from these different sorts of rubber may be very different. Their costs are very different also and depend on different causal factors.

The wages of native labour and the rate of interest prevailing in Ceylon and Indonesia have a large influence on the price of natural rubber, while European and American wages and rates of interest, the cost of establishing high-pressure apparatus and the rate of its wear and tear are the chief items in the cost of synthetic rubber, etc. In the case of regenerated rubber costs of production are made up in a totally different way, payment for scrap rubber appearing here as a new item which, of course, we did not find in the case of natural and of synthetic rubber.

But though this is important when we discuss the problem of substitution prices, it is, in other directions, quite irrelevant. We can, *e.g.*, say: "Britain is able to supply herself with rubber from her possessions in Malaya and Ceylon; the U.S. can satisfy its wants to a large extent by regenerating scrap rubber; Germany could make all the rubber she needs for army purposes in the factories of the *I.G. Farbenindustrie*"—if price and durability are minor points of interest. If, *e.g.*, a country's situation in war or its need for self-sufficiency, involuntary or self-chosen, is to be discussed. We have, therefore, sometimes to take into consideration differences like those mentioned in this particular example, and at other times we may safely neglect them.

§ 2

Many raw materials, by their very nature, satisfy widely-varying wants: by providing us with more than one material for the further processing activities of industry, or by being usable in different ways. Some copper ores, when they are smelted and refined, deliver silver as a by-product.

The oak tree gives acorns for feeding pigs[1] and wonderful timber. In the one case we must leave it standing, in the other we have to cut it down. In some parts of Silesia the leaves of oak trees are systematically picked while they are still green, to make up for a deficiency of hay and straw. In these districts the bare trees, which have served and are still serving as "air-pasture" (*Luftweide*), may be seen on all sides. When they are felled after many years of use in this way the wood of these trees is only good for firewood.

[1] The suitability of acorns for feeding pigs very cheaply was one of the chief economic causes of the Great War, namely, of the long-standing jealousy between the Serbian and Hungarian agriculturists.

Wheat provides us not only with corn, but also with straw. From rye flour we may make bread, or paste for sticking papers on the walls of our houses. Iron is equally necessary for the bayonet of the soldier and the knife of the surgeon.

Where a material in its natural state is a compound of widely differing useful substances, it is generally necessary, first of all, to process it in order to separate the ingredients. Its compound character is not generally, therefore, a source of ambiguity in statistics, because we simply use the statistics of the raw materials resulting from the splitting-up of the compound.

But where a number of different commodities can be used for the same purpose the case is different. Many technical purposes can be achieved by a large assortment of materials, and nearly every substance serves a wide range of purposes. This possibility of multiple substitution leads to serious difficulties when we try to find out which raw materials are important enough to be of interest to us in this study. Flax may be replaced by cotton, and cotton by artificial silk. So the pines of Germany are competitors not only of the flax of Russia but also of the cotton of Alabama. All this competition occurs in order to satisfy, say, the effort of the textile industries of Italy to supply the fashionable dressmaker in Paris working for well-to-do ladies in Mayfair. Hemp is indispensable as a reliable material for ropes for navigation ; but in most of its other uses it may be easily replaced by other fibres. Is, then, the one use in which it cannot be supplanted important enough to justify us in including it in our review ?

§ 3

Human life persists through the consumption of goods and services. O. *Neurath* has divided things consumed into five groups : food, clothing, dwelling, education and amusement. If we add as a sixth group public order (which certainly is, by its very nature, neither educative nor amusing) and transport as a seventh, this list covers indeed the whole field, provided that these terms are used in a wide sense. Are all these groups equally important from the viewpoint of our study ? Obviously not. Which, then, can we exclude ? Under " food " we find necessaries, and also some things which nobody would believe to be vital in any sense to any number of people, though views on what are comparative superfluities change from time to time and vary widely from place to place. Tea is to the Britisher what coffee is to the German and to the American. The requirements of dress vary according to climate (*cf.* those of the Indians and of the Eskimos) or change according to periods (four petticoats were a "moral" necessity in the Victorian age and seem unwearable now). The Japanese idea of a dwelling is thoroughly different from the French one, and at the same time so obstinately enduring that it seems that Japanese people can settle successfully only in districts where the climate allows them to establish the kind of houses they are accustomed to on their main island. The closest approach to a general world opinion as to what standards of consumption ought to be may probably be found in educational matters—though, on the other hand, the standards of existing educational practice vary more than those in any of the other fields of consumption. What, then, is necessary, vital, indispensable? And what is wonderful, nice, good, wholesome, superfluous, a distinct luxury, a pernicious luxury, a vice?

The greatest variety of opinions is to be found as to amusements; and in this sphere opinions change with particular speed. We all have lived through the development of the cinema and of the wireless from far-fetched snobbish luxuries to matters-of-course in the every-day life of at least one half of mankind. Twenty-five years ago it was possible to state seriously that the motor-car was useful for warfare and for ambulances but otherwise a public nuisance of the first order (in Mr. A. P. Herbert's *Uncommon Law* something of this feeling still distinctly survives). To-day the urbanization of the country, the country week-ends of many townspeople, the unveiling of huge unexplored or otherwise "backward" areas, and even the timely prevention of the terrors of local famine all depend on the automobile. Modern life in the U.S. without 25 million automobiles to deal with the enormous distances of the country would seem an impossibility. No young person there understands how life was at all "possible" before the internal combustion motor allowed 50 million people to flit about at will at the rate of 40 miles an hour. Flying also seemed at first important only for warfare. To-day we dust forests threatened with devastation by the nun moth with arsenic potash from aeroplanes; we discover and kill approaching armies of tropical grasshoppers and caterpillars with the help of aviation, and so on. England transports all her letters between important centres by daily air mail.

Nearly equally uncertain are our ideas about what is necessary, what is pleasant, and what is obnoxious in the maintenance of public order. What a variety of ideas there are about the advantages and disadvantages of war, from some statesmen's panegyrics in favour of it to other politicians' bans upon it! What gauge of public order is common to Lord Baldwin, General Franco and Mr. Stalin?

Things seem to be rather chaotic, what with so many philosophies of life, so many hierarchies of values in consumption. Think of the ensuing variety of producers' goods needed for all these commodities for final consumption! We have, therefore, either to base our study on a purely individual choice as to what raw materials shall be included, or we have to try something which seems scarcely less arbitrary, but which is, nevertheless, rather more hopeful: let us take as a basis the existing consumption in kind and quantity; let us leave a loophole for certain probable developments; let us, finally, look at those raw materials which are used, or might be used in the near future, to maintain consumption at the present rate, and to increase it on account both of the probable increase of population and of urgent and widely called-for extensions of individual consumption of goods and services. These are the factors which we have, in fact, tried to make the basis of this study.

§ 4

I felt sorely tempted, for the sake of shortness, to exclude from our inquiry all raw materials used for feeding human beings, vegetable as well as animal. There is at least a *prima vista* case for doing so. In principle we have in their case three possible situations as regards production and sale: (*a*) equilibrium of production and consumption; (*b*) lagging of production behind actual consumption or, if this is deemed unduly low, behind what consumption should be; (*c*) surplus of production (or possible production) over consumption. Each of these situations exists in a number of countries; and where one or other of the two possible types of disequilibria obtains, we can really see no remedy for this state of things by changing the distribution of productive resources. The allocation of more of the wheat area of the Argentine to Great Britain, *e.g.*, might take one of two possible forms: (*a*) the institution of political domination by Great Britain over the Argentine; or (*b*) the transplantation of an adequate proportion of the inhabitants of the British Isles to the Gran Chaco and Patagonia. Conquest or migration? We shall discuss these possibilities later.

In fact the volume of production of edible things varies widely from country to country, and this is true not only for foodstuffs as a whole but for individual foodstuffs. Great Britain and Germany are, *e.g.*, on the whole, large net importers of food (though these net imports, expressed in calories and in units of protein, form a very different proportion of the whole quantity actually consumed in each case). But Britain is not an exporter of a surplus of any important kind of food, though Germany is (or has been, in the recent past) in this position with regard to some foodstuffs. The German statistics of foreign trade show the following examples:

TABLE T53.

EXPORTS AND IMPORTS OF CERTAIN FOODSTUFFS; GERMANY, 1930–1935

	Year.	In Metric Tons. Imports.	Exports.
Living pigs	1930	23,554	26,994
	1931	8,743	21,202
	1932	2,456	5,171
	1933	2,444	3,767
	1934	3,446	990
	1935	11,211	14
Fresh potatoes	1930	319,933	99,898
	1931	118,515	494,650
	1932	125,538	202,087
	1933	71,220	34,262
	1934	111,829	38,676
	1935	60,172	17,083
Sugar	1930	34,070	321,703
	1931	14,278	368,006
	1932	34,328	4,281
...	1933	29,275	19,054
	1934	20,799	4,430
	1935	30,140	9,775
Rye	1930	59,036	240,208
	1931	101,823	84,909
	1932	646,064	92,627
	1933	238,387	263,179
	1934	52,684	107,272
	1935	219,799	36,666

Do these figures show a clear tendency towards the definite disappearance of international trade in these foodstuffs? The changes shown by them may well lie completely within the range of the shrinkage in international trade during the last slump and depression. After all, the decline in turnover was enormous in nearly all fields of international commerce. Unfortunately, a comparison between the trade of different countries is made difficult by the fact that we have to use the common denominator of money as a gauge, though we know quite well that this is methodologically an awkward procedure. But if we want to soothe our statistical conscience (and we want it badly in this case) we can do so by making the helpful and not too improbable assumption that prices fell, on the whole and within certain limits, more or less proportionally to the volume in international trade; this restitutes our right to measure the volume of international trade during the last business cycle by money turnover. I take from the German Statistical Abstract for 1936 a series of figures which covers the exports of countries accounting for 99 per cent. of the world trade. Here we find the following series of indexes for world exports:

TABLE T54.

INDEX FIGURES OF INTERNATIONAL TRADE; EXPORTS ONLY; 1929=100.

Years.	Foodstuffs of animal origin.	Foodstuffs of vegetable origin.	Total food-stuffs.	Raw materials.	Semi-processed materials.	Finished goods.	Provisionally Finished goods.	Definitely Finished goods.	World exports.
1929 ...	100	100	100	100	100	100	100	100	100
1930 ...	89	79	82	74	78	82	78	85	80
1931 ...	67	59	61	49	53	59	57	60	57
1932 ...	44	44	44	34	35	38	39	37	38
1933 ...	38	37	37	36	34	34	36	32	35
1934 ...	33	34	34	37	33	33	34	32	34
1935 ...	34	35	34	37	34	33	33	33	34
1932 ...	117	117	117	87	90	95	100	95	97
1935 ...	97	100	97	106	97	94	94	94	97

It is astonishing how close together the figures are found to be again at the end of this period, as is shown by the first part of our table. The second part illustrates this even more clearly; here the median in each of the two years 1932 and 1935 is taken as equal to 100. The differences, wild enough during the slump from 1929 to 1930 and in the first part of the ensuing depression, had already begun to subside quietly in 1932, when the bottom of the depression was reached and at least some recovery in some raw materials began. The next two years brought such an adjustment that in 1935 the deviation both ways from the median was only 6 per cent.—not a remarkable change from the 1929 levels after such wild convulsions of world economics. *Parturiunt montes. . .* .[2]

The following is the result of finding the index figures for the share of world exports taken by the different classes of commodities. Of the total value the following classes comprised :

TABLE T55.

PERCENTAGE SHARE OF CERTAIN CLASSES OF COMMODITIES IN INTERNATIONAL TRADE, 1929–1934.

	Per Cent.		
	1929.	1932.	1934.
Foodstuffs and beverages	23·2	27·3	23·3
Raw materials and semi-finished goods ...	34·8	31·8	36·4
Finished goods	41	40	39·5

Here again the difference between the state of things at the end of the period and the position in 1929 is not very important. Whereas in some groups quantities particularly declined, prices must have remained firmer, and *vice versa*.

One word more about our Table T53.

A country may be an exporter of some foodstuff in one year and an importer of it in another year. If these oscillations round zero point are only small in proportion to total home consumption (and production) and alternate fairly regularly, they are the natural expression of equilibrium between production and consumption which is never mathematically exact. If they are irregular, large in proportion to home consumption, or show a definite trend they cannot be taken as a sign of such equilibrium. In years of bumper crops a country whose trade shows these features will suffer from a serious glut, and in times of bad harvests it will be at the mercy of politics or foreign

[2] The great imperfection of these statistics is, of course, that they leave out of account the international exchange of services (transport of passengers and goods, etc.). There are no statistics available on the latter subject. It seems that the drop was smaller, *e.g.*, in the carrying of overseas freight and overseas mail, but greater in the carrying of passengers.

producers. Such cases indicate either an erratic disequilibrium (rye) or changing situation (pigs, potatoes, sugar).

When we divide the six years under observation into two periods of three years each and compute the annual averages, our table for Germany becomes as follows :

TABLE T56.

CHANGES IN THE FOREIGN TRADE IN SOME FOODSTUFFS ; GERMANY, 1930/32 AND 1933/35.

	In 1,000 Metric Tons.			
	Imports		Exports	
	First	Second	First	Second
	Period.		Period.	
Living pigs	11⅔	5⅔	17⅔	1⅔
Fresh potatoes	188	81	265⅔	30⅔
Sugar	27⅔	26⅔	258	11
Rye	269	270⅓	139⅓	135⅔

All these commodities are, therefore, characterized by large deviations from the general international trend. The importation of pigs shows a fairly typical behaviour, but not the exportation, the shrinkage here being particularly large.

Fresh potatoes again conform to the general international trend in importation, but exportation is fast disappearing.

Rye shows unusually small changes in both imports and exports ; and the volumes of both are not very important in proportion to the size of the production in Germany.

Sugar likewise shows a small variation in imports, but the flourishing export trade of former years has practically disappeared.

Now the example of Germany is important, because she is one of the countries where, in order to achieve self-sufficiency in foodstuffs, protection has been carried very far indeed ; but the result has been minimal and not clearly in the direction of fuller self-sufficiency. A trend towards greater self-sufficiency may have asserted itself for a few years, but 1932 was clearly a turning point, not only in unemployment but as regards self-sufficiency in foodstuffs, too. Increasing appetites following the increase in employment have put a stop to all hopes of self-sufficiency in foodstuffs without important curtailments of the food consumption per head of a fully-employed population.

§ 5

Refined sugar, though itself the result of processing activities, is always treated as a raw material, in analogy with the usual treatment of metals. The materials from which it is produced —sugar cane, sugar beet, liquid residue of the cellulose industry—are never exported, though parts of them provide useful fodder or fuel material for further processing activities.[3] Just as we treat both ores and the metals produced from them up to the stage of refinement as raw materials for the purposes of these studies, so do we include both wheat and wheat flour in our list of commodities to be taken into consideration.

Among foodstuffs we exclude such things as oranges, lemons, dates, figs, grapefruits, bananas, tea, cocoa, coffee, tobacco from our study. But this is not because it is, at present, scarcely possible to grow them outside quite definite climates. This argument might no longer hold good after a comparatively short time. We have experienced great surprises in similar matters within recent years.

The invasion of the waste plains of Western Canada by wheat came within the lifetime of all those who survived service in the Great War. I have seen the generalization of tomato-growing in Germany, beginning with the culture of an expensive luxury in hot-houses forty years ago and developing into a common and extremely simple branch of suburban gardening. In both cases the breeding of new varieties led to developments of which nobody had even thought previously; the same is true of the cultivation of citrus fruits in Palestine, of sugar cane in large parts of India, of cocoa in the Gold Coast, of rubber trees in Malaya and Indonesia. There is nothing ridiculous in the supposition that it might prove possible to breed a new strain of banana which might ripen with reasonable certainty in Northern Italy, in the Channel Islands and in the Bergstrasse.

We exclude these things from our study for another reason:

[3] The cellulose fibre of sugar-cane, bagasse, is now used for making "artificial" wood—boards and blocks—with valuable technical qualities (resistance to termites, low degree of conductivity for sound and heat). It has been therefore an important article of exportation in recent years. In the same way the empty wooden shells of coconuts, which are left over when the copra is cut out and which formerly were burnt as rubbish, have become a valuable material, because a kind of coal is made from them which is used as being the best gas-absorbent filling for certain types of gas masks.

they come under the heading of mass luxuries for the white population. For the same reason, and to save space and to avoid blurring the more important outlines, we will, furthermore, exclude all those raw materials which come under the headings education and amusement. What we do *not* exclude are those raw materials necessary for building or keeping up the productive apparatus of any kind, even if it also serves to produce food, education or amusement. So we find our first limitation. The series of statistical tables at the end of the book, which we have already discussed in the first chapter, provides us with the necessary data, as far as they are available and fairly reliable, concerning all these materials.

§ 6

As to the reliability of these statistics, we must note that the figures for production are often only estimates, and sometimes private ones, though we find these reprinted in official statistical annuals,[4] etc., because data from more official sources are lacking. Where it is a question of telling us what mineral resources are waiting for exploitation, an estimate (which often enough is not much more than a crafty guess) is obviously the only possible way of knowing anything at all, and some of the results are of small reliability as, *e.g.*, the estimates of coal down to 6,600 feet below the surface, which we have mentioned already. Huge surprises, positive and negative, are quite possible here. A footnote to the table in the German source from which the estimates are quoted raises the estimate for Africa (and for the world) by another 168 thousand million tons. Something of the sound scepticism inspired by this adventure in coal statistics should be applied to all the statistical tables we are discussing here, though the case of coal seams is, perhaps, a rather spectacular one. The Table B2 (1) on geological stocks of oil is open, to a certain extent, to the same doubt, though the information on which it is based is more recent and probably better and more complete.

[4] The best current collection of them is to be found in the German Statistical Year Book, in an international appendix of now nearly 300 pages which has been largely used in preparing this book. Other good sources, only partly overlapping with this and also largely used in compiling our data, are the Statistical Year Book of the League of Nations and the annual publication *The Mineral Industry of the British Empire and Foreign Countries*, published by the Imperial Institute in London.

CHAPTER III

STABILITY AND VARIABILITY IN THE "NATURAL" CONDITIONS OF PRODUCTION

§ 1

CLIMATE is a fairly stable factor in human economic activities. We know of variations of local climate through time, but generally their range is known by experience, and the expectation of extreme (and particularly dangerous) variations is so well defined a probability that the community should be able to make some provision for them with a fair degree of certitude.[1] But for all that, climate is not an unchangeable factor. The natural changes are generally very slow (though in the Tacna-Arica district of Peru and Chile, where the normal

[1] To give an example: the *Indian Statistical Abstract*, 1919–20 *to* 1928–29, gives the following figures for what it calls the "normal" and the "actual" annual rainfall, in inches, in several subdivisions of India:

TABLE T56a.—NORMAL AND ACTUAL RAINFALL IN INDIA, 1919–1928.

	Inches.										
	"Normal."	"Actual."									
		1919.	1920.	1921.	1922.	1923.	1924.	1925.	1926.	1927.	1928.
Madras, Malabar	100·1	112·3	122·5	99	122	120	142·9	110	103·1	102·4	88·1
Bombay, Konkan	109·6	109·6	77	108·4	107·6	112·3	98·5	93·5	121·7	107·9	120·1
Hyderabad, North	34·3	30·4	16·2	29·0	32·5	28·8	29·8	29·8	30·1	31·8	37·3

What a catastrophe the surplus of rain in Madras in 1924 must have been; what terrible droughts those of 1920 in the two other sub-divisions! But most of the deviations are within the limits of safety, in every one of these three sub-divisions only one in ten years was serious; certainly it should have been possible to insure against it, if that task had been undertaken seriously.

The extreme deviations from the "normal" figure are in these cases, expressed as percentages of the "normal" value:

Madras + 43, — 12, range 55 per cent. of "normal"
Bombay + 12, — 29, „ 41 „ „ „
Hyderabad + 9, — 53, „ 62 „ „ „

annual rainfall is less than one millimetre, the spell of wet years which some time ago melted part of the nitrates in the soil was as quick in coming as in disappearing). Adaptation to these slow changes is generally easy and goes on mostly rather automatically. It is so imperceptible that it often appears to the inhabitants simply as better adaptation of life and production to the peculiarities of the local climate.

More important than these natural changes are changes in climate caused by human activities, together with the consequences thereof. The devastation of forests has dried up whole provinces; and in many parts of Africa, in the cotton belt of the United States, etc., shifting cultivation brought about such a denudation of the soil that thousands of square miles of land were sterilized, large rivers silted up and huge swamps created. Afforestation and re-afforestation, if they are undertaken on a large scale and with untiring consistence, can stop, and even reverse, these pernicious developments. Irrigation and drainage are other ways of achieving similar beneficent aims.

There is still much scope for such dodging of climate by human intervention. In many cases the technique is already entirely or partly known, though often important points remain still to be cleared up. It is generally a question of planning and of deliberate diversion of large amounts of capital from other uses to these purposes.[2] The breeding of new species of domestic animals and useful plants, and the introduction of new methods of using the soil, like dry farming, have helped in the dodging of climate. The eradication of epidemic and endemic diseases, of predatory beasts, and the adaptation of the customs of human life to new climatic conditions have had just the same result. "Dodging the drawbacks of climate" has been one of the great chapters of human progress during the last two centuries, and should become an even greater one in the near future.

[2] The plan of Mr. Wallace, the present Secretary for Agriculture in the United States, to buy up 100 million acres of land used for farming, but unsuitable for it in the long run because of the lack of water, and the gradual re-afforestation of these lands, will be a marvellous achievement of this sort, provided that future U.S. governments will proceed with it without a break.

§ 2

The same is true as to soil. Man can influence it in a bad and in a good way. The fertile plains of Western and Central Europe and of the British Isles are not as nature originally offered them : they are the result of centuries of exploitation, often ruthless enough, and of re-fertilization, often, so far, imperfect enough. The original high fertility of the black soil of the Ukraine has dwindled to a mere shadow of what it used to be. But at Tel Aviv in Palestine we have seen wonderful gardens rise on land which twenty years ago consisted only of loose fine sand, entirely bare of any organic substance and blown hither and thither by every fresh breeze—all this achieved by patient fixing of the dunes and the application of green manure year after year. In many countries we see fertile humus being carried up to terraced, steep hillsides for gardening—in China as well as on the Canary Islands, on human shoulders as well as on mule-back. It is again a question of applying deliberately to these problems capital, labour and scientific knowledge or inherited experience. There was a king in Prussia who boasted that he had added a province to his country in peace—by draining swamps. The clearing of trees, bush and rocks ; ploughing, manuring and the rotation of crops : all these change the soil from its uncouth natural state into something more civilized, more sophisticated. Enormous increases in production are the prize shared out among the nations concentrating their investments and endeavours on these works. The discovery of hidden mineral treasure in the soil comes under the same heading.

§ 3

A further " natural " factor in economic life is human labour. But it is even less constant than climate or soil. It varies and may be varied, in quantity and in quality. The variations are partly " Acts of God "—not always in the sense that they may not be foreseen, but in the sense that they " just happen". Epidemics and wars fulfil even the condition that they cannot be forecast ; so do famines and other sudden inroads of mass-death into human society. But it is an old truth that after catastrophes of this sort populations restore themselves very quickly. On the slopes of volcanoes people sometimes sow into the still warm ashes of the last eruption.

Practically more important, therefore, are slower changes, which, for all that, may be the outcome of some human activities. Few only of those who repealed the British corn laws in 1846 wanted to drive British and Irish rural youth overseas and into the big British towns and cities: but these two mass-migrations were the results of their legislation and created the dependence of the United Kingdom on unhampered importation of foodstuffs and raw materials together with the enormous industrial and agricultural growth of the United States of America. The propagandists of birth control, or at least some of them, only wanted to make the supply of human labour rather more scarce in England; many of them did not think of putting a brake on the increase of the population at all, but dreamt (and dream even to-day) only of a more reasonable "spreading-out" of the same number of births over a wider part of married women's lives. The married couples, however, in practising this new technique, thought only of their personal wishes, they "chose the baby-car in place of the baby". So they instigated the slowing-down of the increase of population; and to such an extent has it proceeded that it has become a factor of first-rate importance for the future British labour market.

Let us look at two examples of countries with serious "population problems".

Palestine is one of the few countries showing, during the last ten years, a permanent dearth of labour, chiefly of semi-skilled and skilled labour for the finishing industries, building, growing citrus fruit and rearing cattle. An enormous quantity of capital is brought into the country. Much of it is absorbed by the equally enormous increase of prices for rural and urban land. But much of it lies in the banks and awaits investment. The chief (though not the only) limiting factor to this is the shortage of labour.

We see just the contrary in India. The population has been increasing rapidly since 1920. It has increased during these 17 years by about 60 million or more. The country is chiefly agricultural, but the area under cultivation can extend only very slowly, and capital for the intensification of rural work is lacking. Though in some parts two harvests per year, one in the wet and one in the dry season, are possible, generally much of the possible working time of the labourer is simply unused.[3] In Europe the winter slackness of agricultural work is mitigated by work in connection with live-stock, forest work, etc. But winter work shrinks everywhere in India to the care of cattle and chickens, and for the majority of the population, the Hindoos, even this does not exist. Rural industry (*e.g.*, spinning and weaving) barely holds its own, in fact is probably decreasing. So India fills herself more and more with people fit for labour whose work is, at the present time, unwanted. In spite of this, population is growing with extreme speed.

The first beginnings of deliberate planning for an *optimum* density of population may be observed in many places: the qualitative, though chiefly negative, experiments in "race hygienics" in some states of the U.S. and in National Socialist Germany, and their quantitative corollaries, planning for limitation of increase (Canada, U.S., New Zealand, Palestine) and for enhancement of increase (Italy, Germany, France). We even see scientific research beginning on the subject of what an optimum population *is*; and in Australia[4] the problem as to what is the maximum possible density of population for a country has been the subject of serious scientific inquiry.

On the qualitative side education generally, and professional education particularly, are age-old endeavours to make up for natural shortcomings in skill. The result of long discussions seems to be that we have no reason to assume that so-called "coloured people" have not the capacity for being educated into fitness for high-grade industrial work. Perfectibility of skill does not seem to be the privilege of one or two "races" only.[5] Even the quantity of labour to be extracted from the individual is becoming gradually a subject of planned policy.

Obligatory labour service; limitation of working hours;

[3] See R. K. *Das, The Industrial Efficiency of India.*

[4] See the extremely interesting and in many ways elucidating discussion of this problem in the volume edited by Mr. P. D. *Phillips* and Mr. G. L. *Wood, The Peopling of Australia,* particularly the contribution by Mr. F. C. *Benham,* "The Optimum Size of Population," pp. 246 *seq.*

[5] My professional experience as an instructor at a college for negro boys and girls bears out this view perfectly, in spite of all the handicaps, social, economic and psychic, under which the pupils are struggling. The same applies to my experience with Indian post-graduate students of economics in England.

progressive exclusion of children, young people and women from certain kinds of work or from work at all or at certain times ; the introduction of old-age pensions ; enforced retirement of public servants, judges and teachers : all these work towards the same end : to make the natural factor labour more and more plastic and to strip it more and more of the characteristics of superfluity, shortage or lack of qualification.

§ 4

What, then, is the outcome of all this ?

Certainly that our review assumes a very provisional character. What was true yesterday is, often enough, only a half-truth to-day and may be totally wrong to-morrow. For example, what increased importance wood, as a raw material, has gained from the invention of the cinema and of artificial silk ; rubber from the invention of the bicycle and of the motor-car ; milk from the use of galalith for electrical installation ; steel from railways, machinery, ferro-concrete building ; shellac from the gramophone !

And what is true of invention is no less true of discovery. Let us have a look at the statistics of copper production. The copper produced by refining from copper ores mined in the several countries has been as follows :

TABLE T57.

SHIFTING OF DISTRIBUTION OF COPPER PRODUCTION, 1913–1934.

In 1,000 Metric Tons.

Year.	Canada.	U.S.	Mexico.	Chile.	Northern Rhodesia.	Belgian Congo.	World.
1913 ...	13·9	555·4	43·7	20·2	nothing	7·5	1,018·5
1928 ...	56·6	828·2	45·3	274·9	6	112·5	1,695·1
1930 ...	101·6	632·5	56·4	208	6·4	140	1,577·3
1932 ...	95·1	231·8	35·1	247·7	69	58·9	922·2
1934 ...	151·9	215·9	47·1	247·7	140·1	110·1	1,273·2

These figures reveal an historical drama : First the discovery of new supplies of copper ore in Chile, with the consequent investment of huge sums of capital and the concentration of large numbers of miners in this area, depreciating much of the capital invested, and throwing out of employment many of the miners, in the copper mines of the United States. Second, the opening of the copper mines in Katanga in the extreme south of the Belgian Congo, involving new investment and the roping in of new herds of negro workers—checking, in spite of increasing world consumption, the further growth of mining in Chile and deepening the gloomy outlook in the U.S. Third, we see once more entrepreneurs on the move, pouring their capital into Northern Rhodesia, developing new riches of ore there, attracting negroes from quite different parts of the Dark Continent, putting a check on the development of Katanga, and further depressing copper mining in the U.S., even during the years of quick world-wide recovery. What destruction of productive equipment and, worse even, what frustration of masses of human lives! And all this in little more than twenty years. It is a clear illustration of how totally unexpected changes may cut into the web of our most carefully woven expectations as to the future of the supply of raw materials.

Chance, private individual endeavours, and planned achievements can scarcely be forecast with a fair degree of certainty. All that we say must, therefore, be understood with this enormously important qualification—that we make predictions to the best of our knowledge, but that we are fully prepared to see things go quite a different way from what we now believe to be their probable direction in the near future.

CHAPTER IV

THE EXISTING DISTRIBUTION OF RAW MATERIALS

A.—The Raw Material Resources of the More Important Countries

1.—*Calculation of Index Figures of the Wealth in Raw Materials for 15 Countries.*

We now begin to formulate explicitly the result of the masses of figures we have marshalled in our statistical tables. But before doing so I have to explain the methods on which the last table of our Appendix is based, and to deduce the inferences to which it leads. My endeavour was to try to find out if it is possible, with some real meaning, to measure the strength of the more important countries in terms of a series of comprehensive figures. Of course the argument can be raised that to do this is arbitrary and is, at the same time, something like adding up apples and pigs. All that is quite true, just as it is true that an examiner, by giving marks, inevitably violates realities to some extent, and that giving marks often enough means a wild, though respectable orgy of individualism. But in spite of all these well-founded doubts examinations will continue to be useful; and as in politics the classification of nations under the heads of " Haves " and " Have-Nots " will be used again and again, it seemed worth while trying to bring at least some small amount of method and consistence into the study of these international problems. So I have worked out the following system of giving marks:

(1) For every one of the raw materials 10 marks were shared among the countries producing it, whether the country was mentioned in our table or not; the proportion of the 10 marks

obtained by each producing country was equal to the proportion of the world supply of the raw material in question which the particular country contributed, so that a country contributing 10 per cent. of the world supply received 1 mark, etc. I avoided decimals and rounded off the figures to the next integer, according to the usual system, seeing to it, however, that no vertical column in the table ever showed a sum higher than 10.

(2) In so far as these marks fell to one of the 15 countries appearing in this table these marks were credited to them in Table A. Marks falling to countries not included in this table simply dropped out of our calculation, so that the sum of one vertical column may be (and very often is) less than 10, and may even be zero.

(3) Colonial resources were included in the wealth of the mother country. In the case of the U.K., the Dominions and India were treated as separate countries, so that "Great Britain" in this table means: England and Wales, Scotland, Northern Ireland, the Crown Colonies, Protectorates and Mandated Territories. Burma was treated as part of India; so were the territories of the Indian Princes. The Anglo-Egyptian Sudan was treated as a British colony. In the case of Italy, Ethiopia reckons as a colony (though that has scarcely any importance for our table), and in the case of Japan, Manchuria is treated as part of the Japanese Empire, just like Formosa, Korea, etc. The Philippine Islands are treated as a separate entity, not as colonies of the United States.

(4) This was the simpler part of the whole plan. The more difficult one was the process of weighting these marks. This was and is a very doubtful affair. The weighting of some raw materials depends entirely on whether a country is at peace or at war. Strontium is, only in peace-time, *e.g.*, important for fireworks for amusement purposes. This is so extremely subordinate a purpose that we would not have included this metal in our inquiry at all for this sake; the same is true in regard to the use of strontium compounds in the cane-sugar industry.

But in war-time strontium compounds may be very important, as they were from 1914 to 1918, because the strong red light which they produce when they are burned makes them a very valuable raw material for signalling-rockets. That is why we have included strontium in our inquiry and our table. But should peace-time or war-time importance serve as the basis of weighting?

After much hesitation I decided on the following system of weighting, the results of which I give for what they may seem worth to my readers—I feel very far from being cocksure in regard to this method. I found out, as nearly as possible, what proportion of the total value of world exports the value of the known exports of the material in question formed. This was expressed as a "weighting index" for that product, expressed in thousandth-parts of total world trade. In those cases where it was not possible to find such a figure (they are all cases of "minor" materials) *one*-thousandth was taken. The number of thousandths falling to every raw material in this way has been entered in the Appendix, in Table E, B in the form of integers.

(5) Part C of Table E contains the results obtained by multiplying the figures of Table A by the weighting indexes of Table B, and of adding up the horizontal lines of Table C.

(6) For obvious reasons iron ore, iron and steel were treated as separate items. This seemed to me the best way of evading the difficulty arising from the impossibility of obtaining figures showing the importance of scrap iron in the individual countries. For other metals the problem of scrap did not seem to me of sufficient importance to take particular notice of it in the weighting system. In the case of gold, however, where "scrap" is identical, more or less, with the gold imprisoned in the cellars of the banks, gold in banks and gold production were treated as separate items, the same weighting figure being taken for both.[1]

[1] The tables of lodes of coal, iron and oil in the earth were not taken into consideration.

With this system of marking I reached the following results :

TABLE T58.

UNWEIGHTED AND WEIGHTED MARKS OF 15 COUNTRIES FOR WEALTH IN RAW MATERIALS.

Country.	Unweighted Marks.	Weighted Marks.	Percentage of Total Unweighted Marks.	Percentage of Total Weighted Marks.
Australia	11	75	2	3
Brazil	7	58	1	2
Canada	46	149	9	5
China	18	48	3	2
France	38	123	7	4
Germany	36	140	7	5
Great Britain	48	260	9	9
Holland	13	95	3	3
India	62	260	12	9
Italy	17	71	3	3
Japan	32	151	6	5
Poland	5	28	1	1
Russia	73	422	14	15
Union of South Africa ...	17	81	3	3
United States	112	894	22	32
	515	2,785		

Now let us compare these percentages with the population figures for the countries in question. The latest population figures, in millions, which are known, are :

TABLE T59.

WEIGHTED MARKS OF 15 COUNTRIES FOR WEALTH IN RAW MATERIALS, COMPARED WITH THEIR POPULATION.

Country	Population in Millions.	In Per Cent. of sum of Previous Column.	Percentage of Total Weighted Marks.[1]
1. Australia	7	·4	3
2. Brazil	43	2·4	2
3. Canada	11	·6	5
4. China	444	25·3	2
5. France	106	6·5	4
6. Germany	67	3·8	5
7. Great Britain	104	5·9	9
8. Holland	69	3·9	3
9. India	380	21·7	9
10. Italy	54	3	3
11. Japan	129	7·4	5
12. Poland	32	2	1
13. Russia	170	9·7	15
14. Union of S. Africa	9	·5	3
15. United States	128	7·3	32
	1,753	100	

[1] Repeated from previous table.

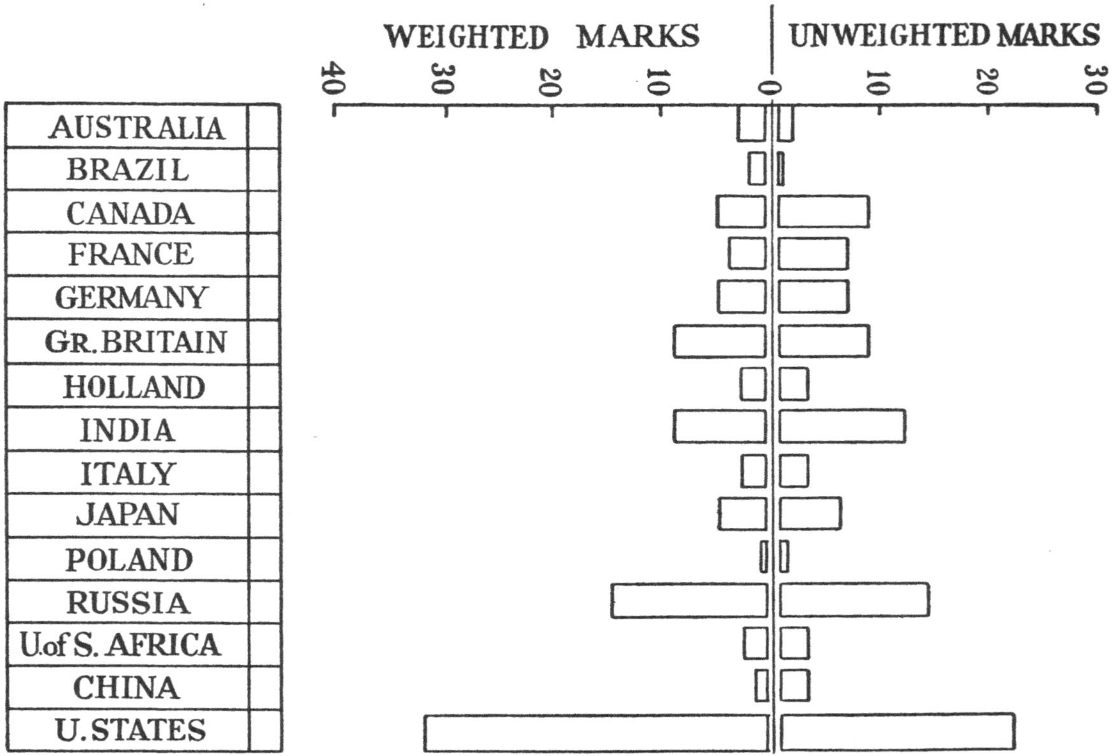

Figure 1: Unweighted and Weighted Marks for 15 Countries. Their Wealth in Raw Materials.
Marks for Wealth in Raw Materials in per cent. of Total Marks.

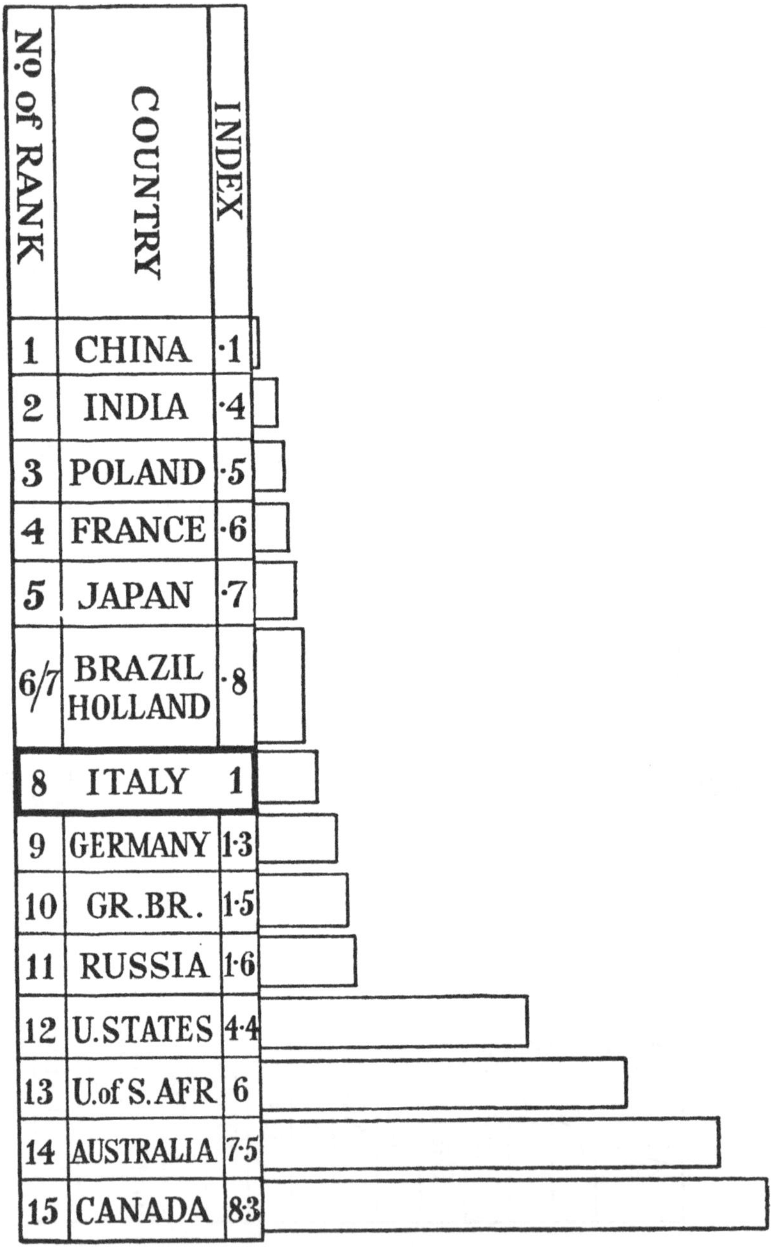

Figure 2: Index Figures of Wealth in Raw Materials.

If we now divide the last column by the second, we get a figure showing how many times the share of raw materials of the particular country is larger or smaller than unity :

TABLE T60.

INDEX OF WEALTH IN RAW MATERIALS FOR 15 COUNTRIES.

Number of country in previous table ...	1	2	3	4	5	6	7	8	9	10	11	12	13	14	15
Index of wealth in raw materials	7·5	·8	8·3	·1	·6	1·3	1·5	·8	·3	1	·7	·5	1·6	6	4·4

And this, as the final result of our long-winded and bothersome, risky, but not quite useless, statistical venture, gives us the following list :

TABLE T61.

RELATIVE IMPORTANCE OF 15 COUNTRIES ACCORDING TO THEIR WEALTH IN RAW MATERIALS.

Rank.		Index of Wealth in Raw Materials.
	Poorest.	
1	**China**	**·1**
2	**India**	**·4**
3	**Poland**	**·5**
4	**France**	**·6**
5	**Japan**	**·7**
6/7	**Brazil, Holland**	**·8**
8	**Italy**	**1**
9	**Germany**	**1·3**
10	**Great Britain**	**1·5**
11	**Russia**	**1·6**
12	**United States**	**4·4**
13	**Union of South Africa**	**6**
14	**Australia**	**7·5**
15	**Canada**	**8·3**
	Richest.	

If we go over this table in a reflective mood its general result does not seem so great a surprise as one might have expected. It makes sense, though some weaknesses are obvious. Among the commodities produced on a large scale and of economic importance in the world are a few which would have influenced the result perceptibly as, *e.g.*, coffee in the case of Brazil, tea in the cases of China and India, cocoa in that of Great Britain, tobacco in the cases of Brazil, Holland and the U.S. ; meat, butter and cheese would have still further raised the already very high indexes for Australia and New Zealand. China with her extremely low place in this table is obviously to a certain degree the victim of the fact that most of her production, though it certainly reaches her 444 million consumers, does not reach statistical tables. The Italian index is *lowered*, unduly, as some will think, by our inclusion of ten million Ethiopians in her population percentage and therefore in the denominator of the fraction determining the value of the index of raw material wealth. Skins and hides, milk, transport services and potatoes are other gaps. On the whole the filling in of these and the avoidance of some of the other flaws we have mentioned would perhaps have raised Italy to 1·2 and other countries to the extent to be seen from the following table, the second line of which gives our result and the third line a very rough estimate of the changed figures which would be the outcome of such a "correction" of the tables :

TABLE T62.

POSSIBLE CORRECTED MARKS OF 15 COUNTRIES IN REGARD TO THEIR WEALTH IN RAW MATERIALS.

Relative importance	1	2	3	4	5	6	7	8	9	10	11	12	13	14	15
Original index ..	.1	.4	.5	.6	.7	.8	.8	1	1.3	1.5	1.6	4.4	6	7.5	8.3
Corrected index ...	.4	.5	.6	.7	.8	1	1	1.2	1.4	1.6	1.7	4.5	6.1	7.7	8.4

The changes are not important, and a change in the relative position of any country is, as far as I can see, scarcely involved in these possible corrections.

A crudity in our method is the use of integers instead of decimal fractions for the weighting indexes and for the unweighted marks. The result of the use of a decimal unit would have been that a number of entries would have appeared in our tables which do not now appear because they were below ·5, and that a number of items would have appeared with fractions between ·5 and 1, 1·5 and 2, and with fractions between 1·5 and 1, etc. The result would have tended, as far as I can see, towards raising the results for Nos. 4 to 11 by ·1 or ·2, and lowering those for Nos. 12 to 15 by about the same amount. The changes, then, would not have been important and would scarcely have involved alteration of the hierarchy. But the use of decimals here would have taken away from the method something of its character of a roughshod statistical cross-country ride which it should, I think, keep, in order to prevent pedantic and dogmatic over-exploitation of this source of information. When you want orange juice with your cornflakes, never press the orange pips until they give juice ; it will spoil your breakfast.

2.—*Discussion of the Real " Haves " and " Have-Nots".*

One inference we may certainly draw with safety from our figures : *i.e.*, that our inquiry into the existing distribution of productive wealth among the 15 countries and empires possessing more than 30 millions of population explodes the myth of the division of mankind into " Have " and " Have-Not " nations. It does not abolish the assertion that some nations are much better off than others in respect to those attributes which interest us here : but the composition of the unfavoured group turns out to be quite different from what we hear so often stated, namely, that Germany, Italy and Japan are those unhappy nations which need a redistribution of raw materials in their favour. The truth is quite different, though certainly, scientifically and politically, no less interesting. The following facts can safely be inferred from our schoolmaster-like system of marks-giving :

(1) *The Plutocrats among the Nations*

There is one group of nations enormously favoured in comparison with the others ; it consists of the United States, the Union of South Africa, Australia and Canada. Three of them have " colonies " of a sort ; but they are very unimportant in territory, population and wealth in comparison with the mother country. None of these colonies contributes to the marks gained by their mother countries in even equal proportion to the amount they add to the respective population denominators (with the exception of Porto Rico, a producer of sugar-cane). If, then (a very doubtful assumption, as we shall see ; but let us assume its truth, for argument's sake), wealth in raw materials means power, the colonies of these three are leakages of power, not sources. And it is perhaps more than a mere coincidence that the highest place is held by that one country among the members of this group which has no colonies at all, viz., Canada.

(2) *The Upper Middle Class among the Nations*

The second best group comprises our Nos. 8 to 11, so to say the upper middle class in the society of nations, consisting of two popularly so-called "Have-Nots" and two "Haves". Among these Russia is rapidly advancing, whilst Great Britain, so long as her retreat from imperialism persists, is gradually approaching more and more the situation of Italy, which is the average situation of all large countries. In the case of Great Britain the disproportion between the size of her colonial empire (big even after all the deductions we have deemed necessary) and her colonies' contribution to the Empire's wealth in raw materials is worth mentioning. It is only about two-tenths of the unit, or 16 per cent. Even Italy, with her "teeming" millions (they always teem when the author wants to give a nice impressive turn to his sentence), and with her poverty in minerals, is not so badly off after all, though her colonies do not contribute an atom towards her raw material position, but are, as yet, like Ethiopia, a distinct source of weakness. How far the possession of Ethiopia may change this in the future is, of course, just as much an open question as so many other questions concerning the future, though what we know so far does not justify any sanguine expectations. Russia has developed during the last ten years by such leaps and bounds that, in spite of her quickly growing population, it is quite possible that she may within the next ten years turn her back on so mediocre a class as the second-best group and rise into the ranks of the monied aristocracy among the great nations of the world.

(3) *The Lower Middle Class among the Nations*

The third group I should like to call the lower middle class among the nations. It comprises, if we follow the results of our inquiry, Holland, in spite of her great, rich and well developed colonies, Brazil, Japan and France, which is, I must say surprisingly, worse off than Japan. It is very interesting to see how colonies are distributed among these countries.

TABLE T63.

MOTHERLAND AND COLONIES OF THREE EMPIRES.

Empire	Area in 1,000 Square Kilometres.			Population in Millions.		
	Mother Country.	Colonies.		Mother Country.	Colonies.	
		Actual.	in Per Cent. of Mother Country.		Actual.	In Per Cent. of Mother Country.
French ...	551	11,910	2,163	41·2	64·5	157
Japanese ...	382	1,913	501	60·3	59·8	86
Dutch ...	34	2,042	6,006	7·9	60·9	771

Though in all these cases the contributions of the colonial possessions to the wealth in natural resources of their three empires are not negligible, it is very doubtful whether they make up for the increase in necessities which their population and territory, of course, demand. This seems to be so particularly in the case of Holland, where the disproportion of colonial territory to the area of the motherland is by far the greatest.

(4) *The Proletarians among the Nations*

The poorest group of countries consists of Poland, India and China. In India it is the fantastic and absolutely extraordinary increase in population during the last score of years which may be regarded as the chief source of the poverty of this country. The fact that these countries have no colonies cannot be deemed very important, in view of the facts we found when looking at the " lower middle class ".

3.—*Particular Questions Concerning the British " Empire."*

One remark may be added : Four of the fifteen countries in our list of indexes of wealth in raw materials are parts of the British Empire. Great Britain's marks have, accordingly, been calculated by excluding from " Great Britain " in our sense the three Dominions : the Dominion of Canada, the Union of South Africa (with her Mandated Territory South-West Africa) and the Commonwealth of Australia (with the territories mandated to it), and also India with Burma. Three more territories which, in view of the smallness of their population, do not appear among our fifteen, viz., the Irish Free State, Newfoundland and New Zealand, have also been excluded. If one counts, weighing one thing against the other, India among the sovereign parts of the British Empire for economic purposes, the Empire is a loose federation of the Motherland, six Dominions and the rather indefinite creation India (and Burma as a further extra now), bound together by tradition, by "allegiance to the British Crown" (as the Statute of Westminster says), whatever that means (as the King acts in the Dominions and in Great Britain on the advice of separate and independent sets of ministers who are responsible to separate and independent parliamentary majorities and to nobody else[2]), and by a bundle of commercial treaties. These are centred round the treaties concluded at Ottawa in 1932[3] and in regard to the future distribution of raw materials are unimportant, because the preferential treatment which these nine units have given one another has been limited in the recent past to importation, whereas no differentiation of an imperial character has taken place with regard to export. And the present tendency is clearly towards further loosening even the economic connection and coherence of the Empire. The history of the Empire since Ottawa seems to me overwhelming proof of this. The most important items in this process may be explained here:

A new constitution for India is gradually coming into operation which subjects the commercial policy of that country in constitutional law, as it has already been subjected in constitutional practice for about 20 years, to the will of the Parliament of India, irrespective of the wishes of the Parliament or the Government of Great Britain. In these matters the Viceroy will have no powers of emergency legislation and no power to override the resolutions of the future Indian legislature. Commercial policy, therefore, falls clearly into that

[2] Since 1936 Burma is no longer a part of India; but it has not returned to the position of a crown colony, protectorate or mandated territory of Great Britain; it has retained its somewhat intermediate position of being no longer a colony but not yet a dominion. In our list, which is based on figures for the past in which the share of Burma cannot be isolated without enormous bother, we have treated Burma as part of India. But its exclusion would not change the index for India perceptibly—perhaps by ·01 or so, one way or the other.

[3] See the discussion on the Ottawa Conference between Lord *Olivier* and the present author in the various numbers of the *Sozialistische Monatshefte* (Berlin), 1932.

sphere of activities for which the Viceroy's ministers are fully responsible to the Indian Parliament.[4]

The situation as regards the other Dominions is very clearly shown in the Memorandum of the Royal Institute of International Affairs[5] which inquires into the importance of colonial possessions for the problem of raw materials. The authors base their treatment of the Dominions, as we do here, in the Statute of Westminster of 1926, and they exclude India also from the British Empire within the meaning of their (and our) inquiry: " Thus India is excluded by her tariff autonomy since the war, quite apart from her membership of the League (of Nations) and other considerations." Though her membership of the League is perhaps not as important as the Memorandum would lead one to believe and the " other considerations " are scarcely more than a vague hint (even if there is anything to hint at), the sole argument of the tariff autonomy which India enjoys has gained in force and goes on gaining force the nearer the full working of the new Indian constitution approaches.

We are drawing the line here, though there is something to be said for the similar treatment of Ceylon, Southern Rhodesia and some other crown colonies. But the fact remains that these *are* still crown colonies, and that the overriding powers of the governors there, against the will of the local parliaments, have been made clear by the enforcement by the British Government of the anti-Japanese textile importation quotas on Ceylon in 1934. The " Memorandum " treats Southern Rhodesia like India. But as the *Dominions Office and Colonial Office List*, 1930 (p. 210), says of the constitution (which indeed gives the country a large measure of self-government, so that its affairs are treated in London by the Dominions Office, not the Colonial Office), the governor " is empowered to assent to a law passed by the legislature, withhold his assent or reserve the law for signification of the King's pleasure." This reservation of overriding powers seems so important that we believe it

[4] In India this does not refer to the whole activities of the government; there are reserved subjects and emergency powers in respect to which the Viceroy (and through him the Emperor) acts on the advice of the Secretary of State for India in London, who is responsible only to the Parliament at Westminster; but these reserved subjects and emergency powers do not concern commercial policy.

[5] See *Raw Materials and Colonies*, pp. 15 *seq.*

better to treat Southern Rhodesia as a colony for the purposes of our inquiry.

Other " border-line cases " are Manchuria, which has been treated here as a part of the Japanese Empire, and Ethiopia, which we must now consider as a part of the Italian Empire. The considerations of international law are clearly against this classification, even more so than in the case of Southern Rhodesia. But whereas the contents of constitutions, treaties, and even gentlemen's agreements are very real factors in matters concerning the British Empire, the same can scarcely be said, to put it mildly, in relation to the Italian and Japanese Empires. The Philippine Islands are, for obvious reasons, not treated as a part of the Empire of the U.S.

The question of status is not so important for the right understanding of the assigning of our marks, because the effects of the colonies on the present distribution of raw materials are not important. If we were to compute an index including India, Canada, Australia and the Union of South Africa into the term " Great Britain," we would find :

TABLE T64.

CALCULATION OF AGGREGATE MARKS FOR THE BRITISH EMPIRE.

	Population in Millions.	Weighted Marks.
Australia	7	3
Canada	11	5
Great Britain	104	9
India	380	9
Union of South Africa	9	3
Totals	511	29

This aggregate population of 511 million forms 29 per cent. of the aggregate population of the 15 countries in our table of valuations. We have, therefore, a very interesting result, viz., that the whole British Empire obtains the index $\frac{29}{29}$ or 1, *i.e.*, shares honours of place with the median country, Italy, and is distinctly lower in rank than Great Britain without the inclusion of these other countries in her index. It is, of course, India with her enormous population which pulls down, in this amusing but also enlightening tug-of-war, the mother country by more than compensating for all the enormous relative wealth of the three great Dominions. As we may fairly safely assume that the poverty of Ireland and Newfoundland would at least compensate for the possibly enhancing influence of New Zealand on our index we may take it as established that this system of giving the four mentioned big parts of the Commonwealth of British Nations separate treatment does not artificially lead to understatement of the wealth of Great Britain in raw materials. If it leads to anything which has the slightest taste of bias at all it is to a moderate measure of *over*statement.

This, I think, is all that can usefully be said about the result of our inquiry at the present stage of the discussion. To draw further positive inferences here and now would mean jumping to unjustified and perhaps quite misleading conclusions. We shall use, however, our results in the further discussion of the problems in their proper places.

B.—The Importance of Raw Materials

"Raw materials are just what their name implies, *i.e.*, materials which are processed into other materials and things, which may be used for any purpose, nice or less nice; and that is the long and short of it." So one might feel tempted to think on reading this heading, and to go on: "Their importance is therefore incommensurable, as without them no production, and therefore no consumption, is possible."

This is quite true. But, all the same, for the purpose of clarifying our minds it is not quite valueless to know what the particular import of some raw materials may be; what their importance is, to express ourselves in a more slipshod, though more popular manner. But the term "importance" is an ambiguous one; we have to distinguish its meanings, and to say how we propose to use it.

Again, we have to go off in a direction which the reader perhaps will think is a tangent: into a discussion of a methodological character. But it just cannot be helped. We have a double purpose here: to exhibit the facts, and to interpret their meaning. It is easy to see what a mess the world has got into through the mixing elegantly and lazily of misstatements of facts and misinterpretations of them; and all signs promise a far more terrible mess to come if this method is not replaced by a better one. So it is natural that our inquiry must proceed by means of statistics (the comparatively most certain way of assembling facts) and discourses on method. Perhaps those sceptics are right who say that even the most watertight case for reason, stated in the most elegant way, will not make people believe in reason and act accordingly. I do not know ; maybe. In any case the " retreat from reason", as Mr. Hogben says, has had such terrible results that it is at least worth trying to appeal to people with the answers which reason gives to our problems. No damage can be done, and there is just a chance that people may come round and behave more reasonably, and with better results. As Father Brown said to Flambeau : " You damned reason ; and that's very bad theology."

Raw materials are interesting to the statesman looking after the interests of the population of his country mainly because they are necessary for the production of all the commodities and the performance of all the services needed for the everyday life of the members of the community. They, therefore, by their quantity and variety, determine the standard of living. In consequence, two more factors regarding raw materials claim the interest of the statesman : *i.e.*, their price and the certainty that they will be available when and as needed. Their prices determine whether they can be used for the satisfaction of consumers' wants at all, and in what quantity they may be able to contribute to the standard of life of the population. On the degree of probability that they will be available as and when needed depends the security of the standard of life.

(*a*) *Security of the Standard of Life.*

Any man who produces a certain material to-day may stop doing so whenever he likes ; or he may vary the quantity he sets out to produce. In a sense a nation may act, in this respect, as if it were an individual. " Production " of a raw material in the international sense means something which is closely akin to the original meaning of the Latin verb *producere*, viz., to bring forth, to hold out to possible foreign purchasers. It depends on the will of the government of a country (whatever this will may depend on) whether a country, while growing, *e.g.*, sugar all the time produces sugar in the sense of producing it for international exchange. The government can allow or disallow the exportation of raw materials, can limit the quantity exported to any positive fraction of the total quantity produced annually, etc. Nor is this only theoretically possible. In war-time it is a matter of ordinary experience that governments prohibit the exportation of certain materials they deem particularly indispensable for purposes of defence (every country involved in a war is always and all the time fighting in defence) or the free exportation of which they believe would favour the enemy or enable neutrals to escape some nicely-prepared plan for rubber-shoe blackmail. But there is no necessity to fall back on war-time conditions for an example. Even in undisturbed peace restrictions of this sort have been quite frequent. For centuries Spain, Portugal and other European nations forbade the export of gold and silver from their territories even in peace-time. In recent times the exportation of grafting or planting material or of the seed of newly-bred, very perfect varieties of sugar-cane from the Dutch Indies was made illegal. The Peru Government does not allow the exportation of guano until what they believe to be the needs of their planters of sugar-cane and cotton are satisfied year by year. The prohibition of the export of gold is quite the peak of elegance in fashion among modern statesmen. We shall speak later of the system of putting a quantitative limit to the export of quite a number of raw materials, introduced by governments for the purpose of manipulating prices, etc. If somebody would take the pains to make a complete list of such government activities the resulting catalogue would, probably, surprise many people by the number and the importance of its contents.

One of the very important points here is whether such limitations are applied in a manner one might feel tempted to call impartial to the whole outside world, or whether differentiation takes place. It is clear that differentiation might be, sometimes, a rather important feature of such a policy. Let us imagine an example. There was a great dearth of coal in Europe immediately after the Great War, because so many mines had been destroyed and the rest had been pitilessly overworked during the war years. If, then, a country in Europe had forbidden the exportation of coal to, *e.g.*, Spain, this would have been serious. At best it would have meant that coal would have had to have been bought from producing countries which could have delivered it only at the cost of enormous expenditure on transport, *e.g.*, from the United States; the second best possibility would have required the additional investment of much expensive or perhaps unavailable capital. The third and worst possibility would have been that, for a time at least, Spain would have had to go without coal or any substitute. For a large number of the former consumers this worst possibility of all would certainly have happened, because their incomes, their selling prices, etc., would not have permitted them the enormously-increased expenditure occasioned by the first two possibilities and the large additional investment demanded by the second one.

Since the war, still entirely the prisoners of war psychology, many European politicians have lived under the obsession of possibilities of this sort. They have spread their hysteria among the public, and so the struggle against such a danger has become an important feature of European politics. In spite of all experience to the contrary, this hang-over of the war is still quite alive and chirpy. Newspapers, speeches and popular books are full of it, and practical politics are largely shaped by the obsession of politicians, pressmen and populace that their country might be "starved" of "vital" raw materials in peace-time, and that therefore governments should see that they created an industry producing the particular raw material within their country's own economic frontiers (colonies, if any included).

I took part, as a journalist, at the end of the war in the discussion on Germany's obligation to deliver coal in kind to France to help in the reconstruction of north-eastern French territory which had been so thoroughly devastated by more than four years of warfare. Most German politicians were then of the opinion that it would cripple Germany's own recovery were she obliged to deliver the quantity of coal, stipulated in the negotiations at Spa (Belgium) at 26·2 million tons annually. I tried to show that, under certain conditions, Germany would be able to deliver this quantity and even more, and I concluded my part in the debate with the words:

> "It would have been in the interest of the alleviation of Germany's obligation to contribute to reparations if Germany had managed to transform the *right* of the Allied Powers as

laid down at Spa, to get such quantities of coal delivered into an *obligation* on those powers to take this coal."[6]

This shows how necessary it may be at times to make it clear that a policy of restriction of exports in peace-time is wrong, and how difficult it may be to make this clear to all those concerned. There are situations when restriction of exports for the purpose of better provision at home or discrimination against some nation or other for the purpose of damaging it exercises a great attraction on those deciding on important questions of economic policy. In view of this it seems to me all the more remarkable that all my endeavours to find a case of discrimination against a nation or a group of nations by a policy of restricting exports of raw materials in peace-time have been entirely without result. Nothing of the kind of at least fairly recent date (say after 1920) could be found, and it is remarkable that authors who do not discard the fear of such an eventuality always gloss over, more or less skilfully, the difficulty when it comes to giving examples from experience. We may take it as established, therefore, for our further discussion, that such discrimination has not been part of modern experience. Though that does not make it impossible in the future (there are no *a priori* limits to what madness can do) it makes it at least extremely improbable.[6a]

This does not mean that restriction of exports of important raw materials without discrimination among buying nations is equally improbable. Quite the contrary; it is a frequent modern experience. But what does it come to?

[6] See H. *Kranold*, "Die Kohlenfrage in Spa" and "Wie bezahlen wir die Milliarden an die Entene" in *Die grossen Wirtschaftsfragen* (Hannover), I, pp. 1 *seq.* and 25 *seq.* (1921.)

[6a] I have already mentioned in Chapter I the exception of tin. Two more cases, also obsolete now, appeared as fruits of my enquiries: (1) In 1916 Nigeria passed an act discriminating by means of an export tax on palm kernels in favour of those exported to be processed in the British Empire; the discrimination came into force in 1919 and was repealed in 1922. (2) For some years, from 1919 onwards, India gave a rebate of two-thirds of the export duty of 15 per cent. *ad valorem* on hides and skins on those exported to be processed within the British Empire. In 1923 the tax was reduced to a flat rate of 5 per cent. for all destinations, and the preference in favour of the British Empire was abolished. (See *Bastable-Gregory*, pp. 66, 171, 199, V. *Anstey*, p. 347, B. M. *Das* in *Current Science* (Bangalore), November, 1936, p. 261, and J. H. *Richardson*, pp. 136–137. All these exceptions were unimportant except in so far as their short lives, and, in the case of tin, their lack of effect, have shown the futility of such a policy.

Our statistical tables show us, and the table which sums up the whole of our statistical work does so in a particularly impressive manner, that at least among the 70 raw materials we have taken into consideration here there are scarcely any of which we could say that one country enjoys a total monopoly of its production at the moment. The cases coming comparatively nearest to such a production monopoly of a raw material of some importance are the following:

Nickel, Canada; palladium, Canada; "other" platinum metals, Canada; molybdene ore, United States; strontium minerals, Great Britain; hempseed, Russia; jute, India.

Most of these cases are not, it is obvious, of particularly great importance in peace-time; even a dire scarcity of red rockets on July 4th in the U.S. and on July 14th in France, should the United Kingdom abuse her quasi-monopoly of the production of strontium minerals, would be a tolerable evil, after all. . . . And our table shows that only one of these raw materials gives its producing country unweighted marks of 10, viz., jute in India; so that only this index shows an approach to a real monopoly. But here the temptation to extort high prices from other countries by a temporary embargo on exportation or to starve other nations of sackcloth by a permanent embargo is very small, because there are so many substitutes for jute fibre which would be produced elsewhere in enormous quantities following a comparatively slight rise in the price of jute. What else could the Indian Government do with the surfeit of jute on their hands than to repent in sackcloth over their mistaken policy?

In all the other cases limitation of export is a matter for concerted international action (rubber, coffee, cotton, sugar) which has been tried again and again with remarkable results, as we shall see later on, in recent times, but with results rather out of line with the arguments of those who take the expectation of embargoes on the exportation of important raw materials in peace-time into consideration as an item affecting their plans for an economic policy.

There remains only the case where a country gives preference to its own citizens' needs of a material as against those of the inhabitants of other countries, like Peru with her policy of forbidding the export of guano under certain circumstances. But cases of this sort have made so slight an impression (because of the intervention of substitutes) that this instance itself is almost unknown and scarcely mentioned in the literature on the subject.

(*b*) *Price and Range of Consumption.*

In quite a number of cases governments have arranged plans for either increasing the price of a raw material which is an important item in the export trade of their country or for curtailing the volume of exports, generally with the intention of bringing about such an increase in price by a roundabout way. Actions of governments are not always positive; sometimes they only "favour" or even merely tolerate certain behaviour on the part of their subjects or groups of subjects. In other cases either concerted action by several governments or favourable or at least tolerant treatment of the activities of international capitalist private organizations are found. The question whether a particular case comes under the heading of government action or of favouring or toleration is of minor interest. We may take it for granted that the most private efforts at price-raising and restriction by the most private capitalists are not done without their government throwing a kindly eye on their undertaking.

The list of examples is long and quite recent; many of the restriction plans are still in operation,[7] and it is not probable that this policy of restriction will disappear soon from international business life.

In 1922 the so-called Stevenson plan, which we have already mentioned, was introduced, which endeavoured to enhance the price of rubber by restricting exports from the British territories producing rubber (British Malaya, British Borneo, Ceylon, etc.). The consequences were at first an enormous rise in the price of rubber, then the growth of powerful outside production, then a great breakdown of price.

These developments took several years. During these years the rubber producers everywhere had a fat time, but not only was outside production stimulated, the working-up of scrap

[7] The international tin syndicate was extended for a further number of years, in February, 1937; the share of Siam was cut down a bit; otherwise no important changes seem to have been made. Bolivia is now a participant in the plan.

rubber became profitable, the production of rubber from coal-tar derivatives came near to being profitable on a large scale, and even the collection of wild rubber in Brazil (where reserves of untapped *Hevea* rubber trees are estimated at 300 million or more) and elsewhere was revived for a time. The chief profits went to the outsiders who enlarged their plantations and gardens of rubber trees enormously and tapped every tree which was even half mature. Consumers had, for a few years, to pay "through the nose", which made them extraordinarily irate, but later, when prices slumped again, they quickly recovered their losses.

After another period of extremely low prices a new international arrangement for the restriction of output came into force. This time the important outsiders were included (chiefly Siam and the Dutch Indies) and the restriction of exports was now handled so cautiously that prices could not again rocket sky-high. The prices at which wild rubber, artificial rubber and recovered scrap rubber became able to compete with new plantation rubber (2s., 2s. and 1s. 6d. or so per lb. respectively) were respected in the price policy of the new corner. A mild degree of profit was obtained by those producers who had survived the second slump, rationalization and cheapening of their production methods was encouraged, and the consumer paid a price which on the whole must be called perfectly bearable. After all the consumer of a commodity cannot very well expect a producing industry to supply him permanently at prices which cause it to lose its capital. Our tables concerning rubber prices show all these features quite clearly.

Let me give two more examples of the effects on prices of international restriction of important raw materials: steel in Europe, and tin all the world over.

The world market for steel is divided into two parts; one of them is served chiefly by the heavy industry of the United States, the other by that of north-western Europe: Great Britain, Holland, Belgium, Luxemburg, France and Germany. The territories on which these two groups actually compete are of minor importance. It was, therefore, not an impossible idea to restrict production in the European field alone for the purpose of improving the prices of steel in their particular selling areas. The European Iron and Steel Agreement of September

30th, 1926, was signed by German, French, Belgian, Luxemburg and Saar industrialists. Of the whole quantity to be produced, Germany and France obtained quotas of 40 per cent., and smaller shares were allotted to the minor members of the group. Prices were not fixed, nor were markets shared out to the several partners. The only factor to be manipulated was the aggregate production. Since then the agreement has undergone many changes in detail, it has been temporarily stopped, Great Britain and some new minor partners have become associated with it, but the principle of regulation of the market by manipulating the quantity produced has remained unchanged. The outcome is shown in our table of the course of the prices of iron and steel—A1 (8). If we make 1913 = 100, we get, for some important iron products in comparatively unprotected areas like Great Britain and Belgium, the following price index figures:

TABLE T65.

PRICE MOVEMENTS OF IRON AND STEEL IN WESTERN EUROPE, 1929–1936; INDEX FIGURES.

1913=100.	1929.	1932.	1936, July.
Pig iron, Great Britain	119	71	78
Iron bars, Belgium	112	48	62
Girders, Belgium	88	39	54

The fact that this trend of prices, in the teeth of the quickly-increasing wave of international rearmament requiring enormous quantities of steel, led even in 1936 to prices which were only one-half or three-quarters of what they had been in 1913, seems to me proof that the government-favoured monopoly policy of these cartellists was remarkably cautious. The price level of 1929 was not particularly high. The slump was rather deep, and recovery in prices slow and small. It would have cost the consumers of iron and steel many, many million pounds more to buy the quantities of steel they bought in 1934/1936, had they had to pay anything like the prices they had to pay and did pay ungrudgingly before the Great War.

Another important international output restriction scheme designed to "improve" prices was (and is) that in respect to tin. Here the producers on British territory (Great Britain, Nigeria, British Malaya) and some others like Siam have arranged for the restriction of the quantities of this metal offered on the world market. Our tables enable us to assemble the following instructive figures :

TABLE T66.

STATISTICS OF MARKETS FOR TIN, 1929–1936, WITH INDEX FIGURES.

	1929.	1932.	1935.	1936. June.	1936. July.
Production of tin ores in 1,000 metric tons of tin content	195·1	98	149·8		
Index (1925=100)	132	66	101		
Stocks of tin on world markets, in 1,000 tons ...	28·3	59·1	17·4	15·7	
Index (1925=100)	117	244	72	65	
Price of tin in London, in RM. per 100 kg. ...	411·67	196·92	271·85		229·14
Index (1925=100)	79	38	52		44

Here again it seems as if the lessons of previous restriction schemes for other raw materials had been well learned. Though restriction had by 1932 brought output down to half what it had been at its peak in 1929, this was the result, obviously, of a very conservative policy. Stocks increased, so that one cannot say that a particularly high degree of scarcity of this important metal was created. Later on stocks fell below the level of 1925, but prices remained remarkably moderate, at least well into 1936. No substitutes and no newcomers were encouraged, and one cannot say that the consumers have been hit hard by a policy which involved these prices.

Not all the plans for the restriction of output of raw materials for the purpose of stabilizing (or, better, buttressing) prices show the same features. Hope of profit has, often enough, led the leaders of such organizations seriously astray. Indeed, we find among these " valorization " schemes some which, in their endeavours to skin the consumer while keeping him alive, are suspiciously similar to simple corners in one or the other commodity such as from time to time are organized on the commodity markets of the world. But it would be unjust to think that this describes the mentality from which most of the valorization schemes spring. What happens when such valorization schemes are tried ?

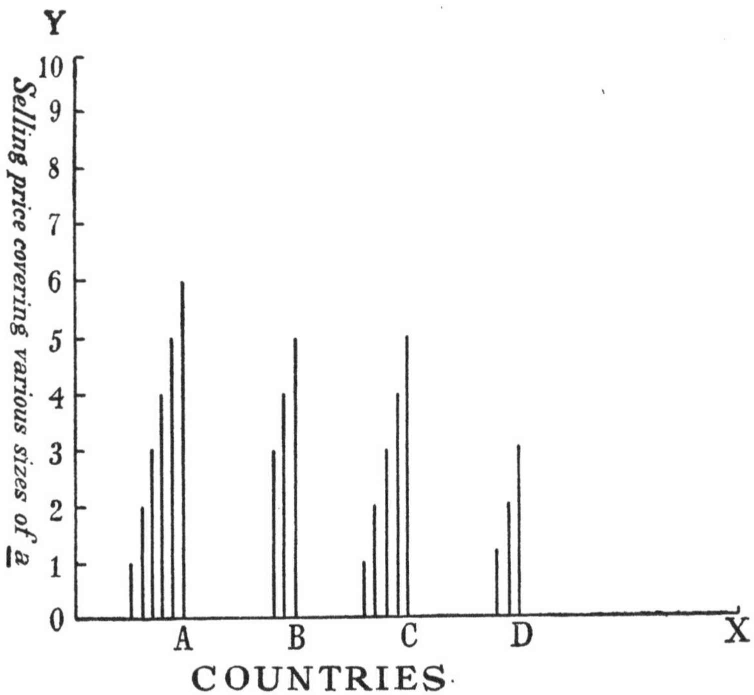

Figure 3: Influence of Overhead Charges on Survival of Competing Firms in Different Countries.

Let us assume that a number of countries, A, B, C, D. . . produce some commodity which is liable to suffer from enormous variations of price and demand on the world market. Production will either follow the law of diminishing or of increasing returns ; the first case will probably be the one which interests us most, because the extractive industries (like mining) and agriculture mostly follow that type. We shall, however, treat only the case of diminishing returns, as what we prove for this case is *a fortiori* true for the opposite case.

The equation for the cost of production will be, if we assume that it is linear in type, *i.e.*, that the elasticity of the curve is everywhere the same, of the form :

$$y = a \pm bx$$

where : y : cost of production per unit ;
x : quantity produced ;
a : a constant of the general overhead charges ;[8]
b : a constant characterizing the angle which the curve makes with the x-axis.

The sign before bx will depend on whether we have a case of increasing or diminishing returns ; in the first case its sign will be negative, in the second case positive.

There is no necessity for any factory, plantation or mine to have the same a and b as any other factory, plantation or mine.

Now let us look at the meaning of different sizes of a for a given b. Figure (3) shows in the form of straight lines the several selling prices which are necessary, when the productive capacity of the enterprise is fully used, to allow the enterprise to work without a loss. We then see very simply that all enterprises can work when the price is 6·5, that a few make losses when the price is 4, etc.

As the several classes of enterprises with different a's contain

[8] a must be understood as representing all cost items which are independent, in their absolute size, of the quantity produced and which, therefore, increase in weight per unit produced when the quantity produced decreases. b is the constant on which it depends whether in a particular enterprise a decrease or increase of the quantity produced makes for a quick or slow increase or decrease of cost per unit. Our equation is an artificial simplification ; the real equation will probably never be linear ; it will have additional terms of the form $\pm cx^2$, $\pm dx^3$. . . . But we simplify to save unnecessary mathematical calculations, the result of which would not be different, in principle, from the simple case we are analyzing here ; and we limit ourselves to a qualitative analysis, which is also sufficient for our purposes.

varying numbers of members from country to country, some countries have to disappear from production entirely at certain price levels, in others some enterprises close down, etc.

After a time the accumulated stocks which drove the price down become exhausted, consumers fear running short of supply, confidence returns, consumers of the raw materials accept larger orders, and prices rise again so that they cover the costs of all the classes which had to stop production while prices were low. If, in the meantime, the works or plantations have been simply lying idle, they may be reopened and begin production again. But this will rarely be the case, when low prices have persisted over a fairly long time. In these cases mines will have been drowned in water, plantations may have become wildernesses of weeds and obnoxious plants, parasites and pests will have multiplied luxuriantly, factories may have been pulled down, become dilapidated or obsolete, in short, a new investment on a large scale is necessary to restore production to its original size, and consumers will have to pay for this. They will recuperate later, and they will have been compensated for some of this cost by previous profits while prices were low. But this is true only if we take "*the* consumers" as a unit, not when we look at the fact that the individuals composing this group will have changed and will further change. The one then pays for the gains of the others, etc. There is no strict solidarity of interests between "*the* consumers."

To a certain extent the producers who work under conditions of decreasing returns will be able to meet the heavier and heavier burden their overhead charges mean for them when prices fall by curtailing their production; but this is true for all enterprises, and so in the ensuing competition their gain from a falling incidence of bx will be over-compensated by the increasing weight of an absolutely invariable a.[9]

A different development will follow if production is curtailed in such a way that the fall in prices is mitigated. In this case losses will be distributed more equally over the various enter-

[9] The result of this antagonistic interplay of a and b will depend on their relative size, when the sign bx is positive. The case of $-bx$ (law of decreasing returns) does not make a and b antagonistic; the effect of both of them works then in the same direction, unfavourable when prices fall and favourable when prices rise.

prises, those which have a favourably low *a* will bear part of the losses, those which have an unfavourable *a* will get off lightly, and more, or even all, enterprises will survive into the next period of better prices, so that new investment to re-establish full producing capacity at the previous level will not be necessary and will not have to be paid for by the consumers. Some consumers will forgo speculative gains, others will avoid speculative losses ; prices will be kept within a narrower range of variations, and that will make for stability and safety in the raw material industry as well as in those industries which process the raw material in question. Governments which have an interest in stable employment and taxation returns will naturally favour such a development.

The indispensable condition for all this is that the organization which puts the brakes on the fall in prices should enjoy a stable monopoly ; otherwise it will favour the intrusion of outsiders, whose production will, in due time, bring down prices with a bump in spite of all endeavours to buttress them, driving out of production many members of the monopolistic coalition.

If the elasticity of the curve of cost is low, curtailment of production will have to be done on a large scale ; the larger this scale, the nearer the conditions of the regulated market will come to the conditions of the unregulated market, and the less stabilizing will be the influence on prices and on the survival of weak enterprises.

Consumption at definite price levels varies in this world in accordance with the way in which business conditions vary between brisk, intent business and high degree of employment and periods of depression, inactivity and widespread unemployment. If demand is to be satisfied at all in the peak boom period it is inevitable that at the bottom of the slump a considerable volume of unused capacity of production should exist. This is quite all right for factories with a low *a*, but pernicious for those with a high *a*.

I think that governments interested in stability, industrialists, planters, etc., interested in factories, plantations, etc., with high *a*'s, and, if they are provident and cautious also capitalists interested in enterprises with low *a*'s, may find the idea of spreading the loss in profits over all enterprises, by preventing, to a certain extent, the fall in prices, and of keeping alive as many of the enterprises as possible through the slump period, very attractive.

Even consumers may find it to their advantage not to reap the full profit accruing to them temporarily (often only too temporarily) as a result of the drop in prices, thus avoiding later scarcity and a high price period. Their position, of course, depends on how strongly the syndicate would put on a brake on prices. But those syndicates which have learnt the lessons offered by experience of valorization during the last twenty years will know:

1. That to restrict production too much means heavy losses;
2. That it is not a wholesome policy to encourage, by particularly high prices, the intrusion of outside producers.

So their interest, if they understand it correctly, and particularly if the governments involved understand theirs correctly, should lead them to a conservative scaling down of production. By trial and error, by *tâtonnement*, they should find the best medium course to adopt. Experience seems to show that, as the years go on, valorization schemes adapt themselves more and more to the dictates of wisdom; and on the whole it seems to me that the consumer does not fare badly through such a policy.

Whether such a policy is feasible is, of course, quite a different question. In cases where a medium price allows outsider production to raise its head, in cases where some governments and/or industries with fairly low *a* costs remain outside the scheme and in cases where even a medium price still favours the large-scale production of substitutes, the thing cannot be done. The restriction of output will in these cases have to be small and the price must be allowed to sag rather considerably. But the more the price drops in this way towards the level which would be reached under free competition, the more similar the general consequences of a policy of concerted restriction become to those of a competitive regime, and the less worth while it becomes, therefore, to undertake the whole valorization plan.

We can enumerate quite a number of valorization schemes which belong to this "non-feasible" type; to name a few examples: the first Stevenson plan in rubber; the government's coffee valorization in Brazil; the co-operative wheat pooling policy in Canada; the government limitation of the area under cotton cultivation in the United States. It is characteristic that all these examples show restriction of production in only one or a few of the producing countries in which the production of the particular raw material is actually or potentially of importance. Sometimes sheer luck saves such schemes at the last moment; those involved have a hair-breadth escape, like the Canadian growers, co-operative societies, banks and governments connected with the Canadian wheat valorization. But sometimes the whole economic structure of a country may be shaken, as, *e.g.*, the case of the coffee valorization in Brazil shows.

Enterprises of this sort, if undertaken without success, or continued beyond the first period, before the coming in of outsiders (this first period always shows splendid success and induces people to give the thing up either too late in the day or not at all) have the nasty knack of involving more and more deeply the general business life of the country in which they are worked. Stocks increase; producers or their co-operative societies or governments borrow on the "security" of these stocks; the existence of the stocks, known to all the world, drives prices farther down and keeps them down, so that the collateral security no longer covers the loans; selling-out of the stocks to cover the margins begins and the market slumps farther and farther for a period. Producers, co-operatives, bankers, depositors and the government suffer huge losses. The crowning mistake is made when stocks are destroyed; the peak of bad luck is climbed when stocks turn bad and have to be destroyed. The security for the loan is then burnt or thrown into the ocean; the credits based on them have to be written off, and many people's savings and employment go overboard with the spoiled goods.

Sometimes a "fortunate" series of bad harvests may save the valorization, as this seems to have happened in the present case of wheat owing to the poor harvest of 1936 and the heavy buying by frightened governments anxious to lay in stocks as insurance against famine in case of war. But what are one or two such lucky escapes at the last minute compared with the experiences in the majority of such cases, where this kind of *deus ex machina* does not provide a happy ending to the adventure ?

To sum up : It may be that consumers have to pay " through the nose " in cases of restriction of production of a raw material. But they will get their own back with a vengeance. Adventures like the first Stevenson scheme or the Brazilian coffee valorization have made the frequent recurrence of such cases very improbable. And " mark my words " : discrimination against any particular purchasing country has been a totally unknown feature in all cases of this sort.

C.—Non-Economic Uses of Raw Materials.

The provision of the belligerent powers with raw materials in war-time is quite a separate question. This is naturally the concern of politicians, statesmen and pressfolk. It is perhaps equally natural that, with the memory of the last war still alive in their heads, and with the permanent danger of a new general conflagration providing the headlines of their papers every day, the public at large think of all problems connected with the international distribution of raw materials in the first place in terms of war. And indeed, if self-sufficiency in these materials has any importance at all, it is certainly when strategical interests become vital.

The ardent interest of a wide public in this question has been precisely the cause of a terrible inundation of sheer bilge into popular and political discussions of the matter. Pride and prejudice have rarely had such a heyday in economic writing as when Sir Samuel Hoare's speech at Geneva in the autumn of 1935 drew, efficiently though involuntarily, a big red herring across the trail which leads to truth. A dispassionate statement of the facts is, therefore, all the more necessary and valuable.

Much of the work necessary in this field has been done by an extremely interesting book by Mr. Brooks Emeny (*The Strategy of Raw Materials*). It goes into the question systematically. It has a profuse outfit of impressive graphs. It gives statistical material of interest. And, together with our own studies, it enables us to make quite definite statements concerning things as they actually are.

Mr. Emeny, in general, limits his inquiry to seven states : the

United States, Great Britain, France, Germany, Italy, the U.S.S.R., and Japan, the " Great Powers", the " Big Seven", as we might say. I think that he is quite right in doing so, as to take into account the details concerning smaller countries might only create a maze of facts among which the Ariadne thread of real understanding might get entangled and even break. His list is really not so much smaller than ours of 15 countries, since he includes Canada, India, South Africa and Australia in his term Great Britain. So our list of fifteen includes beyond his list really only Poland, China, Brazil and Holland, countries on whichever, if any, side they may be found will not be of very great significance in case of war as producers of raw materials.

In another direction we cannot quite approve of Mr. Emeny's method. He distinguishes, quite rightly, between Mother Countries and Empires. But when speaking of the British Empire he uses this term so as to include the Dominions and India. Now it is true that for some of the Dominions a patriotic all-British revival may be expected in case of war, which even may lead these Dominions to take part in it on the side of the United Kingdom. At least it is probable that neutrality may be operated so as to withhold raw materials of military importance from her enemies. But I should think that the list of such " certs." is exhaustive if we put on it Australia and New Zealand. Canada and Newfoundland may be only slightly dubious, but dubious they will be, particularly if the United States keeps out of the conflict and boycotts the export of war materials to the United Kingdom, her allies and her enemies with beautiful impartiality. The Union of South Africa seems a very dubious factor, and the Irish Free State and India can scarcely be considered as more than sources of additional trouble. It seems to me, therefore, that probably five and possibly all the seven of the Dominions should be eliminated from the assets of the Mother Country.

The commodities with which Mr. Emeny is concerned are :

Metals: iron (ore), copper, lead, aluminium (ore), zinc, manganese, nickel, chromium, tungsten, antimony, tin, mercury.

Other minerals: coal, petroleum, nitrates, sulphur, potash, phosphates, mica.

Organic materials: cotton, rubber, wool, and occasionally: "food," "power."

(*a*) *Peace-time Production is not Sufficient in War-time.*

There is one assumption underlying the whole review of Mr. Emeny's which, though it is a very moot point in all these discussions, is difficult to avoid. "Self-sufficiency" for war-time is taken as being a result of two conditions.

It is believed that the absence of net imports of one or a number of raw materials over a number of characteristic years, or the presence of net exports in peace-time, will constitute self-sufficiency, *i.e.*, that the demands of the belligerent state will not be higher than those of the same state in peace-time. Even had Mr. Emeny taken years when, in the pursuance of large-scale armaments, the Big Seven were building up reserves of raw materials, this would still have been a very bold assumption. But in view of the fact that Mr. Emeny's statistical data end generally with 1932 or even an earlier year, the assumption becomes particularly dubious. The years he has taken as his basis are those years before the craze for armaments gripped the world. It is idle to assume a general percentage by which the peace-time figures ought to be increased in order to make up for the increase of consumption resulting from a war, and to inquire in what cases self-sufficiency would still then remain. The percentage would, in all probability, be extremely different from material to material and might vary in the course of a lengthy future war just as unexpectedly and unequally as it did during the last war. But we must not forget, because it is impossible to correct the error, that an error it is, and a serious one, I believe.

(*b*) *Peace-time Production cannot go on in War-time.*

Peace-time production, on the whole, can be assumed, at least, to be not larger than the war-time requirements of strategically necessary raw materials in a belligerent country. In this respect it is characteristic that the word "Labour" does not appear in Mr. Emeny's index. But war means a serious deficiency of labour all over the body economic, human as well as animal, and of power both mechanical and electrical. How such a shortage affected Germany's agricultural production, together with the deficiency in materials for manuring the fields, can be seen from the following table:

TABLE T67.

INDEX FIGURES OF TOTAL HARVESTS IN GERMANY, 1914–1918.

1913 = 100.

Year.	Wheat.	Rye.	Oats.	Potatoes.	Sugar Beets.	Rough Fodders.
1914	86	85	93	85	100	99
1918	55	66	49	56	59	72

Already the second year of the war (1915) brought the harvest of oats down to 62, of sugar beet to 65, of hay and other dried green fodders (rough fodders) to 79 and of rye to 75. After one year, therefore, the decline in production was more than a quarter of the whole. The number of cattle fell between December 1st, 1914, to December 1st, 1918, from 21·8 to 17·2 million, and that of pigs during the same four years from 25·3 to 10 million. The losses in the average weight of these animals (excluding calves) were 41 and 65 per cent. respectively. This gives us for cattle an index (1914 = 100) of 41 and for pigs of 14 for 1918 ! Though scarcely any part of Germany producing coal was in the war zone at any time, the production of coal diminished in this way :

TABLE T68.

GERMANY'S PRODUCTION OF COAL AND PIG IRON, 1913–1918.

	In Million Tons.		
	1913.	1915.	1918.
Coal	190	147	158
Pig iron...	19·3	11·7	9·2

These results occurred in spite of feverish endeavours to produce, with the help of millions of prisoners of war, as much as possible of these foodstuffs, fodders and vital raw materials. Here again losses of 17 and 52 per cent. were experienced.

Again we cannot apply a definite general percentage to the decrease of production of vital raw materials. But the fact remains though its elusive character allows it to escape our calculations.

(*c*) *The War-time Outlook for the Big Seven.*

Self-sufficiency in peace-time can, therefore, be assumed to persist in war-time only subject to the following qualifications :

(1) Self-sufficiency in war-time cannot be expected unless
  (*a*) Peace-time imports will not be cut off ;
  (*b*) Peace-time net exports form at least 20 to 30 per cent. of home consumption, or unused capacity to produce amounts to a similar percentage.

(2) Self-sufficiency cannot be assumed to persist in war-time unless it is independent of imports from countries or " possessions " which will probably be neutral.

We shall have to revise the lists given by Mr. Emeny in this light. He gives a long table of raw materials in which the United States will be fairly well off in case of war, and we agree with this list. Mr. Emeny's list for Germany is : power, iron, chemicals, coal, iron ore and nitrates, but I should feel inclined to put a question mark against power and nitrates and to strike iron and iron ore from the list.

Mr. Emeny's list for *Great Britain :*	My list :
Power, iron, chemicals.	Power, iron (?), chemicals.
Coal, iron ore, copper.	Coal, iron ore (?).
Lead, nitrates, aluminium.	Nitrates, aluminium (?).
Zinc, rubber, manganese.	Rubber.
Nickel, chromium, tungsten.	
Wool, tin, mica.	Wool (?), tin, mica.
For *France :*	
Food, power, chemicals.	Food (?), power, chemicals.
Iron ore, nitrates, aluminium.	Iron ore, [9] nitrates (?), aluminium.
Nickel, chromium.	Chromium.
Potash, antimony.	Potash [9], antimony (?)
	Iron [9].
Russia :	
Food, power, iron and ore.	Do.
Chemicals, coal, petroleum.	Chemicals, coal, petroleum (?).
Copper, lead, sulphur.	Lead, sulphur.
Cotton, zinc, manganese.	Do.
Mercury, mica, chromium.	Do.
Wool, potash, phosphates.	Potash, phosphates.
Italy :	
Food, power, chemicals.	Food (?), power (?).
Lead, nitrates, sulphur.	Lead, nitrates (?), sulphur.
Aluminium, zinc, mercury.	Zinc, mercury.
Japan :	
Food, power, coal.	Food (?), power.
Copper, nitrates.	Copper (?), nitrates.
Sulphur, mica.	Sulphur, mica.

[9] Depending on the non-invasion of Lorraine by an enemy.

In the cases of Germany, France, Italy and Japan, Mr. Emeny's list is already not a very imposing one, and our revision makes it extremely poor. It reduces even the better position of Great Britain to quite an appreciable degree. Only the United States and Russia make a better show. But many materials of distinct war-time importance do not appear on any of these lists; and if the scepticism expressed in our question marks is justified we find that of 26 items in our list (counting iron and iron ore as separate items) we find a positive result in the following numbers of cases:

United States	21	France	7 (of which 3 conditional)
Germany...	3	Russia	16
Great Britain	7	Italy	4
		Japan	4

And even more significant than the list of positive cases and the mere numbers is the following list of a few important clearly negative cases (disregarding "question-mark" and "conditional" cases):

Germany: food, iron ore, iron, petroleum, cotton, aluminium, rubber, manganese, nickel, tin, wool.
Great Britain: food, petroleum, cotton, manganese, nickel.
France: petroleum, cotton, manganese, rubber, nickel, tin, wool.
Italy: the same, and: aluminium, chromium.
Japan: the same.

The list is clearly an important one. Of course it does not tell the whole tale. There is, within certain limits, the possibility of the use of substitutes. The light liquid fuels and the heavy oils burnt in aeroplanes and other vehicles of military importance driven by internal combustion motors may be produced from coal in several ways, by liquefied hydrogen and other combustible gases, and so on. But there is a wide gap between an industry established on a small experimental stage and an industry functioning on the certain and large scale which a war might demand. There are stocks on which a country may draw largely in war-time: nickel coins may be melted down, copper roofs may wander into the melting-pot, etc. But if artificial silk and other textile fibres are to take the place of cotton *and* wool, while cellulose is required at the same time as a substitute for dozens of materials the country can no longer import, then an inroad into the country's forests and labour market may become necessary on such an enormous scale as to be an impossibility.

(*d*) *Shortage of Labour in War-time.*

The shortage of human labour in a belligerent country is particularly remarkable. Let us sketch out a case.

Germany[10] had a male population, between the ages of 15 and 65 years, in 1933, of 21·6 million. The number of male persons employed of the ages 16 to 65 was 19·3 million. For the female population the same figures were 23·3 and 10·8 million respectively. This leaves at best the following "reserves":

TABLE T69.

GERMANY'S LABOUR RESERVES.

	Males.	Females.	
Persons not employed in peace-time	1·9		12·5
Of which we have to deduct:			
Mothers in families with more than 3 children		3	
Mothers with birth in that year ([11]) ...		·7	3·7
Net reserve	1·9		8·8

[11] Of all women between 15 and 65, 5·7 per cent. had a confinement in 1935; so this figure represents 5·7 per cent. of 12·5 million.

This brings the net reserve to 10·7 million people. From this we have further to deduct all people who are in any way unemployable, say ten per cent. or 1·1 million, which reduces the reserve for employment or military service to 9·6 million. If, then, 10 million soldiers are needed and 2 million extra people for work to make substitutes for missing imports, there will be already a surplus of demand over supply. But even this is still too optimistic a picture; we have to make a further deduction, to make up for the fact that women generally are not quite as efficient in male work as men if they have never done that work before and do not usually take to it. We assume for this fact a discount of 20 per cent. The new requirements are 12 million people, and all reserves really available may be calculated by the formula

$$1{\cdot}9 - \frac{1{\cdot}9 \times 10}{100} + \frac{(8{\cdot}8 - {\cdot}9)80}{100} = 1{\cdot}7 + 6{\cdot}3 = 8 \text{ million.}$$

[10] I take the figures for Germany because they happen to be at hand; the case is fundamentally the same for all European countries.

So the maximum strength for army service plus additional labour for war-time production would be only 8 and not the required 12 million—and if a larger number of men is put into one of the two groups of war service the other category will have to go short by a corresponding amount. As this does not take into account any losses or increase of mortality from other sources the deficiency of 4 million may safely be taken as a minimum figure.

Our point is that this shows that the development of the use of substitutes cannot go on indefinitely. In this self-sufficiency-ridden world of ours substitutes which are not used in peace-time are not used largely because they require too much work. If we assume that they require, for the same degree of satisfaction of needs, 50 per cent. more work in investments and current employment together we shall be not so very far away from the truth.

So we find that a country can use substitutes ; it can create one or a dozen substitutes in certain quantities of medium size. But it cannot use them in war-time indiscriminately without either stopping important other industries or draining its army of fighters. All this is true even if we totally disregard, as we have done, destruction of civilian life and of factories, etc., by air attacks. This reasoning goes, I think, quite a way already towards proving that the idea that self-sufficiency in peace means something very "comfortable"[12] in the way of self-sufficiency in time of war is erroneous.

(*e*) *The Bunkum of "Control"*.

If this pricks a nice bubble, another one is not less worth while pricking. Namely that of the "control" of raw materials.

It is a very handy word, control, and used, flippantly or seriously, by many people. There is often (though not always) some meaning behind it ; though it is important, if not easy, to find out how much there is behind it in each case. Again we have to distinguish between control of a raw material in peace-time and in war-time.

[12] A word Mr. Emeny frequently uses !

(1) *Control in Peace-time.*[12a]

Here control of, *e.g.*, coal in Belgium, may mean that some person or group of persons or some public authority can decide what quantities of the one or the other or of all sorts of coal are to be produced and/or marketed within a certain period of time, in a certain area, at certain prices, possibly even to certain consumers only. This, obviously, does not contribute anything to our subject, though it is important enough in other respects.

Again, a group of Belgian capitalists may own the majority of the shares in one or several coal mines outside Belgium. They can then decide to import that coal into Belgium or to sell it elsewhere in certain quantities, to offer it at certain prices, to curtail or enlarge its production, etc. This may be important in case a particular quality of coal is necessary for some special purpose and can be safely expected to be available in the necessary quantities at the right time only from this source. In other cases " control " of an enterprise, at home or abroad, may mean the possibility of manipulating its shares, of making it sell to particular customers at a loss or at least an unjustifiably low profit, etc. But all this has no importance for the provision of raw materials in international life. This would not be true, however, if, for example, the control of the copper mine *Aleph Alpha* in *Chamberlainisia* by the *Morning* interests would mean preventing the *Evening* interests controlling the

[12] The futility of the usual meaning of " control " of a raw material comes out very clearly in the following boastful statement by Sir Edward Mackay *Edgar*, sometime president of a group of British oil capitalists. Messrs. E. H. *Davenport* and S. R. *Cooke* have gleaned it from an article of Sir Edward's in the September, 1919, issue of *Sperling's Journal* and quote it in their book: " The British position is impregnable. All the known oil fields, all the likely or probable oil fields, outside the United States itself *are in British hands or under British management or control or financed by British capital.* America . . . will have to purchase from British companies. . . . We hold in our hands the secure control of the future of the world's oil supply. We are sitting tight on what must soon be the lion's share of a raw material indispensable to every manufacturing country . . . *the future has in store for us to hold up the entire world to ransom. . . .*" Is it to be wondered that the uncritical reader takes such an outbreak of " exuberant " spirits seriously ? But what is the relevance of the *argument ?* The possibility of exploiting the foreigner in peace-time by making him pay " through the nose " does not carry with it any political power of providing oneself with a necessary raw material in war-time. And would Sir Edward let off the British consumer more cheaply than the American customer, or would he propose to " hold him up to ransom " also ? (Italics in the quotation mine.)

mine and refusing to sell copper to people in whom the *Morning* group took a lively interest, especially if these people had no other possibility of buying copper. It is obviously possible that an international monopoly, created with or without government help, of the production of some raw material might restrict production or quantity sold, enable minimum or maximum prices to be fixed, the division of markets among its members, etc. But as curtailment of turnover is costly, it will be kept strictly within the limits of what seems indispensable ; and to discriminate against the industry of one or the other country would scarcely be a sport cultivated by people enjoying such " control "—simply because arbitrage would make such endeavours futile. " Control " in this sense is a very interesting business proposition on which opinions are widely divided ; but it is scarcely of interest in regard to the international distribution of raw materials.

The last possibility is that governments, exercising " control " in quite another sense, by legal powers, by persuasion or by intimidation, should prohibit the exportation of some raw material to foreigners at large. Here again, however, the web of connections in international trade has so many and such complicated meshes that a government would scarcely think it worth while to discriminate against the one or the other country by refusing to sell to it whilst freely selling to others.

(2) *Control in War-time.*

Here " control " of a sufficient quantity of a raw material again means that somebody, generally a government or a group of allied and associated governments, may decide where the raw material shall go, in what quantities and at what prices. The history of the last war provides many examples, and the next one will probably do so again. But the essential element in this form of control is not ownership, but military and sea power. The Allies of 1914 to 1918 controlled nearly all the raw materials of the world (with the exception of those produced between the German–Austrian–Hungarian–Bulgarian–Turkish front lines) because they " ruled the waves ". Control during a war of a raw material is, therefore, secured when two (and only two) conditions (or their equivalent, as, *e.g.*, successfully blackmailing or bribing neutrals) are fulfilled :

(1) Production must be outside the reach of the other party to the war, and if possible within one's own reach, from a military standpoint.

(2) Transport must depend on the would-be controlling power or group of powers only.

It is only a negative form of this if a country, without being able to get any of the material in question for herself, is able actually to cut off the enemy's supplies by sinking his ships, frightening or bribing neutrals to enforce embargoes on exportation, etc.

So control in war-time boils down to geographic and military factors. Ownership, holding of share majorities or influential minorities has scarcely anything to do with it. Iron ores from German-owned mines in Morocco went freely to France during the Great War; the "enemy capital" was ousted from its "control" in a moment. So the owners had not even to decide whether they preferred to be good patriots or good business men. Seizure of their capital in enemy territory protected them from all the tortures which men have to suffer who must choose between such a Scylla and Charybdis.

(*f*) *Security of Transport in War-time.*

Before leaving the subject under discussion at the moment, viz., the self-sufficiency of certain powers in certain raw materials, we have to add one thing more.

Our lists are based on the assumptions:

(*a*) That every country, even during a war, rules the whole of her territory and enjoys liberty and security of transport within that territory;

(*b*) That those countries depending for supplies, partly or entirely, in peace-time, on their colonies, enjoy free and safe transport from the colonies to the mother country.

These assumptions are certainly unreal to a certain extent. Experience alone can show to what extent. Let us hope that the point will remain open for ever, because of lack of future experience!

(*g*) *Stocks and Scrap Materials.*

A country preparing for the possibility of a war, and believing that it may be cut off from important raw materials, can, of course, lay in a stock against such a contingency. To a certain extent this is done automatically by the normal activities of peaceful business life. Every branch of industry holds certain stocks at all times and does not live from hand to mouth. Much metal invested in peace-time in nickel coins, brass buttons, copper roofs and jewellery (gold, platinum) may be seized or collected by the government and used for new purposes. The more investment takes place, the more a long period of peace makes nations wealthy, the better will they be able, in war-time, to live on scrap materials like wedding rings, copper cables for long-distance transmission of electric power, statues of conquering generals,[13] etc.

Mr. Emeny gives a number of interesting and meritorious data on the importance of scrap material as one of the sources of these metals to the United States in the case of a forthcoming war or in the case of that country becoming involved in other people's wars and so cut off from foreign resources. He calculates, *e.g.*, the requirements in manganese metal for a two-year emergency at 1·58 million long tons of ferro-grade (metallurgical) manganese ores. Of these he assumes, following official American estimates, 100,000 tons of metal to be available from bonded warehouses. He adds 30,000 tons in the hands of consumers, so that he balances these 130,000 tons of metal against the 643,000 tons of metal content of the ores required. For nickel he computes the quantity necessary for two years of war at 48,000 tons of metal. As against this Mr. Emeny puts :

TABLE T70.

NICKEL IN WAR-TIME IN THE U.S.

Stocks in hand	12,500 tons	
Recovery from coins and ferrous alloys ...	9,500 tons	(29% of the whole requirements)
Recovery from steel scrap	14,000 tons	(29% ,, ,, ,,)
	36,000 tons	(or 75% of the whole requirements)

For tin the total requirements are given as 70,000 tons, of which 60,000 or six-sevenths can be got from scrap materials. For antimony the requirements are 84,000 tons, secondary recovery 31,000 tons, etc.

[13] This is why it is so much more patriotic to erect artistic atrocities in the shape of monuments to dead heroes and rulers in bronze than in marble. The time is past when cannon balls could be turned out from stone, at a pinch.

Now what is true of a country with such a fantastic use of metals as the United States is not necessarily true, to the same extent, of other countries. Though Mr. Emeny is cautious in his endeavours not to underestimate the war-time needs, we cannot be sure either if his assumptions are true or if his "two-years" emergency will be sufficient. But whatever the opinion of the critic as to the figures of the individual case, it is certain that scrap material is at least an additional factor affecting security in all calculations of supplies of war-time materials.

Another item must be mentioned here, though it proves still more elusive the moment we try to grasp it quantitatively: the laying-in of stocks by governments, directly or indirectly. They do not tell us, of course; but it is probable that most of the governments of the Big Seven cannot entirely have missed the golden opportunity of the years 1931 to 1936, when metals were dirt cheap, to pile up some stocks. Though their size is an unknown magnitude, these stocks are a factor which should not be totally skipped in a review of the situation.[14]

One last remark, and we are through. Our statistics of production have the one great drawback, however reliable they otherwise may be, that they do not tell us of those cases where lodes of an important ore exist in a country and which were not mined because at the prices prevailing from 1919 to 1937 it was not good business to mine them (low-grade, inaccessible or difficult ores) but which were used to a large extent during the four war "emergency" years and may be used, together with others not mined during this time, in the next "emergency". It will cost money, materials and men to develop such productions again. It will take time; but done the thing can be, and in so far as this is so the situation, as given by our peace-time statistics, is, perhaps, in some cases slightly, in other cases totally leading us astray. We know quite well that a nasty source of error looms here in all our inquiries; but though we know it we cannot do anything else than be so well prepared as not to be surprised by a surprise.

[14] This applies to wheat and some other foodstuffs also. What a boon and a blessing might it not have been to the Canadian farmers, banks and governments, had the British Government bought up the Canadian carry-over of wheat on December 31st, 1934, to the tune of 5,800,000 metric tons at the then prevailing price of RM. 70 per ton. It is quite possible to-day to think of a thing like this; see further.

D.—The Unreality of It All.

We have taken use in war-time as the prototype of the use of raw materials for non-economic purposes. It is certainly by far its most important form. Perhaps some reader will think that "non-economic" is a misnomer. In a sense it is; and if I had had to coin the terms used in this inquiry for the first time I (so I hope at least) should not have made it. But it is there; is widely used; is not particularly misleading—and contains even a useful hint of what the investment of raw material in armament and warfare really is. And I should like to say that in this regard the expression seems to me to sin on the side of understatement in a very serious sense. For this whole discussion, necessary as it is because it employs the minds of so many and so influential people, is truly totally unreal and absolutely misleading.

We have now heard something from the mouths of eye-witnesses in Ethiopia and Spain about what aeroplanes can do even when used in small numbers and hampered by scarcity of ammunitions and fuel and by dispersion of objectives. There was a time when Mr. Haldane and Miss Woker could fight publicly on whether the new weapon was devastating or not. These things are clear now, cleared up by experience. What the aeroplanes seem *not* to do with certainty is to shorten war if they are used in something like equal numbers on both sides; but when they swoop down on large towns they will blow them to smithereens and burn them in huge pyres. They will cut off inland transport, bring down factories, incinerate pitheads, sink ships and drive mankind from towns and cities into the starvation of comparative scarcity in the country where there are no targets worth a bomb and a gallon of petrol. It is, indeed, as Mr. C. E. M. Joad, always an outspoken, but also always a conscientious author, says in his review of a book in the *New Statesman* of February 20th, 1937:

> "Within a few days . . . the gas and electric light systems will have broken down, there will be no ventilation in the tube tunnels, the drainage system will have been thrown out of gear and sewage will infect the streets, large parts of London will be in flames, the streets will be contaminated with gas,

> and hordes of fugitives will spread outwards from the city, without petrol for their cars or food for their stomachs, pouring like locusts over the country."

A real modern war will extinguish victor and vanquished alike ; it will be only a minor anxiety whether or not their raw materials will hold out for two or more years, for just one week longer than those of the enemy. Who knows which country will be conquered by the other ? Perhaps the wide areas of Russia or the remoteness of the United States may make it possible for them to survive. But they will have lost the sources of innumerable purchases, the buyers of enormous exports. They will survive like overgrown heads on the body of mankind that has dwindled to dwarfish smallness. A new war will be an *auto-da-fe* of the most fantastic kind of European and, probably, Indian, Chinese and Japanese mankind. After a century somebody will dig up a copy, surviving by a mere whim of fate, of all our wise inquiries into the impact of the international distribution of raw materials, and as none of our contemporaries will survive *and* read scientific books afterwards, nobody will be the wiser, and nobody will find out by experience whether we were right or wrong in our endeavours to forecast that impact.

All this glib talking of self-sufficiency, whether or not it will be there in war-time, even that of the most sober, the most critical sort, has one distinct danger : it helps to keep up the atmosphere of unreality which is created by taking such problems seriously. The moment the occasion for these problems really turns up it will abolish the brains to which they are problems and without which all problems are just dead letters mouldering deep under smouldering ashes.

This whole debate on raw materials in the next war rests on a total impossibility, turns round and round an entirely empty fiction. Not even the historic statue of the " economic man ", Mr. Gradgrind in Dickens' *Hard Times*, is such an empty show. All this is a tale, told by an idiot . . . signifying nothing, though chock-full of sound and fury.

E.—The Cluster of Real Problems

We believe we have dealt with some of the more important fallacies of our subject ; to mention only a few, we will remind the reader of the following :

(*a*) The importance of colonial productions ;
(*b*) The particular poverty of the " Have-Nots " ;
(*c*) Exploitation of the consumers by restriction of output ;
(*d*) Damaging the consumers by embargoes on exports ;
(*e*) Export discrimination against some nations in peace-time ;
(*f*) The meaning of " control ".

Our list of proved red herrings is, as we see, quite a nice one already. But an important task still remains, viz., to show the real problems underlying the state of deep-rooted and terrifying uneasiness as to raw materials in international life. There is quite a cluster of such problems, and to exhibit them and to show in which direction possibly their solution may be found becomes doubly necessary after this first pricking of a few bubbles.

CHAPTER V

THE RATIONALIZATION OF THE DISTRIBUTION OF RAW MATERIALS

History often moulds human affairs in a manner which we, looking at things afterwards, feel to be extremely unreasonable. History is stupid. Well, history, after all, is an abstraction only, and to accuse an abstraction of stupidity or vice is certainly no more than child's play. But underneath this hardly sensible vituperation against a mere abstraction lies, dim but real, the *ex-post* understanding that endless bloodshed, epidemics and starvation, with all their ensuing unhappiness, might have been avoided, if history had been formed by the actions of human individuals and nations in a more reasonable way.

Now it is, to a certain degree, comparatively easy to know in the aftermath of an historical period what might have prevented the swooping down upon us of a "*great time*" (great times meaning, generally, times with a particularly high quota of bloodshed and starvation). It is true that conjectural history *ex-post* is speculative and uncertain also, to a degree. But as long as this speculation does not take the form of ruminating over such questions as what might have happened had not Madame de Pompadour enjoyed the favours of royalty in 1755, such a review of the past has at least one fact in its favour: viz., that the historian is sometimes able to know important facts better than the persons acting at the time.

All the same, if people refuse the advice of reason in the conduct of their day to day affairs, they throw away opportunities of avoiding catastrophies. Now it is certainly not the fashion to-day to believe in the ultimate usefulness of reason, because we have learnt that reason is sometimes extremely weak, almost powerless. But does the state of the economic and political affairs of the world look as if the retreat from reason (as Mr. L. Hogben has called this supreme vice of the present) had brought humanity nearer to paradise than the old, dry, unfeeling, reckoning way of crafty politicians ? It was popular, for a long time, to disparage the wisdom of the method of regulating Europe created by the Congress of Vienna. But does not that method of regulation, with its comparative stability and peacefulness, compare rather favourably to-day with the outcome of the one-sided conferences of the Allied and Associated Powers at Versailles ? And do not tell us that the statesmen did not know, could not know, what they were doing at the latter conferences. Never, as far as our knowledge goes, was the voice of reason raised so clearly, so insistently as by the leading economists of the day, with Mr. J. M. Keynes as their choragus. Never was their advice so wilfully, so deliberately spurned, as by the Big Five in their clandestine brooding over the problem of how a cluster of splendid principles, the principles proffered by Mr. Woodrow Wilson, might, by typical sham rationalization, be used as a mask for the most shameful and headlong race for electoral successes. Reason, in this case, has taken a terrible revenge.

The retreat from reason is the real cause of the economic and political mess in which the world is sunk to-day. And it is a mess. Let nobody be deceived by the fact that a new boom of the old sort is just in course of following the great depression. This boom will be just as short-lived as the last one. It will not be controlled in time. It will bring happiness and wealth to a few only, and it will rush us onwards headlong into the next slump. Now capitalism has shown a power of survival which has, rightly, astonished many a politician and economist. But its power of resistance is not unbounded. Even many people who, like the author of this booklet, do not fear but positively want a socialist transformation of society, do not wish to reach a very doubtful form of dictatorial socialism by way of an earthquake, a violent disruption, do not hope to see more helpless hecatombs slaughtered on the altar of equality. They hope passionately for a reasonable and, if necessary, slow transition from a system which, though unjust and in many regards exploitative, has certainly not been sterile even for the poorest of its members. They do not believe in the gospel of "After us the deluge of the great bliss of equality," because, after all, they do not even feel sure that they may see that great bliss emerging from the deluge. So the policy of blazing a trail towards socialism through a series of slumps and depressions does not attract them. A policy of peaceful, gradual transformation remains for them the best one, even if the author of the slogan of the inevitability of gradualness forgets his own gospel for a moment when he dwells under the dazzling light of the Russian upheaval.

In economics the appeal of reason should perhaps be stronger than anywhere else. Let me say this in the words of Lionel Robbins (*An Essay*, etc., p. 157):

> " . . . in the last analysis Economics does depend, if not for its existence, at least for its significance, on an ultimate valuation—the affirmation that rationality and ability to choose with knowledge is desirable. If irrationality, if the surrender to the blind force of external stimuli and unco-ordinated impulse at every moment is a good to be preferred above all others, then it is true the *raison d'être* of economics disappears. And it is the tragedy of our generation, red with fratricidal strife and betrayed almost beyond belief by those who should have been its intellectual leaders, that there have arisen those who would uphold this ultimate negation, this escape from the tragic necessities of choice which has become conscious. With all such there can be no argument. The revolt against reason is essentially a revolt against life itself."

All those who stand for a greater measure of planning as the foundation of the economic order of the future will, I hope, understand, that they cannot damn reason in the morning and expect all their hopes to be fulfilled by it in the evening. So the question of what would be a rational international distribution of raw materials, under present conditions in this world naturally, is the next step in our inquiry.

Rationality concerns, in the first place, production. Technical progress over the last few scores of years has been so astonishing that, in a literal sense, we can make almost anything anywhere, provided we are allowed and able to do it irrespective of cost. We can grow bananas in hothouses near the polar circle—if we are prepared to pay for it; we may see oranges ripen in the hothouses in Kew Gardens, certainly far outside the "natural" limits of citrus-cultivation. We can produce substitutes of entirely satisfactory quality for nearly any important raw material, if we do not grudge the money required.

But it is certainly not economically rational to do these things. There is a sort of substitute rationality, however. For example, let us take the case of a country without coal of its own, but which could produce electricity cheaply with the help of imported coal which it can easily buy. Such a country may very well resolve to do nothing of this kind. It may decide to make electricity with the help of water and wind—at three times the price it is true, but in independence of the importation of coal which might be interrupted in war-time leaving the power stations without steam. Safety in war-time is a very important non-economic element in "substitute rationality," and we shall not overlook it ; we shall discuss its impact on our problem later on. But in the meantime we have to discuss the rationality of production from the narrower, more elementary viewpoint of economics. The same is true for rationality of use. Maybe in the end we shall find that rationality from the economic point of view is not the decisive factor, that other "substitute rationalities", distinctly irrational from the economic point of view, take pride of place. But the economic inquiry comes first ; if we throw it to the winds, let us know at least whether we throw away a bushel of chaff or of grain, and how valuable the grain is we are tipping into the dust-bin.

One of the factors of rationality which we must not forget is the economic interest in comparative stability. There is, of course, an economic policy aimed at the cultivation of stability for its own sake ; and with all its advantages it may become too expensive, it may become too overwhelming, it may degenerate into stagnation. But though this danger is certainly more than a mere day-dream, stability is not quite the sterile nightmare which one might at first suppose. The enjoyment of life as well as the achievement of great enterprises depends, to a large extent, on whether, in our economic forecasts which we, perhaps a bit too proudly, call economic plans, important factors in the near future can be counted on with a reasonable degree of probability. If we widen the term stability somewhat so that it includes the possibility of forecasting inevitable future changes with a fair degree of reliability, the idea of stability in economic relations and conditions becomes one of the leading features of our investigation.

A.—Rationality of Production

Ores of the same metal occur, as we have seen, often in only a few, but widely separated parts of the earth. And in some such cases our need for these metals may be so strong that we wish to see all these places develop their production fully. But there are other cases where many countries have supplies, but where we have a choice between two possibilities: (*a*) the development of production on the basis of the lowest cost, or (*b*) its development on the basis of stability.

The first will increase the possible range of consumption, but at the same time the districts of cheap production may be fully able to provide for even this increased consumption. The production of copper is a case in point. There seems no doubt that even the least favoured copper ore mines in Northern Rhodesia can produce copper as cheaply as the lowest-cost mines in other districts. The full use of the "best source" seems to be of common interest to mankind, and we find that this theory of far-reaching international division of labour swept the field in the battle for free trade between 1800 and 1850. Then the idea was prevalent that, if we would only go deeply enough into the matter, we would always find that every country had a few things which, for "natural" reasons, it could produce better, *i.e.*, more cheaply, than any other country in the world. The inference was—let each country concentrate its producing activities on those industries, and let each exchange her surplus of these products for those which other countries, on their side, can produce more cheaply. Nobody would advise a country, the free-traders used to say in a manner sure of its impressiveness, to develop expensive coal mines in one province if it had large, adequate, low-cost coal mines in another province. Why should we think wrong, in the case of international division of labour, what we think right in the case of division of labour within the same country? Frontiers are, after all, only artificial things, nearly, if not quite, fictitious, though they cost us enough; let us, they said, be reasonable at least in matters economic, let us disregard frontiers at least in these matters, let us produce cheaply, as cheaply and therefore as abundantly as possible everywhere, and equalize the natural inequalities in production costs by international exchange on the largest scale necessary.

All this is true. I think that in principle this case cannot be disproved within the field of economic rationality, provided that in comparing costs the full cost is counted on both sides, and that no important items are forgotten. There are two items which seem particularly important, though it seems to be rather difficult to appraise them numerically. This difficulty, however, does not justify those who simply neglect them.

1.—*Dis-investment; the Gospel of the Cheapest Field.*

It is not only sentimentally difficult to scrap an existing producing unit when it becomes weak in competition; the loss of investments is generally rather a serious one. And the loss on investment is far from being limited to the capital immediately serving the production in question. Let us take one example only, but one which has been and is still of very far-reaching importance for the economic policies of the world.

The production of grain for food and for fodder is much more expensive now in those parts of Europe where it is cultivated on a large scale, under technical conditions of extremely intensive production and high yields per area unit, but at the same time under the economic conditions of the law of diminishing returns than in many countries outside Europe which have developed into large-scale competitors, working under entirely different technical and economic conditions. The latter produce with the application of a minimum of capital, and farm extensively. They do not restore to the soil either by the application of organic manure or of fertilizer what they take out of it by the annual harvests. They "mine" the soil by cultivation, and they export its mineral wealth and its organic richness in the shape of the corn, cotton, wool and skins overseas. The European producers of surplus grain and wool did the same themselves—several centuries ago. This devastation of the natural wealth of the soil does not appear as an item in the costs of capitalist agricultural production. As long as an increasing population is one of the qualities of a capitalist society the increase in money value of the land compensates, and for quite a time even more than compensates, the loss of value due to the decrease of natural fertility. As long as this condition persists, the territory where the soil is " mined " by cultivation is a very strong competitor of the territory where all the arts of modern conservative agriculture have to be applied and all the money necessary for the application of these devices has to be spent.

There are two possibilities open to countries where the soil has reached a naturally low level of fertility: either the country can begin a well-ordered and consistent retreat from agriculture, or it can try to keep it in existence.

The first system was followed in Great Britain. There the less good soils (which, of course, felt the competition of America first and worst) went gradually out of cultivation and only the better soils were worked. As time went on the " poorer " soils in this sense became a larger and larger, and the " better " soils became an ever smaller, proportion of the total arable area of England. The retreat was a gradual one, and in order to achieve it Great Britain had naturally to export something. She exported at first the surplus and then the substance of the agricultural population of Ireland, and then began to export the surplus and later the stock of the rural population of England herself. She could do this without creating artificial crises of the first order, because she had a century or so to do it in; but a long chain of individual bankruptcies, and a huge account of individual misery, were the inevitable concomitants of this development. Whatever the political implications may have been (we shall discuss them later), the social consequences were that England paid for this retreat from agriculture with an urbanization of her population which is deeply regretted by many, and with the silent, but for all that very real, misery of millions of emigrants. After a century of such experience the British nation was, to say the least, thoroughly dissatisfied with it, and we see now hectic endeavours being made to turn the tables and to reconstruct a rural, *i.e.*, an agricultural, population comprising a higher (as some like to say, a " more natural ") proportion of the British nation. It is difficult to say whether this endeavour will be successful, and at what cost. But it is quite certain that anything which may be achieved will be extremely expensive and will take a very long time.

The same choice which lay before the British statesmen in

1846 had to be made in Germany in 1878. But Germany made a different choice : she chose to keep her agricultural population alive "artificially" as best she could. For that purpose, she drove up the level of selling prices of all sorts of agricultural produce so that these covered the cost of producing under the new technique of intensive cultivation, subject to the law of diminishing returns. She built a huge fence of protective duties round herself, and the consumers had to pay while they ate for keeping a large peasantry and semi-feudal aristocracy alive and at work. Many people now advise the Germans to pull down the fence or at least lower it, and to allow foreign food and fodder to compete in German markets on equal or nearly equal conditions with German-grown food and fodder. This advice certainly has its attractions. It would simplify and ease the economic situation of the world to a large extent if Germany opened her frontiers to U.S., Canadian and Argentine grain, fed her population at less than half the price at which they are fed to-day, and could lower her industrial protection as a result of this great decrease in an important item in the cost of her industrial production. But nothing is gratis in economic life ; a price must be paid even for the most wholesome reform. And the price in this case would be the immediate exportation of many millions of her agricultural population. But this could not be done. It would be extremely expensive, and would really, in its political implications, be the beginning of a revolution which would certainly not secure the necessary political support, not to mention all the other reasons why such a mass export of Germany's peasantry is absolutely out of the question. To do it gradually, to spread the misery over a century, is not economically possible to-day. The British example and the deep disappointment with its results after a century of pride and jubilation is certainly not an encouragement to imitation, especially in the absence of the most important condition which enabled comparative success in the British case, viz., the possibility of spreading the movement over a century.

And if we imagine agriculture as it will be in the world of 2000 A.D., is it so sure that it is the right thing to make, over and over again, whole nations rush to and fro from the cheapest producing area of to-day to the cheapest producing area of to-morrow? After all, even American soil is not inexhaustible. Every attentive observer in the United States can see that it is becoming rather quickly exhausted. Where is the agriculture of New England to-day? Where are the deep fertile soils of the cotton belt? Mr. Secretary Wallace and his scientific helpers think of taking a hundred million or more acres out of agriculture, because the soil is already so exhausted that it cannot any longer be worked profitably under the conditions of extensive cultivation. Where is the natural fertility of the *Chernosiom*, formerly so famous? Gone, gone, gone; eaten up by the inhabitants of Western Europe to whom the Russian *mujik* exported the wheat and rye which the Tsarist régime extorted from him. This game with Nature, this robbing of the soil, goes on till the soil is empty. Then cultivation simply has to be stopped, or at best it can be shifted. Shifting cultivation is regarded as one of the most characteristic features of native African, as we like to say "backward", tribes; well, is there really much difference between the shifting cultivation of the Shilluk and the shifting cultivation of the Alabama share-cropper? Is it really very different, when the Shilluk goes a few miles farther into the primeval forest and leaves the field he had cultivated denuded, exhausted and a prey to large-scale erosion, and when the white or coloured farmer cultivates the plains of Georgia, Alabama, Mississippi, robs them, and leaves them denuded, exhausted and the victim of large-scale erosion and passes on to Oklahoma and Western Texas? The only difference is that, whereas only a few thousand Shilluk are at work in this way, millions and millions of American people have adopted this procedure. Within the last forty years, Canada, the Argentine, Australia and New Zealand have been attacked in just the same way as the plains of the Middle West and South in the U.S. Are we too enterprising in our speculations if we say that probably in forty or sixty years' time mankind, growing at the rate of 1 or 2 per cent. per year, will have exhausted the natural fertility of these areas and will be faced with the end of virgin soils on the globe? There will then be reached a new phase when the existence of widespread, old-established experience of the most intensive forms of cultivation will be a question of life and death for millions and millions of mankind. But where would this experience be found, if in the meantime the plough seeks the areas of cheapest production and the farmer follows the plough ?

2.—*Mono-Cultivation ; the Gospel of Specialization.*

Some countries have had outstanding success in the production of particular commodities and have, therefore, more or less thoroughly specialized in them. Sheep on the plains of Australia, grain on the plains of the Middle West of the U.S., cotton in the Old South, cotton in Egypt, cocoa in the Gold Coast : these are some examples. This tendency towards specialization would probably, in quite a number of cases, have been effective to a much larger extent, had not the intentional activities of governments diverted the development of many districts from their " natural " course. The reason for these governmental activities was that it is never very wholesome, economically, to have all your eggs in the same basket. It is true that most branches of human productive activity pass, from time to time, through critical phases as, *e.g.*, during the last slump and depression. But in quite a number of cases depressions have hit only one or the other branch of agriculture, mining, etc., at a time, so that a district or country which enjoyed a certain diversity of economic activities did not find itself with all its population simultaneously unemployed, near bankruptcy and in need of relief. This is doubly true of agricultural districts, where the fact that ordinary foodstuffs of everyday consumption are grown enables the population, even in times of extreme distress, to get along without the most severe sufferings. International division of labour, driven to its last extreme, would increase the number of instances of mono-cultivation to an unreasonable extent. Thus additional centres and periods of acute distress which could be avoided by diversification would probably be created. It does, of course, cost money deliberately not to develop exclusively that branch of economic activity which pays by far the best, but to devote part of the capital, the soil and the labour of the population to the production of commodities which, in the ordinary course, are less remunerative but which are beneficent buffers in periods of difficulty and which may even, sometimes, prevent the occurrence of terrible famines, etc. Such a policy is of great importance from the political point of view, even for nations which remain neutral in a great conflict. Good earnings in " normal " times do not always fully compensate for the enormous risks and dangers consequent upon extreme international division of labour.

One may, if one likes to, call the cost of this uneconomic " artificial " diversification (I am quite prepared to allow any disparaging adjectives people like to apply to such an activity) the cost of insurance. It certainly is very similar in principle; and by simply stating this analogy it becomes clear that, if the principle is allowed, its consequences must also be accepted. Here again people can have the apple only when they do not eat it.

One of the consequences, often enough, is, that the types of production which are fostered for safety's sake pay only under " artificial " conditions, namely, with a level of prices buttressed artificially by subventions from the public exchequer, etc.

The principle that only the best productive resources should be used is one which, in international life, must be subject to certain limitations. How far one or the other country is prepared and even willing to carry this interference with strictly economic activities will depend largely on the opinion of the moment. But it is not even certain that such interference really is " uneconomic". Postponed cost is not avoided cost.

B.—Economizing Labour

There was a time when people believed the funds of labour available for satisfying the economic necessities of society, at least in peace-time, to be practically inexhaustible. Now it is quite certain that to some extent this is true even for the present, and it was even more true for the past. Economic history does not provide many examples where a shortage of labour has been important, though some examples are certainly spectacular. But if we inquire into the reasons why this is so, we find that in the past there were at work at least two factors which no longer operate so much as a matter of course.

The first one is that people did not very much object in former times to the average quantity of labour done by man, woman or child being increased beyond the usual limit when their increased activities were provoked by increased wages. In this respect things have changed since the well-being of even the majority of the working class has so much improved that the marginal utility of additional wages has definitely decreased. For to-day public opinion views the matter quite differently. The reasons may vary; some people think of the danger of spoiling a full harvest of sturdy recruits for the army; others think more of human dignity, etc. But whatever the motive may be, it is quite certain that the simple extension of the working day according to the current necessities of economic life beyond a certain maximum is no longer approved of, and that even the attraction of extraordinarily high wages may often fail to provoke that increase of the fund of labour which those offering the better pay want.

The other element which does not fit into the well-known and here certainly very necessary formula: "other things being equal," is that population does not respond in the old manner to the stimulus of high wages by undergoing a corresponding increase. Birth control is revolutionizing the world. There was a time when scientific discussion of whether it was true that improved wages meant only increased breeding of the working class and increased survival of their offspring was not quite without meaning. Nowadays, the number of children has become small enough in many countries to inculcate into the most boneheaded governments the fact that it may be good business to spend taxation money on seeing that children, once conceived and born, do not die prematurely, before having contributed by their own work to the necessities of society. And I think the class of workmen's wives who bear children as often as the men's sexual strength and the women's physical strength will allow them is dying out very quickly. It may be that, within certain limits, additional income encourages the conception of a child here and there which otherwise would have remained unborn. Positive evidence in this direction is, so far, rather scarce and contradicted by much other experience, though the last word has, I think, not yet been spoken on this subject. But it is quite certain that if increased income tends to increase the number of children born to the working population, the margin of indifference to increases in income is also rather wide. Extraordinarily high wage increases are therefore necessary to provoke an even grudging response in the way of more children.

The old elasticity of the reservoir of working power has gone. It has become much more rigid, and will continue to do so in the near future as far as we are able to form any clear idea on this point. The necessity for economizing labour is, therefore, quickly becoming a very important and rather general feature of modern economic life.

It shows itself in many ways ; in the necessity for using the fittest labour for every kind of work, avoiding unnecessary transport of workers, day by day, etc. From it arise two problems which will come into the foreground more and more.

1.—*The Problem of the " Rest".*

One of the most popular features in modern economic life is the careful selection of workers according to their faculties and the employment, wherever possible, of only the pick of possible candidates. The Taylor system provides an example of only one form of selection, though certainly the most impressive one. It is clearly to the advantage of productivity that every kind of industrial work should be done only by people particularly well gifted for it. But what becomes, once this principle is introduced into industry everywhere, of that large group of people who are certainly not particularly gifted for any special kind of work, but who, quietly plodding along, do work of quite undistinguished quality ?

2.—*Stability of Employment.*

The selection of workers according to their particular physical and intellectual gifts will have very different results at different times for the same individual ; the highest degree of rationality may, therefore, mean a large measure of instability in the lives of millions and millions of people. They may develop the psychology of eternal examination candidates.

All this poses new and enormous problems. If the interests of maximum productivity (which in most societies, even exploitative ones, is also, to a certain degree, an interest of the exploited class) prevail, its realization will mean the introduction of new sources of insecurity. So we find that the attainment of maximum productivity and of security of existence may become and are already to a large extent incompatible.

Between these two goals, therefore, reason has to choose its way. It certainly will have much to do to solve all the problems arising; problems which may sometimes be the same for large parts of the world, and sometimes very special ones concerning particular countries or districts. Rationality may lead to different forms of production, and to different patterns in its international distribution; moreover, ideas as to what is rational will change as time goes on, making obsolete to-day what yesterday was brand-new and the last word in masterful adaptation. When ideas concerning rationality in production conflict, shall we be content, in the future as in the past, to leave the decisions to chance, to the survival of the stronger competitor, or even to the arm stronger and more resolute in wielding the sword? Or shall we try to avoid decisions by any of these means and to set deliberate and considerate planning in their place? Shall we, courageously facing the accusation that we arrange matters economic "artificially" (artificial in economic life always means what someone else does), try to find a middle way between mere wealth and mere security, between mere productivity and mere equality, when these aims conflict with one another?

The world has given, I think, a good and fair trial to the system of free competition among nations as well as between individuals. There is no doubt that this system of "simple freedom" (not quite as simple, though, I am afraid, as Adam Smith thought) has contributed enormously to the development of the productive powers, inventiveness, adaptability and thoughtfulness of mankind. But if it has done something to increase our powers of thinking forward for more than half a year, it has certainly also taught us to see, in the nick of time, that the system is about to overreach itself, that the unfettered forces of free competition have now such a choice and quantity of means of destruction at their disposal that self-destruction in a supreme victory threatens to be the ultimate outcome. We have managed to progress so much that progress threatens to manage us, to pull us helpless towards the destruction of the roots of our existence. We shall have to do something to stop this, be it even at some cost in productivity and rationalization. Features which can be expressed in terms of somebody's profits can claim no monopoly of rationality. Not all important items appear on even the most truthful and complete balance sheet of an enterprise. The fact that we cannot express the yearning of the masses for security and a quiet life in £ s. d. does not detract at all from their vital importance.

C.—Rationality of Use

The appeals for freer access to certain raw materials which some nations make with untiring propaganda may or may not withstand cool criticism: their moral and political importance should, and perhaps will in the near future, depend largely on how the nations asking for such an improvement of their position want to use the raw materials. Of course, they will all use them only for peaceful purposes or at the worst for defence. No war is possible nowadays in which every party does not fight for defence, for the whole defence and for nothing but defence. Maybe in a regrettable moment of absentmindedness they swallow the vanquished enemy's territory as at Brest and Bucharest, at Versailles and Trianon. But, to my mind, the time has come when we do no longer want to run the risk of absentminded victory, when we do not want any longer to see victors, to hear or read of victory, when we want to live in peace and to prosper as far as a dearly-bought peace will allow us.

This is the first conclusion as to rationality of use: in future no demand for raw materials shall be fulfilled with the help of a future international organization unless the materials are credibly destined to be used only for peaceful purposes. Strategic reasons for wanting to have access to certain sources of raw materials are typically irrational and should carry no weight at all. If it were possible to arrange the international territorial distribution of raw materials so that every great power would be totally lacking in at least one material absolutely indispensable for modern warfare, it would be a good thing to reshuffle the maze of political frontiers so as to ensure such a crippling of every great, or would-be great, power as to make it impossible for them all, the whole rabble of them, to "defend" themselves. But this is only a dream, though perhaps a beautiful one. One of the terrible achievements of technical progress is that substitutes can do the service of formerly "indispensable" things in war-time. So we have to discard this positive side of the idea of introducing rationality in use as an organizing principle for the new distribution of raw materials. Only the negative principle that nothing should be given to anybody merely because they need it " for defence " can be applied in trying to solve our problems.

As regards the processing of raw materials, the advantages and disadvantages possessed by the various nations in processing are very different. Some countries are particularly fitted for certain industries because they have developed a well-trained body of workmen and technicians and business men over a long period. Naturally the relevant raw materials would be used to the greatest advantage by these countries. But it is very questionable whether it would be right to help a country to achieve a monopoly or quasi-monopoly of production when it had in any case an advantage over its competitors. Monopolies in private hands sometimes sow the spirit of exploitation even in people who before were not so minded ; and nations in international strife have, through their statesmen, a nasty habit of acting like individuals in this respect.

Another point in this connection concerns natural advantages in marketing. Marketing at the lowest possible cost is one of the few cases in which the interests of the producer and the consumer are generally identical or at least very similar. Every natural advantage in this direction should, therefore, be developed carefully by international action. Wherever private or national interests stand in the way of this rationalization they should be overruled. The problems of unemployment which would arise from such regulations would not generally concern large groups of people.

Here, again, we are not interested so much in the question as to whether natural advantages should be fostered so that rationality in the use of raw materials is increased far beyond what it is now, we are much more interested in those disagreeable and unfortunately rather numerous cases where interests of rationality come into conflict with one another. Then we have to choose between them, just as we have to choose whether motor-cars in a country shall use the left-hand or the right-hand side of the road, and the choice will be the more difficult if, in addition to the many other niceties involved, a certain degree of incommensurability exists between the conflicting interests.

(1) *Distribution of Investments.*

Where home production of a certain raw material is small or non-existent and purchase of the material might become difficult, investment of capital as a means of securing a supply has been, and still is, popular with many capitalists and statesmen. There have been cases when this method has been of some importance, and it might well be so again. But these cases will be exceptional. Those of which we have heard in recent times have been instances in which other interests, real enough, but certainly not connected with the international distribution of raw materials, have been the true reasons for such investments —for instance, the endeavour of some group of capitalists to acquire political control over a country. In such cases governments have favoured the foreign investments of their subjects. The history of oil exploitation has been made up of investment partly or entirely influenced by ideas of this sort. The interest of the British Government in Persian oil has been founded on the idea of securing a plentiful supply of oil for the Navy. But in view of the relative purchasing powers of the several countries competing for oil it is very doubtful whether one drop of oil has been diverted from the course it would anyhow have taken.

Another factor comes into play here: namely, that for the last forty years or so, with very few exceptions, the situation in peace-time has been basically the exact opposite of a shortage of raw materials. The few exceptions (the shortage of coal in Europe, 1919–1924, *e.g.*) should not be forgotten, but it must be made clear that they were really exceptions and chiefly aftermaths of some war situation. In general, we may say that for the last two score of years or more now the world problem has been in no wise one of how to secure free access to raw materials to everybody who wanted to buy and had the wherewithals to pay, but how to get rid of the raw materials produced. The one important peace-time exception has been in the case of grain when occasional simultaneous bad harvests have occurred in all the important production centres. But though a serious shortage might have led to the limitation of exports to a particular country such a thing has not happened so far —and it is very improbable that it will ever happen. If, *e.g.*, Chile should want to withhold her nitrates from Portugal in peace-time and if, consequently, she should put an embargo on their exportation to Portugal, the consequence would only be that Portugal would appear as a buyer on the London market. Even if the Chilean Government were such good friends with the British Government as to make the latter forbid the exportation of Chilean nitrates from the British Empire to Portugal, this country would only have to direct her demand to Paris or Rome or any other propitious country. As long as nations are not involved in war (and scarcely then, with international collaboration as weak and hesitant as it is now, as the example of the sanctions against Italy has shown), it is hardly possible to withhold a raw material from any country which is willing and able to pay for it. At the same time it is extremely rare for a country producing any raw material not to be utterly indifferent as to which of the several competitors for it get it in the end. Chile will certainly not jeopardize her good commercial relations with Portugal for the mere pleasure of favouring any country which wants, with the help of such a discriminating anti-Portuguese embargo, to buy Chilean nitrates more cheaply than she would be able to when facing normal Portuguese competition at Tacna instead of at Liverpool.

But in another sense the existing distribution of investments influences the distribution of the production of raw materials quite considerably: namely, in so far as the owners of investments throw good money after bad money to rescue former investments. In this regard it is necessary to think of the many agreements between capitalists (and often governments) which may be called international, because the capitalists who are parties to them belong to different nations and the enterprises themselves are situated in the territories of different nations. Here the entrepreneurs (and their governments, sometimes) may try to prevent changes in what are the centres of most efficient production from leading to shifts in the centres of actual production. This is the more understandable as very often new units of production owe their superiority in competition, at least partly, to the fact that some of the expenses incurred in order to enable them to start producing do not appear among their costs of production. Within the framework of capitalist society there are at least four such factors of great frequency which must be mentioned here:

(*a*) *Previous Bankruptcies.* In Bernard Shaw's *Heartbreak*

House poor Mr. Mangan gives some short, impressive lectures on the philosophy of bourgeois *entrepreneurial* economics from one of which we will quote the following:

> "Your father's business was a new business; and I don't start new businesses: I let other fellows start them. They put all their money and their friends' money into starting them. . . . They're what you call enthusiasts . . . in a year or so they have either to let the whole show go bust, or sell out to a new lot of fellows for a few deferred shares. . . . As likely as not the very same thing happens to the new lot. They put in more money and couple of years' more work; and then perhaps *they* have to sell out to a third lot. If it's really a big thing the third lot will have to sell out, too, and leave *their* work and *their* money behind them. And that's where the real business man comes in: where *I* come in."

It is one of the characteristics of capitalist money economics that the losses of all Mr. Mangan's predecessors do not reappear in the bill of cost when Mr. Mangan works the thing; though they are real losses (or, to look at it the other way round, part of the necessary total investment), they are borne by people who "do not count".

(*b*) *Depreciation of Debts* through depreciation of the purchasing power of money may have something to do with the difficulties of old-established enterprises and the advantages of new ones in competition, but this factor will generally work the other way round, the older business being probably more deeply in debt and therefore more likely to profit from falls in the purchasing power of money.

(*c*) *General Development Expenditure* will very often not appear at all, or at least only as a very modest quota of its real size on the costs bill of a new enterprise, particularly when such enterprises are located in newly-developed parts of the world. The expenditure involved in opening up the Katanga and Northern Rhodesian districts for copper mining has been borne largely by the Belgian, British and native taxpayers, and only to a very modest extent, at least during the years of development of copper mining there, by the entrepreneurs of these mines. Old-established mines, however, have to bear to the full their share in the tax requirements of the state in which they are situated, and even taxes not immediately imposed on them may find their way back to them by the shifting processes to which taxation is prone. The wages, *e.g.*, which an old-established mine has to pay will somehow and to some degree make up for the direct taxes paid by the workman and for the indirect taxation he has to pay in the prices of what he consumes, etc.

(*d*) *First Robbing of the Soil.* The factor just mentioned is more or less of a temporary character, and so is a fourth one which is generally very important when new production is being established in a new place: *i.e.*, the phase of the first robbing of the soil. Nearly everywhere this recklessness in skimming the natural fertility of the soil, the natural cheapness of local labour, the natural richness of the best parts of a lode will enable the new business to show a bill of costs which will enable it to live even through lengthy periods of bad prices without coming seriously to grief, while the old-established centre may break down if it has to bear the unbroken brunt of the storm.

Nothing is more attractive, therefore, and even from the viewpoint of the interests of the community more reasonable, than to try to tide over these critical periods by artificially ensuring to the old enterprises at least a certain proportion of trade which allows them to stand the crisis. After all, the handicap under (*d*) is only a passing one, that under (*a*) does not affect the real cost of the new enterprise to the community, and (*b*) works, in the long run, nearly always both ways. This is why it is so difficult to blame all the international agreements of producers of raw materials in mining, industry, etc., for the establishment of monopolistic price policies and consequently for the stabilization of prices and enterprises, as long as their policy is one of reasonably forward-looking capitalist selfishness and not of reckless pocketing of momentarily seductive exploitation hauls.

(2) *The Web of Financial Obligations.*

This policy of tiding over difficult times by "artificially" buttressing prices by way of international limitation of production is made possible by the existing entanglement of financial obligations. It is not the best policy for a capitalist to put all his eggs in the same basket; it is not the best policy for him to stick to his money in South American copper and to disregard the new developments in Rhodesia. Whenever he hears of a new, really promising centre for the production of the raw material, he is interested in it. The best policy, naturally, for him is to put his finger into that pie also, be it even at the price of liquidating part of his former investments in the older copper mines. Then he can exercise his influence in the business policy of the new as well as of the old centre. What he may lose temporarily under the one head he will regain under the other head. It is really a form of hedging which we see at work here : maybe one forgoes some possible gains of a highly speculative nature, but one also avoids very serious risks, and the cost of the operation, if undertaken early (before the price to be realized by the sale of part of the old shares falls heavily), is not worth mentioning ; an insurance premium must be paid, if one wants to be safe.[1]

This book is not meant to be a defence of the doctrine that the egotism of the enlightened capitalist is really conducive, in most cases, to the common good ; indeed, I feel very far from thinking this. But it is not good policy to deny that there are cases where this relation between the egotism of the entrepreneur and the common weal actually does obtain. In these cases the experience of the experiment in stabilizing the international prices of certain raw materials by private " conspiracy " (if you want to use the word ; I am not afraid of it) with the help of one or more governments is extremely valuable as a step towards the concerted international action which I think should provide a solution of our real problems. The real problems are : insecurity of prices and profits, and waste of limited valuable resources. It is quite certain that these two problems (which will, I hope, emerge as the real ones from this inquiry) cannot

[1] The point is well illustrated by a contribution by Mr. J. H. *Hammond* to Mr. *Crowther's* book (p. 86). He gives an enumeration of the spread of investments in the copper mining industry, from which I glean the following details : (*a*) The Anaconda group had (in 1932) copper mines in Montana and Arizona, U.S., in Chile and Mexico. (*b*) The Kennecott group had copper mines in New Mexico, Arizona, Nevada, Utah, U.S., in Alaska and in Chile. (*c*) The Phelps-Dodge group had copper mines in Arizona, U.S. and Mexico. (*d*) The American Smelting and Refining group held interests in copper mining in the U.S., Mexico and Peru. (*e*) There existed in the same year a certain American interest in copper-mining in Katanga. In addition to this one must take into account the fact that many minority blocks of shares in these groups may be held by people not included in those groups of capitalists which appear here as the " group." All this gives a picture, full of criss-cross lines, of the spread of interests in copper mining all the world over.

be solved for more than a moment except by a concerted and, to tell the truth, complicated and difficult international policy and organization.

But there is not the slightest doubt that these investment interests and financial obligations, though quite clearly private interests of a profiteering nature, are not only private profiteering interests and nothing more. They may be in sharp contradiction to the rational use of natural advantages in processing and marketing and to the existing distribution of skill and labour. Though this may be so, however, this simple fact of a contradiction between private and common interests is not sufficient reason for disregarding the one and respecting only the other complex of the conflicting interests; they are all different factors of rationality in the production and use of raw materials. They must, therefore, all be taken into account by an international organization which functions impartially as a court of arbitration and carefully smoothes out those conflicts between the individual and the communal interests of mankind which stand in the way of a considered compromise.

All this is only a sketch of the framework of business life. It does not give any ready-made solution of any definite special problem, it does not even state definite problems. It would be much too early to do so, for two reasons: first, we do not know enough so far, for lack of a planned collection of material, about the individual problems, and secondly, their leading characteristics tend to change so quickly just now that even the truth of to-day may be the error of to-morrow. Only a court of arbitration of the kind already mentioned can do anything of a more concrete character, and even its existence presupposes the solution of some particularly recalcitrant problems which we shall mention in a later part of this essay.

The next step in our inquiry is bound to be a difficult one. We have, so far, more or less disregarded the political implications of our subject. But we cannot do that permanently. After all, economic activities are not, or at least should not be, entirely an art for art's sake. And many of the political implications of our subject are not only nasty manifestations of human unreasonableness which one has to deal with willy-nilly; quite a few of them are reasonable in themselves and need to be taken into account in a serious and impartial way. A realistic policy in these things does not only require that facts of a political kind, nasty as they may be, should be taken into account, but it also requires that the real impact of political complications should be clearly seen and respected in trying to blaze a trail towards a solution of these problems. We shall study the problems of peace and of war separately, including the problem of armaments in peace-time under the heading of war-time problems.

CHAPTER VI

THE POLITICAL PROBLEMS OF RAW MATERIAL SUPPLIES

A.—Raw Materials in Peace-Time

We have seen that during the last forty years it has, most of the time, been at least as difficult to sell raw materials as to buy them. There are, therefore, two sets of complaints to be considered: those of the people who want to buy more than they actually can, and those of the people who want to sell more than they actually can. Let us take the first set first.

Many factors co-operate in determining what quantities of any raw material a nation can buy. The most important are the following:

(*a*) The extent of their purchasing power;
(*b*) The prices at which the materials can be bought;
(*c*) The competition of wants for the limited amount of purchasing power at the disposal of any nation.

Now these factors are not quite independent of one another, nor are they primary factors at all.

1.—*International Purchasing Power.*

The international purchasing power of a nation depends, in the long run, on what it can sell or has already sold on the world's markets, the latter factor being of account only so far as the earlier sales were sales on credit. It is, of course, necessary to include services (like shipping services, tourist facilities, etc.) with the commodities sold. In some cases there is a third factor to be taken into account, namely, the obligation of one nation to pay another or others sums in money, or to deliver goods or labour in kind without getting anything in return or without having received anything on credit previously. The amounts involved must be subtracted from a nation's purchasing power in international commerce. The most important such case is that of war reparations (in money or in kind).

A few years ago this item was a very important handicap on the international purchasing power of some nations, particularly Germany. But in 1932 Germany practically repudiated her reparations debt and is very unlikely to recognize it again at any time in the future ; so improbable is it, in fact, that we will disregard reparations as a factor affecting the future. The same is true of reparations as a source of possible international purchasing power. They did form such a source to a certain extent after 1919, but are so no longer and will not be so again. We may even take a further step. One of the ticklish points worrying many people in the United States is the future of inter-allied war debts. Huge sums are owed to the United States by the former European Allied Powers, but nothing (if we except Finland) is being paid or has been paid for quite a long time, and it is very improbable that payments will be made in the future to any extent worth mentioning.[1] It is quite easy to understand that a fact like this is hard to swallow, but our inquiry would only be muddled if we did not take as our basis the only view of the future which seems probable ; namely, that the United States will have either to write off the capital invested in loans to their former allies or go on carrying them from balance sheet to balance sheet as a perhaps decorative, but certainly bad, asset. In my mind it is always better to throw a bad egg into the dust-bin ; but if people prefer to have its smell in the larder there is no means of deciding who is right.

Nevertheless, the fact remains that the purchasing power of the nations in international commerce depends on their sales

[1] There is a big difference between paying for armaments and war by means of loans raised at home and loans raised in foreign countries. The choice is in both cases between paying, though with some postponement, out of the proceeds of taxation—and repudiation. Repudiation of a loan at home damages many subjects in the indebted state and creates unpleasant perturbation in the home capital market; a government will take this course only as an ultimate refuge. To pay off a foreign loan would be equally difficult on account of all the complications and drawbacks connected with the one-sided large-scale transfer of money which would emerge, while repudiation would damage only other states' citizens, and the shock to international credit of the repudiating country, as experience has clearly and often shown, would be soon forgotten. Ultimately, of course, the capital of a public debt is hardly ever paid back. But it is quite clear that the possibility of borrowing abroad is an incentive to war.

and on their debts and assets ; and in some cases, for a longer or shorter time, on their credit. All these rivers pour their water into the same ocean of international currency relations.[2]

2.—*Payment of International Debts.*

The payment of debts in international life can be effected, in principle, in four ways :

(*a*) *By Migration.*

Migration of wealthy people from the creditor to the debtor countries may be mentioned first. It is a thing which, on a large scale, has never taken place and is quite unlikely to occur.

(*b*) *By Transfer of Currency Metal.*

The transference of precious metals is the second method of settling international debts. This method has been much used during the last 17 years. Its results may be summed up by saying that, after some wandering, the gold of the world is now collecting more and more in the treasury and bank cellars of the United States. The latter, since they have no other use for it, bury it as deeply as possible, not daring even to use it for the purpose of coining golden money or of issuing bank

[2] The extent of international purchasing power depends largely on the quantity of goods a country is able to sell abroad, and this quantity again depends to a large extent on the level of costs. Low costs help to sell a commodity or service easily in international competition on a large scale ; high costs are prohibitive in this regard unless they are lowered by all sorts of subsidies or other dumping arrangements. Now one of the large items in the costs of production of any industry is the level of taxation in the country of production, and this again depends partly on the purposes for which taxation is used. I take from Mr. *Bradley's* book (pp. 19–20) a few figures of the expenditure of important countries for military purposes in 1929, *i.e.*, *before* the mad race for armaments of these last years set in : Germany, RM. million 691 ; France, fr. million 10,969 ; Great Britain, £ million 99 ; Italy, lire million 4,934 ; Japan, yen million 268 ; Russia, rubles million 1,125 ; U.S., $ million 703. These figures are now, of course, quite obsolete and far behind present expenditure, and they were probably incomplete even for 1929 (the figure for Japan, *e.g.*, is incredibly small). But they show that of these Big Seven not one has a right to complain of a lack of international purchasing power as long as it prefers armament and a high level of taxation to the other alternative. It is quite clear that only concerted international action, coupled with reliable international treaties, can offer a way out of this deadlock ; it is absolutely beyond one country's power to break away from it at its own risk.

This point has been worked out, with admirable clearness, in Dr. C. Delisle *Burns'* article "Guns and Grievances" in *One and All* of July, 1937, p. 131 *seq.*: "I fail to see why there should be any international conference on raw materials to consider the claims of the "have-nots" while Italian and German policy in Spain and Japanese policy iu China is what it is."

notes against the full amount of gold cover.[3] As the quantity of gold existing in the world is finite, and as its production, as we have seen, is chiefly limited to a few countries, some of which (India in " normal " times, Russia even during the depression) manage to retain what they produce, this procedure will be bound eventually to stop to a large extent. Only a small quantity, such as is produced annually, may go on trickling into the United States in the long run. This will be so, of course, only so long as the U.S. does not resolutely turn over a new leaf and spend some of its gold in international commerce, so that the gold may return to it after a spell of playing truant.

(c) *By Sale of Commodities and Services.*

The next point to be discussed is the sale of commodities and services on the world market. In the long run this is the only means of acquiring international purchasing power. No

[3] The international movements of gold, though still rather meandering, have shown since the end of the war a distinct one-sided tendency. Allow me to give a picture of the state of things and an example of how these things may be totally misunderstood by authors and by the public with the help of the following quotation and criticism of it. Mr. Samuel *Crowther* says in his otherwise quite interesting, though often much too sweeping, book *America Self-Contained* (the italics in the quotation are mine ; pp. 218–219) :

" In 1900 the world's stock of monetary gold was two billion dollars, in 1913 if was four billion dollars, and in June of 1932 it was 10 billions—using the nearest round figures. Of this stock the United States in 1900 held 511 million, in 1913 it had 1,290 million, and in 1932 it held 3,610 million dollars. *Thus the proportion of the world's gold held by this country has not varied greatly in the last quarter century.* That is not true of France. That country in 1900 had 451 million, in 1913 had 679 million, and in 1932 had 3,218 million dollars. Great Britain, in spite of being forced off the gold standard, has 663 million dollars in gold as compared with only 139 millions in 1900. Germany is the only one of the major nations which now has proportionately less gold than in 1900—198 million dollars as against 119 millions."

This quotation contains many dubious assertions, and the figures really need investigation. But besides this and taking the figures on faith, there is a lot to be said about Mr. Crowther's inferences. I have assembled in the following tables : (a) the figures contained in Mr. Crowther's text ; (b) a number of complementary figures ; these figures, marked a, I have taken from *Die Wirtschaft des Auslandes*, 1900–1927, those marked b from the same Office's Abstracts for 1936, and those marked c from the Abstract for 1935 ; (c) index figures for the absolute figures calculated by myself. These index figures tell us among other corrections of Mr. Crowther's assertions (32 years by the way, are nearer to a third than to a quarter of a century) that : (a) In 1932 four of the seven " major nations " had gold stocks which had grown at a slower rate than world stocks had grown since 1913 (a comparison 1900–1932 being impossible because of the lack of some data for Japan and Italy), and three of them showed even a clear absolute decrease. (b) In the same year three " major nations " showed increases of their gold stocks at a greater rate than the increase in world gold stocks. The largest index in that year was that for France. But since then she has lost much of her gold ; at the end of 1935 the amount was down to 2,643 million $ gold, while gold stocks in the U.S.

country which is not able to sell is able to buy. No country which refuses to accept other people's commodities and services can expect to get payment for its exports. Fundamentally, in spite of some minor complications which slightly (but only slightly) modify the working of the principle in practice here and there, it remains true that imports can be paid for only with exports, and *vice versa.* The quantity of any nation's exports does not, of course, depend only on the willingness of others to allow importation. The level of prices is another important factor in the problem. Every nation that wants to sell something will see that the volume of its sales depends on two possible price policies :

(1) *For exports of monopoly goods* the quantity sold will depend on the price, *i.e.*, the problem will be to find the

had further risen to $5,977 million, so that we get (even without the further losses of France and the further gains of the U.S. in the meantime in spite of their being forced off the gold standard) the following second table.

TABLE T70a.—INTERNATIONAL DISTRIBUTION OF GOLD STOCKS, 1900–1932.

	In $ Million.			1900 = 100.		1913 = 100
	1900.	1913.	1932.	1913.	1932.	1932.
WORLD	2,000	4,000	10,000	200	500	250
U.S.	511	1,290	3,610	252	706	279
France	451	679	3,218	151	714	474
Great Britain	139	a 175	663	126	477	379
Germany	119	c 245	198	206	166	81
Japan (million yen)		a 286	a 426			149
Russia (million RM.)	b 2,256[2]	a 3,369[1]	c 1,600	149	71	48
Italy (million RM.)		a 1,542[3]	c 1,290			84

[1] 1912; including a small amount of foreign bills. [2] 1898 *and* 1903. [3] Including gold in State Exchequer, against which State Notes were circulating.

TABLE T70b.—GOLD STOCKS IN U.S. AND FRANCE, 1900–1935.

	1935. $ Million.	1900. = 100	1913. = 100
France	2,643	573	389
United States	2,977	1,168	463

From this it is quite clear that France's great treasure in 1932 was only a passing phenomenon, caused by the fact that she was, at that particular moment, slightly less distrusted in currency matters by capitalists than other countries. In the meantime the index figures for France have probably decreased to something like 400 and 200 respectively and those for the U.S. risen to something like 1,300 and 600 or so. But even disregarding the developments after 1932 (which Mr. Crowther might have guessed at, but could not have known) the first table, if we fill in the gaps left by Mr. Crowther's arbitrary choice of data and if we look closely enough at the figures to see their real significance, shows in nearly every point the contrary of what Mr. Crowther says in his text.

optimum monopoly price. This price can be found only by *tâtonnement*, by " trial and error", and the trial will have to be made again and again, because the demand schedule of the purchasing nations will change often and sometimes unexpectedly, and because the competition of substitutes, again a matter of price levels, may change in the same way.

(2) In the case of *exports of competitive goods* the price level will decide who, among the competitors, captures the markets. Success can be achieved either by curtailing home production costs as far as is necessary to capture the foreign market, or by selling deliberately at a loss, in the beautiful and not always unjustified confidence that either the home consumer or the home taxpayer, or both together in honourable co-operation, will fill the gap in the profit and loss account. A prevalent name for this last practice is " dumping " (but in international economic life a bad name does not hang a dog). " Dumping," in discreet and indiscreet forms, is a widespread practice in respectable bourgeois as well as in disreputable bolshie countries. The granting of particularly cheap railway rates for coffee in Kenya, for which the natives have to pay in enhanced freights for their necessities, is in principle just as much an aid to dumping as the formerly popular payment of export premiums to manufacturers by the exchequer.

Many states have done much to try to " put their export price level right", by means of pressure on wages, and on the employers to make them rationalize their methods of production and marketing, as well as by giving, more or less chastely, export premiums to those of their export industries which they wanted to develop. But other countries have, again and again, " called their bluff". Protective duties, embargoes, import quotas, anti-dumping legislation, anti-sweating legislation concerning foreign trade : all these are now like many stops on a complicated organ ; the virtuoso knows when to use the basses or the *vox humana*, and he plays all the time, throttling imports, whatever the price levels in his and the other countries may be, exactly down to that particular point which he believes to be the optimum. So we have reached a point in international commercial policy where all the several technical features designed to overcome protective walls are frustrated by the art of wall-building. We may say without risk of being disproved by experience that, if the protectionist states insist on using their protective powers till they die, nobody can prevent them by economic means.

3.—*Dodging the Currency Problem by Annexations.*

In the modern world nothing can be bought without money. In national economic life money is either earned or made. In international life the finest art of currency manufacture is of no avail unless you print banknotes of other countries; and in spite of all the usual crudity of modern economic battling it does not seem likely that anybody will seriously think of doing this.[4] But there is a substitute for the making of money for the purpose of creating artificial purchasing power in international life, namely, the annexation of territory. If government A wants to buy some raw materials from territory B it may annex this territory if it feels that it cannot otherwise buy any or sufficient of the raw material in question. The technique of creating purchasing power would then become applicable, because the producing territory would be part of the currency area of its new master. This is why those governments which speak for the "dissatisfied" nations are thinking of annexations and speaking of them as a vital right and are pursuing a practical policy in this direction whenever they dare. This is where our analysis of the first chapters of this booklet can usefully clear up the problem. We may confidently say that short of annexing half the world not one of the "dissatisfied" nations would be able to bring into her currency territory all those sources of raw material after which they hanker. If they were to try such a policy of radically remedying their lack of raw materials by indiscriminate annexation, the three chief dissatisfied powers would find that they were after the same thing in the sense that they would have to decide between them with respect to many a raw material which of them should get it and which of them go without it. This would only create a new set of "dissatisfied" nations, and instead of a new play being

[4] The faking of other nations' (the enemy's, of course) money was a device not unpopular with famous kings in former centuries. But nowadays it has lost its attractions even in the most passionate wars; it is a weapon which too dangerously cuts both ways. The only example where something of the sort seems to have been planned (though in peace-time) concerned Hungary; and that attempt was killed in the bud.

given on the old, rather dilapidated stage, we should simply see the same play beginning a fresh run with another set of actors. And what about those not entirely negligible powers which are as yet unworthy, so it seems, of the name of great powers, but which might become worthy of it rather soon, namely, China, India, Brazil, Poland? They are, as our analysis has shown, individually in any case particularly badly off as regards their supply of raw materials. It is only a question of time before they will appear behind the footlights asking for an interesting and well-paid part if the old play is to go on. There is only one form of annexation which is in some sense "possible" (namely, in the sense that one can imagine it really happening, though the imagination must penetrate into rather dim precincts), the annexation of everything by everybody, the creation of a world state, and in respect of our immediate subject the creation of one world currency.

4.—*International Currency.*

Well, let us assume, for a moment, that instead of having as many currencies as sovereignties we manage to achieve a state of things wherein sovereignty is neatly separated from currency regulation; wherein a separate authority regulates all the legislative and administrative acts of all the world relating to currency, and wherein the making of money, the holding of reserves, etc., is regulated in one and the same manner for the whole world from one centre, whatever that centre may be.

(*a*) The Central Authority (hereafter called C.A.) would establish as its currency a particular unit, with certain sub-units, represented concretely by notes, coins or tokens. The unit could be either an artificial unit or a unit of some precious material. In both cases the C.A. would have to decide how many of the tokens should be produced (the decision might, of course, be—as many as the amount of precious metal presented for the purpose to C.A.'s mints allows). And the C.A. would have to go a step farther, either regulating the quantity of the currency metal to be produced in the future (probably only a maximum, not a minimum regulation being possible), or regulating how many tokens of intrinsically worthless material might be made and put into circulation. It would have to allot a quota of these to every state and prevent any state making more than its quota. Whatever the currency policy of such a C.A. might be: inflatory, deflatory, gold standard, silver standard, bi-metallic, or what not, the consequence of having a world currency would be that the individual sovereign states would have to forgo the powers of regulating, managing and manipulating the currency within their own territory according to their own wishes and persuasions. If the monetary policy of the C.A. were inflatory the governments favouring deflation would have to tolerate a policy which disagreed fundamentally with their plans, and *vice versa*. No local political pressure would be able to influence such a government. The international applicability of the C.A. policy would have to be enforceable, if need be, up to the hilt.

All this is not a fundamental argument against the possibility and usefulness of a world currency. It only shows that it will take a long time to come, if it comes at all, and that a thoroughgoing change of mentality all the world over will be necessary if people are to avoid creating the permanent danger of the internal catastrophic disruption of this new system.

I do not propose to discuss further this idea of a world currency; not that it seems too Utopian to me. We have seen so many "Utopias" safely located on this globe now that this would be no real argument. But it is clear that what makes such a proposition appear so Utopian nowadays is the glaring incongruity between the spirit of sweet reasonability, which is its one unchallengeable condition, and the absolutely supreme spirit of egotistical unreasonableness which rules the world to-day. And the fundamental side of this proposal will turn up again when we try to work out the necessities for, and possibilities and means of, introducing a thoroughgoing education in reason.

(*b*) But do not let us forget that it does not follow as a matter of course that such international regulation of currencies would penetrate to the roots of the "evil" (if evil there be). Even under such a régime a nation might find that it was suffering from a lack of purchasing power for certain raw materials and that it could not acquire it except by creating additional money. Would the C.A. then allow that country in "distress" to create the "necessary" money? Even if quite a number of governments were to urge the C.A. to grant such permission, because they were in similar difficulties or because they wanted to sell more, such a policy (not meant to be inflatory but which just could not help being inflatory) might go absolutely against the policy of the C.A. Even those who would be inflationists under certain conditions should not forget that the measure of inflation which they would find propitious might be the subject of differences of opinion between themselves. They also should not forget that we cannot absolutely eliminate from future possibilities a C.A. which would not be inflationistically-minded under any circumstances.

(*c*) There is, even from the point of view of the inflationist, very serious doubt as to whether the measure of actual inflation achieved should be allowed to depend on pot-luck, *i.e.*, on how much is necessary for the realization of purposes which have nothing, or very little, to do with the purposes and ideas which should regulate currency policy generally. Very few people would go, I think, as far as to welcome inflation wherever it raises its head. Inflationists may be divided, I think, into two groups: There are those who want inflation to be used as a general fillip to economic life in periods of (as they believe) money-caused depression. And there are those who, without going as far as that, propose inflationary measures because they want to anticipate future purchasing power and to finance the creation of additional employment. Though they do not want inflation for its own sake, they are prepared to put up with it if they cannot otherwise get what they believe to be a vital necessity for human society as a whole. But I do not think that there is any serious economist who when asked: "But how can we pay for building a dozen new water-power stations; the government has not got the money, cannot borrow it on reasonable terms and does not dare raise taxation to the necessary degree?" would coolly answer: "Well, let them print the money, and the devil take the consequences."

After the experience of the last twenty years it seems to me that the old theories of "sound money" are rather a sad heap of ruins, and that there is at least a *prima vista* case for believing that manipulation of the currency may, at times, be very useful and not over-dangerous. But no case has ever been put up for haphazard inflation; and this would be a necessary piece in the intellectual armour of those who expect from the establishment of a world currency a fundamental improvement in the difficulties concerning the international purchasing power of any nation.

One side of the currency problem still remains to be discussed here, and one of very practical importance for the present day: namely, whether it is possible and how it is possible to improve the situation by making it easier for those who are too poor in international purchasing power to buy all the raw materials they believe to be vital for their economic well-being, nay, as they assure us, for their very existence, to acquire it by increasing their exports and/or restricting their imports of other things, in short by changing their balance of international payments.

5.—*Protectionism and Free Trade.*

Some ideas in economics are so simple, and such strong instincts work in their favour, that they always find an open ear. The case for free trade is one of them; and it is a case which has been reinforced by quite a lot of experience extending over long years.

Some of the basic ideas of the philosophy of free trade have, it is true, lost their splendour in the course of time.

We no longer believe in the natural superiority of the stalwart average blockhead over a well-informed administration, and we know that even the most rabid free trader is bound to find that some economic activities will not be carried out at all unless the government does them. But this is not the plane on which the fight for and against free trade is fought to-day.

Now it would swell this book unboundedly and make it one more of the many rather unattractive tracts on free trade *versus* protectionism were I to try really to discuss the subject. But I think that three points are clear to-day and really beyond discussion:

(*a*) Much of the potential world production of raw materials must remain unused and unenjoyed henceforth if the present general system of blocking out others from one's home market is to be continued. This dog-in-the-manger attitude may be easy to understand; it may be very convenient for those who do not like to overstrain their brains by trying to understand the elements of the mechanism of international trade; it may go perfectly with the mental state of the average successful politician, as politicians go nowadays, in democracies as well as in dictatorial régimes. But all the same it is true that if those countries which have positive balances in international trade insist on not accepting payment of these balances in kind they will not get anything and will rush the world headlong into a new crisis at least as deep as the last one was. I am thinking mainly of the United States, though not by any means of them alone. The story of the U.S. is told by the following table:

TABLE T71.

IMPACT OF IMPORT DUTIES ON U.S. TRADE, 1929–1935.

In Million Dollars.

		1929	1930	1931	1932	1933	1934	1935
A	Merchandise imported:							
1	Free of duty ...	2,843	2,051	1,381	879	878	991	1,206
2	Dutiable ...	1,556	1,010	709	444	571	645	835
A1	In per cent. of total imports of merchandise ...	65	67	66	67	61	61	59
A2	Do.	35	33	34	34	39	39	41
B	Customs revenue of U.S. Government	602	587	378	328	251	313	343
B1	B in per cent. of dutiable imports	38	58	53	76	44	49	41
B2	Do. of all imports	14	19	18	25	17	19	17
B1	1929=100 ...		153	139	200	116	129	108
B2	Do.		136	129	179	122	136	122

The figures of this table include fiscal as well as protective duties. But all the same the figures are simply exorbitant. With the coming of Mr. F. D. Roosevelt came a pleasant tentative change of policy, but after the first wave the development stopped and at the moment there does not seem to be the slightest hope of further improvement.

The response of the other countries to the lowering of the tariffs in the U.S. in 1933 was more than poor. But this is neither a question in which polite acknowledgment of the other party's politeness may be expected, nor one in which the other countries can, as easily as the U.S., go forward on this way. To turn this into a question of whether the weak ones follow the strong leading man sufficiently quickly would mean killing all hope of an early improvement.

(*b*) In a number of cases some countries simply cannot lower their protection of some industries as long as they are not able immediately to offer to the masses of unemployed and of ruined business people new fields of activity. The chief case in point is that of agriculture in Europe, though a number of overseas manufacturing industries are in the same plight, *e.g.*, the textile and iron industries of India. Here the choice lies between three possibilities: (1) mass emigration; (2) quick creation of new large industries with a ready-made market; (3) continuance with the system of protection, hoping for the best from the equalizing effects of the further growth of the world population.

The first of these three possibilities must be discarded for many reasons: there are no countries able to receive quickly really large masses of immigrants. Any country which might try its hand at such a game would thoroughly and speedily be thrown out of gear; and the experience of the mass transplantation of Greek people from Asia Minor into Greece was certainly not encouraging. The expense would be enormous and certainly not much less than the cost of establishing new industries, as our second possibility involves. But money enough is scarcely available in the really urgent cases, and even were it squeezed out of the taxpayer or forced as a rather violent loan from the recalcitrant capital market there would be no market for the additional industrial produce created in this way.

(*c*) The only remaining possibility for countries in this position is to continue their protective policy, though on no account to increase it. At the same time, nowhere in the world should a government encourage the development of new industries by help of any kind, be it ever so well veiled or indirect. If a kind of truce in these things could be reached by all those countries which are not strong enough to lower their protectionist walls for the time being, there would be a certain hope that the increase in world population might allow the present day surplus of industrial and agricultural productive power gradually to be absorbed.

This fact that the population of the world is growing all the time is often overlooked, because the white nations, for obvious reasons, are more hypnotized by their own population movements. Nearly all of these show quickly-decreasing frequencies of births, most of them, as Mr. Robert Kuczynski has shown,[5] have reached a stage where, other things remaining equal, their population is bound to decrease in the near future at no negligible rate. But this is not the state of affairs in the rest of the world. Even allowing for all the uncertainties in our knowledge of population movements in a number of countries it is quite certain that a rough estimate of 1 per cent. as the annual rate of increase of world population is more probably an under- rather than an overestimate. This means an annual increase of more than 20 million new consumers. If we assume that the raising of consumption in India, the French and Dutch Indies, Brazil, China, Central Africa and some other countries to present-day levels in Europe and the U.S. will take no more than thirty years, then a further growth at the rate of 1½ per cent. in the world's consumption of goods produced by modern industrial and agricultural methods may safely be expected, on the average, for the years to come. This annual expansion of the world market for modern products is really important. At present it refers to the industries of at most half the human population of the world. A rate of increase of 2½ per cent. in world population is a rate of increase of 5 per cent. in relation to this half. Such a rate should remedy the existing cases of over-production within a period of five or six years—if the truce should hold good over that period.

This is no panacea; it cannot heal all the wounds of the last twoscore years of unreasonableness. Alone it cannot help at all, because alone it cannot be worked at all. There must be reached, at the same time, other international agreements of a general character, and some other changes must take place in the mentality and behaviour of certain powers. Of these we shall speak presently. But taken together with these agreements and changes in mentality it is not blind optimism to hope that the mere growth of mankind will help the world's consumption to overtake its production.

Part of this policy would be a series of credit operations and a temporary international stabilization of the production of certain raw materials and foodstuffs. The chief problems are two:

(1) Our technique of storing raw materials and foodstuffs,

[5] See R. R. *Kuczynski, Population Movements, passim.*

with the exception of the most perishable among the latter, is now so advanced that in times of surplus it is quite possible to lay in stocks which may be drawn on in times of shortage. The world is now consuming certain metals for armament purposes as quickly as possible, and a serious shortage of some of them may come within a relatively short time. The same is true of certain foodstuffs, the prices of which have risen very quickly since the middle of 1936. The present moment is, therefore, one at which intervention for the purpose of absorbing stocks which press on prices, and thereby prevent recovery, might be necessary only in a few cases. But if once the principle of international action had been established in a few " minor " cases it would quickly become a standing feature, so that the next glut of wheat or cotton would find it in working order and the apparatus necessary for financing such a procedure organized and supplied with the necessary means.

(2) An indispensable feature of this policy would be that it should be the policy of governments, and that all governments should accede to it and in their legislation and administration implement it to the full. As it can hardly be expected that, from the first moment and in every case, all countries will take part, international agreements concerning the more important raw materials should be concluded from time to time by the governments chiefly interested. The crucial question is, of course, whether those governments which do not represent actual, but only possible producers, would take part in such arrangements. Mild pressure might help a lot, and a cautious price policy on the part of the monopolistic organizations created in this way, clothed in the robes of international governmental help and supervision, would go a long way to prevent a Cadmus seed of outsiders arising. The organizations should give a wide measure of influence to the consumers in the shape of the governments representing them, when the fixing of prices or of quotas of production or similar things turned up. It should not be necessary for every international organization of this kind to make its own Stevensonian blunders. But then nothing is such good propaganda as success. When some industries, some branches of agriculture, some countries have experienced in one way or another the blessings of " artificial " stabilization of production and prices, others will become

friendly towards the idea in their particular fields of interest; and when some countries have shown an improvement of their economic situation under such a system, one after the other will try to take part in the scheme, after the total deadlock reached under the at present prevalent method of protection of everything and retaliation at any price. Drive in the thin edge of the wedge; and others will only be too willing to drive in the rest of it.

All this would, of course, be possible only in an atmosphere of mutual confidence and of peaceful co-operation. Against a desire for territorial gains, and attempts to subject other nations to blackmailing tactics, the most reasonable policy cannot thrive. But this leads us to the next subject of our inquiry, viz., the emergency situations caused by wars and periods of feverish all-round preparation for war.

6.—*The Present Boom.*

It seems, some people might think, ridiculous to think of stabilizing the production of raw materials in a period of renewed activity, marked by a rapid increase in the numbers of people employed. Accumulated stocks, remainders from former periods of glut, are being speedily consumed, prices are rising with great speed, and in some cases even begin to soar sky-high. But such a period is just the right time to think of the future and to provide for it. Is there anybody who can see how the development of 1937 apes the development of 1925 with feelings other than the deepest misgiving? After the period of consumption of stocks and of rising prices we shall see as the next stage, just as twelve years ago, a mad rush for the extension of the means of production. Is this to be the only outcome of our bitter experience? We should not overlook how much of the present boom is due merely to the crazy armaments race into which mankind has recently plunged. This is bound to overdevelop certain industries and parts of the world and to leave others lagging behind. Now armaments have, among other qualities, a very nasty one. There comes a time when armament requirements are satisfied, when either the stocks of war materials must be "consumed" or the industries producing them must reduce their activities to the small scale of renewing those implements and ammunition which either become technically obsolescent (*e.g.*, aeroplanes) or unsafe to hold in stock any longer (explosives). The choice is then between war and unemployment. This is a terrible choice, and one must do in time all that is possible to prevent it from arising. I quite understand that at the moment rearmament cannot be stopped. It is sad, but it is true. But there is all the more reason why statesmen should see to it that at this fateful time their nations should have a third alternative. It is easy to ask people to make sacrifices, even of wealth and of profits, when business booms, when they are wallowing in riches. The time to provide for lean years is in the fat years. Nations which forget this in the frenzy of their orgy of brisk business will suffer for it.

Sceptics may doubt whether the economist has any chance of being heard when he raises the voice of reason during such a time ; but the duty of the economist is quite clearly to speak in time. He would not be a real asset to mankind were he to hold his tongue when his word might possibly be heard. To be wise after the catastrophe is a sad pleasure and cannot revive a corpse.

B.—Raw Materials in War-Time

Two features are characteristic of the part which raw materials play in war-time and in the preparation for it : (1) compared with peace-time they are necessary in larger quantities and in different proportions ; (2) they serve, to a large extent, different technical purposes, that is, a substitution of uses takes place. The first makes the creation of stocks in peace-time the focus of interest, the second the development of new technical features which may serve armament purposes immediately, but which may create new technical foundations for peaceful production also. The history of industrial progress during the last century has been, to an important extent, the history of the development of substitutes ; and it is probable that the technical development of the years to come will consist to an even larger extent of progress in this field. Warfare and armaments, unpeaceful as they are meant to be and as their chief and immediate achievements in the fields of economics and technique are, have proved many a time, and will prove so in the future, strong levers of progress for non-military purposes.

1.—*War-time Production of Raw Materials.*

We have shown already that the quantitative achievements in the production of raw materials, foodstuffs and fodders of which a nation may boast in peace-time will not always hold good during war-time. The change-over from peace- to war-time production means quick new investment on a large scale, even if none of the existing industrial body is destroyed or put out of gear by inimical action. Munitions may have been produced in large quantities against a coming war, but once " consumption " begins it is up to production to maintain the supply. No general ever complained of a surfeit of shells. The size of the stocks determines the tactics of warfare, not the tactics the requirements in ammunition. The productivity of industrial labour and the numbers of the army become mutually limiting factors.

Most of the raw materials will be necessary just as they were for peaceful purposes, though the production of some of them will be more vital than of others, while the production of some goods which serve " only " civilian purposes will be pushed into the background. The number of these key materials, in the positive and in the negative sense, is, however, not very large. Some may, however, offer serious difficulties to those countries which have not developed satisfactory substitutes, do not produce them themselves in sufficient quantities and are not able to get them from abroad. War leaves behind it, even in victorious countries, industries in a sad state of depreciation and disproportion. But the aftermath of the next great war is scarcely an object for our scientific interest at the present moment.

There exists, however, a connection between some raw materials and the possibility of preventing war.

Many people have been sorely disappointed by the poor results of the activities of the League of Nations in aid of Ethiopia. I quite understand this feeling, and to a certain extent I share it. It was a shameful experience to see the whole of white humanity, with very few exceptions, wanting passionately to stop the war and to save the Ethiopian sovereignty from extinction but being unable to do it. The conquest of Ethiopia was an enterprise of deliberate brutality. It would have been a wonderful thing had the League of

Nations been able to save the Ethiopians. But the fact that the League's endeavours were not successful cannot destroy our hopes for the future.

This enterprise of the League was a first attempt in an entirely new field. It faced difficult problems which, in such a trial case, could have been solved only by quite extraordinary wisdom, energy and discipline. Which were the key points in regard to raw material supplies ? An economic and diplomatic technique for mastering these problems had to be built up. The astonishing thing was not that these problems were not solved in time, but that some of them were solved, though too late, at all, and that the strong endeavours to stop this war became, gradually, surprisingly popular in many countries. After all, Mr. Mussolini had a close shave. His guesses came out right, but in spite of the unheard-of favour of the political, military and economic situation, with an astonishingly narrow margin. Now dejection and hopelessness prevail among the friends of the idea that war might and should be prevented by economic boycott, backed by military power. But such despondency is not justified by the facts of the case. The League of Nations will be powerless in the next case only if and when her friends give up or when her apparent friends double-cross her. Many people all the world over are prepared to follow a policy which deprives even their home industries of big chances of temporary profits and employment provided that such a sacrifice seems to offer a real chance of avoiding or shortening bloodshed or of protecting weakness in distress.

This is particularly true of the United States. It would be quite wrong to think that the idea of those who take an interest in politics is to save their own skins at any price. They know only too well that Europe, after a new great war, would be no good as a customer. They have already suffered from the experience that Europe does not pay her war debts to America and understand that the condition of Europe after a war may mean the breakdown of normal, peace-time employment of large numbers in the U.S. The form in which this knowledge expresses itself in terms of legislation resembles the groping movements of a blind man in an unknown place. But I think that any country which takes the possibility of war seriously into account will have to reckon on total passivity in the U.S.

The industry and agriculture of this country will not provide any country which is at war with anything it needs or wants on credit, and probably not even for cash, and the government and public opinion of that country will not allow any belligerent government to borrow there.

2.—*Transport of Raw Materials.*

On the whole a boycott by important countries like the U.S. against belligerent nations would bear impartially on whoever might be fighting, including " satisfied " as well as the " dissatisfied " nations. But one factor will work chiefly against countries like Germany, Italy and Japan: namely, the insecurity of transport to them from those parts of the world which might be willing to play the hateful rôle of black-legs in an international selling strike against countries at war. If we look at the results of our inquiries from this angle, we find that Russia hardly depends at all on transport which might be easily interrupted by enemy activities. France may count on the raw materials she can obtain from her colonial empire: not much, but certainly a help. The same is true of the British crown colonies, protectorates and mandated territories. It is not certain how far this applies to the raw materials Britain might buy from the Dominions and India. But as things stand now it is more than probable that at least Canada, Newfoundland, Australia and New Zealand would not take part in an international selling boycott against Great Britain, so long as the goods were paid for without loans raised in these Dominions themselves. The investments of Britishers in all these Dominions are still very large. Mr. J. H. Richardson estimates them for 1933 at £2,260 million, and those in the U.S. —including Central America—at only £220 million. To buy these back would probably be deemed sufficient payment by these Dominions. As to India it is, of course, not sure whether the foundations of British power are secure enough to keep that country out of such a boycott or from revolt. If they are, certainly British investments in India are large enough to pay for a large volume of raw materials and foodstuffs from India in time of war. (The British investments in India are included in Mr. Robinson's total.)

For France and England the question is only whether ocean

transport will continue to bring them the things they may buy overseas. I am not an expert in these matters, so I do not feel very competent to press my personal opinion about this ; but I think that it will be found true that even a pessimistic view of this question shows Britain and France to be in a much better position than Italy, Japan or Germany.

But whatever the opinion of the experts may be, it seems certain that to organize safe conduct over the sea for goods on the necessary enormous scale, and to provide the equally enormous quantity of tonnage will require a great deal of time. This is where the laying-in of stocks may prove decisive. It seems hardly possible to lay in stocks of a size sufficient for a long war : the investment would have to be enormous. It could not be done on such a large scale in secret. Really large purchases would be a sort of public announcement that a country expected war within a short time. Such a thing might be done openly by a country which nobody believed to want, or to be prepared for, a war. Countries which rightly or wrongly are suspected of being on the look-out for a good chance to begin a victorious war cannot undertake such a thing without giving their hand away. All they can do is to lay in some small or middle-sized stocks clandestinely. But even stocks of medium size will be of vital importance during the period of organizing mass transport and huge *convoys*. In this respect Great Britain and France are incomparably better off than the other big powers.

Germany, Italy, Japan, indeed, have all the odds against them in this matter as long as the other nations do not sleep or deliberately look the other way. Their purchasing power on the world market is not large, neither is their credit. Both are already overstrained owing to the purchases they have had to make for current rearmament on a large scale. Germany has already had seriously to hamper the nutrition of her population. A country which, according to the words of its leading politicians, has even in peace-time reached a stage where it has to choose between butter and bombs, will certainly not be able to count on sufficient food and material when the consumption of these things really begins on a war-time scale. Even were Germany able to buy abroad its international purchasing power would be small, as its foreign investments are not large. It would scarcely be able to bring over its borders such goods as it might be able to buy in neutral countries. An occasional "commercial" submarine boat, not very large, might slip through, but this would hardly cause any remarkable alleviation of the scarcity, particularly of the two really crucial classes of materials which are bulky, viz., petrol (and coal, in the case of at least Italy) and foodstuffs. The country would have to manage with the stocks it had in hand when war broke out, plus what it might possibly capture (it would not a second time find the warehouses of a captured ocean port bulging with wool and cotton), plus what neighbouring neutrals would let them have. This would not be much, for the technique of preventing neutrals inside a blockade line providing blockaded powers with materials and food was worked out between 1914 and 1918, and a new war would find it applied without the hesitations which marked those years.

The situation of countries like Germany is so hopeless that one can only wonder why the policies of these states are not framed with reference to these realities. It is quite possible that the responsible politicians know all this quite well, but try to bluff, believing that their bluff will not be called. . . . But this leads us into the realm of politics and away from the subject-matter of this essay in applied economics.

3.—*Planning.*

War and preparation for war cannot, under modern conditions, be undertaken thoroughly without a large measure of planning. When Mr. J. M. Keynes was able, a few years ago, to say that the end of *laisser-faire* had come, the reason why he found so much agreement with this bald statement was partly that all governments had been taught the above truth by the bitter experience of the last war. The planned economic system which has grown up since the war has disappointed many an observer and critic in the rank and file of the economists. The blunders of uncontrolled bureaucracy have not been negligible, and every mistake made by a public authority has been subjected to the widest measure of publicity, often consisting of criticism and comment far beyond the limits of truth. So we have liberal outbursts of all kinds, and these are certainly not always the outcome only of wounded prejudice. All the same it is certain that private initiative can scarcely hope to enable any modern industrial country to hold its own in a modern war even for one month. Already in peace-time armament is beginning to force planning on all nations which seriously want to prepare for their defence. Even liberals who oppose protectionism with convinced passion proclaim the necessity of hoarding in the United Kingdom at least one year's supply of wheat, dispersed in specially-built underground warehouses. The next step is clear. This wheat would have to be sold each year and replaced by fresh wheat, so that before anyone knew what was happening governments would find themselves ankle-deep in the wholesale wheat trade. The necessity for, and possibility of, large-scale governmental planning is becoming self-evident, even though economic theoreticians remain unconvinced. Gradually even more sophisticated observers are recognizing that the blunders made by an experienced bureaucracy are certainly not worse than those made in ordinary private business.

This is important for two reasons.

(*a*) Under such conditions the necessity for state planning and state direction of production, transport and consumption would present no serious difficulty to any government involved in a future war.

(*b*) If the maldistribution of raw materials is to be remedied in peace-time and for peaceful purposes, governments will have to plunge deeply into economic activities. A tentative dip will no longer do. They will be able to do this wholeheartedly and with fair prospect of success because they are accumulating such a stock of varied experience and building up an adequate technique for an apparatus applying it. War and armaments are in this respect not only the great taskmasters, but also the successful teachers of mankind. But in the pleasure of this discovery do not let us forget that they are nasty and dangerous teachers.

CHAPTER VII

RAW MATERIALS AND INTERNATIONAL PLANNING

NOT all nations are equally wealthy ; but not every miser is poor. A country cannot at one and the same time spend all its money on materials for armaments and on materials for civilian purposes. Apart from this we have seen that no problem of *access* to raw materials exists. The lack of international purchasing power from which some countries suffer is, in its bearing on the raw material situation, just as much a problem of selling up to the full production capacity of existing industries. In some cases rather successful compromises concerning price control, limitation of output and division of markets have been reached by private, though government-tolerated and sometimes government-helped, agreements among producers. There would not be much point in giving a descriptive catalogue of existing organizations of this sort ; the details frequently change and such a list would soon become partially obsolete. We will therefore hurry on to a discussion of those problems connected with a policy of deliberately developing these modest beginnings, attributable mostly to private initiative, energy and reasonableness, into a properly organized plan. What, then, are the conditions of successful international planning in the field of the distribution of raw materials, and how is it possible to imagine them being implemented in our actual world ?

A.—SCIENTIFIC PREREQUISITES OF INTERNATIONAL PLANNING

The first requisite is a knowledge of the facts with which we have to deal. We are not absolutely ignorant in this respect. The official and private statistics of many countries contain quite a lot of valuable information, which allows certain conclusions to be drawn with a good measure of certainty. We have made use of these sources ourselves, in so far as one individual's knowledge of languages and time for calculations have allowed; and the author of this book feels decidedly that he, at least, has learned a good deal about the subject, and that the additions to his knowledge concern points of real practical interest. He hopes that the reader may feel the same. But the studies we have made have shown, I hope, how many contradictions and other uncertainties the material still contains, how many gaps remain to be filled, and how much the lack of comparable data makes itself felt in a rather exasperating way. Quite a lot of the work to be done in order to further international planning would consist in forecasting. But this is quite impossible, as far as the future demand for raw materials is concerned, so long as we know little about the elasticity of the demand and supply curves of the different materials. The beginnings of such statistical work can be seen in many places; we have used this work freely and found that it is valuable. The League of Nations already plays an important part here, and so also does what we might call the British League of Nations. But this is not enough; inquiries of this sort will be really conclusive only when they are made at the instance of one international authority, when the statistical offices of all important countries adapt their methods of collecting and presenting their data to the requirements of international comparability, and when the control of the accuracy of these statistics is itself international, so that no suspicion can disparage the value of the data.

All this will be politically and technically difficult, and also expensive. It must be undertaken, however, in spite of all these difficulties; but it is not necessary to wait for perfect achievement in this field before making endeavours in other directions.

B.—A Central Economic Planning Authority.

One of our proposals, made above, was that an international truce in the opening up of new, and the expansion of existing, industries with the help of governments should be introduced, so as to give the normal peace-time consuming power of mankind an opportunity to catch up with productive capacity. This disparity is at present a permanent source of local distress and of serious general disturbances of economic life. If this proposal were adopted, one of the first problems to be handled would be that of trying to stabilize the business cycle so far as the production of raw materials is concerned, thereby increasing the feeling of security and diminishing the objective damage brought about by fluctuations in prosperity, which always tend to lead not only to desperate steps in wholesale protectionism but also to serious political troubles. Another object of such an organization would be the restoration of a reasonable distribution of international purchasing power. A start has already been made along these lines, *e.g.*, with the Free Trade régime in certain parts of central Africa.[1] It should be possible to encourage similar developments, to influence national protectionist policies and to make countries apply protective measures in such a way as to injure as little as possible the economic interests and susceptibilities of other nations. Another function of such an international planning centre would be to give advice to those nations wanting to establish plans for their internal economic development. The International Labour Office has certainly not fulfilled all the optimistic hopes which greeted it when it was established. Too many of the international agreements drafted by it have remained unratified by many important nations. But some progress has been made, and at least in the non-dictator countries the findings of the conferences and committees of the office have exercised some influence by morally educating authorities, scientists and public opinion. The eight-hour day has lost its bad name, thanks to the respectability with which it has been invested owing merely to the fact that the governments affiliated to the I.L.O. have taken it seriously, even in countries where public opinion is not favourable to such measures of " rank bolshevism ".

[1] An example of the possibility of smoothing out ominous international conflicts of interests and jealousies by sitting round a table in time and with good will is provided by the International Congo Act. By this Act the so-called conventional Congo Basin was made an area of free trade where all nations were treated on an equal footing. The clauses of the Covenant of the League of Nations and of the several Mandates for Mandated Territories providing for the same treatment for all member states of the League are further proofs of the organizing power of good will. The fact, too, that discrimination against Japan and Germany was not reintroduced in these Territories when these states left the League and thereby lost their right to equal treatment in the Mandated areas is again a proof of the possibility of doing things reasonably in public life even at the cost of some sacrifice on the part of those who might easily play the role of dog-in-the-manger.

Another field of activity would be an impartial inquiry into the effects of protection and its alternatives in special cases. Such work as this also, and much more which might have been mentioned here,[2] has been undertaken already, or is about to be undertaken, either by the I.L.O. or by the League of Nations itself.[3] But it has all been done without the necessary measure of co-ordination, in an unsystematic way, when particular problems came to the fore and generally only after some crisis had occurred. This business of planning must itself be planned.

The ultimate aim would be for the Central Authority to pursue a policy of promoting international agreements not only concerning certain raw materials, but also concerning the financing of sales and the redistribution of international purchasing power. On the strength of international advice and of confidence in international control, the credit resources of the world might again be used systematically instead of in the present piecemeal way.

C.—Political Conditions

All this would mean a great deal of interference in the affairs of individual governments. It cannot be denied that sovereignty would be at a discount under a policy of this sort. This is a serious difficulty. A government which wants to take part in such work of reorganization must not only take part in the deliberations and debates, but must apply by its national legislative powers the resulting suggestions, recommendations and rules. The argument that one or the other measure would infringe on sovereignty would be totally incompatible with these ideas. All the activities of a really active political and economic world organization inevitably infringe on sovereignty. The activities recommended here will do so no more than those caused by the Washington Naval Agreement, the Washington Agreement on the Eight-Hours Day, and many another agreement. The mere existence of the League of Nations and of the International Labour Office is a permanent and strong challenge to the sacrosanctity of sovereignty.

[2] A splendid example of work of the kind is the inquiry of the International Labour Office on Forced Labour.

[3] See the inquiry of the League of Nations mentioned in the Preface of this essay.

I shall not here go into the several purely political implications of such plans. They are obvious, and they lead far away from the field of an economic inquiry. But it is quite clear, to mention only a few examples, that the measure of armament which a country would be free to undertake could not fall outside the scope of such regulation. The powers wishing to bring order into the world would have to tolerate such regulation. And if certain nations refuse to take part and to implement the international decisions, those countries which are prepared to implement them must develop plans for acting on their own account and for leaving the others outside—literally in the cold. If, *e.g.*, metals necessary for armaments can be bought even for alleged or actual non-military purposes only by states which subscribe to such an international order; if international loans are given only to nations which qualify in the same way; and if foodstuffs are sold only to nations which fulfil these obligations: then it will not take very long to bring order out of chaos and to stop large-scale waste of the produce of precious human labour and thriftiness on internationally mischievous objects.

D.—Psychological Conditions

There are grave difficulties in the way of such a development. The past policy of some régimes has been quite incompatible with such an objective. Such régimes will have to choose between either an adaptation of their ideology and propaganda to these new needs, or the consequences of being left out in the cold. The restitution by international action of purchasing power to those nations seriously short of it can be expected only if these nations give the necessary guarantee: not merely on paper, but in a way that is open to impartial international control. Against such a development many cheap and sophisticated philosophies will be mobilized as well as many instincts, valuable or nasty, as the case may be. As long as *sacro egoismo* is a respectable philosophy in national and international life; as long as hymns are sung after a successful act of cheating, blackmail or violence against another nation, such a development is impossible.

The old battle between emotionality and rationality will have to be re-fought. As long as nations believe in adventures whilst complaining that adventures may be dangerous, as long as they believe that domination is healthier, more productive of great ideas, and more virtuous than comradeship, all endeavours to smooth out economic difficulties by reasonable organization will be hopeless. Ultimately the problem is one of education in co-operation and obedience to the rules of an international administration ; education in international virtue. But this is a subject for a whole further book, and so we will break off here with the words of Mr. Hogben :

> The greatest obstacle to lucid discourse in these matters is the psychological anti-vaccinationist who uses the word freedom to signify the natural right of men and women to be unhappy and unhealthy through scientific ignorance instead of being healthy and happy through the knowledge which science confers. Haunted by a perpetual fear of the dark, the last lesson which man learns in the difficult process of growing up is " ye shall know the truth, and the truth shall make you free. . . . Knowledge which hath a tendency to use is the only proper preparation of a race of young men and women provided against the next age."

APPENDIX

Statistical Tables

Most of the figures in these tables have been taken

either from the German Statistical Abstract,

or from the Statistical Year Book of the League of Nations,

or from *The Mineral Industry of the British Empire and Foreign Countries.*

In some cases conversions of data given in various measures have been converted into one system of units by the author, and additions and computations of percentages added.

When figures from several sources have been combined into one table or when figures have been taken from other sources this is stated.

A.—METALS

1.—IRON.

(1) World Production.

In Million Metric Tons.

	1913	1922	1925	1926	1927	1928	1929	1930	1931	1932	1933	1934	1935
Iron ore ...	177	105	153	154	173	176	203	181	119	76	89	119	?
Pig iron ...	79	56	77	79	87	89	99	81	56	39	49	62	74
Raw steel	80	70	92	95	103	111	122	96	70	51	68	82	99

(2) Lodes of Iron Ore.

(Only countries where the lodes comprise more than 1,000 million metric tons.)

(a) According to a German Compilation of 1913[1].

Continents. / Countries.	In Million Metric Tons. Certain Lodes. Iron Ore.	Percentage of Metal.	Content of Metallic Iron.	Possible Further Lodes.
Europe	22,598	41	9,307	16,818
Asia	4,402	62	2,734	20,855
Africa	1,344	50	678	10,000
America	26,866	53	14,249	119,947
Oceania	2,602	54	1,403	43
TOTALS, WORLD ...	57,812	49	28,371	167,663
France	8,164	39	3,184	4,090
Germany	1,317	39	517	2,843
Great Britain	5,970	33	1,986	6,199
Sweden	2,203	63	1,387	674
Spain	1,216	51	571	273
U.S.S.R.	2,057	49	1,009	617[2]
India	3,326	65	2,170	20,500
Union of South Africa ...	1,095	50	544	2,000
Brazil	7,000	66	4,620	?
Cuba	3,159	41	1,308	12,000
Newfoundland	4,000	53	2,120	4,000
U.S.	10,452	47	4,949	83,728

[1] Following a compilation of the *Verein für die bergbaulichen Interessen* at Essen, 1913.
[2] Excluding new lodes found in the district of Kursk of between 15 and 40 thousand million metric tons of a content of iron between 30 and 50 per cent.

(b) According to an American Estimate[1]

Known Iron Ores.	In Million Metric Tons.	In Per Cent. of World Totals.
France	1,790	18
U.K.	317	3
Sweden	442	4
Germany...	255	3
Spain	353	4
U.S.S.R.	263	3
Total, Europe	3,735	30
U.S.	4,700	40
Brazil	3,000	24
Cuba	1,000	8
TOTALS, WORLD	10,000 and more	

[1] Quoted from *Lippincott*, who follows M. *Roesler*, Bulletin No. 706, U.S. Geological Survey, 1921, Roesler mentions a possible further 424 thousand million tons reserves of iron ores.

(3) Production of Iron Ores by Countries, 1913–1935.

	In Million Metric Tons.					
	1913.	1928.	1932.	1933.	1934.	1935.
Germany	36·9[1]	6·3	1·3	2·6	4·3	6
Luxemburg	7·3	7	3·2	3·4	3·8	4·1
Austria	3[1]	1·9	·3	·3	·5	·8
Hungary	2·1[1]	·2	·1	·1	·1	·2
Czechoslovakia	—	1·8	·6	·4	·5	
Great Britain	16·2	11.4	7·4	7·6	10·8	11·1
France	21·9[1]	49·2	27·6	30·2	32	32·3
Spain	9·9	5·8	1·8	1·8	2·1	2·6
Italy	·6	·6	·4	·5	·5	·6
Sweden	7·5	4·7	3·3	2·7	5·3	7·9
U.S.S.R.	9·2	6	12·2	14·5	21·7	27·1
U.S.	63	63·2	10	17·8	25	31
Newfoundland	1·5	1·5	·3	·3	·5	·7
Cuba	1·6	·4	·1	·2	·2	
Chile	·01	1·5	·2	·6	1	·8
India	·4	2·1	1·8	1·2	1·9	
China	1	2	2·3	2·1		
Algeria	1·3	2	·5	·8	1·3	1·7
Spanish Morocco	—	1	·2	·4	·8	1

[1] Pre-war area. Only those countries have been included (with the exception of Italy) where at least one figure was bigger than 1·0.

(4) Production of Pig Iron and Raw Steel, by Countries.

	In Million Metric Tons.							
	Pig Iron.				Raw Steel.			
	1913.	1929.	1934.	1935.	1929.	1934.	1935.	1913.
Germany, (incl. Saar)	20·7[1]	15·3	10·6	13·1	20·8	18·3	13·7	16·4
Luxemburg ...	2.5	2·9	2	1·9	1·3	2·7	1·9	1·8
U.K.	10·4	7·7	6·1	6·5	9	10·1	9	10·2
France	5·2	10·4	6·2	5·8	5·1	9·8	6·2	6·3
Belgium ...	2·5	4	2·9	3·1	2·6	4·1	2·9	3
Spain	·4	·8	·4	·4	·2	1	·6	·6
Italy	·4	·7	·6	·7	1	2·3	1·9	2·3
U.S.S.R. ...	4·6[1]	4·3	10·5	12·5	·5[1]	5	9·5	12·4
Poland	—	·7	·4	·4	—	1·4	·9	·9
Czechoslovakia	—	1·6	·6	·8	—	2·2	·9	1·2
U.S.	31·5	45·3	16·4	21·7	31·8	57·3	26·4	34·6
Canada	1	1·2	·4	·7	1·1	1·4	·8	1
India	·2	1·4	1·4	?	·06	·6	·8	·9
Japan (incl. Korea and Manchuria)	·2	1·5	2·4	2·7	·2	2·3	3·7	4·4

[1] See note [1] at the foot of Table (3).

(5) Iron in International Commerce; Exports of All Countries.

	In 1,000 Metric Tons.				
	1929.	1930.	1931.	1932.	1933.
Iron ores, including pyrites	50,149	44,306	29,268	20,535	24,631
Scrap iron, scrap steel ...	2,978	2,179	1,743	1,633	2,716
Pig iron and semi-finished goods of iron	5,010	4,259	3,618	2,436	2,894
Tubes and pipes	1,761	1,280	930	675	872
Iron in bars	6,070	5,101	4,629	3,496	3,444
Iron wire	1,389	1,063	1,059	777	835
Tinplate	908	801	600	629	751
Other sheet iron	4,052	3,192	2,503	2,018	1,921
Rails for railways and tramways	1,352	1,137	889	399	546

(6) International Trade in Iron Ore and Pig Iron.

	In Million Metric Tons.											
	Iron Ores.						Pig Iron.					
	1929.		1932.		1934.		1929.		1932.		1934.	
	Imp.	Exp.	Imp.	Exp.	Imp.	Exp.	Imp.	Exp.	Imp.	Exp.	Imp.	Exp.
Germany	17	·1	3·5	·02	8·3	·08	·2	·4	·06	·07	·09	·2
Belgium and Luxemburg	14·1	·8	9·5	·4	10·3	·7	·7	·1	·2	·04	·2	·04
France	1·1	16·4	·3	10·1	·9	12·6	·04	·6	·07	·2	·07	·2
U.K.	5·8		1·8		4·4		·1	·5	·1	·1	·1	·1
Czechoslovakia ...	1·6	·4	·2	·08	·3	·09	·06					
U.S.S.R.		·5		·3		·3						
Sweden		10·9		2·2		6·9	·09	·07	·04	·03	·08	·07
Spain		5·6		1·3		1·8						
Japan	2·3		1·6		2·3		·8		·7		·8	
Algeria		2·1		·5		1·4						
Spanish Morocco ...		1		·2		·8						
Chile		1·8		·2		1						
Newfoundland ...		1·4		·5		·4						
Canada	2·5		·8		1		·04					
U.S.	3·2	1·3	·6	·09	1·5	·6	·2	·05	·1		·1	
British Malaya ...		·8		·7		1·1						

Only countries are mentioned where at least one item runs up to at least 1·0 in this table.

(7) PRICES.

In R M. per ton.

	Annual Averages									Monthly Average
	1913	1928	1929	1930	1931	1932	1933	1934	1935	July, 1936
Iron Ore: U.S., old range Bessemer, Lake Superior ...	?	18·80	19·59	19·84	19·84	19·84	15·63	11·83	11·77	11·76
Pig Iron: U.K., Middlesborough Cleveland III	59·49	66·15	70·76	67·31	54·79	42·36	42·60	41·39	40·80	46·12
Iron Bars: Belgium, barres, f.o.b. Antwerp	103·04	114·54	115·81	97·20	69·37	49·26	57·05	63·89	64·09	64·09
Girders: Belgium, poutre normal, f.o.b. Antwerp	114·10	97·43	101·87	92·64	64·34	44·23	51·77	60·62	61·83	61·83
Sheet Iron: U.K., Middlesborough, ship plates, exp. f.o.b. ...	?	153·74	153·36	155·82	145·17	112·23	106·06	96·25	93·17	96·09
Tinplate: U.K., Cardiff, f.o.b. ...	?	379·91	386·37	372·61	281·68	234·77	237·91	224·55	234·14	241·65
Scrap Iron: U.K., heavy steel, N. Engl.	55·12	56·09	64·57	52·98	38·40	26·24	29·25	31·33	31·48	35·36

(8) German Consumption of Pig Iron.

	1913.	1917.	1925.	1929.	1932.	1934
Pig iron consumed in million tons	18·6	13·7	10	13·2	3·9	8·7
Population in million ...	67			63·1		

1913 to 1929: decrease of population 3·9 million or 6 per cent.; decrease of consumption in pig iron 5·4 million or 29 per cent.

(9) Production in the U.S.S.R.

	In Million Metric Tons.							
	1913.	1929.	1930.	1931.	1932.	1933.	1934.	1935.
Pig iron	4·2	4·3	5	4·9	6·2	7·1	10·4	12·5
Raw steel	4·4	5	5·9	5·6	5·9	6·9	9·6	12·4
Rolling-mill produce ...	3·5	3·9	5	4·4	4·3	4·9	6·7	8·2

(10) Development of Heavy Industries in Western Europe.

(a) *Production of Coal and Coke.*

	In Million Metric Tons.				
	1913.	1930.	1929.	1932.	1934.
Coal:—					
Germany[1 3]	141	108	163	105	125
Saar territory	—	9	14	10	11
Belgium	23	22	27	21	26
France	40	24	54	46	48
Great Britain	292[4]	233[4]	262	212	225
Netherlands	2	4	12	13	12
Coke:—					
Germany[3]	32	25	39	20	21[2]
Saar Territory	2	1	2	2	2
Belgium	4	2	6	4	4
Netherlands	?	?	2	3	3[2]

(*b*) *Production of Iron Ore, Pig Iron and Raw Steel.*

	In 1,000 Metric Tons.				
	1913.	1920.	1929.	1932.	1934.
Iron Ore :—					
Germany[7] ...	2,353	1,919	2,080	443	137[5]
France ...	21,918	13,921	50,731	27,599	32,000
U.K.	16,248	12,881	14,014	7,446	10,757
Luxemburg ...	7,333	3,704	7,571	3,231	3,834
Pig Iron :—					
Germany ...	10,900	6,000	13,400	3,900	8,700
Saar Territory	1,371	644	2,105	1,349	1,826
Belgium ...	2,485	1,116	4,040	2,749	2,907
France ...	5,207	3,344	10,362	5,537	6,155
U.K.	10,425	8,174	7,711	3,631	6,074
Luxemburg ...	2,548	693	2,906	1,960	1,955
Netherlands ...	—	—	260	233	258[2]
Raw Steel :—					
Germany ...	11,800	?	16,000	5,600	11,900
Saar Territory	2,080	740	2,209	1,463	1,950
Belgium[6] ...	2,467	1,253	4,011	2,758	2,898
France ...	4,687	2,706	9,717	5,640	6,174
U.K.	7,787	9,213	9,791	5,346	9,002
Luxemburg ...	1,335	570	2,702	1,956	1,932

[1] Bituminous coal and anthracite, excluding brown coal. [2] 1933. [3] Excluding Saar Territory.
[4] Including Irish Free State. [5] Probably a misprint in the (German) source. [6] Excluding ingots.
[7] Metal content of iron ores mined.

General Note to the Statistical Tables on Iron.

The above figures are taken chiefly from the German Statistical Abstract.

The Statistics of the League of Nations differ from the German figures in some cases seriously. To give a few examples :

	1913. Production of					
	Iron Ores.		Pig Iron.		Raw Steel.	
	G	LN	G	LN	G	LN
	in Millions of Metric Tons.					
Germany	36·9	28·6	20·7	16·6	20·8	17·6

The differences concern mostly figures for Germany.

2.—ALUMINIUM.

(1) Production of Bauxite.

	In 1,000 Metric Tons. 1913.	1929.	1932.	1934.	1935.
France	309	666	401	528	513
Italy	7	193	87	131	170
Yugoslavia	—	103	67	84	190
Hungary	?	389	112	120	211
U.S.	214	372	98	160	238
British Guiana	?	220	85	66	?
Dutch Guiana	?	215	127	101	110
World		1,951	1,026	1,270	?

The peak years of production were in Hungary and the U.S. in 1928, in Dutch Guiana in 1930.

(2) Production of Aluminium Metal.

	In 1,000 Metric Tons. 1913.[1]	1929.	1932.	1934.	1935.
Germany	1	33	19	37	71
U.K.[5]	10	8	10	11[4]	15.1
Norway	2	29	18	16	16
Switzerland	10	21	9	8	11·7
France	14	29	15	16	21·8
Italy	1	7	13	13	14
U.S.[2]	21	146	69	76	?
Canada	6	39	18	16	20·6
World[3]	65	277	154	170	259·2

[1] League of Nations figures for 1913: *Germany*, ·8; U.K., 7·6; *Norway*, 1·5; Switzerland, 9·2; France, 14·5; *Italy*, ·9; *U.S.*, 20·9; *Canada*, 5·9; World totals, 63·3. The countries the names of which are not given in *italics* show serious differences.

[2] Including "secondary production." [3] Excluding "secondary production" of the U.S. [4] 1933.

[5] The *Statistische Zusammenstellungen der Metallgesellschaft A.G., Frankfurt a. M.* give the following series: 1913, 7·6; 1929, 13·9; 1932, 10·2; 1934, 12·9.

(3) International Commerce in Aluminium (Exports only).

	In 1,000 Metric Tons. 1929.	1930.	1931.	1932.	1933.	1934.	1935.
Bauxite	545	510	383	379	380	533	766
Aluminium ...	101	75	67	40	57	61	62

(4) PRICES.

	In RM. per Kg.								
			Annual Averages.						July
	1913.	1929.	1930.	1931.	1932.	1933.	1934.	1935.	1936.
Germany, "Hütten," 98–99 per cent. ...	170	190	185·71	170	160	160	157·33	144	144
U.S., New York ...	?	222·23	218·06	212·04	212·04	171·04	119·82	113·61	109·72

2a.—BARIUM MINERALS.

PRODUCTION.

	In 1,000 Long Tons.					
	1928.	1929.	1930.	1933.	1934.	1935.
Germany	254·1	281·6	232	145·4	349·2	341·8
U.S.	240·7	247·6	209·8	130·7	159·3	194·7
U.K.	49·9	57·1	58·7	66·6	74	18·1
Italy	26·7	25·5	19	23·1	31·9	40·5
France	29·6	—	—	13·5	18·1	—
Korea	—	—	—	4·9	5·8	10·9

A figure for world production is not available. The various barium minerals in this table contain very different percentages of the metal.

3.—CHROMIUM.

PRODUCTION OF CHROME ORE.

	In 1,000 Long Tons.					
	1928.	1929.	1930.	1933.	1934.	1935.
Southern Rhodesia ...	195·9	261·7	202·4	34·5	71	104·2
Union of S. Africa ...	31·2	63	13·5	33·5	60·4	89
India	45·5	49·6	50·7	15·5	21·6	39·1
Japan	9·7	9	11·2	19·7	26·8	?
Greece	20·6	23·8	16·8	14·6	30·2	31·5
Yugoslavia	16·4	42·3	50·6	25·1	46·6	59·5
Russia	40·7	28[1]	65[1]	110·9	127·2	?
Cuba	28·7	39·8	35·9[2]	21·8	57·3	47·7
Turkey	11·7	9·9	27·7	74·2	118	148·1
New Caledonia	50	49·9	52·7	49·1	54·3	54·4
World	440	580	530	403	618	?

[1] Incomplete. [2] Only exports to the U.S.

4.—COPPER.

(1) Production of Copper Ores.

	In 1,000 Tons of Content of Metallic Copper.				
	1913.	1929.	1932.	1934.	1935.
Germany	26·8	29·1	30·9	26·1	28·3
Yugoslavia	?	20·7	30·2	44·4	39
Norway	10·6	19·1	16·7	22	20·5
Spain	44·9	63·7	35	33	30
U.S.S.R. in Europe ...	33·7	25	30	40	55
India	?	7·6	11·4	11·8	11·3
Formosa	?	6·1	3·5	4·5[1]	?
Northern Rhodesia ...	—	5·6	88·6	140	?
Union of S. Africa	—	9	9·4	7·9	10·7
South-West Africa ...	?	12·6	2·4	—	—
Canada	34·9	112·5	112·3	166·5	189·9
U.S.	555·4	905	216	217·1	335·2
Mexico	52·6	86·6	35·2	44·3	39·4
Cuba	3·4	15	5·9	6·2	—
Chile	42·3	320·6	103·2	256·7	267·5
Peru	27·8	54·4	115	27·6	29·6
Australia	52·1	13	14·9	12·2	17·5
World Totals	990·4	1,947·6	900·8	1,287·3	1,491·7

[1] 1933.

(2) Production of Copper.

Countries.	In 1,000 Metric Tons.				
	1913.	1929.	1932.	1934.	1935.
Germany	49·5	93·4	129	104·8	116
Belgium	1·3	68·2	86·2	151·6	?
Great Britain	52·2	22·4	13·2	11·5	15·5
France	12	1·4	1	1·3	1
Spain	31·3	53·4	33·1	27	?
U.S.S.R.	29	33·5	46·6	53·6	63
Yugoslavia	6·4[1]	20·7	30·5	44·4	39
Japan	66·5	75·5	71·9	67·8	69·8
U.S.	732·6[2]	1,242·9	308·9[3]	407·1[3]	537·5[3]
Canada	13·9	72·9	95·7	151·9	140·1
Mexico	43·7	66·2	35·1	44·3	41·2
Chile	20·2	303·2	97·5	256·9	270·7
Northern Rhodesia ...	—	5·6	69	140·1	148·2
Belgian Congo	7·5	137	54·1	110·1	108
Commonwealth of Australia	43·8	11	13·5	8·1	16
World Totals	1,018·5	1,894·7	929·1	1,273·2	1,497·5

[1] Serbia. [2] Excluding "secondary copper." [3] Refined copper only.

(3) International Commerce.

	In 1,000 Metric Tons. 1929.	1930.	1931.	1932.	1933.	1934.	1935.
Total exports of copper ore	1,447	1,209	866	615	399	474	
Total exports of copper ...	1,284	1,136	976	755	870	1,158	1,329
Goods of copper exported, value, mill. RM.	815	718	475	289	260	265	265

(4) International Trade in Raw Copper.

	In 1,000 Metric Tons. Imports.		Exports.	
	1932.	1934.	1932.	1934.
Germany	131	180	45	12
Belgium and Luxemburg ...	39	74	60	61
France	93	94		
U.K.	146	255		
Italy	53	63		
U.S.S.R.	12	11		
U.S.	149	175	101	238
Yugoslavia			26	36
Belgian Congo			60	44
Northern Rhodesia			74	132
Canada			92	97
Chile			121	239
Mexico			?[1]	?
Peru			23	26

[1] 1931: 43.

(5) Stocks and Prices of Copper.

	Annual Averages. 1925.	1926.	1927.	1928.	1929.	1930.	1931.	1932.	1933.	1934.	1935.	Monthly Average July, 1936.
Stocks: 1,000 metric tons	374	368	351	278	382	530	597	704	692	590	568	548[1]
Prices: RM. per 100 Kg.— Great Britain, London:												
Electrol.	147·20[2]	132·13	125·31	139·56	172·20	126·12	81·02	53·22	50·71	41·70	42·91	50·94
Standard	137·45		112·02	128·15	152·10	110·12	71·99	46·06	44·58	37·66	38·34	45·82

[1] December, 1935. [2] 1913.

5.—GOLD AND SILVER.

(1) World Production and Price of Gold and Silver.

	1928.	1929.	1930.	1931.	1932.	1933.	1934.	1935.
Gold	603	609	648	695	751	818	860[2]	946[2]
Silver	8,022	8,117	7,735	6,094	5,129	5,007	5,772	6,230
Price of silver, RM. per Kg. ...	79·12	72·38	52·28	40·22	37·99	36·57	38·79	47·40[1]
Units of silver equivalent to one unit of gold ...	35·19	38·45	53·25	69·22	73·28	76·13	71·77	

[1] July, 1936: 32·76. [2] Excluding China.

(2) Production of Gold, by Countries, 1929–1935.

	In Kg.			
	1929.	1933.	1934.	1935.
Yugoslavia	575	2,194	2,305	2,445
France	1,795	2,930	3,157	?
Rumania	2,213	3,732	3,468	3,509
U.S.S.R.	33,760	114,600	132,600	175,000
Sweden	900	8,978	7,673	5,600
Europe	40,000	136,500	149,700	191,300
Belgian Congo ...	5,377	9,794	11,672	13,000
Rhodesia	17,465	20,064	21,563	22,600
Tanganyika	282	1,230	1,325	1,550
Union of South Africa	323,860	342,565	325,960	335,109
Gold Coast	6,465	9,551	10,140	11,050
Africa	354,000	380,000	378,800	393,000
Canada	59,977	91,736	92,443	102,351
U.S.	64,042	71,653	86,430	98,484
Mexico	20,274	19,836	20,572	21,223
Central America ...	1,655	2,708	4,043	4,666
Brazil	3,415	3,919	3,449	3,706
Chile	1,028	4,526	7,392	8,562
Colombia	4,268	9,277	10,704	10,233
Ecuador	2,094	1,887	2,066	2,177
French Guiana ...	1,522	1,493	1,476	1,555
Peru	3,734	3,010	3,075	3,421
Venezuela	1,446	2,977	3,392	3,577
America	163,848	215,421	237,878	261,614
China	2,700	4,666	?	?
Japan and Dependencies	16,437	26,814	28,618	?
India	11,318	10,454	10,018	10,100
Dutch Indies	3,412	2,452	2,232	2,120
Philippines	4,996	9,215	10,585	13,400
Asia	39,700	51,000	54,100[1]	59,000[1]
Australia	13,286	25,824	27,577	28,530
New Zealand	3,500	5,136	7,065	8,290
Papua	1,420	4,098	4,984	?
Oceania	18,206	35,058	39,420	41,200
World	615,754	817,979	859,898[1]	946,114[1]

[1] Without the production of China.

(3) PRODUCTION OF SILVER, BY COUNTRIES, 1929–1935.

	In 1,000 Kg.			
	1929.	1933.	1934.	1935.
Germany	171	197	185	195
Yugoslavia	11	54	60	57
Europe	392	494	443	
Canada	720	472	511	517
U.S.	1,830	719	1,020	1,485
Mexico	3,380	2,118	2,306	2,351
Central America	93	149	109	93
Bolivia	193	170	162	192
Peru	660	228	323	490
America	7,026	3,911	4,506	5,211
Africa	11	124	146	161
India	227	189	181	181
Japan and Dependencies ...	163	205	249	254[1]
Asia	459	433	464	500
Commonwealth of Australia ...	313	336	353	386
Oceania	326	350	365	400
World	8,274	5,312	5,924	?

[1] Incomplete.

(4) SILVER: STOCKS.

Figures for India and Shanghai [stocks in warehouses and afloat], U.S. and Canada [stocks held by producers], in 1,000 Kg.

Annual Averages.										Monthly Average.
1925.	1926.	1927.	1928.	1929.	1930.	1931.	1932.	1933.	1934.	March, 1935.
12,016	13,909	15,602	15,064	17,047	19,217	20,166	20,406	23,024	22,898	17,867

(5) Stocks of Gold in the World.

Visible stocks of banks and estimated gold in monetary circulation.[1 2]

In million Kg.

1913.	1926.	1927.	1928.	1929.	1930.	1931.	1932.	1933.	1934.	1935.
15	16·2	16·5	17	17·4	17·1	17·7	18·7	18·4	19·7	20·1

[1] From 1930, excluding gold in circulation.

[2] Converted from tables in *Statistisches Jahrbuch fuer das Deutsche Reich*, 1928–1935, at the rate of RM. 1,392=500 gr. of gold.

(6) Production of Gold During the Post-War Period.

In 1,000 Kg.

	1913.	1920.	1921.	1922.	1923.	1924.	1925.
Europe	47	2	3	7	10	21	31
Asia	44	35	34	36	36	35	33
Africa	312	288	281	249	316	330	329
America ...	287	148	151	160	164	174	178
Australia ...	80	34	28	28	28	25	22
World... ...	768	507	497	481	553	586	593

6.—LEAD.

(1) Production of Lead Ores in the World by Countries.

Lead Content of Ores Mined; in 1,000 metric tons.

(*a*) *in the World.*

1913.	1925.	1926.	1927.	1928.	1929.	1930.	1931.	1932.	1933.	1934.	1935.
1,229	1,435	1,565	1,639	1,599	1,684	1,598	1,337	1,186	1,145	1,287	1,341

(*b*) *by Countries.*

	1929.	1932.	1934.	1935.
Germany	52·5	45·3	52·9	54·2
U.K.	18·9	33·4	54·7	39·8
Yugoslavia	14·7	49·5	70·2	
Spain	116·5	100	63·1	66
India	103·7	80·1	90·2	90·8
Canada	148·1	116·1	157·1	153·8
U.S.	587·9	265·6	260·1	300
Mexico	248·4	137·2	166·3	184·2
Australia	197·1	213·9	233·5	225·4

(2) Production of Lead.

	In 1,000 Metric Tons. 1929.	1932.	1934.	1935.
Germany	124	106	124	136
Belgium	83	64	75	60
Spain	143	105	73	68
U.S.[1]	1,008	561	487	294[2]
Canada	148	115	143	149
Mexico	231	137	166	180
Burma	82	72	73	73
Australia	180	189	199	278
U.S.S.R.	6	19	27	45
World	1,742	1,152	1,323	1,368

[1] Including, [2]excluding, " secondary production."

(3) Lead in International Commerce.

	In 1,000 Metric Tons. 1929.	1930.	1931.	1932.	1933.	1934.	1935.
Total exports	825	291	290	601	658	730	777

(4) Stocks and Prices.

	1913.	1927.	1928.	1929.	1930.	1931.	1932.	1933.	1934.	1935.	1936.
Stocks, in 1,000 tons					65[2]	136[2]	240	279	304	302	294[1]
Price, RM. per 100 Kg.; Gt. Britain, London, raw, standard ...	40·06	51·49	45·09	49·44	36·33	24·24	17·21	15·94	13·47	17·11	19·50[3]

[1] June. [2] Only U.K. and U.S. [3] July.

(5) Scrap Lead Production in Germany.

	In 1,000 Long Tons. 1928.	1929.	1933.	1934.	1935.
Production of primary lead ...	85·6	96·4	114·8	118	120·4
Secondary lead (from scrap) ...	26·7	18·3	15·2	4	9·6
Total lead produced	111·7	114·7	130	122	130

(6) Balance Sheet of Lead for some "Have-Not" Nations.

In 1,000 Long Tons.

[p=production, i=imports, e=exports,[2] b=balance for consumption or addition to stocks.]

	Germany.					Italy.					Japan.				
Years	p	i		e	b	p	i		e	b	p	i		e	b
1928	111·7	148·3	260	47·3	212·7	20·9	27·2	48·1	15·1	33	4·3	63·2	67·5	2·2	65·3
1929	114·7	136·9	251·6	55·8	194·8	22·3	24·8	47·1	10·8	36·3	3·6	62	65·6	2·1	63·5
1930	127·1[1]	86·2	213·3	70·4	142·9	24	18·6	42·6	12·9	29·7	3·6	56·4[3]	60	2	58
1933	130	48·7	178·7	46·2	132·5	24	9·3	33·3	4·3	29	7·5	68	65·5	3·1[3]	72·4
1934	122	48·4	170·4	23·7	146·7	47	6·6	43·6	4·2	49·4	9	95·9	104·9	4·9[3]	100
1935	130	54·1	184·1	24	160·1	42	6·6[4]	48·6	4·2[4]	44·4	9	91·8	100·8	4·8	96

[1] Estimate. [2] Metal content of ores assumed to be 73 per cent. of weight of ore.
[3] Slightly incomplete. [4] Figure for 1934 repeated, as that for 1935 is not yet available.

7.—MANGANESE.

(1) Production of Manganese Ore.

	In 1,000 Metric Tons. 1929.	1932.	1934.	1935.
Germany[1]	182	21	129	192
Czechoslovakia	97	34	59	
U.S.S.R.	1,184	826	1,820	2,378
U.S.[1]	1,321	44	253	
Brazil	293	20[2]	2[2]	61[2]
India	1,010	216	413	225
Egypt	192	3	1	1
Gold Coast[2]	426	52	345	405
World	3,658	1,270	2,967	

[1] With widely-varying contents of metal. [2] Exports.

(2) Manganese Ore in International Trade.

	In 1,000 Metric Tons. 1929.	1930.	1931.	1932.	1933.	1934
Total exports	2,696	2,110	1,402	769	1,360	1,660

8.—NICKEL.

(1) Production.

	In 1,000 Metric Tons. (a) Nickel Ores.			(b) Nickel Metal.			
	1929.	1932.	1934.	1929.	1932.	1934.	1935.
Greece	4	20	29	4	20	22	
New Caledonia... ...	136	92	118[1]	136	92		
Canada	1,807	717	1,392[1]	50	14	58	63
Norway	24	23	24[1]	24	23	29	

[1] 1933.

(2) Prices.

	In RM. per 100 Kg. Annual Averages. 1930.	1931.	1932.	1933.	1934.	1935.	July, 1936.
Nickel, Great Britain, London ...	342·39	351·86	346·16	320·41	262·88	243·44	249·06

9.— QUICKSILVER (MERCURY).

Production.

	In 1,000 Kg. 1929.	1932.	1934.	1935.
Spain	2,476	816	1,096	1,232
Italy	1,998	1,016	441	972
U.S.S.R.	120	200	267	
U.S.	816	435	532	604
Mexico	83	235	158	216
World	5,583	2,831	2,089	3,378

10.—TIN.

(1) Production of Tin Ores.

	Metal Content in 1,000 Metric Tons. British Malaya.	Dutch Indies.	Siam.	Bolivia.	Nigeria.	U.K.	World.
1913	52·2	20·9	6·9	26·7	3·9	5·4	135·5
1923	40	29·6	7·8	30·2	6	1	131·1
1924	47·7	32·1	7·9	32·1	6·3	2	143
1925	48·9	33·2	6·9	33·1	6·6	2·4	148·1
1926	48·5	33·5	7·6	30·1	7·2	2·4	145·2
1927	55	35·9	7·7	34·4	7·7	2·6	159·3
1928	65·4	35·5	8·6	41	9·3	2·5	178·8
1929	70·5	31·2	11·1	47·1	10·9	3·3	195·1
1930	65	35·1	12·1	38·8	8·7	2·5	177·5
1931	55·8	27·8	11·3	31·2	7·2	·6	149·6
1932	30·2	17·1	9·8	20·9	4·4	1·4	98
1933	25·3	12·7	10·7	15	3·8	1·6	89·4
1934	34·7	20	10·8	21	5·1	2	118·1
1935	43·3	25	9·9	27·6	7·1	2·1	149·8

(2) Production of Tin

In 1,000 Metric Tons.

	Germany.	U.K.	Holland.	China.	Dutch Indies.	Straits Settlements.	U.S.	World.
1913	12	22·7		6·1	20·5	65·6		132·5
1923	2·4	31·5		8·9	74		34·2	125·6
1924	2·5	36·6		7·1	88		28·8	135·9
1925	1·5	39·6		8·5	90·7		28·1	146·1
1926	2·3	42·7		6·6	93·5		30·3	147·7
1927	6·2	43·7		6·2	99·1		23·5	158·1
1928	4·7	53·2		6·9	14·2	100·4	32·5	185·1
1929	2·7	56·3	·7	6·9	13·6	107·2	31·1	195·1
1930	2·9	48·1	1·9	6·6	14·6	98·5	23·8	179·6
1931	3·7	36·2	2·6	6·8	13	88·9	18	156·2
1932	1·9	29	3·8	7·1	8·2	50·7	13·4	107·4
1933	1·7	18·5	5·1	7·7	9	47·7	20	101·3
1934	2·2	26·9	13·6	8·2	10·7	50·4	22·6	124·2
1935	2·1	30·5	15·9	9·9	11·5	61·5		146·4

(3) Foreign Trade in Tin Ores and Tin Metal.

Exports in 1,000 Metric Tons.

	1929.	1930.	1931.	1932.	1933.	1934.	1935.
Tin ores ...	147	131	109	77	64	92	
Tin metal ...	170	159	131	94	121	111	141

(4) Foreign Trade in Tin in Some Countries.

In 1,000 Metric Tons.

i=imports; e=exports; aa=annual average.

		1913.	1919.	1920.	1921.	1922.	1923.	1924.	1925.	1926.	1927.	1928.	1929.
Germany[5]	i ...	14		5	5		6	9	13	11	16	13	18
	e ...	6		2	6		2	3	3	4	6	6	5
U.K. ...	i[4] ...	46	23	29	12	25	14	17	16	14	14	16	15
	e[4] ...	12	15	13	10	13	20	18	26	27	27	23	30
U.S.[1] i ore	...				aa 5,812					aa 1926/30 194[2]			
i[3]	...				aa 132					aa 1926/30 177			

		1930.	1931.	1932.	1933.	1934.	1935.
Germany i		15	14	12	15	13	
e	...	5	5	3	4	2	
U.K. i[4] ...	...	12	12	4			
e[4] ...	...	23	12	13			
U.S.[1] i (ore)	...		30[2]	17[2]	24[2]	22[2]	
e[3] ...	...		148	78	143	90	

[1] Quantitative statistics of exports not printed in Statistical Abstract. [2] Tin content.
[3] In million lbs.; bars, blocks, pigs, etc. [4] Blocks, ingots, bars and slabs.
[5] Raw, scrap and compounds.

(5) Stocks of Tin on World Market.

In 1,000 Metric Tons. Annual Averages.

1925.	1926.	1927.	1928.	1929.	1930.	1931.	1932.	1933.	1934.	1935.	June, 1936.
24·2	17·6	16·2	19·9	28·3	43·8	57·2	59·1	43·7	21·8	17·4	15·7

(6) Price of Tin.

	In RM. per 100 Kg. Annual Averages												
	1913.	1925.	1926.	1927.	1928.	1929.	1930.	1931.	1932.	1933.	1934.	1935.	July, 1936.
London : blocks	405·65	522·37	582·10	576·92	456·00	411·67	285·59	221·97	196·92	265·46	286·11	271·85	229·14
New York	415·76	535·66	604·08	596·68	466·68	418·15	293·71	226·86	203·98	277·32	288·06	276·86	236·21

11.—ZINC (Spelter).

(1) Production of Zinc Ores.

	Metal Content of Ores ; in 1,000 Metric Tons.											
	1913.	1925.	1926.	1927.	1928.	1929.	1930.	1931.	1932.	1933.	1934.	1935.
Germany ...	244	49	79	111	117	125	131	99	72	85	105	108
Italy ...	63	69	71	85	85	87	70	42	32	25	40	50
Norway ...					—	1	8	7	9	10	7	6
Poland ...	—	122	116	97	90	94	97	75	25	42	53	45
U.S.S.R. ...					11	11	18	20	17	22	32	46
Sweden ...	17	19	21	24	14	30	30	29	25	25	29	30
Spain ...	67	49	53	47	43	53	50	39	35	35	32	33
India ...	4	43	46	61	65	56	62	46	42	56	56	59
Indochina	15	21	25	22	22	19	16	8	5	5	5	4
Algeria ...	37	24	26	26	15	15	8	4	2	3	2	2
Northern Rhodesia	—	2	1	—	13	23	20	7	—	19	20	21
Canada ...	7	81	99	102	124	141	121	108	78	90	136	145
U.S. ...	375	645	703	652	631	657	540	372	259	349	399	469
Mexico ...	7	46	105	137	162	174	143	151	88	89	125	136
Australia ...	220	141	153	174	150	157	122	175	118	126	139	151
World ...	1,139	1,312	1,558	1,585	1,565	1,704	1,511	1,164	929	1,144	1,374	1,493

(2) Production of Zinc.

Excluding Zinc Dust; in 1,000 Metric Tons.

	1913.	1921.	1922.	1923.	1924.	1925.	1926.	1927.	1928.	1929.	1930.	1931.	1932.	1933.	1934.	1935.
Germany	279	102	42	35	41	63	74	90	105	108	101	49	45	51	71	123
Holland...	24	6	13	16	18	21	25	26	27	26	23	19	16	19	20	14
Belgium	204	66	112	147	162	171	190	202	206	198	176	135	96	137	175	184
France	68	24	40	49	58	64	75	83	93	87	87	57	46	56	51	52
U.K.	66	6	19	32	39	39	18	43	56	59	49	22	27	46	55	64
Norway	9	2	2	4	5	7	5	6	—	6	35	40	39	45	45	45
U.S.S.R.	8				1	2	2	2	3	3	4	10	15	17	27	46
Poland	—	6	85	96	93	114	124	150	162	169	174	131	85	83	93	85
Italy		1	3	4	6	7	8	7	11	16	19	17	18	23	25	28
N. Rhodesia	—	—	—	—	—	—	—	—	10	12	18	7	—	19	20	21
U.S.	360	213	384	522	523	573	650	598	682	697	542	330	231	359	390	382[1]
Canada	3	24	26	27	45	50	68	75	74	78	110	108	78	83	123	136
Mexico	7	5	3	19	18	1	6	6	11	17	19	35	30	28	27	40
Japan	2	10	13	14	14	17	17	17	19	22	25	25	27	31	32	32
Australia	4	2	24	42	47	47	48	49	51	53	56	55	45	55	56	69
World	1,001	437	708	948	1,006	1,135	1,233	1,418	1,403	1,457	1,400	1,001	783	988	1,172	1,335

[1] Incomplete.

(3) World Exports.

	In 1,000 Metric Tons.						
	1929.	1930	1931.	1932.	1933.	1934.	1935.
Zinc ores ...	1,258	1,192	916	708	923	1,004	970
Zinc metal ...	452	440	445	358	398	450	446

(4) Stocks and Prices.

	Unit.	1913.	1925.	1926.	1927.	1928.	1929.	1930.	1931.	1932.	1933.	1934.	1935.
Stocks[1] ...	1,000 tons									303	253	224	
Price, U.S., New York, spot ...	R.M. per 100 Kg.	43·40	73·98	71·20	61·02	58·98	63·24	42·22	34·17	26·46	29·07	22·96	23·80

[1] Only those of the International Zinc cartel, U.S. and U.K.

12.—METALS OF THE PLATINUM GROUP, PRODUCTION.

	1928.	1933.	1934.		1928.	1933.	1934.
A. Platinum				B. Palladium			
U.S.S.R. ...	3,110	3,110		Canada ...	370	965[2]	2,610[2]
Columbia ...	1,665	1,429	1,703	U.S. ...	160	29	
Canada ...	328	770	3,615	C. Osmium and Iridium			
Union of S. Africa ...	736	74	1,174	Union of S. Africa ...	176	209	158
Ethiopia ...	101	100		Australia ...	57	18	
Sierra Leone	17[1]	13	15	U.S. ...	66	60	
Japan ...	3	6		D. Other Platinum metals			
U.S. ...	1,616	1,549					
Australia ...	11	4		Canada ...	53		
New Zealand	1	1		U.S. ...	11	3	

This table comprises only primary productions.

[1] 1930. [2] Including Osmium, Iridium, Rhodium, Ruthenium.

13.—MINOR METALS.

A. Antimony.

PRODUCTION; METAL CONTENT OF ORES.

	In Long Tons.					
	1928.	1929.	1930.	1933.	1934.	1935.
Austria	1,125	700	—	—	—	
Czechoslovakia ...	1,189	684	378	1,341	1,142	1,900
France	1,138	1,200	1,300	379	261	
Italy	282	378	413	358	346	446
French Morocco ...	221	177	nothing[3]			135
Mexico	3,521	2,667	2,984	1,919	2,626	4,498
U.S.[1]	37	nothing		524	361	39
Bolivia[2]	3,487	3,719	?	1,866	1,182	3,348
China	20,741	23,581[2]	18,060[2]	13,100	15,200	18,000
World[4]	30,000	31,000	27,000	21,000	22,000	30,000

[1] Excluding recovered metal. [2] Exports. [3] Spanish Morocco, 1934 : 309. [4] Estimates.

B.—Bismuth.

(1) PRODUCTION, BISMUTH ORE.

	In Cwts.					
	1928.	1929.	1930.	1933.	1934.	1935.
Australia ...	152	66	83	53	279	470
Germany ...	1,610	940				
Rumania ...				—	—	280
Spain ...	2,539	2,323		1,516	3,543	
Argentine ...	417	145		—	180	

(2) PRODUCTION, BISMUTH CONTENT OF ORES, OR METAL.

In addition to (1).

	In Cwts.					
	1928.	1929.	1930.	1933.	1934.	1935.
Canada	125	1,735	114	699	2,265	123
Germany				—	—	80
Spain	469	219	?	512	905	
Mexico				923	2,033	4,204
Bolivia (exports) ...	2,679	2,974		37	993	412
Peru	—	613		5,756	5,368	
China				350	570	
Japan	633	984	1,079	1,124	991	

C.—Cadmium, Production. *D.—Cobalt, Production.*

	In 1,000 lbs. Avoirdupois.			In 1,000 Cwts.		
	1928.	1929.	1930.	1933.	1934.	1935.
Cadmium.						
Canada	492	774	457	246	294	581
Australia	387	446	510	357	380	490
France	104			88	—	267
Germany[1]	100	100	100			
U.S.	2,116	2,915	3,094	2,678	3,344	3,985
U.S.S.R.					6	26
Mexico	779	1,413	1,208	1,107	848	1,317
South West Africa				—	140	320
Belgium	11[2]	5[2]	11[2]	355	498	333
Norway				308	302	260
Poland	9	8		114	316	248
Italy			27[1]	16	18	35
Cobalt.						
Canada	8·5	8·3	6·2	4·2	5·3	6·1
India	·2	2·2		2·3	3·5	4·3
Australia	·2	·4	·1	·1	·2	
Belgian Congo ...	9	13·9	14	12·2		
N. Rhodesia ...				2·3	11·4	8·2
French Morocco ...				1·4	3·3	8·2

[1] Estimates. [2] Exports.

E.—Molybdene, Production. *F.—Radium.* *G.—Strontium, Production.*

(*a*) MoS_2 content of ores.
(*b*) Ores.

Radium content of compounds produced.

		Unit.	1928.	1929.	1930.	1932.	1933.	1934.	1935.
E.	Canada (*a*)	cwt.	—	258	—				
	Australia (*b*)	cwt.	40	10	105		208	89	212
	Norway (*a*)	cwt.	3,287	3,478	4,193		8,149	4,793	12,736
	Fr. Morocco (*a*)	cwt.	787	20			3,700	2,850	3,230
	Mexico (*b*)	cwt.					1,303	15,315	22,528
	U.S. (*a*)	cwt.	29,725	34,863			84,554	139,315	171,310
	Japan and Korea (*b*)	cwt.	609	582	520		2,070	2,136	2,077[1]
F.	Czechoslovakia	gr. ...		3·5		3·8	3·3	7·8	
	Belgian Congo	gr. ...		60		6	6·7		
G.	U.K.	long tons ...	7,126	5,329	5,141		3,862	9,440	4,510
	Germany	long tons ...	857	717	359		148	341	182
	Tunisia	long tons ...			500				

[1] Incomplete.

H.—Thorium.

Production of Monazite in Long Tons.

I.—Titanium.

Production of Titanium Minerals in 1,000 Long Tons.

	1928.	1929.	1930.	1933.	1934.	1935.
Thorium.						
India	103	180	14	139	1,009	3,819
Ceylon	85					
Brazil	100	88	15	401		
Egypt						11
Titanium.						
Canada	2	2·2	·4	—	1·8	2
India	25·3	23·7	28·8	53	75·6	127·1
British Malaya				·2	·1	3
Norway	7·9	7·8	7·5	22·9	26·1	37·5
Portugal	·7	·1	·8	·4	·3	
French Senegal	6·9	8	5·2	·3	·5	12
Argentine				2·6	1	
Brazil	1·5	6·3	·1	·1	·1	·3

J.—Tungsten (Wolfram). Production.

(a) Ores; (b) concentrates (about 60% WO_3 content); (c) WO_3 content; in 1,000 Long Tons.

K.—Uranium Minerals.

Production in Cwts.

L.—Vanadium.

Production of Ores in Long Tons.

	1928.	1929.	1930.	1933.	1934.	1935.
Tungsten.						
India (a)	·8	1·3	2·5	2·1	3·3	3·8
British Malaya (b) ...	·1	·5	1	1	1·6	1·7
Portugal (b)	·1	·3	·5	·4	·7	1·1
U.S. (b)	1·1	·7	·6	·8	1·8	2·1
Bolivia (b)		1		·2	·8	1·3
China (a)	7·3	8·7	8·6	5·6	6·2	
French Indichina (c) ...	·1	·1	·1	·1	·2	·3
Japan and Korea (c) ...				·1	·3	
Uranium.						
Canada				300[1]	250[1]	
Czechoslovakia (U_3O_8 content)	378	316	259	236	236	
Portugal	2,815			1,233	791	117
U.S. (U_3O_8 content) ...		232		18	70	232
Vanadium.						
South West Africa ...	5,033	3,036	4,461	177	324	1,570
World[1]	5,160	5,000	5,000	220	330	2,000

[1] Estimates.

B.—NON-METALLIC MINERALS

1.—COAL.

(1) Geological Stocks down to 6,600 feet.(a)

(a) Estimate of the XIIth International Geological Congress, Toronto, 1913.

In 1,000 Million Metric Tons.

	Certain.	Certain and Probable.		Certain.	Certain and Probable.
Germany	89[1]	181[1]	China	19	217
Belgium	7	11	India		78
France	5	17	French Indochina		20
Great Britain ...	141	190	Japan and Korea ...	1	8
Netherlands ...	3	5	Russian Asia ...		352
Poland	10	158	Asia	22	680
U.S.S.R.		64[3]	Oceania	3	148
Spain	6	8	Belgian Congo ...		·5
Norway		9	Rhodesia	1	1
Czechoslovakia ...	7	25	Union of S. Africa ...		56
Europe	270[2]	671[2]	Africa	1	57[4]
Canada	185	666	Total non-European territories ...	722	4,316
U.S.	511	2,736	World	992	4,989
Chile	2	3			
America	698	3,434			

[1] Later estimate only 26 and 44. [2] id. 203 and 534. [4] id. 225.

(a) In these tables on coal, brown coal has been converted into coal at the rate of ·402 : 1.

(b) *American Estimate.*

In 1,000,000 Millions.

North America ...	4·97	Australasia	·17
Asia	1·40	Africa	·06
Europe	·76	South America ...	·04
World	7·40		

(2) Production by Countries.

	In Million Metric Tons.						
	1913.	1928.	1929.	1930.	1933.	1934.	1935.
U.K.	292	232·5	258	243·9	207·1	220·7	222·3
Union of S. Africa	8	12·4	12·8	12	10·5	12	13·4
Canada	14	15·7	15·6	13·3	10·6	12·4	12·4
India	16	22·6	23·4	23·8	20·3	22·7	23
Australia	13	13·4	12·1	9·5[1]	11·7	12·2	13·1
Belgium	23	27·1	26·5	27	24·9	26	26·1
Czechoslovakia ...	—	34·5	38·5	33·1	25·2	25·4	25·8
France[2]	41	41·6	54·1	54·2	47·2	47·9	47·3
Germany[3] ...	238	324·4	346	297·1	243·2	269·1	287·5
Italy		·8	1	1	·8	·8	1
Holland	2	10·7	11·6	12·2	12·5	12·2	11·8
Poland	—	40	45·6	36·9	26·9	28·8	28·1
U.S.S.R. ...	37	35·2	38·1	45·7	74·7	82·5	102·2
U.S.	517	514·4	541·2	474	342·1	371·9	375·3
China		25	25		18·5	20·6	1·2
Japan[4]		34·8	35·3	31·9[1]	45	51·4	
World	1,268	1,440	1,430	1,390	1,150	1,260	1,290

[1] Incomplete. [2] Without Saar. [3] Including Saar.
[4] Including Asiatic possessions and, for 1933 and 1934, Manchuria.
Source: "The Mineral Industries of the British Empire," etc.

(3) World Production of Coal.

In Million Metric Tons.								
1909–13 Annual Average.	1913.	1920.	1921.	1922.	1923.	1924.	1925.	1926.
1,098	1,268	1,193	993	1,057	1,201	1,188	1,188	
1927.	**1928.**	**1929.**	**1930.**	**1931.**	**1932.**	**1933.**	**1934.**	**1935.**
1,357	1,335	1,421	1,298	1,149	1,023	1,057	1,156	1,260

Source : German Statistical Abstract.

(4) Prices.

	Annual Averages							
RM. per to	1913.	1930.	1931.	1932.	1933.	1934.	1935.	July, 1936.
Germany: Rheinisch-Westf. FettfœrderKohle, f.o.b. mine	12·34	16·76	15·40	14·21	14·21	14·05	14	14
U.K.: Cardiff, best Admiralty, f.o.b.	21·11	21·11	18·73	14·12	13·34	12·11	11·72	11·99

(5) WORLD EXPORTS.

	1929.	1930.	1931.	1932.	1933.	1934.	1935.
Coal.							
Quantity, million tons	155	141	124	101	103	111	112
Value, R.M. million ...	2,825	2,586	2,042	1,352	1,205	1,138	1,095
Brown Coal.							
Quantity, million tons	3·6	2·8	2·4	1·8	1·9	2·1	2
Value, R.M. million	56	43	36	20	19	19	18

(6) EXPORTS AND IMPORTS, BY COUNTRIES, 1934.

In 1,000 Metric Tons.

Countries.	Net Imports.	Net Exports.	Countries.	Net Imports.	Net Exports.
Germany ...		17,075	Austria	2,587	
Belgium and Luxemburg ...	670		Sweden ...	5,265	
Denmark ...	3,801		Poland ...	9,880	
France	13,720		U.S.S.R. ...		2,167
Great Britain ...		53,997	Switzerland ...	1,900	
Irish Free State...	2,343		Japan[1]		3,322
Italy	11,781		Canada	11,462	
Holland	2,762		U.S.		11,638
Norway	2,065				

[1] Including Manchuria; 1933.

2.—OIL.

(1) GEOLOGICAL STOCKS.

(*a*) *Estimate by V. R. Garfias*, 1933.

Countries.	Probable Capacity of Production of Fields worked at the end of 1932 in Million Metric Tons.	Future possibility of Production at the Rate of 1932. Years.	Countries.	Capacity of Production in Million Metric Tons.	Future possibility of Production at the Rate of 1932. Years.
U.S.	1,715	15	Trinidad ...	13	9
U.S.S.R. ...	429	20	Poland ...	7	12
Irak	357	?	Japan	6	20
Iran	314	52	Sarawak ...	4	14
Venezuela ...	286	17	Canada	1	14
Dutch East Indies	143	29	Egypt	1	7
Rumania ...	71	10	Germany ...	1	7
Colombia ...	57	29	Ecuador ...	1	7
Mexico	43	11	France	·7	10
India	14	12	Other Countries	1	2
Peru	14	9			
Argentine ...	14	7	WORLD	3,495	19

(*b*) *Estimate of the American Petroleum Institute.*

Published after the War.

In Million Metric Tons.

Countries.	Estimated Resources.	Per Cent. Totals.	Countries.	Estimated Resources.	Per Cent. Totals.
South and Central America ...	1,322	23	Balkans ...	162	3
U.S.	1,000	17	Indonesia ...	142	3
U.S.S.R.	964	17	Canada	142	3
Near Orient ...	833	14	Africa	132	2
Mexico	646	11	WORLD ...	5,774	
India	431	7			

This does not include the resources of Persia.
An estimate published in 1920 by Mr. David White enhances the total quantity to 8,000 million metric tons.

(2) PRODUCTION OF OIL.

(*a*) *World Production*, 1913–1935.

In Million Metric Tons.

1913.	1920.	1921.	1922.	1923.	1924.	1925.	1926.	1927.	1928.	1929.	1930.
53	99	107	120	142	141	148	152	174	183	207	197

1931.	1932.	1933.	1934.	1935.
190	181	197	208	226

(*b*) *Production in Important Countries.*

In Million Metric Tons.

	1913.	1928.	1934.
U.S.	34	124	123
Mexico	4	8	6
Venezuela	—	16	20
Peru	·3	2	2
Argentine	—	1	2
Colombia	—	3	2
Trinidad	—	1	2
Iran	·2	6	8
Dutch East Indies	2	4	6
India	1	1	1
Sarawak	—	1	·3
Japan and Formosa	·3	·3	·2
Northern Sachalin (Japanese Concession) ...	—	·1	·3
U.S.S.R.	9	12	24
Rumania	2	4	8
Germany	·1	·1	·3
Poland	?	·7	·5
WORLD	54	184	209

(3) World Exports.

Quantities in 1,000 Metric Tons ; =q.
Value in RM. Million ; =v.

		1929.	1932.	1933.	1934.	1935.
Crude Petroleum	q ...	31,038	27,061	29,170	33,645	
	v ...	1,006	608	571	691	
Light fuel oil	q ...	12,339	11,750	10,537	10,762	11,023
	v ...	2,044	910	700	616	624
Lighting oil	q ...	5,988	4,175	3,917	4,128	3,949
	v ...	661	241	197	164	156
Heavy fuel oil	q ...	14,250	15,826	17,485	19,808	
	v ...	501	337	373	406	
Lubricating oil	q ...	2,154	1,527	1,795	1,857	1,910
	v ...	583	296	276	233	239
Totals, value in million RM.		4,795	2,392	2,117	2,110	

(4) International Trade, 1934.

I=Imports ; *E*=Exports.

In 1,000 Metric Tons.

	Crude Petroleum.		Light Fuel Oil.		Lighting Oil.		Heavy Fuel Oil.		Lubricating Oil.	
	I.	*E.*	*I.*	*E.*	*I.*	*E.*	*I.*	*E.*	*I.*	*E.*
Germany ...	277		1,158		98		956		322	72
Belgium-Lux....	226		268		28		327	269	200	106
France... ...	4,322		1,054		38		516	295	156	
U.K.	1,939		3,682	186	784		3,230	143	394	
Italy	143		348		150		1,122		66	
Holland ...	141		336		188		379	50	45	
Austria ...	166		48							
Sweden ...	63		351		95		253		48	
Czechoslovakia	121		121							
Rumania ...		274		1,958		1,085		3,117		62
U.S.S.R. ...		459		1,120		436		1,951		305
Denmark ...			256		80		237			
Irish Free State			115		60					
Norway ...			108				301			
Switzerland ...			219				163			
Spain			440				352			
Hungary ...	229									
Poland and Danzig				56		31				
Greece ...							140			
Egypt	113		13	28	265		163	64		
Algeria ...			126							
Union of South Africa ...			301				110			

In 1,000 Metric Tons.

	Crude Petroleum.		Light Fuel Oil.		Lighting Oil.		Heavy Fuel Oil.		Lubricating Oil.	
	I.	*E.*	*I.*	*E.*	*I.*	*E.*	*I.*	*E.*	*I.*	*E.*
Japan	2,958		613							
Iran		1,565[1]		1,524[1]		445[1]		3,741[1]		
Dutch Indies ...		484		1,455		573		2,253		
Sarawak ...		15		93		14		535		34[1]
British Malaya			412	326	93	55	353	250		
China			110		360		409			
Manchuria ...			54		75				35	
Philippines ...			75		56		288			
India					235		445		71	
Argentine ...	170		61				917	119	18	
Canada ...	4,264		210				236		40	
Dutch West Indies ...	13,954[1]	1,203[1]		2,210[1]		281[1]	929[1]	9,855[1]		110[1]
U.S.	4,972	5,716	16	2,689		1,210	2,133	5,596		1,007
Colombia ...		2,351								
Ecuador ...		172								
Mexico ...		1,641		264[1]		750		1,116		46
Peru		1,351		389				196		
Venezuela ...		18,780						805		
Brazil			265		93		452		28[1]	
Chile			53[1]				213[1]			
Cuba	24[1]		32[1]				248[1]			
Trinidad and Tobago		65		303				996		
Uruguay ...	80[1]						183[1]			
Australia ...	532		690		112				46	
New Zealand ...			214				173			

[1] 1933.

(5) Stocks of Petroleum and Processed Products, in Hands of Producers in U.S.

In Million Hektoliters.

1925.	1926.	1927.	1928.	1929.	1930.	1931.	1932.	1933.	1934.	1935.	June, 1936.
858	839	895	981	1,059	1,095	1,015	981	951	925	883	866

(6) Prices.

	In RM. per 100 l.							
	1913.	1930.	1931.	1932.	1933.	1934.	1935.	July, 1936.
Crude Petroleum:								
New York, Pennsylvanian, free well ...	6·47	6·37	4·70	4·81	3·17	3·38	2·96	3·41
Lighting Oil:								
New York, standard white, spot, in chests	?	18·43	17·76	18·47	14·56	10·75	10·70	10·68
Benzine:								
New Orleans, 60/62 Bé	?	9·46	5·20	4·78	3·74	3	3·25	3·54

3.—ASBESTOS, PRODUCTION, BY COUNTRIES.

	In 1,000 Metric Tons.						
	1928.	1929.	1930.	1931.	1933.	1934.	1935.
Southern Rhodesia ...	35·7	38·1	33·7	21·8	26·9	28·8	38
Union of South Africa ...	24·2	28·7	23·1	11·7	15·2	16·2	18·2
Cyprus	16·3	14·1	7·3		3·5	7·1	7·5
U.S.S.R.	26·1	29·1	56	64·7	73	91	100
Canada	265·5	294·8	251	137·2	147·2	143·4	190·6
World	379	414	379	243	279	303	374

4.—SALT, PRODUCTION.

In 1,000 Metric Tons.

Africa	580	U.S.S.R. ...	2,900	Italy	1,054
		Oceania ...	112		
U.S	6,899			Poland ...	450
Rest of America	562	Europe outside U.S.S.R. ...	10,380	U.K.	2,402
India	1,740	Germany ...	2,268	World ...	24,800
Rest of Asia ...	1,610	France ...	2,130		

5.—MINERAL FERTILISERS.

(1) PRODUCTION.

Countries.	Potash Content of K_2O.		Natural Phosphates.		Super-phosphate.		Basic Slag.		Natural Guano.	
	In 1,000 Metric Tons.									
	1928.	1934.	1928.	1934.	1928.	1934.	1928.	1934.	1928.	1934.
Germany ...	1,432	1,179			792	720	1,639[2]	1,400[3]		
France ...	407	379	180	71[1]	2,265	1,324	1,594	988[1]		
Spain ...	24	110			895	967[1]				
Poland ...	58	58[1]			240	90				
U.S.	54	131	3,580	2,720	4,071	2,602				
U.S.S.R. ...			122	712[1]	151	850				
Algeria ...			876	532						
Tunisia ...			2,789	1,766						
French Morocco			1,268	1,199						
Egypt ...			201	438						
Dutch West Indies			104	86[1]						
Xmas Island			114	130						
Japanese Empire			138	150	976	1,083				
Nauru and Ocean Island			552	558[1]						
Paumotu Islands			187	77						
U.K.					507	494[1]	222	266		
Belgium and Luxemburg					400	290[1]	1,554	1,003[1]		
Holland ...					645	559				
Italy					1,151	1,083				
Australia ...					732	759[1]				
Chile									3·2	11·1[1]
Peru									125·5	162·4[1]
India[4] ...									10·7	4·7
Union of South Africa									9·2	5
Seychelles[4] ...									15·4	12·3

[1] 1933. [2] Saar: 330. [3] Saar: 323. [4] Exports.

In addition to the materials mentioned in this table Chile produced the following quantities of *Sodium Nitrate:* 1928, 3·1; 1934, ·5 million metric tons.

(2) PRODUCTION OF NATURAL NITRATES IN CHILE; NITRATE OF SODA.

	In 1,000 Long Tons.					
	1928.	1929.	1930.	1933.	1934.	1935.
Production	3,113	3,186	2,403	528	1,115	1,201
Exports	2,788	2,851	1,757	659	1,274	1,269
Increase (+) or decrease (—) of home stocks	+325	+335	+646	—131	—159	—68
Total	+ 1,306			— 358		

(3) Production of Guano.

	In 1,000 Metric Tons.										
	1913.	1920.	1921.	1922.	1923.	1924.	1925.	1926.	1927.	1928.	1929.
Peru ...	29	51	64	63	111	137	126	80	78	125	151
World	57	79	100	107	147	185	171	120	131	154	177

	1930.	1931.	1932.	1933.	1934.
Peru ...	133	95	134	162	148
World ...	163	115	170[1]	211[1]	

Figures before 1932 from the Statistical Year Book of the League of Nations, afterwards from the German Statistical Abstract.

[1] Including Indian "fish guano."

(4) World Exports of Some Mineral Fertilisers.

	In 1,000 Metric Tons.						
	1929.	1930.	1931.	1932.	1933.	1934.	1935.
Raw phosphates ...	7,039	6,961	4,330	4,437	5,194	5,799	5,436
Superphosphate and basic slag	3,866	3,627	3,291	2,478	2,345	2,696	2,552
Sodium nitrate (Chilean saltpetre)	3,002	1,886	1,550	519	804	1,394	1,342
Potash compounds ...	2,452	2,370	1,864	1,317	1,717	2,366	2,475
Ammonium sulphate ...	1,756	1,537	1,772	1,706	1,591	1,457	1,656

(5) Prices.

	Annual Averages; in RM. per 100 Kg.									
	1913.	1928.	1929.	1930.	1931.	1932.	1933.	1934.	1935.	1936.
Great Britain, London, Chile saltpetre	23·86	25·98	24·32	22·57	19·55	13·18	11·50	9·75	9·36	9·53[1]
Basic slag, 15% P_2O_5, Aachen, Germany ...	132	91·36	88·98	83·40	78·77	73·18	70·08	67·50	65·25	71·00[2]

[1] Monthly average, July. [2] Idem, June.

6.—SULPHUR.

(1) Production of Brimstone and in Pyrites.

	In 1,000 Metric Tons. Brimstone.					Sulphur Content of Pyrites Mined.				
	1928.	1929.	1932.	1934.	1935.	1928.	1929.	1932.	1934.	1935.
Italy	328	345	234	251	329	257	306	238	372	
Germany ...						146	150	75	97	118
France ...						92	92	87	69	
Greece ...						45	64	42	23	
Yugoslavia[1] ...						64	60	16	23	80
Norway ...						322	324	319	425	396
Portugal ...						122	193	112	102	100
U.S.S.R. ...						152		242[2]	382	
Sweden ...						12	32	50	104	
Spain ...	21	24	17	43		1,572	1,815	1,219	1,320[3]	
Cyprus ...						124	149	81	101	
Japan ...	70	66	85	128	152	270	280	330	491	
Canada ...						35	39	48	5	13
U.S.	2,014	2,400	905	1,450	1,659	115	122	68	170	
Chile	16	16	12	21	21					

[1] Pyrites without regard to proportion of sulphur contained in them. [2] 1930. [3] 1933.

(2) Sulphur Balance Sheet of the "Have-Not" Powers.

	In 1,000 Metric Tons.								
	Germany.			Italy.			Japan.		
	1933.	1934.	1935.	1933.	1934.	1935.	1933.	1934.	1935.
Production: pyrites, sulphur cont.	80·3	95·4	122·5	330·4	366	372	409	500	605
Imports: pyrites, sulphur cont.	334	388	401	48·4	47·2	47·2[1]			
Production: brimstone	24·5	27	34	395	360	324	116·2	140	157
Importation: brimstone... ...	45·6	52·1	60·1				2·8	2·5	·5
	484·4	562·5	617·6	773·8	773·2	743·2	528	642·5	762·5
Exports: pyrites, sulphur cont.	13	7·4	8·6	119·6	126·3	77·4			
Other sulphur	29	28·9	24·4	217·5	215·2	242·8	32·3	45·7	54·5
Total exports	42	36·3	33·4	3 7·1	341·5	320·2	32·3	45·7	54·5
Balance	442·4	526·2	584·2	436·7	431·7	432	485·7	596·8	708

[1] Figure for 1934 repeated, as figure for 1935 is not yet available.

7.—MINOR NON-METALLIC MINERALS, PRODUCTION.

	Graphite Stone in 1,000 tons.		Mica in 1,000 Kg.		Silicious Earth (Diatomeæ Earth) in 1,000 Kg.	
	1928.	1933.	1928.	1933.	1928.	1933.
Germany	18	20	269	73		
Austria	24	15				
Czechoslovakia	32	1				
Italy	7	3				
France	1				10,000	9,130[1]
Sweden			12	68	721	650
U.S.S.R.	1		1,493		12,220	
Great Britain					4,312	4,062
Denmark					35,561	21,337
Hungary[1]					3,547	1,266
Spain					250	1,229
Ceylon[2]	15	6[1]				
Japanese Empire	23	17[1]	29	20[1]	203[3]	3,042
India[2]			4,851	2,932		
Madagascar	17	3[1]	861	178[1]		
Union of South Africa ...			3,629	358		
Southern Rhodesia ...			186	4		
Tanganyika			34	11		
Algeria					9,000	11,000
U.S.	5		7,803	8,104	117,497	100,529
Canada	1	4	3,320	856	334	1,623
Mexico	5	3				
Australia			12	43	1,382	2,895

[1] 1932. [2] Exports. [3] 1929.

C.—VEGETABLE AND ANIMAL RAW MATERIALS

1.—GRAINS (CEREALS), INCLUDING WHEAT, FLOUR AND RICE.

(1) Production of Cereals in Important Countries.

(a) *Wheat.*

In 1,000 Metric Tons.

No.	Countries.	1913.	1920.	1921.	1922.	1923.	1924.	1925.	1926.	1927.	1928.	1929.	1930.	1931.	1932.	1933.	1934.	1935.
1	*Europe*	53,653[8]		47,924[9]				56,068								75,291	75,267	
2	Germany	7,972[6]	2,248	2,934		2,897	2,427	3,217	2,597	3,280	3,854	3,349	3,789	4,233	5,003	5,604	4,532	4,667
3	France[1]	8,692	6,609	8,994		7,500	7,684	8,956	6,308	7,739	7,655	8,705	6,208	7,338	9,077	9,861	9,000	7,755
4	Great Britain ...	1,482	1,549			1,618	1,449	1,440	1,388	1,518	1,354	1,354	1,150	1,028	1,187	1,700	1,899	1,780
5	Italy	5,835	3,847	5,248		6,119	4,631	6,555	5,329	5,329	6,221	7,097	5,717	6,748	7,537	8,100	6,333	7,715
6	Poland		497	960		1,354	885	1,573	1,281	1,476	1,612	1,793	2,240	2,265	1,346	2,174	2,080	2,011
7	Russia[2]	12,189[3]				8,976	9,107	15,706	22,035	20,400	21,590	20,110	29,500	[5]	20,250	27,727	30,410	31,330
8	*America*	29,404[8]		32,128[9]				35,990								31,842	29,235	
9	Argentine	5,400		4,620		6,723	5,220	5,202	6,010	6,509	8,365	3,740	6,422	6,149	6,406	6,978	6,550	3,920
10	Canada	6,306	7,163	8,977		12,906	7,133	11,196	11,325	11,987	15,424	8,152	11,449	8,277	12,058	7,341	7,508	7,548
11	U.S.	20,776	22,672	21,634		21,702	23,751	18,217	22,652	23,724	24,899	21,950	23,356	24,284	20,251	14,354	13,538	16,968
12	*Asia*	14,232[8]		11,440[9]				11,470								15,596	12,410	
13	India	9,870	10,284	6,817		10,142	9,911	8,836	8,844	9,092	7,916	8,595	10,637	9,397	9,169	9,601	9,582	9,884
14	Japan[7]	710	770	759		773	691	1,090	1,060	1,042	1,072	1,055	1,049	1,085	1,086	1,282	1,549	1,596
15	Russian Asia ...	5,496[4]																
16	*Africa*	2,762[8]		2,568[9]				3,122								3,330	4,138	
17	Union of S. Africa	148	221	237					231	181	189	291	253	384	289	315	418	550
18	*Australia*[6]	2,659	4,117	3,862[9]		3,511	4,600	3,049	4,606	3,217	5,545	3,241	6,011	4,944	6,110	4,967	3,792	4,039
19	WORLD, without U.S.S.R.	83,271[8]					85,230	91,857	93,005	99,805	109,980	96,998	104,593	103,750	103,467	103,350	94,430	
20	TOTAL, WORLD ...	106,701[8]		97,921[9]			94,337	107,563	115,040	120,205	131,570	117,108	134,093	?	123,717	131,077	124,843	

Note.—Under 1935 is included 1934–35, where this is the harvesting year, etc. [1] After 1919, including Alsace-Loraine. [2] After 1919, territory of U.S.S.R. in Europe and Asia. [3] Annual average 1915–17, excluding Poland, but including the later Baltic States and Bessarabia. [4] Annual average 1915–17. [5] Including New Zealand. [6] 1914. [7] After 1924 including Korea. [8] Annual average, 1909–13. [9] Annual average, 1920–24.

(*b*) *Rye.*

Countries.	1913.	1920.	1925.	1926.	1927.	1928.	1929.	1930.	1931.	1932.	1933.	1934.	1935.
	In 1,000 Metric Tons.												
Europe ...	44,009[2]	34, 09[7]	44,705		42,093[8]						49,672	43,091	
Germany ...	9,585[1]	4,934	8,063	6,406	6,834	8,522	8,155	7,679	6,680	8,364	8,727	7,608	7,478
Poland ...	5,711[2]	1,901	6,539	5,011	5,688	6,110	7,010	6,958	5,702	6,111	7,073	6,464	6,617
Czecho-slovakia	—	837	1,476	1,166	1,25	1,464	1,834	1,729	1,388	2,176	2,085	1,523	1,638
U.S.S.R. ...	19,172[4]	9,337	19,498	22,030	23,700	19,900	20,220			22,020	24,190	20,130	21,380
Asia	200[2]	100[7]	116		101[8]						341		
Africa ...	16[2]	19[7]	18		21[8]						35	28	
America ...	990[2]	1,537	1,180	1,017	1,725[8 9]		1,056[6]		276	284	898	961	
Australia ...	6[2]				2[8]								
World:													
Incl. U.S.S.R.	42,240[3]	36,618[7]	46,565		44,840[8]		36–48 million[3]		40–50 million[3]		50,950	44,082	
Excl. U.S.S.R.											26,760	23,950	

See note to Wheat Production (C1 1(*a*)); also for explanation of territory covered.

[1] Annual average, 1911–13. [2] Annual average, 1909–13. [3] Very rough German estimates.
[4] 1914. [5] 1913–1932 and 1934 only U.S. [6] Annual average, 1926–30.
[7] Annual average, 1920–24. [8] Annual average, 1926–28. [9] Whole American continent.

(c) *Maize.*

In 1,000 Metric Tons.

	1909/13.[1]	1924.	1925.	1926.	1927.	1928.	1929.	1930.	1931.	1932.	1933.	1934.	1935.
Europe	16,454	14,410[7]	20,413								20,481	22,854	
Italy	2,549[3]	2,684	2,793	3,000	2,220	1,659	2,530	2,997	1,946	3,015	2,591	3,193	2,520
Yugoslavia	762	3,795	3,791	3,410	2,109	1,819	4,178	3,465	3,203	4,793	3,578	5,154	3,028
Rumania	2,730[3]	3,949	4,159	6,083	3,533	2,753	6,386	4,520	6,063	5,993	4,554	4,846	5,379
Hungary	1,506[4]	1,883	2,235	1,944	1,736	1,101	1,794	1,407	1,518	2,432	1,809	2,098	1,436
U.S.S.R.	1,335	2,395	5,024	3,705	3,780	3,320	4,210	[5]	[5]	3,430	4,800	3,840	3,260
Asia	4,586	4,688[7]	5,100								7,920	6,305	
India	2,105[5]	1,716	1,904	1,950									
Africa	3,185	4,076[7]	3,760								5,490	5,320	
Egypt	1,540[6]	1,716	1,961			1,990		1,775	1,986	1,932	1,476	1,572	1,689
Union of S. Africa ...	754[6]	2,192	988	1,715	1,962	1,743	1,763	1,473	1,389	866	2,168	1,722	1,407
America	82,263	87,437[7]	84,529								76,000	55,700	
U.S.	68,897	58,746	74,094	67,186	70,153	72,138	66,606	52,231	65,212	73,867	59,735	35,072	55,954
Argentine	4,869	4,732	7,670	8,153	7,700		5,886	10,510	7,454	6,700	6,526	11,500	9,650
WORLD:													
Including U.S.S.R. ...									100–130 million[2]		110,000	90,443	
Excluding U.S.S.R. ...	103,558	95,940	114,789	110,098	108,600	106,357	109,287	97,914	110,899	120,458	105,200	86,600	

Maize statistics are very incomplete and full of later corrections of figures for earlier years.
[1] Annual average. [2] Very rough German estimate. [3] Pre-war territory. [4] Annual average, 1911–15. [5] Annual average, 1911–13.
[6] Annual average, 1910–13. [7] Annual average, 1920–24.

(*d*) *World Production of Rice.*

In Million Metric Tons.

Annual Averages 1909–13.	1920–24.	1924.	1925.	1926.	1927.	1928.	1929.	1930.	1931.	1932.	1933.	1934.	1935
78·2	83·2	86·3	87·7	85·2	84·6	87·6	85·4	90·8	88·3	88·7	90·1		82·5

These figures exclude U.S.S.R., China, Irak and Iran.

(*e*) *World Harvest of Grains,* 1933.

	In Million Metric Tons.						
	Wheat.	Rye.	Barley.	Oats.	Maize.	Rice.[2]	Totals.
Europe[1] ...	75,291	49,642	24,755	43,548	20,881	975	214,692
Asia	15,596	341	7,190	435	7,920	79,253	110,735
Africa ...	3,330	35	2,350	864	5,490	1,599	13,668
America ...	31,842	898	5,890	16,370	76,000	803	131,803
Australia ...	4,967		16	60			5,043
WORLD ...	131,077	50,950	40,380	61,030	110,000	82,630	476,067

[1] Including whole of U.S.S.R. [2] The figure for rice in Asia is certainly much too low.

(2) INTERNATIONAL TRADE IN GRAINS.

(*a*) *World Exports,* 1929–1935.

	In Million Metric Tons.						
	1929.	1930.	1931.	1932.	1933.	1934.	1935.
Wheat	19·1	16·3	19·9	17·3	15·4	13·9	13·9
Rye	1·3	1·5	1·8	1·3	1·2	1·1	1
Barley	3·9	4	4	2·7	2·7	2·8	2·5
Oats	1·6	1·7	1·5	1·3	·9	1·1	1
Maize	9·6	8	12·1	10·6	9·6	8·3	9·4
Rice	6·7	6·7	7·1	7·3	7	7·6	
Wheat Flour	3·8	3·6	3·1	2·7	2·8	2·7	2·6
Other milling products from cereals and rice	·7	·7	·7	·7	·7	·8	·7

(*b*) *World Trade in Grains, etc., by Countries.*

I = Imports ; *E* = Exports.

		In Million Metric Tons.													
		1913	1923	1924	1925	1926	1927	1928	1929	1930	1931	1932	1933	1934	1935
Wheat:															
U.K.	*I*	5·4	5·1	6	4·9	4·9	5·6	5·2	5·6	5·3	6	5·3	5·7	5·2	5·1
	E				·1										
Germany	*I*	2·5	·5	·7	1·7	2·2	2·6	2·5	2·1	1·2	·8	1	·8	·6	·2
	E	·5			·2	·3		·3	·3		·3	·5	·5	·2	—
France...	*I*	1·6	1·4	1·5	1·2	·3	2·2	1	1·4	1	2·3	2·1	·8	·7	·7
	E									·4				·3	·8
Italy	*I*	1·8	2·8	2·1	2·2	2·1	2·3	2·7	1·8	1·9	1·4	1·1	·5	·5	·5
	E														
India	*I*							·6	·4	·2	·3		·1		—
	E	1·2	·6	1·1	·2	·2	·3	·1		·2					
U.S.	*I*		·5	·4	·4	·4	·3	·5	·4	·5	·4	·2	·3	·5	1·1
	E	2·5	2·7	4·5	2·4	3·8	4·6	2·6	2·5	2·4	2·2	1·5	·2	·5	—
Russia	*I*	·1													
	E	3·3	·3	·3	·4	1	·8			2·5	2·5	·6	·7	·2	·7
Rye:															
Germany	*I*	·4	·9	·5	·4	·2	·8	·3	·1		·1	·6	·2	·1	·2
	E	·9			·2	·3	·1	·4	·6	·2	·1	·1	·3	·1	—
U.S.	*I*														
	E		·8	·9	·7	·3									
Russia	*I*				·2		·9	·4							
	E	·6	1·2	·6	·2	·2	·4			·6	1·4	·4	·2	·1	—
Wheat Flour:															
U.K.	*I*	·6	·6	·6	·5	·5	·6	·5	·5	·6	·5	·4	·5	·5	·4
	E	·1	·2	·3	·4	·2	·2	·2	·2	·2	·2	·2	·2	·1	
Germany	*I*		·1	·6	·4	·1	·1								
	E	·2			·1	·1		·1	·1				·2	·2	
France...	*I*													·1	
	E			·1						·3	·4	·1	·2	·2	·2
Canada	*E*	·4	1	1	·9	·9	·8	1	·9	·7	·5	·5	·5	·4	4
Argentine	*E*	·1	·1	·2	·1		·2	·2	·1	·1	·1	·1	·1	·1	·1
U.S.	*E*	1	1·5	1·4	1	1·1	1·1	1·1	1·2	1·2	·9	·5	·4	·4	·3
Barley:															
U.K.	*I*	1·1	1	1·1	·8	·6	·8	·7	·6	·8	·8	·5	·8	·8	·9
Germany	*I*	3·2	·3	·6	·9	1·7	2	1·9	1·8	1·5	·8	·5	·2	·6	·2
France...	*I*	·1	·1	·1					·1	·2	·4	·4	·2	·2	·2
Canada	*E*	·3	·3	·5	·7	·8	·7	·8	·4	·1	·5	·2		·2	·2
Rumania	*E*	·4	·8	·3	·2		·7	·4	1·2	1·4	1	·5	·6	·3	·2
U.S.	*E*	·4	·3	·5	·6	·3	·8	1·1	·6	·2	·2	·2	·2	·1	·2
Russia	*E*	3·9	·2	·2	·5	·7	?	?	·2	1·2	1·0	·4	·6	·2	·6
Maize:															
U.K.	*I*	2·5	1·8	1·9	1·4	1·6	2·1	1·6	1·7	1·6	2·6	2·5	2·6	3	2·9
	E		·1	·1	·1	·1									
Germany	*I*	·9	·3	·4	·6	·7	2·1	1·3	·7	·7	·5	·8	·3	·4	·3
France...	*I*	·6	·6	·6	·5	·6	·8	·7	·8	·8	1·1	1·2	·7	·6	·6
Italy	*I*	·4	·4	·1	·2	·5	·4	·9	·8	·7	·7	·6	·1	·2	·2
Argentine	*E*	4·8	2·9	4·5	2·9		8·3	5·4	5	4·7	9·8	7·1	5	5·5	7·1
U.S.	*I*			·1			·1							·1	
	E	1·2	1·1	·5	·3	·6	·3	·9	·9	·2	·1	·2	·1	·1	
Russia	*E*	·6		·2	·1	·3	·1			·1	·1	·3	·1	·1	

		1913	1923	1924	1925	1926	1927	1928	1929	1930	1931	1932	1933	1934	1935
Oats:															
U.K.	*I*	·9	·5	·5	·4	·4	·3	·4	·4	·5	·4	·3	·3	·2	·2
Germany	*I*	·5		·1	·4	·3	·3	·2	·1						·2
	E	·7		·1	·1	·1	·1	·3	·5	·4			·1		
France...	*I*	·6	·1	·1	·1	·1	·1		·1	·1	·1	·2			
Argentine	*E*	·9	·5	·7	·4		·6	·3	·4	·5	·6	·7	·4	·5	·4
Canada	*E*	·5	·4	·5	·7	·2	·1	·2	·1		·2	·2	·1	·2	·2
U.S.	*E*	·5			·5	·2	·1	·2	·1			·1			
Russia	*E*	·6	·1				·1			·4	·4		·1	·1	·2
Rice:															
U.K.	*I*	·2	·2	·2	·2	·1	·1	·1	·1	·1	·1	·1	·1	·1	·1
Germany	*I*	·5	·2	·4	·5	·3	·3	·4	·3	·3	·4	·4	·3	·3	·2
	E	·2		·2	·2	·2	·1	·1	·1	·1	·1				
India	*E*	2·5	2·2	2·3	2·6	2·1	2·2	1·8	2·4	2·3	2·2	2·2	1·9	1·4	1·7
Italy	*E*	·1	·1	·2	·2	·2	·3	·2	·2	·2	·2	·2	·2	·2	·1
Indo-China	*E*		1	·9	1·1		1·5	1·6	1·3		·9	1·1	1·2	1·4	1·7
U.S.	*I*					·1									
	E		·1	·1			·1	·1	·1	·1	·1	·1	·1		·1

(*c*) *Foreign Trade in Rice.*

	In 1,000 Metric Tons.								
	1927.	1928.	1929.	1930.	1931.	1932.	1933.	1934.	1935.
(1) *Imports*:									
British Malaya	858	820	811	816	704	605	609	636	672
Ceylon	486	510	513	470	461	470	458	485	566
China ...	1,275	765	655	1,203	650	1,360	1,295	771	1,296
Manchuria							337	741	80
Formosa	122	46	84	12	2	35	7	1	
Japan ...	1,812	1,505	1,238	1,180	1,765	1,693	1,748	2,069	1,822
Dutch Indies	470	570	735	627	608	424	334	279	387
(2) *Exports*:									
British Malaya	296	281	234	210	177	187	163	169	188
Formosa	407	328	316	297	412	528	544	727	615
Korea ...	877	955	788	700	1,228	1,018	1,079	1,348	1,108
Siam ...	1,540	1,320	1,006	928	1,202	1,518	1,530	1,863	

(*d*) *Japanese Balance of Foreign Trade in Rice.*

	In 1,000 Metric Tons.								
	1927.	1928.	1929.	1930.	1931.	1932.	1933.	1934.	1935.
Imports ...	1,934	1,551	1,322	1,192	1,767	1,728	2,192	2,811	1,902
Exports ...	1,284	1,304	1,147	1,089	1,839	1,617	1,652	2,164	1,794
Balance ...	—650	—247	—175	—103	+72	—111	—540	—647	—118
Annual averages	—202						—594		

Note.

Total production of rice in the Japanese Empire, 1929 to 1935 ... 96·5 million metric tons.
Import surplus ... ... 2·5 ,, ,, ,,

Total consumption ... ... 99·1 ,, ,, ,,

Net importation in per cent. of total consumption ... ... 2½ per cent.

(3) PRICES.

	In RM. per 100 Kg.											
	Annual Averages.											July,
	1913.	1926.	1927.	1928.	1929.	1930.	1931.	1932.	1933.	1934.	1935.	1936.
(a) WHEAT.												
Germany: Berlin, " märkisch " ...	18·81	26·81	26·71	23·40	22·78	25·64	24·88	22·95	18·71	19·61	20·74	21·94
France: Paris, home wheat	23·18					24·51	28·42	24·23	18·18	19·61	12·97	17·94
Great Britain: London, Plata, Rosario, spot	14·86	25·05	23·24	20·23	19·88	16·29	10·83[3]	8·57[3]	7·30[3]	6·08[3]	6·90[3]	
U.S.: New York, red winter II, spot	15·92	26·11	23·03	25·97	22·23	17·42	12·37[1]	9·90[1]	10·52[1]	9·50[1]	9·56[1]	11·35
Canada: Winnipeg, North Man. I, spot	13·61	23·07	22·85	20·81	20·70	14·57	8·73[2]	7·56[2]	6·78[2]	6·94[2]	7·69[2]	8·54
(b) WHEAT FLOUR.												
Great Britain: London, stand. ex mill						25·71	16	13·33	12·46	10·92	11·88	13·75
(c) RYE.												
Berlin: " märk."	15·55	19	24·90	23·91	19·24	16·19	18·28	17·85	16·04	16·31	16·82	17·13
Poland: Poznan, home, spot	15·64	13·78	19·98	19·22	13·39	9	10·89	9·80	7·66	7·21	6·27	6·27
(d) OATS.												
Berlin: " märk."	15·97	18·46	21·60	22·63	18·42	15·25	15·60	14·75	13·29	16·44	?	?
Buenos Aires: home	9·78	11·82	13·07	15·90	12·73	6·95	5·52	5·70	4·33	3·91	4·78	5·64[4]
(e) BARLEY.												
Winnipeg: Western III, spot... ...	8·90	11·98	15·46	15·40	13·95	7·61	5·74	5·93	7·90	5·34	4·78	5·87
(f) MAIZE.[5]												
New York: mixed II, spot	?	14·37	16·30	17·35	17·72	15·78	11·12	6·82	6·41	7·14	9·43	9·91
(g) RICE.												
Bombay: Rangoon	17·15	26·89	25·56	22·84	21·80	18·84	11·17	10·39	9·26	6·23	7·66	7·52

See footnotes at bottom of opposite page.

(4) Visible Stocks of Grains.

	In Million of Metric Tons.					
	Wheat.[1]	Rye.	Barley.	Oats.	Maize.	Rice.
1925	6·99		·23	·1	·60	
1926	6·71		·22	·07	·64	
1927	7·94		·24	·08	1·04	·25
1928	9·89	·26	·63	·44	1·39	·21
1929	13·29	·42	·88	·7	1·37	·14
1930	13·74	·72	1·04	·64	1·26	·15
1931	15·90	·76	·77	·55	1·85	·17
1932	14·45	·54	·45	·55	1·98	·22
1933	15·58	1·2	·86	·88	2·63	·17
1934	15·65	1·54	·94	·79	2·77	·14
1935	13·47	1·73	·77	·72	1·76	·16

[1] Up to 1927, inclusive, these figures comprise only: U.S., Canada, Australia, Argentine, the ports of the U.K., stocks afloat.

Further included from 1928 ... Union of South Africa.
1929 ... Hungary.
1931 ... Rotterdam, Antwerp and France.
1933 ... Germany.
1934 ... Italy.

This qualification applies also to the statistics for rye, oats, barley and maize.

2.—SUGAR.

(1) Production of Sugar Cane.

	In Million Quintals.		
	1925–29.	1933.	1935.
India	?	?	
Dutch Indies	231	115	46[1]
Formosa	55	47	73
Philippines	?	?	
Egypt	17	23	21
Mauritius	22	22	16
Union of South Africa	22	29[2]	30[1]
Argentine	51	39	38
Cuba	406	178	203
Mexico	40	28	28[1]
Peru	34	33	34
Puerto Rico	56	65	58
U.S.	17	26	27
Australia	38	38	46
Hawaii	66	78	?

[1] 1934. [2] 1932.

	1931.	1932.	1933.	1934.	1935.
[1] In cents per 60 lbs.	80·13	64·13	86·97	103·24	104·33
[2] ,, ,, ,, ,, ,, ...	58·72	55·59	60·94	74·79	84·40
[3] In shillings and pence for 480 lbs. ...	21/6	25/3	21/10½	20/11¾	24/7

[4] Monthly average, October, 1935.

	1913.	1926.	1930.	1934.	1935.
[5] Argentine maize, Buenos Aires, yellow	9·30	11·21	8·75	4·79	3·88

(2) PRODUCTION OF SUGAR BEET.

	In Million Quintals.		
	1928–32.	1933.	1935.
Germany	112	86	106
Belgium	17	15	15
Bulgaria	2	3	2
Denmark	11	17	19
France	72	75	87
Great Britain	21	33	32
Irish Free State	1	2	5[1]
Italy	28	1	23
Yugoslavia	8	5	5
Latvia	—	2	3
Holland	18	19	15
Austria	9	11	11
Poland	39	19	25
Rumania	7	7	6
Sweden	11	18	19
Spain	20	20	23[1]
Czechoslovakia	56	29	37
Hungary	13	9	7
U.S.S.R.	98	90	162
Asia	?	5	2
Canada	4	4	4
U.S.	74	100	72
WORLD	?	540	653[1]

[1] 1934.

(3) PRODUCTION OF SUGAR, BY COUNTRIES.

	In Million Metric Tons of Raw Sugar.		
	1913–14.	1934–35.	1935–36.
Germany	2·2	1·7	1·7
Czechoslovakia	—	·6	·6
U.S.S.R.	1·4[1]	1·4	2·5
France	1	1·2	·9
U.S.[2]	·8	1·5	1·5
Hawaii	·6	·9	·9
Cuba	2·6	2·6	2·6
India	2·4	3·1	3·6
Java	1·4	·5	·6
Japan and Formosa	·2	1·1	1·1
TOTAL, beet sugar	9	9·8	10·3
TOTAL, cane sugar	10·1	14·7	16·1
TOTAL SUGAR	19·1	24·5	26·4

[1] Territory of Tsarist Russia.

[2] U.S., including Hawaii and Puerto Rico: 1913–14, 1·9; 1934–35, 3; 1935–36, 3·3.

(4) Total World Production.

	In Million Metric Tons of Raw Sugar.		
	Beet Sugar.	Cane Sugar.	Total Sugar.
1912/13	8·9	9·5	18·4
1913/14	9	10·1	19·1
1929/30	9·3	17·8	27·1
1930/31	11·9	16·4	28·3
1931/32	8·7	16·7	25·4
1932/33	7·9	15	22·9
1933/34	9	15	24
1934/35	9·8	14·7	24·5
1935/36	10·3	16·1	26·4

(5) International Trade in Raw and Refined Sugar, by Countries.

	In Million Metric Tons.			
	1929.	1932.	1934.	1935.
A. Imports:				
Great Britain	2·1	2·4	2	2
Japan	1	·9	·8	1
U.S.	4·4	2·6	2·7	2·7
France	·5	·4	·4	·4
India	·9	·4	·2	·2
China	·4	·4	·2	·3
B. Exports:				
Dutch Indies	2·4	1·5	1·1	1
Philippines	·7	1	1·2	5
Cuba	5	2·7	2·4	
Czechoslovakia	·5	·4	·2	·2
Japan and Formosa	1	1	·8	1·1

(6) Total International Trade in Sugar, Exports.

	1929	1930	1931	1932	1933	1934
Quantities, in million metric tons	13	11·3	9·7	9·6	8·5	8·5
Values, in RM. million ...	3,022	2,283	1,662	1,295	1,018	858

(7) Stocks.

Million Metric Tons.									
1927	1928	1929	1930	1931	1932	1933	1934	1935	June, 1936
4·9	5·3	6·1	7·1	8·8	9	8·7	8·2	7·4	5·8

(8) NET SUGAR EXPORTS OF CERTAIN COUNTRIES.[1]

	In 1,000 Metric Tons.				
	1931	1932	1933	1934	1935
Germany	341	56	−1	−13	−9
Belgium	2	−1	20	−14	10
France	−68	−127	240	248	−106
Holland	−81	−118	−55	−23	−64
Poland	345	185	114	101	107
Hungary	52	17	22	40	13

[1] Figures with negative sign = net imports.

(9) PRICES.

	In RM. per 100 Kg.							
	Annual Averages.							
	1913	1930	1931	1932	1933	1934	1935	Dec. 1935
Great Britain, London, Java White, cif. India ...	22·16	18·36	15·08	11·58	10·11	7·50	7·52	7·98
								July, 1936
Czechoslovakia, raw, 88° ...	18·06	11·73	9·33	7·20	7·16	5·58	5·11	4·66
U.S., N. York, Cuba, 96° centr. excluding duty ...	20	14·07	12·41	8·61	8·89	9·35	17·87	15·37

(10) HOME CONSUMPTION IN CERTAIN COUNTRIES.

	In 1,000 Metric Tons of Raw Sugar.									
	1913/14	1929/30	1931/32	1933/34	1934/35	1929	1930	1931	1932	1933
Germany ...	1,430	1,655	1,449	1,506	1,547					
Great Britain		1,813	2,102	1,920						
Italy		355	313							
U.S.		4,513	5,466							
Belgium ...						200	211	198		
France ...						942	901	968	959	965

3.—RUBBER.

(1) WORLD PRODUCTION, STOCKS AND PRICES.

	1913	1920	1925	1928	1929	1930	1931	1932	1933	1934	1935	June, 1936
World *production*, 1,000 tons	114	347	510	673	882	839	812	721	863	1,034	887	
Stocks, 1,000 tons ...			137	271	311	442	588	621	664	733	721	561
Amsterdam, stand. plant, *price*, RM. per 100 Kg.	709			202	189	108	54	30	41	71	68	86

(2) Changes in Stocks During Stevenson Scheme.

In 1,000 Metric Tons.				
1925	1926	1927	1928	1929
137	174	282	271	311

(3) Production, in Certain Countries.

	In 1,000 Metric Tons.																
	1913	1920	1921	1922	1923	1924	1925	1926	1927	1928	1929	1930	1931	1932	1933	1934	1935
British Malaya ...	33	174	151	216	168	168	201	299	246	304	464	451	430	413	453	475	424
Dutch Indies	5	79	68	89	118	168	193	211	233	233	259	245	261	214	285	384	288

(3a) Production, by Countries.

	In 1,000 Metric Tons.		
	1920	1925	1934
Africa	6	8	3
Mexico	—	4	—
South America	33	31	9
British Borneo	6	15	29
Ceylon	40	46	80
India	6	11	12
Dutch Indies	79	192	384
French Indo-China	3	8	20
British Malaya	174	213	475
Siam		5	18
Total Asia	308	490	1,018
Oceania, including Philippines ...		1	1
World Totals	347	534	1,031
Colonial		483	992
Non-Colonial		51	39

(3b) Plantation and Wild Rubber, Production.

	In 1,000 Metric Tons.							
	1913	1920	1921	1922	1923	1924	1925	1935
Plantation rubber ...	51	311	274	368	342	377	466	869
Total, including wild rubber	63	36	24	28	28	30	38	18

(4) INTERNATIONAL TRADE: WORLD EXPORTS OF RUBBER, GUTTAPERCHA AND BALATA.

	1929	1930	1931	1932	1933	1934	1935
Quantities, in 1,000 metric tons	1,139	1,058	1,005	875	1,111	1,308	1,111
Values, in RM. million ...	1,723	1,038	485	234	358	679	590

(5) NET IMPORTS, 1934.

In 1,000 Metric Tons (— = net exports).

Germany	64	Japan	71
Belgium and Luxemburg	15	India	−11
France	58	Ceylon	−81
Great Britain	160	Dutch Indies	−385
Italy	22	Brazil	−12
U.S.S.R.	48	Canada	29
British Malaya	−472	U.S.	446

4.—TIMBER.

(1) FOREIGN TRADE.

		In 1,000 Metric Tons. 1929.	1932.	1933.	1934.
A. IMPORTS *I. Hard Wood, unsawn*	Germany ...	479	210	235	324
	Belgium and Luxemburg ...	275	177	192	174
	France	?	65	105	113
	Great Britain ...	102	50	43	63
	Holland	67	55	52	57
	Switzerland ...	53	50	41	55
	Czechoslovakia ...	15	45	31	40
	China	87	105	148	122
	Japan	42	—	4	9
	Canada	23	9	28	82
	TOTALS	1,143	766	879	1,039
II. Pit Prop Material	Germany ...	285	86	28	81
	Belgium and Luxemburg ...	576	435	568	417
	France	165	198	239	259
	Great Britain ...	2,073	1,476	1,494	1,754
	Holland	145	132	180	120
	Czechoslovakia ...	132	25	1	—
	Hungary	114	78	65	64
	TOTALS	3,490	2,430	2,575	2,695
III. Wood for Pulp and Paper	Germany ...	2,534	1,200	2,472	3,018
	Holland	340	84	259	323
	Sweden	62	42	23	19
	Czechoslovakia ...	147	56	48	49
	Canada	81	82	33	27
	U.S.	2,934	1,408	1,571	2,109
	Norway ...	—	267	139	81
	TOTALS	6,098	3,139	4,525	5,626

		1929.	1932.	1933.	1934.
IV. Other Soft Wood, unsawn	Germany ...	1,623	300	372	986
	Denmark ...	76	30	32	24
	Finland	158	241	253	360
	France	491	140	136	116
	Great Britain ...	328	327	258	312
	Italy	442	221	254	321
	Holland	361	120	195	207
	Sweden	138	90	93	126
	Switzerland ...	157	166	134	108
	Hungary	311	134	145	251
	China	244	207	177	140
	Manchuria ...	—	—	161	122
	Japan and Korea	934	587	512	462
	U.S.	443	172	213	106
	Norway ...	197	267	?	?
	Czechoslovakia ...	182	32	—	—
	TOTALS	6,085	3,034	2,935	3,641
V. Hard Wood, sawn	Germany ...	159	16	17	58
	France	17	29	13	9
	Great Britain ...	662	584	594	720
	Holland	57	39	43	47
	Austria	35	14	6	7
	Sweden	—	9	8	15
	Switzerland ...	57	51	35	38
	Czechoslovakia ...	35	27	17	15
	Hungary	31	6	3	10
	China	34	31	33	34
	Canada	167	41	39	47
	U.S.	162	29	51	39
	TOTALS	1,416	876	859	1,039
VI. Soft Wood, sawn	Germany ...	1,645	583	583	1,039
	Belgium and Luxemburg ...	1,005	669	627	554
	Denmark ...	409	257	391	481
	Finland	—	54	125	104
	France	1,285	775	726	591
	Great Britain ...	4,009	3,246	4,300	4,843
	Irish Free State	81	74	110	?
	Italy	1,194	835	976	931
	Holland	1,392	851	1,279	1,140
	Norway ...	190	97	49	67
	Spain	591	348	303	320
	Hungary	461	221	210	274
	Union of South Africa	224	117	182	272
	China	428	193	344	311
	Manchuria ...	—	—	74	94
	Japan and Korea	1,064	466	423	396
	Canada	172	26	22	43
	U.S.	2,008	484	438	345
	Commonwealth of Australia ...	459	162	245	257
	Czechoslovakia ...	139	17	4	1
	TOTALS	16,756	9,475	11,411	11,263

		1929	1932	1933	1934
VII. Wooden Sleepers	Germany ...	237	6	3	20
	Belgium and Luxemburg ...	93	22	53	70
	Denmark ...	31	9	4	5
	France	15	11	7	5
	Great Britain ...	284	171	177	233
	Holland	91	81	30	27
	Spain	114	23	13	4
	China	—	83	133	167
	Manchuria ...	—	—	141	173
	Canada	57	10	7	10
	U.S.	63	29	31	29
	Austria	41	1	—	—
	Hungary	60	1	—	—
	New Zealand ...	16	—	—	—
	Totals	1,102	447	499	743
B. Exports *I. Hard Wood, unsawn*	Germany ...	86	93	76	57
	Yugoslavia ...	114	29	30	51
	Poland	197	75	92	102
	U.S.S.R. ...	95	62	33	2
	French Equatorial Africa	?[1]	264	303	353
	French West Africa	83	38	58	61
	Totals	965	561	592	626
II. Pit Prop Material	Germany ...	373	299	304	217
	Finland	991	946	1,006	1,266
	France	868	256	173	190
	Latvia	384	135	135	116
	Poland	416	104	48	45
	Portugal ...	70	268	266	376
	U.S.S.R. ...	521	784	765	901
	Sweden	454	228	276	205
	Czechoslovakia ...	112	72	49	38
	Totals	4,189	3,092	3,022	3,354
III. Wood for Pulp and Paper	Finland	740	121	475	800
	Latvia	108	58	180	145
	Lithuania ...	177	75	124	134
	Austria	179	37	98	199
	Poland	1,172	152	337	352
	U.S.S.R. ...	1,477	1,304	1,693	1,798
	Czechoslovakia ...	196	428	434	520
	Canada	2,813	1,149	1,416	2,005
	Sweden	181	5	19	42
	U.S.	114	62	23	26
	Totals	7,157	3,391	4,799	6,021

		1929	1932	1933	1934
IV. Soft Wood, unsawn	Germany ...	287	204	172	99
	Finland	276	61	93	193
	Yugoslavia ...	253	85	122	129
	Austria	581	145	209	349
	Poland	396	62	150	284
	U.S.S.R. ...	776	664	556	476
	Sweden	300	99	141	168
	Czechoslovakia ...	535	210	247	608
	Brazil	104	82	84	?
	Canada	683	330	435	390
	U.S.	566	174	215	322
	France	201	44	50	54
	TOTALS	4,958	2,160	2,474	3,072
V. Hard Wood, sawn	Yugoslavia ...	324	186	230	236
	Poland	154	74	96	116
	Rumania ...	104	62	67	81
	U.S.S.R. ...	12	79	107	187
	Canada	176	84	111	133
	U.S.	762	400	487	463
	TOTALS	1,532	885	1,098	1,216
VI. Soft Wood, sawn	Esthonia	169	45	129	218
	Finland	3,165	1,881	2,491	2,719
	Yugoslavia ...	722	272	356	414
	Latvia	396	213	369	386
	Austria	1,044	549	574	576
	Poland	830	441	789	785
	Rumania ...	1,007	518	436	601
	U.S.S.R. ...	2,301	2,600	2,799	2,816
	Sweden	2,579	1,617	1,892	1,969
	Czechoslovakia ...	256	118	109	238
	Canada	2,598	1,039	1,511	1,986
	U.S.	3,507	1,182	1,294	1,386
	Norway ...	132	72	48	45
	Australia ...	114	58	34	30
	TOTALS	18,820	10,578	12,831	14,169
VII. Wooden Sleepers	Yugoslavia ...	—	17	12	43
	Poland	219	54	77	157
	U.S.S.R. ...	177	171	167	86
	U.S.	362	76	137	222
	TOTALS	758	318	393	508

[1] 1930: 390.

(2) SUMMARY OF FOREIGN TRADE IN TIMBER.

			In 1,000 Metric Tons.			
			1929	1932	1233	1934
A. IMPORTS	I	... Hard wood, unsawn	1,143	766	879	1,039
	II	... Pit prop material	3,490	2,430	2,575	2,695
	III	... Wood for pulp and paper	6,098	3,139	4,525	5,626
	IV	... Soft wood, unsawn	6,085	3,034	2,935	3,641
	V	... Hardwood, sawn	1,416	876	859	1,039
	VI	... Soft wood, sawn	16,756	9,475	11,411	11,263
	VII	... Wooden sleepers	1,102	447	499	743
		TOTALS	36,090	20,167	23,683	26,106
B. EXPORTS	I	... Hard wood, unsawn	965	561	592	626
	II	... Pit prop material	4,189	3,092	3,022	3,354
	III	... Wood for pulp and paper	7,157	3,391	4,799	6,012
	IV	... Soft wood, unsawn	4,958	2,160	2,474	3,072
	V	... Hard wood, sawn	1,532	885	1,098	1,216
	VI	... Soft wood, sawn...	18,820	10,578	12,831	14,169
	VII	... Wooden sleepers	758	318	393	508
		TOTALS	38,379	20,985	25,209	28,966

5.—WOOD PULP, PRODUCTION.

	In 1,000 Metric Tons of Dry Weight.	
	1925	1933
Canada	2,455	2,703
U.S.	3,594	3,898
Asia	422	647
U.S.S.R.	75	472
Rest of Europe	5,890	8,030
Germany...	1,650	1,700
Finland	624	1,379
Norway	812	855
Sweden	1,733	2,563
TOTALS	12,610	16,020

6.—OIL SEEDS, ARRANGED ALPHABETICALLY.

(1) Copra.

(a) *Production, by Countries.*

In 1,000 Metric Tons.

	1922	1923	1924	1925	1926	1927	1928	1929	1930	1931	1932	1933	1934	1935
Africa	35	38	42	49	50	47	50	51	54	54	57	61	64	
British Col. Africa ...	20				28			26			28		27	
French Africa	1				2			4			3		4	
Colonial Africa	35				50			51			57		64	
British Central America[1]	6	10	8	8	14	12	19	20	18	15	13	15	11	
Asia	968	886	929	958	1,067	1,013	1,248	1,304	1,092	1,104	1,083	1,370	1,363	1,330
British Colonial Asia ...	250				299			311			257		367	
French Asia	7				12			13			5		5	
Oceania	140	144	147	158	169	171	203	205	201	179	172	183	178	
British Colonial Oceania	44				69			87			54		38	
French Oceania	24				14			31			21		30	
World	1,150	1,079	1,126	1,175	1,300	1,243	1,519	1,579	1,365	1,352	1,324	1,629	1,646	1,580
Colonial[2]	1,127				1,300			1,579			1,005		1,044	
Non-Colonial	23				—			—			319		572	

[1] Including British Guiana. [2] The Philippines counted as colonial, prior to 1930.

(b) *Prices.*

In Gold Francs per 100 Kg.; end of Year.

	1923	1924	1925	1926	1927	1928	1929	1930	1931	1932	1933	1934	1935
London, Ceylon copra	73·78	71·80	78·35	69·02	72·43	64·99	60·02	41·99	29·31	27·57	17·24	17·28	20·89[1]

[1] June.

(2) Cotton Seed.

(*a*) *Production.*

In 1,000 Metric Tons.

	1923.	1924.	1925.	1926.	1927.	1928.	1929.	1930.	1931.	1932.	1933.	1934.	1935.
Africa	726	853	961	906	745	996	998	977	827	724	1,070	1,031	1,120
Non-Colonial Africa	611	677	745	711	565	745	790	762	583	455	784	692	760
North America	4,084	5,489	6,486	7,247	5,224	5,838	5,978	5,616	6,896	5,245	5,264	3,885	4,380
Central America	102	117	119	198	104	155	123	91	106	57	120	105	110
Colonial Central America ...	2	2	2	4	3	3	4	6	3	1	1	2	
South America ...	390	406	430	399	434	403	513	426	479	410	725	1,014	1,170
Asia[1]	3,420	4,036	4,261	3,482	4,062	4,365	3,976	4,301	3,629	4,098	4,508	4,741	4,960
Colonial Asia ...	66	69	73	76	78	84	85	91	66	75	80	82	105
Europe	9	11	12	62	38	69	64	52	57	31	82	104	150
Oceania	6	8	5	4	6	4	7	6	8	6	9	7	
Colonial Oceania	1	1	2	1	1	1	1	1	1				
World	8,740	10,920	12,274	12,300	10,610	11,820	11,660	11,470	11,950	14,560	11,720	10,820	11,900
Colonial	184	248	293				298			345	367	423	467
Non-Colonial ...	8,556	10,672	11,981				11,362			10,215	11,253	10,397	11,433

[1]Including U.S.S.R. in Asia.

(b) Prices.

	In Gold Francs per 100 Kg; end of Year.								
	1927	1928	1929	1930	1931	1932	1933	1934	1935
London, Sakellaridis	28·63	23·65	19·93	14·07	10·11	12·22	6·72	9·06	9·64

(3) Ground-Nuts (Pea-Nuts).

(a) Production.

Countries.	In 1,000 Metric Tons.							
	1922	1925	1928	1929	1932	1933	1934	1935
Africa	610	917	1,140	1,270	1,260	1,390	1,380	
Colonial Africa ...	595			1,248	1,230		1,358	
U.S.	287	317	388	434	471	411	482	573
Mexico	9	8	8	6	5	5	7	
South America ...	51	79	57	74	90	115	100	
Asia	1,797	2,753	3,550	3,110	4,050	4,130	2,720	2,900
Colonial Asia[1] ...	310			550	792		493	
Spain	21	22	27	26	20	21	21	
Australia... ...			3	4	1	2		
World	2,770	4,090	5,170	4,920	5,900	6,070	4,710	
Colonial[1] ...	905			1,798	2,022		1,851	
Non-Colonial ...	1,865			3,122	3,878		2,859	

[1] After 1925, including Manchuria, after 1930 excluding the Philippines.

(b) Prices.

	In Gold Francs per 100 Kg., End of Years.									
	1923	1925	1928	1929	1930	1931	1932	1933	1934	1935
London, Coromandel, shelled	56·58	53·66	49·75	44·67	26·99	22·72	22·12	15·40	17·47	20·46

(4) Hemp-seed.

(a) Production.

Countries.	In 1,000 metric tons.						
	1921	1925	1928	1929	1932	1933	1934
Europe	266	600	603	464	329	269	325
U.S.S.R.	218	550	560	410	280	219	277
World	268	604	605	465	329	270	325

Without China, which is a very important producer; no reliable statistics exist.

(b) Prices.

	In Gold Francs per 100 Kg., End of Years.									
	1923	1925	1928	1929	1930	1931	1932	1933	1934	1935
London, Manchurian ...	36·75	50·87	37·22	28·54	20·20	17·52	15·65	13·32	10·80	17·07

(5) Linseed.

(a) Production.

Countries.	In 1,000 Metric Tons. 1921	1925	1928	1929	1932	1933	1934	1935
Africa	16	25	15	13	13	8	15	12
North America	308	728	579	457	367	194	159	420
Mexico		1	1	1	4	2	2	
South America ...	929	9,160	2,044	1,353	1,614	1,665	2,110	1,367
Asia	292	521	357	331	427	430	416	470
Europe	378	791	777	964	906	868	845	
U.S.S.R. ...	347	576	600	710	800	740	690	
Oceania	3	2	1	5		8	1	
World			3,770	3,120	3,330	3,170	3,550	

(b) Prices.

	In Gold Francs per 100 Kg., End of Years. 1922	1925	1928	1929	1932	1933	1934	1935
Buenos Aires, 4% extraneous matter...	35·26	36·39	33·65	42·19	11·97	13·24	12·10	12·40

(6) Olive Oil, Production.

Annual Average.	In 1,000 Quintals. 1909–13	1920	1930	1933
Colonial Africa	604	868	535	786
U.S.	1	1	10	?
Colonial Asia	200	422	370	166
Europe	5,023	6,712	3,620	6,830
World	5,830	8,005	4,540	7,790
Colonial	804	1,290	905	952
Non-Colonial	5,826	6,715	3,635	6,838

(7) Palm Oil and Palm-Kernel Oil, Raw, Net Exportation.

	In 1,000 Quintals. Annual Average. 1909–13	1921	1930	1933
Liberia	—	5	?	56
Colonial Africa	2,651	2,155	4,628	4,434
Brazil	2	35	55	3
Dutch Indies	—	—	537	1,267
World	2,653	2,195	5,220	5,760
Colonial	2,651	2,155	5,165	5,701
Non-Colonial	2	40	55	59

(8) Rape Seed.

(a) *Production.*

	In 1,000 Metric Tons.							
	1921.	1925.	1928.	1929.	1932.	1933.	1934.	1935.
Asia[1]	970	1,309		925	1,133	1,151	1,066	1,031
Europe[1]	208	174		160	138	92	137	230
World[1]	1,178	1,483		1,085	1,219	1,243	1,204	1,260

[1] Without: China, U.S.S.R. and from 1921 to 1925 Germany; *i.e.*, without nearly all important producers.

(b) *Prices.*

	In Gold Francs per 100 Kg.; End of Years.									
	1922.	1925.	1928.	1929.	1930.	1931.	1932.	1933.	1934.	1935.
Hull: Toria	39·81	51·18	47	45·91	26·79	21·16	20·18	15·57	17·59	19·67

(9) Sesamum.

(a) *Production.*

	In 1,000 Metric Tons.							
	1922.	1925.	1928.	1929.	1932.	1933.	1934.	1935.
Africa	40	40	51	67	67	57	67	
French Africa	3	3		5	5	7		
British Colonial Africa[1] ...	5	31		42	46	36		
Italian Africa	?	2		2	—	?		
All Colonial Africa ...	40	35		63	62	51		
Mexico	5	10	15	11	16	13	14	
Asia	582	476	582	574	614	619	513	600
British Colonial Asia	4	3		5	1	—	3	
Japan and Colonies[2] ...	9	8		8	14	30	45	
All Colonial Asia	11	11		19	17	31		
Europe		13	41	55	46	46	46	
World	640	539	689	707	743	734	640	720
Colonial	51	46		82	79	82		
Non-Colonial	589	493		625	664	652		

Note.—Chinese production large but size unknown; in some important colonial countries only exports are recorded; these and Chinese exports are included in the table.
[1] Including the Anglo-Egyptian Sudan. [2] Including Manchuria.

(b) *Prices.*

	In Gold Francs per 100 Kg.; End of Years.								
	1927.	1928.	1929.	1930.	1931.	1932.	1933.	1934.	1935.
London: Chinese	60·89	55·64	45·40	33·11	24·01	24·69	18·38	20·89	22·56

(10) Soya Beans.

(a) *Production.*

	In 1,000 Metric Tons.							
	1922.	1925.	1928.	1929.	1932.	1933.	1934.	1935.
Japanese Empire[1]	185	133	5,735	5,754	5,148	6,160	4,122	
World	1,617	5,533	6,117[2]	6,100	5,193	6,787	4,880	

[1] Including Manchuria after 1925. [2] Changed statistical method.

(b) *Prices.*

	In Gold Francs per 100 Kg.; end of Years.									
	1923.	1925.	1928.	1929.	1930.	1931.	1932.	1933.	1934.	1935.
Hull, Manchurian ...	30·62	31·33	29	25·44	17·06	12·76	12·14	9·79	9·53	11·12

(11) Whale Oil, Production.

	1920–21.	1925–26.	1928–29.	1929–30.	1930–31.	1931–32.	1932–33.	1933–34.	1934–35.
No. of whales caught ...	12,174	28,193	27,896	37,674	42,874	12,797	28,668	32,167	39,056
Production of oil, in 1,000 tons	79·8	195·2	319·4	474	624·3	155·1	439·7	435·7	454·5

7.—COTTON.

(1) Production (Excluding Linters and Seed).

	(a) In Million Quintals.			(b) Percentages of World Harvest.		
Type of Cotton.	1913–14.	1920–21.	1926–27.	1913–14.	1920–21.	1926–27.
American	33·6	31·6	43·4	59	58	65
Indian	9·3	9·5	9·1	16	17	14
Egyptian	3·4	2·7	3·9	6	5	6
All Sorts	56·8	54·5	66·5	Others ... 19	20	15
Country of Production.	1927–31.	1934.	1935.	1927–31.	1934.	1935.
U.S.	31·8	20·9	23·1	56	42	43
India	9·5	8·7	10·4	17	17	19
Egypt	3·4	3·5	3·8	6	7	7
World	56·6	50	53·5	U.S.S.R. 5	8	16
				Others ... 16	26[1]	15[2]

[1] Brazil, 3. [2] Brazil, 4.

(2) Exports.

(a) *Exports from Certain Countries; Raw Cotton, including Linters.*

	In 1,000 Metric Tons.					
	1913.	1925.	1929.	1932.	1934.	1935.
Egypt	313	289	343	301	385	384
India	530	757	713	291	621	571
U.S.	2,069	1,989	1,806	2,179	1,428	1,467
Proportion of Indian to U.S. cotton	1 : 3·9	1 : 2·6	1 : 2·5	1 : 7·5	1 : 2·3	1 : 2·6

(b) *Whole Volume of World Exports of Raw Cotton.*

	Unit.	1929.	1930.	1931.	1932.	1933.	1934.	1935.
Quantities	1,000 tons	3,333	3,040	3,015	3,157	3,278	2,999	3,079
Values ...	RM. million	5,908	3,994	2,581	2,158	2,182	1,958	2,025

(3) Consumption.

(a) *In Million Bales.*

[One bale=230 Kg. for American; 180 Kg. for Indian; 340 Kg. for Egyptian; 135 Kg. for other cotton.]

	U.S.-American.			Indian.			Egyptian.			All Types.		
	1913.	1930.	1934.	1913.	1930.	1934.	1913.	1930.	1934.	1913.	1930.	1934.
Germany	1·3	·9	1·1	·2	·3	·2	·1	·08	·1	1·7	1·3	1·5
Belgium	·2	·2	·1	·1	·2	·1				·3	·5	·3
France	·8	·7	·7	·1	·2	·2	·1	·1	·2	1	1·2	1·1
U.K.	3·7	1·5	1·5	·05	·2	·2	·4	·3	·4	4·3	2·5	2·5
Italy	·6	·7	·6	·2	·3	·1		·05	·08	·8	1·1	·9
U.S.S.R.	·5	·03	·06	·02	·2	·03	·1	·05		2·5	2·1	1·9
Spain	·3	·3	·3	·03	·1	·06		·03	·05	·4	·4	·4
Czechoslovakia ...	?	·3	·2	—	·1	·03		·02	·03	?	·5	·3
Europe	8·4	5·5	5·4	·9	1·6	1·1	·8	·7	·9	12·6	10·4	9·9
China	?	·3	·3	?	·5	·2				?	2·3	2·4
India	·1	·04	·04	2·1	2·2	2·2				2·2	2·4	2·5
Japan	·4	1·1	1·8	1	1·7	1·2				1·6	3	3·3
Asia	·5	1·4	2·2	3·1	4·4	3·6		·06	·1	3·8	7·7	8·1
U.S.	5·5	5·8	5·6	·1	·06		·1	·1		5·8	6·1	5·7
Brazil				·1						·5	·4	·5
America	5·7	6	5·8	·2	·06		·1	·1	·08	6·6	6·9	6·6
World	14·6	13	13·5	4·2	6·1	4·8	·9	·9	1·1	23	25·2	25·1

(b) *In* 1,000 *Metric Tons.*

	U.S.-American.		Indian.		Egyptian.		Totals.	
	1913.	1934.	1913.	1934.	1913.	1934.	1913.	1934.
Germany ...	299	253	36	36	34	34	379	341
Russia ...	115	14	4	·5	34	—	411	227
Great Britain	851	345	·9	·36	136	136	1,020	572
Asia	115	506	558	648	—	34	694	1,479
U.S.	1,265	1,288	18	11	34	—	1,321	1,303
WORLD ...	3,358	3,075	756	864	306	374	4,856	5,082

(4) STOCKS.

	In 1,000 Metric Tons.											
	1925.	1926.	1927.	1928.	1929.	1930.	1931.	1932.	1933.	1934.	1935.	1936.[1]
All types ...	1,039	1,276	1,527	1,313	1,344	1,646	1,966	2,087	2,070	1,822	1,411	1,230
American only	740	955	1,188	909	880	1,124	1,470	1,688	1,671	1,332	1,036	812

[1] End of June

(5) COTTON SPINDLES IN SOME IMPORTANT COUNTRIES AND IN THE WORLD.

	In Millions of Spindles ; July 31st.					
	1913.	1925.	1929.	1932.	1934.	1935.
Germany	11·2	9·5	11·3	10·2	10·1	10·1
France	7·4	9·4	9·9	10·1	10·2	10·2
U.K.	55·7	57·1	55·9	51·9	45·9	42·7
Italy	4·6	4·8	5·2	5·4	5·5	5·5
Austria	7·9[1]	1	1	·8	·8	·8
Russia	7·7[2]	7·2	7·5	9·2	9·8	9·8
Spain	2	1·8	1·9	2·1	2·1	2·1
Czechoslovakia	—	3·5	3·7	3·6	3·6	3·6
Belgium	1·5	1·9	2·2	2·2	2·1	2·1
Europe	99·5	101·1	104·3	101·4	96·2	92·9
China	?	3·4	3·6	4·3	4·7	4·8
India	6·1	8·5	8·7	9·3	9·6	9·6
Japan	2·3	5·3	6·3	7·8	9·1	9·9
Asia	8·4[3]	17·1	18·8	21·4	23·4	24·4
Brazil	1·2	2	2·8	2·7	2·7	2·7
U.S.	32·1	37·9	34·8	31·7	30·9	30·1
America	34·9	42	39·6	36·5	35·7	34·8
WORLD	143·5	161·4	164·2	161	156·9	153·8

[1] Including Czechoslovakia. [2] Excluding Poland and Finland. [3] Excluding China.

(5a) Cotton Looms, Excluding those Driven by Hand.

In Thousands.

Countries.	1913.	1920.	1933.	Countries.	1913.	1930.	1933.
Germany ...	230	224	223	Czechoslovakia	—	125	105
Belgium ...	24	54	55	India	94	180	190
France	108	200	198	Japan	21	188	277
U.K.	805	693	588	U.S.	696	699	614
Italy	140	147	147	Brazil	50	78	82
Holland... ...	40	55	56				
Austria	170[1]	14	13	Europe ...	1,875	1,914	1,847
Hungary		12	13	Asia	121	401	515
U.S.S.R. ...	213	159	250	America ...	804	842	766
Spain	55	81	67				
				World	2,807	3,159	3,130

Austro-Hungarian Monarchy.

(6) Prices.

	In RM. per 100 Kg.								
	1913.	1929.	1930.	1931.	1932.	1933.	1934.	1935.	July, 1936.
Egypt, Alexandria, Sakellaridis, futures	175·76	311·31	223	126·85	91·02	86·15	89·89	84	101·21
India, Bombay, Oomra I	85·03	127·57	80·79	65·19	60·52	52·59	51	55·34	54·92[1]
U.S., New York, middling upland, spot	118·76	177·13	125·74	79·26	59·63	62·41	68·14	65·37	71·94
Cotton yarn, U.K., Manchester, 32' ...	?	?	220	157	122	117	119	115·03	126·29

[1] June.

(7) Russia: Present Territory of the U.S.S.R. in Europe and Asia

	Unit.	1913.	1920.	1929.	1930.	1931.	1932.	1933.	1934.
Production of cotton ...	1,000 tons	740	10	860	1,110	1,290	1,270	1,315	1,320
Production of cotton piece goods	million metres	1,625	[5]	3,183	2,515	2,541	2,690	2,701	2,711
Imports of raw cotton ...	1,000 tons	196·9	—	115	57·9	53·7	24·3	22·5	22·6
Exports of raw cotton ...	" "	?	?	2·5	10·1	40·2	17·9	·6	11
Exports of cotton piece goods	" "	17·2	—	3·2	13·4	15·9	18·8	15·3	20·8

(8) PRODUCTION OF GINNED COTTON, ANNUAL AVERAGE, 1925–1929.

In 1,000 Q.

French Africa	96	Total, Central and South America ...	2,551	U.S.S.R.	2,158
Belgian Congo	57			Europe	267
Egypt	3,442	China[1]	4,465	Australia	16
Portuguese Africa ...	25	India	10,243	WORLD	57,700
British colonial Africa ...	403	Iraq	6	Colonial	921
Italian Africa	9	Iran	175	Non-colonial[2] ...	56,779
Anglo-Egyptian Sudan...	272	Siam	7		
Union of South Africa ...	25	Dutch Asia	10		
Total, Africa	4,330	Br. colonial Asia ...	5		
U.S.	33,104	Korea	298		
British West Indies ...	8	French Asia —	3		
Non-colonial Central and South America	2,543	Total, Asia	15,245		

[1] Very incomplete. [2] Proportion, 1934 : colonial, 1,100 ; non-colonial, 48,900 (roughly).

8.—MINOR TEXTILE FIBRES.

A.—Flax.

(1) PRODUCTION.

In 1,000 Quintals.

	Annual Average 1925–29.	1934.	1935.		Annual Average 1925–29.	1934.	1935.
Egypt ...	10	14		Rest of Europe	2,260	1,480	
Asia	37	24[1]					
U.S.S.R. ...	2,980	5,300	5,500	WORLD ...	5,290	6,800	9,691

[1] 1933.

(2) QUANTITY IN INTERNATIONAL TRADE.

In 1,000 Metric Tons.

1929.	1930.	1931.	1932.	1933.	1934.	1935.
406	316	265	272	246	280	305

(3) PRICES.

In RM. per 100 Kg.

	1913.	1930.	1931.	1932.	1933.	1934.	1935.	July, 1936.
Great Britain, London, Riga flax, spot ...	66·72	103·29	65·78	65·63	70·12	75·16	94·78	67·59

B.—Hemp.

(1) Production in Certain Countries.

	In 1,000 Quintals. Annual Averages 1925–29.[1]	1929–33.[2]	1934.[2]	1935.[2]
Chile	23			
Japanese Asia	293	280	258	
Philippines	1,855			
Total, Asia	2,166			
U.S.S.R.	3,189	2,278	1,565	
Rest of Europe	1,950	1,456	2,960	1,453
World	8,180	4,148	3,415	

[1] Including manilla hemp. [2] Excluding manilla hemp.

(2) International Trade: Exports of European Hemp.

In 1,000 Metric Tons.

1929.	1932.	1933.	1934.	1935.
127	69	78	85	90

(3) Prices.

	In RM. per 100 Kg.; Annual Averages. 1913.	1931.	1932.	1933.	1934.	1935.	July, 1936.
London, Man. J.2, futures	62·82	35·04	26·99	21·75	18·38	23·59	34·47

C.—Silk

(1) Production of Cocoons.

	In 1,000 Metric Tons. 1929.	1930.	1931.	1932.	1933.	1934.	1935.
Japan and Korea ...	398	417	382	355	401	350	329
China[1]	121	92	82	47	54	38	
France	2·5	1·8	1	1	·9	1	·7
Italy	53	53	34	38	35	29	18
Greece	2·5	1·9	1·7	1·9	2·2	2·6	
Turkey	1·8	1·6	1·4	1·2	1·9	1·9	
Bulgaria	2·4	2·3	1·1	1·3	1·4	·3	1·2
Yugoslavia	1·3	1·3	·8	·5	·7	·4	
Syria and Lebanon ...	3·5	3·7	2·8	1·7	1·8	1·2	·7
U.S.S.R.	15	19	20	10	14	15	18

[1] Exports.

(2) Production of Raw Silk.

In 1,000 Tons.

Countries.	1929.	1932.	1933.	1934.	1935.	Countries.	1929.	1932.	1933.	1934.	1935.
Korea and Japan	43·4	42·8	42·8	47	41	Rest of Europe	5·8	4·5	4·1	3·8	2·4
China[1]	10·2	4·2	4·6	3·5	4·6						
Total, Asia ...	54·3	47·3	48·7	50·8	45·9	World ...	61·4	52·6	54·2	56	49·9
U.S.S.R. ...	1·3	·9	1·2	[5]	1·5						

[1] Exports.

(3) Stocks and Prices.

	1925.	1926.	1927.	1928.	1929.	1930.	1931.	1932.	1933.	1934.	1935.	1936.
Stocks, in 1,000 tons	7	7·1	8·1	8	9·1	13·7	15·2	15·2	15·7	16·9	13·3	11·2[3]
Prices; Great Britain, London, Japanese silk; RM. per 100 Kg.[1]						34·97	23·83	15	12·25	7·88	9·57	9·73[2]

[1] 1913: 36·03. [2] June. [3] April.

(4) International Trade, Exports.[1]

	Unit.	1929.	1930.	1931.	1932.	1933.	1934.	1935.
Values ...	RM. million ...	2,327	1,391	1,068	602	467	290	366
Quantities	1,000 metric tons	56	47	52	44	43	41	45

[1] Excluding silk waste.

D.—Jute.

(1) Production.

In 1,000 Quintals.

	1913.	1920.	Annual Average 1925–29.	1929.	1933.	1934.
Japanese Empire ...			48			
French Indo-China ...			4			
India	16,140	10,730	18,688	18,750	14,490	15,480
Nepal			113			
World			18,853			

(2) Exports from India.

	Unit.	1913.	1920.	1929.	1932.	1933.	1934.
Raw jute	1,000 tons ...	781	480	820	572	760	765
Jute piece goods ...	Million metres	970	1,237	1,509	925	962	972
Jute bags	Million ...	369	534	522	415	402	423

(3) Exports in International Trade, All Countries.

	In 1,000 Tons.						
	1929.	1930.	1931.	1932.	1933.	1934.	1935.
Raw jute ...	886	649	692	519	755	750	824

(4) Prices.

	In RM. per 100 Kg.							
	1913.	1930.	1931.	1932.	1933.	1934.	1935.	July, 1935.
Great Britain, London, nat. I, futures ...	61·17	42·39	32·09	24·40	21·13	19·23	22·17	20·43

9.—WOOL.

(1) Production.

	In 1,000 Metric Tons.						
	1928.	1930.	1931.	1932.	1933.	1934.	1935.
Germany	15·3	14·7	14·7	14·3	14·2	14·6	16·5
France	21·4	26·1	25·4	24·6	24·4	24·3	24·3
Great Britain	51·7	50·3	51·3	54	54·4	51·7	49·9
Italy	14·5	21·8	20	19·1	18·6	16·3	
Yugoslavia	12·3	12·3	12·6	13·4	13·5	13·7	12·5
Rumania	25·6	23·8	24·7	25·2	25	26	29·6
Spain	38·1	36·3	34·9	35·4	35·4	33·1	29·9
Turkey	19·2	16·7	18·9	18·7	17·6	17·1	19·7
U.S.S.R.	177·8	137	98·9	64·9	61·7	64	75·8
Europe	427·2	388·1	352·7	310·1	318·1	314	328·8
China[1]	41·1	25·7	29·5	13·5	27·8	41	55
India	45·4	45·4	45·4	45·5	45·4	45·4	45·4
Iran	22·2	20·4	22·2	22·2	22·2	22·2	22·2
Asia	130·6	112·9	118·2	100·5	113·6	127·8	143
French Morocco	12·7	12·7	10·5	12	12·2	12·8	15
Union of South Africa ...	131·6	137	142·4	149·7	128·8	100·7	113·4
Africa	175·2	187·3	180·5	105·5	175·2	146·3	
U.S.	174·1	197·1	210·7	199·8	208·6	204	204·6
Argentine	157·4	163·7	171·4	176	174·6	170·6	163·3
Brazil	15·2	15·7	15·9	15·3	16	16·5	
Chile	15·4	12·1	12·9	15·3	12·7	12·7	
Uruguay	62·6	75·3	47·2	50·8	43·1	53·1	47·6
America	448·3	491	482	481·1	478·3	480·4	468·1
Australia	439·2	} 536·7	584·9	612·4	583·1	587·8	554·3
New Zealand	123·4						
World	1,744·4	1,716	1,718·3	1,709·6	1,668·3	1,656·3	1,656
Colonial...					78·6		
Non-colonial					1,589·7		

[1] Exports.

S

(2) STOCKS.

	In 1,000 Tons.								
	1928.	1929.	1930.	1931.	1932.	1933.	1934.	1935.	1936.[2]
Raw wool	?	?	?	?	?	189	223	199	135
Tops ...	23·1	25·5	21·4	22·3	25·8	30·7	28	21[1]	

[1] October. [2] June.

(3) PRICES.

	RM. per 100 Kg.							
	1913.	1930.	1931.	1932.	1933.	1934.	1935.	July, 1936.
France, Le Havre, Buenos Aires fine, futures ...	157·95	139·22	96·89	76·41	87·43	89·93	85·09	91·30

(3a) WORLD PRODUCTION, 1909–1935.

Annual Average	In 1,000 Metric Tons.						
1909–13.	1922.	1923.	1924.	1925.	1928.	1933.	1935.
1,463	1,214	1,236	1,296	1,329	1,744	1,669	1,656

(4) WORLD EXPORTS.

	1929.	1930.	1931.	1932.	1933.	1934.	1935.
Quantities, in 1,000 tons							
Raw wool	1,004	918	946	961	1,114	904	1,015
Tops	55	52	56	55	63	53	60
Values, in RM. million							
Raw wool	2,905	1,657	1,190	884	998	1,174	938
Tops	368	255	197	155	177	162	160

(5) EXPORTS, BY COUNTRIES.

In 1,000 Metric Tons.

	1931.	1934.	1935.		1931.	1934.	1935.
Great Britain ...	16	25	36	Chile	10	11	10
Union of S. Africa...	107	87	118	Uruguay ...	66	24	50
India	18	18	23	Australia ...	369	367	386
China	15	15	20	New Zealand ...	96	103	101
Argentine ...	141	113	136				

(6) PRODUCTION OF WOOLLEN GOODS.

	Year.	Woollen Yarns, in 1,000 tons.	Woollen Cloth, in 1,000 tons.	Id., in million metres.
Germany ...	1927 1928 1933	61·2 61·7 64		
France	1913 1926/27	88 106·7	55 73·6	
Poland	1930 1933	23·2 23·6	8·6 6·6	
Sweden ...	1930 1933	10·2 10·8	8·4 8·2	
Great Britain ...	1907 1912 1924 1930	202·3 256·3 251·5 175·1		416 440 398[1] 288[1]
U.S.	1925 1927 1929		151·6 145 143·4	
U.S.S.R. ...	1931 1934	73·3		122·6 88·2
Japan[3]	1929 1930 1931 1932	29·2 25 35·2 38·5		205·6 198·8 215·2 ?
Australia ...	1929/30 1932/33	3·5 4·6		14·5[2] 28·1[2]

[1] Qm. [2] Excluding rugs, carpets and shawls. [3] Rugs, million: 1929, ·9; 1930, ·9; 1931, 1·2.

10.—ARTIFICIAL SILK (RAYON).

(1) WORLD PRODUCTION.

In Million Lbs.

1892.	1902.	1912.	1919.	1921.	1929.	1932.	1933.	1934.	1935.
·031	5	20	40	65·5	442·4	489·4	670·7	795·4	1,017·6

(2) PRODUCTION BY COUNTRIES.

	In 1,000 Metric Tons.						
	1929.	1930.	1931.	1932.	1933.	1934.	1935.
France	16·8	18·1	20	23	25·5	32·1	32
Germany ...	26·5	26·8	28·1	28·2	32·8	41·6	62
Great Britain ...	25·8	22·1	24·8	32·9	38·1	42·2	49·1
Italy	32·3	30·1	34·6	32·1	37·2	48·3	
Japan	12·2	16·6	22·3	31·6	44·7	69·2	98·6
U.S.	55·3	49·9	65·5	61·2	94·6	95·4	116·4
WORLD	198·9	192·6	224·6	240·2	349·7	413·8	462

(3) PRICES.

	In RM. per Kg.							
	1913.	1930.	1931.	1932.	1933.	1934.	1935.	July, 1936.
Germany, Krefeld, 120 den. Schuss	12·50	6·74	5·15	5·08	5	5	5	4·85

(4) EXPORTS OF RAYON AND RAYON YARNS.

(*a*) *World Exports.*

In 1,000 Metric Tons.						
1929.	1930.	1931.	1932.	1933.	1934.	1935.
61	63	66	64	69	89	88

(*b*) *By Countries.*

	In 1,000 Metric Tons.				
	1931.	1932.	1933.	1934.	1935.
Germany	8·5	9·1	9·6	7·4	6·4
Belgium and Luxemburg	2·8	2·5	2·7	3·5	3
France	8·5	8·3	10·4	12·5	8·3
Great Britain	4·1	6·8	7·3	8·1	8·3
Italy	22·5	18·7	19·1	30·1	24·8[1]
Holland	10·1	8·4	8·3	8·1	7·6
Switzerland	4·6	3·7	4·7	4·5	3·5
U.S.		·3	·5	1·1	1
Japan		3·3	4	10	13·6

[1] January–September.

D.—ELECTRICAL ENERGY

(1) PRODUCTION.

	In Million Kwh.		
		Last Year for which Figures Available.	
	1925.	Year.	Figure.
Algeria	59	1933	174
Morocco	?	1934	141
Union of South Africa ...	1,761	1934	3,309
Canada	10,110	1935	23,404
U.S.	90,300[1]	1935	99,384
Newfoundland	?	1930	795
Mexico H.	1,262[1]	1935	2,064
Argentine T.	?	1933	1,630
Chile	214	1934	356
Uruguay	84	1932	158
French Indo-China	?	1934	56
Japan	8,172	1934	19,108
Dutch Indies H.	?	1933	231
British Malaya T.	57	1934	228
Philippines	65	1934	115
U.S.S.R.	2,925	1935	25,900
Germany	20,328	1934	30,727
Belgium T.	2,274	1935	4,875
Bulgaria	32	1934	137
Denmark T.	380	1933	751
Spain H.	1,611	1935	3,270
Esthonia T.	—	1933	39
Finland	541	1935	2,000
France	10,222	1935	15,600
Greece T.	?	1932	140
Hungary T.	441	1933	729
Irish Free State H. ...	?	1933	185
Italy	6,545	1935	13,118
Latvia T.	?	1933	100
Norway H.	?	1934	7,143
Holland	1,004	1935	2,207
Poland T.	1,668	1935	2,810
Portugal	?	1933	250
Austria	2,140	1934	2,465
Rumania	243	1933	594
U.K.	11,278	1935	18,944[3]
Saar Territory T.	504	1935	990
Sweden H.	3,673	1935	6,900
Switzerland H.	3,665	1935	5,692
Czechoslovakia T.	1,955	1935	2,970
Turkey T[2]	?	1933	89
Yugoslavia	?	1931	392
Australia	1,537	1934	2,910
New Zealand H.	340	1934	916

[1] 1926. [2] Only Istambul. [3] Only public works.
H—only hydro-electric power. T—only thermal-electric power.

(2) Developed Water-Power of the World, Jan. 1st, 1932.[1]

In 1,000 H.P.

Canada	6,125	France	2,300
U.S. (incl. Alaska) ...	14,921	Germany	2,000
North and Central America	21,800	Italy	4,840
Brazil	640	Norway	1,000
Total South America ...	900	Spain	1,000
		Sweden	1,675
America	22,700	Switzerland	2,300
Japan	3,500	Europe	18,400
Asia	4,000	World	46,000
Africa	33		
Oceania	370		

[1] From *The World Almanac*, 1933.

E.—TABLE OF MARKS OF INTERNATIONAL WEALTH

(A) Unweighted Marks

No. of Country.	Iron Ore. 2	Iron. 3	Steel. 4	Bauxite. 5	Chromium Ore. 6	Copper Ore. 7	Gold Stocks in Central Banks. 8	Gold Production. 9	Silver. 10	Lead Ores. 11	Manganese Ore. 12	Nickel Ore. 13	Quicksilver. 14	Tin Ore. 15	Zinc Ore. 16	Platinum. 17	Palladium. 18	Osmium and Iridium. 19	Other Platinum Metals. 20	Antimony Ore. 21	Cadmium. 22
1 Australia									1	2					1						1
2 Brazil ...																					
3 Canada ...						1		1	1	1		9			1	1	9		8		
4 China ...																				7	
5 France ...	4	1	1	4	1		2					1									1
6 Germany		2	1												1						
7 G. Britain	1	1	1	1	2	1	1				1			4							
8 Holland ...				1										2							
9 India ...					1					1	1										
10 Italy ...				1									2								
11 Japan ...					1																
12 Poland ...																					1
13 Russia ...	2	2	1		2			1			6		1			3					
14 Union of S. Africa ...					1			4										7			
15 U.S. ...	3	3	3	1		2	5	1	1	2	1				3	2		2	2		6

B.—Weighting Index Figures.

	2	3	4	5	6	7	8	9	10	11	12	13	14	15	16	17	18	19	20	21	22
	5	4	4	1	1	1	10[1]	10[1]	1	3	1	2	1	7	2	1	1	1	1	1	1

[1] See explanation in text.

No. of Country.	Cobalt. 23	Molybdene Ore. 24	Bismuthum Ore. 25	Strontium Minerals. 26	Thorium Ore. 27	Titanium Ore. 28	Vanadium Ore. 29	Tungsten Ore. 30	Uranium Ore. 31	Radium. 32	Coal. 33	Oil. [illegible]	Asbestos. 35	Salt. 36	Potash. 37	Natural Phosphates. 38	Superphosphate. 39	Basic Slag. 40	Natural Guano. 41	Sulphur. 42	Graphite Stone. 43	Mica. 44
1																1	1					
2					3	1																
3			2										5									1
4								5														
5							1							1	2	4	1	3				
6			4	1							2			1	6		1	4			3	
7				9			3				2		1	1				1				
8																						
9	1				7	6		2						1					1			3
10																	1			1		
11			3														1			1	2	
12																						
13											1	1	3	1		1	1			1		
14							3															
15		9					2	1	1		3	6		3	1	3	2			3		6

B.—Weighting Index Figures.

	23	24	25	26	27	28	29	30	31	32	33	[illegible]	35	36	37	38	39	40	41	42	43	44
	1	1	1	1	1	1	1	1	1	1	29	46	1	1	2	2	1	1	2	1	1	1

No. of Country.	Silicium Earth. 45	Wheat. 46	Rye. 47	Maize. 48	Barley. 49	Oats. 50	Rice. 51	Sugar Cane. 52	Sugar Beets. 53	Rubber. 54	Timber. 55	Wood Pulp. 56	Cotton Seed. 57	Copra. 58	Ground-Nuts. 59	Soya Beans. 60	Sesamum. 61	Hempseed. 62	Rape-seed. 63	Linseed. 64	Palm Oil, Palm-Kernal Oil. 65	Olive Oil. 66
1 ...														1								
2 ...													1									
3 ...	1					1					2	1										
4 ...													1		1	1	1					
5 ...	1					1			1					1	1						2	
6 ...		2			1	1			2			1										
7 ...						1	1		1	6				3	1						4	
8 ...								1		4				3							2	
9 ...	1				1		5						1		2		6		1	1	1	
10 ...	1																					8
11 ...							2	2											1			
12 ...		2				1					1					8						
13 ...	2	5			2	3			3		2		1					9		3		
14 ...																						
15 ...	1		4		1	2		3	1		1	2	4		1							

B.—Weighting Index Figures.

	45	46	47	48	49	50	51	52	53	54	55	56	57	58	59	60	61	62	63	64	65	66
	1	20	1	8	3	1	13	9	9	13	24	10	1	2	4	2	1	1	1	4	2	3

No. of Country	Cotton.	Flax.	Hemp.	Silk.	Jute.	Wool.	Rayon.	Electrical Energy.	Total Marks.
	67	68	69	70	71	72	73	74	75
1 ...						2			11
2 ...	1							1	7
3 ...								1	46
4 ...				1		1			18
5 ...							1	1	38
6 ...		1					1	1	36
7 ...							1	1	48
8 ...									13
9 ...	2				10				62
10 ...				1			1	1	17
11 ...				8			2	1	32
12 ...									5
13 ...	2	8	4			1		1	73
14 ...						1		1	17
15 ...	4					1	3	1	112

B.—Weighting Index Figures.

	43	3	1	8	3	20	4	10[1]	

[1] Estimated.

C. Weighted Marks.

No. of Country.	2	3	4	5	6	7	8	9	10	11	12	13	14	15	16	17	18	19	20	21
1 ...									1	6					2					
2 ...																				
3 ...								10	1	3		18			2	1	9		8	
4 ...																				7
5 ...	20	4	4	4	1	2	20					2								
6 ...		8	4												2					
7 ...	5	4	4	1	2						1			28						
8 ...				1										14						
9 ...					1					3	1									
10 ...				1									2							
11 ...					1															
12 ...																				
13 ...	10	8	4		2			10			6		1			3				
14 ...					1			40										7		
15 ...	15	12	12	1		5	50	10	1	6	1				6	2		2	2	

No. of Country.	22	23	24	25	26	27	28	29	30	31	32	33	34	35	36	37	38	39	40
1	1																2	1	
2						3	1												
3				2										5					
4									5										
5	1							1							1	4	8	1	3
6				4	1							58			1	12		1	4
7					9			3				58			1				1
8																			
9		1				7	6		2						1				
10																		1	
11				3														1	
12	1																		
13												29	46	3	1			1	
14								3											
15	6		9					2	1	1		87	276		3	2	6	2	

No. of Country.	41	42	43	44	45	46	47	48	49	50	51	52	53	54	55	56	57	58	59
1 ...																		2	
2 ...																	1		
3 ...				1		20				1					48	10			
4 ...																	1		4
5 ...					2	20				1								2	4
6 ...			3				2		3	1			9			10			
7 ...										1	13		18	78				6	4
8 ...												9	9	52				6	
9 ...	2			3		20			3		65						1		8
10 ...		1				20													
11 ...		1	2								26	18							
12 ...							2			1					24				
13 ...		1				40	5		6	3			27		48		1		
14 ...																			
15 ...		3		6		20		32	3	2		27	9		24	20	4		4

No. of Country.	60	61	62	63	64	65	66	67	68	69	70	71	72	73	74	Total Weighted Marks
1													60			75
2								43							10	58
3															10	149
4	2	1									8		20			48
5						4								4	10	123
6									3					4	10	140
7						8								4	10	260
8						4										95
9		6		8	4	2		86				30				260
10							24				8			4	10	71
11	16			1							64			8	10	151
12																28
13			9		12			86	24	4			20		10	422
14													20		10	81
15								172					20	12	10	894

F.—SUPPLEMENTARY TABLES

1.—POTATOES.

(a) Production, 1921–1935.

	Annual Average, 1921-25.	In 1,000 Metric Tons. 1929.	1932.	1933.	1934.	1935.
North America ...	13,249	11,583	11,565	10,695	12,710	11,490
Europe		189,733	189,056	185,724	200,229	203,240
Germany	35,502	40,072	47,016	44,071	46,781	41,016
France	12,284	16,618	16,484	14,822	16,653	14,019
Poland	26,535	31,750	29,975	28,330	33,470	32,502
U.S.S.R.		47,850	45,120	49,250	51,010	69,740
World		206,000	205,890	202,050	218,150	220,702

(b) Prices, 1926–1935.

	In Gold Francs per 100 Kg.; End of Year. 1926.	1927.	1928.	1929.	1930.	1931.	1932.	1933.	1934.	1935
Berlin, red	7·75	7·98	7·05	5·88	6·42	4·18	3·26	3·80	5·93	5·56
Czechoslovakia, for consumption	10·83	5·27	6·51	4·76	4·38	4	4·16	5·08	4·90	5·63

2.—PRODUCTION OF GRAPHITE, ASPHALT AND NATURAL GAS IN THE "HAVE-NOT" COUNTRIES, 1928-1935.

Country.	Commodity.	Unit.	1928.	1929.	1930.	1933.	1934.	1935.
(a) *Germany*	Graphite ...	Long tons ...	17,188	21,012	24,602	19,443	17,258	21,321
	Asphalt rock	1,000 long tons	156	143	115	43	64	71
(b) *Italy* ...	Graphite ...	1,000 long tons	6·9	7·4	5·8	3·1	3·8	5·1
	Natural gas ...	Million cubic feet	226	247	307	487	529	436
	,, asphalt	Long tons ...	2,144	904	286	301	313	719
	Asphalt rock	1,000 long tons	238	216	220	49	133	146
	Oil shale ...	Long tons ...	7,271	8,101	10,923	10,875	4,642	12,440
(c) *Japan*	Natural gas ...	Million cubic feet	970	?	?	1,657	1,664	?
	Graphite ...	Long tons ...	435	303	226	855	954	

INDEX

For Product Safety Concerns and Information please contact our EU representative GPSR@taylorandfrancis.com Taylor & Francis Verlag GmbH, Kaufingerstraße 24, 80331 München, Germany